Case Studies in Social Entrepreneurship and Sustainability
The oikos Collection Vol. 2

CASE STUDIES IN
SOCIAL ENTREPRENEURSHIP AND SUSTAINABILITY

The oikos collection
Volume 2

Edited by Jost Hamschmidt and Michael Pirson

with a Foreword by Marina Kim, Ashoka

Greenleaf
PUBLISHING

© 2011 Greenleaf Publishing Limited

Published by Greenleaf Publishing Limited
Aizlewood's Mill
Nursery Street
Sheffield S3 8GG
UK
www.greenleaf-publishing.com

Printed in Great Britain on acid-free paper by
CPI Antony Rowe, Chippenham and Eastbourne

FSC
www.fsc.org
MIX
Paper from
responsible sources
FSC® C013604

Cover by LaliAbril.com

British Library Cataloguing in Publication Data:
    Case studies in social entrepreneurship and sustainability.
        -- (The oikos collection ; v. 2)
        1. Social responsibility of business. 2. Sustainable
        development.
        I. Series II. Hamschmidt, Jost. III. Pirson, Michael.
        338.9'27-dc22

    ISBN-13: 9781906093471

Contents

Acknowledgements

This book is the result of a fruitful collaboration between oikos and Ashoka. We would like to express our gratitude to Marina Kim and her team from the Ashoka University Program, who enthusiastically supported our collaboration from the very first moment. Furthermore we thank the donors of the oikos Foundation: Avina Foundation, Ernst Schweizer AG, Fondation Looser, Fondation Andre Hoffmann, Helvetia, Knecht & Müller AG, Mercator Foundation Switzerland, Rhomberg Bau, UBS AG and Stiftung Drittes Millennium. Their support for oikos in general and the oikos Global Case Writing Competition in particular have provided the platform on which to build the collection of cases for this book. In that context, a special thank you goes to Evelyn Braun, Nadine Felix, Andre Hoffmann, Randolph Koller, Christian Leitz, Hubert Looser, Peter Müller, Sindy Schmiegel, Hansruedi Schweizer and Hansruedi Zulliger, whose commitment to oikos has always been and continues to be a strong encouragement and driver for our work. Thank you! At the same time, we are indebted to all the members of the oikos Case Writing Competition's Social Entrepreneurship Track award committee—their ongoing support provided a strong academic base for this publication: Leo Bartlett, AISE Brisbane, Australia; Gabriel Berger, University of San Andres, Argentina; Marie Lisa M. Dacanay, AIM, The Philippines; Gregory Dees, Duke University, USA; Anil Gupta, IIM, India; Roberto Gutiérrez, University de los Andes, Colombia; Kai Hockerts, CBS Copenhagen, Denmark; Kate Kearins, Auckland University of Technology, New Zealand; Johanna Mair, IESE Barcelona, Spain; Patricia Márquez, University of San Diego, California; Sharon Oster, Yale University, USA; Francesco Perrini, Bocconi University, Italy; Jim Phills, Stanford University, USA; Madhukar Shukla, XLRI Jamshedpur, India; Chris Steyaert, University of St. Gallen, Switzerland; Mark Swilling, University of Stellenbosch, South Africa; Phil Auerswald, George Mason University, USA; Julie Battilana, Harvard Business School, USA; David Cooperrider, Case Western Reserve, USA; Minna Halme, Helsinki School of Economics, Finland; Cheryl Kernot, CSI, Australia; Roger L. Martin, Rotman School of Business, Canada; Alex Nicholls, University of Oxford, UK. Liudmila Nazarkina added tremendously to the project. Many thanks!

List of Contributors

- Bala Chakravarthy, IMD Lausanne
- Imran Chowdhury, ESSEC Business School
- Mary Christiansen, William Davidson Institute/Ross School of Business, University of Michigan
- Lisa Jones Christensen, Kenan-Flagler Business School, University of North Carolina
- Eva Collins, University of Waikato Management School
- Charles J. Corbett, University of California, Los Angeles
- Sophie Coughlan, IMD Lausanne
- J. Gregory Dees, Fuqua School of Business, Duke University
- Hadiya Faheem, IBS Center for Management Research, Hyderabad
- Saji Sam George, IBS Center for Management Research, Hyderabad
- Jacen Greene, Portland State University
- Michael Gordon, University of Michigan
- Vivek Gupta, IBS Center for Management Research, Hyderabad
- Aytha Harish, IBS Center for Management Research, Hyderabad
- Rebecca Henn, University of Michigan
- Andrew J. Hoffman; University of Michigan
- Kate Kearins, Auckland University of Technology
- Benoit Leleux, IMD Lausannne

- Ted London, William Davidson Institute/Ross School of Business, University of Michigan
- Scott Marshall, Portland State University
- Ramalingam Meenakshisundaram, IBS Center for Management Research, Hyderabad
- V. Namratha Prasad, IBS Center for Management Research, Hyderabad
- William G. Powell, University of California, Los Angeles
- Debapratim Purkayastha, IBS Center for Management Research, Hyderabad
- Filipe Santos, INSEAD Fontainebleau
- Besta Shankar, IBS Center for Management Research, Hyderabad
- Jessica Thomas, Kenan-Flagler Business School, University of North Carolina
- Helen Tregidga, Auckland University of Technology

Foreword

Marina Kim, Director, Ashoka U

Interest in Social Entrepreneurship has been rising dramatically over the last 15 years. Since the first course debuted at Harvard Business School in 1995, the number of colleges and universities teaching and researching social entrepreneurship has exploded. In 2008, Ashoka co-developed the "Social Entrepreneurship Teaching Resources Handbook," showcasing over 350 faculty members from 122 universities pursuing social entrepreneurship teaching and research.

As the largest global network of social entrepreneurs with over thirty years' experience in the field, Ashoka has been recognized as a convener, a catalyst, and a facilitator of quality social entrepreneurship education. Ashoka formally launched the University Network for Social Entrepreneurship (UNSE) in 2005, in partnership with Oxford's Skoll Centre for Social Entrepreneurship, the EMES European Research Network and the Social Enterprise Knowledge Network (SEKN). UNSE compiled and mapped out the diverse and fragmented resources and networks related to social entrepreneurship education.

In 2008, Ashoka launched the "Changemaker Campus Initiative" which applies Ashoka's rigorous criteria to select and support universities as they develop and implement a comprehensive social entrepreneurship plan. Through the lessons learned from this network, and with input from our broader global network of those experienced in the field, our goal is to set a new standard for social entrepreneurship education. Indeed, despite the rising demand, there remains a dire need for quality coursework and global teaching case studies. Social entrepreneurs—and the pressing challenges they solve—are not bound by geographic borders or a single political environment, yet we lack the materials necessary to equip students with the skills and mindset required to catalyze systemic social change.

What few high-quality case studies do exist typically highlight social entrepreneurs within the United States. The cooperation with oikos within the Social Entrepreneurship Track of the annual oikos Global Case Competition is a critical vehicle for tackling that challenge. As a result of this effort, more locally relevant case studies are being written, peer-reviewed and judged than ever before, and are able to make their way into the hands of global audiences eager to adopt them into their courses.

Building social entrepreneurship skills and problem-solving abilities are best practiced and honed using real-life examples and strategic challenges—not just learning theories in a vacuum. Case studies provide this exposure and real-time training in systemic problem-solving. Through these teaching cases, students learn that social entrepreneurship is about identifying root causes of problems and applying a solution that tackles the system. As study upon study has shown, the band-aid approach does not work. To effectively address a social problem, the solution must continually adapt and evolve based on market feedback about what works and what needs to change in the model.

As we seek to integrate these case studies and other innovative learning materials into the fabric of higher education coursework and research, it has become increasingly clear that we are in the midst of a new wave of creation and innovation. Questioning the role of higher education in preparing tomorrow's change leaders is now part of the agenda.

Social entrepreneurship is one of the key threads that resonates with university faculty, students, administrators, and, increasingly, with university presidents. One example is the recently created annual meeting of university presidents committed to supporting social change and social entrepreneurship through the Clinton Global Initiative's University Program. There is new and urgent demand for applied learning, applied research and the opportunity to develop skills and knowledge that can be directly applied after graduation. This invites us all to step up and improve the teaching materials that currently exist, while using a comprehensive approach to build an enabling environment at colleges and universities everywhere to provide resources, role models, and a community of like-minded individuals to foster and support the next generation of changemakers.

Please join us in our journey to improve the quality and quantity of social entrepreneurship education. We need more faculty members who are able to blend theory and practice in a way that doesn't lose rigor of thought. We need more case-studies written to demonstrate real-life examples and contextualize them for students from all over the world. We need more courses that go beyond frameworks and theories, so we can allow students to grapple with the problems and solutions in a real-world context.

In short, we need more of the thinkers and doers whose extraordinary work will appear in future editions of this invaluable collection of case studies in social entrepreneurship and sustainability. We hope you'll join us.

Part I
Introduction

1.1
Preface

This book is the second volume resulting from the oikos Global Case Writing Competition—an annual program launched in 2003 to promote the publication of high-quality teaching cases in Corporate Sustainability and Social Entrepreneurship. The first volume titled *Case Studies in Sustainability Management and Strategy: the oikos collection* was successfully published in 2007.[1] Numerous positive feedbacks since then have underlined our conviction, that there is a growing need for tested case teaching materials. Against this background, the second volume expands the collection with strong cases in the rapidly growing field of Social Entrepreneurship and Sustainability. The selection includes winning cases of the oikos Global Case Writing Competition's Social Entrepreneurship Track[2] for which oikos has teamed up with Ashoka, the leading global Organization for Social Entrepreneurship.[3] The nucleus of our cooperation dates back to Harvard Business School's 2008 Social Entrepreneurship Conference, where the editors met with Marina Kim, an enthusiastic personality dedicated to bringing Social Entrepreneurship topics into the classrooms of leading Business Schools. We joined forces, expanded the international judging committee of the program to add professors in the field of social entrepreneurship and launched the first call for Social Entrepreneurship cases in November of 2008. The call gathered more than 20 submissions from leading business schools. We are happy to present the best of these cases within this volume, along with best cases of the subsequent 2010 competition edition.

---

1 Jost Hamschmidt, *Case Studies in Sustainability Management and Strategy: The oikos collection* (Sheffield, UK: Greenleaf Publishing, 2007; www.greenleaf-publishing.com/oikos).
2 For more information on this competition please consult Chapter 6.4 or www.oikos-international.org/projects/cwc.
3 See: www.ashoka.org.

oikos aims to strengthen management competence for sustainable development among tomorrow's decision makers by integrating pressing issues into teaching and research at the world's faculties for economics and management. The oikos Case Collection reflects this objective and aims to add relevant content to education at management schools worldwide. Both oikos and Ashoka regard the case method as one important teaching concept that is able to intertwine theoretical concepts with hands-on experiences, based on real-life organizations. We believe that this is a method that prepares the business students of today to deal with contemporary and future challenges.

In view of the growing importance of various sustainability trends, management schools are increasingly challenged to adapt their Entrepreneurship and Business curricula. Management education needs to reflect the trends and provide a broadened understanding of value creation. Sustainability is a concept that demands organizations to consider the legitimate expectations of different stakeholders in their value creation processes. At the same time, it underlines the fact that many sustainability trends offer new business opportunities that entrepreneurs will seize. As a result, value creation processes need to be reorganized in order to create economic capital while developing social capital and preserving natural capital.

Indeed, entrepreneurial organizations are increasingly dealing with these challenges. The fifteen case studies in this book explore both the opportunities and pitfalls entrepreneurs face in targeting sustainability issues and how their values and core assumptions impact their business strategies.

We are aware, that this volume can only be a start to explore the rich field of entrepreneurial social impact strategies applied by an increasing number of organizations—currently we see a growing number of groundbreaking initiatives evolving and we would be happy if scholars will cover the impact of these movements with new teaching cases in the future. We have also just launched the oikos case teaching initiative in order to bring innovative teaching cases into the classrooms of the management schools of the world.

As an incentive, the reader will find in Chapter 1.2 an introduction to the characteristics of excellent cases, but also hints on avoiding the most common mistakes in case writing. For this part we screened the written feedbacks of our case-writing judging committee, searching for patterns of the most often cited pitfalls. And in Part 6 we provide up-to-date information on external sources dealing with the case-writing process, international case competitions and case collections.

We hope that this volume will both stimulate the use and the production of Social Entrepreneurship and Sustainability Cases.

Jost Hamschmidt, St. Gallen
Michael Pirson, New York
January 2011

1.2

Cases in Social Entrepreneurship and Sustainability
What Makes an Excellent Case?

The case method of teaching was developed by Faculty of the Harvard Business School[1] and the Ivey School of Business in the 1920s. The basic idea was to simulate real business challenges in the classroom in order to breathe life and instil greater meaning into the lessons of management education. Case studies can be important tools for creating learning processes on different levels—students are forced to struggle with exactly the kinds of decisions and dilemmas managers confront every day. In this reflection of reality, the values and goals of the student are systematically challenged. Uncertainty is key: students are asked what they think, how they would act, and what challenges they feel are important. The use of a case study should create a classroom in which students succeed by exercising the skills of leadership and teamwork in the face of real problems. Facts, figures and theories play an important role; but contexts, emotions and value judgments have a large influence, too. Guided by a faculty member, students cooperate, analyze and synthesize conflicting data and points of view. The objective is to define and prioritize goals, to persuade and inspire others who think differently, to make tough decisions with uncertain information, and to seize opportunities in the face of doubt.

These attributes are especially valuable in the context of social entrepreneurship, sustainability and strategy; organizations are now continually forced to value

---

1 This introductory paragraph is based on information available at www.hbs.edu/case and McNair and Hersum 1954.

the different aspects of sustainability and their interrelations: How do social issues impact the economic bottom line? How can an environmentally sound strategy create a positive impact on employee motivation and thus have a measurable impact on economic performance? What comes first and why? These are just some of the many questions that may arise.

What makes an excellent case in social entrepreneurship? There are multiple case "recipes" available, e.g. via the Internet, and a vast literature about case writing and teaching.[2] Many of these tips and hints can be applied to social entrepreneurship and sustainability cases. In this section we propose 11 features of an excellent case, which are derived from experience with the oikos Global Case Writing Competition. They also echo the lessons of a classic article by Clyde Freeman Herreid.[3]

1. **An excellent case provides a learning opportunity on a relevant topic.** The case should tackle a decision situation with impact on the future of an organization and implications for corporate strategy. It should be a real case, not just a story. And it should identify clear-cut management decisions (i.e. merge or not; compete or cooperate).

2. **An excellent case tells an engaging story. It should have an interesting plot that relates to the experiences of the target audience.** It needs a hero, a dilemma and a solution. The solution may not exist yet; it will be what the students need to supply once the case is discussed.

3. **An excellent case is accompanied by teaching goals and a teaching note.** It should be explicit which audience is being addressed with the case. Undergraduates have a different background compared to MBA students. What does the case do for the course and the student? Which theories are employed? How should the students be involved (e.g. group works, student preparation, class interaction)? Cases can be choreographed with role-plays and/or voting. Students need to be systematically challenged to argue. Excellent cases provide suggestions for frameworks and literature for faculty and students.[4]

4. **An excellent case is based on a recent situation.** To appear real the story should have the trappings of a current challenge. If a student has just seen the problem mentioned in the media, so much the better. Thus, a case on corporate strategies to deal with climate change will arouse the students' interest more than one on Shell's Brent Spar Platform disposal challenge.

5. **An excellent case includes quotations.** Digital technology has made the life of case writers easier; nowadays it has become simple to produce a

2 See e.g. Heath 2006; Leenders *et al.* 2001.
3 Herreid 1997.
4 For more information see also chapter 1.3 in this volume and additional hints including a sample teaching note at www.oikos-international.org/academic/cwc/what-makes-an-excellent-teaching-note.html.

short film on the "hero" of a case. A face and a voice is the best way to gain empathy for the leading characters: let them speak in their own voices. If this is not possible, use quotations and add life and drama to the case. Quotations from other sources, e.g. leading newspapers, advertisements or internal documents, should be used as well. They make your case more authentic.

6. **An excellent case is relevant to the audience.** Cases should be chosen that involve situations that the students know or are likely to face. This improves the empathy factor and makes the case clearly something worth studying. Thus, for a graduate student in finance, a case involving George Soros's opinion on Tobin taxes might be of greater interest than barter trade in Papua New Guinea.

7. **An excellent case is debate-provoking.** It should provide food for thought and should leave room for different interpretations. It should fuel the debate on an issue. Take, for example, the Procter & Gamble case in this book (pp. 204-27): is this pure philanthropy or a strategic investment of a multinational company?

8. **An excellent case is decision-forcing.** Not all cases have to be dilemmas that need to be solved, but there must be an urgency and a seriousness in such cases. Best-practice cases are often boring for the reader whereas, in dilemma or decision cases, students are forced to face challenges head-on. Provide a time-line and sufficient data in order to enable well-reasoned options.

9. **An excellent case has generality.** Cases should be of more use than addressing a minor or local problem; they should have general applicability. The case writer should make sure that the case provides useful generalizations and clear take-aways. Patterns should be recognizable and key insights should be aimed for—for on-the-job application or for confidence in mastering similar challenges in the future. Take, for example, the Better Place case in this book (pp. 292-316): what could be the implications for the global automotive industry?

10. **An excellent case is as short as possible.** This is basically a matter of attention span. Cases should be long enough to introduce the facts of the case but they should be carefully designed in order to keep interest high. Complexity can be introduced in stages. Case series can help in structuring the information. Data can be provided accompanied by some questions and a first decision point before additional information is introduced. Remember that the average person is not able to digest more than three pieces of information at a time. Take, for example, the Gram Vikas case in this book (pp. 43-68): why is it structured as it is?

11. **Finally: an excellent case is one that is revised after a first try in class.**
    Very often case writers take implicit knowledge for granted and the per-
    ception of the case presented in class is different from what was expected.
    Different mental models and understandings of the foundations of man-
    agement might also hinder the applicability of cases in different geograph-
    ical and cultural contexts. This is a growing challenge in a world economy,
    where regional contexts are often key to understanding markets and soci-
    ety in order to guarantee long-term business success.[5] At the same time,
    this represents a great opportunity, since an explicit description of busi-
    ness models and dilemmas in a specific context does contribute to a better
    understanding of cultural foundations and underlying values of the envi-
    ronments in which the featured organisations are operating.

5 See e.g. Friedman 2001.

1.3
Teaching Notes
Combining Contents with Concepts

Excellent cases are always linked to learning objectives, which include concepts, theories and methodologies. However, the underlying conceptual ideas are sometimes not wholly explicit in the case; therefore, teaching notes provide the means for an educator to explore the full learning potential of a case in class. Within the oikos Competition we have observed a surprisingly widespread lack of knowledge concerning concepts, goals and contents of case teaching notes. In this section we therefore provide a brief description of what useful teaching notes should look like.[1]

Teaching notes should provide useful background information in order to better understand a case. According to the European Case Clearing House,[2] which holds the world's biggest case collection, only about 50% of their registered cases are accompanied by teaching notes. However, 80% of the 50 most popular cases do provide teaching notes. This leads us to the assumption that teaching notes confer important benefits to case instructors.

All of the cases included in this book have excellent teaching notes, which are available for faculty, some free of charge, by request from Greenleaf Publishing at the following link:[3]

www.greenleaf-publishing.com/oikos2_notes

1 See also Lapierre and Cardinal (2003): "Guidelines for Writing Teaching Notes. HEC Montreal". Online resource available at: hec.ca/en/casecentre/case/guide_redaction_np_a.pdf.
2 See www.ecch.com/about/writing-teaching-notes.cfm; see also the information in Chapter 6.3.
3 Please note: if you would like teaching notes for cases 8 and 15, please contact GlobaLens directly. Contact details are in the footnotes on pages 178 and 370.

Basically, teaching notes are guidance documents that enable potential case instructors to teach a case, providing a case summary, teaching goals, key issues, concepts, open questions and potential approaches to the case. While the style, length and design of a teaching note may vary widely, we consider here the following elements:[4]

- **Case summary.** The case summary is a short version of the case and highlights the major points. What is the context and storyline? Who are the main players? What issue is framed by the case? The aim is to provide the case instructor with the key elements of the story as concisely as possible.

- **Case teaching objectives, target audience, targeted courses.** A teaching note explicitly clarifies the teaching objectives (e.g. concerning content and theoretical concepts) and target audiences (e.g. undergraduates, MBA or executive MBA students). It should also mention the courses in which the case can be applied. Is the case suitable for a mainstream marketing, strategy or management course or should it be taught in an environmental management or CSR course? What knowledge base is needed in order to successfully deal with the case?

- **Sources of the case material.** The case author should explain how the case was developed, including the steps involved in information gathering and data collection (e.g. interviews with company representatives and/or stakeholders, annual reports, media reports, Internet searches, press coverage, internal documents, scientific articles, etc.).

- **Teaching approach and didactic elements.** The teaching note should enable the transfer of knowledge. Cases are question-oriented and the teaching note should systematically help the instructor to raise relevant questions in order to promote a learning experience. It should also provide possible answers to questions that are likely to arise during in-class discussion. Questions can be developed to prepare students for in-class discussion, in order to open or to advance the discussion. It might be helpful to develop an ideal structure for this, where each issue is allocated a certain amount of time. These guidelines serve as a starting point for the instructor and will have to be adapted to suit particular circumstances. Other didactic elements can be the introduction of additional information during the course, the use of the blackboard, online research during class, suggestions for group work, role-plays, or student assignments in order to consolidate the learning process.

- **Analysis and methods.** Of course, the questions posed in a case require answers. Therefore, the teaching note should include the necessary links to concepts and theories and provide comprehensive response options to the

---

4 The proposed elements include the standard elements of ECCH requirements for a teaching note; see www.ecch.com/uploads/teachingnote.pdf.

questions. The frameworks provided should also help the students to develop their personal synthesis and should encourage further reflection. It should be noted that an excellent case will have multiple "solutions" to business challenges. Teaching notes should therefore reflect possible trade-offs among competing alternatives (e.g. how to evaluate a short-term cost reduction against a long-term reputational risk). The identification of trade-offs and the understanding of the logic of these trade-offs will improve the students' strategic perspective on business challenges in a sustainability context.

- **Further reading, references, media support.** A further reading and reference list, useful in mastering the concepts and theories addressed by the case, should be provided. Suggestions for reading assignments for students are helpful; and references to relevant websites and other sources of information are becoming increasingly important. The use of additional multimedia support, if available, should be briefly outlined.

- **Feedback and perspectives.** Teaching notes should also communicate any tips or hints the author has gained from their personal teaching experience with the case. What has worked well and what has not and for what reasons? If there is information available on the real outcome of a case, it should be included in the teaching notes. Also helpful are suggestions for other possible avenues of exploration, which could provide the basis for a more detailed study or some form of knowledge transfer in other contexts.

These are some basic suggestions for constructing teaching notes. We also acknowledge that there are a variety of other valid approaches. In essence, however, the user of teaching notes will be well served if they are: brief (a maximum of ten pages), well structured and comprehensive.

1.4
Introduction to the Cases

According to management luminary Sumantra Ghoshal[1] management schools need to reconsider the basic foundations of their management approaches and curricula. Ghoshal asks that business education be much more in tune with societal trends and not just seek narrow goals at the expense of the well-being of the world community. This calls for a broadened understanding of value creation. The following fifteen cases deal with this challenge. They describe new patterns of value creation, new alliances and the challenges of dealing with existing paradigms. In this chapter we briefly introduce the cases and their core characteristics. This volume does contain a majority of cases on social entrepreneurship, but also a number of sustainability cases portraying entrepreneurs practicing innovative ways of doing business by integrating environmental and social questions into the core of the business model. We see that new ways of doing business are substantially shaping markets and society. While we do not want to engage in an academic discussion on the distinction of Social and Sustainability Entrepreneurship[2] we would rather encourage the reader to realize the conceptual variety of practices illustrated in this volume—these cases cover organizations with for-profit, hybrid and non-profit business models—but all of them share a common objective of maximizing social impact.

1 Ghoshal 2005; see also Mintzberg 2005, Hoffman 2004 and Zell 2005.
2 Schaltegger and Wagner give a comprehensive overview of Sustainable Entrepreneurship and related Social Entrepreneurship concepts in their contribution "Types of Sustainable Entrepreneurship and Conditions for Sustainability Innovation: From the Administration of a Technical Challenge to the Management of an Entrepreneurial Opportunity" in R. Wüstenhagen *et al.*, *Sustainable Entrepreneurship and Innovation* (Edward Elgar, 2008), pp. 27-48. See also the recent overview from Tina Dacin *et al.*: P.A. Dacin, M.T. Dacin and M. Matear, "Social Entrepreneurship: Why We Don't Need a New Theory and How We Move Forward From Here", *Academy of Management Perspectives* 24(3) (2010).

Part II: Understanding the Nature of the Social Entrepreneur

Starting out our volume are introductory cases to social entrepreneurship. We thank Greg Dees for sharing his thoughts on "The Meaning of Social Entrepreneurship". Dees is providing a *tour d'horizon* on the foundations of Social Entrepreneurship and develops a base for a shared understanding of the nature of the social entrepreneur. We are convinced that this classic article will guide students of Social Entrepreneurship in their understanding and analysis of social enterprises.

The first teaching case by Michael Gordon, University of Michigan, can be used as a further introduction to the concept of social entrepreneurship. "So you want to be a Social Entrepreneur: Starting Out, Scaling Up, Staying Committed" presents an excellent overview of the challenges and problems faced by budding social entrepreneurs. The case focuses on the global water crisis—a topic covered by several other cases in this book—which does not attract the same level of attention as airline accidents or plummeting economic statistics. Yet its toll is far more staggering: more than 3 billion illnesses and 2 million deaths result from drinking contaminated water each year. These casualties take place almost exclusively in the developing world, and the rural poor bear the brunt of the burden. The organization in case, Hippo Water International (HWI), is a US-based nonprofit organization that aims to improve access to water by implementing sustainable solutions to the global water crisis. HWI's flagship product is the Water Roller, an innovative water transportation tool that carries water inside its "wheel", transforming 200 pounds (90 kg) of water to an effective weight of just 22 pounds (10 kg). HWI's director, Cynthia Koenig, founded the organization with the intention of assisting the manufacturer/distributor of the Water Roller bring the product to new international markets. But what began as a project to occupy her spare time as she searched for full-time employment soon took centre stage, with Cynthia taking on responsibility for marketing, fundraising, product redesign, and day-to-day operations. This case sheds light on the process of social entrepreneurship and the daily challenges faced by a social entrepreneur. As such it provides an excellent opportunity for the discussion of life plans, personal ambitions, and the pitfalls of a calling.

In a similar way, the case on Gram Vikas by Filipe Santos at INSEAD and Imran Chowdhury of ESSEC Business School allows for the examination of the meaning of social entrepreneurship. The Gram Vikas case especially allows for a comparison between traditional entrepreneurship and social entrepreneurship. It therefore builds a nice platform for more general discussions about the realm of entrepreneurial opportunities. Gram Vikas is an organization that develops comprehensive water and sanitation systems in rural villages in India. Case A describes the story and development of Gram Vikas. Case B focuses on the challenges of scaling up social innovations by transferring them to other organisations, a common challenge in any innovation process. The case conveys the central elements of the very distinct management approach of the Indian social entrepreneur, based on the notions of empowerment of the beneficiaries and sustainability of the solutions provided. The case thus helps to understand the essence of social entrepreneurship and its distinctiveness when compared to commercial entrepreneurship or charity work.

The third case, on KickStart International Inc., features a Kenya-based nonprofit organization which developed innovative ways to distribute irrigation pumps. Kick-Start was founded in Kenya in 1991 by Martin Fisher and Nick Moon, two visionary social entrepreneurs. In an innovative approach to fighting poverty, they sought to develop and sell tools and low-tech pump technologies that could be utilized by entrepreneurial poor people to establish small businesses, earn a steady income and eventually overcome poverty. In 2009, KickStart claimed that through the usage of its pumps about 439,000 people were able to overcome poverty, 88,600 profitable new businesses came into existence and new revenues equivalent to 0.6% of Kenya's GDP were generated. For their efforts to alleviate poverty, the organization and its founders also won many awards and prizes from several international entities, including the "Social Capitalist Award" of Fast Company (2008), the "European Hero Award" of Time Magazine in 2003 and the Peter F. Drucker Award for Non-Profit Innovation.

We conclude Part II with a snapshot from New Zealand on "Kapai New Zealand—Eat Your Greens", about a small company that had grown from an idea to two salad stores with two more on the way, and ambitions for national and international expansion. It features two case protagonists, James Irvine and Justin Lester, who are keen to start a successful business and to promote both their country and healthy eating. Despite their big ambitions, they were resource-poor, both in time and money. The case describes the challenge of developing a franchising system, which needed to not only be good for business, but to stay true to their values and lifestyles and to be practicable as well. It is a case on sustainability entrepreneurship, strategy and social innovation. It can serve as a model, how personal and professional values can be aligned in an entrepreneurial business model.

Part III: Entrepreneurial Action for Developing Inclusive Markets

Part III builds on the insights gained about the nature of social entrepreneurship and deepens some of the learnings by examining the development of inclusive markets. Examining the case of Fabio Rosa by Aytha Harish and Vivek Gupta (ICMR), we can gain insight into Rosa's efforts at providing rural families living in Brazil with access to electricity. About 25 million people lacked access to electricity in Brazil, most of them residing in rural areas as of late 2006. The adverse impact of lack of electricity resulted in high costs of cultivation, lower farm yields, high expenditure on non-renewable and hazardous energy sources, and poor living conditions. Rosa, an agronomic engineer, started working for the government as secretary of agriculture for Palmares, a municipality in Southern Brazil in 1983. Looking for ways to improve the living conditions and income levels of low-income rural families, Rosa realized that lack of electricity was the root cause for low-income levels for several rural families. He found out that high capital investment for setting up distribution networks was one of the reasons behind the exclusion of several rural families from access to electricity. On conducting further research, he came across an electricity distribution model, mono-phase, which was developed by an academic researcher in Brazil, that could bring down the cost of distribution drastically. Using the new distribution model, Rosa helped farmers in Palmares to cut the cost of cultivation and improve the yields. Rosa founded a private organization, Sistemas de Technologia Adequada Agroeletro (STA), in 1992 and worked towards his mission of rural electrification. After initial success, Rosa faced the challenge of scaling up his business to cover the whole of Brazil and expand to other developing countries. Specifically, the government's efforts to extend the electricity grid to rural areas posed a threat to Rosa's business model. The case nicely demonstrates some of the challenges of a highly replicable idea in the context of a developing market.

Moving from Brazil to India, the case on Dr. Reddy's (www.drreddys.com) provides a great example of a large-scale social entrepreneurial approach. Stories about inclusive business models have typically focused on exploiting business opportunities at the bottom of the pyramid (BOP)—the business case is the driver and a social good follows. This case is about finding a business model to support a social cause. It describes the development of a polypill to provide an effective treatment for cardiovascular disease (CVD), the number one killer worldwide, at a price tag of $25 per annum—a sum that even a poor person earning $2 a day could afford. The pill is estimated to avert 8 million deaths over a ten-year period, single-handedly contributing 75% to the World Health Organization (WHO)'s goal of reducing the death rate from chronic diseases by 2% each year from 2005 to 2015. Bala Chakravarthy and Sophie Coughlan from IMD Lausanne (Switzerland) illustrate in the "Dr. Reddy's: Medicine is for People, Profits Follow" case the fascinating approach of Dr. Anji Reddy, the founder and chairman and Raghu Cidambi, a senior advisor on strategy and intellectual property. Reddy firmly believed that developing drugs for unmet patient needs and making the drugs accessible and affordable would eventually benefit shareholders as well. The case presents impressive numbers: Dr. Reddy's was the second-largest pharmaceutical company in India in 2009, having grown from humble beginnings to become a $1.4 billion multinational in the space of 25 years. The case details the dilemmata that Cidambi faced in pursuing the Red Heart Pill (RHP) (as the polypill was called at Dr. Reddy's) project and his struggles at finding a convincing business model.

Delving deeper into the social entrepreneurial context, Jacen Greene and Scott Marshall, Portland State University, present the case of a prototypical social enterprise: ALTIS, a microfinance startup in Nepal. The case describes the issues and dilemmas facing a social entrepreneur in a developing country with rather uncertain political circumstances. Although the Nepalese government supports microfinance models, a recent civil war severely disrupted government services and worsened poverty. Covering the recent political history of Nepal, the case also covers the condition of the country's capital markets, the ALTIS concept and the competitive landscape. In the case we follow the protagonist, Sanjay, as he is seeking to establish the microfinance enterprise in the poorest and most neglected regions of Nepal. Sanjay possesses much of the expertise, a high level of motivation and many key stakeholder relationships to help him establish the microfinance enterprise. He has given a lot of thought to the funding needs, financial and technical services components of the client model and the initial management structure. However, there remain a number of issues he has yet to fully consider and he has not developed a clear strategic plan for implementing the enterprise. The case is designed to highlight the inherent uncertainties of new enterprise launch, the particular challenges of starting a social enterprise in a developing country, and the role of a variety of stakeholders in influencing the potential success of such as startup.

We conclude Part III with the winning case of the 2008 oikos Global Case Writing Competition: "VisionSpring: A Lens for Growth at the Base of the Pyramid"[3] by Molly Christiansen and Ted London from the University of Michigan. Vision-Spring sells affordable reading glasses to the poor at the base of the pyramid through Vision Entrepreneurs and, more recently, through franchise partners. The case explores how best to scale VisionSpring's approach to serving the poor. As an innovative social enterprise VisionSpring (www.visionspring.org) is dedicated to reducing poverty and generating opportunity in the developing world through the sale of affordable eyeglasses. The company has been internationally recognized by The Skoll Foundation and is a three-time winner of Fast Company's Social Capitalist Award. The case provides a rich description of the company's business model, facts on its financial performance and societal impact and the aspirations of its founders.

Part IV: Topic Spotlight: SE Approaches for Tackling Water Challenges

As one of the most pressing challenges of the 21st century is the safe supply of potable water, we present more cases of organizations that deal with the water crisis in innovative ways. In the first case, a perspective on the provision of safe drinking water is provided by Lisa Jones Christensen and Jessica Thomas from the Kenan-Flagler Business School, University of North Carolina. They describe the approach of the multinational Procter & Gamble (P&G) to develop solutions in their teaching case "Procter & Gamble's PuR Water Purifier: The Hunt for a Sustainable Business

---

3 Note that the case title has changed due to the fact that in 2008 the Scojo Foundation changed its name to Vision Spring.

Model". The case features Dr. Greg Allgood, director of the Children's Safe Drinking Water Program at P&G. Within the program P&G has helped to distribute 65 million PuR packets, that have been used to purify 650 million litres of water, most often in rural locations. Over time, and through a variety of deliberate partnerships that Allgood cultivated in ten countries, P&G has tested three different sales and distribution models: commercial marketing, social marketing and disaster relief—each with varying degrees of success. Drawing from past successes and failures, Allgood is considering how to fulfil P&G's aggressive commitment to providing 135 million litres of safe drinking water in Africa and how to achieve long-term behaviour change. This case presents the range of business models that P&G has explored for the sales and distribution of PuR (see www.purwater.com). The case also presents the risks and hurdles inherent in these projects, as well as implications for their potential scalability to other countries/regions. Through this case, students may gain insight into both the challenges and significant opportunities in addressing the needs of low-income consumers in emerging markets.

Next Debapratim Purkayastha (ICMR) highlights the approach taken by Trevor Field and the PlayPumps in Southern Africa. In the 1980s, Trevor Field, a UK-born advertising professional who had emigrated to South Africa, had chanced upon a child's roundabout (merry-go-round) fitted with a pump that could pump water as it turned. Field worked with the inventor of this roundabout to bring about improvements in the system, and later developed the PlayPump Water System that was attached to a high-capacity storage tank and a tap. The four surfaces of the storage tank were used as billboards for commercial and public education/social messages (such as HIV/AIDS prevention). Revenue earned from the advertising helped maintain the water systems for up to a decade. Field co-founded a for-profit organization with a social mission, and Roundabout Outdoor Party Ltd. were instructed to install and maintain these PlayPumps in various parts of Southern Africa. By the end of 2007, more than 1,000 PlayPumps had been installed in four countries in Southern Africa. However, Field faced a number of challenges in scaling up further as he aimed to install 4,000 PlayPumps in ten African countries by 2010. The case examines (1) the difficulties of starting up a venture and managing its growth; (2) ways in which a social entrepreneur can build a sustainable business in developing and emerging markets—especially with respect to serving the base-of-the-pyramid population—and (3) challenges faced by social entrepreneurs in sustaining innovation and also in sustaining the enterprise financially. In the light of recent news on the PlayPump System[4] this case offers also an important learning opportunity to realize how narrow the line of success and failure can be.

In the final case Hadya Faheem and Debapratim Purkayastha outline a different solution in a very similar context. Their case "WaterHealth International: Providing Safe Drinking Water to the Bottom of the Pyramid Consumers" presents a for-profit social enterprise aiming to decrease the risk of water-borne diseases. The case introduces Ashok Gadgil, an Indian-born physicist at Lawrence Berkeley

---

4 See e.g. www.casefoundation.org/blog/painful-acknowledgement-coming-short.

National Laboratory, who came up with an innovative and breakthrough technology that disinfected water from harmful pathogens and microbes with the help of ultraviolet light. In 1996, Gadgil licensed the UVW technology to WHI, set up by Ghana-born entrepreneur and Johnson & Johnson veteran Tralance Addy. As the CEO of WHI, Addy played a crucial role in refining the business model. WHI helped arrange loans for communities to finance the installations of its water systems and the beneficiaries had to pay a nominal user fee to avail of the service. The company also offered a franchise model to entrepreneurs where they received a return on investment within 12 to 18 months. The proceeds were enough to cover the expense of the UVW system, cost of installations, and maintenance of the equipment. WHI was successful in attracting commercial financing for setting up its water systems. As of mid-2009, more than 600 WaterHealth Centers (WHCs) had been installed in many countries including India, the Philippines, and Ghana, providing safe water to more than one million people around the world. While experts appreciated WHI's efforts to provide potable supply of water to underprivileged communities in developing countries, they pointed out that certain aspects of its water systems and business model needed to be changed to make it more relevant to the target segment. The case explores these challenges as well as the issue of securing financial support for further growth.

Part V: Scaling, Legitimacy and Profit Challenges for Mission-Driven Organizations

The issue of sustainable mobility is of high actuality—in this context the case "Business Model Innovation by Better Place: A Green Ecosystem for the Mass Adoption of Electric Cars" provides an excellent learning opportunity. It discusses the innovative business model of Better Place, which proposed to offer transportation services to consumers through miles-per-month subscription plans on electric cars, with the cost of the car being subsidized based on the tenure of the plan. The case protagonist, Shai Agassi, started Better Place with the ambition of setting up an ecosystem—including a "smart grid" of charging stations and battery swapping facilities—for electric cars. These charging stations were to be powered by electricity generated from renewable sources to eliminate indirect emissions due to the operation of electric cars. Better Place also partnered with governments, parking lot operators, and companies to install charging stations. This ecosystem was expected to eliminate the barriers to the mass adoption of electric cars for personal transportation. It received support from the regulatory authorities in Israel, Denmark, Australia, Japan, and some states of the United States and Canada. However, it remained to be seen whether the proposed ecosystem and business model would encourage widespread adoption of electric vehicles, reduce the dependence on fossil fuels, and contain the levels of environmental pollution. While the company intended to make the world a better place by accelerating the transition to sustainable transportation, was its business model sustainable in the long run? The case provides detailed information on a highly relevant business model—and can definitely serve as a base for discussion in the classroom.

The case by Benoit Leleux (IMD, Lausanne) on Noir/Illuminati II (www.noir.dk) presents the dilemma of a mission-driven for-profit business that is struggling to defend its model towards the more traditional investor world as well as the more socially minded customers. The case focuses on Peter Ingwersen who founded the two companies: Noir designed and produced luxury clothing for women, while Illuminati II was set up to produce high-quality, fair-trade, organic cotton fabrics of the highest quality both for Noir and other leading fashion brands. Together, they should provide the basis for a totally new concept in fashion. Over the years, Peter had attended many fashion shows all over world and had become both aware and very concerned by the total lack of "social substance" of many of the major fashion companies. Conceptually Noir/Illuminati II would define socially responsible affordable luxury clothing, but would customers buy the story and would there be enough investors to support him? The case allows for an in-depth discussion of legitimacy and profitability in an industry that is known for the lack of social concern. How could one company make a credible difference, and what was needed for the business model to really do so?

While almost all cases describe a growth-related issue, our final case will highlight some of the strains and challenges faced by organizations called to grow. In "The ReUse People: Turning Scrap into Sales", William G. Powell and Charles Corbett (University of California at Los Angeles) present a social enterprise that specializes in deconstruction of buildings, with the aim of reusing as much of the materials as possible, hence keeping them out of landfill. While the main focus is based on the environmental aspects, the success soon calls for an expansion of the social services the organization should provide. The case presents an opportunity to discuss the problems of mission creep, and the growing demands on social enterprises to take on more problems. While the mission of The ReUse People is squarely environmental and the organization rather successful, it is increasingly called to provide social benefits by reaching out to community organizations and providing employment opportunities as well. In addition, the organization is facing a classical growth-related dilemma: should it grow organically, keeping most of the work in-house but hence limiting its growth rate, or should it "franchise" its deconstruction approach by certifying other companies in the deconstruction process? As such, this case presents a rich opportunity to discuss the curses of success and allows one to examine strategies to ensure sustainable success.

Energy consumption in construction and housing is, next to mobility, one of the key issues when it comes to environmental sustainability challenges. Rebecca Henn and Andy Hoffman from the University of Michigan's Ross School of Business provide a number of stunning facts on the challenges in the United States: in their case they quote statistics that, for example, the average size of a single-family home in the United States increased 2.5-fold from 1950 to 2006, while at the same time the average number of occupants per household decreased by more than 20%. The case outlines the state of both the housing industry and the green building industry in 2007. Students will learn about the environmental impacts of buildings, North American certification programs to build green buildings, and the critical elements of creating a sound business that capitalizes on the green building industry. The authors feature the case protagonist Steve Glenn, a successful internet startup entrepreneur, who returned to his love of architecture and commitment to sustainability by creating the company "Living Homes" (www.livinghomes.net) which would provide signature, green, prefabricated homes to the "cultural creative" market. The case can be used in environmental business, competitive strategy, entrepreneurship, marketing, or green building classes.

Part VI: Resources

The cases in this book offer only a glimpse of the radical transformations we are currently observing in business practices and the changing landscape of doing business on a finite planet. We would also wish to encourage scholars to produce new innovative cases reflecting new phenomena such as shared value business models, collaborative entrepreneurship and corporate approaches to dealing with risks and climate change. In Part VI we have therefore collected a number of resources for case writers which might be helpful not only for developing cases but also for marketing theses cases and bringing them into classrooms. Finally, we shed some light on the project behind this case collection and introduce the reader to the oikos Global Case Writing Competition concept and judging committee.

## Part II

Understanding the Nature of the Social Entrepreneur

2.1

The Meaning of Social Entrepreneurship[1,2]

J. Gregory Dees

Fuqua School of Business, Duke University

The idea of social entrepreneurship has struck a responsive chord. It is a phrase well suited to our times. It combines the passion of a social mission with an image of business-like discipline, innovation, and determination commonly associated with, for instance, the high-tech pioneers of Silicon Valley. The time is certainly ripe for entrepreneurial approaches to social problems. Many governmental and philanthropic efforts have fallen far short of our expectations. Major social sector institutions are often viewed as inefficient, ineffective, and unresponsive. Social entrepreneurs are needed to develop new models for a new century.

The language of social entrepreneurship may be new, but the phenomenon is not. We have always had social entrepreneurs, even if we did not call them that. They originally built many of the institutions we now take for granted. However, the new name is important in that it implies a blurring of sector boundaries. In addition to innovative not-for-profit ventures, social entrepreneurship can include social purpose business ventures, such as for-profit community development banks, and hybrid organizations mixing not-for-profit and for-profit elements,

1 Copyright © J. Gregory Dees. Originally published in 1998, revised in 2001. This version merely adds footnotes and makes minor textual corrections.
2 The Kauffman Foundation provided the funding for this chapter. The chapter benefited tremendously from comments and suggestions by the members of the Social Entrepreneurship Funders Working Group, particularly Suzanne Aisenberg, Morgan Binswanger, Jed Emerson, Jim Pitofsky, Tom Reis, and Steve Roling.

such as homeless shelters that start businesses to train and employ their residents. The new language helps to broaden the playing field. Social entrepreneurs look for the most effective methods of serving their social missions.

Though the concept of social entrepreneurship is gaining popularity, it means different things to different people. This can be confusing. Many associate social entrepreneurship exclusively with not-for-profit organizations starting for-profit or earned-income ventures. Others use it to describe anyone who starts a not-for-profit organization. Still others use it to refer to business owners who integrate social responsibility into their operations. What does 'social entrepreneurship' really mean? What does it take to be a social entrepreneur? To answer these questions, we should start by looking into the roots of the term 'entrepreneur'.

Origins of the Word 'Entrepreneur'

In common parlance, being an entrepreneur is associated with starting a business, but this is a very loose application of a term that has a rich history and a much more significant meaning. The term entrepreneur' originated in French economics as early as the 17th and 18th centuries. In French, it means someone who 'undertakes', not an 'undertaker' in the sense of a funeral director, but someone who undertakes a significant project or activity. More specifically, it came to be used to identify the venturesome individuals who stimulated economic progress by finding new and better ways of doing things. The French economist most commonly credited with giving the term this particular meaning is Jean Baptiste Say. Writing around the turn of the 19th century, Say put it this way: "The entrepreneur shifts economic resources out of an area of lower and into an area of higher productivity and greater yield".[3] Entrepreneurs create value.

In the 20th century, the economist most closely associated with the term was Joseph Schumpeter. He described entrepreneurs as the innovators who drive the 'creative–destructive' process of capitalism. In his words, "the function of entrepreneurs is to reform or revolutionize the pattern of production".[4] They can do this in many ways: "by exploiting an invention or, more generally, an untried technological possibility for producing a new commodity or producing an old one in a new way, by opening up a new source of supply of materials or a new outlet for products, by reorganizing an industry and so on".[5] Schumpeter's entrepreneurs are the change agents in the economy. By serving new markets or creating new ways of doing things, they move the economy forward. It is true that many of the

---

3 Quotation taken from Peter F. Drucker, *Innovation and Entrepreneurship: Practice and Principles* (New York: Harper & Row, 1985), p. 21.

4 Joseph Schumpeter, *Capitalism, Socialism, and Democracy* (New York: Harper & Row, 3rd edn, 1950), p. 132.

5 Ibid.

entrepreneurs that Say and Schumpeter have in mind serve their function by start-ing new, profit-seeking business ventures, but starting a business is not the essence of entrepreneurship. Though other economists may have used the term with vari-ous nuances, the Say–Schumpeter tradition that identifies entrepreneurs as the catalysts and innovators behind economic progress has served as the foundation for the contemporary use of this concept.

Current Theories of Entrepreneurship

Contemporary writers in management and business have presented a wide range of theories of entrepreneurship. Many of the leading thinkers remain true to the Say–Schumpeter tradition while offering variations on the theme. For instance, in his attempt to get at what is special about entrepreneurs, Peter Drucker starts with Say's definition, but amplifies it to focus on opportunity. Drucker does not require entrepreneurs to cause change, but sees them as exploiting the opportunities that change (in technology, consumer preferences, social norms, etc.) creates. He says, "this defines entrepreneur and entrepreneurship: the entrepreneur always searches for change, responds to it, and exploits it as an opportunity".[6] The notion of 'oppor-tunity' has come to be central to many current definitions of entrepreneurship. It is the way today's management theorists capture Say's notion of shifting resources to areas of higher yield. An opportunity, presumably, means an opportunity to create value in this way. Entrepreneurs have a mind-set that sees the possibilities rather than the problems created by change.

For Drucker, starting a business is neither necessary nor sufficient for entrepre-neurship. He explicitly comments, "Not every new small business is entrepreneur-ial or represents entrepreneurship".[7] He cites the example of a "husband and wife who open another delicatessen store or another Mexican restaurant in the Ameri-can suburb"[8] as a case in point. There is nothing especially innovative or change-oriented in this. The same would be true of new not-for-profit organizations. Not every new organization would be entrepreneurial. Drucker also makes it clear that entrepreneurship does not require a profit motive. Early in his book on *Innovation and Entrepreneurship*, Drucker asserts, "No better text for a *History of Entrepre-neurship* could be found than the creation of the modern university, and especially the modern American university".[9] He then explains what a major innovation this was at the time. Later in the book, he devotes a chapter to entrepreneurship in public service institutions.

6 Peter F. Drucker, *Innovation and Entrepreneurship: Practice and Principles* (New York: Harper & Row, 1985), p. 28.
7 *Innovation and Entrepreneurship*, p. 21.
8 *Innovation and Entrepreneurship*, p. 21.
9 *Innovation and Entrepreneurship*, p. 23.

Howard Stevenson, a leading theorist of entrepreneurship at Harvard Business School, added an element of resourcefulness to the opportunity-oriented definition based on research he conducted to determine what distinguishes entrepreneurial management from more common forms of 'administrative' management. After identifying several dimensions of difference, he suggests defining the heart of entrepreneurial management as "the pursuit of opportunity without regard to resources currently controlled".[10] He found that entrepreneurs not only see and pursue opportunities that elude administrative managers; entrepreneurs do not allow their own initial resource endowments to limit their options. To borrow a metaphor from Robert Browning, their reach exceeds their grasp. Entrepreneurs mobilize the resources of others to achieve their entrepreneurial objectives. Administrators allow their existing resources and their job descriptions to constrain their visions and actions. Once again, we have a definition of entrepreneurship that is not limited to business start-ups.

Differences between Business and Social Entrepreneurs

The ideas of Say, Schumpeter, Drucker, and Stevenson are attractive because they can be as easily applied in the social sector as the business sector. They describe a mind-set and a kind of behavior that can be manifest anywhere. In a world in which sector boundaries are blurring, this is an advantage. We should build our understanding of social entrepreneurship on this strong tradition of entrepreneurship theory and research. Social entrepreneurs are one species in the genus *entrepreneur*. They are entrepreneurs with a social mission. However, because of this mission, they face some distinctive challenges and any definition ought to reflect this.

For social entrepreneurs, the social mission is explicit and central. This obviously affects how social entrepreneurs perceive and assess opportunities. Mission-related impact becomes the central criterion, not wealth creation. Wealth is just a means to an end for social entrepreneurs. With business entrepreneurs, wealth creation is a way of measuring value creation. This is because business entrepreneurs are subject to market discipline, which determines in large part whether they are creating value. If they do not shift resources to more economically productive uses, they tend to be driven out of business.

Markets are not perfect, but over the long haul, they work reasonably well as a test of private value creation, specifically the creation of value for customers who are willing and able to pay. An entrepreneur's ability to attract resources (capital,

---

10 Howard H. Stevenson, "A Perspective on Entrepreneurship", in William A. Sahlman, Howard H. Stevenson, Michael Roberts and Amar Bhide (eds.), *The Entrepreneurial Venture* (Boston: Harvard Business School Press, 2nd edn, 1999), p. 10.

labor, equipment, etc.) in a competitive marketplace is a reasonably good indication that the venture represents a more productive use of these resources than the alternatives it is competing against. The logic is simple.

Entrepreneurs who can pay the most for resources are typically the ones who can put the resources to higher valued uses, as determined in the marketplace. Value is created in business when customers are willing to pay more than it costs to produce the good or service being sold. The profit (revenue minus costs) that a venture generates is a reasonably good indicator of the value it has created. If an entrepreneur cannot convince a sufficient number of customers to pay an adequate price to generate a profit, this is a strong indication that insufficient value is being created to justify this use of resources. A redeployment of the resources happens naturally because firms that fail to create value cannot purchase sufficient resources or raise capital. They go out of business. Firms that create the most economic value have the cash to attract the resources needed to grow.

Markets do not work as well for social entrepreneurs. In particular, markets do not do a good job of valuing social improvements, public goods and harms, and benefits for people who cannot afford to pay. These elements are often essential to social entrepreneurship. That is what makes it social entrepreneurship. As a result, it is much harder to determine whether a social entrepreneur is creating sufficient social value to justify the resources used in creating that value. The survival or growth of a social enterprise is not proof of its efficiency or effectiveness in improving social conditions. It is only a weak indicator, at best.

Social entrepreneurs operate in markets, but these markets often do not provide the right discipline. Many social-purpose organizations charge fees for some of their services. They also compete for donations, volunteers, and other kinds of support. But the discipline of these markets is frequently not closely aligned with the social entrepreneur's mission. It depends on who is paying the fees or providing the resources, what their motivations are, and how well they can assess the social value created by the venture. It is inherently difficult to measure social value creation. How much social value is created by reducing pollution in a given stream, by saving the spotted owl, or by providing companionship to the elderly? The calculations are not only hard but also contentious. Even when improvements can be measured, it is often difficult to attribute them to a specific intervention. Are the lower crime rates in an area due to the Block Watch, new policing techniques, or just a better economy? Even when improvements can be measured and attributed to a given intervention, social entrepreneurs often cannot capture the value they have created in an economic form to pay for the resources they use. Whom do they charge for cleaning the stream or running the Block Watch? How do they get everyone who benefits to pay? To offset this value-capture problem, social entrepreneurs rely on subsidies, donations, and volunteers, but this further muddies the waters of market discipline. The ability to attract these philanthropic resources may provide some indication of value creation in the eyes of the resource providers, but it is not a very reliable indicator. The psychic income people get from giving or volunteering is likely to be only loosely connected with actual social impact, if it is connected at all.

Defining Social Entrepreneurship

Any definition of social entrepreneurship should reflect the need for a substitute for the market discipline that works for business entrepreneurs. We cannot assume that market discipline will automatically weed out social ventures that are not effectively and efficiently utilizing resources. The following definition combines an emphasis on discipline and accountability with the notions of value creation taken from Say, innovation and change agents from Schumpeter, pursuit of opportunity from Drucker, and resourcefulness from Stevenson. In brief, this definition can be stated as follows.

Social entrepreneurs play the role of change agents in the social sector, by:

- Adopting a mission to create and sustain social value (not just private value),

- Recognizing and relentlessly pursuing new opportunities to serve that mission,

- Engaging in a process of continuous innovation, adaptation, and learning,

- Acting boldly without being limited by resources currently in hand, and

- Exhibiting heightened accountability to the constituencies served and for the outcomes created.

This is clearly an idealized definition. Social sector leaders will exemplify these characteristics in different ways and to different degrees. The closer a person gets to satisfying all these conditions, the more that person fits the model of a social entrepreneur. Those who are more innovative in their work and who create more significant social improvements will naturally be seen as more entrepreneurial. Those who are truly Schumpeterian will reform or revolutionize their industries. Each element in this brief definition deserves some further elaboration. Let's consider each one in turn.

Change agents in the social sector

Social entrepreneurs are reformers and revolutionaries, as described by Schumpeter, but with a social mission. They make fundamental changes in the way things are done in the social sector. Their visions are bold. They attack the underlying causes of problems, rather than simply treating symptoms. They often reduce needs rather than just meeting them. They seek to create systemic changes and sustainable improvements. Though they may act locally, their actions have the potential to stimulate global improvements in their chosen arenas, whether that is education, health care, economic development, the environment, the arts, or any other social field.

Adopting a mission to create and sustain social value

This is the core of what distinguishes social entrepreneurs from business entrepreneurs even from socially responsible businesses. For a social entrepreneur, the social mission is fundamental. This is a mission of social improvement that cannot be reduced to creating private benefits (financial returns or consumption benefits) for individuals. Making a profit, creating wealth, or serving the desires of customers may be part of the model, but these are means to a social end, not the end in itself. Profit is not the gauge of value creation; nor is customer satisfaction; social impact is the gauge. Social entrepreneurs look for a long-term social return on investment. Social entrepreneurs want more than a quick hit; they want to create lasting improvements. They think about sustaining the impact.

Recognizing and relentlessly pursuing new opportunities

Where others see problems, social entrepreneurs see opportunity. They are not simply driven by the perception of a social need or by their compassion, rather they have a vision of how to achieve improvement and they are determined to make their vision work. They are persistent. The models they develop and the approaches they take can, and often do, change, as the entrepreneurs learn about what works and what does not work. The key element is persistence combined with a willingness to make adjustments as one goes. Rather than giving up when an obstacle is encountered, entrepreneurs ask, 'How can we surmount this obstacle? How can we make this work?'

Engaging in a process of continuous innovation, adaptation, and learning

Entrepreneurs are innovative. They break new ground, develop new models, and pioneer new approaches. However, as Schumpeter notes, innovation can take many forms. It does not require inventing something wholly new; it can simply involve applying an existing idea in a new way or to a new situation. Entrepreneurs need not be inventors. They simply need to be creative in applying what others have invented. Their innovations may appear in how they structure their core programs or in how they assemble the resources and fund their work. On the funding side, social entrepreneurs look for innovative ways to ensure that their ventures will have access to resources as long as they are creating social value. This willingness to innovate is part of the *modus operandi* of entrepreneurs. It is not just a one-time burst of creativity. It is a continuous process of exploring, learning, and improving. Of course, with innovation comes uncertainty and risk of failure. Entrepreneurs tend to have a high tolerance for ambiguity and learn how to manage risks for themselves and others. They treat failure of a project as a learning experience, not a personal tragedy.

Acting boldly without being limited by resources currently in hand

Social entrepreneurs do not let their own limited resources keep them from pursuing their visions. They are skilled at doing more with less and at attracting resources from others. They use scarce resources efficiently, and they leverage their limited resources by drawing in partners and collaborating with others. They explore all resource options, from pure philanthropy to the commercial methods of the business sector. They are not bound by sector norms or traditions. They develop resource strategies that are likely to support and reinforce their social missions. They take calculated risks and manage the downside, so as to reduce the harm that will result from failure. They understand the risk tolerances of their stakeholders and use this to spread the risk to those who are better prepared to accept it.

Exhibiting a heightened sense of accountability to the constituencies served and for the outcomes created

Because market discipline does not automatically weed out inefficient or ineffective social ventures, social entrepreneurs take steps to ensure they are creating value. This means that they seek a sound understanding of the constituencies they are serving. They make sure they have correctly assessed the needs and values of the people they intend to serve and the communities in which they operate. In some cases, this requires close connections with those communities. They understand the expectations and values of their 'investors', including anyone who invests money, time, and/or expertise to help them. They seek to provide real social improvements to their beneficiaries and their communities, as well as attractive (social and/or financial) return to their investors. Creating a fit between investor values and community needs is an important part of the challenge. When feasible, social entrepreneurs create market-like feedback mechanisms to reinforce this accountability. They assess their progress in terms of social, financial, and managerial outcomes, not simply in terms of their size, outputs, or processes. They use this information to make course corrections as needed.

Social Entrepreneurs: A Rare Breed

Social entrepreneurship describes a set of behaviors that are exceptional. These behaviors should be encouraged and rewarded in those who have the capabilities and temperament for this kind of work. We could use many more of them.

Should everyone aspire to be a social entrepreneur? No. Not every social sector leader is well suited to being entrepreneurial. The same is true in business. Not every business leader is an entrepreneur in the sense that Say, Schumpeter, Drucker, and Stevenson had in mind. While we might wish for more entrepreneurial behavior in both sectors, society has a need for different leadership types and styles. Social entrepreneurs are one special breed of leader, and they should be recognized as such. This definition preserves their distinctive status and ensures that social entrepreneurship is not treated lightly. We need social entrepreneurs to help us find new avenues toward social improvement as we enter the next century.

Case 1

So You Want to Be a Social Entrepreneur?

Starting Out, Scaling Up and Staying Committed[1]

Michael Gordon
University of Michigan, USA

Introduction

Haven't we all wished for a few extra hours in the day—more time to spend with family, finish up a project we've been putting off, or get more accomplished at work? In the spring of 2009, Cynthia Koenig was in exactly that situation. She was working at a full-time job while pursuing an MBA and, in her spare time, running Wello, the nonprofit she had founded eighteen months earlier.

As Cynthia sat on the tarmac, waiting for her return flight from Delhi, India, to depart, she leaned back in her seat and closed her eyes. She had been out of the office field testing Wello's new product for the past two weeks, and work for her 'real' job, as well as her MBA courses, had no doubt piled up. As Wello grew, it was becoming more challenging to manage on a part-time, volunteer basis. But she couldn't afford to quit her job, and without a reliable source of funding, Wello couldn't afford to hire her.

A few months earlier, Cynthia had applied for an Echoing Green Fellowship. This support would give her mentorship from experts in the field, access to legal,

1 This case © Michael Gordon, University of Michigan.

tax and business planning resources, and seed capital, including the funding to work on the project full time. To Cynthia's surprise she continued to round after round, making the cut from 950, to 300, then 100 applications. "If I'm not selected for Echoing Green," she thought, "there's no way I can continue to work full-time, go to school, AND run Wello." She was expecting an email from Echoing Green any day with the results.

She let out an audible sigh. "Everything ok?" inquired her seatmate. "I'm just realizing that I took a two-week vacation from work to do more work!" said Cynthia. "You sound like me. Max Dreyer," he said, holding out his hand. "So what is it that brought you to this part of the world?" Cynthia smiled. "It's a long story," she said. "Well, then it's a good thing we have 18 hours," Max replied. Cynthia began by giving him some background on the problem Wello worked to address.

The Global Water Crisis

The global water crisis is a complex and pervasive problem. Unlike wars, natural disasters, and economic downturns, the global water crisis does not make headlines or rally concerted international action, despite the fact that more than 3 billion cases of illness and 5 million deaths—the majority children—can be attributed annually to unsafe water.[2]

Access to safe drinking water is critical to human health and well-being. For most of us, clean water comes with the twist of a faucet. However, more than a billion people lack access to clean drinking water. Many more must struggle to meet their daily needs for water—or pay high costs for this essential commodity.

As part of its Millennium Development Goals, the United Nations expressed its commitment by 2015 to reduce by half the proportion of people without "sustainable access to safe drinking water."[3] However, effective technological solutions to the water crisis are few and far between, and interventions carried out by governments, aid, and non-governmental organizations have failed to achieve widespread success. A population's inability to access a sufficient amount of clean water is due to a number of factors, including poor public policy, political and ethnic conflict, gender and other forms of inequality, and limited resources. To be more specific, water networks are aging, rapid population growth is increasing demand faster than networks can expand, many people live in water-stressed regions and water sources are being polluted by industrialization, agricultural runoff, and lack of sanitation

---

2 World Health Organization. 2007. *Combating waterborne disease at the household level.* www.who.int/water_sanitation_health/publications/combating_diseasepart1lowres. pdf, accessed October 23, 2009.

3 United Nations. *United Nations Millennium Declaration.* General Assembly Resolution 55/2. New York: 15 October 2009. www1.umn.edu/humanrts/instree/millennium.html, accessed 12 September 2009.

services. Compounding the problem is the fact that water quality, distribution, and access can vary dramatically, even within a single country. In short, there is no technological silver bullet or amount of monetary aid that would simultaneously address all of these underlying issues quickly, effectively, and universally.

The water crisis is most acute in developing countries, particularly in sub-Saharan Africa and South Asia. However, it isn't confined to a particular region of the world. A third of the Earth's population lives in water-stressed regions, such as the Middle East, North Africa and sub-Saharan Africa, and that number is expected to rise dramatically over the next two decades.

Water and Human Health

Water is fundamental for human health and survival. The United Nations Development Programme suggests that humans require 20 liters, or approximately 5 gallons, of water every day to maintain reasonable levels of personal health and domestic hygiene.[4] Factoring in bathing and laundry needs raises the personal threshold to about 13 gallons per day. But most of the 1.1–1.4 billion people who lack easy access to water only have access to 5 liters, an amount equal to a single flush of the toilet.[5] As a point of comparison, the average American uses approximately 100 gallons per day.[6]

Nearly 2 million people die each year from diseases associated with unclean water and poor hygiene. In addition, many infectious skin and eye diseases, such as scabies and trachoma, are related to poor hygiene and inadequate water supplies. Children are especially vulnerable. The lack of clean, safe drinking water is responsible for the deaths of an estimated 4,500 children per day.[7] Current research suggests that 88% of the deaths resulting from unclean water and poor hygiene could be avoided each year by improving access to safe drinking water, sanitation and hygiene.[8]

Tens of millions of people suffer from chronic poor health as a result of dehydration or illnesses that result from drinking contaminated water. Economic opportunities are routinely lost when ill health strikes. Children who are in poor health have lower cognitive potential, miss school more frequently, and are more likely to

4 United Nations Development Report (UNDP). *Human Development Report 2006. Beyond Scarcity: Power, Poverty and the Global Water Crisis.*

5 Ibid.

6 US Geological Survey. *Water Use at Home.* ga.water.usgs.gov/edu/qahome.html, accessed 26 October 2009.

7 UNICEF/WHO. *Water for Life. Making It Happen,* 2005.

8 World Health Organization. *Combating waterborne disease at the household level.* 2007. www.who.int/water_sanitation_health/publications/combating_diseasepart1lowres. pdf, accessed 23 October 2009.

drop out early. For example, in India, the economic burden that results from lack of access to clean water is estimated at US$600 million per year.[9]

Social norms in most parts of the world dictate that women and girls are responsible for water collection, a task that takes African women approximately 8 hours of their time per day. In the dry season, water is scarcer, and women and young girls trek further from their homes to retrieve water for their families.[10] Collecting water often means waiting in long lines at a water source, and making multiple trips. For the sick and elderly, it's a nearly impossible task. Due to the large time burden associated with this daily chore, women are prevented from maintaining their households or earning additional income. Water collection also takes a physical toll, damaging the head, neck, and spine over time, often leading to dangerous complications during pregnancy and childbirth, and stunting children's growth.[11] The daily task of water collection dominates children's lives and leaves them little time for school or play.

The United Nations considers universal access to clean water a basic human right, and an essential step towards improving living standards worldwide.[12] Water-poor communities are typically economically poor as well, their residents trapped in an ongoing cycle of poverty. Access to clean water is a necessary first step to enable families to achieve a better standard of living. Research shows that when women have extra time, they choose to spend it on activities that boost family income and well-being. In addition, women with even a few years of basic education have been shown to have smaller, healthier families, are more likely to be able to work their way out of poverty, and are more likely to send their own children to school. Female education is accepted as an effective strategy to break the cycle of poverty.

Wello

Wello manufactures and distributes a product that significantly reduces the physical and time burdens associated with traditional water collection. This tool, known as a 'WaterWheel,' makes it possible to collect 20 gallons of water—approximately four times the amount possible using traditional methods—in less time and much more easily.

9 Kassalow, J.S. (2001) *Why health is important to US foreign policy*. Council on Foreign Relations and Milbank Memorial Fund, New York, NY.

10 United Nations Department of Economic and Social Affairs. 2004. "A Gender Perspective on Water Resources and Sanitation." www.un.org/esa/sustdev/csd/csd13/documents/bground_2.pdf, accessed October 23, 2009.

11 Ibid.

12 United Nations Development Report (UNDP). 2006. *Human Development Report 2006. Beyond Scarcity: Power, Poverty and the Global Water Crisis.*

The WaterWheel is manufactured from a high-quality, durable plastic and has a large screw cap, which allows users to thoroughly clean its interior. WaterWheels are a major improvement on the toxic, repurposed fuel containers ('jerry cans') that are typically used to collect water. One WaterWheel carries enough water to meet the basic needs of four people per day. Access to sufficient amounts of water enables people to practice better hygiene and stay healthy.

Back at 19,000 feet, Max was all ears—he recognized a good business opportunity when he heard one. "How did you get involved with this in the first place?" he wondered.

Cynthia founded Wello in January 2008. However, her involvement actually began nine months earlier, when she participated in a University of Michigan course that focused on emerging market economies, and included a trip to South Africa.

In the spring of 2007, Cynthia completed a Master's degree in environmental studies. A post-graduation fellowship gave her the opportunity to spend several months in South Africa, where she lived in a rural community, and learned about the challenges people faced on a daily basis. For example, due to the devastating impact of HIV/AIDS, it was not uncommon for a family to adopt one or more orphans, or for grandparents to take responsibility for raising their grandchildren. Economic opportunities were few and far between. With an unemployment rate hovering around 80%, many families survived on the pension of a single family member. In many cases, one or both parents would migrate to urban centers for work for months at a time, leaving their children behind in the care of friends or relatives. Rural areas, like the one Cynthia lived in, often lacked basic services, like health care, higher education, electricity and physical infrastructure.

The community Cynthia lived in was typical of rural South African communities—only a few water wells served the population, so access to clean water was very limited. Each family had one day per week when it could visit the tap—provided it was in working condition. Typically, one child from the family would line up with his or her containers early in the morning, and the other siblings and their mother would arrive later in the day to carry the containers home. On non-tap days, women and children collected water from open water sources that were shared with animals and often contaminated. During the dry season, surface water was harder to find, and even the wells ran dry as the water table dropped.

It was in South Africa that Cynthia first learned about the concept of 'rolling water.' A handful of private and nonprofit organizations manufacture and distribute 10–25 gallon drums that literally roll water as an alternative to carrying smaller quantities on the head. She was immediately intrigued.

Conventional wisdom led her to believe that people needed products and services to disinfect their water. Certainly this was the approach taken by the vast majority of the organizations focused on global water issues. However, people in South Africa repeatedly told her that they knew how to make their water safe to drink; what they wanted was more water. Cynthia saw the evidence of this first-hand—even with multiple family members collecting water, it was difficult to provide five gallons per person each day, the UN minimum for maintaining a basic level of health. Furthermore, water collection is a long and strenuous process, one that kept children out of school and prevented women from carrying out other household or income-generating activities.

"By the time I left South Africa," Cynthia explained, "I was convinced that the concept of rolling water had the potential to make a positive impact on a global scale. However, existing efforts to distribute such tools were very localized and donor-dependent. I had a few ideas about what a business model should look like for this type of product, but not much confidence to back up my vision."

"I fell back on skills I already had in order to get started. Once I returned to the US, I started the lengthy process to establish a 501c3 nonprofit organization that could offer tax exemptions for charitable contributions from individuals or foundations. I wasn't sure that nonprofit status was the right choice, but it offered the best access to patient capital."

"But what was your real motivation for getting involved?" asked Max. "From what you've told me, it seems as though you didn't have a particular interest in water issues before you launched your organization."

"True," said Cynthia. "For the past ten years, I've worked in the field of sustainable development with a focus on environmental sustainability. But I'm fortunate to have had the opportunity to travel widely, and have spent long periods of time living and working in rural communities where conveniences like water and electricity were not always readily available. As a result, I know what it means to wake before sunrise, walk to the nearest water source (in Mexico, a 25-foot deep *cenote*; in Guatemala, a murky pool of water with a thick film of algae and family of resident crocodiles), and trudge home trying not to spill the entire contents of a 5-gallon bucket before I arrived. But my experiences of these hardships were short-lived—I was always able to return to my comfortable life where water conveniently flows from the tap and opportunities abound. I can only imagine what it's like to collect water every day. I've never had to wonder where my next meal will come from, or been told that my dreams were unattainable simply because of my gender."

"I love hearing about how people turn issues they're passionate about into careers," said Max.

"Well, not exactly," replied Cynthia. "My fellowship only provided a stipend for a few months. When I got back to the US, I started working full-time, and enrolled in an MBA program a few months later."

"It sounds like there were a lot of moving pieces to deal with when you started out—no funding source, no business plan and probably not much free time to work on this! Why did you decide to launch Wello when you did?" asked Max.

"There were a few reasons," explained Cynthia. "Launching Wello was a way for me to stay focused and motivated. It was also a result of advice I had been given by a professor who teaches a course on social entrepreneurship at my university. As my graduation neared, I asked him if he knew of any job opportunities in the field. I expected him to help me brainstorm a list of potential employers. Instead, he encouraged me to follow my north star, and work to address an issue I really cared about. At the time, I didn't think it was very helpful advice. Although I cared about a lot of issues, I didn't feel as though I had the solutions to any of them. In fact, I realized later, when I launched Wello, how practical this advice was. No one launches a venture with a perfect concept—most of the time, it's just an idea, and little by little, you do what it takes to keep moving it forward and developing it."

"I think the ability to stay committed in the start-up phase is a good test of the viability of the business. Creativity, adaptability and patience are important skills early on. Of course, this changes—you can't stay patient for too long, otherwise you never make any progress! Getting started was the hardest part for me—Wello didn't have any funding—or even any real funding prospects. On top of all this, I was planning to launch operations in India, though work and school commitments meant that I would have to remain in the US for the next two years. In order to cover my travel expenses and our state filing fees, I took advantage of a promotion my bank was running—$250 for each new account you opened … I opened several."

Max nodded. "I'm sold. It sounds like the need for a product like the WaterWheel exists. But where do you get the funds to run the organization?"

Fundraising

Cynthia's fundraising efforts started out small—and snowballed into a much larger project very quickly. Initially, she envisioned raising some funds to improve the living conditions in water-scarce communities. However, having worked for a nonprofit, she knew that grants could be far more lucrative than individual donations—and both were more easily achieved by incorporating as a 501c3. So, she started the tedious, months-long process of incorporating and applying for tax-exempt status with the federal government.

But before Cynthia felt comfortable launching a fundraising campaign, she felt that it was important for the fledgling organization to look professional. A web presence was a necessity. But with zero web design skills, and exactly that much money in the bank, Cynthia was at a loss. In an attempt to grow the fledgling organization she asked people to support Wello by donating their time and talents instead of cash. To her surprise, responses came pouring in. However, Cynthia quickly learned that pro bono support, although always well-intentioned, sometimes created more problems than it solved. For example, she found that volunteers came and went, sometimes even in the middle of a project. Finally, after a few false starts, she was introduced to FreeWorld Media, an Atlanta-based design and marketing firm that took on the task of rebranding and a complete website redesign.

A few months into the website design process, Cynthia received an unusual email from Google. The message said they were about to celebrate their tenth birthday by holding a competition for world-changing ideas. They had learned about Wello and wanted to feature it when announcing the competition.

Cynthia assumed the email was spam, but curiosity eventually got the better of her. She followed up, and Google confirmed that, yes, they were holding a competition; and, yes, they wanted to use Wello as a way of illustrating the type of world-changing ideas they were seeking. With only a few weeks until Google's announcement of Project 10^100, the FreeWorld team kicked into high gear. The new website site went live with just hours to spare. Thanks to mentions in Google's press release, on CNN, and other news coverage, inquiries and donations began to roll in.

"What a great stroke of luck," exclaimed Max. "That's the kind of thing a new business dreams about! But—correct me if I'm wrong—it sounds like you were still formalizing your business plan. When did you finally sit down and formalize the plan in writing?"

Business Evolution

Cynthia laughed. "Actually, during the first two years, things changed so quickly that I couldn't keep up. Our business plan was only written recently! Putting it on paper for the first time was intimidating, but in retrospect, I wish I had started even earlier, because it really pushed me to answer tough questions and further develop and fine-tune our strategy."

The original concept for Wello was that it would purchase water transport tools from existing manufacturers, then work with community-based organizations to educate end users to use the tools to generate revenue. However, exorbitant shipping costs and already high price points for these products made Cynthia question the viability of this model. It simply wasn't scalable.

"In most parts of the developing world, recycling and trash collection isn't available. As a result, there is a tremendous amount of waste everywhere. Plastic bottles, like the kind soft drinks come in, are especially prevalent. People often reuse them several times, but once cracked or broken, they ended up littering the streets."

Cynthia continued: "I had this crazy idea that we could have people gather up this trash, then bring it to a mobile manufacturing unit where we would mold a WaterWheel for them on the spot. "As it turns out, it isn't possible to re-engineer soda bottles in this way, but the idea of manufacturing and distributing a new water transport tool stuck with her.

"People all over the world were writing to me to ask about how they could get water transport tools," said Cynthia. "I thought that if we could make an affordable, high-quality product available globally, we could meet this need and have a tremendous impact on the health and well-being of millions of girls and women and others in their communities."

Max scratched his head. "You said you were pursuing an MBA, but this sounds very technical. Where is the engineering expertise coming from?" he asked.

Cynthia admitted that she had no engineering experience. In addition, she had little experience to prepare her for a career as an entrepreneur. She majored in Anthropology and Environmental Studies as an undergraduate, and earned an MS in Natural Resources Management, with a focus on community-based conservation strategies. Rather than let this get in her way, she recruited a team of volunteers to optimize the design of the WaterWheel. "In our case, the business model came first, and guided the design for the product. Key considerations included affordability, durability, and quality," explained Cynthia. "Ultimately, my lack of engineering expertise was actually a good thing, because it meant that I often asked silly questions that the designers weren't asking themselves. So while I often drove the designers crazy by insisting on things that weren't technically possible, there were a few instances where my insistence led to great breakthroughs."

"It sounds like you're spending a lot of time on this," exclaimed Max. "How do you manage to work AND run Wello?"

Time Management

"Its true, I don't have much free time …" said Cynthia. The fact that she had a full-time job and schoolwork to focus on meant that she had to be very reactive, focusing primarily on whatever was demanding her attention at the moment.

"For example, the purpose of this trip was to coordinate logistics on behalf of our operations team. We were conducting willingness-to-pay studies, reaching out to potential partners and following up on manufacturing leads.

In the weeks leading up to the trip, Cynthia spent more and more time on Wello-related projects: organizing travel plans and logistics, lobbying airlines for free tickets, and running a fundraising campaign to cover the remaining costs.

"Since I don't have much time, I try to focus on things with the most potential. That said, we've only been speaking about the opportunities I've pursued that have worked out—for each lead that actually turns into something, there are probably five dead ends that suck up a lot of time and never materialize. There are also times when I have to turn down projects I'd love to pursue, but I simply don't have the time to invest in something without a clear payback. I'm always thinking about funding. It takes a long time to research funders, find a good fit, develop a relationship and present a proposal. That's why fellowships offered by organizations like Draper Richards and Echoing Green are so attractive. With a fellowship, I'll have the financial support to focus completely on Wello, and begin to work more strategically on scaling up," explained Cynthia. "Now, with the chance for funding so close, it seems unthinkable to continue running the organization as I have been, focusing my attention on it in fits and starts, reacting to opportunities rather than seeking them out."

"Something I realized recently is that so much of my work takes place in a vacuum—I don't meet many other social entrepreneurs, so I don't often have the chance to bounce ideas off people who are struggling with similar issues. Websites like Ashoka's Changemakers, Skoll's Social Edge and Change.org are great places to learn about different issues and approaches, but for me, making connections with other people is so much more beneficial. In 2009, I was a StartingBloc Fellow, and it was really exciting to meet other social entrepreneurs—for me, that made the whole community much more real. The experience opened my eyes to how much energy there is in the social enterprise space, and now I'm always looking out for experiences like that."

"I have to give you credit," said Max. "I can't think of too many people who would volunteer to run a business in their spare time. How much time do you spend on this?"

"It really varies. Probably an average of twenty-five hours—though I've definitely had more than a few forty-hour weeks," said Cynthia. "But honestly, seeing how much of a difference WaterWheels make in people's lives really does make it all worthwhile. A WaterWheel symbolizes innovation and optimism, the hope for an easier, healthier, better life."

Developing a Scalable Business Model

"You've put a lot of work into developing a brand, creating awareness, and developing the product," said Max. "But tell me, what is the market like for something like this?"

"It's a challenge," said Cynthia. "The target market for the WaterWheel—people living on less than $2 per day in developing nations—can't afford expensive products. It's crucial that any investment they make pay for itself in a few months. The WaterWheel saves time and energy, but does it generate sufficient income to make it a worthwhile investment? Lately, I've been thinking more and more about income-generation ... what if we worked with micro-entrepreneurs who used the WaterWheel to sell clean water?" In fact, people in many parts of the world purchase water from vendors. A 2007 report by the World Resources Institute measured the Base of the Pyramid[13] water market in several countries across Africa, Latin America, Asia and Eastern Europe and the Caribbean. They estimated the water market across these five regions to be US$20 billion, which accounts for the spending of 3.96 billion people.[14]

---

13 The term "base of the pyramid" (or BoP) refers to the four billion people who live on less than $2 per day, typically in developing countries.

14 World Resources Institute. 2007. "Water: The Next 4 Billion." www.wri.org/publication/the-next-4-billion, accessed 12 October, 2009

"Now this is getting really interesting," said Max. "It sounds like there's a real market for the WaterWheel. You mentioned that your motivation was to expand the availability of the product. Have you been able to make progress in that area?"

"Yes! The plan is to manufacture the WaterWheel in the countries where we plan to distribute in order to create local jobs and minimize shipping costs as much as possible," explained Cynthia.

By pairing a simple product design with an innovative business model, Wello aims to improve global access to water and reduce the physical and time burdens of water collection. However, in order to reach the greatest number of people, it was clear that Wello had to think creatively about addressing affordability.

Wello's starting point is the Business in a Barrel strategy, which empowers end-users to use the WaterWheel as an income-generating tool. For example, a water entrepreneur might use the WaterWheel to collect large quantities of clean water and sell smaller amounts to her neighbors, making a small profit on each trip. Conservative estimates suggest that a water entrepreneur could easily earn more than $80 a month, which represents a 33% increase over the average income of people living on approximately $2 per day.

Wello's goal is for the WaterWheel to pay for itself in the short term, making it accessible to the people who are most in need of it, but have the least ability to pay. In the long term, it can provide them with a sustainable income while improving their health as well as the health of their communities. An added benefit of the WaterWheel is that it has the potential to carry much more than water—it can carry all kinds of goods to and from market. A simple, inexpensive modification to the design could add refrigeration, which would allow farmers to sell milk at better prices, since they wouldn't have to sell at the cheapest price once they got to market for fear of the milk going bad. A WaterWheel would also enable a micro-entrepreneur to purchase goods like kerosene, rice, or gasoline in bulk (at cheaper prices), then easily transport the load back to his or her village where a small profit could be made on each transaction.

The Business in a Barrel strategy addresses one aspect of affordability. However, in order to produce a product that retails at a price point well under the average microloan, local production is key. Wello plans to fill large orders by contracting with manufacturers located as close as possible to the delivery point. For smaller orders and direct sales to end users, Wello is developing an innovative mobile manufacturing strategy. A 40-foot rail container will be modified into a self-contained manufacturing unit that contains the tools necessary to manufacture the Water-Wheels. This significantly reduces the price for the end-user by eliminating the high cost of shipping individual units. "At $34 per WaterWheel, this strategy enables us to cut manufacturing costs significantly," explained Cynthia. "The idea is to ultimately work with local franchisees who can further penetrate our target markets." Because the mobile manufacturing unit can be easily transported by rail, manufacturing can move to new locations according to regional demand.

Cynthia glanced at her watch. "I can't believe three hours have gone by!" she exclaimed. "I should get some sleep—I'm heading in to work as soon as we land. It was nice chatting with you."

Max nodded. "Likewise. Thanks for telling me your story—I should have mentioned this at the start, but I work for a social venture capital firm, and we're always looking for new investment opportunities." He handed Cynthia his card. "Stay in touch."

Fifteen hours later, Cynthia turned on her smartphone in the Detroit airport. She quickly scanned her inbox, looking for a specific message. Her heart skipped a beat when she saw the words, 'Echoing Green.' Would it be good news? What would she do it if wasn't?

Teaching notes for this case are available from Greenleaf Publishing. These are free of charge and are available only to teaching staff. They can be requested by going to:

www.greenleaf-publishing.com/oikos2_notes

Case 2
Gram Vikas[1, 2, 3]

Imran Chowdhury
ESSEC Business School

Filipe Santos
INSEAD, France

Case A: Social Entrepreneurship in Rural India

Scene 1: 8:30am, Monday, March 16, 2009: Prologue

The scene is set on the head office campus of Gram Vikas, an NGO involved in rural development projects in the Indian state of Orissa. The campus is located in Mohuda, a village in Orissa's Ganjam District (see Appendix).

1 Copyright © 2010 INSEAD.
2 This case was written by Imran Chowdhury, PhD Candidate at ESSEC Business School, and Filipe Santos, Associate Professor and Director of the Maag International Centre for Entrepreneurship at INSEAD. It is intended to be used as a basis for class discussion rather than to illustrate either effective or ineffective handling of an administrative situation.
3 We gratefully acknowledge the editorial support of Charlotte Butler, Senior Researcher at INSEAD. We are thankful for funding provided by the INSEAD R&D Committee and the APAX Social Entrepreneurship Fund. The research project underlying this case is being developed in partnership with the Schwab Foundation for Social Entrepreneurship. The INSEAD Social Entrepreneurship Initiative is housed within and supported by the Social Innovation Centre and the Maag International Centre for Entrepreneurship.

A man approaches the main office entrance. He is Gobardhan Sen. He is obviously unsure about his surroundings, and fiddles nervously with his watch as he waits for someone.

Gobardhan Sen is indeed feeling nervous. An MBA graduate of the famed Indian Institute of Management–Ahmedabad, he has recently made the career shift that has brought him to Gram Vikas. And today is his first day in this new job.

Ever since his time as an economics student in Calcutta, Gobardhan had been drawn to the idea of working in the field of rural development. However, after his MBA he had followed the path his family expected and got a good job with an IT services outsourcing provider to Western companies. But then the worldwide economic crisis struck and suddenly his future looked less secure. Rather than wait to be fired, as many of his fellow junior executives had been, Gobardhan decided to seize the opportunity to change direction and quit his job. Shortly after, a chance conversation with a former classmate at a party led him to Gram Vikas, a social organisation focused on developing water and sanitation projects in rural villages. Following a meeting with Joe Madiath, the charismatic (and persuasive) Executive Director, Gobardhan agreed to join Gram Vikas as Expansion Manager.

He arrived in Mohuda on Friday and spent the weekend getting used to life on a rural campus (Exhibit 1). Living in Mohuda was completely different from the life he left behind in the rich, busy city of Hyderabad. While he had everything he needed—food, a nice (if basic) apartment and some new friends—it was strange not to have 24-hour access to the internet, digital TV or to be able to eat in expensive restaurants. "Oh well … it's easy to adjust if you really believe in what you're doing," Gobardhan told himself.

Now it is Monday, his first real day at work. He is due to have breakfast with Abhimaniu Mohanty, one of Gram Vikas' most effective field managers. Gobardhan hopes to learn a lot about the organisation from him, and in particular get an idea of how exactly the field programmes work. After all, how can he help the organisation expand if he doesn't understand what he is trying to expand?

At that moment another man walks towards the main office, stops, looks at Gobardhan with a puzzled face and then smiles. He approaches holding out his hand. He is Abhimaniu Mohanty.

Abhimaniu Mohanty is a happy man, doing a job he loves. Every morning he wakes up eager to get to work. It will be a long day like so many others, but that doesn't matter to him. Today is no different. He has to visit a village that he is sure will sign up with Gram Vikas. He can't wait to have breakfast and get out on the road again. He walks towards the main building.

And then he remembers: there is a new recruit to meet and begin training. Abhimaniu has heard that the newcomer is a native of Calcutta, the capital of West Bengal, and a graduate of several prestigious schools. "An educated man for sure, but with no experience of village life," as a colleague told Abhimaniu. How will such

Exhibit 1 **Picture of Gram Vikas Campus Main Entrance**

Source: Imran Chowdhury (2009)

Exhibit 2 **Photo of Main Office**

Source: Imran Chowdhury (2009)

a man adapt to doing this kind of work and to this way of life? Well, hopefully the training will be done quickly so he can make his field visit in the afternoon. He smiles and walks towards the young man standing nervously by the door.

Scene 2: 9:15am: The Initiation

After breakfast, the two men walk to the main office (Exhibit 2). They enter a workshop room on the second floor. It is a big room, but they are alone. Abhimaniu turns on an old projector and the first slide comes up on the screen. It is headed 'Gram Vikas—the early years'.

Abhimaniu begins: So, Gobardhan, I think the best introduction would be to go through the history of Gram Vikas. I know you are keen to learn about our fieldwork, but you can't really understand that until you know where the organisation has come from—where its roots lie.

Gobardhan: Sure, I am here to listen and learn. All of this is new to me ...

Abhimaniu: OK, we start almost 30 years ago in 1971. Our founder, Shri Joe Madiath, was actually a university student in Chennai then, but he took time off to lead a group of volunteers up here to Orissa to help deal with a refugee crisis. At that time, Bangladesh was fighting for its independence from West Pakistan. Refugees were flowing into India to get away from the fighting and, at the same time, a huge cyclone hit Orissa and the Western part of the Bay of Bengal. Those two events created a huge humanitarian crisis. Over a million people were made homeless from the cyclone alone.

So as you see, Gram Vikas' roots were in the voluntary movement that sprang up in India in the 1960s and 1970s. Many students became social volunteers then and Joe led a group called the Young Students Movement for Development (YSMD) which came to Orissa. The group was highly motivated by the idea of social equity and wanted to do something for the countryside. In fact they were following the dream of the 1947 Indian independence movement when the slogan was 'Go back to the villages'. And that was what they did.

After the 1971 crisis was over, some of the volunteers, including Joe, decided to stay in Orissa and help with rural development activities in the state. For the next few years they experimented with various activities to help the poor, mostly in irrigation technology and agriculture. However, they felt dissatisfied because the underlying social conditions that kept the people poor remained unchanged. In the course of their work they spoke to all kinds of people throughout the state (villagers, government officials, business people), and came to realise that one of the major, unaddressed needs was the condition of the so-called adavasi, or tribal people of Orissa. So when the district authorities here in Ganjam invited Joe's group to set up a dairy co-operative for the tribal people, they accepted. Soon afterwards, in January 1979, they officially set up as a separate organisation, Gram Vikas. And

Gram Vikas, as I'm sure you know, means 'village development' in both Hindi and Oriya, the local language in Orissa.

Gobardhan: So essentially Gram Vikas was founded to help tribal people. I guess Joe thought that the organisation would work on water and sanitation activities within a smaller population, before expanding to serve a larger group across the whole state?

Abhimaniu: Well, that would seem the natural progression but it's not how it worked out. Social entrepreneurs tend to focus on the most pressing problems of the populations they serve. So Gram Vikas at first focused on two major problems: alcoholism and the high levels of indebtedness among the tribal families. These problems were often interlinked, and Gram Vikas' staff members discovered that a health focus was useful as an entry point. They realised that over 95% of all tribal assets and property were mortgaged or used to pay landlords, liquor merchants and moneylenders. Even people were mortgaged! Often when tribal members had finished paying off their debt, their young sons and daughters were bound to work for these people for years and years.

So tackling these problems took up the first few years of the organisation's life. Then after a period of initial success in reducing alcoholism and indebtedness, yet another opportunity came up. The government of Orissa was set on bringing energy to the villages. Not electricity, which is quite expensive. Instead their goal was to develop a series of biogas projects as demonstrations. If these proved successful, they would scale up to the entire state. Coincidentally, Gram Vikas already had experience with biogas. We had a demonstration farm here in Mohuda and our staff members had built a biogas generator to power it, since there was no electricity. The plant converted cow dung and water mixture into gas—clean fuel—and staff used it for their own cooking and lighting needs. Interestingly, the plant also became a model for local people in the surrounding area. People from other villages would flock to see it when they heard about the plant. They asked us: "What is this? Why don't you come and do this in our villages?"

The Orissa state government knew it didn't have enough expertise in biogas and there were very few other organisations in the state with any experience, so Gram Vikas was lucky. Because of its experience, the Orissa government asked Gram Vikas to do the initial demonstration projects for the state. This was a critical moment in the life of Gram Vikas because until then we had not worked with the government on any large projects. But Joe and the other leaders had an ambitious vision and, even though they were a small team, they took up the challenge. They made an intensive drive to build biogas generators throughout the state, training a lot of people as the project progressed because it required a different skill set from the one that even most masons possessed. So as a result, one big stream of activity within Gram Vikas became biogas—highly technical projects. And then there was another stream that concentrated on tribal projects, including education, health, and so on. That is how the organisation moved into biogas a few years after its creation. For about a decade biogas was our main activity.

Gobardhan: This is fascinating … But why did Gram Vikas move into something outside its core focus on tribal people? We seemed to be very successful with the tribal work. We were making an impact on alcoholism and indebtedness. Why change focus?

Abhimaniu: You must understand that the perception of NGOs [non-governmental organisations] in India at that time was that they were small-time players in a world of huge challenges. The general feeling was that they showed "islands of excellence" but on a large scale were ineffective. And even if NGOs could implement on a large scale, government officials and business leaders believed they were a more expensive option than if government or private-sector agencies developed the project.

When Joe heard this he was determined that Gram Vikas would prove them wrong. Biogas presented the perfect opportunity. We had been invited in by the government and we knew the technology. Thus Gram Vikas began recruiting people and developing biogas projects across Orissa. Ultimately, with about 15% of the funds spent on biogas projects in Orissa we built 85% of all the plants in the state, while the government with 85% of the funds built 15% of the plants. So we went ahead doing this for about a decade until, at a certain point, the leadership realised that Gram Vikas had become an excellent implementing agency with the ability to scale up: if we wanted to prove an NGO could scale up these biogas projects effectively, we had done it. At this point, we began to wonder whether we would implement biogas all our life—or was there something else that we should do.

In the meantime, we lobbied the government to give out an incentive of as much as 500 rupees to anybody who would set up a biogas project and guarantee that it would work for at least five years. When the government agreed to implement this scheme, we felt we had reached our final goal. We went to our colleagues, employees and workers and said: "Well there is a government biogas programme now. You can remain with Gram Vikas but you will make much more money if two or three of you get together and go out and build some biogas units. Since we have some influence with the government, we can locate areas where you can implement the projects. You construct these biogas plants and you'll earn pretty good money." Initially, there were very few people willing to take the offer. So we gave biogas employees an option: those who went out would be on leave for two years—meaning no salary but the possibility of returning after that time. If someone did come back, they re-entered the organisation at the same level they had left. If they did not return after two years then they were on their own. Between 1992-93 about 600 people left to work on biogas projects, and only about six or seven ultimately returned.

Gobardhan: So in effect Gram Vikas spun off the biogas programme to its own employees! But … (*he looks confused*) that doesn't seem to make a lot of sense. It was your core activity!

Abhimaniu: That is absolutely true. By the time we decided to phase out the biogas programme we were working in about 6,000 villages and there was a general sense that Gram Vikas should continue to work in these villages. Our credibility was good, people wanted us, we were delivering results. So we thought long and hard before making a final decision.

Gobardhan: I don't get it. According to everything I have been taught, that is a flawed strategy! Imagine if my former company leaders said to their employees: "Here are all these profitable contracts awarded to us. Now you take them, go out and create little businesses and take the profits yourselves. And if it doesn't work we'll take you back if you wish." A manager needs to protect a company's core business—not give it away …

Abhimaniu: You really don't get it, do you? Look, you need to understand the mindset of social entrepreneurs, how they think about problems in society and their own role. Their aim is not to create a large organisation and capture value from its activities. Their aim is to identify a pressing and neglected societal problem which, if solved, can lead to many positive spill-overs for society. Then they devise a sustainable solution to the problem, demonstrate that it can be done and scale it up. This proves to society, to governments and large companies that it is an important problem that needs to be tackled, and that there are cost-effective solutions to it. Once social entrepreneurs achieve this aim, their goal is to deliver the solution to society for wider adoption and then refocus on the next neglected problem.

The thinking of Joe and other senior managers was that Gram Vikas' work in the biogas programme was done. It was successful; a solution was now widespread and subsidized by the government. It was time to move on since this problem was no longer neglected by society. We could have more impact working on other, more pressing areas.

Gobardhan: I think I am starting to get it … but it is so different from the companies I worked at, and from everything I learned in business school. The mantra was that business is all about focusing your efforts on a profitable set of activities, becoming the best in the world at doing it and then protecting what you have and using it to build the next set of advantages. You just don't go out and give your advantage away … But I see that here there is a direct goal of having an impact on society, which doesn't exist in the same way in for-profit firms.

Abhimaniu: Exactly! In addition, the biogas project did not allow Gram Vikas to work with the really exploited section of the rural population —the extreme poor. Our goal has always been about achieving social equality. The question Gram Vikas' leadership asked was: how do we address, on a larger scale, the issue of inequality in India? We did a study in 100 villages to find out what was the most pressing problem faced by rural people in Orissa. We found that it was the lack of proper sanitation facilities. When we looked at morbidity in rural areas we found that over

80% of diseases in rural areas were caused by the poor quality of the water. When we looked further, we found that this poor quality was due to our abysmal attitude to the disposal of human waste: raw human waste was often found in bathing and drinking water. Then it struck us that this might be an idea for the next phase of the organisation's life—a way to focus on social inclusion and equality in Orissa's villages. Because the waste disposal habits of even one person can affect the water quality of the whole village—it is the one area where we can argue for total inclusion of all village members, regardless of class or caste differences.

So that was the genesis of our water and sanitation programme—the Movement and Action Network for the Transformation of Rural Areas (MANTRA) (Exhibit 3).

Exhibit 3 **The Elements of MANTRA**

Source: Imran Chowdhury (2009)

With MANTRA it is clear that water and sanitation are the entry points for our work on social inclusion. Under MANTRA we ensure there are toilets, bathrooms and a supply of piped water to all the families of a village. Water is pumped from a safe source, mostly deep tube wells (Table 1 and Table 2, Appendix) and stored in an overhead water tank (Exhibits 4 and 5). Every family can access this source and is given three water-taps: in the toilet, bathroom, and in the kitchen. Every family has to contribute to a village fund to ensure the maintenance and growth of the system in perpetuity as the village population grows.

Exhibits 4 & 5 **Photos of Completed Overhead Water Tank & Tank Under Construction**

Source: Imran Chowdhury (2009)

Gobardhan: In perpetuity? Paid upfront by such poor people? Those are very stringent conditions. Surely many people cannot afford it and will be left out of the system?

Abhimaniu: No, listen carefully because these are the two non-negotiable conditions in Gram Vikas' MANTRA approach. The first is there must be 100% coverage involving all families in the village. The second is that the village must raise a corpus fund made up of on average 1,000 rupees [approximately €15 in July 2009] from each family to sustain the system in perpetuity. We may compromise on other issues, but never on these core principles. They are there because they ensure the social impact and sustainability of our solution.

By now, Abhimaniu is becoming very excited. He points at Gobardhan with the pointer he is using to emphasise key words in the slides and continues.

And it is doable! We have already achieved these goals in over 500 villages. Adult men and women are motivated to come together at the start of the project and they form a village general body. They then elect a representative executive committee with an equal number of men and women. The amount collected towards the corpus fund is placed in a savings account, with the President, Secretary and Treasurer of the elected committee as signatories. The interest earned by the corpus fund is reserved for supporting the future building of toilets and bathrooms for new families in the village.

So we have proved it can be done … but it is true that it is a long process. In fact, it can take a few years for MANTRA to be up and running in a village from the first meeting when we tell villagers about our work, to when we consider that our work there is complete.

Of course, we would like water and sanitation to be just the entry point. We are interested in carrying out other programmes—aiding health, education or economic development. But in reality MANTRA ends up being such an intensive and demanding programme that it is difficult to plan for the next stage. So in most cases we are not able to go beyond water and sanitation. We want to do more, but it can only happen step by step. And keep in mind that we have been focused on scaling up the programme locally, mostly within Orissa. Even to this day less than 20% of the rural population in Orissa has access to protected water, less than 1% to a piped water supply, and less than 5% to sanitation facilities.

Gobardhan: OK, now I think I understand how MANTRA works, at least in theory—but, in practice, how do you get villagers to join up with such a scheme? Caste barriers, class differences, poverty—these are really powerful forces in the villages.

Abhimaniu: Oh yes … you are absolutely right. I could talk about that for ever. But I have a better idea—why don't we go out and see how this works in practice? There's a meeting scheduled this afternoon in a village that is considering joining our network. It is near my project office at Rhudapadar. You should come with me and see how we do it.

Gobardhan: That sounds great—let's go!

Abhimaniu: Good! It's a long drive, five hours from here. Let's make an early start now and have our mid-day meal when we reach the project office at Rhudapadar. From there we can go straight on to the village.

Scene 3: 4:00pm: The Village Meeting

Abhimaniu and Gobardhan reach Rhudapadar after a long, hot and dusty drive. They stop at the project office for a hasty lunch and then continue on, by motorcycles now instead of a jeep, towards Bahalpur Village. They travel for about another hour, mainly bumping over dirt roads. Finally they reach the village main square. Many of the villagers have already gathered and there is a hubbub of noise as people greet each other. The women and men sit separately (Exhibits 6a and 6b).

Exhibits 6a & 6b **Photos of a Village Meeting in Progress**

Source: Imran Chowdhury (2009)

Village headman: I'll open this meeting with a few very brief remarks. As you know, Mr. Mohanty from Gram Vikas has come today to speak to us about his organisation. Mr. Sen, who is standing next to Mr. Mohanty, is a new member of Gram Vikas and he is here to learn about our village.

The reason that I have invited our guests today is to explain their project and how it can improve our lives. When I visited one of our neighbouring villages, Vikaspur, some months back, I was amazed! It is not much bigger than Bahalpur—they have 60 families, and we have 50—but in every household they have clean water for bathing, cooking, and using the toilet. They don't have to go and get water far from their houses, and the fields around the village are clean. It was all a very big surprise to me. When I spoke to the headman there he told me that they had been working with Gram Vikas for several years. Gram Vikas has shown them how to install the water system, helped them maintain it, and are now involved in several other activities in the village as well.

This made me think: why can't the same thing happen in our village? So I invited Mr. Mohanty to speak to us and explain what is involved in joining the Gram Vikas network. Please give him your full attention.

As Abhimaniu stands up and begins, the villagers listen attentively:

Abhimaniu: Thank you very much, dear sir. We are all gathered here today at Bahalpur Village to discuss something very important. As your village headman, Jagdish Pradhan, has told you, my organisation, Gram Vikas, wants to work with you to bring running water supply and toilets to every household in Bahalpur. This means that you won't have to walk more than a few metres from your home to get water, and that you will have both privacy and cleanliness any time of the day when using the toilet. As I understand it, most of you don't have toilets in your houses and use the fields surrounding the village as the common toilet (Exhibits 7a and 7b).

Exhibits 7a & 7b A Village without Access to Clean Water and Sanitation Facilities

Source: Gram Vikas

A young woman in a brightly patterned sari puts up her hand. The village headman motions her to speak. She clasps her hands together and addresses Abhimaniu.

Young woman: Oh sir—I think this would really help us so very much. At the moment it is difficult for me as a young woman to even use the toilet. As you know, we are modest people. A woman going out of the village during daylight can be seen by anyone. So we prefer to go at night, when we will not be noticed. But this is not always easy.

A second village woman is too excited to wait for permission to speak. She rushes in:

Second woman: Yes, it is very, very difficult for us women, whatever our age. In the morning I have to walk a long way to get water for cooking and washing and carry it home. Sometimes I have to do it again in the evening. Having water at our home would really help me and my family.

Abhimaniu nods to them and replies: These are indeed important reasons for installing the water and sanitation system that Gram Vikas has in mind. But you should also think about other serious health concerns: defecating in the fields is very unhygienic. It can lead to the spread of disease and contaminate your water supply. It is very important to have a clean, reliable, source of drinking water. The source of the water should not be close to any place where people are bathing, cooking, going to the toilet and so on.

As he finishes, one of the male elders of the village, who has been frowning during Abhimaniu's explanation, stands up to speak.

Village elder: Mr. Mohanty, what you are saying is quite correct. Most of us in this village don't have our own source of water—we use the local well. You are also correct that we don't have private toilets, but rather use the big fields surrounding Bahalpur, as our ancestors did and as we have always done. But I don't think this change is a pressing need, and our experience with such schemes in the past has shown that they are not always useful.

As an example, let me tell you the following story. About ten years ago there was a government effort to introduce toilets into the village—much as you are doing. One day out of the clear blue sky, a group of officials, masons, and construction men appeared in Bahalpur. They decided that we should have four toilets for our village of 300 people and then they built them. They were not as complicated as the ones you suggest with running water and all, but they were built quickly. And do you know what happened? After a few months no one was interested in using them any more. They were dirty. A terrible smell came out of them. We can show you those toilets if you like—they are still here, though I don't think anyone has used them in years. It is much nicer to use the fields. Why do you think it would be different with your scheme?

Abhimaniu replies quickly over the noise of the villagers nodding and agreeing with the village elder:

Abhimaniu: Sir, I am glad you have brought up these points as they bring me to the most important part of my explanation—the difference between our scheme and the one you experienced in the past. Let me tell you loud and clear—it is the comprehensive nature of our actions. We are not just going to come and build you these toilets—no, not at all! There has to be some very active involvement in this project by all the village members. In fact, it is more correct to say that the village will own the project, and that the people of the village must decide if it is right for them. We at Gram Vikas will just act as facilitators.

When the government constructed the four toilets for your village, I don't think they consulted you very much. It was a technology they just 'dropped' into Bahalpur. And, not surprisingly, after the novelty of the new technology was gone and the inconveniences associated with it were apparent, people stopped using it.

This can never happen with the system Gram Vikas is offering you. First of all, this system is integrated. There will be water to flush your toilets so they will remain clean, as will the water for bathing, water for your cooking and even for irrigating your fields if you need it. We will not just jump in and construct a toilet without considering the system which has to be built around it for it to continue to function properly.

Secondly, for sanitation purposes we insist that 100% of families in Bahalpur—all 50 households—participate in the programme. Without 100% involvement it cannot go forward. This is a MUST! This means that not only will all families have toilets and running water in their households, but also that every family must contribute to the construction of these facilities in their own household, and in the village at large. The village as a whole must source the local materials—the bricks, cement, mortar, etc. Villagers must also work towards the construction of the facilities. If there is a local mason, we will train him to do the specific construction required for the water tank, toilet and running water facilities. Village leaders must also ensure that a corpus fund is raised to support the ongoing maintenance of the system once construction has been completed. This amounts to an average of 1,000 rupees per household. If some families are richer, they may contribute more. Poorer families can contribute less, but they must make up the difference by working on the construction of the facilities. But in the end we must raise an average of 1,000 rupees per household for the fund, which means 50,000 rupees for Bahalpur village.

In this way we will be sure that the village is really committed to the project. We will provide the technical expertise and bring in materials that are not available locally to aid the construction projects. Local staff from our field office in Rhudapadar will visit regularly and make sure things are going well, and help you with any problems you might have. I, too, will be available for you any time you need me. But ultimately the responsibility will be yours—each and every household in Bahalpur must be actively involved to make this programme a success.

By the time Abhimaniu has finished, the village elder is once more on his feet.

Village elder: What you have said makes things much clearer now. It is a far bigger undertaking than I thought. But I am not sure that we can do all that you ask, and I am especially sceptical about the 100% requirement. You know, I think we will have no problem getting perhaps about 45 families to agree to your scheme. But there are some families who will be very hard to get involved in the project. They have never taken any interest in these kinds of communal schemes, and indeed there is no one from any of these households at this meeting. They are just not bothered about any improvement. But we cannot sacrifice the wishes of the majority of the village just because some people are not interested or willing to participate, Mr. Mohanty.

Abhimaniu: With all due respect, sir, this is where I disagree with you. The 100% requirement is the most important part of our programme. We cannot have health and proper sanitation for the village unless everyone is involved! Just take one example: if 45 households get toilets and running water facilities, and five households continue in the way they have always done, there will be no reduction in the spread of disease through contaminated water and similar routes. Indeed, transmission of disease in this way could actually increase! Because although most families will have clean water and toilets, other families will still be defecating in the fields and using sources of water which are subject to contamination, bringing the danger of cross-contamination. The waste from the fields, produced by this minority, may seep into the water sources of the majority and thus help spread disease.

At this, the village elder begins to nod his head.

Village elder: I see … I wasn't aware that it was so easy to spread disease when only a few people are not involved in the sanitation scheme.

Abhimaniu: Yes, most definitely it is true.

He turns to address the whole village.

For all of you in Bahalpur, we want to construct one of the most advanced water supply systems available; one that will be free from contamination. In some of our villages, where feasible, we have established water supply systems powered by electricity. However, I know that Bahalpur does not have access to electricity. While alternative power generation is possible, based on an initial survey of the area around the village we think that a gravity flow supply of water is most appropriate for your village.

Essentially, we will use the water from nearby perennial springs via a pump that will be built at the water source. Water will then be diverted through pipelines using the principles of gravity flow and siphoning to traverse the small hills along the way and reach an overhead water storage tank in the village. From there it will go to individual homes. (Exhibit 8). This system has proved successful in many villages in this area, some not very far from Bahalpur.

Exhibit 8 **Schematic of a Gravity Flow Water Supply System**
Source: Gram Vikas

In total, Gram Vikas has successfully implemented this system in nearly 80 villages, covering over 3,000 families. Of course the village will take full responsibility for maintenance of the entire water supply system, including safety of the pipeline. Although the initial investment is high, due to the length of pipeline to be built and the size of the storage tank, the recurring costs will be small because gravity flow eliminates the need for a pump and its associated maintenance expenses.

The village headman gets up, looks around at all the assembled villagers and speaks.

Village headman: Mr. Mohanty, thank you very much for this information. It is a lot for us to think about. I don't think we are ready to make a decision yet about joining the Gram Vikas network. That will happen after much discussion amongst ourselves. But we appreciate that you have come here with other Gram Vikas staff members such as Mr. Sen to discuss your project with us.

Abhimaniu: It is no trouble at all, sir. When you are ready, we will be available to help. If for one reason or another you decide not to join us, that is fine too. We just ask that you take into consideration that the system we are offering, though it will certainly require much work and effort, is ultimately for the benefit of everyone. If you would like to visit some of the other villages, apart from your immediate neighbours, who have joined our scheme, don't hesitate to ask. We will gladly come on our motorcycles and take you to see some of these projects.

The meeting finishes and the villagers gather in small groups and chat excitedly amongst themselves.

Scene 4: 9:30pm: The Debriefing

The two men are back in the Rhudapadar project office. They are drinking tea and discussing the meeting. (Exhibits 9a and 9b)

Abhimaniu: So, Gobardhan, I think that you've now got a pretty good picture of what Gram Vikas is about, isn't it?

Gobardhan: Yes, Abhimaniu, that was a very enlightening discussion with the Bahalpur villagers. But something is puzzling me. This is so difficult, this MANTRA thing—the demands that you impose on the villages, the corpus fund, providing the materials, etc. Gram Vikas could easily go to the government or donors and ask for the necessary resources. This way you could implement water systems in each village much faster. I am afraid that, to my mind, the Gram Vikas model does not seem very efficient … maybe because it is an NGO and competitive pressures are weaker.

Abhimaniu: You are quite wrong there. Completely wrong! It is not about the resources or about efficiency. It is about empowerment and engagement. It cannot be OUR solution; it has to be THEIR solution! Only then will they believe in

Exhibits 9a & 9b **Photos of Rhudapadar Project Office**
Source: Imran Chowdhury (2009)

it, invest in it, make sure everyone adopts it, and maintain it with as much care as they maintain their own homes. You heard the story about the government toilets … It just does not work if something is given from the top. It is not sustainable. And these people don't need our charity. They are poor but have dignity. And they are smart and resourceful. They just need the right framework, some training, someone to show them the most technical parts. Our goal is not to give them anything. It is to provide a framework that empowers them to take full control of the solution. Empowerment is the key concept here. If we do our job well, in three years our staff can leave this village and never return because the villagers will have taken the solution into their own hands. They will have a functioning system, used by everyone and capable of growing and being maintained forever. Our system will be so embedded in village life that there will be no turning back for them. That leaves us free to focus our attention on the next village or on the next pressing problem. Again, this is the spirit and the approach of the social entrepreneur. You need to understand and assimilate it to be able to do your job well.

Gobardhan: I am amazed … this is so different from what I expected. I thought: "Well Gram Vikas is an NGO so the pressure from any competition will be less and the concern for social impact higher. But the rest will be the same …" I mean, how you implement projects, how you manage people … But this is so different. It is a totally different approach to business and management. You are not trying to build a strong, enduring organisation—you are trying to build sustainable solutions for your beneficiaries. Then you give it away. And then you start from scratch in another area. It's insane!

Abhimaniu: Well, we never start from scratch. Gram Vikas is infinitely more credible and wiser as an organisation than it was 10 or 20 years ago. We know how to implement these community empowerment projects. We use a similar approach each time, just focused on a different type of problem. But yes, it is a different approach to business. If you ask me, it is a better approach; one focused on creating value for society, not capturing value for the organisation.

Gobardhan: You have given me a lot to think about. All of this is new to me and seems so different. I thank you very much for the time you spent with me. I feel I learned more today than in a whole year at school. And, by the way, I think you did a great job at the village meeting. It seemed to me that by the end, they were all interested in joining Gram Vikas.

Abhimaniu: Yes, it looks like it, but I think there are still significant barriers to overcome. This village is a small one, only 50 families, and the caste differences aren't so great. We have had greater difficulties in larger villages where the caste differences between members can be quite strong. Often the higher caste members don't want to share water facilities with the lower caste groups or Dalits—who, as you know, have traditionally been called upon to do tasks which other caste members consider "dirty".

Our MANTRA model offers a way for everyone to share the same technology. But even then there is resistance—some people think: "Why should I, a rich and high-caste person, have the same facilities as lower caste and poorer groups?" This kind of thinking is still entrenched and we are trying to change it. We are trying to promote greater equality. But saying this directly isn't necessarily the best policy. When everyone has the same facilities there is at least some degree of equality.

Gobardhan: Yes, I see what you mean. After the meeting, I spoke briefly with some of the village members and I got the sense that they were receptive. I hope that the village will agree to join our programme. But I also got a sense that these barriers are not just particular to Ganjam District, or to Orissa State in general. Indeed, I know they are India-wide. It is something I will have to deal with in my role as Expansion Manager, I imagine.

Abhimaniu: Having spent the day with you, I do believe you are equipped to do this job. You have come here and seen how we work, how we operate. I hope you will spend more time in the coming weeks studying our programmes in depth. Do this even as you visit other organisations to discuss whether or not they are interested in adopting MANTRA in their own regions.

Gobardhan: Thank you, that's good advice. My first assignment is to visit the Comprehensive Rural Health Project (CRHP), in Maharashtra, on the other side of India. I am scheduled to go there in a month's time, and I understand they have already started to implement MANTRA. I'm very keen to see how it is going!

Case B: Scaling Up
Social Innovations

A month has passed since Gobardhan joined Abhimaniu to visit Bahalpur village and observe the MANTRA programme up-close. Since then, Gobardhan has learned more about Gram Vikas' work. He has spoken to many managers at headquarters and in the field, and has visited project villages where MANTRA has been successfully implemented. For his first field trip outside Orissa, Gobardhan goes to visit the Comprehensive Rural Health Project (CRHP) in Jamkhed, Maharashtra—a six-hour drive to the east of Mumbai (Bombay) (Appendix). His task is to assess the progress of the Gram Vikas–CRHP partnership that began several months ago, and see how the implementation of MANTRA is working out at CRHP. He begins the assessment by meeting Dr. Shobha Arole, CRHP's Associate Director.

Scene 1: 10:00am, Monday, April 20, 2009: CRHP Meeting

Gobardhan knocks and enters Dr. Arole's office at the Comprehensive Rural Health Project. (Exhibits 1a and 1b). It is simply furnished with two chairs, a cupboard and a wooden desk covered in papers and plans. A large map of the area covers one wall. A noisy fan circles overhead as they talk.

Exhibits 1a & 1b **Photos of CRHP Office**

Source: Imran Chowdhury (2009)

Gobardhan: Dr. Arole, thank you for receiving me here in Jamkhed. It is a pleasure to be able to see your organisation at first hand. As you know, I was hired by Joe Madiath to serve as Expansion Manager for Gram Vikas. I'm here today to note any progress or problems related to the joint project between our organisations, specifically the transfer of the MANTRA programme to a model village within the CRHP network.

Shobha: You are most welcome, Gobardhan. And, please, do call me Shobha. As you probably know, we have been partnering and exchanging knowledge with Gram Vikas for a few years now. We work in complementary areas—Gram Vikas in water and sanitation, and CRHP in providing a comprehensive public health programme for villages around Jamkhed, where we were invited in by the local community in 1970. My parents, Drs. Raj and Mabelle Arole, started CRHP back then. Compared with Gram Vikas, we are a much smaller, focused programme serving around 70 villages. Gram Vikas is now present in 500 villages I believe.

Gobardhan: Yes, that is correct, we reached over 500 villages in March 2008.

Shobha: Good. But even though there have been exchanges, we only set up a formal partnership about a year ago to bring the MANTRA programme to our villages here in Jamkhed. The idea was that a well-known programme like Gram Vikas could serve as a reference for a successful programme in our area. We have not really focused on sanitation and water supply in the programmes CRHP has run over the past four decades. Here and there we have put toilets into villages, but nothing has been done systematically. We liked Joe's idea that you must collect 1,000 rupees from each household for the corpus fund, and that this will be put on deposit and used by the villagers themselves for future building, emergencies, repairs, etc. We really appreciated the philosophy behind the scheme and the idea of 100% inclusion.

Gobardhan: Yes, Joe told me that you were very enthusiastic about MANTRA. So what has happened in the past year since Gram Vikas and CRHP signed the partnership agreement? I have heard bits and pieces from staff members at our headquarters, but I would appreciate hearing your thoughts.

Shobha: For the most part we believe we have been successful. About ten months ago, a team of five villagers from our proposed model village, Sharadwadi, went along with two CRHP staff members to Orissa to visit the project villages and learn about MANTRA. Among the group was a mason from Sharadwadi. He was trained by Gram Vikas staff in techniques for constructing the water tower, toilet and shower facilities, and the like. The villagers and staff got to know the Gram Vikas programmes and also received instruction on implementing the MANTRA programme here in Jamkhed. We then came back and everyone was very enthusiastic. They wanted to have toilets and bathing facilities in their own households too!

But since then not everything has gone smoothly. About two-thirds of the villagers in Sharadwadi, which has about 90 families, have paid into the corpus fund. Most have also given some materials such as bricks and cement towards the construction effort. But a third of the families have still not participated. Either they have not given materials or they have not paid into the corpus fund. We are at a loss as to what to do.

Gobardhan: This is the first I have heard of the problem here. Why do you think some of the villagers haven't contributed? Is there a money problem?

Shobha: I think it is more complicated. We have repeatedly made visits and urged them to come together as a community, but they have offered many excuses. For instance, many of the men in Sharadwadi migrate for several months of the year to work in the nearby sugar cane factories. It is a source of cash income for them in addition to any money they may get from raising and selling their crops. It is very common in this area. They go during the Diwali festival time in October and come back in the summer before the monsoon rains begin.

As of now, many men are still away in the factories. And most of the non-contributors have withheld money, not materials. Maybe when the men return they will be more willing to pay the 1,000 rupees for the corpus fund. We may just have to wait. But this lack of full participation may also be due to another reason.

Gobardhan: Which is …?

Shobha: Well, we have worked with these communities for many years, and empowered them to help themselves through various training programmes and projects. But we have never undertaken a programme of this sort, where 100% of villagers must participate. We have selected some of the most capable people of the village, or rather they have selected themselves, and provided them with the means for self-improvement, and the improvement of the overall health of the village. But MANTRA requires that everyone be involved, and everyone be involved equally. It does not take into account the differences in capability and motivation of the various inhabitants of a village. Maybe it is just not possible to get 100% participation in our state of Maharashtra. Maybe the conditions are very different from those in Orissa.

Gobardhan: What do you think we should do? Is there any way people can be persuaded to join the programme?

Shobha: As I said, maybe we have to lower our expectations. Getting 100% participation may be difficult, but having 75% of the villagers involved is not too bad. In Sharadwadi, where there are 90 families, this would mean about 68,000 rupees, which is not a small sum! We could help the participating families build the toilet and bathing facilities, and maybe then the remaining villagers would be persuaded to join.

Gobardhan: I see your point. But I'm afraid that the 100% inclusion requirement is really a central element in the philosophy behind the work we do. I'm not sure it is something that we should ever change, whatever the circumstances. I'll have to speak to Joe about this. Let me call him after we finish our site visit. Then we can talk about this again when we meet tomorrow. Thanks very much for your time, Shobha.

Scene 2: 8:00pm: The Phone Call

Gobardhan returned from his visit to Sharadwadi having heard first hand from Dr. Shobha and seen with his own eyes that the village is only partially ready to go forward with the MANTRA programme. That evening, from his room in the CRHP Guest House, he calls Joe Madiath, Executive Director of Gram Vikas, to ask for advice.

Gobardhan: Hello, Joe? This is Gobardhan, calling from Jamkhed.

Joe: Gobardhan, very good to hear from you. How did your first field visit outside Orissa go? I hope progress has been good at Sharadwadi.

Gobardhan: Well, sir, there have actually been a few problems. While most of the families—about 60 out of a total of 90—have actively been involved in gathering the materials for construction and also contributed to the corpus fund, the remaining families have not been so co-operative. Either they have not contributed to the corpus fund or not gathered materials for construction or both. It's a tricky situation.

Joe: Hmmm … this is not good news. Did Shobha say why this was happening? When the villagers came here to Orissa they seemed very excited about going back to Sharadwadi to start work on their own programme.

Gobardhan: Shobha told me that she believes it will be very difficult to get 100% participation in the village. First of all there is a custom of seasonal migration to the sugar cane factories which has probably slowed things down. Second there might be some cultural differences between villagers in Orissa who participate in our programme and the CRHP villages. They have not really engaged in activities requiring 100% participation before as the villagers in the Gram Vikas network have done. Shobha suggests that maybe we should relax the 100% participation requirement in this case. She thinks they will be able to get 75%, and that the others will join in after the programme has been launched.

Joe: Impossible, Gobardhan! I thought you understood how important the 100% requirement is to our programme. We simply cannot relax it—no exceptions. Remember, our programme is not just about building toilets, showers and water tanks. We are in the business of building dignity for everyone in the village, from the headman down to the poorest families. If we allow this requirement to be relaxed it will be the most marginalised who suffer, who will once again be excluded. And, of course, how can you have clean water for everyone in the village if there are still some villagers who are defecating out in the open? There will be a strong chance of contamination. We simply can't have the programme run any other way. Our 100% inclusion requirement is non-negotiable. You should know that.

Gobardhan: Yes, sir, I see that now. But what should we do? Do you have any suggestions?

Joe: Yes, I have a suggestion. You must go back to Shobha tomorrow morning and tell her that there must be 100% inclusion by all villagers in Sharadwadi to make the programme work. Otherwise it will not be sustainable and will not have the same impact. You can work with them to figure out how this can be achieved. I have faith in you—you will find a solution that will make it possible.

Gobardhan: Thank you for your confidence in me. I will do my very best. Please, have a good evening.

Joe: You, too, Gobardhan. Good night and good luck!

Gobardhan puts down the phone. He is sweating and it is not just because of the humidity and the heat. He is feeling nervous again. Joe is intense and can be rather overpowering, even at the end of a phone line. What should he do next? Is there any way he can work with Shobha to implement the MANTRA model as developed at Gram Vikas, with the 100% inclusion requirement? Is this requirement really so essential? What solution can he offer Shobha when they meet again tomorrow morning to make this innovation transfer succeed?

Teaching notes for this case are available from Greenleaf Publishing. These are free of charge and are available only to teaching staff. They can be requested by going to:

www.greenleaf-publishing.com/oikos2_notes

Appendix

Map of India and Orissa

Source: Gram Vikas

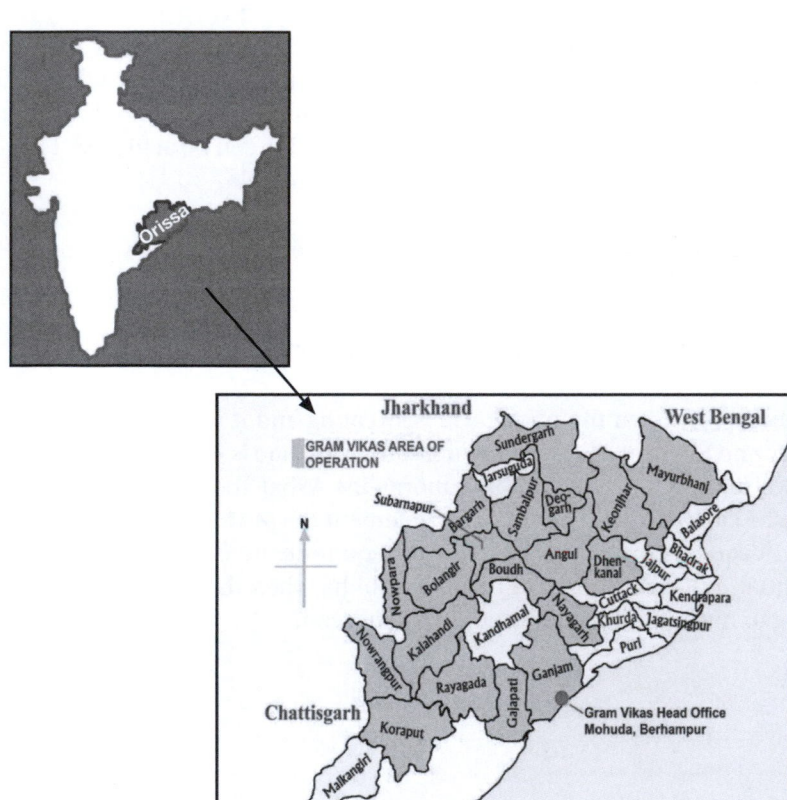

Table 1 Water and Sanitation Coverage under MANTRA

Source: Gram Vikas

Period	State	Villages Covered	Households Covered	Toilet and Bathing Room Units Constructed	Water Tanks Constructed
1992–1998	Orissa	40	3,089	3,127	40
1999–2002	Orissa	27	2,074	2,089	26
2002–2003	Orissa	38	3,021	3,034	38
2003–2006	Orissa	184	14,214	14,216	122
2006–2007	Orissa	72	4,452	4,452	12
2007–2008	Orissa & Madhya Pradesh	160	8,572	8,572	58
Total		521	35,422	35,490	296

Note: Total toilet and bathroom units constructed includes common units in schools, community halls, and individual village households constructed after the withdrawal of Gram Vikas.

Table 2 Sources of Water Supply to Villages under MANTRA

Source: Gram Vikas

Period	Villages Covered	Bore Well	Dug Well	Gravity Flow Water System	System to be Identified
1992–2002	101	97	4	0	0
2003–2008	699	214	40	173	272
Total	800	311	44	173	272

Location of Jamkhed, Maharashtra in India
Source: CRHP

Case 3

KickStart

A Business Model to Tackle Poverty[1, 2]

Saji Sam George and V. Namratha Prasad

IBS Center for Management Research, Hyderabad, India

> The vast majority of development is about giving things away, and most development agencies see the poor as victims asking for help. At KickStart, we have a very different opinion of them. We see them as entrepreneurs. We see them as extremely hardworking people seeking the opportunity to get out of poverty.[3]
>
> Martin Fisher, CEO and co-founder of KickStart International, Inc., in 2008

In creating KickStart, Martin (Fisher) has created a model that is, by design, sustainable and easily replicated nearly anywhere in the world where people suffer grinding poverty. Because of the quantum leap in

---

2 This case was written by V. Namratha Prasad, under the direction of S.S. George, IBS Center for Management Research (ICMR). It was compiled from published sources, and is intended to be used as a basis for class discussion rather than to illustrate either effective or ineffective handling of a management situation.

3 "Inventor's Irrigation Pumps Help Lift African Farmers out of Poverty," web.mit.edu, accessed 2008.

ICMR
IBS Center for Management Research
www.icmrindia.org

income brought about by these technologies, the journey out of poverty is a one-way trip.[4]

Frances B. Emerson, Vice President of corporate communications at Deere and Company,[5] in 2008

Introduction

In early 2009, KickStart International, Inc. (KickStart), a Kenya-based non-profit organization, launched a marketing campaign called "Farming is My Business", to sell its range of irrigation pumps. Talking about the campaign, Martin Fisher (Fisher), the CEO and co-founder of KickStart, said, "We realized that we needed to do more than just sell our pumps, or even selling the "dream" of success, we needed to sell farming as a viable and profitable business. The results have been phenomenal since we launched that new message—an 800 percent increase in sales."[6]

KickStart was founded in Kenya in 1991 by Martin Fisher and Nick Moon (Moon), two visionary social entrepreneurs. In an innovative approach to fighting poverty, they sought to develop tools and technologies that could be utilized by entrepreneurial poor people to establish small businesses, earn a steady income and eventually overcome poverty.

Initially, KickStart developed low-tech devices like a soil block press for making low-cost building blocks and an oil seed press for extracting cooking oil. Later, they developed and introduced the MoneyMaker Pumps, a series of hand- and foot-operated water pumps that could irrigate about 1 to 2 acres of land and cost between US$35 and US$100. One of the unique aspects of KickStart was that in spite of being a non-profit organization, it did not give handouts. Instead, it sold its various devices to the poor, to create a sustainable and profitable private-sector supply chain for its devices. Moreover, the organization operated under the assumption that people were more likely to use and maintain the devices if they were purchased with their hard-earned money.

In 2009, KickStart claimed that through the usage of its pumps about 439,000 people were able to overcome poverty, 88,600 profitable new businesses came into existence and new revenues equivalent to 0.6% of Kenya's GDP were generated. For their efforts to alleviate poverty, the organization and its founders also won many awards and prizes from several international entities.

---

4 "Fisher Receives Lemelson-MIT Award," blogs.physicstoday.org, accessed April 23, 2008.
5 Deere and Company, established in the US in 1837 is a leading global manufacturer of agricultural machinery. It sold tractors, balers, planters/seeders, lawn mowers, string trimmers, chainsaws, etc.
6 "The Old Ways of Ending Poverty are Not Working," us.oneworld.net, accessed January 27, 2009.

While KickStart developed the various devices, manufacturing and retailing were outsourced. However, the marketing and promotion of the devices remained Kick-Start's responsibility, and consumed a significant proportion of its resources. The organization faced a lot of hurdles in selling its devices to poor African farmers who were risk-averse, isolated and ignorant of modern farming methods. Moreover, the organization sometimes found it difficult to raise funds because of its innovative business model.

As of 2009, KickStart sold its irrigation pumps in several African countries. It planned to expand its operations gradually and eventually sell its devices throughout the world. In addition, more and more social entrepreneurs were incorporating KickStart's market-based model in their development projects. Fisher said, "When we first started, the idea of using business models to solve social problems was considered crazy—if not complete heresy. Today social enterprise is the most vibrant sector in philanthropy."[7]

Background

Martin Fisher was born in England in 1958 and moved to the US with his family when he was eight years old. In 1979, he received a bachelor's degree in mechanical engineering from Cornell University. Later, he obtained a masters degree in mechanical design and a PhD in theoretical and applied mechanics from Stanford University.

In 1985, after finishing his studies, Fisher decided to travel. He visited Peru in South America, and was intensely affected by the poverty he witnessed. He saw that the people there were still using rudimentary, outdated tools to carry out everyday tasks, and seemed to have no knowledge about the simple, new technologies that were available for performing these tasks. He thought that these people would be able to improve their lives if they had access to the new technologies.

Fisher applied for a Fulbright Fellowship[8] to go back to Peru and work on the poverty problem, using his engineering and design knowledge. However, when he learnt that he needed to know Spanish to work in Peru, Fisher decided instead to

---

7 "Winners Chosen for the Drucker Award for Nonprofit Innovation," www.reuters.com, accessed September 24, 2008.

8 The Fulbright Fellowship program seeks to increase mutual understanding between the people of the US and other countries. It provides funds for students, scholars, and professionals to undertake graduate study, advanced research, university teaching, and teaching in elementary and secondary schools in countries outside the US. The program is administered by 50 bi-national Fulbright commissions, US embassies, and cooperating organizations.

go to Kenya, where knowledge of English was enough. He arrived in Kenya with the objective of studying the 'appropriate technology movement'[9] in action.

At the end of his 10-month Fellowship, Fisher decided to stay on in Kenya. He began working at a British non-profit organization called 'ActionAid' that believed in integrated rural development. ActionAid utilized the money it received as donations on developmental work in Kenya. It developed low-cost building materials and later trained local artisans in using them in building schools and other structures. In addition, it built community-owned wells, dams, etc., in poor villages. ActionAid also built and ran a rural workshop to manufacture low-cost ploughs and carts, which were donated to poor farmers. It also provided training to women and youth to enable them to start their own businesses.

Fisher worked at ActionAid for five years and there he met Moon, a skilled carpenter and entrepreneur. Moon, who was born in Bombay and later studied and worked in London, had been doing social development and community work in Kenya for several years.

Over time, Fisher and Moon came to believe that give-away aid programs, though life-saving in the short-term, were not sustainable in the long run. They observed that most of the developmental projects they had worked on did not last long once their involvement ended. Talking about his experiences, Fisher later said, "Nonetheless, the water sources we built would fall into disrepair after a few years of use; youth groups we trained to start productive enterprises would fall apart because they were not cohesive or entrepreneurial; our manufacturing workshop competed unfairly with local businesses, and when the project ended, our improved farm equipment was no longer available. No doubt we were teaching the local communities how to manage a large amount of development aid, but it was much less clear if we were having any lasting impacts on poverty—or if we were simply making the local people less self-sufficient and more dependent on our aid."[10]

Fisher and Moon thought that giveaways didn't work because people tended to give away what they wanted to give, rather than what was actually needed. Fisher said, "We need to get past our love for the "cool and clever" and the "warm and fuzzy" to find those efforts that are doing proven, cost effective, sustainable and scalable things. There is too much of "us" giving "them" what "we" think "they" need. Or worse, "us" giving only what "we" want to give regardless of what's needed."[11]

Fisher and Moon felt that the socialist philosophy common in developmental work, which favored community ownership of projects and went against the creation of personal property, money, and business, was the reason for the failure of such projects. Fisher said, "Africa is literally littered with hundreds of thousands

---

9 The appropriate technology movement that began in the early 1970s was based on the idea that advanced technology was often inappropriate for undeveloped countries and that an intermediate level of technology, based on locally available materials was often better.

10 "Income Is Development," www.mitpressjournals.org, accessed February 23, 2006.

11 "Innovative Ideas for Ending Poverty," www.gather.com, accessed January 28, 2009.

of broken down community water points. It is the "tragedy of the commons" that makes community systems so hard to maintain—why should I maintain it if you are going to use it, and why should you if I am?"[12]

After a few years, frustrated that the conventional developmental initiatives were not making a significant impact on poverty, Fisher and Moon decided to adopt a different approach. Believing that groups were not effective enough in sharing and maintaining productive assets, they decided to focus on the individual and develop tools and technologies, which a poor person with an entrepreneurial spirit could utilize to start a profitable new business.

They felt that with a reliable source of income, poor people could gain access to food, shelter, education and healthcare. Fisher said, "A poor person's number one need anywhere in the world is actually a way to make more money. The other thing you realize about the poor is that they're extremely hard working, and extremely entrepreneurial. They're not looking for handouts; they're looking for opportunities to get ahead, just like we are. If we're going to solve poverty, we have to find a way to enable literally millions and millions of people to make a lot more money."[13]

In July 1991, Fisher and Moon quit 'ActionAid' and rented a run-down house in Nairobi to start ApproTEC (Appropriate Technologies for Enterprise Creation), a Kenyan non-profit, in collaboration with APT Enterprise Development, a British NGO. Later, it received a grant from the British Department for International Development (DFID). In 2001, a fundraising office was opened for ApproTEC in San Francisco, US ApproTEC was renamed KickStart in 2005. Fisher said, "Nick and I built KickStart to overcome some of the basic and profound failures we found in both the philosophical approach (seeing poor people as victims) and practical effort (community owned assets, giveaways)."[14]

KickStart's Initiatives and Products

Fisher and Moon adopted a businesslike approach to the problem of poverty. Moon said, "Well I think I can't do better than to describe myself as a social entrepreneur. Meaning that we're trying to find new and effective ways to make the market work for society as a whole, people at the bottom of society's pyramid here. So we're try-

---

12 "The Old Ways of Ending Poverty are not working," us.oneworld.net, accessed January 27, 2009.

13 Britt Bravo, "Tools to End Poverty: An Interview with Martin Fisher of KickStart," havefundogood.blogspot.com, accessed August 20, 2008.

14 "The Old Ways of Ending Poverty are not working," us.oneworld.net, accessed January 27, 2009.

ing to achieve social equity and economic growth through the application of business methods."[15]

The founders developed a five-step market-based model for KickStart. The organization would research markets and identify profitable business opportunities which a large number of people could start; design tools and equipment to create those business opportunities; train manufacturers and establish a sustainable supply chain; develop the market by promoting the technologies; and monitor impact, end subsidies and create a profitable private-sector supply chain.

Initially, KickStart developed several low-tech devices like a machine for making low-cost building blocks from soil and cement (Stabilized Soil Block Press) and an oil seed press (Cooking Oil Press). Both the machines were priced between US$300–450. According to Fisher and Moon, even though it was a very large investment for a poor person, people who had purchased those machines were not only able to create profitable new businesses, but were also able to provide employment to several other people.

Over time, KickStart turned to developing tools that farmers could use. Fisher said, "We asked ourselves, well, we're working in Africa, what business can your average African start? Now, your average African is a poor, rural farmer. In fact, 80% of the poor in Africa are poor, rural farmers."[16]

The founders recognized that a poor rural farmer had one asset—a small plot of land—and one basic skill—farming. They decided that irrigation technologies would provide the greatest help to farmers. Fisher said, "We soon realized that if we were going to have a major impact on poverty we had to focus on new business opportunities for poor rural farmers. For them, by far the best business to start was one that would move them from subsistence rain-fed farming to commercial irrigated farming."[17]

KickStart soon learnt that inexpensive and practical irrigation technologies were not available to poor farmers in Kenya. Irrigation equipment that utilized petrol cost about US$3,000. Electric pumps were comparatively cheaper, but less than 10% of the population in Africa had access to grid electricity, and solar electricity was far too costly. The only remaining option for a farmer was to manually draw water from a well or a stream, with a bucket and a rope. Not only was this method primitive and strenuous, it was also highly inadequate, as two people could irrigate only about 1/8 of an acre per day.

The founders observed that most Kenyan farmers had access to water—either surface (pond, lake or river) or ground water—on their small farms. Even those who did not have water sources on their land could lease plots with water sources, or make arrangements to harvest rainwater. Seeing that availability of water was not

15 "Nick Moon: Development Entrepreneur in Kenya," www.dw-world.de, accessed October 6, 2009.

16 Britt Bravo, "Tools to End Poverty: An Interview with Martin Fisher of KickStart," havefundogood.blogspot.com, accessed August 20, 2008.

17 "Income is Development," www.mitpressjournals.org, accessed February 23, 2006.

an issue, KickStart began to think about developing manually-operated micro-irrigation pumps that could easily move the water from the source to the fields.

In the mid-1990s, KickStart introduced a manually operated treadle pump[18] costing US$100. The pump had the capacity to draw water from a surface source and direct it to where it was needed to irrigate crops. The design of the pump was inspired by a kind of treadle pump, mostly used in Bangladesh and India. The original pump design was modified by Fisher, to make it suitable for use in Kenya. The pump was made portable, so that it could be locked up at night. It also had a shorter tread, so that Kenyan women, who generally wore long skirts, could use it without any discomfort.

However, the price of US$100 was considered too high for a Kenyan farmer, who made only about US$300 annually. KickStart refused to give out the pump as a handout, as its aim was to bring in a new model of development and "to create dignity rather than dependency and to leave in place a sustainable and dynamic private sector."[19]

To ensure that the supply chain was self-sustaining, the price of the pump included a profit margin for KickStart and its distributors/retailers. Also, if the manufacture and sale of the pumps was a profitable business, there would be others interested in making the pumps even if KickStart were to exit the business. The organization also felt that, with a viable supply chain, the pumps would be available to all those who wanted them, without any scope for patronage or favoritism.

KickStart claimed that the farmers who bought the pumps could get their investment back in three to six months. Speaking on why the pumps were not distributed free, Martin Rogena, an employee of KickStart, said, "If you did that, the farmers would just stick them in a corner and not use them."[20] The farmers were more likely to use and maintain the pump well if they purchased it with their hard-earned money.

However, despite its best efforts, KickStart was able to sell only a few hundred pumps. According to the organization, the reasons for this were the poor portability of the pumps—farmers claimed that the pump was bulky to carry—and the absence of an efficient supply chain.

In 1995, Bob Hyde, a former marketing executive, joined KickStart. He persuaded Fisher and Moon to reconsider the design of the pump, as he felt that while they had identified the right business opportunity, they had not yet designed the right product. Fisher later said, "For cost-effective distribution and mass marketing we

---

18 A treadle pump uses a lever device called a treadle that is pressed by the foot to power the pump.

19 "A Moneymaking Water Pump: Tools for Poor Farmers," www.time.com, accessed May 1, 2007.

20 Rory Cellan-Jones, "Day Two: Water or the Web?" www.bbc.co.uk, accessed September 15, 2009.

needed a much smaller, lighter-weight irrigation pump. Bob also helped us greatly improve our distribution, sales, and marketing functions."[21]

In 1996, KickStart introduced the Super MoneyMaker Pump that at 21 kg (45 pounds) was lighter and more portable than the previous design. The treadle pump, costing about US$100, had the capacity to draw water from a depth of 23 feet (7 m). It could also push water through a hosepipe for about 656 feet (200 m) on flat ground and could be used to irrigate up to two acres of land.

In October 1998, a modified version of the pump called the Super MoneyMaker Pressure Pump was introduced (See Exhibit I for more about the design of the Super MoneyMaker Pressure Pump). Apart from the features of the previous pump, the new pump had the capability to pressurize the water being pumped and spray it to a height of over 46 feet (14 m) above the pump. The new pump was developed in response to the demand by farmers for a pump that could push water uphill, and could be used on steeply sloping land with the water source at the bottom. The new pump could also be used for sprinkler irrigation (it could power five sprinklers) and filling overhead water tanks, as well as with nozzles and sprays attached to the end of the delivery hose.

In July 2001, KickStart introduced the MoneyMaker Plus Pump, a pressure pump priced at US$55. The small treadle pump had one piston and one cylinder and had the capacity to pull water from a depth of 23 feet (7 m), a pumping head of 69 feet (21 m) and could be utilized to irrigate about an acre.

In 2006, KickStart launched the MoneyMaker Hip Pump priced at US$35 and weighing 4.5 kg (10 pounds). The unique pivoted design of the Hip Pump allowed the user to pump water using an easy-to-use rocking motion. It could irrigate up to one acre and power three sprinklers. Talking about the affordability of the new pump, Fisher said, "Lowering the barrier to entry is a big goal for us. While the $35 Hip Pump is a great entry point, we'd love to lower the cost, so we can sell it for $25."[22] The pump had the capacity to pull water from 23 feet (7 m) and had a pumping head of 46 feet (14 m).

Over the years, it was observed that the devices developed by KickStart had some common characteristics. All the machines were manually operated; required a maximum of two people to operate; were ergonomic, durable and easily repairable (because they had few moving parts). Fisher said that while developing the devices, KickStart did not follow the western notion that tools and technologies had to save time and manpower. Fisher said, "Saving labor is good, right? Well not if that "labor" is someone's job. We love to save time because it feels so scarce and precious. But in the developing world, time and labor are a poor person's greatest assets—they

21 "Income Is Development," www.mitpressjournals.org, accessed February 23, 2006.
22 "The Old Ways of Ending Poverty are not Working," us.oneworld.net, accessed January 27, 2009.

have them in abundance and they can be quite valuable. That's why our designs are focused on turning time and labor into cash rather than "saving" them."[23]

KickStart's pumps were designed in such a way that they did not require any tools for assembly and maintenance, with inexpensive parts that could be replaced easily when they wore out. The pumps were also designed to be safely used barefoot.

Exhibit I KickStart's Super MoneyMaker Pressure Water Pump

Source: www.nextbillion.net, www.designnews.com and design4dev.wetpaint.com.

The treadle pump that served as an inspiration for KickStart was invented by American engineer Gunnar Barnes in 1985. It consisted of two metal cylinders, fixed above a shallow tube well with a piston attached to two bamboo treadles. The user of the pump stepped back and forth between the treadles, thereby drawing water from the well into the irrigation channel that distributed it to the crops.

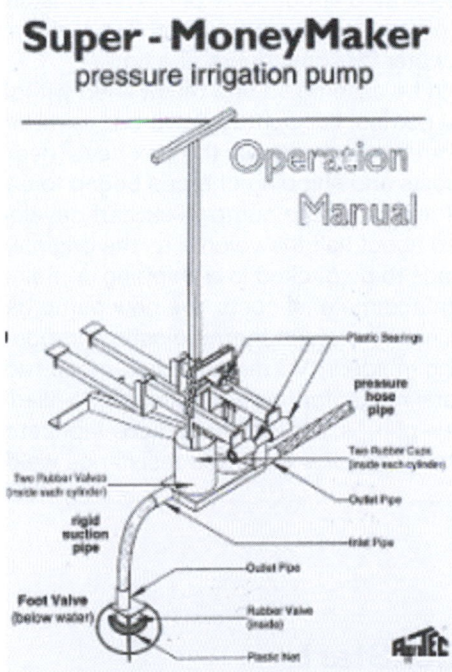

A US non-profit organization, International Development Enterprises (IDE), successfully adopted a market-based approach to manufacture and sell the treadle pumps in Bangladesh and India. Over two million pumps

23 "Interview with KickStart: Making the Anti-Poverty Pump," shakeoutblog.com, accessed March 11, 2009.

were sold in less than 20 years with each pump on an average generating US$100 per year in new net income for the users. KickStart claimed to have been inspired not only by the design of the treadle pump, but also IDE's approach of providing the pumps.

The Super MoneyMaker Pressure Pump used a mechanism similar to the one used in hand pumps—with a piston and a handle to pump the water. The Super MoneyMaker Pressure Pump that resembled the stair climber exercise equipment commonly seen in gyms had two pedals for the operator to push up and down with his/her feet, while he/she held onto a handle. The up and down motion of the user's feet powered the pump, driving a piston into a cylinder, and enabling the drawing of water through an inlet pipe.

The pump was about three feet high and a foot wide. The maximum pumping rate was 1.5 liters/second and the pump had the capacity to irrigate up to 2 acres in 8 hours. Depending on the individual farmer's power input and the pump head (about 7 to 8 m), the pump had an efficiency ranging from 75 to 80%.

The pump was portable and had the capability to withstand relatively high forces day in and day out. Its duty cycle also involved long periods of use—its users generated about 80 W of power constantly for five or six hours. The testing process to gauge the reliability of the pumps involved the pumping of sandy water for some hours at a time.

The pumps could be assembled and maintained without tools. In contrast to commercial pumps, the pump's valve box components could be serviced entirely from the inlet side, so the box never needed to be opened.

As rising steel costs and shipping charges began to eat away into the already small profit margin on the pump, KickStart developed a folding pump that occupied about half the volume as the original, enabling two times as many pumps to be packed in a shipping container.

To reduce weight and material costs, the new pump used more pre-fabricated steel and injection-molded thermoplastic components. The changes made included using molded PVC instead of stamped rubber for valve discs and changing a metal rocker for the pump treadle to filled thermoplastics. Moreover, in the new pumps, KickStart used pre-fabricated metal parts, and newer welding technologies like laser and resistance welding.

Features of KickStart

A significant portion of KickStart's resources were invested in its Tech Development department. It had engineers, fabricators and technicians—some of them locals—to design and develop its various devices. In addition, KickStart provided training to local manufacturers to make the tools it created, so that the skill-sets to mass-produce them became available locally. Moreover, the local manufacturers were trained in quality control, to ensure that their products were reliable and long-lasting.

Initially, KickStart manufactured its water pumps at a factory near Nairobi. However, later, to ensure better quality, higher productivity in mass production and cost effectiveness, the organization outsourced manufacturing to China. Fisher said, "Manufacturing in China opens so many more options for manufacturing that just don't exist in Kenya. We can also ship to anywhere in the world more easily from China. Like everyone else, we can manufacture more cheaply in China, which means we become more self sufficient."[24]

KickStart did not sell directly to farmers, but through local retailers. It was working with some microfinance institutions (MFIs) to find a way to provide credit to farmers. Fisher said, "We don't sell directly to the farmers. They buy from a local retailer, some of whom do offer layaway or credit. We are working to institute a lay-away program that would be available at all of our retailers."[25]

However, the marketing of the devices, especially its best selling product—the Super MoneyMaker Pressure Pump—was handled by KickStart itself, which organized pumping competitions, handed out flyers and advertised on radio, TV, newspapers and billboards. In addition, it offered a product guarantee and had a sales force that worked on commission, to bring in the customers to see the demonstrations.

KickStart also employed trainers and promoters to explain the benefits of its water pumps to farmers through demonstrations at shops and farms. Fisher added, "The pumps come with an instruction manual. We have reps at the store who will demonstrate. We even have a customer service line people can call (a cell phone will be one of the first things people buy when they have the means)."[26]

Over time, KickStart began selling its water pumps in countries like Tanzania (2000) and Mali (2005). Fisher said, "When we expanded into Tanzania, we were told that a long history of socialism had killed any entrepreneurial spirit and that our model wouldn't work. They were wrong! We were told that we couldn't work in Mali—far too poor. And yet we are thriving there, too."[27]

KickStart had received funds from DFID for expansion into Tanzania, and USAID[28] for expansion into Mali. The funds were used to establish a wholesale and retail network in each country. KickStart also expanded its reach to other African countries, including Senegal, Sudan, Tanzania, Uganda, Mozambique, Burkina

24 "Interview with KickStart: Making the Anti-Poverty Pump," shakeoutblog.com, accessed March 11, 2009.
25 "Innovative Ideas for Ending Poverty," www.gather.com, accessed January 28, 2009.
26 "Poor Farmers who Buy Basic Tech become Entrepreneurs," www.progress.org, accessed October 6, 2009.
27 "Innovative Ideas for Ending Poverty," www.gather.com, accessed January 28, 2009.
28 The United States Agency for International Development (USAID) provides a large portion of the US non-military foreign aid. It advances US foreign policy objectives and it receives overall foreign policy guidance from the US Secretary of State.

Faso and Zambia, where it had a few private sector wholesalers/distributors for its water pumps.

KickStart also sold its water pumps to other NGOs. These sales constituted a major portion of its total sales. In 2009, Fisher said, "About half of our annual sales in the past two years (and a total of more than 30,000 units to date) have been sold to other NGOs (and UN agencies such as the WFP and the FAO) who use them in their programs. We've ramped up production to meet this large and growing demand. We can ship to anywhere in the world."[29]

KickStart attempted to measure the impact of its product on the economy of a country and tried to assess if the farmers were benefitting from the use of the water pumps. It also collected information about the impact of its products to satisfy donor requests to evaluate the impact of their funds. The impact measurement exercise also provided critical market intelligence and feedback for improving each step of the five-step market-based model.

KickStart collected and stored some information—like names and locations—on the people who purchased its products. From this database, a few purchasers who were selected for more detailed study would be interviewed by a small team from KickStart. The team—usually a man and a woman—questioned the farmers about the kind of crops they were growing, how much area they had under cultivation, the amount of income made from the farm during the previous year, etc. KickStart also gathered other information from the pump owners like children in school, social standing, and family health. The team would revisit the farmers after 18 months and 36 months, to repeat the process.

Speaking about the impact created by their products, Fisher said, "I think some of our most powerful impacts are the ones hardest to quantify, but the ones we hear often—increased marital harmony, sense of pride and accomplishment, positions of leadership within a community, and the profound relief of a parent knowing that they can feed and clothe and educate their family without struggling."[30]

Contribution to Society

As of September 2009, KickStart claimed to have sold about 136,000 pumps from the MoneyMaker series. In addition, the organization declared that the usage of the pumps had lifted 439,000 people from poverty, created 88,600 profitable new businesses (at the rate of about 800 a month), 60,500 new wage jobs, and around US$88.7 million per year in new profits and wages. It also claimed that the users of

---

29 "The Old Ways of Ending Poverty are not Working," us.oneworld.net, accessed January 27, 2009.
30 "The Old Ways of Ending Poverty are not Working," www.whatjefflearnedtoday.com, accessed January 27, 2009.

the pumps had generated total new revenues equivalent to 0.6% of Kenya's GDP and 0.25% of Tanzania's GDP.[31]

Pump owners were also said to have increased their expenditure on other farm inputs—like seeds and fertilizers—by about 2000%. It was observed that while some of the pump owners sold their produce to middlemen who in turn sold it to retailers in the cities, others sold it to exporters. Some others set up plant nursery businesses, growing seedlings and selling them to local farmers. About 30% of the pumps were also lent out by the owners to their family members or neighbors, who used them on their farms. The pumps were also used to set up businesses such as vehicle washing and drinking water supply.

Fisher stated that with the ability to irrigate their farms without having to depend on rains, which came only once or twice a year, the farmers were able to grow and harvest crops throughout the year. Instead of the one or two crop cycles that were likely with rain-fed agriculture, use of the pumps ensured three or four crop cycles a year. Fisher said, "You can grow high-value crops like fruits and vegetables. You can get very high yields because you have the right amount of water. And most importantly, you can bring these crops out in the long, dry season when nobody else has any crops at all, and the price is very high at this time."[32]

According to Fisher, a farmer using the Super MoneyMaker Pressure pump could expect to grow enough produce to earn a profit of up to US$1,000 per year, and one using the MoneyMaker Hip Pump could make a profit of up to US$650 annually. He added, "One thousand dollars a year profit is a huge amount of money because these families are typically living on something like $400 to $500 per year, before they buy a pump. All of a sudden now, they're living on $1400–$1500 a year. This literally takes them from below the poverty line into the middle class. For the first time, not only do they have enough to eat, and they can feed their kids, and they don't have to worry about where the next meal comes from, they can also send all their kids to primary school, including their sons and daughters. They can afford basic health care. They have enough clothes, and they have a decent house to live in. Most importantly, they have a little bit of money left over to invest in the future."[33]

The pump owners used the money they were able to save on diversifying or starting new businesses. Fisher said, "KickStart really captures what we are trying to do—to stimulate economic growth. A lot of people think that these farmers climb up to some plateau and stay there. In reality, these people continue on this upwards spiral of prosperity—growing their businesses, diversifying, creating jobs and hiring. So yes, there is a ripple effect."[34] The organization also stated that half the

31 "Our Impact," www.kickstart.org/what-we-do/impact, accessed October 19, 2009.

32 Britt Bravo, "Tools to End Poverty: An Interview with Martin Fisher of KickStart," havefundogood.blogspot.com, accessed August 20, 2008.

33 Britt Bravo, "Tools to End Poverty: An Interview with Martin Fisher of KickStart," havefundogood.blogspot.com, accessed August 20, 2008.

34 "Interview with KickStart: Making the Anti-Poverty Pump," shakeoutblog.com, accessed March 11, 2009.

water pumps were being operated by women and these pumps had created a way for women to work in the fields and help irrigate crops.

KickStart believed that by developing technologies and markets, and providing opportunities to entrepreneurial local people to start businesses, it was reducing dependence on aid. Fisher said, "Once we have finished the "market development" and our technologies are as commonly known as bicycles and sewing machines, the local private sector will continue to make money selling the technologies and no more donor funds will be required at all."[35]

KickStart claimed that its water pumps did not have any adverse affect on ground water levels. Fisher said, "Our pumps pull from surface sources or shallow aquifers, and both of these are recharged by the annual rainfall. Because our pumps are human powered, there is a built-in limitation to overuse … the "pressurized hosepipe irrigation" ensures that the watering itself is very water efficient. So no one pumps any more water than they need!"[36] KickStart's water pumps were also estimated to use much less water per acre than even the low-cost drip irrigation systems, commonly used in other parts of the world for water conservation.

KickStart also claimed that it's various tools, including the water pumps, were highly energy efficient and good at converting human power to mechanical power. This utilization of human power was particularly useful in countries like Kenya, where conventional energy sources were not available everywhere. The devices were also non-polluting.

Awards and Recognitions

In 2002, KickStart was nominated for the Tech Awards[37] in the Economic Development category, and subsequently went on to win the award. Ken Wiemar, Senior Development Officer of KickStart said later, "To be a Tech Awards nominee—and better yet to win—gave us credibility. We were still small, but we had big friends."[38] After this win, it began receiving major support from organizations like the Skoll Foundation, the Bill and Melinda Gates Foundation, and the Morgan Family Foundation.

---

35 "The Old Ways of Ending Poverty are not working," us.oneworld.net, accessed January 27, 2009.

36 "Innovative Ideas for Ending Poverty," www.gather.com, accessed January 28, 2009.

37 The Tech Awards is an international awards program that honors innovators who apply technology to benefit humanity. Awards are presented in five categories: Health, Education, Environment, Economic Development, and Equality. Three entities in each category are honored and one entity in each category receives US$50,000.

38 "As Partners with The Tech Awards, USAID Pumps up Innovators," www. globaldevelopmentcommons.net, accessed July 21, 2009.

Fisher and Moon were honored by many prominent non-profit organizations and international agencies. They were given the Schwab Foundation's 2003 'Social Entrepreneur of the Year' award and the 2005 Skoll Award for Social Entrepreneurship (See Exhibit II for more about the awards won by KickStart, Fisher and Moon). Fisher also served on the board of the non-profit organization BuildChange, and the advisory boards of the non-profit prize institute XPrize, and the Global Social Benefit Incubator at Santa Clara University.

In 2008, Fisher was honored with the Lemelson-MIT Program's[39] Award for Sustainability, with prize money of US$100,000. After he won the award, David M. Kelley, IDEO chairman and founder of the Hasso Plattner Institute of Design at Stanford University said, "The MoneyMaker pumps Martin designed are inspirational on many levels. The inventions are remarkable in the huge impacts they have had on poverty and the lives of hundreds of thousands of poor farmers in Africa. They are an exceedingly simple solution to a very complex problem."[40]

Exhibit II **Awards and Recognitions**

Sources: various

Award	Year	Given to
Peter F. Drucker Award for Nonprofit Innovation	2008	KickStart
Design News, "Engineer of the Year"	2008	Fisher
Fast Company/Monitor Group, "Social Capitalist Award"	2005, 2006, 2007, and 2008.	KickStart
Index Award	2005	Fisher
Newsweek magazine, "Inventions that Will Change the World"	2003	KickStart
TIME Magazine, "European Hero Award"	2003	Fisher and Moon
IDEA Design Gold Medal	–	Fisher
Beacon Prize for Outstanding Achievement in Social Enterprise	2003	Fisher and Moon
United Nations AGFUND Prize for Pioneering Development Projects	2003	Fisher and Moon
Gleitsman Award of Achievement for Commitment & Leadership in Initiating Social Change	2003	Fisher and Moon

39 The Lemelson-MIT Program at the Massachusetts Institute of Technology was constituted in 1994. Funded by the Lemelson Foundation, it recognizes outstanding inventors who provided sustainable new solutions to real-world problems.
40 Joseph Ogando, "The Power of Pumps," www.designnews.com, accessed September 21, 2008.

Challenges

According to Fisher and Moon, one of the greatest challenges they faced was one which every manufacturer encounters, while introducing a new product in the market—marketing the product effectively. KickStart spent a significant portion of its donor funds not on product development, but on marketing and distribution (See Exhibit III for KickStart's financials). Using donor funds for marketing enabled KickStart to skip the early, low-volume phase of product introduction, when prices are usually the highest, to directly enter the high-volume phase, when prices are at their lowest.

Exhibit III **Financial Information on KickStart (in US$)**

Source: www.universalgiving.org.

Year	2007	2005	2004
Total Revenue	4,834,963	2,788,593	1,319,937
Expenses:			
Program Services Expenses	2,437,951 (69% of total)	1,944,903 (83% of total)	946,272 (73% of total)
Management & General Expenses	734,439 (21% of total)	193,688 (8% of total)	133,059 (10% of total)
Fundraising Expenses	361,127 (10% of total)	210,591 (9% of total)	216,112 (17% of total)
Total Expenses	3,533,517	2,349,182	1,295,443

Moreover, the founders pointed out that it had taken years for new products like cell phones, TVs, etc. to become mainstream products even in wealthy countries, with strong marketing infrastructure and high levels of consumer awareness. In a poor country, without well developed channels of information dissemination like newspapers and television, creating awareness about a new product was even more difficult. KickStart also found it difficult to reach most of its prospective customers as they lived in remote areas with no proper means of transport.

In addition, KickStart had to deal with the fact that its target customer—the African rural farmer—not only had a low income, but was also highly risk-averse. Fisher said, "What we're talking about is selling a very expensive, big-ticket item. These pumps are something like a quarter to a third of somebody's annual salary. They don't have any savings, and they don't have any credit. They're now going to buy this thing and if it fails, they're going to go hungry for months. It's a technology they've never seen before. It's something that they have never even dreamed could exist. What we're doing is saying, 'Go out and buy these things.' "[41] KickStart

---

41 Britt Bravo, "Tools to End Poverty: An Interview with Martin Fisher of KickStart," havefundogood.blogspot.com, accessed August 20, 2008.

stated that it also sometimes encountered farmers who were accustomed to receiving such devices as part of aid and were reluctant to buy them thinking, 'If I wait around long enough they'll just give it to me.' "[42]

The absence of institutions which offered finance to low income customers also had an adverse impact on sales. Explaining why microfinance was not an option, Fisher said, "It works well in cities, but not so well in rural areas, where the acquisition cost of each new customer can be as high as US$300 per person."[43] KickStart also claimed that it sometimes took up to nine months to convince a farmer to purchase a pump.

On the other hand, KickStart, like many other social entrepreneurship initiatives, found it difficult to raise funds. Fisher said, "There's still a shortage of funds, and the funds that are there are still very hard for social entrepreneurs to get. Every social entrepreneur I've met is spending far too much of their time working to raise money."[44]

KickStart also faced some criticism from aid agencies and large aid providers, who did not approve of its business model. These organizations argued that KickStart was wrong to make people in poverty, pay for technology and products, which were far beyond their means. Fisher said, "We do work with other NGOs, supplying them with pumps for their programs, but getting funding from big guys like the World Bank, bilaterals, and even some of the larger, more traditional foundations has been very hard. They like our pumps but don't 'get' our model. We had one bilateral head tell us 'we love your results; we just don't like your methods.' As if one occurred without the other."[45]

As of 2009, KickStart had 260 employees in four African countries and about five employees in the USA. On KickStart's growth, Fisher said, "The big limitations in our growth are time and money. We could do a lot more with a lot more money. Money 'buys' additional staff, which would increase the 'time' we have. Over the past few years, we've transitioned out of our startup mode where most of the planning and decisions and management were done by Nick and me. We've brought on a lot of excellent senior managers, but time is still scarce."[46]

42 "Interview with KickStart: Making the Anti-Poverty Pump," shakeoutblog.com, accessed March 11, 2009.

43 "KickStart: Social Entrepreneurs use Technology (and More) to Eradicate Poverty in Africa," www.socialedge.org, accessed October 6, 2009.

44 Nicole Wallace, "Social Entrepreneurs Seek New Investments to Reach a 'Tipping Point'," philanthropy.com, accessed March 30, 2007.

45 "The Old Ways of Ending Poverty are not working," us.oneworld.net, accessed January 27, 2009.

46 "The Old Ways of Ending Poverty are not working," us.oneworld.net, accessed January 27, 2009.

Outlook

In 2009, Fisher said that he was working on a concept for a human-powered lighting system and a small-scale electricity generation system to be used in Africa. Irrigation solutions too had a lot of potential for growth, as only 3% of the arable land in Africa was under irrigation. By the end of 2009, KickStart planned to develop a 'Deep Well Pump' that had the capability to draw water from a depth of more than 30 feet.

Talking about the future projects, Fisher said, "We have just scratched the surface on what is possible with our pumps. There is a worldwide potential for over 40 million pumps and we've sold 125,000 (as of March 2009). There is a lot of room for growth. We've got some allied technology, like a pretty effective well-drilling technology that we'd love to get out on the market, and I've got a few other ideas I'd love to pursue, but for the foreseeable future, KickStart will continue to be about irrigation."[47]

KickStart stated that it aimed to create mass awareness about its pumps in Africa. Fisher said, "Eventually what will happen, of course, is that these pumps will hit a tipping point where everybody knows about them, and they become as well known in Africa as, say, a sewing machine or a bicycle. You will no longer have to tell people, 'This is an irrigation pump. This is what it is used for.' We are hoping to get to this tipping point in any particular country in about 10 to 15 years."[48] According to KickStart, this tipping point would be reached when the sales reached 15% to 20% of the total market potential.

KickStart believed that its promotional activities would enable it to reach the tipping point faster. Fisher said, "We are probably about five years from this point in Kenya and a bit further in Tanzania and Mali. We are also proving in an experiment—with intensive marketing in a small region of Kenya—that we can greatly accelerate knowledge and sales of the pumps thru more intensive promotion activities."[49] KickStart believed that it could cut its marketing costs drastically after the tipping point was reached, thus improving profitability, and allowing the profits to be reinvested in developing new markets and new technologies.

KickStart also planned to introduce some services to assist the farmers who purchased their pumps. Fisher said, "As we reach out to the next group of 'adopters,' we expect that the average increase in income will fall (we suspect that these later adopters will be less entrepreneurial), so we are considering adding some addi-

---

47 "Interview with KickStart: Making the Anti-Poverty Pump," shakeoutblog.com, accessed March 11, 2009.

48 Rob Katz, "Market Creation at the Base of the Pyramid: It Isn't Easy," www.nextbillion.net, accessed August 30, 2008.

49 "Innovative Ideas for Ending Poverty," www.gather.com, accessed January 28, 2009.

tional services (like basic farming advice) to help these farmers earn the maximum return on their investment."[50]

Fisher believed that the global inflation with rising food and energy prices had adversely affected the poor and brought the issue of affordable irrigation systems to the forefront. In the future, KickStart planned to expand its operations in the countries in which it was operating, enter new countries, and continue to work with NGOs, worldwide. The organization had plans to raise enough funds to expand to two new countries each year.

KickStart had also patented its pump designs and Fisher had plans to license the designs in the developed world. He believed that the pumps would be a viable replacement for inefficient hand pumps in marine, sporting goods and residential pumping applications.

Fisher and Moon claimed that their private sector market-based model was being adopted by more agencies for their developmental projects. Fisher said, "When we started in 1991, the idea of using private sector models to address poverty was still heresy. Now it's the Social Enterprise movement. So it is very gratifying to see these methods adapted to a wide range of geographies and sectors—including health care and education."[51]

References and Suggested Readings

1. Joshua Kurlantzick, "Rescue Mission: Can American Entrepreneurs Help Solve Social Ills?" www.entrepreneur.com, August 2005.
2. "Productivity Tools Designed for the Poor," www.defeatpoverty.com, March 24, 2006.
3. David Louie, "Local Invention Hopes to Kick Start Africa's Economy," abclocal.go.com, September 14, 2006.
4. Kathryn Martorana, "KickStart: Providing Effective Tools to End Poverty," www.iijd.org, August 3, 2007.
5. Phoebe (Yat) Wu and Sheila Doshi, "Money Maker Pump," design4dev.wetpaint.com, February 21, 2008.
6. "Inventor of the Week Archive—Martin Fisher," web.mit.edu, June 2008.
7. Peter Smith, "A Water Pump for the People," features.csmonitor.com, July 23, 2008.
8. "Martin Fisher's Irrigation Pump for the People," aquadoc.typepad.com, July 31, 2008.
9. Kathy Gaertner, "As Partners with the Tech Awards, USAID Pumps Up Innovators," www.globaldevelopmentcommons.net, July 21, 2009.
10. Rory Cellan-Jones, "Kenya: Water or the Web?" washafrica.wordpress.com, September 15, 2009.
11. "KickStart: Winner's Statement," www.fastcompany.com, accessed October 8, 2009.
12. Suzanne Ridgway, "Martin Fisher, Nick Moon and KickStart," www.workingworld.com, accessed October 8, 2009.

50 "Poor Farmers who Buy Basic Tech become Entrepreneurs," www.progress.org, accessed October 6, 2009.
51 "The Old Ways of Ending Poverty are not working," us.oneworld.net, January 27, 2009.

13. "Super MoneyMaker Pump," other90.cooperhewitt.org, accessed October 8, 2009.

14. "Meet the New Heroes—Nick Moon & Martin Fisher," www.pbs.org, accessed October 8, 2009.

15. "Visionaries—KickStart," www.ki-rin.com, accessed October 8, 2009.

16. "Winners' Circle: Martin Fisher," web.mit.edu, accessed October 8, 2009.

17. "Investing in Social Innovation: Harnessing the Potential for Partnership," www.hks.harvard.edu, accessed October 8, 2009.

18. "Expanding Possibilities at the Base of the Pyramid," www.mitpressjournals.org, accessed October 8, 2009.

19. Pamela Hartigan, "Living on the Edge—and Thriving," www.sustainability.com, accessed October 8, 2009.

20. www.KickStart.org.

21. www.socialedge.org.

22. www.schwabfound.org.

23. www.skollworldforum.com.

Teaching notes for this case are available from Greenleaf Publishing. These are free of charge and are available only to teaching staff. They can be requested by going to:

www.greenleaf-publishing.com/oikos2_notes

Case 4

Kapai New Zealand
Eat Your Greens![1]

Helen Tregidga and Kate Kearins
Auckland University of Technology, New Zealand

Eva Collins
University of Waikato Management School, New Zealand

By August 2007, Kapai New Zealand Limited had grown from an idea to two salad stores with two more on the way, and ambitions for national and international expansion. James Irvine and Justin Lester had returned from their travels abroad, keen to start a successful business, and to promote both their country and healthy eating. Despite their big ambitions, they were resource-poor, both in time and money. James was doing daily management of the salad stores, and Justin, who had a day job elsewhere, was working after-hours on strategic and operational plans. Franchising struck them as a good way to quickly grow the salad store business ahead of competitors also planning expansion—and to ultimately free up more time for soccer and personal relationships. The pair needed to update their business plan, seriously consider the criteria for future store locations, and decide on other revenue-enhancing activities to make Kapai a more attractive franchise proposition. James and Justin wondered how they could enhance Kapai's environmental and social sustainability without detracting from potential franchisee interest. Whatever options they chose, they needed to not only be good for business, but to stay true to their values and lifestyles and to be practicable as well.

---

1 This case previously appeared in *Business Case Journal* Issue 17 Volume 1 (2010), pp 50-69. Copyright © 2010 Society for Case Research. Reprinted with permission.

*   *   *

Two energetic young Kiwis[2] came home from overseas to start a business. By August 2007, the well-travelled 28-year-olds, James Irvine and Justin Lester (see Figure 1) had opened their second salad store in downtown Wellington, and had plans for more. They wanted to establish Kapai New Zealand as a "leading nationwide retailer of healthy fast-food" (Kapai New Zealand, 2007a, p. 4).

The idea of going into business together had been a long-time dream for these soccer-playing mates from school. James, a geography graduate, took care of Kapai's day-to-day operations. Justin, a qualified lawyer, retained his day job for a property management company and worked after-hours on business development. Proud of their national heritage and having learned from their overseas experience, the Kapai boys wanted to grow a strong New Zealand business they could take to the world. They had little doubt that the Kapai salad store business concept was good enough—but were debating how they should continue to roll it out, with whom, how fast and where next?

Figure 1 **Kapai Owners, James Irvine and Justin Lester**

---

2   The term 'Kiwi' is often used nationally and internationally to refer to a New Zealander. It is perhaps the most prominent and widely known way in which the New Zealand people gain a sense of identity through drawing on nature (Bell, 1996).

Developing a distinctly New Zealand business concept

James and Justin came up with the Kapai salad store business concept in August 2004. They adopted the name Kapai, a term originally used by New Zealand's indigenous Maori, and now in more common use among New Zealanders, meaning 'good', 'well done'. The name Kapai evoked a relaxed national attitude to things, suggesting everything will be ok. James and Justin's hope was that everything would be ok—if people ate healthy food, presented by a business that really did have their and the country's interests at heart.

The Kapai boys had returned to New Zealand, aware of a gap in the market. Their business plan pointed to:

> the lack of healthy, reasonably-priced food in the New Zealand market. We recognized that while New Zealand culinary restaurant and café trends had changed dramatically over the past decade, the fast-food market had largely remained stagnant. At home New Zealanders had access to and were making use of some of the freshest, highest quality produce in the world. But within our business districts the healthy options were restricted, at best. We sought to change this by bringing some hearty greens into the mainstream fast-food market (Kapai New Zealand, 2007a, p. 3).

Justin had worked in downtown Wellington and knew what was available, "and it was pretty much stodge … You can get sushi, and outside of sushi there wasn't a lot on offer." With James, he wanted to "create a New Zealand iconic food outlet" that was both healthy and unique. Justin reflected:

> We've got McDonald's and Subway and we've got what the rest of the world's got. Great—but not that interesting. Whereas with Kapai, rather than mimic what other people are doing, we wanted to create something of our own.

Kapai was based on the values of great food which was made in New Zealand for New Zealanders (see Figure 2).

The Kapai concept involved a New Zealand identity, a social consciousness, and an environmental awareness.

Kapai's New Zealand image and cultural identity was evident in the name and logo, which incorporated the native flora of a 'koru' (see Figure 3) or "unfurling fern frond symbolizing new life, growth, strength and peace" (Wikipedia, 2007). The Kiwi version of DIY (do-it-yourself)[3] was an important attribute of the business. During his travels, Justin had thought about what made up New Zealand culture: "You

---

3 The Kiwi DIY mentality refers to the tendency of New Zealanders to have a go at doing things themselves rather than paying an expert to do something for them. There is a resultant sense of pride in the personal achievement that this brings.

Figure 2 **Kapai Values**

Source: Kapai New Zealand, 2007a, pp. 6-7

Kapai values determine the way our stores are operated. To ensure the ongoing success of Kapai we focus on the following:

Great Food

Our primary concern is the health and the welfare of New Zealanders. We aim to promote healthy living and fitness by increasing awareness amongst all New Zealanders of the value of eating real food produced in our own backyard. Our definition of real food is pretty basic in that we require it to be sourced from the earth and grown conventionally.[a] We will use our best efforts to supply only local products that are produced without chemical or genetic modification.

We also consider it fundamental to provide our products at prices that are accessible to all persons. We believe that wholesome food is not a commodity to be enjoyed only by a select few; instead it has to be available to everybody.

Made in New Zealand

Kapai recognizes the distinct employment, economic, environmental and social benefits of buying locally made products and services and will endeavour to do so wherever we can.

For New Zealanders

We believe there is no greater measure of success than the worth an organization is able to create within the community. For this reason we will use our resources to contribute to our immediate living environment.

Kapai adopts socially responsible business practices that recognise the value of community return and will:

- Aim to return a portion of net profits to the local community
- Aim to be a socially responsible employer
- Promote sustainable environmental practices

---

a Justin explained the term "conventionally" referred to food "grown naturally, without modification or any processing."

think of Maori, and the All Blacks [national rugby team], sheep, clean, green environment, and outdoors-living." But he felt there was more: "a New Zealand cultural renaissance going on, where people are proud of their New Zealand identity." He and James wanted to do something good for New Zealand and New Zealanders.

Figure 3 **Kapai Logo**

Social consciousness was inherent in Kapai's effort to "move away from processed, high-fat content foods towards freshly made and nutritious products." Kapai provided healthy and delicious food that also met convenience needs. For James, the emphasis was on "providing good-quality and affordable products that are quick and easy." Along with offering a healthy alternative to 'traditional' fast-food at an affordable price, the Kapai boys were keen to support the local community through buying locally, being good employers, connecting with their customers, and giving to local causes. Kapai's business plan stated the aim:

> to maintain moderate pricing at all times. Kapai wishes to be accessible to all walks of life. No single menu item shall cost more than the minimum wage hourly rate[4] for an adult (Kapai New Zealand, 2007a, p.11).

With a lot of Kapai's prices ending in 95¢—and New Zealand having phased out its 5¢ coin—cash transactions were rounded up, with the 5¢ bonus going to the Karori Wildlife Sanctuary, one of the Kapai boys' favorite local places. According to James, "it's a great spot ... we wanted to give back and do something that we're proud of and our friends and employees are proud of." Promotional material for the wildlife sanctuary sat prominently on store counters.

James and Justin also wanted Kapai to be environmentally responsible but Kapai did not have any formal systems in place to assess environmental performance. As James stated, "We love nature, both of us ... love the outdoors. So we're trying to be environmentally friendly." They were feeling their way and had not sought outside help on the environmental side.

Also, like many other New Zealand business-owners, James and Justin saw that an important element of the Kapai brand, particularly if they were to successfully take the Kapai concept to the rest of the world, was New Zealand's clean, green image.[5] Justin noted:

---

4 The minimum wage in New Zealand in 2007 was $11.25 an hour.
5 The phrase "clean and green," while its accuracy is debated, is often heard when talking about New Zealand's natural environment. While many New Zealand businesses and industries leverage off this image (e.g. the tourism and dairy industries), it is arguable as

> Basically we want to make as small an impact on the environment as we possibly can, so that by developing Kapai we're not adversely affecting our wider environment, or nature, so whether it be, for example, having biodegradable packaging, recycling, having a zero waste policy and other things like using environmentally friendly cleaning products to lessen our impact.

Armed with a business concept, a set of values and an enthusiasm for healthy living, James and Justin set out to bring "some hearty greens to the mainstream fast-food market" (Kapai New Zealand, 2007a, p. 3).

Store location, decor and layout

Rolling out the stores

James and Justin lived with their respective partners in Wellington, and had picked that city's central business district as the location for Kapai's first salad stores. As New Zealand's political capital, and reputedly also its cultural capital (Wellington City Council, 2007a), Wellington boasted a regional population of nearly 450,000 in 2006 (Wellington City Council, 2007a). The city itself had favorable demographics. Unemployment was considerably lower than the national average of 7.5%. A greater percentage of the population than the national average was working age, earning on average considerably higher than the median income. A high proportion identified as professionals (Statistics New Zealand, 2001).

Kapai's business plan noted "visibility, foot traffic and surrounding population [as] key drivers for determining the likely success of a site" (Kapai New Zealand, 2007a, p. 8). Considerable thought had been given not only to location, but to getting the first store up-and-running as a model for those to follow. Kapai's first store opened in October 2006. It was centrally located in the basement level of Lambton Square, a small mall with access from Wellington's main shopping street which boasted the highest pedestrian count in the country (Katipo, 2003). The area was dominated by commercial office towers and government offices.

The second downtown Wellington store opened less than a kilometer away in August 2007. The location in the Willis/Bond Quarter of the city was the second busiest street in the city, also home to a large number of businesses and "somewhat limited in its choice of eateries in comparison to other areas of Wellington" (Kapai New Zealand, 2007a, p. 8). There were plans for another downtown store, a little further along in the Manners/Cuba quarter, identified as having the highest weekend foot traffic in Wellington, and at fifth place during the week (Kapai New Zealand, 2007a, p. 8). This area attracted fewer professionals and already had many

---

to how many businesses and industries really add substance to the image through activity and action.

eateries. James and Justin chose their sites carefully, but the reality was that New Zealand city centers had many other cafes and restaurants, including fast-food outlets. They were banking on there being none quite like Kapai.

This idea of something different and the potential to get in early with an exciting new business opportunity appealed to one of Kapai's customers who approached James and Justin about taking on a franchise. Franchising had always been on the Kapai boys' minds as a good way to grow the business fast without the need to take on a lot of debt. The approach had come a little early, however. According to Justin:

> We said "We're not ready to franchise yet, we don't have an ops manual, we haven't necessarily documented everything that we do." And they said, "we'll run with what you've got"—and away they went. And so they've been in relatively close contact; they're taking a lot upon themselves to get up and running. And they've had retail experience in the past, and they're doing a fantastic job of it so far.

The first franchise store was to be located in Westfield's Queensgate shopping centre about 15 km from Wellington's CBD in Lower Hutt City, the largest mall in greater Wellington. This shopping center had around 8 million customer visits per annum to its more than 140 retailers including its major retail anchors

With two stores now running, a third planned, plus the first franchise due to open in September 2007, the Kapai boys were extremely busy. Justin was writing the operations manual at nights. And, they were finding one of the best times to talk about business was before and after their soccer training and matches. While franchising involved a lot of up-front work for them, they thought that it would ultimately leave James free to undertake more of a general management role and Justin to concentrate on more strategic matters.

Styling the stores

Kapai's two stores had a distinct décor based on the Kapai boys' interpretation of a New Zealand environmental theme. For James, the subtle greens and browns were inspired by New Zealand's landscape—and linked to the salad product as well: "our fertile pastures where the vegetables are grown." Natural timbers featured in the decor. For Justin, there was "quite an earthy feel to the store." The colors, the name Kapai, the logo and slogans on the walls, the staff's brown T-shirts incorporating the koru design all contributed to this feel. The customers "love the colors, and they love the furniture, its smooth and funky lines—they just love seeing something different," commented James. The plan was to use similar décor in Kapai's future stores, with perhaps a twist here and there.

The stores had a large menu board above the servery counter where all the salad ingredients were on view. Cold beverages were available for self-selection from an adjacent fridge. Fairtrade coffee was available for pick-up at the end of the salad line. The emphasis was on simple, fresh and largely unprocessed ingredients, served without undue fuss or packaging.

The first store had its own customer seating area, for around 20 people. Regular café-style tables and chairs as well as more comfortable lounge style seating were available. Daily newspapers and Kapai newsletters were on hand. The overall ambiance was a cross between a fast-food outlet and a regular café. The second store was located in a food-court which had its own seating. The majority of customers across both stores were take-away customers. Store opening hours were 8 am–4 pm Monday to Friday and 10 am–2 pm on Saturdays for the first store, and an hour less each day for the second in its start-up phase.

Menu choices and prices

James and Justin crafted the Kapai menu with the aim of developing food which was both nutritious and fast. Salads were the main fare on the Kapai menu (see Appendix 1). James noted the emphasis on "giving the customer control … DIY, do-it-yourself salads so the customer can choose exactly what goes in, and knows exactly what they're getting."

The salad base was a choice of mesclun, baby spinach, cos lettuce, or rocket (also known as arugula) lettuce. There were 22 'regular fillings' (e.g., roasted pumpkin, cucumber, field mushrooms, and sundried tomatoes), 8 'gourmet fillings' (e.g., chilli chicken, honey ginger beef, and grilled bacon), and 11 dressings (e.g., lime, chilli and soy, balsamic, and blue cheese and chive). Customers could combine these as they liked, with prices starting at NZ$6.50[6] for a small salad. Alternatively, they could choose an advertised salad, or 'Kapai Favorite.'

For larger appetites, Kapai allowed customers to have a choice of salad in toasted pidé bread. Prices for these started at NZ$6.95. Kapai also offered soup served in a freshly-baked hollowed bread bowl, and breakfast food options to cater for the early pedestrian crowd. The soup choice, priced at NZ$6.95, was designed as a salad alternative for the cooler winter periods. Breakfast included honey hotcakes, yoghurt and fruit and muesli. Also available were juice, coffee and a range of teas.

Along with DIY, other Kapai values influenced the menu. The salads were served in biodegradable potato pack containers while the bread-casings were entirely edible. For take-aways, bread bowl soups were wrapped in paper, and brown paper bags were given on request. Coffee was served in cardboard cups, as recyclable cups were not readily available in New Zealand.

---

6 In August 2007, NZ$1 was valued at approximately 0.5 euros and around US 70 cents.

Operations

Management and staffing

From the beginning, James and Justin took on different roles. As General Manager, James focused on getting the first store up and running. He had since hired a manager for the first store, and was busy getting the second store fully operational. He spent time sourcing ingredients, cooking and preparing food in the new offsite kitchen, and managing staffing. Justin, as Business Development Manager, concentrated on strategic development. He noted sometimes the day-to-day reality was a bit different: "I do payroll and invoicing and the like as well, but more focusing on growing the company as quickly as we can." James saw this arrangement as working well:

> We really liked the idea of working together, and still do. We complement each other quite well. Justin is very much an ideas sort of man; I'm sort of more at-the-coalface, getting things done. So we balance each other well.

It had been tricky at first making sure they had the right number of staff to deal with the increasing customer numbers in the beginning months, until customer numbers settled. But staffing was now "quite stable" and James was extremely happy with the Kapai employees.

> I think we attract people who are young, and vibrant. They are into healthy food, and into the outdoors and are well-educated. I think they just sort of like what we're doing and I think they see it as being quite a funky sort of place as well.

Many Kapai staff were university students wanting part-time work. They suited Kapai, which needed flexible staff willing to work short 2–4 hour shifts over the busy lunch period. Justin felt that "the vibe at Kapai stores often attracts the type of people we want" and also noted that "a lot of new staff come via word of mouth—through other satisfied staff members."

Getting supplies

In line with the Kapai values, social responsibility and environmental awareness were considered when getting supplies. Kapai sourced many of its products from within New Zealand. "Where we can, we try to support local," James said. However, he did have to balance this aim at times with his desire for quality:

> Like 90% of it is local, but then there's the odd thing, like at the moment, it's very difficult to get decent New Zealand tomatoes, so there's some tomatoes over from Australia, but you just can't really not do that.

Getting quality produce required James' constant attention "because of the large amount of greens we have." He considered that Kapai had established a good relationship with a local produce supplier, and recognized that new relationships with other suppliers would likely be needed when the business grew into different regions.

Drinks available at Kapai were also sourced with a social conscience. Fairtrade coffee was chosen. Preservative-free fruit juice was made by a small producer, just north of Wellington. As Kapai was its only major customer of bottled juice, it supplied the juice in glass bottles with Kapai labels. James and Justin were satisfied with these arrangements but were unsure how long this producer could continue to supply the amount of product that Kapai required. The producer would either need to grow with Kapai or the Kapai boys would have to investigate other suppliers of preservative-free, and even possibly organic beverages.

Sourcing biodegradable packaging for the salads had not been straightforward. The packaging was originally obtained through a supplier from a Malaysian company. It was difficult to ensure continuous supply. With the Kapai boys wanting to support local suppliers and reduce the miles behind their product in an age of increasing food miles consciousness,[7] an international company was not their first choice. As James stated "there's a New Zealand place called Potatopak who we wanted to go with, but the containers didn't have any lids, which is kind of crucial for us."

With the third store on the way, Kapai had reached a capacity where it was feasible for Potatopak to produce potato-based containers and lids for Kapai. Working with a small local producer had once again resulted in opportunities for Kapai. It now had a reliable supply of biodegradable containers and, as the lids had been made for Kapai, its logo was embossed on the top of the container. Getting these economies of scale helped Kapai's finances as well.

Money matters

While traveling and working overseas, James and Justin had each managed to save some money which helped finance their first store. They were equal partners in the business, and had two smaller shareholders, each with a 5% share. With James and Justin doing a lot of the set-up work themselves, they had also reduced the amount of start-up capital needed. At their stage of life, establishing Kapai was a relatively big investment.

The first Kapai store performed better than originally forecast (Kapai New Zealand, 2007a, p. 11). The location had proved effective, at times exceeding 300 customers a day. On average, customers spent NZ$8.82. Earlier in 2007, monthly turnover figures were approximately NZ$63,569 with around NZ$10,806 of that

---

7 Food miles (the distance food travels from the place of its production to the consumer) is a topic of international debate and an issue receiving significant attention in New Zealand due to its potential trade implications for exporters. For further information and a New Zealand perspective on the topic see Landcare Research (2007).

being profit (Kapai New Zealand, 2007a, pp. 10-11). James drew a salary as a company employee; Justin did not.

The business plan outlined a number of operational assumptions developed by researching industry best practice (see Figure 4) and Kapai's own financial analysis. These functioned as a guide to the set-up of future stores and a means to assess the performance of existing stores. Operational assumptions were:

- Rent costs should account for no more than 12% of turnover;

- Stock and raw materials will account for no more than 33% of overall costs;

- Staff costs should account for no more than 30% of turnover;

- Daily store customer numbers should reach 200 people at a minimum; and

- Average customer sale will be no less than NZ$8.30 (Kapai New Zealand, 2007a, p. 12).

Figure 4 **Restaurant and Cafe Cost Structure 2005**

Item	%
Salaries and wages	28.17
Food and beverage purchases	32.80
Other purchases and operating expenses	22.12
Rent and rates	6.41
Depreciation	3.78
Interest and indirect taxes	2.01
Total costs	95.29
Operating profit before tax	4.71

Note: Figures are derived from Statistics New Zealand and were obtained from The Restaurant Association of New Zealand. Statistics are an amalgam of data from all sorts of operations (e.g. *à la carte*, buffet, over the counter service and table service) and are provided to indicate industry averages. Individual establishments could vary significantly from these figures. The authors thank an anonymous reviewer for suggesting this table.

Attracting customers

Marketing was another DIY affair for Kapai. Its business plan stated:

> We do not intend to use paid advertising campaigns in the media as we believe that any benefits are disproportionate to the costs. We believe that there are more effective ways to advertise, such as guerrilla advertising that draws attention to the store in the store's vicinity through antics, art and innovative ideas (Kapai New Zealand, 2007a, p. 10).

It was difficult to know what antics the pair had in mind—but they had been clever with their wall art (see Figure 5). The walls and cabinets of the stores were sparingly decorated with Maori proverbs and quotes from early New Zealand settlers. These had attracted attention in the news articles on Kapai.

Figure 5 **Kapai Wall and Cabinet Art Samples**

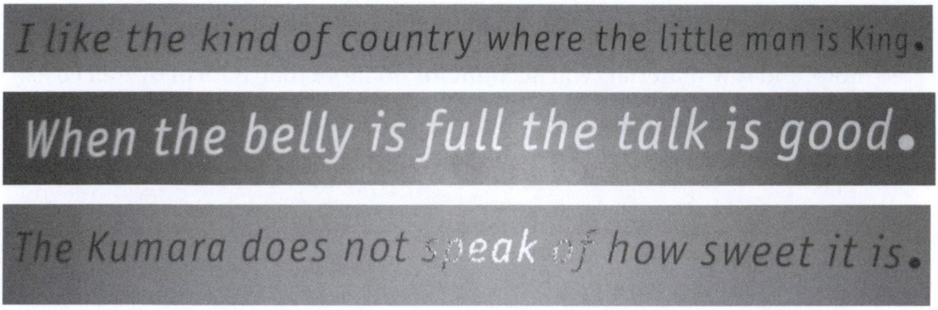

I like the kind of country where the little man is King.

When the belly is full the talk is good.

The Kumara does not speak of how sweet it is.

Note: Kumara is New Zealand's native sweet potato.

James and Justin had done several newspaper, magazine and radio interviews. Their plan was "to gain exposure in all forms of the media through our exuberance, vitality and unique ideas" (Kapai New Zealand, 2007a, p. 4).

Getting customers involved was another Kapai strategy. A monthly competition for best salad combination invited customers to further develop the 'Kapai Favorite' menu. A Kapai newsletter covered relevant global and New Zealand issues, along with recipes and events.

Kapai's website came up at the top of many keyword searches,[8] was professionally presented and contained information targeted mainly at customers such as menus and basic nutritional content. The website had "received more than 130,000 hits and 2,000 visitors within the first six weeks of opening" (Kapai New Zealand, 2007a, p. 4) and continued to attract good patronage.

Fast-foods and salad stores in New Zealand

Justin saw Kapai as "an alternative fast-food to fish and chips, hamburgers, pizzas and the like." Kapai was a new entrant operating in the established fast-food industry and the emerging salad store segment. It was just a tiny business up against some major competition.

8 Google New Zealand keyword searches with which Kapai New Zealand features either first, or on the first page of results, include "kapai," "eat your greens," and "salad bar."

The fast-food industry

Whether the actual food was good for them or not, approximately 50% of New Zealanders regularly consumed fast-food (The Food Industry Group, 2006, p. 16). 'Branded' fast-food stores could be found throughout the country, and small owner-operated outlets were also popular.

Burger chains dominated New Zealand's fast-food landscape. McDonald's golden arches could be seen in all major cities and many towns. McDonald's New Zealand boasted 139 stores, with 19 in the Wellington region (McDonald's, 2007a). Burger King, another franchised chain, had 67 stores throughout New Zealand (Burger King, 2007). Burger Fuel, a gourmet burger store, had 21 New Zealand stores (Burger Fuel, 2007) and was quickly expanding since listing on the New Zealand Stock Exchange. Wendy's Old Fashioned Hamburgers had yet to expand beyond Auckland. Other burger offerings came from smaller branded stores and locally-owned operations, including from fish and chips shops in virtually every city and town.

Other major fast-food segments included pizza and, to a lesser extent, chicken. Restaurant Brands was a prominent company in the New Zealand fast-food industry in both these segments. It operated Pizza Hut, KFC and Starbucks, in New Zealand. Pizza Hut had 101 stores throughout the country (Restaurant Brands, 2007). Other big competitors in the pizza market included Domino's with 65 stores (Domino's Pizza Enterprises Ltd, 2007, p. 3) and New Zealand-based sensation, Hell Pizza with 67 stores (Hell Pizza, 2007). Competitors to Restaurant Brand's 86 KFC restaurants (KFC, 2007) included Oporto's six Auckland stores (Oporto, 2007) and countless smaller chicken joint operators.

Then there were the fish and chips and pie segments of the industry. Both were traditional Kiwi favorites linked to New Zealand's British heritage. The vast majority were single owner-operated businesses. Notable exceptions were LJS Seafood Restaurants with 15 franchised fish and chip outlets in shopping malls, and Jesters Pies (Jesters Pies, 2007), a franchise based on healthier pies, expanding throughout the country.

These mainstream fast-food offerings of burgers, pizzas, fried chicken, fish and chips, and pies faced expanding competition from food-courts, ethnic restaurants and take-away bars (The Food Industry Group, 2006, p.16). Many of these alternatives catered for the more health-conscious convenience buyer. In city centers, sushi bars were common, as were sandwich stores. Subway, the world's largest submarine sandwich franchise, had obtained a big market presence with 193 outlets in New Zealand (The Food Industry Group, 2006, p. 16). Subway was located in cities and large towns as well as in rural towns positioned on major highways. Subway's menu was made up of a range of sandwiches and salads. On a smaller scale, but with multiple channels, Wishbone targeted health-conscious convenience buyers with a gourmet sandwich selection and ready-made meals including salads (Wellington City Council, 2007b). Wishbone had quickly grown to 9 stores in Wellington and 3 in Auckland (Scoop, 2006), predominantly in busy CBD areas. It planned to open more stores, in other New Zealand cities (Unlimited, 2004), and internationally. Wishbone also supplied ready-to-heat meals to supermarkets and in-flight catering for New Zealand's national airline, Air New Zealand.

The 'health conscious' consumer was beginning to be taken notice of, by a variety of players.

Health concerns and industry responses

With more than 50% of New Zealand adults being overweight or obese , and this percentage having doubled between 1977 and 2003 (Stuff, 2007), diet and health was a major concern reflected in national health policy and the promotion of healthy eating guidelines.

Many major fast-food chains had made attempts to 'balance' their menus with a range of salad products, low fat mayonnaise, diet drinks and water (The Food Industry Group, 2006, p. 16). However, 'healthy' offerings on most menus were limited, with KFC offering only one salad priced at NZ$7.00. McDonald's had revamped its menu adding a range of salads (NZ$6–NZ$8), deli rolls (NZ$5–NZ$6), cereals and yogurts, fruit snacks and beverages (McDonald's, 2007b). Nutritional and allergy information was available on most of these fast food chains' websites; sport and community sponsorship and social marketing programs were also part of these companies' health and social campaigns.

Many customers still did not routinely make healthy fast-food choices. LJ Seafood admitted its healthier options—such as grilled not fried, battered or crumbed fish, and its salad offering were not really profitable items as yet (Lord, 2007). Despite the efforts of fast-food chains and others, there was still work to be done to make the words "fast-food" and "healthy" go together.

Salad store competitors

Like Kapai, others had noted that gap in the market. Many cafés now provided salads, both eat-in and take-away. And while Kapai had been the first mover in the fast-food salad market in Wellington, other New Zealand entrepreneurs had the same idea.

Auckland, New Zealand's largest city and its commercial capital, was home to fast-food salad stores, Saladworks and Toss. Each had two stores. Unlike Kapai, Saladworks and Toss had chosen stand-alone stores (as opposed to food-courts or malls), but were similarly placed in relation to high pedestrian counts and proximity to office buildings. Their menus also featured house and DIY salads, soup, breakfast items and a range of beverages. Saladworks was lower priced on some items (salads ranging from NZ$6.50–NZ$7.00) and had received a number of accolades.[9] Toss, with salads priced at around NZ$9.50–NZ$10, had a comprehensive

---

9 Awards included the *New Zealand Herald on Sunday* 2006 #1 Gourmet Health Food Takeaway and New Zealand Retailers Association Top Shop 2006 Award (Saladworks, 2007).

on-line ordering and delivery system but did not yet have nutritional information available for its products. Neither business had an environmental or social focus beyond providing an alternative to high-fat fast-food. Toss's menu included several 'less-healthy' items such as chocolates and cookies. Saladworks and Toss had not publicly indicated plans for expansion.

Reload started out as a coffee and juice bar. In 2005, it introduced a salad menu creating what it called a 'HEALTH.fuelstop.' Reload now had two stores in Dunedin and two in Christchurch, and was set to launch in Singapore and China in 2007 (Reload, 2007). According to its website, "Reload is New Zealand's most innovative fast-food outlet. Reload prides itself on offering something unique in the fast-food industry" (Reload, 2007). While salads were a key menu item, juice options were prominent. Health supplements could be added, with Reload suggesting the addition of Wheatgrass to juice in order to 'drink your greens' (Reload, 2007). Reload stores were situated in street-front locations and in malls and food-courts. The company aggressively promoted expansion through franchising. Reload had extensive franchise information available on its website and featured in the *Franchise New Zealand* magazine.

Between these salad store companies and other one-store businesses, salad stores had begun to establish a presence in at least four major New Zealand cities. An Australian-based franchise Sumo Salad was also looking at entering the New Zealand market (Franchise Business, 2007). The question was which company would grow to capture the biggest share of this emerging market.

The economics of taking Kapai forward

Profit margins were often hard to achieve in café and fast-food businesses. The Kapai boys knew that a close eye on overheads and other costs was essential. They recognized that the operational assumptions in their business plan needed to be considered further, especially with their plans to franchise and the need to offset franchise costs and ensure a profit for both Kapai and franchise owners. Similar fast food franchises in New Zealand ranged from around NZ$100,000 to NZ$350,000.[10] James and Justin were deliberating the price of a Kapai franchise.

Getting the right locations was key. However, they came at considerable cost. Kapai's operational assumptions set a maximum rent cost of no more than 12% of turnover, noting rent as a major expense and indicating the preference for good locations. Rent prices in central Wellington were averaging NZ$800–NZ$2,600 per m², with similar prices in Auckland. Other locations such as Whangarei, Hamilton,

10 Two fast-food salad store franchises were listed on the Official Directory of the Franchise Association of New Zealand website. Reload Salad and Juice Bar franchise was listed in the NZ$100,000–NZ$250,000 category while Sumo Salads was priced higher at NZ$300,000–NZ$350,000 (Franchise Business, 2007).

Tauranga, Christchurch and Dunedin carried a much lower price tag (averaging NZ$400–NZ1,000 per m²), according to property industry sources. James and Justin wondered whether the maximum rent cost could be reduced to 8–10% bringing it more in line with the industry norm,[11] while still locating stores in the prime real estate positions required to meet their other operational assumptions. Or perhaps they should take a risk on the higher rents being offset by turnover.

Stock and raw materials, as with all food operators, also represented a big expense for Kapai. The fluctuating cost of produce between seasons needed to be considered, although it could potentially be minimized in the future through agreements with some suppliers to set a standard price across the entire year. Supporting local produce growers could limit the economies of scale Kapai could achieve through expansion.

Menu item prices and staff costs were also important. Kapai's social responsibility included an aim of having no menu item priced higher than the current minimum wage. Could prices be sustained and ensure future profitability for both Kapai and franchisees or would they need to be increased to offset franchise fees? Would staff costs be able to be reduced from a maximum of 30% in other locations? These were just some of the issues the Kapai boys needed to consider as they looked at opportunities for growth.

Opportunities for growing Kapai

James' and Justin's long-term objectives for Kapai included it becoming "New Zealand's signature fast-food outlet with stores across New Zealand, an iconic brand that New Zealanders are proud to call their own" (Kapai New Zealand, 2007a, p. 5). Both were keen for the business to grow.

> We have put significant effort into the development of the Kapai brand to distinguish us from competitors and create a concept that we and our customers are proud of … Through our marketing and physical environment we have also positioned ourselves as a uniquely New Zealand alternative amongst retail food operators, which we believe will offer us a significant advantage in the domestic market (Kapai New Zealand, 2007a, p. 2).

James reflected: "It was always the idea to go bigger, although you have to take steps, one step at a time, and basically the first store, we saw that as being our first step, but then our aim was to have three stores open within a year. And we're going to achieve that." The current business plan pointed to a further "5–10 stores nationally within the next three years" … and noted seeking strategic partners "to work

11 Industry averages are identified in Figure 4, which indicate rent and rates to be 6.41%; arguably, a more realistic target for Kapai New Zealand is 8–10% due to the nature of the operation and the location requirements (i.e. high pedestrian count and visibility).

with to grow the business and ensure its continued success" (Kapai New Zealand, 2007a, p. 2). Beyond that the plan was silent.

The priority was to finalize the operations and franchise details for the new Queensgate franchise operation and get that store and the third Kapai store up-and-running effectively. Then, the Kapai boys intended to actively seek people interested in both master franchises for different areas, or single store franchises. Justin noted:

> We'll actually put up on the website if people are interested in franchising, they should contact us; we'll start advertising locations where we want to set up Kapai stores … such as Christchurch, larger towns and cities in New Zealand, initially. We've got people quite keen to do something in Queenstown … it would work quite well, because you've got that fast moving public, a lot of tourists eating and they want something different as well. They don't want to go to McDonald's. Yes, Christchurch and Auckland, Hawkes Bay, Palmerston North perhaps.

James mentioned a preference, too, for the bigger centers for future stores but was also hopeful that they would get into "the likes of Invercargill and Blenheim." They had a lot of contacts, even a mate in London who was keen to try the idea out there at a later stage. They were keen on having at least one international store within the next five years.

There needed to be some research done on which New Zealand cities and towns to take Kapai next (see Figure 6)—and also internationally in places like London or Sydney where there were a lot of expatriate New Zealanders. Decisions needed to be made on general locations. Should Kapai focus on space in food-courts or malls, or stores in city-center or suburban blocks, or stand-alone stores, maybe even mobile outlets? In terms of specific locations there would have to be a strong eye kept on rent levels. The Kapai boys felt that the opportunities were there, but they needed to move ahead of other competitors in getting the best locations.

Meanwhile, there were plenty of other things to think about. Maybe the Kapai menu could be altered by adding or deleting ingredients and product offerings. There were some product line extensions that could boost sales. Healthy food items such as a range of condiments had been considered. Clothing (e.g. the brown staff t-shirts featuring the logo or some variation), salad bowls and servers were other ideas. Catering for office lunches was an option too—it was advertised on the website but had only moderate take-up of one or two orders a week.

The Kapai boys also wondered whether their premises could be made to work outside breakfast and lunch times. Options for the stores included providing quick take-home salads for commuters after work, opening later for dinners, or especially for community groups or other meetings. They could even rent out their kitchen.

Another possibility was to move more into organics. James and Justin thought their customers sometimes saw their business as more organic and more environmental than it perhaps was. Because of the limited supplies of organic produce available locally, going wholly organic was not going to be easy and the boys

Figure 6 **Main New Zealand Urban Area Populations**

Source: Statistics New Zealand, 2006.

City (by geographical position north to south)	Population
Auckland Region	1,074,507
Hamilton	138,792
Tauranga	95,694
Rotorua	52,608
Taupo	20,310
Napier	54,537
Hastings	59,139
New Plymouth	47,763
Wanganui	39,423
Palmerston North	72,681
Wellington	292,530
Nelson	53,688
Blenheim	26,550
Christchurch	334,107
Queenstown	8,538
Dunedin	107,088
Invercargill	46,305

wondered if it could end up causing more problems if they could not consistently deliver on it. There was an option to buy key supplies in bulk and redistribute them. This approach might have worked for the disposable wooden forks and biodegradable cups available overseas but which were simply not economic right now in the small quantities Kapai needed.

And then there were all the other great extension ideas the pair had for the Kapai brand … But it was early days, and would-be investors were not falling over themselves yet. James and Justin were also keen to decide on the model they wanted to use to expand before pursuing further enquiries.

Updating the business plan and moving forward

James and Justin recognized Kapai as having a bit of a first-mover advantage in Wellington at least. But they didn't necessarily think that advantage would last long, or exist everywhere. James acknowledged, "There was room for competition—but we're just trying to stay ahead of them in terms of rolling out ours as quickly as we can." It was time to update Kapai's business plan to provide important details on where the business should go next, when, and with whom it might partner. There was also the problem for the energetic yet time-strapped Kapai boys of deciding which of their ideas they should hold on to or let go of.

The Kapai boys saw franchising as the way to grow faster as they "don't have to be actively involved on site doing all the nitty gritty work for each store," according to Justin. "It'll be alright if things keep going to plan, but one never really knows," he said. For James, opening stores throughout New Zealand and then taking Kapai international was the ultimate goal—but "whether or not it happens is another story."

James and Justin were examples of what had been referred to as New Zealand's brain-drain generation—skilled graduates leaving the country to travel with many never returning. However, they had chosen to come home and settle with, as James put it, "better skills and different ways of looking at things." Would their mix of skills and ideas be good enough to help them stand out in a market awash with global fast-food giants, established local players and emerging salad-store competitors? There was an issue about how they could grow the business while still holding true to the Kapai values and maintaining work–life balance. James and Justin wondered how they could enhance Kapai's environmental and social responsiveness without detracting from potential franchisee interest. Whatever options they chose, they needed to not only be good for business, but to stay true to its Kiwi spirit and to be practicable as well.

Teaching notes for this case are available from Greenleaf Publishing. These are free of charge and are available only to teaching staff. They can be requested by going to:

www.greenleaf-publishing.com/oikos2_notes

Appendix 1 Kapai Menu

Source: Kapai New Zealand, 2007b

References

Bell, C. (1996). *Inventing New Zealand: Everyday Myths of Pakeha Identity*. Auckland: Penguin.

Burger Fuel. (2007). "Store Info." www.burgerfuel.com, accessed 1 November 2007.

Burger King. (2007). "Locations." www.burgerking.co.nz, accessed 1 November 2007.

Domino's Pizza Enterprises Ltd. (2007). *Annual Report 2006–2007*.

Franchise Business. (2007). "Buy a Franchise." www.franchisebusiness.co.nz, accessed 30 October 2008.

Hell Pizza. (2007). "Stores: Hell Hole Locations." www.hell.co.nz, accessed 1 November 2007.

Jesters Pies. (2007). "About Jesters." www.jesters-pies.co.nz, accessed 1 November 2007.

Kapai New Zealand. (2007a). "Kapai New Zealand Business Plan." (Confidential document made available to authors and quoted with permission).

Kapai New Zealand. (2007b). Menu. www.kapaisalads.co.nz, accessed 13 September 2007.

Katipo. (2003). "CafeNET Lambton Quay Extension Launched Today." 5 December 2003.

KFC. (2007). "KFC Store Location." www.kfc.co.nz, accessed 1 November 2007.

Landcare Research. (2007). "Landcare Research Manaaki Whenua." www.landcareresearch. co.nz.

Lord, S. (2007). "Healthy Eating Franchises Offer Fresh Options." *Franchise New Zealand*, 15(3), 5pp. www.franchise.co.nz/article/view/414, accessed 20 October 2008.

McDonald's. (2007a). "Inside McDonald's." www.mcdonalds.co.nz, accessed 14 November 2007.

McDonald's. (2007b). "Our Food." www.mcdonalds.co.nz, accessed 14 November 2007.

Oporto. (2007). Oporto Home Page. www.oporto.co.nz, accessed 1 November 2007.

Reload. (2007). Reload Home Page. www.reloadhealth.com, accessed 31 October 2007.

Restaurant Brands. (2007). "Company Profile." www.restaurantbrands.co.nz, accessed 1 November 2007.

Saladworks. (2007). "Saladworks Because." www.saladworks.co.nz, accessed 1 November 2007.

Scoop. (2006). "Wishbone Onboard at Wellington Airport." 4 October 2006. www.scoop.co.nz/ stories/BU0610/S00057.htm, accessed 7 December 2007.

Statistics New Zealand. (2001). "Wellington City Community Profile 2001." www.stats.govt. nz, accessed 11 September 2007.

Statistics New Zealand. (2006). www.stats.govt.nz, accessed 2 November 2007.

Stuff. (2007, November 1). "Obesity, Inactivity 'Strongly Linked to Cancer'." www.stuff.co.nz, accessed 1 November 2007.

The Food Industry Group. (2006). *2nd Annual Report to the Minister of Health*. October 2006.

Unlimited. (2004). "The Woodward Group (Wishbone)." 15 September 2004. www.unlimited. co.nz, accessed 7 December 2007.

Wellington City Council. (2007a). "About Wellington." www.wellington.govt.nz/aboutwgtn/ glance/index.html, accessed 11 September 2007.

Wellington City Council. (2007b). "Innovation Capital, Cuisine: Wishbone." www.wellington. govt.nz/aboutwgtn/innovation/details/wishbone, accessed 7 December 2007.

Wikipedia. (2007). "Koru." www.wikipedia.org/wiki/Koru, accessed 11 September 2007.

Part III
Entrepreneurial Action for Developing Inclusive Markets

Case 5
Fabio Rosa
Bridging the Electricity Divide in Brazil[1,2]

Aytha Harish and Vivek Gupta[3]
IBS Center for Management Research, Hyderabad, India

Fabio Rosa is one such entrepreneur, and while his name may not be as well known as many of today's brightest minds, he is the man who brought light to rural Brazil. This may seem an overstatement, but for the farmers living without the benefit of electricity—up to 70% of the rural population—this is no small thing. In fact, it has made a world of difference.

Niel Peterson, Head of Edge Foundation,[4] in June 2009[5]

1 This case © 2010, IBS Center for Management Research. All rights reserved.
2 This case was compiled from published sources, and is intended to be used as a basis for class discussion rather than to illustrate either effective or ineffective handling of a management situation.
3 This case was written by A. Harish, under the direction of Vivek Gupta, IBS Center for Management Research.
4 Edge Foundation is a charitable organization that provides personal coaches for children with Attention-Deficit/Hyperactivity Disorder. It was founded in 2006 in the US.
5 Niel Peterson, "The Case of Fabio Rosa: How Social Entrepreneurs Take on the World," www.nielpeterson.com, June 27, 2009.

Providing Electricity to Rural Masses

In February 2008, Fabio Rosa (Rosa), a social entrepreneur based in Brazil, was awarded The Leapfrog Fund Award[6] sponsored by The Schwab Foundation for Social Entrepreneurship[7] and the Lemelson Foundation.[8] This was the second time that Rosa was receiving the award, the first being in 2006. The award, among many others, recognized Rosa's efforts at providing rural families living in Brazil with access to electricity (refer to Exhibit I for awards received by Fabio Rosa).

Exhibit I **Awards Received by Fabio Rosa (1988–2008)**

Compiled from various sources.

Year	Award
2008	• "Leapfrog Fund Award" from The Schwab Foundation for Social Entrepreneurship and the Lemelson Foundation.
2006	• "Leapfrog Fund Award" from The Schwab Foundation for Social Entrepreneurship and the Lemelson Foundation
2004	• "Fast 50 Winner", Fast Company Magazine, USA • "The World Technology Award: Social Entrepreneur Category", The World Technology Network, San Francisco, CA, USA
2002	• "Avina Foundation Leader" from Avina Foundation. Miami, USA • "Outstanding Social Entrepreneur", The Schwab Foundation for Social Entrepreneurship" from the World Economic Forum 2002, New York, USA
2001	• "Technology Personality 2001", São Paulo State Engineers Society, São Paulo, Brazil • "Award of Appreciation", Embassy of United States of America/ United States Agency for International Development—USAID/Energy Program, Brasília, Brazil • "The Tech Museum of Innovation Awards: Economic Development Category Winner", The Tech Museum of Innovations, Center for Science, Technology & Society; Santa Clara University, CA
2000	• "Social Entrepreneurship Prize 2000: ASHOKA/McKinsey" Innovative idea in Fundraising, São Paulo State, Brazil

6 The Leapfrog Fund Award was presented by the Schwab Foundation for Social Entrepreneurship and the Lemelson Foundation. The Leapfrog fund supports the transfer and adaptation of technological innovations developed by social entrepreneurs. Winners were awarded grants worth US$75,000 over a 36-month period to facilitate technology transfer.

7 The Schwab Foundation for Social Entrepreneurship was established in 1998 in Geneva, Switzerland. Its purpose was to advance social entrepreneurship and to foster social entrepreneurs as an important catalyst for societal innovation and progress.

8 Established in 1993 in the US, the Lemelson Foundation supports projects in the US and developing nations that nurture innovators and unleash inventions to advance economic, social, and environmentally sustainable development.

Year	Award
1994	• "The ASHOKA Society Memberlife Fellow", Ashoka Social Entrepreneurs, Washington DC, United States of America
1988	• "Merit of the Imperial Bridge", for relevant services rendered to the community of Palmares do Sul; City Hall of Palmares do Sul, Rio Grande do Sul, Brazil

Note: the list is not exhaustive.

Rosa had been working since the year 1983 toward rural electrification in Brazil. According to him, as of November 2006, there were around 25 million people in Brazil who lacked access to electricity (refer to Exhibit II for a note on Brazilian economy and its power sector). Rosa realized that access to electricity would provide many ways to these people to increase their income levels. However, his attempts to find solutions that would allow them access to electricity met with several obstacles.

Exhibit II **A Note on Brazilian Economy and its Power Sector**
Compiled from various sources.

Brazil is the largest country in Latin America and the fifth largest in the world, going by surface area. Because of large surface area and good agricultural climate conditions, Brazil is a dominant player in production and trade of agricultural commodities. Brazil's GDP grew by 5.1% in the year 2008 and reached US$1.573 trillion in year 2008. Though Brazil is a prominent producer of agricultural commodities, the agriculture sector contributes only around 5.8% to its GDP. Brazil's services sector contributed the highest, 65.8%, to its GDP followed by the industrial sector, contributing 28.7%, in the year 2008. The GDP per capita of Brazil in 2008 was US$10,100.

The Brazilian economy had been witnessing a steady growth since 2000 with declining unemployment, strong exports, moderate inflation, healthy external accounts, and reductions in the debt-to-GDP ratio. In 2008, some of the major credit rating agencies upgraded Brazilian sovereign debt to investment grade despite the ongoing global economic slowdown. Brazil is open to foreign investment and was the largest receiver of foreign direct investment (FDI) in Latin America in 2008. However, several investors required Brazil to simplify its tax code and improve its regulatory environment to attract more FDI.

Brazil had around 100.8 million strong labor force in 2008 of which 20% were employed in the agriculture sector, 14% in the industries, and 66% in the services sector. The unemployment rate was estimated to be around 8%. The inequality in distribution of income in Brazil has been one of the highest in the world, with the country ranking 9th on Gini coefficient index in 2008.[a] Brazil population in 2008 was 198 million of which 86% lived in urban areas. About 31% of population in Brazil lived below the poverty line. Around 85% of the electricity generated in Brazil was hydro-electric power.

The Brazilian government had been spending the biggest portion of its budget—up to 50%—on social security and personnel to address issues like poverty and high income inequality. These measures were financed by higher taxation, which was not favorable for FDI. Poor infrastructure in Brazil was also a hindrance to its economic growth.

In late 2006, there were around 25 million people in Brazil without access to electricity. The Brazilian government targeted at providing 10 million people with electricity by the end of 2008 and to everyone by 2015. The main obstacle to providing access to low-income families, both in rural and urban Brazil, was the characteristic of these markets—low consumption per unit. Lower consumption per unit significantly increased the recovery period of investments. This problem was severe in rural areas because of low population density which required high capital investments, relative to the number of users, in setting up a distribution network. One more issue in extending the electricity grid to rural areas was poverty. Electric companies faced several problems like illegal connections, tampering with meters, corruption of meter readers, and defaults by customers which further increased the losses.

Though Brazil's power sector was state owned till the late 1990s, this particular drawback had resulted in the exclusion of several rural areas from the electric grid. The power sector was privatized in the late 1990s and rural electrification was given the least priority as maximizing return on investments was the motive of private distribution companies. There were not enough incentives for private distribution companies that could encourage them to go in for rural electrification. Agriculture, one of the main occupations in rural Brazil, was severely impacted because of lack of access to electricity. Without electricity, the efficiency of farming came down, impacting crop yields and hence the income levels of rural families. Lack of access to electricity also resulted in high expenditure on non-renewable energy sources for rural families.

a The Gini index calculates the inequality in distribution of income between rich and poor people within a country.

Rosa started off working as a part of the government to bring electricity to the rural areas in Brazil. He teamed up with several people like local politicians and academicians who helped him in overcoming some of the obstacles that lay in the way of achieving rural electrification. Rosa was keen on bringing about a significant positive difference in low-income families living in the rural areas in the country. He observed that there was a major exodus of people from the villages to the urban areas in search of better incomes and life styles. Through his efforts, he wanted to attract migrants from rural areas back to their villages.

Rosa changed his strategy and business model whenever he came across a barrier that could not be overcome. However, his goal remained the same—to improve the income levels of the rural families living in Brazil by providing them with access to electricity. In 1992, Rosa established a private firm, Sistemas de Technologia

Adequada Agroeletro[9] (STA), to pursue his goal of rural electrification. In STA, Rosa focused on using solar energy in combination with a few other techniques to improve the income levels of rural families in Brazil. He developed STA's business model in such a way that the majority of the rural families in Brazil could afford solar energy which otherwise would be expensive for them.

In the late 1990s, Rosa started a non-profit organization, Instituto Para O Desenvolvimento De Energias Alternativas E Da Auto Sustentabilidade (IDEAAS),[10] to develop business models targeted at low-income families that could not afford to access solar energy at STA offered prices (market rates). Through IDEAAS, Rosa developed business models where low-income families were provided with means to improve their income levels. Rosa felt that subsidizing the cost of solar energy would not be a sustainable solution for the low-income families. He realized that if they were provided with the means to generate more income, they would be able to afford solar energy at market rates. IDEAAS continued to develop sustainable business models using renewable solar energy through its learning center.

Rosa's dream was to ensure access to electricity to the two billion people all over the world who lacked access to electricity. He said,

> We have millions of people without energy, just like we did 10 years ago, just like we did 20 years ago. Brazil has this problem. India has this problem. China has this problem. Bangladesh has this problem. Two billion people have this problem. At the moment, we have a mature technology, but technology is only one part of the business. So what are we doing? Instead of focusing on commerce first, we are focusing on service. Commerce will come—but not in the way that people are thinking.[11]

However, some analysts pointed out that though Rosa had started pursuing his goal in 1983, he was not able to cover the whole of South Brazil even by late 2009. His business model required extensive market research to provide solutions as the products he provided his customers through IDEAAS were dependent on the type of terrain. Being a lean organization, it would take a long time for Rosa's team to customize solutions according to the requirements of each area, create awareness among beneficiaries, and provide training to them on how to use those products to augment their incomes, they said. Rosa's dream was to cover Brazil first, then provide similar solutions to other developing nations where millions of people lacked access to electricity. The cash flow in Rosa's business models was low, most of it contributing to recovering the capital invested. In such a business model, hiring more personnel required additional funds from the private investors or donations. Analysts felt that Rosa needed to tie up either with the respective governments or with

---

9 The English translation of Sistemas de Technologia Adequada Agroeletro is Agroelectric Adequate Technology Systems.

10 In English, it translates as Institute for the Development of Natural Energy and Sustainability.

11 "Fabio Rosa: Making the Sun Shine for All," www.globalenvision.org, February 7, 2006.

other non-governmental organizations (NGOs) to scale up his rural electrification efforts.

Background Note

Fabio Rosa (Rosa), an agronomic engineer, graduated from the Federal University of Rio Grande do Sul State, Brazil. In 1983, on an invitation from a friend, Rosa visited Palmares, an area in the Southern state of Rio Grande Do Sul. His friend's father, Ney Azevedo (Azevedo), was elected Mayor of Palmares at around the same time Rosa visited it. After conversing with Rosa about his ideas to improve the lives of the villagers, Azevedo offered him the post of Secretary of Agriculture for Palmares. Rosa accepted the offer and started working out of a church as there were no facilities like office premises, staff, or pickup van for the newly created post. Rosa spoke to several villagers to get a grip on the problems they faced. He realized that the politicians in Palmares were making promises about building roads whereas the priority of the villagers was on provision of better education, nutrition, and living conditions for their children and families. The poor productivity of farms was one of the most pressing issues for the local farmers. In search of better earnings, many farmers had started fleeing to urban areas.

After studying the area, Rosa understood that the primary source of income of Palmares was cultivation of rice. Rice requires plenty of water but most of the channels for water like dams were controlled by the wealthy landlords. These landlords had set such a high price for water that a quarter of the cost of production for the poor farmers was for the purchase of water. That was three times the world average. Rosa did some research and found that artesian wells could solve the water problems faced by the farmers. However, to pump the water to the ground, electricity was required. Rosa then realized that lack of access to electricity was the main reason for the problems faced by the people of Palmares. He conducted a survey and found that 70% of the rural population in Palmares had no access to electricity. Brazil's poor planning had led to expensive technology being used, which in turn meant that the cost of providing electricity to rural households was prohibitively high. Utility companies designed electric grids with excess capacity and hence the costs were high and could only be afforded by large farms and industries. In the early 1980s, the capital investment incurred by an electricity distribution company in Brazil to provide electricity to one rural household was US$7,000.

Rosa's First Project

Rosa conducted further research to find a way to bring down the cost of access to electricity in rural areas. He found out that Prof. Ennio Amaral (Amaral) of the Federal Technical School of Pelotas, Brazil, had developed a simple and low-cost rural electrification model. Rosa said, "With cheap electricity, poor farmers could drop wells and irrigate their land. Then they would be free from the tyranny of water."[12]

Rosa met Amaral to learn more about his model. Amaral's model used less material, which was also relatively inexpensive compared to the model followed by the utility companies for transferring electricity during that time. His model used a single high-tension wire (mono-phase) instead of three wires (three phase), which are usually used for transferring electricity. Mono-phase electricity was sufficient for the modest electricity needs of people in the rural areas such as for operating small bulbs and radios. The model used wooden poles instead of cement poles and steel instead of copper wires. Several such modifications resulted in reducing the cost of providing electricity to a rural household from US$7,000 to US$500. Despite being fully operational, Amaral's model was restricted to a test site by forces like cement and aluminum cartels which were benefiting by the then existing model of electricity distribution.

Rosa conducted geological tests at Palmares to find out the groundwater level. He found that there was abundant water available at around 22 meters depth. To experiment with a new model of electrification, Rosa required authorization from the state electric company. Azevedo used his political influence to get Rosa the required permissions. Under the guidance of Amaral, Rosa started off with the project. Amaral sent Ricardo de Souza Mello (Mello), one of his students, to help Rosa.

Mello focused on the technical details while Rosa had to meet the farmers to convince them to help him set up the system. The farmers, who had been promised electricity by the local authorities and politicians many times and had yet to see any signs of it, were understandably sceptical about Rosa's claims. However, they assured Rosa that if the poles, wires, and transformers were ready then they would help him in setting up the equipment.

The next issue that Rosa faced was in digging wells which required drills that operated only on three-phase electricity. Mello and Rosa found an alternative by using water pressure pumps that operated on diesel and forced polyethylene tubes down to the water level. The next challenge that came up was that the motors used to pump water out of the wells too required three-phase electricity. As they dug a few wells, they realized that the natural ground pressure pushed water up to an average depth of four meters from the ground. From that level, a mono-phase motor was sufficient to pump water out. Rosa faced another problem in the form of red rice,[13] which had an adverse impact on the rice yield[14] of farmers. He advised

---

12 "Changing the World on a Shoe String," www.theatlantic.com, January 1998.

13 Red Rice is like a weed and its seeds multiply quickly. If the land is cultivated continually, red rice spreads all over and destroys the desired rice crops.

14 To prevent red rice from spoiling the whole land, farmers cultivated only a quarter of their land every year and kept the remaining three quarters uncultivated. They rotated cultivation among the four quarters.

them to use a technique called water seedling.[15] Though water seedling was an existing technique, farmers in Palmares had not been able to use it earlier as water was expensive. Using Rosa's mono-phase model, farmers could have inexpensive access to water and use the water seedling technique for cultivation. This would help increase their farm yield.

Rosa presented his plan to Banco Nacional de Desenvolvimento Econômico e Social (BNDES),[16] seeking finance for the project. Aluysio Asti (Asti), one of the project analysts at BNDES, strongly supported Rosa's project. Asti said, "Just to have an agricultural development department in a small municipality in Rio Grande do Soul was itself an innovation. Especially an agricultural department that actually worked with small farmers."[17] Asti was impressed at the research work that supported Rosa's data in his presentation like the cost of the project, expenditure, and yields for farmers. According to Rosa's analysis, the bank's investment in the project could be repaid within four years. Asti recommended that BNDES finance the project.

Rosa sought political support for his project by meeting the mayors of neighboring municipalities. He also met journalists, to secure media support. He hired a technician through the mayor's office, contracted two companies to manufacture transformers that supported Amaral's electrification model, and purchased other material. Farmers supplied trees from their properties to build the wooden poles required for Amaral's electrification model. Mello scheduled installations. Just when everything seemed to be in place, Rosa received a letter from the board withdrawing its permission for the project. After several meetings that involved negotiations, both friendly and hostile, among several parties including Azevedo, the Governor of Rio Grande Do Sul, BNDES, the state electricity board, and Rosa, the state electricity board finally gave the required permissions for Rosa to implement his project in the year 1986.

By 1988, Rosa and Mello had delivered electricity to 420 rural families at a cost of US$400 per family. Rosa was encouraged by the fact that one third of the 420 families benefited were those who had returned to Palmares from cities because of their project. With these 420 families being provided with access to electricity, Palmares became the first municipality in Brazil to have 100% access to electricity. The income of farmers who implemented water seedling rose from US$50 and US$80 a month to between US$200 and US$300 a month. However, trouble again reared its head. Azevedo's term ended in 1988 and a new mayor was elected for Palmares.

---

15 Rosa advised farmers to flood their fields before they planted the rice and to let the field saturate when the rice grew. Then they could use pre-germinated seeds from the prepared beds and transplant them to the submerged paddies. As the fields would have been deprived of oxygen, the red rice seeds would not have been able to germinate.

16 BNDES is a federal public company in Brazil, linked to the Ministry of Development, Industry, and Foreign Trade. It was established in 1952 with the goal of providing long-term financing for projects in various sectors that aimed at enhancing Brazil's development.

17 *How to Change the World: Social Entrepreneurs and the Power of New Ideas*, by David Borenstein.

The new mayor closed down Rosa's department, dismissed his technicians, and diverted the loans that Rosa had negotiated with banks.

On the instructions of the Rio Grande Do Sul state government, Asti coordinated meetings between the state electricity board and Rosa and Mello to discuss rural electrification throughout the state. The state electricity board initially refused to recognize Rosa's technical standard as a legal standard for distribution. However, Rio Grande Do Sul's newly elected governor, Pedro Simon, supported rural electrification and BNDES was ready to offer loans for the expansion of Rosa's rural electrification project. In 1989, the state electricity board gave in and recognized Rosa's technical standard as a 025 Norm, a legal standard for electricity distribution in Brazil.

After gaining recognition, Rosa and Mello met the mayors of 42 municipalities to implement their business model. The terrain in each municipality differed and Rosa made changes to the model to suit each. He identified local technicians to carry out the project. Between 1990 and 1994, Rosa and Mello worked on Pro Luz (Project Light), to make electricity available to 6,200 low-income rural families (about 31,000 people). To achieve this, Rosa had to build 2,400 kilometers of low-cost grid. Rosa got low-cost loans of US$2.5 million from BNDES for this project. Due to inflation, the cost of installation went up to US$600 per household during that period.

In 1991, BNDES instituted a special credit line to promote rural electrification based on the 025 Norm. Several states of Brazil started showing an interest in implementing the 025 Norm because of its simple and low-cost model besides the availability of credit. Both with political support and the financial support of BNDES, it appeared that rural electrification all over Brazil was going to happen. However, in 1992, the Brazilian economy faced challenges like high inflation and interest rates coupled with political uncertainty. Under the guidance of the International Monetary Fund (IMF), the Brazil government tightened liquidity. Social spending was slashed and BNDES terminated its credit line for the rural electrification projects.

Rosa was discouraged by the government's withdrawal of support to his low-cost, socially important project. Having faced several obstacles in working with government support, he decided that it was time he set up a private firm to continue his efforts for rural electrification.

Inception of STA and IDEAAS

In 1992, Rosa started STA which focused on using solar energy for rural electrification. Rosa recognized that the major drawback in using solar energy was its high cost. To make it cost effective, Rosa decided to package the solar energy system with some utility just like he had packaged the mono-phase system with irrigation in Palmares. Rosa observed that Brazil had a vast stock of cattle and one of the major problems in rural Brazil was the inadequate fencing for animal grazing. As conventional fencing was expensive, small farmers could not afford it. Poor fencing resulted in the cattle overgrazing on farmers' lands, leading to lower farm yields and degradation of pasture lands.

Rosa traveled across Brazil to identify the problems faced by different farmers and also researched for solutions. He found that the Brazil government, through its land reforms program, had distributed millions of hectares of land to more than half a million families but could not provide electricity and solutions to their problems. Rosa came across a technique called managed grazing[18] invented by André Voisin (Voisin), a French farmer, in the mid-1900s. Even though the managed grazing technique was implemented in Brazil in the 1970s, using electrical fences, the system was not customized for Brazilian conditions and hence was discontinued. However, there was no evidence of any authority examining the details for the failure of this system. Rosa found that the electrical fencing systems had been imported from Europe and were not effective in Brazilian subtropical conditions as plants in Brazil grew taller, as compared to European countries. They touched the fence and drained the current.

Rosa researched and found that the minimum current in an electric fence for cows should be 2,500 volts and for cattle it should be 3,500 volts. In the existing fences, the current dropped to 2,000 to 1,000 volts when the plants touched them and made them ineffective. Rosa designed an electrical fencing system in which the current would not fall below 5,500 volts. Rosa had to make a few more modifications to the system for it to work effectively in Brazil, which had one of the world's highest incidences of lightening and was home to a number of species of cattle.

Rosa used a combination of poly-wire and fiber glass posts in designing an inexpensive, solar powered, electric fencing system. Rosa's fencing system was 85% less costly than conventional fencing. Rosa's idea for higher yields, and in turn higher income, was to use his inexpensive fencing system in combination with the managed grazing technique. Rosa observed that by implementing his model of electric fencing, the yields of cattle farmers had gone up by 100 to 200%. In fields which had been degraded because of poor grazing management, the yields after Rosa's system was implemented went up by around 500%. By the late 1990s, Rosa had installed 700 electric fencing systems in several states of Brazil and had gained nation-wide recognition as a leader in delivering low-cost solar energy (refer to Exhibit III for visual of electric fence).

---

18 André Voisin observed that the key factor in managed grazing is the grazing time animals spend in the same area. He found that if animals spent too much time or returned too early to the same area for grazing, they overgrazed. The solution was to divide the grazing land into different parts and to let the animals graze in each part for only a limited time in rotation. By doing this, grazed land would be used evenly and plants would get the time to grow. This technique was shown to increase yields, decrease soil erosion, and also improve the health condition and productivity of animals.

Exhibit III **Visual of Electric Fence**

Source: www.changemakers.net.

Using the managed grazing technique helped the cattle farmers do away with artificial cattle feeds as the grass on well managed pastures provided healthy feed for the cattle. Cattle farmers using Rosa's electric fencing and managed grazing technique were able to produce organic meat and milk products which had good demand the world over. In 1997, Rosa decided to develop self-sustainable business models in the field of alternative energy and agriculture in his efforts to help low-income rural families improve their income levels. For this purpose, he started a non-profit organization, IDEAAS. IDEAAS intended to use efficient, low-cost technologies to develop sustainable business models using renewable energy that would help low-income rural families improve their income levels.

While Rosa was working for STA, he also worked as a consultant for several state governments that showed an interest in using the 025 Norm for rural electrification. Some of the Brazilian states worked on using Rosa's mono-phase electric distribution model for rural electrification though the BNDES credit line was not available. However, in 1999, under the guidelines of the IMF, Brazil had to privatize its utilities sector. That resulted in privatization of electric companies which terminated the supply of power to mono-phase systems, which were less profitable for them when compared to serving urban areas through the three-phase model.

Renting Solar Energy

With the success of the solar-powered electric fencing systems, Rosa decided to use solar power for rural electrification instead of persuading private electric companies to support his mono-phase distribution model. Rosa conducted research in that direction in the late 1990s. The STA conducted an extensive market study in six villages for eight months. They found that 65% of rural families spent at least US$11 per month on non-renewable energy sources like kerosene, diesel, and batteries whereas the remaining 35% could not afford to spend over US$10 a month. Rosa realized that the 65% of rural families could afford solar energy at the same cost (US$11 a month) but the high cost of the solar energy kit was an obstacle. Brazil's sales tax structure drove the prices even higher by 50%. Then the idea of renting solar energy came to Rosa's mind. He said, "What does it mean to buy solar panels? It means to buy energy for the next 25 years. Who buys food for the next 25 years? You buy food for the next week or month. It should be the same with electricity."[19]

In 2001, Rosa decided to step down as a director of STA and to focus more on IDEAAS. STA helped Rosa to survey the market, develop, test, and refine practical models using solar energy. According to STA's survey, 35% of rural families could not afford market rates and hence needed a subsidy. STA being a for-profit organization could not provide such subsidies. Hence, Rosa formed a team of technicians, businessmen, lawyers, and journalists and discussed the issue. They came to the conclusion that they could follow a hybrid model by operating through both STA and IDEAAS. About 65% of rural families who could afford market rates would be served by the STA whereas the remaining 35% would be served by IDEAAS at subsidized rates.

Rosa's team launched two projects—The Sun Shines For All (TSSFA) and Quiron. TSSFA was to be executed under STA and Quiron was to be executed under IDEAAS. The basic idea behind the two projects was to rent out solar energy kits to the households in rural areas.

The Sun Shines For All

The TSSFA project was based on a business model where the customers would get solar home systems (SHS)[20] on lease for a particular period of time and pay monthly rentals in addition to a small installation fee. The maintenance of SHS was the responsibility of STA. By getting SHS on lease, the customers could avoid high sales tax but get the same benefits of buying a solar energy kit.

The next two years went in studying several existing business models based on solar energy, analyzing the market, identifying the competition and risks, conducting sensitivity analysis,[21] and projecting cash flows and income for the next 10 years. By 2003, the business plan was ready.

Rosa started off in Encruzilhada do Sul (Encruzilhada), one of the poorer municipalities in Brazil, where at least 25% families (around 1,000) lacked access to electricity. He teamed up with Maria Inez Azevedo (Maria), a social psychologist with

19 "Fabio Rosa: Making the Sun Shine for All," www.globalenvision.org, February 07, 2006.
20 Solar Home System is a kit consisting of solar panels, wires, battery and few electric appliances.
21 Sensitivity analysis is a technique used to determine how different values of an independent variable will impact a particular dependant variable under a given set of assumptions.

years of experience working in rural areas as a community motivator. Maria was supposed to handle marketing communication. Rosa hired a local electrician Dariel Ferras Soares (Soares), who founded his own electric shop in 1996, to handle the technical aspect of the installations. It took 2–3 hours for one installation and Soares earned US$30.73 to US$34.15 per installation. Talking about the business opportunity that TSSFA had provided to him, Soares said, "It presented a good opportunity to do business. And it's a great satisfaction to bring electricity to people who don't have it."[22] Rosa met Conceio Deromar Krusser, the then Mayor of Encruzilhada, who offered help in overcoming any political obstacles and also in identifying families without electricity.

STA conducted a pilot project in May 2003 by installing the SHS at three test sites in one of the poorer municipalities in Brazil, to assess the performance of the system. The tests made them realize that it was important for the battery to be protected in a tamper-proof container. Since the responsibility for providing the battery and its maintenance lay with STA, it was important for it to ensure that it was not tampered to cut down on service and replacement costs. They therefore placed the battery of the solar energy kit in a tamper-proof plastic box, even going to the extent of attaching a small ceramic saint to the batteries to remind its users to regard the batteries with respect. Brazilians, predominantly Catholics, considered saints as sacred. This move demonstrated Rosa's attention to detail and his understanding of the market. Though using plastic containers increased the costs marginally, it paid off in the long term by savings in servicing costs.

The product mix and pricing was based on what the target market was spending on non-renewable energy sources. Three different packages priced at monthly rents of US$10, US$16, and US$24 were designed. Pricing was done keeping in mind that the investment should be recovered in four years by providing a 29–30% internal rate of return (IRR). As the business model was capital-intensive, an attractive return was important for raising funds. The basic package, US$10 a month, included a 60-watt photovoltaic solar panel, a high-powered battery, 4 florescent lights, a 12-volt electric outlet, necessary wiring, and a battery change after three years. The other two packages included more outlets and more lights as per charges. Customers had to sign a contract for three years of service and there was an installation cost of US$150 which could be financed over the first 12 months of service. Customers were to be charged an un-installation fee if they opted to stop using the service before three years.

Rosa faced resistance to this project from rural families just as he had in Palmares where people were sceptical about the promise of electricity. Some did not believe that electricity could be generated from sunlight. STA conducted information sessions to convince them about the technology and its impact on their lives. On learning about Rosa's information sessions, electric utility companies made announcements about extending their grids to those areas. Rosa promised customers that they would not be charged any un-installation fees if electric utility

---

22 "Fabio Rosa: Making the Sun Shine for All," www.globalenvision.org, February 7, 2006.

companies extended their grid during the contract period. Rosa convinced customers that his efforts were to provide them with access to electricity but not to compete with the electric utility companies.

Rosa identified local champions, early adopters who understood the model well and could motivate others to use his system, to spread the message about TSSFA's services. STA also tied up with local stores for spreading the message about these services. It relied heavily on word-of-mouth publicity, which was very effective. The first year of service was received rather poorly with only 10% of the target market subscribing to the services. However, with the service making a visible impact on subscribers' lives, the subscriptions went up to 30% in the second year. Maria said, "We needed to build trust and confidence. It takes time to establish credibility. It's all a matter of how you talk to people. You have to ask a lot of questions. It's important to understand why people change or why they don't change. If you understand that, then you can deliver things to people in the way they would like to receive them."[23] (Refer to Exhibit IV for visual of SHS installed in a rural home in Brazil.)

Exhibit IV Visual of SHS Installed in a Rural Home in Brazil

Source: www.changemakers.net.

In late 2004, TSSFA Phase I was launched in nine municipalities of Rio Grandee Do Sul where 150,000 families lacked access to electricity. Phase I planned to cover 6,100 families by covering 1,000 families in the first year, 1,500 in the second, 1,720 in the third, and 1,880 in the fourth year. Phase I was expected to break even in the fourth year after it had 6,100 customers. Rosa received grants of US$60,000 from the Solar Development Foundation (SDF) and an additional commitment of US$50,000. SDF's grants to the STA were conditional—if STA found an investor, then the grant would become a debt for STA. SDF also agreed to provide loans for the purchase of solar panels, which would act as collateral for the loan. Besides, STA invested US$45,000 of its own funds for research and development (R&D).

STA had a lean organizational structure. It hired local electricians to handle the installations and took the help of local champions for marketing the services. On an average, each electrician could handle two installations per day.

Quiron

The project Quiron, executed under the non-profit organization IDEAAS, was targeted at families which could not afford US$11 a month to gain access to electricity. Rosa planned to develop a business model where IDEAAS could provide these low-income families with the means to generate income as a loan. The loan would be paid back by the beneficiaries from the additional income they generated. This project was based on micro-credit. Rosa realized that by improving their income levels, they would be able to afford solar energy at market rates. That would create a market for TSFFA in the longer term and make both his projects financially self-sustainable.

The goal of project Quiron was to increase the income of the rural poor through the use of decentralized renewable energy and appropriate micro-technologies. Conserving the environment which had become degraded because of deforestation in Brazil was also considered important while developing the business plan for Quiron. IDEAAS conducted viability studies of various ideas and developed a business plan with the assistance of Avina,[24] Canopus Foundation,[25] and the Horus Institute for Environmental Conservation and Development.[26] The business plan consisted of three products—Livestock, Grape Vineyard, and Sustainable Forestry.

---

24 Founded in 2000, Avina is a Latin American not-for-profit organization that contributes to sustainable development in Latin America by encouraging productive alliances based on trust among social and business leaders, and by brokering a consensus around shared agendas for action, with the support of people and institutions from around the world (source: www.avina.net).

25 Founded in 1997 in Germany, the Canopus Foundation promotes private social investment and social enterprise in order to fight poverty and environmental degradation, and provides business development assistance for social entrepreneurs in developing countries working in the field of clean energy technologies (source: www.canopusfund.org).

26 The Horus Institute for Environmental Conservation and Development is a Brazilian foundation with a mission to develop alternatives in environmental conservation

In the Livestock plan, IDEAAS provided each customer with five pregnant milk-producing buffaloes. The customer would be provided training in the managed grazing technique combined with electric fences. The customers would be able to generate an income by selling buffalo milk right from day one. After 10–12 months, the customer would return those five non-producing buffaloes which would then be inseminated and calves would be raised for sale. Customers would again receive five pregnant milk-producing buffaloes in return. This rotation would go on and the customer would be able to generate an annual income of US$576 by selling buffalo milk. Customers who wanted to invest their income on expanding the business further could buy more buffaloes and produce processed milk products like cheese which would boost their income further.

In the Grape Vineyard plan, IDEAAS provided seeds and other resources for planting and cultivation of grapes. Small areas which were unused were selected for plantation. IDEAAS supported them in cultivation by conducting soil tests and providing training. It tied up with wineries which agreed to purchase grapes from IDEAAS customers. The project was to generate an income after three years. Though the amount of income depended on several factors like the price and quality of the grapes, it was estimated that from the fourth year, annual income from the business could be around US$3,000.

In the Sustainable Forestry plan, the customers were to be provided with seedlings of several species of trees. The income through this venture would be generated by selling certified sustainable forest products. IDEAAS was to assist its customers by conducting a survey of species for their potential use and a survey of carpenters and sawmills for their requirements, and by identifying preferred species and available species in the market. IDEAAS was also to conduct soil analysis, provide training in planting, get the customers registered for selling forest products, and do periodical reviews. Income was expected to be generated after seven years as the fastest growing tree would take seven years whereas the slowest growing tree would take 40 years to become marketable. The estimated annual income from this plan was US$27,000 from the completion of the seventh year. However, the customers could grow firewood and any secondary products on the same land to generate small incomes in the meantime.

All the beneficiaries of Quiron were provided with SHS on STA's terms and conditions. As the beneficiaries were able to generate an additional income, they were able to afford these services. The means for income generation like livestock, seedlings, and other services that IDEAAS provided to Quiron beneficiaries were on the micro-credit system. The cost IDEAAS incurred on Quiron project was recovered from the beneficiaries in small and periodic repayments. The repayments, though small, also covered the operational costs of the Quiron project, funds for future deployments, market development, and research. The additional finances required

integrated with social and economic development, production systems, and the daily life of the people.

to expand the Quiron project were raised from several NGOs like Avina and the Canopus Foundation.

Social and Environmental Impact

The TSFFA and Quiron projects improved the quality of life of their beneficiaries. Without access to electricity, people had had to use other sources of energy like candles, kerosene, and diesel. Breathing in the smoke emanating from kerosene lamps took a toll on their health. By having electricity, people were able to use appliances such as radios and mobile phones which kept them connected to the world. Prior to TSSFA and Quiron being implemented, people had to travel to a nearby town to recharge their mobile phone batteries by paying a certain amount. Also, with access to electricity, the exodus from rural to urban areas came down. In fact, many of those who had migrated to urban areas were coming back. Otila Maria Rosa Dos Santos, a customer of STA, said, "My son had told me he didn't want to continue living in the dark. He was going to leave home. Now he will stay. I don't believe I lived my entire life without the grid, and now I have electricity."[27]

The environmental impact of using SHS was huge. STA estimated that providing solar energy to 12,900 families would save 9 million liters of kerosene, 4.6 million kilos of liquefied petroleum gas (LPG), 46.4 million wax candles, 9.3 million radio batteries, and 23.2 million liters of diesel. These savings would translate into a reduction of carbon emissions, which in turn, would mean contributing less to global warming. With a better environment, the farm yields would also increase, resulting in an increase in farmers' income levels.

Rosa's efforts had created an additional source of income for several people in the areas where SHS were being installed. STA had developed electronic payment systems that were installed at several places including pharmacies, general stores, and banks in the area where TSSFA and Quiron were being implemented. These electronic payment systems eased the rental payment process for the customers of both STA and IDEAAS. The stores where these systems were installed were paid a commission of US$0.24 per payment, which added to the income of the storekeeper once he recovered his investment on the system. Several stores started selling electronic appliances that worked on 12 volts power since solar energy supported only appliances that would work on 12 volts. These had not been available earlier.

Quiron helped its beneficiaries increase their income by around 240% and also provided them with better lifestyles because of access to electricity. Through the sustainable forestry plan, Quiron helped in the reforestation of several areas which had grown degraded because of deforestation. Through planting a mix of trees with different growth rates, the sustainable forestry plan was able to create consistent

27 "Fabio Rosa: Making the Sun Shine for All," www.globalenvision.org, February 7, 2006.

cash flows for the beneficiaries. Besides generating an income for the beneficiaries, the Grape Vineyard plan also addressed the lack of supply of grapes for the wineries in Brazil to a certain extent. Brazil had been a net importer of wines for a long time and so there was huge scope for indigenous wineries to grow.

Strengths and Challenges

The key strength of the STA and IDEAAS projects was the motivation of Rosa and his team to move forward despite having had to face several obstacles. Rosa's ability to convince the key stakeholders like politicians, bankers, local champions, and customers played a major role in the progress of STA and IDEAAS. Rosa's other strengths included his understanding of the local market, ability to understand and implement new technologies, innovation in using technology, capability to execute projects, and patience and perseverance in getting things done. His attention to detail and obsession with data were the reasons behind thorough market research being done before a business model was developed. According to the analysts, the planned approach that Rosa followed like spending time on pilot projects helped STA in improvising on the product offerings.

Rosa collaborated with 16 NGOs in Brazil to form RENOVE—Brazilian Network for the Use of Renewable Energy. The conferences held by RENOVE helped participating individuals and companies in sharing knowledge on the latest technologies and initiatives in the field of renewable energy. The leasing model followed by TSSFA and Quiron removed the concerns of improper disposal of the SHS into landfills. Customers would return the SHS at the end of the contract period, or when they became dysfunctional, to the STA, which followed better disposal/recycling methods that minimized the impact of disposals on the environment.

STA and IDEAAS followed a leaner business model by hiring local electricians who would be paid from the installation fees and depending more on local champions for marketing the services. To achieve its target of a minimum of 1,500 installations per annum, STA faced the challenge of keeping the electricians and local champions motivated to perform consistently. According to analysts, scaling up the business to expand across Brazil and beyond with a lean organization structure was tough. They felt that finding people motivated to work for social causes was necessary to build the human capital.

Another major challenge that Rosa faced was from electric utility companies. There were chances of the electric companies extending their grid to the rural areas where STA and IDEAAS were operating. Rosa's business model was dependent on future cash flows to achieve break-even and the customers were given an option to stop using their services if the electric grid was extended to them. If the electric grid was extended to the rural areas where TSSFA and Quiron were being implemented, then STA and IDEAAS would lose significant amounts on their investments.

Analysts felt that this challenge would also act as a barrier to private investments in the project.

Another challenge faced by Rosa's team lay in dealing with foreign exchange (forex) fluctuations. STA had been importing solar panels from the US and hence was exposed to forex fluctuations. Analysts felt that STA would have to build a team internally to handle forex management or outsource that function. However, both the options required a significant amount of investment. STA and IDEAAS also faced the risk of default from customers. Though a thorough background check was conducted on customers' credit-worthiness before they were offered SHS, the post-paid method of business always faced the risk of default.

The Road Ahead

As of mid-2008, STA was involved in manufacturing the components required for SHS besides going ahead with the TSSFA project. IDEAAS expanded its activities to include more research work on all renewable energy sources. It had set up a learning center in the Santo Antonio da Patrulha municipality of Rio Grande de Sul. The learning center carried out research on renewable energy sources like wind, solar, and hydro power. The center also provided training and guidance to entrepreneurs interested in clean energy ventures. Different business models were developed and tested at the learning center, which itself was powered by renewable energy sources.

While IDEAAS was working toward creating several sustainable business models in its learning center which could be scaled up to become an incubator for new entrepreneurs, it faced issues of succession. In late 2008, the Brazil government announced that it aimed to bring electricity to all the citizens of the country by extending the grid to even rural areas by the year 2015. Even though such moves were desirable, for STA and IDEAAS, it meant finding an alternative source of income to pay back their loans. About the challenge IDEAAS faced, Francisco Noguera, Managing Editor of NextBillion.net,[28] said,

> In spite of their success in becoming a reference for rural electrification in Brazil and worldwide, IDEAAS faces challenges related to government policies in Brazil and strategic questions related to the true scale potential and profit motive of its operation. In effect, the federal government in Brazil recently announced an aggressive initiative to bring "energy to all" in Brazil, through traditional centralized generation systems. Although that's great news in its own right, it leaves no space for private sector solutions like IDEAAS, unless utilities decide to partner with them in the purpose

28 NextBillion.net is a website and blog bringing together the community of business leaders, social entrepreneurs, NGOs, policy makers, and academics who want to explore the connection between development and enterprise (source: www.nextbillion.net/about).

of reaching remote areas like the state of Amazonia in the far north of the country.[29]

Industry observers said STA and IDEAAS had to work toward getting a standard norm status for their solar energy distribution model and tie up with private electric companies to expand geographically. As private electric companies had a strong financial status, teaming up with them would help IDEAAS and STA to a great extent.

Rosa's vision was to provide access to electricity to the entire rural communities living in Brazil and then to expand this project to include other countries like Bangladesh, China, and India where there were millions of people without access to electricity. According to analysts, theoretically, TSSFA and Quiron could be replicated anywhere but in practice, several issues needed to be considered. To expand to other nations, it would take considerable investments into conducting market research, customizing solutions, creating awareness, developing a supply chain, managing forex, and working according to domestic policies and following those nations' tax structures. However, the favorable aspect of Rosa's business models was that they were focused on implementing renewable energy sources, something which all nations favored as they aimed to bring down their carbon footprint. According to some analysts, Rosa could focus on trading in carbon credits to generate additional revenues but he required skilled human resources and technology to carry this out successfully.

Rosa's rural electrification efforts till mid-2009 were mostly concentrated in the southern part of Brazil whereas the majority of people who did not have access to electricity lived in the northern part of the country (refer to Exhibit V for a map on the density of power transmission lines in Brazil). Though IDEAAS teamed up with some NGOs operating out of the Amazon region in early 2007 to implement the Quiron project there, it was estimated that a significant amount of investment was required to conduct market research and implement the project there. Looking at the pace at which Rosa's rural electrification projects was progressing, analysts felt that he needed to raise more investments, hire more employees, and tie up with several private organizations if he was to achieve his dream of providing access to electricity for two billion people worldwide.

29 Francisco Noguera, "A Visit to IDEAAS: Clean Energy Solutions for Brazil's Poor," www.nextbillion.net, May 27, 2009.

Exhibit V **Map of the Density of Power Transmission Lines in Brazil**

Source: www.geni.org.

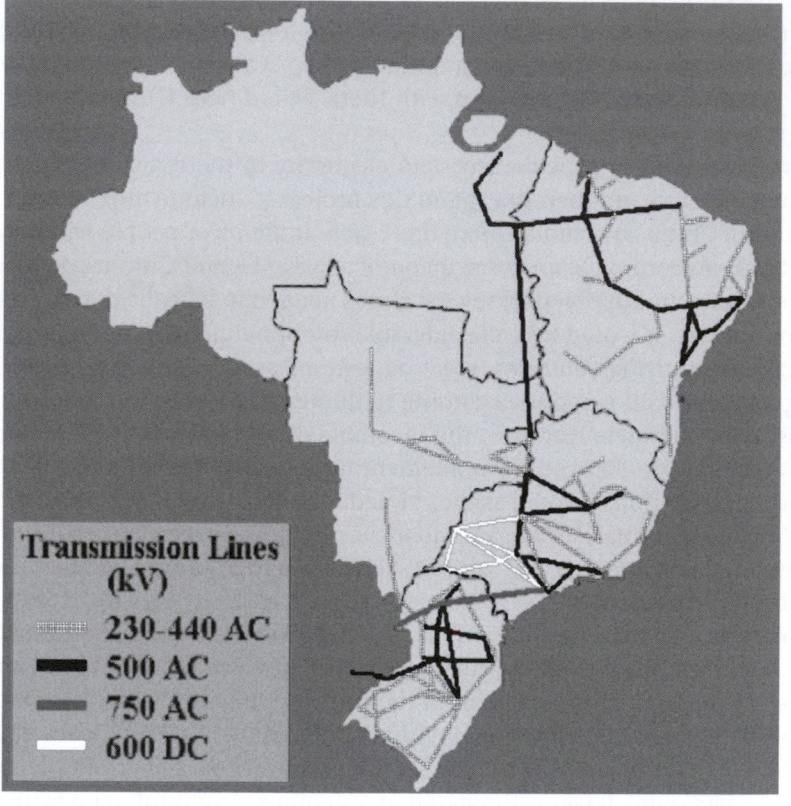

Teaching notes for this case are available from Greenleaf Publishing. These are free of charge and are available only to teaching staff. They can be requested by going to:

www.greenleaf-publishing.com/oikos2_notes

References and Suggested Reading

Book

David Bornstein *How to Change the World: Social Entrepreneurs and the Power of New Ideas* (Second Edition, Oxford University Press, 2007)

Internet Articles

Ethan Arpi, "With Fabio Rosa, Brazil Goes Solar," www.nextbillion.net, June 23, 2006
ASHOKA, "Fábio Luiz de Oliveira Rosa," www.ashoka.org.
Canopus Foundation, "The Quiron Project," www.canopusfund.org.
John Elkington, "Enter the Social Entrepreneurs," www.johnelkington.com, April 28, 2004.
Global Envision, Mercy Corps, "Fabio Rosa: Making The Sun Shine For All," www.globalenvision.org, February 07, 2006.
Global Giving, "IDEAAS: Bring Renewable Energy and Sustainable Electricity," www.globalgiving.org.
Global Philanthropy Forum, "Fábio Luís de Oliveira Rosa," www.philanthropyforum.org.
Francisco Noguera, "A Visit to IDEAAS: Clean Energy Solutions for Brazil's Poor," www.nextbillion.net, May 27, 2009.
PBS, "Meet the New Heroes," www.pbs.org.
Neil Peterson, "The Case of Fabio Rosa: How Social Entrepreneurs Take on the World," www.neilpeterson.com, June 27, 2009
Red Herring, "Clean Tech Empowers Poor," www.redherring.com, December 27, 2005
Regional Office for Asia and the Pacific, United Nations Environment Programme, "Towards Triple Impact," www.roap.unep.org.
St. Bede's Church, "Social Entrepreneur 5: Fabio Rosa," bedesblog.wordpress.com, March 18, 2009
Mike Shanahan, "Brazilian Wins 'Social Entrepreneur' Technology Prize," www.scidev.net, October 20, 2004.
Sustainable Design Update, "Rural Solar Power in Brazil," sustainabledesignupdate.com.
The World Technology Network, "2004 World Technology Awards Winners & Finalists," www.wtn.net.
Tony Wang, "Hidden World of Social Entrepreneurship," www.solutionsmag.net, June 16, 2004
Water for Humans, "Fabio Rosa," www.waterforhumans.org.
William Davidson Institute, University of Michigan, "IDEAAS," www.wdi.umich.edu.
William Davidson Institute, University of Michigan, "Understanding People's Needs Is First Step," www.wdi.umich.edu, November 09, 2006
YouthXchange, "Fabio Rosa: The Sun Shines For All," www.youthxchange.net.

Websites

Fast Company: www.fastcompany.com
Instituto Para O Desenvolvimento De Energias Alternativas E Da Auto Sustentabilidade (IDEAAS): www.ideaas.org.br
World Business Council for Sustainable Development: www.wbcsd.org

Case 6

Dr. Reddy's

Medicine is for People, Profits Follow[1,2]

Bala Chakravarthy and Sophie Coughlan
International Institute for Management Development, Lausanne, Switzerland

> Our vision for the next five years is to ensure that no patient goes without treatment because one is not able to afford it.[3]
>
> G.V. Prasad, Chief Executive Officer, Dr. Reddy's

Dr. Reddy's was India's second largest pharmaceutical company, with revenues of US$1.4 billion in 2009. Founded in 1984, the company owed its success in large part to the sale of generic drugs to markets in North America and Europe, and to the sale of branded formulations in India, Russia and other emerging economies. Its long-term ambition was to be a discovery-led pharmaceutical major.

Dr. Anji Reddy, the founder and chairman of Dr. Reddy's, liked to quote George W. Merck (founder of Merck & Co.):

> We try never to forget that medicine is for the people. It is not for profits. The profits follow, and if we have remembered that, they never failed to appear.

He firmly believed that developing drugs for unmet patient needs and making the drugs accessible and affordable would eventually benefit shareholders as well.

Cardiovascular disease (CVD) was the number one killer worldwide. By 2015, Indians were projected to make up 60% of the world's cardiac patients.[4] Dr. Reddy's was seeking to combine four proven ingredients for cardiac care in one little Red Heart Pill (RHP), to help prevent CVD patients from having another heart attack or stroke, as well as preventing individuals at low to moderate risk of developing acute CVD from having a first heart attack or stroke. The aim was to offer this treatment for less than $25 a year, a price that even the poor could afford. The company's CEO, G.V. Prasad, was counting on his team to develop a strategy for the RHP that would make it accessible and affordable to the poor and profitable for the company.

A Magic Pill to Fight Cardiovascular Disease

Cardiovascular disease (CVD) was the broad term used to describe a variety of related illnesses like aneurysm, angina, atherosclerosis, cerebrovascular accident (stroke), cerebrovascular disease, congestive heart failure, coronary artery disease and myocardial infarction (heart attack). CVD accounted for 30% of global deaths in 2005, killing a total of 17.5 million people—7.6 million due to heart attacks and 5.7 million because of strokes. These numbers were expected to climb rapidly because of an aging population in many developed economies and a lack of access to proper medical care in low- and middle-income countries. Exhibit 1 shows the worldwide burden of CVD.

CVD in India

Over 2 million people died from coronary diseases every year in India. This number was expected to rise dramatically by 2015, when Indians were projected to make up 60% of the world's cardiac patients.

Indians were 3 to 4 times more at risk of developing CVD than Caucasians, 6 times more than Chinese and 20 times more than Japanese. Increased CVD risk in India was the result of nutrition habits (especially high salt intake), tobacco use and decreasing physical activity. Genetics also played a role. The average age for heart patients in India was 57, much lower than the global mean of 66.

The prevalence of CVD in urban areas was higher than in rural areas, but it was difficult to measure the incidence of CVD in rural areas with any precision. Many

4 According to the World Health Organization (WHO).

at-risk people in rural India remained undiagnosed, since CVD was often asymptomatic until it caused a cardiac event. Since traveling to a hospital often cost more than the treatment itself, the rural poor tended to delay seeking treatment until a condition became serious,[5] generally when a heart attack or stroke had already occurred. Also, it was often difficult for people to get to a hospital—even when it was necessary—because they had to cover long distances by bus, tractor, truck, three-wheel rickshaw, or even taxi, if one could be found. Most had no health insurance, paid for treatment themselves and could not afford preventive check-ups. In the few cases that were diagnosed and treated early, patients often did not comply with the treatment prescribed (mainly because they could not afford the medicines or did not appreciate the importance of precise compliance with a complex treatment regime). Cardiac events (heart attacks and strokes) often sent victims' family members into a downward spiral of poverty.

A Polypill for Treating CVD

The dominant treatment paradigm for heart disease was to treat CVD risk factors (such as blood pressure, blood cholesterol, and the like) individually and manage each with great precision—prescribing medications on an individual basis. This approach depended on screening high-risk individuals. As a consequence, treatment was limited only to those already using healthcare services.

In 2003 two British scientists, N.J. Wald and M.R. Law, published a controversial article in the *British Medical Journal* (BMJ) in which they claimed that the use of a regimen of six well-known cardiac drugs (a diuretic, a beta-blocker, an ACE inhibitor, a statin, aspirin and folic acid) in the form of a fixed-dose combination pill (or polypill) could largely prevent heart attacks and strokes.

The cumulative benefits of taking several active ingredients were argued to be substantial. It was claimed that each drug caused a proportional risk reduction that was unaffected by the presence or absence of the other medicines. The net benefit of the combined treatment was estimated to lower the risk of a heart attack or stroke in high-risk patients by 55% over a five-year period (refer to Exhibit 2). A combination pill was expected to avert 8 million deaths over a ten-year period. This in itself would help meet 75% of the World Health Organization (WHO) goal of reducing the death rate from chronic disease by 2% each year between 2005 and 2015.

Although the medications had some side effects, these were estimated to affect only 0.6% of patients (refer to Exhibit 2). Among high-risk individuals, the benefits of the medications in terms of avoiding a major CVD event far outweighed the side effects.

---

5 "The Health Market" in *The Next 4 Billion* (2007) World Resources Institute, pdf.wri.org/n4b_chapter2.pdf.

Bridging the Treatment Gap

For patients who had already experienced a heart attack or stroke, the polypill could help prevent recurrence. All major treatment guidelines in the world recommended a post-event treatment with four agents (a statin, both a beta blocker and an ACE inhibitor to reduce blood pressure, and aspirin). However, prescription data in India (see Table 1) showed that barely 8% of patients who had survived a heart attack were prescribed all four agents, partly because the hospital specialist in India also worried about the patient's ability to pay for the four medicines and adhere strictly to the doses prescribed.

Table 1 **Drug Classes Prescribed in India Post Heart Attack, February 2008 to January 2009**

Source: ORG–IMS Medical Audit

Drug Class	% of prescriptions
Statin	49
Aspirin/Aspirin+Clopidogrel	54
ACE Inhibitor	25
Beta blocker	42
All 4 classes	8

In the US, over 90% of patients discharged from hospital after heart attacks were prescribed all four agents. However, adherence was very poor. For example, only 46% of patients with CVD reported consistent beta-blocker use within one year of a severe heart attack, and only 50% of the patients adhered to their prescribed statin use. Fewer than 20% of all heart attack patients used all four of the recommended agents.[6] It was the same story in Europe.

The polypill would be globally relevant as it would not only close the treatment gap but also improve compliance rates (because it was a single capsule as opposed to four distinct pills). Patients who were prescribed multiple medications for their CVD did not always adhere to their prescriptions. Sometimes the regimen was too complex and they simply forgot. There was also a degree of stigma attached to taking four or five pills per day, and many simply missed a dose especially when they were in company. And in a few cases, especially among the poor who could not afford to pay for all of the medications, those who had received prescriptions for four different medications purchased only the cheaper ones. There was a 5% to

6 Choudhry, N.K., A.R. Patrick, M.A. Elliott and W.H. Shrank (2008) "Cost-Effectiveness of Providing Full Drug Coverage to Increase Medication Adherence in Post-myocardial Infarction Medicare Beneficiaries." *Circulation* 117(10): 1261–68, circ.ahajournals.org/cgi/content/abstract/117/10/1261.

10% increase in the risk of non-compliance with each additional drug prescribed. A more convenient preparation was expected to improve compliance.

Primary Prevention

For individuals with one or more CVD risk factors, such as high blood pressure or high cholesterol, care depended on their access to a health center. The polypill was estimated to lower the risk of a first heart attack or stroke by 55% in this low- to moderate-risk population.[7] Even in richer patients, a single risk factor was commonly either not treated or treated with only one medication. In poorer patients, the early warning signs of CVD typically went undiagnosed. Considering the growing risk of CVD in India, the demand for polypill in primary prevention was also expected to be huge.

An Indian Champion

One of the early proponents of the polypill in India was Professor Srinath Reddy, a world-renowned CVD expert. Professor Reddy headed the elite panel of doctors entrusted with the care of the Indian Prime Minister. He was the head of cardiology at the All India Institute of Medical Sciences (AIIMS), India's leading medical school. But his interests had widened:

> I am no longer working only as a cardiologist. I want to focus on public health. And public health is multi-disciplinary. Prevention of diseases is important and we are looking at strengthening systems.

Professor Reddy took leave of absence from AIIMS to head the Public Health Foundation of India (PHFI), a public–private partnership devoted to the prevention of chronic diseases in India. He noted that the economic burden that CVD placed on India was huge—an estimated $236 billion over ten years, due to both loss in productive working days and treatment costs. India lost more than five times as many years of economically productive life to CVD than the US and this was projected to increase.

Professor Reddy approached his friend Dr. Anji Reddy and asked him to produce a polypill for the Indian market. Anji Reddy agreed—the polypill fitted very nicely with the company's commitment to providing accessible and affordable medicines for the poor.

Dr. Anji Reddy, a PhD chemist, had founded two pharmaceutical companies in 1984 that were subsequently merged in 2000 to create Dr. Reddy's Laboratories, or simply Dr. Reddy's. Anji Reddy stepped down that year from an active role in managing the company. While he continued as chairman, his son-in-law G.V. Prasad became the vice chairman and CEO, and his son Satish Reddy became the MD and

---

7 Estimate provided by Dr. Anthony Rodgers, Professorial Fellow, University of Sydney's George Institute for International Health.

COO. Since 2000, Anji Reddy had devoted more of his time to Naandi, a not-for-profit development institution he founded to help eradicate poverty; and to Dr. Reddy's Foundation for Human and Social Development, a social arm of Dr. Reddy's Labs.

Dr. Reddy's: A Brief History

Dr. Reddy's began by supplying active pharmaceutical ingredients (APIs) and intermediates to other pharmaceutical companies for formulating their drugs. Soon thereafter, the company started formulating its own drugs and supplying them as branded formulations in the Indian market and as generic drugs in the US.

In the 1970s the Indian government had chosen to adopt a process patent regime for the Indian drug industry, whereby a manufacturer could produce any drug whose product patent was still valid, as long as the process used to manufacture the drug differed from that of the innovator/patent holder. Dr. Reddy's took advantage of this opportunity and began formulating several drugs whose patent had not expired. Since all Indian competitors provided the same molecule, Dr. Reddy's had to brand its products and market them successfully against domestic competitors. Hence the name "branded formulation." In 2005 the Indian parliament enacted legislation that made it illegal to copy patented drugs, but by then the generics market had begun to boom. Dr. Reddy's used its marketing and distribution clout to continue branding its generic drugs where it could. The company generated INR15.24 billion (Indian rupees) in revenues from branded formulations in 2008, with a substantial portion coming from India, Russia, China and other emerging economies.

Another core business for Dr. Reddy's was generics, where it was fast emerging as a top ten player in the world. It had world-class factories for producing quality drugs at low costs. The world market for generic drugs was exploding given the push in the US, the European Union and Japan to curb the rising cost of healthcare. New legislation had been proposed in each of these regions, facilitating the entry of generic drug makers like Dr. Reddy's into the US, European and Japanese markets. Over $129 billion of branded pharmaceuticals were expected to go generic between 2008 and 2013. The opportunities for Dr. Reddy's were huge. However, the generics market was also a very fragmented one. The top ten generics companies accounted for just 28.5% of the global market in 2007. Competition for Dr. Reddy's came both from other generics manufacturers (Indian and foreign) and from innovators licensing or selling their own authorized generics.

Dr. Reddy's was also involved in the discovery of new drug molecules in a few specific clinical areas: cancer, metabolic disorders and cardiovascular. By 2009, it had five new drug molecules in the pipeline, one for the treatment of diabetes in the final clinical trial stage of human testing and four other drugs in the initial stages of development for treating cancer and CVD. Even though drug discovery was a long, expensive and risky process, it was the founder's passion.

By 2009, Dr. Reddy's had revenues of INR69 billion (refer to Exhibit 3). International revenues dominated domestic revenues by a factor of four to one. Revenues from India were INR8.5 billion, compared with INR11.9billion from Europe, INR19.8 billion from North America and INR7.6 billion from Russia and the Commonwealth of Independent States (CIS). The company's business portfolio as of 2009 is summarized in Table 2. Exhibit 4 provides a general comparison between Dr. Reddy's and other leading drug companies.

Table 2 **Dr. Reddy's Business Portfolio, 2008/09 (INR million)**
Source: Dr. Reddy's, 2009

	Revenue	Gross profits*	Gross profit as % of revenue
Pharmaceutical services and active ingredients	18,758	5,595	30
Global generics	49,790	30,448	61
Proprietary business	294	196	67
Others	599	261	44
Total	69,441	36,500	53

Note: Does not include selling and R&D costs or exchange gains and losses.

Launching the Polypill at Dr. Reddy's

The challenge of successfully launching the polypill at Dr. Reddy's was handed to Raghu Cidambi, a senior advisor on strategy and intellectual property (IP). He reported to Prasad, the company's CEO. Cidambi had joined Dr. Reddy's from a media company to help organize the IP function and to advise on strategy matters, which meant he had to postpone his plans to spend more time on social causes. Cidambi recalled:

> There are a number of safe and efficacious medicines already available to the world which, when tweaked into a new formulation and supported by appropriate clinical evidence, could make a significant dent in some of the seemingly intractable health problems like cardiovascular disease. The polypill was one such idea that could do a lot of good for the masses. It excited me.
>
> Also, the polypill requires R&D, legal, manufacturing and marketing capabilities that only a few generics companies have; we are one of them. Big pharma has these capabilities too, but can they descend to the price

points that this product will require? We at Dr. Reddy's need to be globally number one in something. I saw in the polypill that opportunity.

Scope of the Challenge

Cidambi realized immediately that to successfully deliver the polypill he would have to tackle a number of challenges:

1. The polypill was a "new drug" requiring pharmaceutical and clinical development. The costs of such development, while being a fraction of the costs of development of a new chemical entity (NCE), would nevertheless be substantial. Cidambi reckoned that he would need $20 to $30 million to develop the polypill, 20 to 30 times what would be required to launch a new generic.

2. The polypill would be difficult to patent. He fully expected competitors to develop competing formulations in parallel. Dr. Reddy's would need other distinctive capabilities.

3. Being a new prescription product, it would have to be marketed to medical practitioners.

4. In order to make it accessible and affordable, the price would have to be low.

5. Despite the higher costs and lower price associated with the project, it had to be profitable and meet top management's tough return on capital employed (ROCE) criterion.

Seeking External Expertise

The immediate task was to formulate the product and get clinical approval for it. Cidambi approached Professor Anthony Rodgers for help, at the suggestion of Professor Srinath Reddy.

Dr. Rodgers was a world-renowned expert on the design, conduct and analysis of large clinical studies on the causes, prevention and treatment of CVD. He had spent many years at the University of Auckland as the director of its Clinical Trials Research Unit before joining the University of Sydney's George Institute for International Health as a Professorial Fellow to work on developing affordable medicines.

He was the principal author of the 2002 World Health Report that stratified the world by CVD risk (refer to Exhibit 1). He had suggested several ways of mitigating this risk, including stopping smoking and reducing salt intake. He had also advocated the launch of a simple and inexpensive treatment regimen using combination therapy—in essence a polypill idea, even before the publication of Wald and Law's article in 2003.

Dr. Reddy's entered into a partnership with Dr. Rodgers in 2003, to help develop the polypill. Like Cidambi, Dr. Rodgers recognized that the key to the polypill's success would be in developing a robust business model more than tweaking the science underlying it:

> At present, this is "in between" the established business models of "new" medicines priced at \$1 to \$3 per day and generics that are straight copies and priced at 10 to 30 cents per day. This combination pill can be made for near-generic prices, but it is a "new medicine" and needs a new approach … But no one is willing or able to add the massive expense of a traditional pharma marketing and sales campaign. This would push the cost up to approach "blockbuster" prices and hence reduce accessibility. It is also too much risk for a generics company, since a different version of the polypill might come along in a few years and "piggyback" on its investment in marketing.

Dr. Rodgers became a valuable sounding board for the project team, besides helping with the polypill's clinical trials.

Formulating the Red Heart Pill (RHP)

The first step in the project was to formulate the polypill. Dr. Sankara Rao, Dr. Reddy's global head of integrated product development for generics, was given this challenge. He assembled a dedicated team of ten members, led by a project manager, to work on the RHP. The team was encouraged to work across functional silos—R&D, manufacturing and marketing—right from the start and come up with integrated solutions. Rao recalled:

> Just to give you a flavor of the challenge, one of our competitors had tried to combine just two active ingredients—a statin and aspirin. But they had to abandon their venture after two years. Taking the polypill idea from a research paper to an approved pharmaceutical product is hard work.

The formulation developed by Dr. Reddy's contained aspirin, simvastatin and two anti-hypertensive ingredients of different strengths (folic acid was dropped due to limited evidence of its effectiveness). The original design choice of a tablet was changed to a capsule—with each active ingredient in a different compartment within the capsule instead of being mixed in a single formulation. The R&D team worked closely with the marketing department to determine the right size, shape and color for the capsule. The color chosen was red and the capsule was small enough to be swallowed easily, yet large enough to hold the desired quantities of the four ingredients. The capsule was also strong and not easily crushed before being ingested.

Product Portfolio

Dr. Asit Datta was appointed head of the RHP project in 2007. He came to Dr. Reddy's after working for many years with an American drug major. He pointed out:

> The buzz in academic circles was around the potential benefits of the poly-pill for primary care, i.e. preventing heart attacks and strokes in patients with one or more risks of developing CVD. But we saw its potential also in the secondary care market, i.e. for CVD patients who had already suffered a stroke or heart attack and were under treatment to prevent a recurrence.
>
> From the very beginning, we sought to build a product portfolio to address the entire spectrum of CVD risk. We wanted to offer patients the possibility of receiving the best tailored prescription for their medical condition.

The RHP was expected to be offered in two versions, each with a further three titrations (different strengths of the constituent ingredients) (refer to Exhibit 5). The two versions were for (1) the secondary market to treat existing CVD patients and help them avert the next heart attack or stroke, and (2) the larger primary market for individuals with moderate to high risk of developing CVD. Four of these six formulations had to be developed for clinical testing.

Manufacturing

The RHP had to be investigated for potential impurities and added toxicity, caused by the simultaneous release of its active ingredients into the bloodstream. These investigations required a large amount of analytical work. Data on the chemistry, manufacturing and controls (CMC) for the RHP had to be compiled meticulously for the regulators. Cidambi noted:

> We pride ourselves on our excellence in doing these studies. This is one of Dr. Reddy's distinctive capabilities that very few of our generics competitors have. We have shown that the impurity profile of the RHP is no worse than the aggregate of the individual ingredients. This will give us a huge advantage in registering the drug.

Manufacturing a stable formulation was another significant technological challenge. But with world-class laboratories, and manufacturing facilities approved by the US Food and Drug Administration (FDA), Dr. Reddy's was able to produce the RHP to the highest international standards. It was also confident of its ability to manufacture the RHP at a lower cost than its competitors. The team had brought the cost per pill down to INR3 (about $0.05). Since Dr. Reddy's offered other branded generics in the Indian market to treat blood pressure and cholesterol problems, the company chose to use different active ingredients in formulating the RHP. This was to avoid a direct price comparison. With an intended retail price close to the cost price, the RHP would be subsidized for the Indian market.

Packaging was another important consideration. The RHP was to be offered in strips of 15 capsules. This would allow the patient to buy two weeks' supply at a time, with a day's buffer in case of unforeseen delays in getting a refill. The strip would be priced at 15 times INR3, or INR45 (roughly $1), no more than half the daily wage of even a low-paid Indian laborer. The overall cost of treatment was estimated at under $25 a year.

Cidambi went on to add:

> We believe that our method of formulation and manufacture provides a shelf life of over two years—closer to three—for our RHP. This can be an important advantage when distributing the drug to rural markets. We also have ongoing plans to streamline our operations and supply chain. We expect to make money with the RHP even at its low price.

Clinical Testing

The next challenge was to conduct bioequivalence studies. Each RHP formulation had to demonstrate that when released into the bloodstream, it would be absorbed and act in an equivalent fashion to each of the RHP's four constituent ingredients (also known as innovator molecules) when taken separately.

Trials began in 2007 for the secondary care formulations of the RHP in 11 centers in India. These proceeded smoothly, since the RHP served as a straight substitute for people already taking blood pressure and cholesterol lowering drugs. A full clinical trial program was not required. A data package to support use in secondary treatment was submitted to the Indian regulators, with a request for an opinion by mid-2009.

International Trials

Simultaneously, with the help of Dr. Rodgers, trials for the secondary care use of the RHP were beginning in other parts of the world. The cumulative data from these international trials together with those from India were expected to help convince prescribing physicians around the world of the merits of the RHP for secondary treatment of CVD. As Cidambi pointed out:

> Once we register the RHP in India, several international markets will open up for us; and registering it in New Zealand would make it easier to register in Europe. We are getting encouraging signals there. We will get to the US progressively, once we have approval in Europe.

In partnership with Dr. Rodgers, Dr. Reddy's was also preparing to launch trials across all six continents to establish the merits of the RHP for primary care, i.e. in preventing heart attacks and strokes in patients at moderate risk of CVD. These trials were expected to last five years, and the earliest that Dr. Reddy's hoped to register its RHP for primary care of CVD was 2017. Cidambi noted:

> These trials will be expensive and we need external funding. We will have
> to compete for these funds. We are hopeful that our track record to date on
> the RHP will give us the edge. But funding remains a huge uncertainty.

The RHP trials for the primary care formulation of the RHP were different from a typical clinical trial for a new drug in two respects: (1) the large number of patients involved (more than 5,000), and (2) the long time period over which the trials were conducted (more than 5 years). The trial protocols had to be the same across all countries, and the results had to be shared among them. Also, the regulators in each country had to briefed on the key milestones reached. The coordination task was complex and the costs involved would be significant even for a pharmaceutical major. Dr. Reddy's could not afford to take on these costs. It needed an alternate arrangement.

International Steering Committee

With the help of Dr. Rodgers, the company set up an International Steering Committee. The role of this committee was to establish a shared protocol for the trials, find funding for them, and to monitor and share the data from each trial as it progressed. The members of this committee were internationally renowned cardiologists from the US, Netherlands, UK, Australia, New Zealand, China and India. Each had conducted major CVD trials around the world, involving 250,000 participants in total. Many of the International Steering Committee members would themselves be Principal Investigators for the RHP trials in their countries, and would work with

Figure 1 **The International Steering Committee and Co-ordinating Centre**

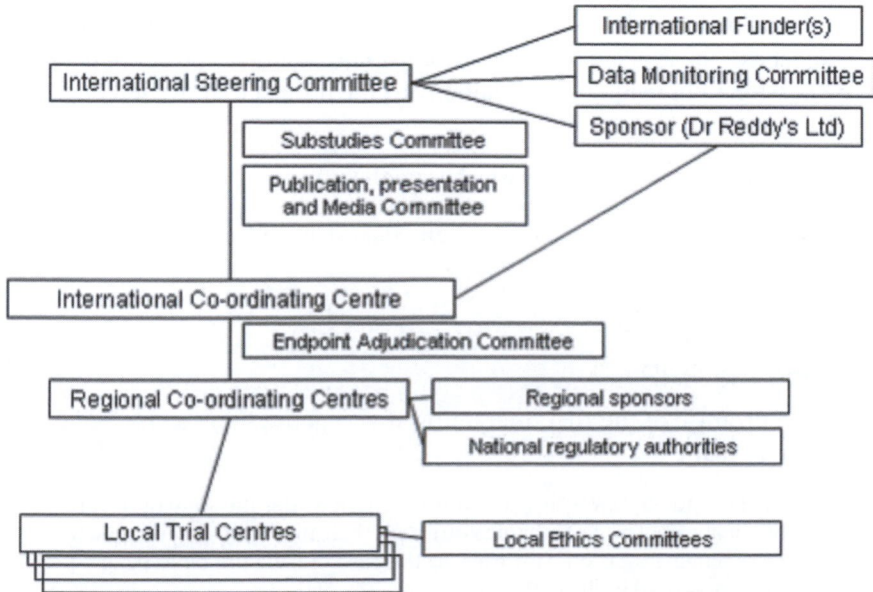

Dr. Reddy's to get external funding for these trials. Dr. Reddy's was the sponsor of the trials, responsible for fulfilling all the legal requirements and documentation, as well as for supplying products for the trials.

The company was also hoping to set up—again with the help of Dr. Rodgers—an International Co-ordinating Centre for the RHP trials, to be housed in the George Institute at the University of Sydney where he was based. This center would help coordinate (through regional centers to be established) information sharing with regional sponsors and national regulatory authorities.

Figure 1 describes the organization that Dr. Rodgers and Cidambi had in mind to administer the RHP trials.

Cidambi was hoping to formalize the roles of the George Institute and the International Steering Committee through appropriate contracts. He pointed out how this special arrangement was a huge win–win for everyone involved:

> Dr. Reddy's interests and those of the collaborators are totally aligned. That is the reason why the arrangement found favor with everybody to start with. They all want the trials done soon. They hope that the findings will lead to a landmark publication. More importantly, they wish that their trial is a success and we can get the drug out into the market as soon as possible and start saving lives. That is what we want as well.

Developing a Strategy for the RHP

By March 2009, the RHP project had already consumed $10 million. A lot had been accomplished but the business model had yet to be proven. Cidambi had run the RHP project as a loose alliance within the company, using his power of persuasion and the passion of individuals associated with the project to move it along. Prasad was getting impatient:

> This is a unique opportunity which is neither a generic, nor quite a true innovator drug. It is a new class. But we have been slow. Perhaps we should have created a dedicated team with the right skills and given it the right incentives to bring in quicker results.

Marketing the RHP

Despite the promise of the RHP, marketing it was going to be a challenge. As Dr. Rodgers pointed out:

> Physicians prefer new drugs, assuming that they offer the state of the art in medical care. Drug companies often pit their new drugs against older ones as patents wear off. However, in the case of CVD the older drugs— like the ones used in the RHP—are just as effective.

> Moreover, experts tend to focus on one risk factor, like blood pressure, and the finer points of managing it. But once a risk has decreased by a certain percentage, the best thing to do is to affect one of the other risks rather than to fine-tune the management of the existing risk. But this is quite a different approach from what I and others in the profession were taught at medical school. The RHP does a better composite job of lowering CVD risks. But convincing physicians to prescribe it will be a challenge.

Dr. Reddy's, like other Indian pharmaceutical companies, had focused its marketing efforts to date on urban centers, where the majority of hospitals and patients with health insurance (i.e. those who could afford expensive drugs and treatments) were located. Also, the country's top doctors practiced in these urban centers. They were the key opinion leaders.

The top cardiologists and vascular specialists in the country needed to be persuaded by the clinical evidence that the RHP had merits for secondary and primary prevention of CVD. Without their endorsement, it was unlikely that other physicians would ever prescribe the RHP. The medical representatives for Dr. Reddy's had excellent contacts with these specialists. But they had typically sold branded formulations of proven innovator drugs in the past. The RHP represented a new drug product and, as such, specialists would need to be convinced of its merits.

The potential demand for the RHP in India was enormous. Sudeep Sheru, an associate director in the Indian generics business, was excited by the opportunity:

> This is the first time that we will have a concept which is innovative and global in nature. It will hasten our quest to jump to the top five from our current tenth place in the CVD market. It will build our brand with top cardiologists.

The aim was to get specialist physicians to prescribe the RHP in the first instance at least to their poorer patients, and thus close the treatment gap. At INR3 per capsule, the RHP was affordable even for the poor. For their richer patients, besides their bias towards newer drugs, physicians were also keen to prescribe tailor-made doses of various CVD medications rather than relying on a standard formulation like the RHP. The attraction of the RHP for richer patients was in its convenience and consequently it resulted in better compliance with the prescribed treatment.

Dr. Reddy's was also seeking to get major consumers of healthcare like government hospitals, Central Government Health Services, the Indian Railways, the Indian Armed Forces and other large public sector institutions to buy the RHP in bulk.

Reaching Rural Markets

Bigger cities (one million inhabitants and over) accounted for close to 29% of the pharmaceuticals market in India, while the rest was in smaller cities and towns (refer to Exhibit 6). Rural markets were projected to grow rapidly because of rising economic prosperity. In both urban and rural areas people generally preferred to pay and seek higher-quality care provided by private physicians rather than use free treatment at public health centers. Private providers covered 80% of outpatient and 55% of inpatient care even in the rural areas nationwide. Private physicians in the rural areas adopted the prescription practices of their urban counterparts.

However, for the poor, especially in rural markets, their only option was to visit a public health center. The government rural health system had three tiers. The primary health centers (PHCs) were intended to cover a population of 25,000 and to provide preventive, curative and rehabilitative care. Each PHC served as a hub for sub-centers, which covered three to four villages and were staffed by a nurse/midwife. From PHCs, more serious cases were referred to Community Health Centers (CHCs), 30-bed hospitals and higher order public hospitals at the taluka (county) or district level. But qualified doctors were reluctant to work in these CHCs, instead preferring the prestige and salaries of urban centers. State-of-the-art medical equipment was primarily limited to urban centers.

R.K. Singh, another associate director in the Indian generics business, felt that selling RHP to the rural poor would need a different approach:

> We need a completely different way in which to reach rural doctors. We are talking about 300,000 rural doctors spread across India, and it can be quite a challenge.

There were three types of doctors who practiced in rural India:

- Medical Management Professionals (MMPs)—qualified doctors;

- Registered Medical Practitioners (RMPs)—licensed to operate but lacked formal qualifications; and

- Traditional medical practitioners—practiced ayurveda or unani medicine.

Singh sought to focus on the MMPs and RMPs, the latter in particular. He had spent two and a half years developing a rural marketing organization, mapping the location of RMPs and developing a process to educate them on disease management. The aim was first to create awareness of CVD and then to upgrade the skills of the rural doctors by providing them with easy-to-use charts for diagnosing and managing the disease. Protocols for diagnosis had to be simplified. For example, getting a lipid test in an Indian village was not easy. It also cost INR250 to INR500 per test. Dr. Reddy's protocol sought to assess the risk of CVD by using simpler measures such as the patient's age (over 55), a bulging waistline and high blood pressure.

By developing the skill base of the RMPs, Singh hoped to earn their trust and win their loyalty towards the RHP. Ten Indian states with a large density of families with incomes of INR1,400 per month or more were initially targeted for this rural marketing effort.

Global Markets

Cidambi realized that global scale would eventually be important to make the RHP a success. Success in India would be an important first step in this journey.

Cidambi expected the RHP to have considerable appeal even in high income countries, where many people did not receive essential CVD medicines long term due to cost, complexity and the stigma of multiple pill therapy. Once Dr. Reddy's had proven the effectiveness of the secondary polypill in India, it would launch it in other developing countries in the ASEAN region, Latin America and Africa, before finally entering the European and North American markets. The RHP for primary prevention would also be launched in the same sequence.

Despite a large patient pool eligible for the medications (about 21 million in Europe with established CVD and a similar number in the US), marketing costs, coupled with the pressures on pricing, were a deterrent. Partnering was one option to address the marketing difficulty. Indeed, GlaxoSmithKline and Dr. Reddy's announced an agreement in June 2009 to develop and market selected products across an extensive number of emerging markets, excluding India. Under the terms of the agreement, GSK would market Dr. Reddy's rich and diverse portfolio and future pipeline of more than 100 branded pharmaceuticals. In certain markets, products would be co-marketed by GSK and Dr. Reddy's.

Another option was to go after major purchasers of healthcare, like the National Health Service (NHS) in the UK or major US health insurers. They were expected to take a more proactive role in the prevention of chronic diseases due to rising costs. Dr. Reddy's hoped to persuade these purchasers to make the prescription of its RHP one of their standard CVD prevention protocols. Here again, there were hopeful signs. The first was when UnitedHealth Group Inc., the top US health insurer, refused to cover GSK's new combination drug for treating migraine, calling the pill overpriced and no better than the two generic drugs that it combined. Large health insurers were becoming interested in combination therapies, but these had to offer benefits to the patient and reduce treatment costs. RHP would be one such drug.

In what was perhaps a sign of things to come, in late June 2009 the US state of Texas passed a landmark bill, the Texas Heart Attack Prevention Bill, mandating health-benefit plans to provide coverage for certain screening tests for CVD. This was the first time a bill had been passed that required health insurance policies to cover heart disease diagnosis in the US. The rate of detection was expected to increase, creating demand for drugs that treated CVD.

Competition

Dr. Reddy's was not alone in seeing the polypill's potential for both primary and secondary care of CVD. There were several competitors in both India and Europe.

The Spanish National Center for Cardiovascular Research (Centro Nacional de Investigaciones Cardiovasculares/CNIC) was trialing for the secondary care segment a three-in-one polypill—with a statin, an ACE inhibitor and aspirin—developed in partnership with Ferrer Laboratories and backed by the World Heart Federation. Trials began in 2008 and were projected to last for a year, followed by a launch in 2010 first in Europe, then in the Americas and Asia.

For the larger primary care market, there were other contenders. Wald and Law, the authors of the BMJ paper referenced earlier, had patented their own version of the polypill. This was being developed for them by Cipla, one of Dr. Reddy's Indian competitors. In its clinical trials, Cipla hoped to show that its polypill would reduce the risk of a heart attack or stroke in healthy adults aged over 55. Another Indian competitor, Cadila, had completed and published the results of Phase II trials in India of its "polycap" formulation that included low doses of three blood pressure medicines, together with a statin and aspirin—a five-in-one combination. The target population was older patients (average age 54) with at least one risk factor for heart disease—high blood pressure, high cholesterol, obesity, diabetes or smoking.

Cidambi acknowledged these competitive threats but felt confident that Dr. Reddy's had several layers of advantage to fall back on:

> It is not any one thing but a combination of strengths that gives us the competitive advantage. Take, for example, the product itself. We follow treatment guidelines scrupulously. Cadila and Cipla use three anti-hypertensives in their formulation, which primary care physicians may find hard to accept. On the other hand, Ferrer has just one anti-hypertensive in its pill. It has eliminated the beta-blocker, which is an anti-hypertensive recommended by all the guidelines.
>
> It would be hard for our competitors to produce a product that matches us on quality, efficacy, affordability and accessibility.
>
> The RHP is also unique in that it offers six different combinations to cover a continuum of risks from mild primary care to acute secondary care. Physicians can better tailor their prescriptions to suit the needs of their patients with our RHP.

Two Recent Developments

A Disappointment

Dr. Reddy's had approached an international charity to help fund its trials for the primary prevention of CVD. Dr. Reddy's proposal was for a trial with 2,500 patients in India (at a cost of $8 million), followed by a trial with 2,500 patients internationally (at a cost of $30 million).

The charity was, however, prepared to fund only up to $8 million and asked Dr. Reddy's to finance the rest. The company could not make such a commitment. Instead it hoped to use the charity funding (if granted) as cornerstone funding to approach others to make up the rest. If unsuccessful within 12 months, Dr. Reddy's would not undertake the trial and return the grant in full to the charity.

Dr. Reddy's learned in June 2009 that the grant had been awarded to another proposal the charity had been considering. Clearly this was disappointing.

Focusing on Secondary Care

Cidambi decide to put primary prevention on the back burner. The focus would be on secondary care. The company wanted to do a trial for 10,000 patients globally, and already had funding for 3,600. It had received funding from the EU, as well as two other grants—one from Australia and the other from New Zealand.

As if to vindicate the company's decision to focus on secondary care, on May 30, 2009, the UK medical journal *The Lancet* published an article calling into question the use of aspirin in preventing a first heart attack. The article suggested that any benefits from aspirin for primary prevention were more than offset by the increased risk of bleeding and hemorrhagic stroke. Clearly, longer trials would be needed to establish the safety of drug cocktails like the RHP in preventing a first heart attack or stroke. A definitive study on aspirin by Bayer was not expected to be complete before 2014 at the earliest.

While Dr. Reddy's waited for the uncertainties around the value of aspirin in primary prevention to lift, it would go ahead with its strategy to serve the millions of patients worldwide who already had CVD. Cidambi was seeking to build a $100 million business for the RHP within five years. The demand in India alone would easily support such a target.

People and Profits

Prasad recognized the good that the RHP could do, especially for the millions of poor in India, yet he cautioned:

> In financial terms, the RHP is not going to be significant over the next few years. But as we develop it globally, it could make a big difference to us financially in the long term.
>
> But the RHP has the cost of an innovator product without its patent protection. It will also need marketing investments. Where is the price premium to recover these added costs? There are many other uncertainties also associated with this project. I am not sure we have made a compelling business case as yet.

Cidambi agreed:

> In our generics business, you can make a decent forecast about the upsides from a patent challenge. For the RHP, it is hard to make any revenue projections confidently because of the technical, regulatory and commercial

risks associated with the project. We are a conservative company and our planning horizons are medium term; RHP is a long-term play.

I firmly believe in our business model. We plan to ramp up this business step by step. And should we fail at any step, the capabilities that we have built through this polypill should come in handy as we explore opportunities for treating other chronic diseases that afflict millions of people around the world. We have to be flexible with our strategy and learn at each step. I am hopeful that if we stay focused on people, profits will indeed follow.

Teaching notes for this case are available from Greenleaf Publishing. These are free of charge and are available only to teaching staff. They can be requested by going to:

www.greenleaf-publishing.com/oikos2_notes

Exhibit 1 **Worldwide Health Burden of Heart Disease and Stroke**

Source: Adapted from WHO, 2009

Country	Heart Disease		Stroke	
	DALYs lost per 1,000 (2003)	Number of deaths (2002)	DALYs lost per 1,000 (2003)	Number of deaths (2002)
Europe	203	811,673	145	505,719
India	20	1,531,534	10	771,067
USA	8	514,450	4	163,768
Rest of World	1,929	4,298,089	1,605	53,425,179
Total		7,155,746		54,865,733

Note: DALY= Disability-Adjusted Live Year

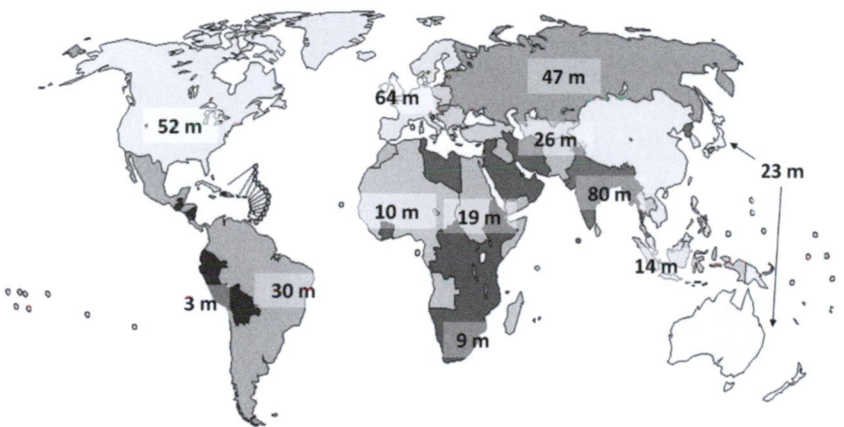

Estimated number of people with previous cardiovascular disease or at over 7.5% in next 5 years by WHO region (WHO Health Report 2002).

Exhibit 2 **Risk of Cardiovascular Events over a Five-Year Period**

Source: Dr. Anthony Rodgers, Professorial Fellow, University of Sydney's George Institute for International Health.

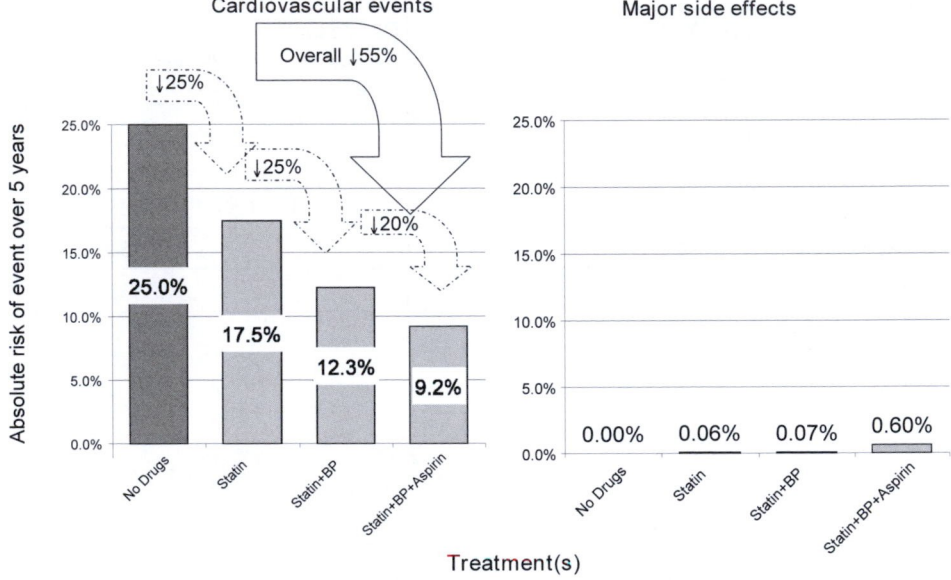

Exhibit 3 **Financial Results, 2005–2009 (INR million)**

Source: Dr. Reddy's, 2009

	2005	2006	2007	2008	2009
(a) Income Statement Data					
Total revenues	19,519	24,267	65,095	50,006	69,441
Cost of revenues	9,386	12,417	34,220	24,598	32,941
Gross profit	10,134	11,850	30,876	25,408	36,500
Gross profit as a % of revenues	52	49	47	51	53
Operating Expenses:					
Selling, general and administrative	7,125	8,449	15,622	16,835	21,020
Research and development	2,803	2,153	2,463	3,553	4,037
Total	9,747	10,167	19,394	23,067	39,334
Operating income	387	1,683	11,481	2,341	(2,834)
Profit before income tax	107	1,887	10,500	2,864	(3,996)
Profit for the year	201	1,629	9,323	3,836	(5,168)
Profit as a % of revenues	1	7	14	8	(7)
(b) Balance Sheet Data					
Cash and cash equivalents	9,346	5,319	18,588	7,421	5,596
Working capital	10,771	1,345	18,832	14,387	12,457
Total assets	29,288	68,768	85,755	85,634	83,792
Total long-term debt, including current portion	25	20,937	17,871	12,698	10,132
Total stockholders' equity	20,953	22,272	42,627	47,350	42,045

Note: INR to US$ rates fluctuated from a high of 0.03974 to a low of 0.01843 in the period from March 31, 2005 to March 31, 2009.

Exhibit 4 **Profile of Pharmaceutical Companies in the World 2008 (US$ million)**

Source: Authors' research (Thomson, company annual reports, SEC filings)

Company	Revenues	Net Profit Margin	Net Property, Plant & Equipment	Working Capital	R&D Expense	Selling, General & Admin Expenses	P/e
Johnson & Johnson	63,747	20.50%	14,365	13,525	7,577	21,490	12.28
Pfizer	48,296	16.78%	13,287	16,067	7,945	14,537	16.45
Bayer	45,759	5.56%	13,195	4,598	3,688	12,432	22.67
GlaxoSmithKline	44,857	18.90%	14,128	10,587	6,569	19,490	12.50
Novartis	42,584	19.17%	13,100	4,338	7,217	14,964	11.72
Roche	42,432	19.66%	17,048	24,836	8,190	18,756	7.34
Sanofi-Aventis	40,623	14.13%	9,812	8,540	6,449	10,602	15.86
AstraZeneca	31,601	19.31%	7,043	2,659	5,179	10,913	10.36
Abbott Laboratories	29,528	18.25%	7,219	5,450	2,688	8,436	12.93
Merck & Co.	23,850	25.33%	12,000	4,986	4,805	7,377	9.16
Wyeth	22,834	19.35%	11,198	16,631	3,340	6,871	13.55
Bristol-Myers Squibb	20,597	25.47%	5,405	8,053	3,224	9,416	12.43
Eli Lilly & Company	20,378	-8.84%	8,626	-656	3,841	6,626	-20.58
Schering-Plough	18,502	13.13%	6,833	5,778	3,529	6,823	17.17
Takeda Pharmaceutical Co.	13,748	n/a	n/a	n/a	2,758	n/a	n/a
Baxter International	12,348	17.09%	4,609	3,513	868	2,698	15.30
Teva	11,085	5.79%	3,699	2,945	786	2,511	44
Astellas Pharma	9,771	18%	1,807	6,960	n/a	4,038	10
Daiichi Sankyo	8,842	11%	2,223	7,354	n/a	4,910	-3.94
Novo Nordisk	8,507	21%	3,480	3,007	1,406	4,197	16.73
Dr. Reddy's	1,244	9%	378	352	88	379	23.19
Cipla	1,000	17%	265	479	54	195	25.57
Cadila Healthcare	565	11%	144	84	36	116	14.58

Exhibit 5 Constituents of the Polypill

Source: Nainggolan, L. (2007) "Clinical Trials of Polypills for CVD Begin" *Heartwire*, 2007, www.medscape.com/viewarticle/551002, accessed 6 March 2009.

Version of polypill	Aspirin dose (mg)	Lisinopril dose (mg)	Simvastatin dose (mg)	Atenolol dose (mg)
Version 1: Secondary Market				
Low-dose	75	5	10	25
Medium-dose	75	10	20	50
High-dose	75	10	40	50
Version 2: Primary Market				
Low-dose	75	5	10	12.5
Medium-dose	75	10	20	12.5
High-dose	75	10	40	12.5

Exhibit 6 Projected Indian Pharmaceutical Market by Geographic Tier, by 2015

Source: Adapted from Kumra, G., M. Palash and C. Pasricha. "Pharma 2015: Unlocking the Potential of the Indian Pharmaceuticals Market." McKinsey & Co., 2008.

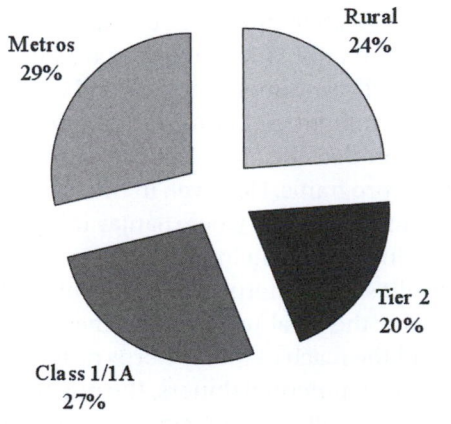

Metros = 1 million+

Class 1-1A = 0.1 million to 1 million

Tier 2 = 5,000 to 100,000

Rural = 5,000 and below

Case 7

ALTIS

A Microfinance Startup in Rural Nepal[1]

Jacen Greene and Scott Marshall PhD
Portland State University, USA

In Sanjay Karki's role as Deputy Director for the Nepal office of Mercy Corps, he had worked on a number of poverty reduction programs. But his current initiative presents the most daunting challenges he has yet faced. One of the most promising innovations in poverty alleviation was the concept of microfinance, the provision of small-scale loans and other financial services to poor entrepreneurs. And although the government of Nepal strongly supported microfinance models, a decade-long civil war ending in 2006 had severely disrupted government services and worsened poverty. In the terai, or plains, of Nepal, government and non-profit microfinance institutions are able to access the population densities and transportation infrastructure necessary to operate poverty relief programs. However, in the rugged and undeveloped mid-mountain and high-mountain regions where Sanjay is hoping to establish microfinance activities, little is being done to help the poor.

Sanjay is considering launching a for-profit social enterprise focusing on agricultural microfinance and technical services for the rural poor, one formed with the assistance of Mercy Corps that could extend the reach of Mercy Corps programs. In a unique approach, and with the full support of potential donors, the organization would start as a non-profit until it became financially self-sustaining, at which time it would transition to a for-profit social business model. Such an organization might be better positioned than the government and private purely for-profit institutions that had previously failed to deliver essential financial services. However, starting a

---

social enterprise was risky even in developed nations, and in a geographically rugged, developing nation recovering from a recently ended civil war, it seemed nearly impossible. Aside from the normal questions of market size, which customers to target, what products and services to provide, how to obtain startup funding, and how to manage competition, Sanjay faced the near total collapse of the national financial system. And yet, some of the very same conditions that increased the difficulty of starting a new business or securing funds spoke to the desperate need for basic financial services. Confronting some of the most daunting challenges to business formation in the world, could a for-profit social enterprise be established to help impoverished farmers improve their livelihoods?

Nepal

Nepal, stretching along the southern slope of the Himalayas between India and the Tibetan plateau, rises from subtropical lowlands to the snow-capped peaks of the tallest mountains on Earth (see Exhibit 1). Although until recently it was the only officially proclaimed Hindu state in the world,[2] Nepal has a rich heritage of ethnic, linguistic, and religious diversity. Nepal's history was strongly influenced by its position between China and India, or as the first King of Nepal famously put it, "a yam between two rocks."

Ten years of civil war between Maoist insurgents and the royal government of Nepal, culminating in the dissolution of parliament by the king, was resolved in 2006 with the signing of a peace treaty and establishment of an interim constitution restoring democratic rule. In 2008, the newly elected Constituent Assembly of Nepal abolished the monarchy, ending more than two centuries of hereditary rule, and proclaimed a federal democratic republic. The nation's first President, Dr. Ram Baran Yadav, was elected in July of that year; the new Prime Minister, Pushpa Dahal, was a Maoist.

The new government faces lingering political instability as well as severe social and economic pressures. With an unemployment rate of 46%, and year-on-year inflation approaching 8%,[3] the economic situation continues to be dire. In 2009 gross national income per capita was US$290[4] and the poverty rate was 31%[5] (those

---

2 "Nepal," *CIA World Factbook*; https://www.cia.gov/library/publications/the-world-factbook/geos/np.html.

3 Ibid.

4 Kiatchai Sophastienphon and Anoma Kulathung, "Getting Finance in South Asia 2009," The World Bank, 2009; siteresources.worldbank.org/SOUTHASIAEXT/Resources/Publications/448813-1231439344179/5726136-1235425345345/GettingFinance2009.pdf.

5 Nepal: Data and Statistics," The World Bank, 2010; www.worldbank.org.np/WBSITE/EXTERNAL/COUNTRIES/SOUTHASIAEXT/NEPALEXTN/0,,menuPK:286961~pagePK:141132~piPK:141109~theSitePK:223555,00.html.

living on less than $0.22 a day, per the national poverty line), placing Nepal among the top 20 poorest nations in the world.[6] Although the Kathmandu valley had a poverty incidence of only 3%, other urban areas averaged 10% and the rate in the countryside was much higher, demonstrating the lack of effective poverty alleviation programs outside of cities.[7]

More than eight out of ten Nepalese live in rural areas and remain dependent on agriculture for their livelihoods.[8] However, the agricultural sector accounted for less than half of the nation's GDP of US$8.05 billion[9] (see Exhibit 3). It is clear that economic development policies and initiatives will need to take into account the important role of rural agriculture to the people of Nepal. The process of structural transformation in Nepalese economy is highly dependent on the process of agricultural transformation from a highly diversified subsistence-oriented production system to more specialized market-oriented agriculture production system. Transforming the agricultural sector is constrained by a number of factors, including weak agriculture marketing organization and technical capacities, inadequate links between rural agriculture production and marketing, the predominant orientation towards production of commodities, and the lack of financing available for growing and processing value-added agricultural products.

Still recovering from the civil war, the government faced major difficulties in meeting the needs of all Nepalese citizens. The rural financial sector, in particular, suffered a near-collapse during the war, and the need for financial services in the mid-mountain and high-mountain regions of Nepal remain almost entirely unmet. It seems clear that a fertile yet challenging market exists for a social enterprise designed to offer low-cost financial instruments to the rural poor of Nepal.

The Market Space

Nepal's position between China and India provides access to two of the world's fastest growing markets, but Nepal is not yet equipped to take advantage of this position, as Sanjay points out:

> [Nepal] has the conditions required to produce food, spice, and medicinal and aromatic crops that are in high demand in both [India and China]. However, Nepal's agricultural sector remains highly under-commercialized due to inadequate organizational, business, and technical practices, and weak input and service markets. [...] If farm enterprises are to

6 Josh Dewald, Former Director of Mercy Corps Nepal.
7 Ibid.
8 ANZDEC Limited, "Nepal Commercial Agricultural Development Project. Final Report," Agrifood Consulting, 2003; www.agrifoodconsulting.com/ai/dmdocuments/Project%20 Reports/NEP%20-%20CADP/CADP%20Final%20Report.pdf.
9 Sophastienphon and Kulathung, "Getting Finance in South Asia 2009."

flourish, smallholder farmers—who cultivate 90% of Nepal's agricultural land—must have access not only to basic inputs and information, but to financial and technical services that provide them with the capital and expertise required to grow, and these services must be provided in a manner that is financially sustainable and commercially viable. Yet no Nepali company currently exists that can provide the required mix of agricultural lending and technical services to the smallholder farmer market in a financially sustainable manner.[10]

In 2006, banks and NGOs in Nepal that served the rural poor accounted for only 2.36% of total financial sector assets, with US$60.6 million in lending.[11] Nepal had only six domestic banks, and the number of branch offices per 100,000 people had declined to a mere 1.73 due to emergency closures during the civil war, with most branches and ATMs located only in cities[12] (see Exhibit 4). Bank deposits and lending showed a linked decline during the same period (see Exhibit 5), and it was estimated that more than 70% of Nepal's people had no access to commercial banks at all.[13] Poor and rural Nepalese faced a crippling inability to access financial services necessary for the most basic aspects of daily life. What few financial services were traditionally available to the rural poor were provided by money lenders or merchants who charged exorbitant interest rates, undermining the effectiveness of such loans in wealth creation and poverty reduction.

Government attempts to expand access to credit were hampered by political instability and endemic corruption. Although Nepal's central bank, Nepal Rastra, introduced corporate governance guidelines in 2005, little progress has been made in achieving the goals set forth in the guidelines.[14] According to the guidelines, commercial banks are required to grant loans or equity of a value between 0.25% and 3% of total loan portfolios to the "deprived sector" of low-income households. But the lack of financial infrastructure in remote areas severely limits the abilities of financial institutions to implement this directive outside of the metropolitan areas.[15] Nepal Rastra has also established five Regional Rural Development Banks to provide financial services to the rural poor, with mixed results. To augment the services of the state and private banking sectors, a number of non-profit organizations formed microfinance banks or stepped in directly to address the financial needs of the poor (see Exhibit 6). Mercy Corps, in particular, has developed a series of offerings that Sanjay is hoping to develop further and integrate as complementary services in his start-up venture.

10 ALTIS Concept Note.

11 Sophastienphon and Kulathung, "Getting Finance in South Asia 2009."

12 Ibid.

13 Thomas, Cherian, "Nepal Asks Lenders to Expand Branches as Maoist Hostility Ends," Bloomberg BusinessWeek, June 22, 2009; www.bloomberg.com/apps/news?pid=newsar chive&sid=apgY6GPJEuXE.

14 Sophastienphon and Kulathung, "Getting Finance in South Asia 2009."

15 Asia Resource Center for Microfinance, "Nepal Country Profile," Banking With the Poor Network; www.bwtp.org/arcm/nepal/I_Country_Profile/nepal_country_profile.html.

Mercy Corps

Founded in 1979 by Dan O'Neil and Ellsworth Culver as an extension of O'Neil's Save the Refugees Fund for survivors of the Cambodian genocide, the non-profit Mercy Corps embraced principles of sustainable development with an emphasis on civic engagement and market-driven efforts (see Exhibits 7 and 8). Headquartered in Portland, Oregon, the organization had delivered over $1.3 billion in aid to more than 107 countries by 2009.[16] Mercy Corps specifically targets nations and communities in transition following major natural or social disasters, with efforts ranging from material relief and assistance to the development of long-term civic and economic programs. With its decentralized management structure, the organization's country directors or representatives spearhead development of regional programs and fundraising in partnership with local organizations, colleague agencies, and the United Nations.

The turmoil in Nepal following the end of the civil war, the abolition of the monarchy, and the establishment of a democratic republic fit well within the scope of Mercy Corps' mission to aid societies in transition. Mercy Corps Nepal was established near the end of 2005. Prior to Sanjay's current effort to establish a rural microfinance entity in Nepal, Mercy Corps had been engaged in a number of projects and partnerships to address unmet needs in agriculture-dependent communities. Examples include Mercy Corps' partnership with the Youth Initiative for Peace and Reconciliation to create youth groups for job training and conflict resolution, its work with the University of Washington to map the value chain of high-value commodities and improve production processes, and its association with Nirdhan Utthan Bank Ltd. (NUBL) to expand access to microfinance services in agricultural communities.[17]

The partnership with NUBL helped Mercy Corps meet some of the critical need for microfinance lending and other financial services in remote agricultural communities. However, Sanjay believes that lending services work best when coupled with technical assistance. By linking Mercy Corps' financial and value chain services together in packaged services, and by moving toward a for-profit model, he hoped to provide a constant revenue stream, offer a greater scope of projects and provide a targeted portfolio of complementary services. He plans to call the new organization ALTIS, or Agricultural Lending and Technical Services Company.

16 Mercycorps.org
17 Ibid

The ALTIS Model

ALTIS is conceived as a non-profit company that will offer micro-loans coupled with technical and agricultural training targeted to the specific needs of small, rural farms (see Exhibits 9 and 10). Loan interest rates would be capped at slightly less than existing microfinance institutions in Nepal, but higher than the 12%–14% average rate from government-subsidized development banks. Although it was necessary for ALTIS to charge a higher rate of interest than government-subsidized banks, Sanjay expects little direct competition in the chronically underserved, remote communities where the company hoped to do business. ALTIS also will be the only agricultural lending institution in Nepal to offer embedded technical services and the first to specifically target high-value crops.[18]

ALTIS's non-profit structure will allow the company to target communities with the greatest need rather than the greatest market potential, to reinvest all profits in expansion, to seek funding from sources not normally available to for-profit companies, and to creatively employ government and non-profit partnerships. Once the company became self-sufficient, it could reorganize as a for-profit social business (see Exhibit 11) relying predominantly on internal revenue to cover operational costs and fund future expansion.[19] One of the biggest risks faced by ALTIS, according to Josh DeWald, Director of Mercy Corps Nepal, is:

> Raising the start-up capital and support funds for its preparatory, inception, and early expansion phases, after which time ALTIS will be self-supporting. This will be difficult because ALTIS, as a concept, falls outside of what is traditionally funded by donors in the humanitarian relief and development field, meaning that fairly non-traditional donors must be identified and convinced of the value of ALTIS as a Nepali institution.[20]

Sanjay estimated that ALTIS needs approximately US$4.16 million in startup capital for the first four years, after which the organization would be expected to quickly achieve profitability (see Exhibit 12). By the tenth year of operation, ALTIS was expected to have a net worth of roughly US$6.75 million, with annual loan disbursements totalling more than US$12 million and total benefits to the agricultural sector of Nepal in excess of US$22 million per year.[21]

Starting with a central office and a pair of branch offices, ALTIS was expected to expand to a total of five branch offices within the first five years. Board members were to be drawn from ALTIS, Mercy Corps, the Nepal Ministry of Agriculture and Cooperatives, the Bankers Association of Nepal, Nirdhan Utthan Bank and Nepal Rastra Bank. It was expected that strategic partnerships could be formed with board member organizations, in addition to the Federation of Nepalese Chambers

---

18 Interview with Josh DeWald, Director of Mercy Corps Nepal.
19 Ibid; ALTIS Concept Note.
20 Interview.
21 All budget estimates altered to maintain confidentiality.

of Commerce and Industry's Agro-Enterprise Center, the Rural Microfinance Development Center, and the Rural Self-Reliance Fund.[22]

By partnering with local NGOs, government institutions, industry organizations and for-profit companies, Sanjay hoped to avoid antagonizing potential competitors and draw on a diversity of experience and expertise to guide the growth of the company. How long such cooperative partnerships could be maintained without devolving into serious competition if ALTIS established a profitable model for serving remote communities, however, remained unknown. ALTIS also faced a number of entrenched alternatives that could either complement or supplant ALTIS operations.

Potential Competitors

Governmental Institutions

National Co-operative Bank, Limited (NCBL)

NCBL was established to provide banking and financial services to Nepal's 7,500 cooperatives, with membership comprising nearly 25% of the nation's population. In addition to providing loans, NCBL was structured to serve as an interface between Nepal Rastra Bank, international financial and aid institutions, and cooperatives. The bank was capitalized with 160 million paid-up shares of capital at 1,000 rupees each, with an additional 160 million issued but unpaid shares, and 320 million authorized but unissued shares.[23]

Agricultural Development Bank, Limited (ADBL)

A government-owned bank with a charter to provide lending to small farmers in addition to traditional commercial financial activities, at the time of this case ADBL accounted for more than 67% of Nepal's institutional credit supply. Under the Small Farmer Development Program, households with a per capita income of fewer than 2,500 rupees or land holdings of less than half a hectare were eligible to receive credit for income-generating activities, participate in group savings programs, and receive business and financial training. An institutional development program to assist with the establishment of self-sufficient farmers' cooperatives was later created to address the lack of growth and high costs of the Small Farmer Development Program. A subsidiary of ADBL, the Small Farmer's Development Bank, was formed

---

22 ALTIS Concept Note.
23 National Co-operative Bank Limited, coopbank.com.np.

in 2002 to further address the needs of rural farmers, with a goal of eventually transferring ownership to farmers' cooperatives.[24]

Microfinance Banks

Nirdhan Utthan Bank, Limited

Nirdhan Utthan was formed as a banking subsidiary of the poverty reduction non-
profit Nirdhan (see Exhibits 13 and 14). Nirdhan Utthan provided a large variety of
loans, as well as banking, microinsurance, and remittance services, but was active
in only a quarter of the Nepal's districts.[25]

Swabalamban Bikas Bank, Limited

Swabalamban Bikas was an offshoot of the Centre for Self-Help Development, a
non-profit organization dedicated to providing financial services in the underserved hill regions of Nepal. In 2006, Swabalamban Bikas had a gross loan portfolio
of US$1,010,436, assets of $2,276,200, savings of $494,548, and equity of $705,775.[26]

Informal Organizations

It was estimated that although roughly 30% of Nepal's citizens had access to traditional financial institutions, only 18% of the population actually borrowed from
such sources.[27] The remainder of the nation's credit needs were served by the informal sector, with 55% of such loans provided by family and friends, 26% by moneylenders, and the remainder by a mix of informal groups.[28] None of these groups
offered the financial, agricultural, and technical services often packaged with loans
offered by microfinance institutions, and a lack of transparency in loan rates and
terms could have crippling consequences on a family's financial stability.

Next Steps

Sanjay believes that ALTIS presents a unique opportunity to serve the financial needs
of poor, rural farmers in Nepal. Traditional governmental and business models fail
to address the needs of the rural poor, and non-profit organizations are not able to

24 Agricultural Development Bank Limited, adbl.gov.np.
25 Nirdhan.com
26 Banking With The Poor network, bwtp.org.
27 Naveen Adhikari, "Determinants of Formal Credit Market Participation in Nepal," *Nep-
    alese Economic Review*, June 14, 2009; www.ner.com.np/vol-1/issue-2/49-determinants-
    of-formal-credit-market-participation-in-nepal.html.
28 Ibid.

maintain long-term planning and scale-up programs due to their dependence on (sometimes fickle) outside funding. Forming ALTIS as a non-profit to broaden funding sources and provide some tax benefits until the company was able to become self-sufficient, then shifting to a for-profit, social business model seemed to offer the best potential, but the company was still highly dependent on a number of major partnerships. Has Sanjay only substituted the demands of investors for the demands of partners? Is a hybrid model combining aspects of both non-profit and for-profit models the best way to reduce the extensive risk faced by entrepreneurs in developing nations, or would the combination prove too unwieldy?

Teaching notes for this case are available from Greenleaf Publishing. These are free of charge and are available only to teaching staff. They can be requested by going to:

www.greenleaf-publishing.com/oikos2_notes

Exhibit 1 **Map of Nepal**

Source: CIA World Factbook

Exhibit 2 **Population of Nepal, Millions**

Source: derived from countrystudies.us, CIA World Factbook, World Bank

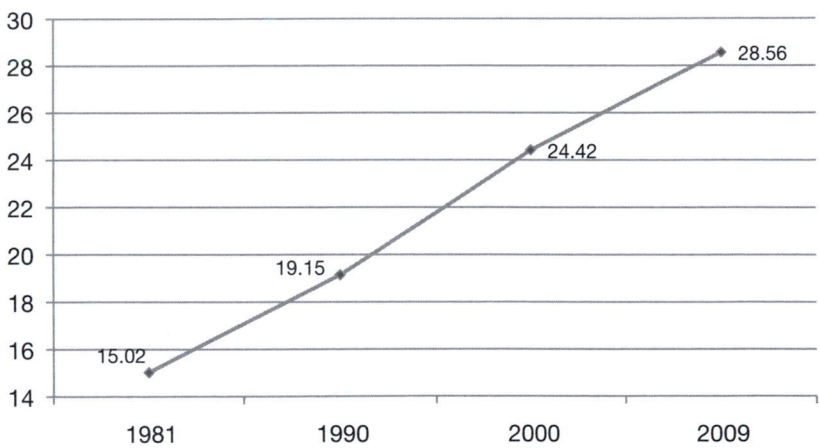

Exhibit 3 **Sector Contribution to GDP in Nepal, by Value Added**

Source: derived from World Bank Nepal factsheet

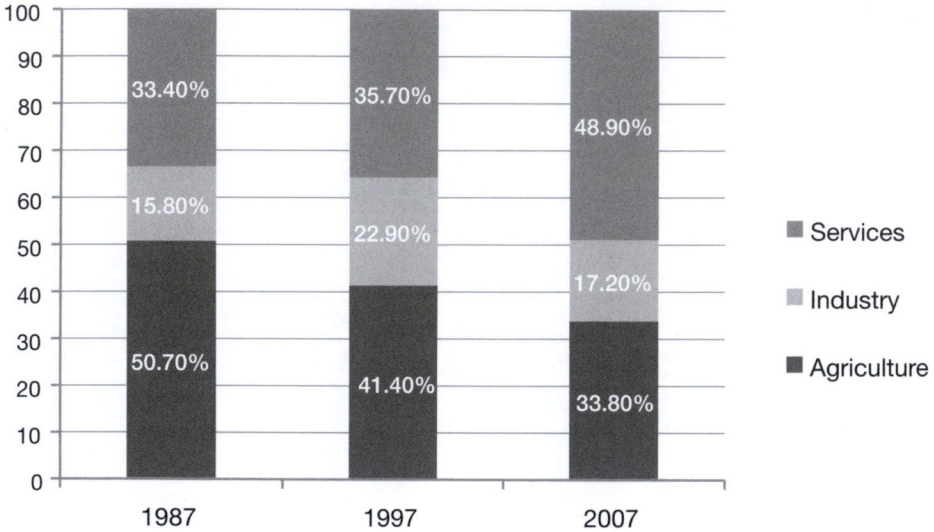

Exhibit 4 **Bank Branch and ATM Penetration per 100,000 People**

Source: The World Bank, "Getting Finance in South Asia 2009."

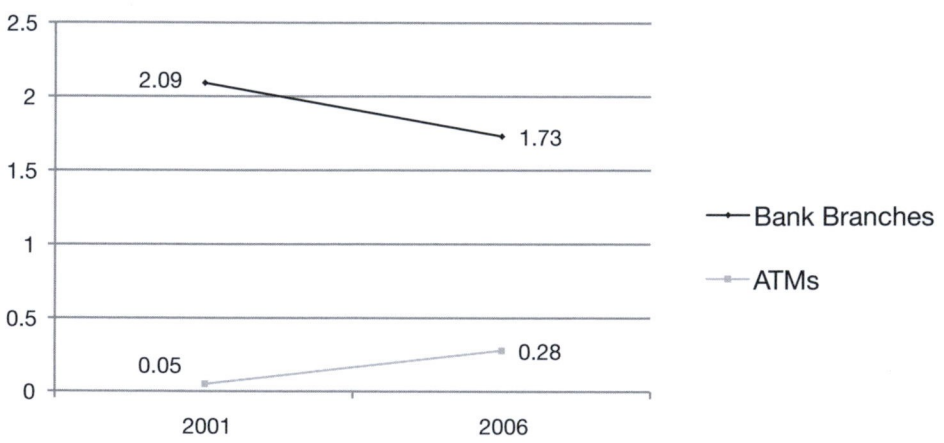

Exhibit 5 **Deposit and Loan Accounts per 1,000 People**

Source: The World Bank, "Getting Finance in South Asia 2009."

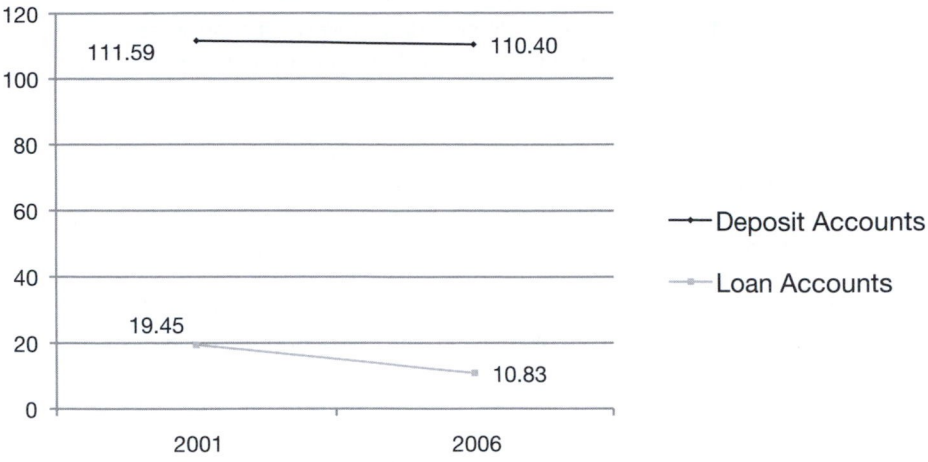

Exhibit 6 **Microfinance Institutions (MFIs) in Nepal**

Source: Nepal Center for Microfinance, "Strategic Plan 2007/08–2009/10"

Institution Type	Number	Inst. Type	Cust. Type	Customers
Grameen Bank Replicators/ Microfinance Development Banks	12,100	Self-managed center	Poor rural women	353,715
	73,120	Groups		
Savings and Credit Cooperatives/Credit Unions	2,672		Clients	310,771
Small Farmers Cooperative Limited/Small Farmers Development Program	47	Intermediary NGOs	Poor	103,000
			Clients	247,000
United Nations Development Program Projects	39,229	Self-help groups	Men	510,676
			Women	523,280
Rural Water Supply & Sanitation Fund Development Board	1,260	Women Technical Support Service Groups	Women	63,000
Total				**2,111,442**
Estimated population, 2005				25,296,537
% of population served by MFIs				8.35%
% below poverty line of those served by MFIs				26.10%
Women served by MFIs				1,233,058

Exhibit 7 **Mercy Corps Strategic Vision, FY 2009**

Source: Mercy Corps Strategic Planning Framework, FY 2009

Mercy Corps' **Mission** is to alleviate suffering, poverty and oppression by helping people build secure, productive and just communities across the globe.

Our **Vision for Change**, based on the Universal Declaration of Human Rights, is that peaceful, secure and just societies emerge when the private, public, and civil society sectors are able to interact with accountability, inclusive participation and mechanisms for peaceful change.

Our **Strategy** is to work in countries in transition, where communities are suffering and recovering from disaster, conflict or economic collapse. Our experience demonstrates that during these times of turmoil and tragedy, there exists the possibility for positive change. We add our greatest value as an international relief and development agency by supporting those kernels of positive change with community-led and market-driven action.

To accomplish our mission, we aim to be a world leader in:

(1) Transforming Transitional Environments Through Community-led and Market-driven Initiatives
Our foundational work is at the community and country level, where we operate rapid relief, long-term recovery and sustainable development pro-grams. In times of crisis or transition, we seek to enable communities to organize for the change they want to see, catalyze the interaction of civil society, government and business, and prompt market-led economic pros-perity. We do this based on our experience working alongside communi-ties around the world that these elements are essential to sustaining the changes communities seek.

We emphasize sustainable solutions that are both specific to the context of each community and scalable for broad impact. These country programs are driven by our significant investments in three areas critical to opera-tionalizing our vision for change: (1) rapid relief assistance that paves the way for longer term recovery programs; (2) initiatives that enable peaceful, community-driven change and linkages between government, business and civic sectors; and (3) market-led development.

(2) Catalyzing Social Innovations
We will have the greatest impact on global problems if we are able to iden-tify, replicate and scale the most innovative solutions that arise from our global team of social entrepreneurs and the communities where we work. Mercy Corps is particularly focused on capturing, "new ideas blending methods from the worlds of business, government and civil society to cre-ate social value that is sustainable and has the potential for large-scale impact." We seek to magnify the influence and impact of our community-led

market-driven programs by reaching for the largest possible impact, with a focus on financial sustainability.

(3) Inspiring Global Engagement

Finally, our experience tells us it is imperative to help create a globally engaged citizenry that can advocate for change and take action in the quest to eliminate global poverty, hunger and conflict. We particularly aim to educate and inspire youth around the world as they represent the hope for the future.

Exhibit 8 **Mercy Corps Financials**

Source: Mercycorps.org

	FY 2008	FY 2007
Support & Revenue		
Proyecto Aldea Global	$2,554,509	$2,526,782
Mercy Corps Scotland	$29,182,552	$34,114,455
Mercy Corps US	$152,883,475	$135,784,173
Material Aid (In Kind)	$59,334,407	$51,148,521
Total Support & Revenue	**$243,954,943**	**$223,573,931**
Expenditures Program		
Proyecto Aldea Global	$2,637,883	$2,090,228
Mercy Corps Scotland	$24,583,110	$30,848,398
Mercy Corps US	$175,436,932	$158,463,970
Total Expenditure	**$202,657,925**	**$191,402,596**
Support Services		
General & Administration	$19,144,523	$16,952,176
Resource Development	$11,227,580	$10,862,768
Total for Support Services	$30,372,103	$27,814,944
Loss	$1,103,410	$2,701,199
Total Expenditures	**$234,133,438**	**$221,918,739**
Net	**$9,821,505**	**$1,655,192**

Exhibit 9 **Rationale for ALTIS**

Source: ALTIS Business Plan

Absence of Technical Capacities

Wider adoption of commercial agriculture requires increased levels of skill and knowledge among farmers as well other stakeholders such as traders, processors, and transporters. The skill and knowledge of actors in the agriculture value chain is inadequate in the changing context of globalization and the WTO. Institutional capacity is also lacking at the local level to foster commercial agriculture.

Lack of Research and Development

The nature of research and development initiatives is still supply-driven and hence less responsive to the needs of clients. Due priority has not been given to the generation and dissemination of location-specific technological packages suitable for the diverse socio-economic and agro-ecological conditions of Nepal. This has resulted in low adoption rates of improved practices.

Decentralized institutional changes are being made to make the extension system farmer-responsible, farmer-accountable and broad-based. However, private-sector involvement in agricultural research and extension activities is currently not receiving much attention.

Lack of Funds and/or Access to Capital

The subsistence nature of much production and low levels of savings have resulted in inadequate funding for farming operations. In addition, high interest rates and difficult access to loans has been a bottleneck in the commercialization of the agricultural sector.

Exhibit 10 **Sample Technical Services Provided by ALTIS**

Source: ALTIS Concept Note

- Agricultural cash flows and lending cycles
- Varietal selection
- Cultivation
- Disease management
- Post-harvest handling
- Low-cost storage
- Grading and processing
- Business planning
- Collective marketing
- Farmers' groups organizational practices
- Global Partnership for Good Agricultural Practice (GLOBALGAP) standards
- Hazard Analysis and Critical Control Point (HACCP) food safety practices

---

Exhibit 11 **Aspects of a Social Business**

Source: Muhammadyunus.org

---

1. Business objective will be to overcome poverty, or one or more problems (such as education, health, technology access, and environment) which threaten people and society; not profit maximization
2. Financial and economic sustainability
3. Investors get back their investment amount only. No dividend is given beyond investment money
4. When investment amount is paid back, company profit stays with the company for expansion and improvement
5. Environmentally conscious
6. Workforce gets market wage with better working conditions
7. … Do it with joy

Exhibit 12 **Disguised ALTIS Financials**

Source: ALTIS Concept Note (figures altered to maintain confidentiality)

The following represents a summary of budget support required during the preparatory, inception, and early expansion phases of ALTIS. This includes four years of operational support for ALTIS, until the point at which the institution will be on sound footing for self-sufficiency and expansion, in addition to Mercy Corps facilitation, support, management, monitoring, evaluation and reporting costs.

The budget provided will lead to the creation of a self-supporting company that will have a net worth of over $6.75 million by its tenth year, with annual loan disbursements of at least $12 million. By its tenth year, this company will provide a conservatively estimated macroeconomic benefit to the Nepali agricultural sector of over $21.9 million per year. This macroeconomic benefit will continue and increase annually thereafter.

Description	Estimated Cost (US$)
Mercy Corps-facilitated 6-month preparation phase	243,926
ALTIS operational losses, Year 1	817,649
Mercy Corps Year 1 support costs	338,771
ALTIS operational losses, Year 2	147,372
Mercy Corps Year 2 support costs	275,010
ALTIS operational losses, Year 3	527,873
Mercy Corps Year 3 support costs	174,600
ALTIS operational losses, Year 4	605,540
Mercy Corps Year 4 support costs	157,539
ALTIS operational losses, Year 5	701,873
Indirect Costs (Applied to Mercy Corps budget component only)	178,476
Total Capital Requirements	**4,168,626**

Exhibit 13 Nirdhan Utthan Bank Quarterly Balance Sheet, April 2009

Source: nirdhan.com

	Amount in '000 Rupees
ASSETS	
Current Assets:	
Cash and Bank balance	244,432
Receivables	24,415
Inventories	1,402
Investments	94,738
Net Loans Outstanding	976,554
Total Current Assets	1,341,541
Total Long Term Assets	56,066
Less Expenses to be written off	-5,775
Total Assets	**1,403,382**
LIABILITIES	
Current Liabilities:	
Inter-Branch Adjustment Account	-23,095
Client Savings	301,500
Other Current Liabilities	51,569
Total Current Liabilities	329,974
Total Long Term Liabilities	894,476
Total Liabilities	**1,224,450**
EQUITY	
Paid up Equity	100,000
General Reserve	11,851
Institutional Development Fund	30,209
Capital Reserve	15,096
Net Profit (Loss) Previous Year	1,196
Net Profit (Loss) Current Year	20,580
Total Equity	**178,932**
Total Liabilities & Equity	**1,403,382**

Exhibit 14 **Nirdhan Utthan Bank Quarterly Income Statement, April 2009**

Source: nirdhan.com

	Amount in '000 Rupees
INCOME FROM INVESTMENTS	
Financial Income:	
Interest from Current and Past Due Loan	122,812
Interest from Investment (Bank Deposit)	6,213
Income from Investment	1,930
Other Income	2,785
Total Financial Income	133,740
Interest on Borrowing	-23,301
Interest on Deposits	-10,818
Gross Financial Margin	99,621
Provision for Loan Losses	-5,334
Net Financial Margin	94,287
INCOME FROM OPERATIONS	
Operating Expenses:	
Salaries and Allowances	62,382
Office Operating Expenses	14,136
Training Expenses	1,780
Loss Sale of Assets	49
Depreciation	1,025
Total Operating Expenses	79,372
Net Income From Operations	14,915
Grant Income	5,665
Net Income (no bonuses or tax)	**20,580**

Case 8

VisionSpring
A Lens for Growth at the Base of the Pyramid[1,2]

Molly Christiansen and Ted London
William Davidson Institute/Ross School of Business, University of Michigan, USA

Jordan Kassalow, Chairman and Co-Founder of VisionSpring,[3] settled into his seat and gathered his thoughts in preparation for the long plane ride back to New York City. VisionSpring uses a market-based approach to sell affordable reading glasses to the poor. He had just spent the last two weeks in India, VisionSpring's fastest growing location. While it had been another successful year for VisionSpring, Jordan knew that the next 12 months would be critical in fulfilling the vision of the organization he and Scott Berrie had founded five years before.

Through the third quarter of 2006, VisionSpring had trained 371 local entrepreneurs in India who collectively had sold over 29,000 pairs of glasses. VisionSpring had primarily distributed its reading glasses through Vision Entrepreneurs (VEs) who marketed and sold the reading glasses in rural communities. In addition to

---

2 This is the winning case of the 2008 oikos Global Case Writing Competition.
3 In mid-2008, the organization changed its name to VisionSpring from Scojo Foundation.

the VE channel, a franchise partner channel had emerged in the past year. In the franchise partner channel, VisionSpring leveraged existing distribution networks of entrepreneurs to sell its reading glasses. Jordan knew that each approach had strengths and weaknesses. He wondered which model would allow VisionSpring to scale more effectively while creating the societal impact and financial sustainability that he and funders were hoping for.

Jordan revisited VisionSpring's mission statement, something to which he had given a lot of thought recently: "VisionSpring improves the economic condition of families in the developing world by broadening the availability of reading glasses and other health products and services. We achieve this through VisionSpring entrepreneurs and other market-based distribution solutions." He wondered whether the emphasis of VisionSpring's mission should be to increase access to reading glasses or to empower entrepreneurs. VisionSpring, itself, could develop a basket of health products and services similar to some of its franchise partners, thus bringing in more business to the entrepreneurs and more products and services to the customers.

In addition, Jordan knew anecdotally that VisionSpring was having an impact in poor communities. However, funders, such as Acumen Fund, were increasingly demanding that VisionSpring find ways to more effectively measure this impact. Jordan was proud of VisionSpring's growth and impact in such a short amount of time. However, he knew that he and his team had their work cut out for themselves. Jordan had to organize his thoughts, consult with his team, and develop some concrete recommendations before meeting with his board and key funders the following month.

VisionSpring's History

The original idea for VisionSpring was driven by the need Jordan and Scott saw for reading glasses in low-income communities in the developing world. Jordan, an optometrist by training, spent a year after optometry school volunteering at the Aravind Eye Hospital in India, one of the most creative models of ophthalmology serving the poor in the world.[4] After working with Aravind, he had split his time between international public health work and an optometric practice in New York City. Scott, a businessman and senior executive of a large family business, was attracted by the idea of combining his interest in entrepreneurship with his passion for public service. On a visit to India in 1998, Jordan and Scott saw first-hand the huge market for reading glasses for the poor.

---

4 Prahalad, C.K. *The Fortune at the Bottom of the Pyramid: Eradicating Poverty through Profits.* New Jersey: Wharton School Publishing, 2005: 131-135.

In 2001, they created VisionSpring (at that time the organization was named Scojo Foundation) to provide affordable reading glasses to people with presbyopia living in low-income communities. Presbyopia is a natural condition whereby the lens of the eye loses its flexibility, resulting in blurry up-close vision (see text box). During this time, Jordan and Scott also formed Scojo Vision LLC, a for-profit company in the United States that targeted the "affordable luxury" niche of the reading glasses market. From the beginning, they designated that 5% of profits from the LLC would funnel into the nonprofit. Jordan felt that he and Scott were a strong team whose skills and experiences complemented one another. Jordan knew about eye care, public health, and fundraising. Scott knew about sales, marketing, and business management. Although they were both integrally involved in designing and building the LLC and the Foundation, they agreed that Scott would take the lead in the LLC and Jordan would run the Foundation.

Presbyopia: Up-close Blurry Vision

Source: Adapted from VisionSpring website

Presbyopia is a natural, progressive vision condition in which the muscles around the lens of the eye lose their flexibility, making it difficult to focus on nearby objects, and thus resulting in blurry near-vision. Presbyopia occurs naturally in most people over 35 and progressively worsens with age. The condition can easily be corrected with simple magnifying "reading" glasses. Left untreated, presbyopia can impede economic productivity and diminish quality of life. Individuals whose livelihoods depend on clear up-close vision such as tailors, bookkeepers, or mechanics become unable to work after they reach a certain age, and they lose their ability to earn an income. Their quality of life suffers too as they become unable to sew, cook, or read newspapers, literature or religious texts.

George Soros' Open Society Institute funded VisionSpring's pilot program in India in 2001. After the pilot, VisionSpring received funding to launch operations in El Salvador in 2002, then expanded into Guatemala in 2004, returned to India in 2005, and launched operations in Bangladesh and Mexico in 2006. VisionSpring India and VisionSpring El Salvador were subsidiaries wholly owned by VisionSpring. VisionSpring worked through franchise partner organizations in Bangladesh, Guatemala, and Mexico. (See Exhibit 1 for VisionSpring Legal and Organizational Structure.) In Bangladesh, VisionSpring partnered with BRAC, one of the world's largest non-governmental organizations (NGOs), to distribute reading glasses through BRAC's network of community health workers. In Guatemala, VisionSpring partnered with Community Enterprise Solutions (CES) to distribute glasses through its network of entrepreneurs. In India, VisionSpring utilized VEs, franchise partners, and a wholesale channel to distribute its glasses.

Since its inception, VisionSpring and its founders have received various awards, including the World Bank's Development Marketplace Award in 2003, Yale/

Goldman Sachs Foundation Partnership on Nonprofit Venture Award in 2003, New York University's Steward Satter Social Entrepreneur of the Year Award in 2006, and Fast Company Magazine's Social Capitalist Award in 2005, 2007, and 2008.

VisionSpring's Micro-Franchise Model

VisionSpring's primary business model was relatively straight forward: select local community members to become VEs, train them in basic eye screenings for presbyopia and other vision-related problems and provide them with a "Business in a Bag," containing the materials, stocks, and information they need to run a business.

Each entrepreneur was a VisionSpring franchisee. VisionSpring took a non-refundable and below-cost deposit of 500 Rs (US$11.11) from each entrepreneur for the "Business in a Bag." The bag included an initial inventory of 40 pairs of reading glasses (given on consignment) of different magnifications and styles, screening materials, marketing materials, and paperwork to manage sales and inventory. Each pair of glasses included a cover and cloth. Reading glasses came in 5 strengths: +1.00, +1.50, +2.00, +2.50, and +3.00. See Exhibit 2 for the contents of each "Business in a Bag."

VisionSpring developed a multi-day training module that taught entrepreneurs to conduct vision screenings, determine the proper power of the glasses needed, market and sell reading glasses, make referrals for additional eye care as necessary, and manage their inventory. When they first met a potential customer, the entrepreneurs were taught to fill out a customer information sheet, including customer name, profession, address, and need for glasses. Then the entrepreneur conducted the distance vision screening test. If the customer failed the distance vision test, they likely had myopia (blurry distance vision, requiring prescription glasses) and were given a referral to a nearby eye hospital for further treatment. The entrepreneur also referred patients with cataracts and other eye disorders to nearby eye hospitals for further treatment. For those that passed the distance vision test, the entrepreneur conducted a near vision test. If the customer had difficulty identifying the lines on the near vision chart, then the customer had presbyopia and needed the reading glasses that the entrepreneur sold. As part of the near vision test, the entrepreneur determined the appropriate power of the glasses. Then the entrepreneur confirmed the power by asking the customer to use the glasses to thread a needle, read, or conduct a similar livelihood activity. Having demonstrated the utility of the glasses, the entrepreneur showed the customer the various models and colors available and hoped to make a sale.

VisionSpring India

VisionSpring India, headquartered in the southern city of Hyderabad (see map of India in Exhibit 3), was VisionSpring's largest and fastest-growing operation. VisionSpring India employed 15 people as shown in Exhibit 4, including an India Country Director, an Operations and Programs Manager, a VE Channel Manager, a Key Accounts Manager, a Training Manager, two VE Identification and Training Managers, six District Coordinators, an Accounts Assistant, and other administrative staff. VisionSpring looked for staff with a blend of experience in business and the civil sector. Arunesh Singh, Regional Director for Asia, served as Programme Director at Appropriate Technology India, a non-profit organization dedicated to sustainable development. Before that assignment he was a manager at one of the largest agricultural products companies in India. Raman Nageswara, Operations and Programs Manager, worked as a Program Officer at Winrock International India, an organization committed to natural resource management, clean energy, and climate change before joining VisionSpring. Previous to Winrock, he lived and worked in the US as an engineer and business consultant to Lucent Technologies and Bell Core Technologies.

VisionSpring India's revenue sources were from eye-glasses sales, grants, and loans. Exhibit 5 shows the financial, operating, and social metrics from the time VisionSpring began operations in India in January 2005 through anticipated figures through fourth quarter 2006. In May of 2006, VisionSpring received a US$100,000 loan from Acumen Fund for its India operations. Acumen Fund is a global non-profit venture fund that invests in scalable and financially sustainable organizations delivering products and services to the poor. Acumen Fund tracks a combination of financial and social returns. With a below market interest rate of 6% annually, the potential to borrow up to a total of US$500,000 and a loan period of 5 years, VisionSpring management hoped that Acumen Fund's loan would provide sufficient capital for them to scale in India. When applying for the Acumen Fund loan, VisionSpring management created a projected balance sheet and income statement through 2010. They anticipated making a profit beginning in 2010. These documents, along with the revenue assumptions used to generate them, appear in Exhibits 6, 7, and 8.

Serving the Base of the Pyramid: A Market for Reading Glasses in India

The base of the economic pyramid (BoP) was a term typically considered to represent the more than 4 billion people in the world living on less than US$4 per day.[5] It was estimated that in India 80% of the population, or approximately 880 million

---

5 Prahalad, C.K., Stuart L. Hart. "The Fortune at the Bottom of the Pyramid." *Strategy + Business* 26 (2002): 55-67.

people, lived on less than US$2 per day.[6] This population was VisionSpring's primary market, of which they estimate more than 92.4 million suffered from presbyopia.[7] These individuals would benefit from reading glasses in terms of improved quality of life and increased productivity. Many people did not know that there was a simple and affordable solution to presbyopia, and therefore did not look for opportunities to buy reading glasses even if they were available. VisionSpring India, therefore, stimulated demand in this market by generating awareness of blurry up-close vision and the benefits of reading glasses.

The majority of rural Indians have limited access to professional eye care. VisionSpring estimates that in India there is an average of one eye care professional per 30,200 people. The majority of these eye care professionals are located in urban areas, which limits access for rural Indians. In addition, the screening and purchase process of an optical visit is expensive for most Indians. It is estimated that a typical rural customer spends somewhere between 250–500 Rs (US$6–US$11) to purchase reading glasses. This amount includes the cost of the glasses, the doctor's visit, and the transportation to and from the doctor's office, and does not include the opportunity cost for workers who lose productive time away from their jobs.[8]

Distribution in India

VisionSpring India distributed reading glasses through three channels: the original VE Channel, the Franchise Partner Channel, and the Wholesale Channel. Each channel had some unique benefits and challenges. Exhibit 5 details VisionSpring India's financial, operational, and social metrics for each distribution channel and Exhibit 6 provides revenue and expenses projections for the next five years. Exhibit 9 illustrates the three distribution channels.

Vision Entrepreneur Channel

In the first three quarters of 2006, VisionSpring India trained and supported more than 100 active VEs through the VE channel in five districts of the south Indian state of Andhra Pradesh: East Godavari, Mahbubnagar, Nalgonda, West Godavari, and Prakasam. In the VE Channel, District Coordinators (VisionSpring India employees)

---

6 "2006 World Population Data Sheet." Population Reference Bureau. Aug. 2006, www.prb. org/pdf06/06WorldDataSheet.pdf.

7 Burke, Andrew G., Ilesh Patel, Beatriz Munoz, Andrew Kayongoya, Wilson Mchiwa, Alison W. Schwarzwalder, Sheila K. West. "Population-Based Study of Presbyopia in Rural Tanzania." *Ophthalmology* 113.5 (2006): 723-727. Approximately 25% of population is over 35, of which 61.7% have presbyopia, of which 70% have "functional presbyopia", meaning they would benefit from reading glasses.

8 Based on field research and estimates by VisionSpring.

provided direct support to the VEs. District Coordinators were responsible for the key aspects of this distribution channel, including identifying and appointing the entrepreneur, initial and ongoing training, sales and marketing strategies, referrals to eye hospitals, and key partnerships.

Identifying the Entrepreneur

Through the VE channel, VisionSpring India employees identified, trained, and supported the VEs. VisionSpring India partnered with local non-profit and government organizations to identify new VEs. VisionSpring India looked at a number of qualities when appointing VEs, including education level, reputation in the community, economic need, connection to the community in which they live, and potential leadership ability. Cultural norms had made it difficult for individual female entrepreneurs because it was often not acceptable for women to travel alone to neighboring villages. Therefore, VisionSpring India often implemented a strategy whereby they appointed pairs of VEs, such as a husband/wife team or two friends to run the business together.

Ongoing Training and Inventory Management

VisionSpring India had developed a multi-day training module for entrepreneurs as described in the micro-franchise section above. VEs also spent several days in the field with a District Coordinator doing onsite training. The District Coordinator then visited each VE approximately once per month to set sales targets and strategies, distribute new inventory, and offer ongoing training. VisionSpring India kept enough stocks for six months in the central office and encouraged each district coordinator to keep two months of stock in hand. Sales data was entered into a web-based sales database (salesforce.com) each month by the District Coordinators, and sales and projections were made for the year to forecast stock requirements.

VisionSpring India gave the reading glasses to VEs on a consignment basis. Typically, they were given 40 glasses of various powers and models in the beginning. At the end of the month the VE paid VisionSpring India for the glasses they had sold.

Sales and Marketing

The VE channel accounted for approximately 30% of VisionSpring India's sales. There were generally two VEs (or VE pairs) assigned to each mandal (county) of each district. Each mandal had a population of about 50,000 and there were approximately 50–60 mandals in each district. A VE sold an average of 14 pairs of glasses per month.

VisionSpring India found that sales increased significantly in the first three months that a VE worked because the VE was selling to their network of family and friends. There was often a drop off in sales after the three-month mark because the VE had exhausted his/her network and had not yet become comfortable approaching people unknown to him/her. VisionSpring India was therefore continually coming up with new sales and marketing strategies to increase revenues for its VEs. For example, sometimes they used an eye camp in which a VE and district coordinator set up a table and screening area in the middle of town, and advertised around the town using a town drummer. Local community members would come to the table to get screened and potentially buy glasses.

In addition, VisionSpring India was promoting a door-to-door strategy for selling glasses, in which a VE approached the village leader first, screened him/her for glasses, made a sale if possible, and then asked for three names of other villagers who might need reading glasses as referrals. The VE then approached those three homes, screened the eligible adults in the home, and then from each of those three villagers looked to get three more referrals, and on and on. One of the benefits of such a strategy was the credibility that the VE attained by associating first with the village leader. Because many rural villages were still stratified by caste, however, villagers were likely to refer the VE to other people of their same caste, which meant that the VE might only have had access to a portion of the community using this strategy.

VE Channel Partners

VisionSpring India partnered with a number of organizations in the VE channel to increase their customer base, connect with potential entrepreneurs, and refer clients for further eye care.

- Government Weavers Cooperatives: VisionSpring India partnered with government weaving cooperatives in Andhra Pradesh to screen large groups of weavers. Many weavers needed glasses to see the fine threads they were weaving and thus relied on reading glasses for their productive activity. In addition, many of the weavers participated in an ICICI Lombard Health Insurance scheme that reimbursed them for the glasses they purchased. VisionSpring India, therefore, had a high yield of sales among these weavers.

- Hindustan Lever Limited (www.hll.com): Hindustan Lever Limited (HLL) is the Indian subsidiary of Unilever, a consumer products goods company. As part of its new ventures group, HLL had trained a network of over 25,000 women entrepreneurs throughout rural India to sell health and hygiene products in rural villages. VisionSpring India partnered with HLL to sell their glasses through these women. VisionSpring India worked on a trial basis with 25 HLL entrepreneurs in the Nalgonda district of Andhra Pradesh, and had plans to expand into other districts of Andhra Pradesh and into new states with this partnership. VisionSpring India considered this partnership and the sales resulting from these entrepreneurs part of their VE distribution channel because VisionSpring India's district coordinators managed the entrepreneurs in this partnership.

- eSeva (esevaonline.com): eSeva is a public–private partnership in the state of Andhra Pradesh to enable rural Indians to pay utilities, get birth certificates, book train tickets and obtain other public services through government-sponsored computer kiosks in individual homes. VisionSpring India partnered with eSeva to train some of the computer kiosk operators to give screenings and sell glasses at the kiosks. The VE in each area managed the relationships with eSeva as a type of sub-franchise. Since eSevas were serviced by VisionSpring India's VEs directly, these were categorized in the VE channel.

Franchise Partner Channel

The franchise partner channel used the same blueprint as the VE Channel, but leveraged existing distribution networks of entrepreneurs, community health workers, or computer kiosk owners to sell its reading glasses. The main difference between the two channels was that for the franchise partner channel, it was the franchise partner who oversaw and managed the network of entrepreneurs, rather than a VisionSpring district coordinator. Through third quarter 2006, the franchise partner channel accounted for about 65% of sales. VisionSpring India looked for organizations that offered a potential distribution network, such as community health workers or computer kiosk owners. These organizations were often interested in providing a larger "basket of products and services" for their entrepreneurs or community health workers to sell, so that they could earn better livelihoods. From VisionSpring India's perspective, the franchise partner channel allowed VisionSpring India to reach more entrepreneurs and BoP customers in a manner that was faster and more affordable than the VE channel.

VisionSpring India partnered with a variety of non-profit, public, and private organizations. When VisionSpring India entered a new state, it looked for potential partners to leverage its limited human resources. Typically, VisionSpring India would train the partner entrepreneurs or community health workers to sell reading glasses, as they would their own VEs. They usually started with a pilot to make sure the partnership was a good fit and then rolled out the program on a larger scale. Unlike the VE distribution channel, the partner organization handled the oversight of the entrepreneurs and supply chain management. VisionSpring India sold the stocks to the partner organization, which then distributed it directly to their entrepreneurs. Partner organizations were charged 2600 Rs (US$57.77) upfront for each "Business in a Bag." Each partner organization could then choose whether or not to charge their entrepreneurs for the "Business in a Bag." The partner organization tracked inventory and requested inventory from VisionSpring India as needed.

VisionSpring India faced different challenges depending on the partner. For example, some of the non-profit partners were not used to operating like a business, and VisionSpring India had to spend more time helping them to track sales and manage their supply chain. In other cases, the partner entrepreneurs had some constraints on their mobility because they ran a shop or kiosk in their home and thus could not move around during the day. Finally, VisionSpring India's market-based philosophy differed from that of some partner organizations. VisionSpring believed that they could maximize their social impact by selling glasses rather than giving them away. In certain cases, the partner organization had wanted to give away or significantly subsidize the cost of the glasses. This arrangement posed challenges for VisionSpring India, its VEs, and its other partners in nearby areas. If VisionSpring India glasses were sold for differing prices in neighboring areas, the entrepreneur selling the glasses for a higher price would quickly lose credibility and sales.

As of the third quarter 2006, VisionSpring India had more than 12 partnerships, in various stages of formation. The following is a description of a few of Vision-Spring India's partners.

- Byrraju Foundation (www.byrrajufoundation.org): The Byrraju Foundation is a non-profit organization that provides healthcare, education, infrastructure, and capacity-building services to 150 villages in five districts of Andhra Pradesh, and in doing so serves over 800,000 people. VisionSpring India has trained approximately 150 Byrraju community health workers since the beginning of 2006, and they have sold 10,000 glasses thus far. Byrraju was VisionSpring India's only partner that subsidized the cost of glasses for its customers. Rather than selling them for 155 or 165 Rs like the VEs, they sold all of the glasses for a uniform price of 90 Rs. Because Byrraju was one of VisionSpring India's first partners, VisionSpring India agreed to this subsidized pricing model. However, VisionSpring India has since made a policy that their partner entrepreneurs must sell the glasses for the same prices as its VEs.

- Drishtee (www.drishtee.com): Drishtee is a for-profit social enterprise that has built a rural network for delivering services and related information to village communities through computer kiosks. The kiosks are run by entrepreneurs selected from the villages. Approximately 50 Drishtee kiosk entrepreneurs sold VisionSpring India glasses (roughly 20 pairs per month). As Drishtee expanded to 3,000 kiosks, new kiosk entrepreneurs would be offered the VisionSpring micro-franchise. VisionSpring India's partnership with Drishtee is being implemented in the states of Assam, Haryana, Uttar Pradesh, and Bihar.

- Vedanta (www.vedantaresources.com): Vedanta is an international mining company with the majority of its operations in India. Through its corporate social responsibility programs, the company works with its employees and the communities where it operates to contribute to the economic development of the region by providing needed health care and education services.

VisionSpring India partnered with Vedanta to distribute reading glasses through its network of community health workers.

Wholesale Channel

Recently, VisionSpring India has begun to sell its reading glasses through retailers and pharmacy chains in urban and semi-urban areas. In December 2005, VisionSpring India made its first sale to Medicine Shoppe, India's second largest pharmacy chain with over 100 pharmacies in India.[9] VisionSpring India trained pharmacists in 20 Medicine Shoppe pharmacies to screen customers for glasses. VisionSpring India was also in the process of training pharmacists in the Guardian and Apollo pharmacy chains.

The wholesale channel targeted middle and upper-middle class customers who shopped at branded pharmacies. The price point of the glasses in the wholesale channel was slightly higher to accommodate the higher margins that pharmacies need to justify the use of display square footage. Similar to their sales practice in the United States, VisionSpring India created a point of purchase display which included instructions for a self-guided vision screening, a mirror, and the display of glasses, which at the same time leveraged VisionSpring India's social brand.

Operations

Pricing

In the VE and Franchise partner channels, VisionSpring India sold its reading glasses for a low price of 95 Rs (US$2.00) to a high price of 165 Rs (US$3.67). VisionSpring India offered four lines of reading glasses, shown in Exhibit 10: Jyoti (tube readers), Kranti (bifocal), Deepti (single-vision), and Usha (low-cost). The average margin for the VE was 50 Rs (US$1.11) per pair of glasses. Interestingly, the most popular model of glasses among customers was not the low-cost model, as seen in Exhibit 11. Actually, the majority of sales were for the glasses priced at 155 Rs (US$3.44) and 165 Rs (US$3.67).

In the wholesale channel, VisionSpring India sold two models of reading glasses (Kranti and Deepti) each priced to the end consumer at 199 Rs (US$4.42). VisionSpring India sold the glasses to the wholesalers for 105 Rs (US$2.33) +4% sales tax, giving the wholesalers a margin of 94 Rs (US$2.08) per pair of glasses.

9 The Medicine Shoppe. 18 Apr. 2008, www.ms-india.com.

Manufacturing

VisionSpring India sourced its reading glasses from manufacturers in China and paid a 17% tariff to import the glasses into India. Although VisionSpring India was looking to source locally, they had yet to find a local manufacturer in India of comparable quality and cost to their Chinese manufacturers. The other components of the "Business in a Bag," such as marketing materials, cords, cases, and the bag itself, were made in India.

Competitors

VisionSpring faced three types of competitors in the reading glasses market: optical professionals, street vendors, and potential new entrants. Optical professionals controlled what little there was of the reading glasses market in India. However, optical retailers were not motivated to sell ready-made reading glasses because of low margins compared to made-to-order prescription lenses and frames. The margin for ready-made glasses ranged from 20–30% as compared to a margin of over 50% for most made-to-order glasses. In addition, optical professionals feared losing their ability to provide higher margin patient eye care services and the recurring revenue stream of multiple check-up visits. Optical professionals that did carry ready-made reading glasses tended to store them behind counters and pull them out reluctantly when pressured by their patients for cheaper alternatives to custom-made products. According to VisionSpring staff, street vendors could also be found selling cheap ready-made reading glasses in urban areas.[10] Finally, there was the potential for new entrants if VisionSpring demonstrated to other companies that this business could be profitable.

Societal Impacts

VisionSpring management recognized the important role that impact evaluation played in the organization. The organization needed to move from the idea phase to a successful model that kept funders interested in them. So far they had sold VisionSpring through their story (see Exhibit 12 for a story on a VisionSpring customer that was displayed on the organization's website), but now there was more pressure to show that the business worked to improve the lives of the poor. They needed to develop metrics to monitor local impacts and better understand the implications of their business model on entrepreneurs and customers. Not only were these kind of metrics increasingly sought after by funders, but they were also

---

10 According to VisionSpring's Business Plan submitted to Acumen Fund, 2006.

needed by VisionSpring in order to maintain and expand support of in-country partners and government officials. In addition, as it scaled, VisionSpring management team wanted to continually evaluate the organization's own performance so that they could improve the business model and maximize local impact.

Looking at the Future

As the plane landed in New York City, Jordan contemplated the future of Vision-Spring. There were a number of decisions he and his team would have to make before the board meeting the following month. Which distribution channel or combination of distribution channels would allow them to most effectively scale their business and best enhance their societal impacts? Should the emphasis of their mission be placed on increasing access to reading glasses or on developing entrepreneurs? This could have important implications for their choice of scaling strategy. And how should they track their poverty alleviation outcomes? In the forefront of his mind, Jordan kept the goal of becoming a self-financing scalable enterprise that was not dependent on donations. How could he best manage the joint goals of societal impact and financial sustainability?

There were several ways in which VisionSpring could develop, but the organization needed to clarify its thinking soon. VisionSpring's on-going success depended on its ability to reach its sales goals, to understand and articulate its societal impact, and to attract new funders and satisfy its existing ones in order to have the capital needed to scale. Jordan and his team had to figure out how to prioritize the critical pieces of the puzzle before his meetings with the board and key funders the following month.

Exhibit 1 **VisionSpring Legal and Organizational Structure**

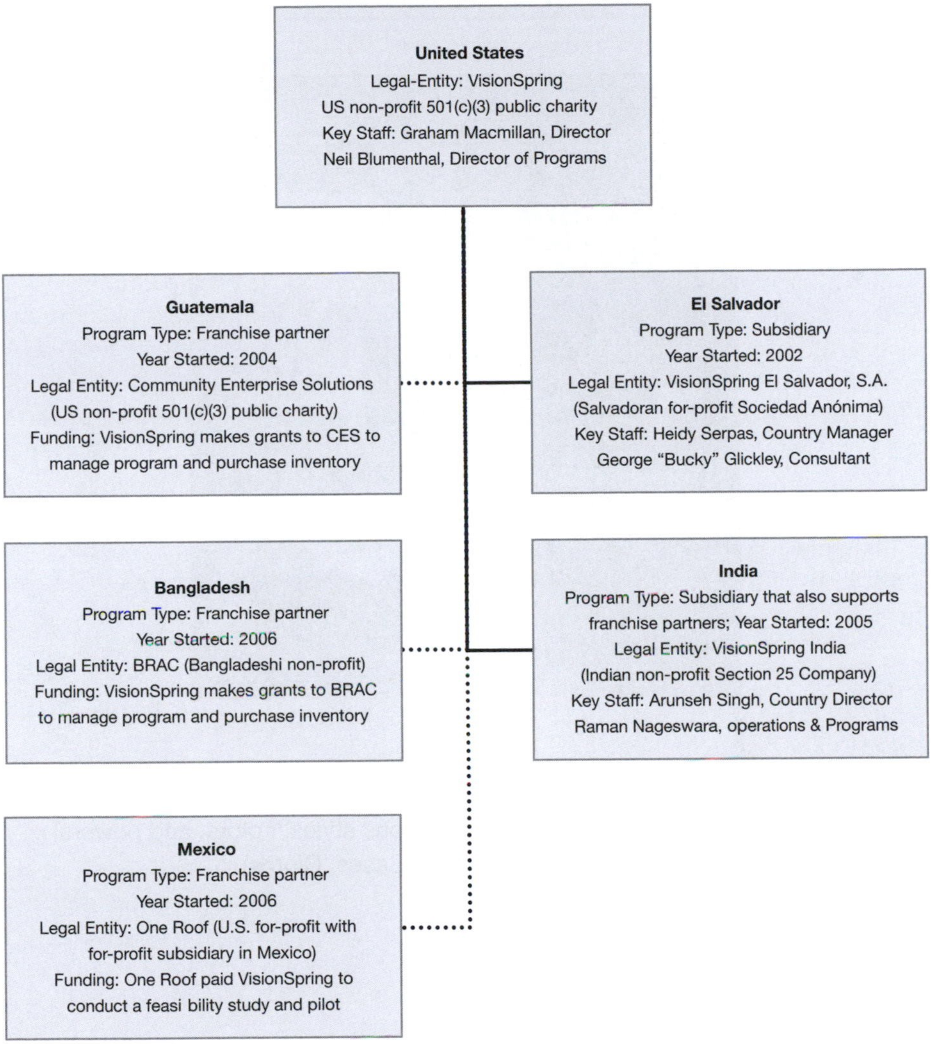

United States
Legal-Entity: VisionSpring
US non-profit 501(c)(3) public charity
Key Staff: Graham Macmillan, Director
Neil Blumenthal, Director of Programs

Guatemala
Program Type: Franchise partner
Year Started: 2004
Legal Entity: Community Enterprise Solutions
(US non-profit 501(c)(3) public charity)
Funding: VisionSpring makes grants to CES to
manage program and purchase inventory

El Salvador
Program Type: Subsidiary
Year Started: 2002
Legal Entity: VisionSpring El Salvador, S.A.
(Salvadoran for-profit Sociedad Anónima)
Key Staff: Heidy Serpas, Country Manager
George "Bucky" Glickley, Consultant

Bangladesh
Program Type: Franchise partner
Year Started: 2006
Legal Entity: BRAC (Bangladeshi non-profit)
Funding: VisionSpring makes grants to BRAC
to manage program and purchase inventory

India
Program Type: Subsidiary that also supports
franchise partners; Year Started: 2005
Legal Entity: VisionSpring India
(Indian non-profit Section 25 Company)
Key Staff: Arunseh Singh, Country Director
Raman Nageswara, operations & Programs

Mexico
Program Type: Franchise partner
Year Started: 2006
Legal Entity: One Roof (U.S. for-profit with
for-profit subsidiary in Mexico)
Funding: One Roof paid VisionSpring to
conduct a feasibility study and pilot

Exhibit 2 **VisionSpring's Micro-Franchise: A Business in a Bag**

Contents of the Business in a Bag

- Glasses (usually around 40 pairs of various styles, colors, and powers)
- Accessories (Cords, Wide Cases, Slim Cases, Cloths)
- Display Boxes for glasses
- File Folder
- VisionSpring t-shirt for entrepreneur
- Pen
- Mirror
- 10 ft. Wire (to measure the distance for the eye charts and testing)
- Needle and Thread (to see if they can thread the needle for vision testing)
- 2 Eye Charts (Near Vision and Distance Vision)
- Carbon Paper
- Banner saying "Authorized Vision Entrepreneur: Trained to conduct free eye screening; Affordable quality reading glasses for Presbyopia," for VE to place outside their home
- VE Invoice Pad
- Eye Hospital Referral Pad

- Rubber stamp of the address of the nearest eye hospital
- Daily Sales Form
- Customer Information Sheet (Includes customer name, village, mandal [county], occupation, gender, age, how did you hear about Vision-Spring, style and power of glasses if purchase made, referral Y/N)
- 25 VisionSpring Promotional Posters
- 100 Promotional Handouts to give out before Vision Camp
- Certificate of VisionSpring Training completion
- Credibility Pack, including letters that demonstrate that VisionSpring's Vision Entrepreneur model is professional and widely recognized.

Note: In mid-2008, Scojo Foundation changed its name to Vision Spring.

Exhibit 3 **Political Map of India**

Source: cyberjournalist.org.in

Exhibit 4 **VisionSpring Organization Chart**

Source: Adapted from VisionSpring's business plan submitted to Acument Fund, 2006

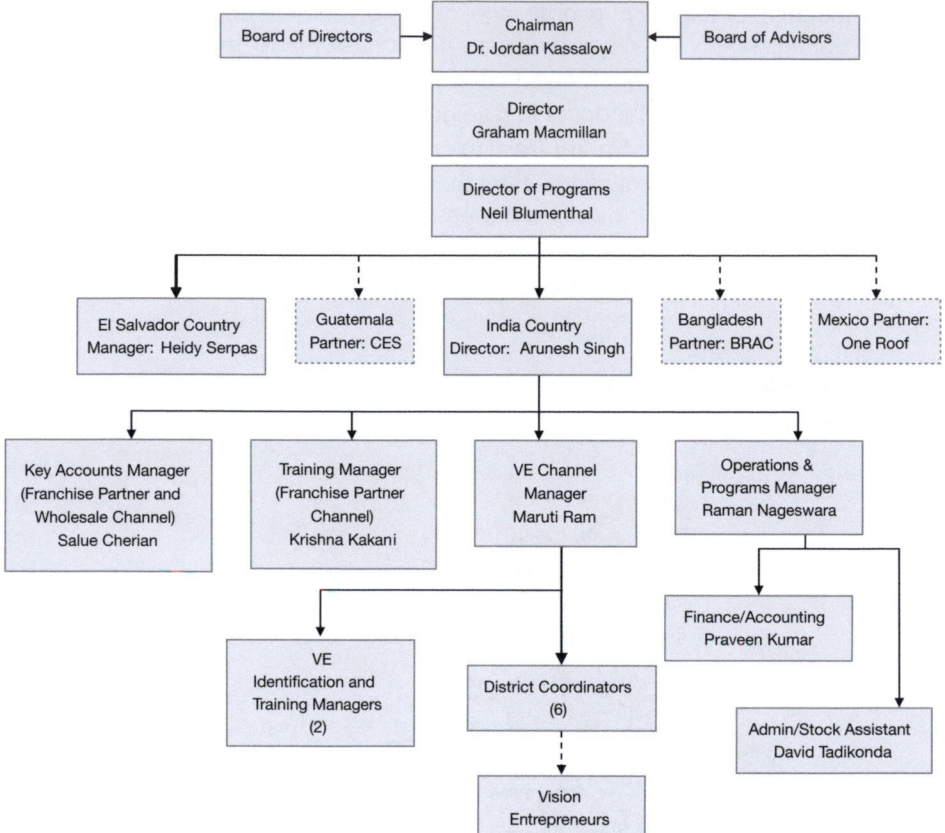

Exhibit 5 **VisionSpring India: Quarterly Metrics in USD**

Source: VisionSpring

	Q1 2005	Q2 2005	Q3 2005	Q4 2005	Q1 2006	Q2 2006	Q3 2006	Q4 2006[a]
Financial data (USD)								
Revenues	$2,467	$1,725	$2,675	$16,285	$21,614	$9,334	$20,090	$15,979
COGS	$1,727	$1,207	$1,873	$11,400	$15,229	$7,116	$14,127	$11,440
OPEX	$14,665	$17,598	$24,160	$22,374	$36,726	$22,697	$35,762	$40,883
Net income	$(13,925)	$(17,081)	$(23,358)	$(17,488)	$(30,341)	$(20,479)	$(29,798)	$(36,345)
Profit margin	-564%	-990%	-873%	-107%	-140%	-219%	-148%	-227%
Operational data								
Total glasses sold	2,019	1,171	1,275	7,081	9,620	3,469	6,472	5,413
# of reading glasses sold	2,019	1,171	1,191	6,777	9,313	3,287	5,797	4,614
# through VisionSpring VEs	2,019	1,171	1,191	1,450	1,802	1,471	1,649	1,487
# through partners				4,725	7,470	1,127	3,890	3,127
# through wholesale				602	41	689	258	
# sunglasses sold			84	304	307	182	675	799
# through VisionSpring VEs			84	245	273	182	127	180
# through partners					24		516	619
# through wholesale				59	10		32	
Days receivable					108	81	101	97
Days inventory					203	380	194	236
# districts in AP with VisionSpring VEs	2	4	5	5	5	5	6	6
# states with partner VEs			1	1	1	5	6	7
Social impact data								
# people served	4,269	3,380	4,564	25,737	40,013	5,394	11,236	6,823
% of customers BOP[b]	100%	100%	100%	91%	99%	80%	96%	100%
# new VEs trained	30	16	30	91	113	46	96	108
# VisionSpring VEs trained	30	16	30	38	18	15	15	37
# Partner VEs trained				53	95	31	81	71
Total VEs employed	30	24	46	131	241	281	371	456

	Q1 2005	Q2 2005	Q3 2005	Q4 2005	Q1 2006	Q2 2006	Q3 2006	Q4 2006[a]
# Current VisionSpring VEs	30	24	46	78	93	102	111	125
# Current partner VEs				53	148	179	260	331
Attrition rate of VisionSpring VEs		73%	33%	13%	4%	6%	6%	21%
% of independent VisionSpring VEs[c]							14%	15%
Avg monthly income from VisionSpring perVE	$82.26	$59.63	$33.88	$26.56	$27.27	$19.81	$19.56	$16.30
# referrals to eyecare clinics	2,220	2,185	3,243	18,525	30,393	1,925	4,764	1,410

a Anticipated metrics for Q4 2006
b % of customers not in wholesale channel
c Independent VE classified as one that operates with minimal supervision from district coordinator

Exhibit 6 **Projected Income Statement for VisionSpring India Operations in Indian Rupees (INR)**

Source: Adapted from VisionSpring's Business Plan submitted to Acumen Fund, 2006

Pro Forma Income Statement	2006	2007	2008	2009	2010	2011	2012
Projected Unit Sales							
# glasses sold (VE channel)	19,656	43,575	77,280	128,380	235,200	235,200	235,200
# glasses sold (partner channel)	34,200	83,250	151,875	232,875	328,500	328,500	328,500
# glasses sold (wholesale channel)	11,400	25,800	51,600	88,200	135,600	135,600	135,600
Total # of glasses sold	65,256	152,625	280,755	449,455	699,300	699,300	699,300
Revenue							
Revenue from VE channel	2,503,192	5,549,276	9,841,608	16,349,193	29,952,720	29,952,720	29,952,720
Revenue from wholesale channel	1,418,730	3,210,810	6,421,620	10,976,490	16,875,420	16,875,420	16,875,420
Revenue from partner channel	3,594,420	8,749,575	15,962,063	24,475,163	34,525,350	34,525,350	34,525,350
Total revenue	7,516,342	17,509,661	32,225,291	51,800,846	81,353,490	81,353,490	81,353,490
COGS	3,941,553	9,220,035	16,959,840	27,146,664	42,223,877	42,223,877	42,223,877
Operating costs from VE channel	2,126,312	3,221,144	4,789,486	7,257,128	10,869,197	10,869,197	10,869,197
Operating costs from wholesale channel	384,200	497,722	1,037,907	2,060,740	3,264,798	3,264,798	3,264,798
Operating costs from partner channel	563,600	1,122,833	1,874,208	3,146,351	4,581,982	4,581,982	4,581,982
Total operating costs	3,074,112	4,841,698	7,701,600	12,464,219	18,715,977	18,715,977	18,715,977
Cost of state offices	0	0	0	1,478,460	1,522,813	1,568,498	1,615,553
Cost of VE regional managers	402,000	422,100	886,410	1,396,096	1,954,534	0	0
Cost of VE state managers	0	0	0	625,118	656,373	689,192	723,652
Cost of executive staff	2,340,000	2,457,000	3,439,800	4,514,738	5,688,569	5,972,998	6,271,648
Cost of support staff	162,000	340,200	535,815	750,141	1,115,835	1,171,626	1,230,208
Total Hyderabad salaries	2,904,000	3,219,300	4,862,025	7,286,092	9,415,311	7,833,816	8,225,507
Total Hyderabad non-personnel costs	1,963,230	1,520,430	1,867,000	2,251,676	3,155,736	1,551,456	2,296,841

Pro Forma Income Statement	2006	2007	2008	2009	2010	2011	2012
Total Costs	11,882,895	18,801,463	31,390,465	50,627,110	75,033,715	71,893,624	73,077,755
EBITDA	(4,366,554)	(1,291,802)	834,825	1,173,735	6,319,775	9,459,866	8,275,735
Depreciation	15,033	35,019	64,451	103,602	162,707	162,707	162,707
EBIT	(4,381,587)	(1,326,821)	770,375	1,070,134	6,157,068	9,297,159	8,113,028
Tax	0	0	0	0	0	0	0
Interest expense	694,073	1,135,756	1,261,951	1,151,897	814,398	814,398	814,398
Net Income	(5,075,660)	(2,462,577)	(491,576)	(81,763)	5,342,670	8,482,760	7,298,630

Note: 1 US Dollar = 45 Indian Rupees (2006)

Exhibit 7 **Projected Balance Sheet for VisionSpring India Operations in Indian Rupees (INR)**

Source: Adapted from VisionSpring's Business Plan submitted to Acumen Fund, 2006

Pro Forma Balance Sheet	2006	2007	2008	2009	2010	2011	2012
Operating cash	5,042,865	8,125,771	9,364,620	3,906,080	1,422,173	1,033,535	9,309,271
Accounts receivable	1,235,563	2,878,300	3,972,981	4,257,604	6,686,588	6,686,588	6,686,588
Inventories	647,927	1,136,717	1,393,959	2,231,233	1,735,228	1,735,228	1,735,228
Other current assets							
Total current assets	6,926,355	12,140,788	14,731,560	10,394,916	9,843,989	9,455,351	17,731,087
PP&E[a]	75,163	175,097	322,253	518,008	813,535	813,535	813,535
Accumulated depreciation[b]	15,033	35,019	64,451	103,602	162,707	162,707	162,707
Net PP&E	60,131	140,077	257,802	414,407	650,828	650,828	650,828
Goodwill/other intangible assets							
Total assets	6,986,486	12,280,865	14,989,363	10,809,323	10,494,817	10,106,179	18,381,915
Accounts payable	161,982	378,906	1,393,959	2,231,233	3,470,456	3,470,456	3,470,456
Accrued liabilities							
Other current liabilities							
Total current liabilities	161,982	378,906	1,393,959	2,231,233	3,470,456	3,470,456	3,470,456
Long-term debt	11,825,000	21,500,000	21,500,000	16,500,000	0	5,406,579	21,500,000
Deferred income taxes							
Total L-T liabilities	11,825,000	21,500,000	21,500,000	16,500,000	-	5,406,579	21,500,000
Equity	(5,000,496)	(9,598,040)	(7,904,597)	(7,921,910)	7,024,362	1,229,145	(6,588,541)
Total liabilities and equity	6,986,486	12,280,865	14,989,363	10,809,323	10,494,817	10,106,179	18,381,915

Note: 1 US Dollar = 45 Indian Rupees (2006)

a Assume PP&E (Property, Plant & Equipment) = 1% sales

b Assume straight line depreciation over 5 years

Exhibit 8 Acumen Fund Business Plan Revenue Assumptions for VisionSpring India Operations

Source: Adapted from VisionSpring Foundation's Business Plan submitted to Acumen Fund, 2006

Revenue Assumptions	2006	2007	2008	2009	2010	2011	2012
Vision entrepreneur channel							
Per Vision entrepreneur							
Number of campaigns per month	2	2	2	2	2	2	2
Glasses sold per campaign per VE	4	5	5	5	5	5	5
Additional sales per month (pairs)	10	10	10	10	10	10	10
Number of VEs per district	20	25	30	35	40	40	40
Number districts with VE sales	7	10	14	20	28	28	28
Number of states with VE sales	1	1	1	2	2	2	2
Annual attrition rate for VE	50%	45%	40%	35%	35%	35%	35%
Months of revenue lost per dropout	3	3	2	2	2	2	2
Partner channel							
Per partner							
Number sales per VE per month	15	15	15	15	15	15	15
Number VEs per partner	150	150	150	150	150	150	150
Number of partners	2	4	7	10	14	14	14
Number months in operation per year	12	12	12	12	12	12	12
Wholesale channel							
Number of accounts	50	100	200	350	550	550	550
Average opening order	84	84	84	84	84	84	84
Average additional order	36	36	36	36	36	36	36
Number of follow-up orders/year	4	6	6	6	6	6	6
Number months in operation per year	12	12	12	12	12	12	12

Exhibit 9 **VisionSpring India's Three Distribution Channels**

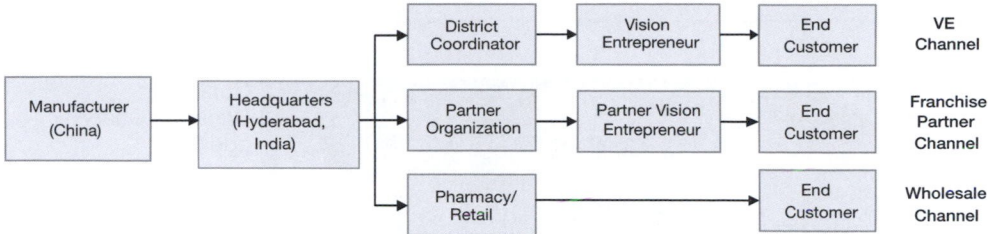

Exhibit 10 **VisionSpring India's Reading Glasses**

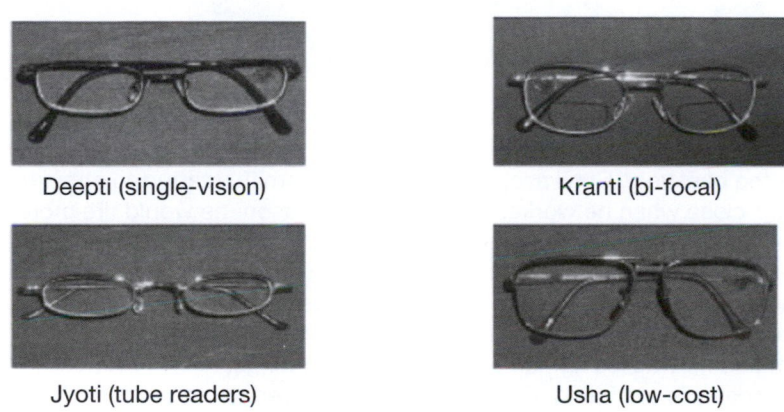

Deepti (single-vision)   Kranti (bi-focal)

Jyoti (tube readers)   Usha (low-cost)

Exhibit 11 **Vision Entrepreneur Margins on Reading Glasses in INR; type of Glasses as % of Sales**

Glasses Type	Price (INR)	VE Margin	% of Sales
Jyoti (tube readers)	165	54	17
Kranti (bifocals)	165	54	62
Deepti (single-vision)	155	49	18
Usha (low-cost)	95	39	3
Sunglasses	165	26	n/a

Note: 1 US Dollar = 45 Indian Rupees (2006)

Exhibit 12 **VisionSpring Customer Story**

Source: www.visionspring.org

Customer:
Srinivasa Chary,
age 36

Photo credit:
VisionSpring

Note: In mid-2008, the organization changed its name from Scojo to VisionSpring.

Over the past year, Srinivasa, a successful goldsmith, started to strain to see up-close when he worked. Unsure of the reason, he would tire more quickly and suffer frequent headaches. Eventually, he stopped being able to work once the sun set due to lack of light. Even with sufficient light, he found it difficult to fit small stones into the jewelry he made. He started to outsource the setting of rings and bracelets to another jeweler he knew. He estimated he was losing half of his potential earnings.

One day, his old friend, Chandra Shekhar, arrived at his shop in a Vision-Spring shirt and offered to give him a free vision screening. The VisionSpring VE quickly determined that Srinivasa suffered from blurry up-close vision and needed a pair of +1.00 reading glasses. Srinivasa purchased the high quality reading glasses for approximately US$3 and thereby doubled his productivity. Now, Srinivasa no longer sends out business to other gold-smiths. He is able to work as hard and as long as he did when he was younger. Currently, it is the wedding season in India, which is his most prof-itable time. Srinivasa often can be found in his shop working until midnight without pain or strain. "I could not imagine that blurry up-close vision had such bad repercussions for me. These glasses have brought a great relief to my life. I am very happy and thankful to VisionSpring for screening and sell-ing glasses at affordable prices right at my doorstep. Also, I am grateful that this has created livelihoods for poor rural youth like Chandra Shekhar whom people here trust more than any stranger who comes and then leaves."

## Part IV

Topic Spotlight: SE Approaches for Tackling Water Challenges

Case 9

Procter & Gamble's PuR Water Purifier

The Hunt for a Sustainable Business Model[1, 2, 3, 4]

Lisa Jones Christensen and Jessica Thomas
Kenan-Flagler Business School, UNC-Chapel Hill, USA

Over recent years, under the leadership of Dr. Greg Allgood, director of the Children's Safe Drinking Water Program, P&G has helped to distribute 65 million PuR packets. These packets have been used to purify 650 million liters of water, most often in rural locations. Over time, and through a variety of deliberate partnerships that Allgood cultivated in 10 countries, P&G has tested three different sales and distribution models: commercial marketing, social marketing and disaster relief—each with varying degrees of success. Drawing from past successes and failures,

1 This case © 2007 Kenan-Flagler Business School, University of North Carolina, Chapel Hill, NC, USA. No part of this publication may be reproduced, stored in a retrieval system, used in a spreadsheet, or transmitted in any form by any means without permission.
2 This case is intended to serve as a basis for class discussion, rather than to illustrate the effective or ineffective handling of an administrative situation.
3 This case presents the range of business models that P&G has explored for the sales and distribution of PuR. The case also presents the risks and hurdles inherent in these projects, as well as implications for their potential scalability to other countries/regions. Through this case, students may gain insight into both the challenges and significant opportunities in addressing the needs of low-income consumers in emerging markets.
4 Available online at www.cse.unc.edu. Clarifications or comments may be directed to cse@unc.edu.

Allgood is considering how to fulfill P&G's aggressive commitment to providing 135 million liters of safe drinking water in Africa and how to achieve long-term behavior change.

Introduction

Greg Allgood watched again the seemingly-magical process of using PuR to purify a bucket of black and dirty water. He was always the first to take a drink of the final product, and this day would be no different—even though uphill from the watering hole where he and the community members had collected the water lay a dead dog. This wasn't the worst Allgood had seen, but it was certainly symbolic of the challenges in creating access to clean drinking water in developing countries.

After he had opened the small PuR sachet and poured the contents into a 10-liter bucket of dirty water, Allgood had stirred the contents for five minutes and watched with others as the dirt and other particles separated out and dropped below the now clear, clean water. Now Allgood strained the water through a clean t-shirt filter and took a long drink for the crowd. His only worry was his knowledge that this process would need to be replicated millions of times to meet his recent commitment to provide 135 million liters of safe drinking water. While Allgood knew how to meet that commitment, he still wondered if his plans for continued social marketing were the best way to achieve household penetration and real, long-term behavior change. As he formed his plans, he reflected briefly on the public promises he had recently made regarding providing safe water, as well as on how far he and his company had already come.

In September of 2006, Procter & Gamble joined with their long-time partner Population Services International (PSI) at the Clinton Global Initiative to announce a commitment to provide safe drinking water in Africa. Working with PSI (and a variety of other partners) as part of their focal philanthropy program—The Children's Safe Drinking Water program—P&G publicly committed to providing 35 million liters of safe drinking water to more than 1 million children. In addition, through PSI's private sector approach and community-based outreach, the team promised to provide another 100 million liters of safe drinking water in Africa. P&G also committed to provide $3.8 million to a variety of other partners focused on water issues. This included a commitment from P&G Retired Officers, funds from a cause-related marketing program in the U.S. sponsored by the PuR® Water Filtration Business, and contributions from the P&G Fund, P&G's philanthropic arm. The total financial commitment was $5 million over three years.[5]

---

5 "Procter & Gamble and PSI announce commitment to provide safe drinking water in Africa," PSI News Release, September 21, 2006.

After 6 years of working on the PuR project, Dr. Allgood, director of the Children's Safe Drinking Water program, had learned a great deal about how to market and distribute PuR by building a diverse web of partnerships. Already, about 65 million PuR packets had purified some 650 million liters of water, most often in rural locations where local populations draw and use their water directly from filthy and foul-smelling lakes and rivers. As P&G prepared to embark on its most significant PuR marketing campaign to date, Allgood considered how to leverage existing partnerships and how to create new partnerships to fulfill P&G's aggressive commitments to provide safe drinking water.

Background on P&G

Established in 1837, the Procter & Gamble Company began as a small, family-operated soap and candle company in Cincinnati, Ohio. In 2007, P&G marketed over 300 brands including Tide, Always, Crest, Braun, Charmin, Duracell, Folgers, Gillette, Pampers, Pringles, Tide, and Wella. With over 135,000 employees working in over 80 countries worldwide, P&G was the world's largest consumer products company.

P&G has always had a strong history of philanthropy, understandable in a company with a mission to "improve the lives of the world's consumers." The Corporate Sustainable Development (CSD) department was formed in July 1999 as a global organization under the leadership of George D. Carpenter. The department focused on defining P&G's overall sustainability policy, identifying emerging sustainability issues, managing corporate sustainability reporting, building external relations and assisting the business units to incorporate sustainable development into their businesses. P&G embraced sustainable development as a potential business opportunity, as well as a corporate responsibility. P&G demonstrated a commitment to the economic and social well-being of a range of stakeholders and to regional, national and international development.[6]

Since 2003, the Children's Safe Drinking Water program has led P&G's effort to provide clean drinking water to families. In its first three and a half years the program distributed enough PuR packets to provide 650 million liters of clean drinking water to children in need and their families around the world. In April 2005, P&G launched the Live, Learn and Thrive (LLT) program focused on the health and development of children aged 0–13. P&G goals for the children are "to help them live by ensuring a healthy start; to provide them with places, tools, and programs to enhance their ability to learn; and to help them develop skills for life so they can thrive."[7] Children's Safe Drinking Water became the signature program for LLT.

---

6 P&G 2006 Global Sustainability & Philanthropy Report, www.pg.com/content/pdf/01_about_pg/corporate_citizenship/sustainability/reports/sustainability_report_2006.pdf.

7 "World Water Day Highlights Around the P&G World," Bea Buyle, Global Sustainability, May 2, 2007.

Why water?

Clean drinking water is one of the world's greatest needs, according to the World Health Organization. Many children in developing countries simply don't have access to clean, safe water in their communities. These children have little choice but to drink from contaminated water sources so filthy and filled with germs that most in the West would not even walk through them, let alone drink from them. Drinking contaminated water can lead to illness such as diarrhoea, typhoid fever and cholera, which can cause death. And, for people in developing countries who have AIDS, drinking contaminated water further challenges their immune systems and is a serious factor in the impact of this disease.

According to a UN study, more than 1.1 billion people in poor nations drink water that has undergone no treatment whatsoever.[8] Each year, 3 million people die due to unsafe water, inadequate sanitation and poor hygiene. A majority of these deaths are caused by infectious diarrhoea. An estimated 5,000 children under 5 years of age die daily due to diarrheal disease, ranked the third-highest cause of morbidity and sixth-highest cause of mortality in the world. Water is the most important route of disease transmission in many countries where there is little or no infrastructure to manage human waste or build appropriate water access and storage.[9] Thus, while work on infrastructure continues, other alternatives such as decentralized and individually-based approaches for water treatment are becoming more and more important.

In-home treatment of existing local water sources, called point-of-use (POU) solutions, allow individuals to control the treatment (and therefore the resulting quality) of their drinking water. POU solutions can vary widely in their approach, effectiveness, and ease-of-use depending on the method of treatment. Ultimately, the cost of POU solutions and their widespread applicability make them a practical short- and long-term complement to water and sanitation infrastructure development.[10]

8 "Making Troubled Waters Potable: An inexpensive water treatment technology is making a difference in poor communities around the world," Ivan Amato, *Chemical & Engineering News*, April 17, 2006, Volume 84, Number 16, pp. 39-40. pubs.acs.org/isubscribe/journals/cen/84/i16/html/8416sci3.html.

9 PuR Marketing Plan, Dominican Republic.

10 Reck, J. & Hart, S., "Water for the Masses: An Assessment of Point-of-Use Water Treatment Solutions," January 2004, Center for Sustainable Enterprise, Kenan Institute.

PuR: The P&G product response to the water issue

During the heyday of the dot-com era, P&G had to grow dramatically to compete. The CEO at the time, Dirk Jager, developed new businesses focused on the largest global problems. According to Allgood, "the focus on global needs made sense strategically for P&G and water was certainly a clear need." The result was an early collaboration with the U.S. Centers for Disease Control and Prevention (CDC). From 1999 to 2001, P&G worked with CDC to conduct village-level trials of a low-cost water filter in Guatemala. Despite the failure of the filter product, P&G and CDC developed a good working relationship.[11] During that time, goals migrated and through a series of events P&G and CDC decided to reverse-engineer the municipal water treatment process and to convert the treatment chemicals into a powdered form. In 2000, PuR® Purifier of Water™ was launched.

The PuR product is a small packet (or "sachet") of a pre-measured compound designed to be mixed with 10 liters of water. The water can be in any state, from fully black and turbid to apparently clear but still contaminated. The packet-water mixture must be stirred for 5 minutes, allowed to flocculate (the pollutants bind to iron and other ingredients included in the sachet), and then the water must be filtered into a new container through a cotton cloth to ensure that all particulates are removed.

The treated water can sit in a household for several days and retain its purity and freshness for that entire period. During product demonstrations and in daily use, the PuR product appears miraculous when it visibly alters the appearance, taste, and quality of brackish, turbid, black water to clear, clean, and good-tasting water. PuR is able to remove pathogens that cause diarrhoea, including viruses, parasites, worms, and bacteria. In addition it removes arsenic, DDT, and other pollutants that make water unsafe.

"Where water is highly turbid, the PuR sachets produce water that looks and tastes better to its users and reduces the risk of diarrheal disease," said Stephen Luby, a former CDC medical epidemiologist. A growing body of field studies, mostly orchestrated by CDC and collectively involving more than 25,000 people, has shown that groups that use P&G's packets suffer only about half of the diarrhoea episodes of groups that use untreated water sources. The chemical technology itself amounts to, in Allgood's words, "putting a mini-water-treatment plant inside a packet."[12]

11 Hanson, M. & Powell, K. (2006). "Procter & Gamble PuR Purifier of Water (A): Developing the Product and Taking it to Market," INSEAD case, p. 7.

12 "Making Troubled Waters Potable: An inexpensive water treatment technology is making a difference in poor communities around the world," Ivan Amato, *Chemical & Engineering News*, April 17, 2006, Volume 84, Number 16, pp. 39-40. pubs.acs.org/isubscribe/journals/cen/84/i16/html/8416sci3.html.

Challenges in finding start-up funding

In 2001, Allgood (who earned a Masters Degree in Public Health and a PhD in Toxi-cology) joined the PuR team. He became the external relations leader for the Per-sonal Health Care team, which included Vicks, ThermaCare and Pepto-Bismol in addition to PuR. Allgood came from the P&G Food and Beverage business where he launched Nutristar, P&G's micronutrient supplement, in Venezuela.[13]

After he joined the PuR team, Allgood's plan was to obtain external funding and to leverage the strengths of other organizations interested in similar goals. He first approached USAID to discuss collaboration to address the global safe drinking water need and to apply for a Global Development Alliance (GDA) grant. In late 2001, P&G submitted a grant proposal for GDA funding in partnership with the Academy for Educational Development (AED) to distribute PuR in very low income markets. The proposal was rejected without feedback.[14] Despite a lack of external funding, village level testing of PuR, funded by P&G, began in Morocco and Paki-stan in early 2002.

P&G concurrently began developing a relationship with Population Services International (PSI). At the time, PSI's expertise was in developing social marketing programs in developing countries.[15] In early 2002, P&G submitted a second grant proposal to GDA combined with a PSI partnership that promised a 20-country roll-out of PuR sachets. The proposal was rejected with the explanation that the scope was too big.

In early 2003, P&G submitted a third proposal to GDA, more scaled down than the second one, in joint partnership with PSI, the Johns Hopkins Bloomberg School of Public Health, and CARE. In August 2003, USAID approved $1.4 million in funding through GDA for the Safe Drinking Water Alliance to provide safe water in Ethiopia, Haiti, and Pakistan. The partners decided to conduct an 18-month pilot to test 3 models that were compelling to Allgood: commercial marketing, social marketing, and disaster relief.[16]

Sally Cowal, a senior vice president with PSI, said of the partnership, "They don't know particularly well how to reach the bottom of the pyramid in the countries we work in; that's what we know really well. But they know things about brands

---

13 "Doing Business with the Poor: A field guide," World Business Council for Sustainable Development, www.wbcsd.org/web/publications/sl-field-guide-reprint.pdf.

14 Hanson, M. & Powell, K. (2006), "Procter & Gamble and Population Services International (PSI): Social Marketing for Safe Water," p. 6.

15 "Conceptual Note Proposal: Haiti: Clean Water, Good Business," Proposal to the Business Linkages Challenge Fund.

16 US Department of State Press Release, 29 April 2004, "Public–Private Partners to Spend $5 Million for Safe Water: Safe Water Alliance will begin work in Haiti, Pakistan." www.america.gov/st/washfile-english/2004/April/20040429164019IHecuoR0.1296656.html.

and brand management and sophisticated marketing and sales techniques that we [can] learn from them."[17]

Declared commercial failure in Pakistan

PuR's first commercial test markets were conducted in Guatemala and the Philippines in 2001 and 2002. Despite the public health benefits of the projects, both were considered failures due to low repeat purchase numbers. In 2002, P&G conducted village-level testing of PuR in Morocco and Pakistan. After a year of testing and public health education, all of the Pakistan village tests were achieving a market penetration rate of about 50%. Despite the promising trial results in Pakistan and the recently received USAID funding, many at P&G still felt that the project required too much public health education infrastructure investment to provide a profitable product line. Said Allgood, "we didn't have the capability to provide education where it was needed and we had to invest a lot to develop it. This resulted in an investment hole that required very high use rates to climb out of."

Allgood argued for emergency relief and social marketing opportunities for the product as well as for the opportunity to leverage the project for employee engagement and for stakeholder relationships. In addition, because the clinical studies showed a dramatic reduction in diarrheal illness, Allgood felt P&G had a real opportunity to make an impact on a critical public health crisis by helping save the lives of many children. As part of his role on the leadership team of PuR, Allgood met with CEO A.G. Lafley on several occasions to assess the product status. After some discussion, Lafley agreed to support launch of a commercial test market in Pakistan and to create a new not-for-profit group within P&G, the Children's Safe Drinking Water program, to allow P&G to provide PuR for social marketing and for emergency relief. At the time, the feeling was that the project would only be pursued long-term if the Pakistan market was successful.[18] Even Allgood envisioned that P&G would provide PuR through social and emergency relief methods with the help of a successful commercial strategy.

With clearance to continue to test the commercial model in Pakistan, in June of 2004, P&G conducted a high profile PuR product launch. PuR sold for the equivalent of about $0.10 a sachet (5 rupees). The launch primarily targeted the urban population in Sindh Province of 15 million.[19] To achieve the aggressive goals of the commercial campaign, P&G partnered with the Pakistan Medical Association

17 "A Clear Solution for Dirty Water," Tim Lougheed, *Environmental Health Perspectives*, Volume 114, Number 7, July 2006. www.ehponline.org/members/2006/114-7/innovations. html.

18 Hanson, M. & Powell, K. (2006). "Procter & Gamble PuR Purifier of Water (A): Developing the Product and Taking it to Market," INSEAD case, p. 10.

19 Ibid. p. 11.

(PMA), Johns Hopkins Bloomberg School of Public Health, PSI and its local affiliate Greenstar.[20] PSI/Greenstar was part of the launch because they were part of the Safe Drinking Water Alliance but they did not have an active role. Allgood included PSI/Greenstar because he respected how well they knew the country and because he saw them as a potential partner in an exit strategy for Pakistan in the event that the commercial launch was not successful. Allgood knew that if the commercial project failed PSI/Greenstar would likely continue to work with P&G on an alternate strategy, such as social marketing or disaster relief.

As part of the launch they created the largest safe water awareness campaign ever held in Pakistan, conducted in collaboration with the PMA. Education teams consisting of 1,400 members went into more than 40 top cities, educating on a one-on-one basis, mothers, children, and heads of families in more than 1.66 million households.[21] The PuR commercial launch was one of the highest profile launches in P&G's ten-year history in Pakistan. The Pakistani Vice President and a number of government officials attended the launch.

Six months later, the Pakistan results were slower than expected (repeat purchase hovered around 5%). In thinking about why the launch "failed" Allgood reflected that P&G experienced several challenges during the launch. A critical element of the success of the village level tests was the education programs in schools; however, the launch of the test market coincided with a teacher's strike preventing implementation of a school education program. In addition, the marketing campaign developed by Hopkins was not released until after the six-month critical launch window. Based on the low repeat purchase rate, P&G was faced with a negative return on investment. The decision was made to end the commercial test market.

Thus, in late 2004 Allgood suggested P&G move PuR from a commercial to a social marketing strategy instead of fully exiting Pakistan. P&G Pakistan donated product, Allgood's group provided technical assistance, and the P&G Fund provided $250,000 to help PSI/Greenstar transition to a social market.

Emergency and disaster relief models in Southeast Asia

While Allgood was already aware of the opportunity to use PuR in disaster relief programs due to its portable, lightweight nature, its effectiveness in heavily contaminated waters, and its 3-year shelf life, the opportunity came more clearly into focus after the devastating Asian tsunami in December 2004. At the time, P&G had already decided to continue to provide PuR as a not-for-profit effort and was early in the launch of the Live, Learn and Thrive program with Children's Safe Drinking

---

20 *Urdu Times*, "Social Sector to Get Major Share in Budget: Soomro," May 28, 2004.
21 "P&G Pakistan, Company Overview 2004."

Water as the signature program. When the tsunami hit, emergency relief personnel from Samaritan's Purse, AmeriCares, and UNICEF called P&G requesting shipments of PuR based on prior relationships. UNICEF and AmeriCares had previously purchased PuR from P&G for use in emergency relief. At the time of the tsunami, Samaritans Purse was already in discussions with P&G to purchase PuR.

P&G had a large stockpile of PuR after the slow results in the Pakistan test market. Initially, P&G sold sachets at cost to aid organizations but once the scope of the disaster became clearer, they decided to donate product. P&G donated a total of $3.1 million in product and cash which resulted in delivery of 13 million packets of PuR for Sri Lanka, Indonesia, and the Maldives.[22] Said Allgood, "P&Gers had made the decision to continue providing PuR prior to the tsunami but the tsunami was really a watershed moment. As we began to help save lives during the tsunami by providing PuR, P&Gers understood on a gut level that we were making a critical contribution to society and that we could turn a commercial failure into a humanitarian success." Thus, P&G entered the disaster relief field with a mixture of product sales (usually at cost) and donations. As a result, P&G created new partnerships and strengthened existing ones with humanitarian organizations.

Testing the social marketing model in Haiti

While Allgood created a disaster relief strategy, he also worked with PSI on a social marketing strategy. Even before the perceived failure of the commercial marketing model in Pakistan, P&G and PSI decided that a social marketing model may be most appropriate in certain markets where economic and infrastructure constraints limit the commercial model. Specifically, the social model involved the use of established social marketing distribution channels by nonprofit organizations as well as a social network approach with local NGOs and Ministries of Health. While P&G had no experience with this approach, PSI had already successfully used this model in parts of the developing world to provide important health products including insecticide treated mosquito nets to prevent malaria and condoms to prevent the spread of the HIV virus.[23] According to Allgood, "In a very important way, we're combining not only the biggest and best social marketing company in the world with the biggest and best consumer products company in the world. Together, we'll make a very important difference for people in the developing world."

In January 2005, the partnership launched its first social marketing campaign for PuR in Haiti. PSI developed a social marketing strategy with assistance from P&G. PuR was sold to wholesalers and NGOs for them to sell to consumers at a

---

22 "A Clear Solution for Dirty Water," Tim Lougheed, *Environmental Health Perspectives*, Volume 114, Number 7, July 2006.

23 "Procter & Gamble, Treating water at its point of use," Case Study, World Business Council for Sustainable Development, 2006.

subsidized price of 3 gourdees (about \$0.08). At the time, P&G had no significant commercial network in Haiti but PSI had been operating there since 1989. PSI Haiti had created a foundation of private-sector infrastructure and NGO partners that could be used to bring diarrheal disease prevention techniques to underserved populations across the country.[24] Diarrhoea was the leading cause of death among Haitian children less than a year old, and the second leading cause of death among children ages 1–5 years, primarily due to the ingesting of unsafe water.[25]

In March 2005, the UK government's Department for International Development (DFID) contributed £224,943 to PSI Haiti for the "Haiti: Clean Water, Good Business" project, through the Business Linkages Challenge Fund. PSI Haiti marketed PuR using a network of women's groups it had worked with in the past. PSI Haiti and P&G provided these women's groups with product and materials, as well as formal training in marketing, sales, and behavior change techniques. Once trained, these women's groups marketed PuR at the community level.[26] Due to the unfolding political crisis, the education campaigns were interrupted. By the end of 2006, Haiti had not met sales objectives. "We couldn't register the product because there was no government," reported Allgood. He continued, "During that time, PSI never left the country when a lot of other NGOs did leave."

"Despite all the difficulties of operating in Haiti, PSI Haiti initially did pretty well with PuR," said Allgood. Within a year of the launch, P&G had delivered 1.6 million sachets: half through social marketing (radio ads, billboards, and reaching people through large events like Carnival) and half through institutional sales. "One of the things we've learned is that large scale events don't result in repeat purchases," said Allgood. "PSI used radio ads and events that reached lots of people and built awareness but these approaches were not by themselves sufficient for people to adopt a brand new health prevention habit." Allgood's goal, as with our other social markets, was to establish a self-sustaining program. When he talks about it he says "In Haiti, we're a long way off. Because of the security issues and lack of infrastructure, it's been difficult for PSI to conduct the community level education and training necessary to create long-term habit change. Despite the challenges, PSI has been able to provide more than 16 million liters of safe drinking water via the PuR sachets in Haiti. In addition, we've learned a lot about where we need to focus and have slowly built relationships with local groups who are beginning to adopt PuR into their programs."

24 "Haiti: Clean Water, Good Business." Conceptual note proposal to the Business Linkages Challenge Fund.
25 MSPP/PAHO, 1998, Analyse de la Situation Sanitaire Haïti: 1999. Port-au-Prince, Haïti.
26 "Haiti: Clean Water, Good Business." Conceptual note proposal to the Business Linkages Challenge Fund.

Transitioning from commercial to social marketing through emergency relief in Pakistan

In early 2005, PSI Pakistan began to transition from the commercial to the social marketing campaign. As Allgood had hoped, PSI worked in close collaboration with its local partner, Greenstar, as well as with several former partners from the commercial marketing attempt. P&G provided the Pakistan project with $250,000 and product labeled in Urdu. Allgood and P&G required a sustainability plan for the social marketing campaign. In the plan, after the initial donated sachets were exhausted, P&G would sell PSI additional sachets at a cost recovery price of $US0.035/packet. The sachets would retail for about $US0.10 to allow for taxes, PSI overhead, and a margin for the distributors, wholesalers, and retailers. Allgood created this "cost recovery" pricing and sales structure as part of his strategy to make the social marketing model sustainable for all parties—including the small-scale retailers in these developing countries.

However, prior to the start of the social market, a large earthquake devastated northern Pakistan. Because PSI and Greenstar had Urdu labeled product and trained teams and because of the outreach conducted with the relief groups as part of the failed commercial attempt, many groups were eager to use PuR to provide safe drinking water to the survivors of the earthquake. PSI and Greenstar were able to provide about 9 million sachets in relief efforts. Allgood used the Safe Drinking Water Alliance to approach USAID's Global Development Alliance and very rapidly used their existing partnership to provide additional funding to support the relief effort and reach 50,000 households.

A different kind of disaster occurred as P&G was increasing production to address demand from the Pakistan earthquake. Arch Chemicals, a global biocides company and the supplier of calcium hypochlorite (the disinfectant active ingredient for PuR) reported that they were no longer making the ingredient to P&G's specifications. The suppliers thought that they could make a different grade of the disinfectant—not realizing that their compound was, in effect, a "secret sauce" in PuR that enabled it to treat a wide range of waters with a single formula. Said Laura Tew, Director of Stakeholder Relations at Arch Chemicals "One of our employees, Bea Pomeraniec, received the e-mail on October 24, 2005 for a product order from P&G. The Arch Charleston plant was just 'ramping up' its production to build inventory for the spring swimming pool season in North America. The calcium hypochlorite characteristics for this application are slightly different from that needed for the PuR formulation. Bea's experience with the P&G procurement team and her natural inclination to be a customer advocate gave her all she needed to escalate the request to the Arch director of manufacturing and the quality team at the Charleston facility. The facility stopped its regular production over the weekend, made the necessary change, and added the special production request to their weekend production plan to meet the PuR required specifications." Arch Chemicals has supplied specialty ingredients to P&G for over 40 years, so the business proposition of working with P&G on the PuR formulation was very important.

Learning from the social marketing experience in Uganda

To continue to increase the availability of clean water and to continue to learn more about how to market and sell the product, Allgood and PSI picked the next country that PuR would enter. They made the choice based on rates of illness and death due to lack of access to clean water. Because PSI was very decentralized they also wanted to find a place where their own country manager was interested in introducing PuR. USAID was already funding PSI with social marketing of condom distribution in Uganda and P&G and PSI agreed informally to continue to work together in Uganda to add PuR to the portfolio of PSI products there.

In 2005, the PSI Uganda country office formally expressed interest in participating in the PuR project. P&G's NGO partner the International Council of Nurses (ICN) was also interested in collaborating. Later in 2005, the group launched a social marketing campaign relying heavily on promotion, communication and education. The plan was a series of 17 product launches across the country. The first day of the launch, PSI met with thought leaders, hospitals and tribal leaders and gave them a seminar on the importance of access to clean drinking water. The next day was filled with a trade blitz and product demonstrations. The third day featured a concert with Ragga D, a popular Ugandan musician.

The same day of the launch for western Uganda, Allgood did an impromptu demo at a water hole with one of the P&G sales representatives. The water was very turbid and the people observing the demo were very excited about the results. One of the observers was a social worker and asked the P&G team to do the same demonstration in his village a short distance away. At the next village, the water was even worse. The social worker got the tribal leaders and a nurse to participate in the demo. Allgood and the PSI sales rep then sold all of the product they had on hand, which ultimately was more than what was sold that entire day at the concert with Ragga D.

"The Uganda launch was executed superbly well but it still didn't work well towards our goal of a sustained social market," said Allgood. "We've learned the hard way that those large scale events don't lead to long-term sustained habit change or even immediate sales." It took over a year, but eventually the partnership in Uganda adapted to focus on grassroots programs to reach more people in rural areas. In late 2005, with some uncertainty around future funding, P&G helped PSI Uganda secure additional funding for the project through a program by P&G UK/Ireland to tie their business success to providing safe drinking water.

In early 2006, PSI lost their USAID funding for the social marketing campaign in Uganda. The safe drinking water work by PSI benefited from the infrastructure provided by the USAID funding. Said Allgood, "A lot of PSI's infrastructure had been supported by USAID. P&G philanthropy provided all of the funding to PSI to launch PuR but the level of funding assumed that there was an existing healthy program. Unfortunately, PSI was not awarded a 5-year extension on its US government funding. This is the way of life in the donor world and we knew this was a possibility. One of the reasons we picked PSI as a partner is the fact that despite these challenges, they have an excellent track record of staying in a country."

With the loss in funding and because the US government had provided the entire funding for the introduction and marketing of most of PSI's other brands, PSI had to turn those brands over to their competitor. According to Allgood, "because PuR was being carried by distributors as part of a line-up of PSI products, this loss in USAID funding meant that PuR lost distribution throughout the country and alternative distributors would need to be identified." This was a setback in Uganda and an alteration of the partnership, but ultimately, by late 2006, some monies were collected to allow PSI to stay in Uganda. Since the launch, PSI has provided more than 2 million sachets of PuR in Uganda. However, the uncertainty of relying on any one country for results suggested to Allgood and others that partnerships be expanded to several countries at once to "hedge" against the kind of situation that occurred in Uganda.

Working with local partners in the Dominican Republic

Thus, also in 2006, PSI requested that P&G bring PuR sachets into the Dominican Republic. In parts of the Dominican Republic, 8 out of 10 people do not have water in their homes. Many people walk 15 minutes or more to collect their water from rivers. Unlike the other countries where P&G worked with PSI, PSI was using their own funds to initiate this market. For Allgood, "It's a bold statement for a non-profit to invest their limited unrestricted funds in our Children's Safe Drinking Water program."

The strategy focused on the commercial market with PSI distributing PuR through three principal channels. The first was Distribuidora Corripio, the largest distributor of consumer products in the Dominican Republic. Because PuR was a P&G product, Corripio donated their services to distribute PuR to *colmados*, the 30,000 small consumer shops across the country. Corripio also donated air time on both radio and television in order to increase public awareness of PuR. Another distribution channel was through Daniel Espinal which served the pharmacy chain Farmax. Daniel Espinal agreed to position PuR in the pharmacies and to cooperate in a donation program in their mid- and high-end stores by providing a collection container for donation of PuR sachets. PSI also distributed PuR through international and local NGOs with which it had prior relationships. Said Allgood "this had pluses and minuses but overall it didn't work very well because the NGO network of PSI had less incentive to provide PuR when it was being provided by Corripio." In the end, the large-scale marketing approach of TV ads didn't work in the Dominican Republic.

The move to school programs in Uganda

In 2006, P&G reached 17 million school children through a variety of educational programs related to hygiene. As a result, the company had developed experience with school programs and had demonstrated that they can be an effective tool in building both trial and longer-term use of a brand as well as contributing to important public health issues. Along with PSI Uganda, P&G agreed on a three-pronged social marketing approach for providing PuR to schools designed to create household behavioral change.

First, they would sample PuR in schools using nurses or teachers as the educators. They would directly engage the parents of these children by providing educational materials as well as an incentive such as a prize or free school fees for a boy and girl in each school. Second, they would build trade awareness of the efforts through the PSI sales reps, who would pick the schools and ensure good product distribution in the surrounding areas. Third, they would conduct a radio campaign to highlight the need for safe drinking water in schools as well as to describe the extensive outreach campaign to provide safe drinking water in schools.

In August of 2006, PSI Uganda completed a pilot, providing safe drinking water education and training in three primary schools in the Soroti District. In each school, children were selected and educated about safe water, hygiene and the use of PuR. After the training, each pupil was given 3 gift sachets of PuR and a leaflet containing information on safe water and hygiene to take home. Pupils were encouraged to demonstrate use of PuR to their parents and to remind their parents to use PuR to treat their drinking water. Parents filled out a questionnaire and children brought back empty sachets to win a prize.

P&G also used PSI staff in Uganda to excite the trade by providing posters and information. PSI was responsible for picking the schools where the product was appropriate, making sure there was distribution near the school and letting the school people know where to get the product. PSI also used mass media, a talk show format in a radio campaign, to talk about unsafe drinking water and convey the message that "PSI will provide 20 million liters of drinking water in Uganda".

Monitoring of this work showed that household use of PuR increased from 5% to 25%. Of the 1,853 pupils trained, 750 brought back coupons with 3 or more empty sachets attached. More than 4,500 used sachets were returned. On average, 6 sachets were returned by each child signifying that 3 additional sachets had been bought by his/her family.[27] "I've learned enough to feel strongly that school programs are critical to the sustainable provision of the PuR sachets, and that they can meet an important public health need" said Allgood. P&G also conducted controlled tests distributing product with and without school programs in Pakistan and Morocco, both eventually indicating high repeat usage through school programs.

Adapting the school model in Kenya

Typically the cost to launch a PuR social marketing campaign in an average-size country ranges from $500,000 to $1 million, although this estimate varies greatly based on the other partners and the characteristics of the country. To launch a new campaign, P&G would provide technical and product marketing expertise. The P&G Fund would often provide cash for marketing materials, infrastructure building and initial product purchase. The goal was that the campaign would become self-sustaining through the cost recovery model.

PSI Kenya initially received $500,000 from the P&G Fund to launch PuR in Kenya February 2006. Thanks to the US PuR Water Filtration cause-related marketing program, PSI received another $800,000 over two years ($600K from the P&G Fund match and $200K from the PuR brand). Prior to the launch by PSI Kenya, P&G had been providing PuR to women's groups through a collaboration with CDC following cessation of a clinical study in which PuR was shown to reduce diarrheal illness and mortality. Because of these two-year demonstration projects, many external partners knew about PuR and were eager to work with P&G.

One of the new partners in the Kenya launch was CFW Shops, run by nurses who provide critical health products in remote and poor areas. The nurses go into the communities to conduct classes in schools, churches, or with community groups. CFW agreed to purchase and provide PuR to the communities where their 55 shops were located. Even though P&G Kenya only had about a dozen employees, they made a commitment to provide more than 1 million liters of safe drinking water over three years working with CFW Shops.

In addition to the three-pronged approach used in Uganda, P&G tested a more in-depth adoption of a school for a semester with Save the Children, CFW, and CARE in Kenya. P&G launched pilot school programs providing safe drinking water using PuR in 3 schools with CARE (later expanded to 20 schools), and with PSI to reach 400,000 children over two years. UNICEF developed plans to provide safe drinking water and hygiene education in schools and communities in the Siaya District.

---

27 Uganda PuR Schools Program, A Nationwide roll-out in 20 districts, PSI Proposal, December 2006.

The Kenyan Nurses Association, in collaboration with the International Council of Nurses, began provision of safe drinking water in 2 orphanages with PuR.[28]

Connecting clean drinking water to HIV/AIDS

P&G also built capacity in Kenya by working with groups focused on HIV/AIDS. SWAP (the Safe Water and AIDS Program), supported by an Atlanta Rotary club, sold a range of goods which included PuR (one of the biggest sellers) as well as bleach, bed nets, water, protein supplement, and other products. Another organization, Village AIDS Clinics, started providing PuR among the Maasai population. There was great need for clean drinking water because of high rates of diarrhoea and lowered immune response to pathogens in the drinking water due to high rates of HIV/AIDS.[29] Initially, Village AIDS Clinics tried to sell PuR at the clinic. But, people were getting free ART and bed nets so it was hard to sell them PuR. Instead Village AIDS Clinics decided to do highly targeted free distribution to people with HIV and AIDS. This included providing PuR along with infant formulation to new mothers who were HIV/AIDS positive in order to prevent the transmission of HIV to the infants via breast milk.

P&G also worked with the International Federation of the Red Cross and Red Crescent Society (IFRC) to address the HIV/AIDS issue. The relationship between the two organizations went back to when the IFRC used PuR in Sri Lanka to help tsunami survivors. More recently, the IFRC worked with the Kenyan Red Cross so that they could leverage their existing infrastructure for providing home-based care for people living with HIV/AIDS. P&G provided funding and the PuR product. The acceptance of PuR was extremely high because the Kenyan Red Cross volunteers took the time to enlist the community. They had a community gathering and asked if people wanted to take part in the effort. They also met with the local chief's council and gained their agreement. Said Allgood after visiting the homes of dozens of the community members, "I hear from each household how critical safe drinking water is in order for people to live positively with HIV/AIDS. I hear about the debilitating, persistent diarrhoea people had before using PuR. They know that people living with AIDS have opportunistic infections and that safe drinking water is preventing waterborne illnesses. "The Kenyan Red Cross reached about 3,500 people with PuR in this area. Because of the existing Red Cross infrastructure, the cost to provide PuR treated water to a person with HIV/AIDS was less than 2 cents per day, but many of these people could not afford a single penny. According to Allgood, "PuR plays a critical role for people with HIV/AIDS and the fact is that this product may have to be provided for free in these circumstances."

28 Commitment Progress Report: September–December 2006, Clinton Global Initiative.
29 Ibid.

The response to PuR inside P&G

Clearly, the PuR team had learned much about when, where, and how to best market and sell this unique product. The response within the company was also one of continual learning and some surprises. Although initially support for PuR was slow to build because of the failed commercial attempts, by 2006 Allgood and his team had managed to generate strong support for the work at all levels of the company and even around the globe. In November and December of 2005, P&G Italy launched a customer relationship marketing (CRM) effort "Pure Water Mission" and donated 70,000 sachets to PSI Pakistan. Support for PuR grew at P&G headquarters. In May 2006, the PuR Water Filtration brand (same brand name but different technology and only available in North America) launched a CRM campaign "Buy PuR, Save Lives" which provided $800,000 over two years through a combination of PuR brand contributions and the P&G Fund.

In the summer of 2005, various retired P&G officers met to review the PuR initiative. At that point, retired P&G Vice President Mike Kremzar, retired Group Vice President Chuck Fullgraf, and retired CFO and Senior Vice President Jim Nethercott spearheaded a program to ask other retired officers to contribute financially to the Children's Safe Drinking Water program. In addition to strategic input and support, 56 retired P&G officers (representing 100% participation) pledged over $680,000 to expand the Children's Safe Drinking Water program in Africa. It was the Retired Officers' personal contributions, along with P&G Fund contributions, that allowed P&G to expand into Malawi and Kenya. The contributions went to PSI.

According to Allgood, "It's been a great honor to work closely with these executives. While showing their heart in making these contributions, they've also given us a tremendous vote of confidence for our efforts and the potential for our program. Along the way, we reviewed our program with retired Chief Executives Ed Artzt, John Pepper, and John Smale. Not only did these legends in business provide useful input to our program, but I was impressed that they each individually took the time to have conversations with me to convey their deep support of the program and their feeling that it was a great and historic decision by the Company to pursue this mission to serve children."

Ed Artzt commented on the retired officers contribution, "This is a wonderful program, and it illustrates not only the ability of P&G alums to come together to do vital work but it also indicates how the special skills of P&G people can be valuable in helping to make a difficult program such as this successful. For example, the money that goes to PSI is used primarily for marketing, training of nurses, radio advertising, and school clinics. As you look at what's being done, what emerges is the skilled-hand of P&G-trained people directing efforts that are efficient, consumer friendly and, in the end, producing results."[30]

30 E.L. Artzt Afternoon Talk—Geneva Alumni Reunion, June 10, 2006.

P&G had definitely received a great benefit from the PuR project. It helped with employee morale and increased the understanding that employees were working at a socially and environmentally sustainable business. When former CEO John Smale found about how much the Children's Safe Drinking Water initiative cost, his response was "The decision to pursue the Live, Learn, and Thrive program is the best decision the company has ever made (in the context of philanthropy)."[31]

According to CEO A.G. Lafley, "Quite frankly, PuR Purifier of Water was not a commercial success. The people who need it most are least able to afford it. But we stuck with the program because we believed it was the right thing to do and we knew we could make a difference. And we created an innovative, market-based distribution model that makes it economically feasible to get this product where it's needed most."[32]

The way forward

P&G was now fully committed to long-term not-for profit sales and distribution working with a variety of partners. "I'm blown away by the level and extent of cooperation," Allgood stated publicly, adding: "we've not seen anything like it in our 170-year history. Since 1991, UNICEF, USAID, CARE, AmeriCares, PSI, Johns Hopkins, the International Council of Nurses, and many other groups have partnered with us to provide safe drinking water in the developing world."[33]

Allgood realized that he and his team and many partners had accomplished a great deal using a range of innovative strategies, but still the commitments he had made loomed large. He knew that prior to 2006, almost 90% of PuR product had been for emergency relief, but that the balance between social markets and emergency relief was shifting. In fiscal year 2006, 50% of volume was actually for social markets albeit much of this provided for emergency use. Thus, despite the great progress, Allgood was plagued with the questions: how he could meet the goals he had set to expand the reach of PuR? What was the most important step at this stage to build the PuR Purifier of Water brand? More specifically, he pondered three questions related to his desire to achieve long-term household-level behavior change:

1. P&G is now considering further exploration into the connection between HIV/AIDS and clean drinking water. Where should they go? How can they

31 P&G Commitment Progress Report: September–December 2006, Clinton Global Initiative.

32 P&G 2006 Global Sustainability and Philanthropy Report, www.pg.com/content/pdf/01_about_pg/corporate_citizenship/sustainability/reports/sustainability_report_2006.pdf.

33 "Making Troubled Waters Potable: An inexpensive water treatment technology is making a difference in poor communities around the world," Ivan Amato, *Chemical & Engineering News*, April 17, 2006, Volume 84, Number 16, pp. 39-40, pubs.acs.org/isubscribe/journals/cen/84/i16/html/8416sci3.html.

leverage existing partnerships and build new partnerships to address this new market? What have they learned from their successes and failures that will allow them to successfully assess this new market?

2. What strategy would allow P&G to best meet the aggressive Clinton Foundation commitments? What new markets or new countries should they investigate or enter? What would be the strategic approach? Will this result in long-term habit change and a self-sustained market?

3. Based on the very positive reception and use P&G has seen when the product is donated (like with the Kenyan Red Cross), the company is considering additional focus on free distribution instead of social marketing. This is similar to issue with insecticide treated bed nets that were socially marketed for years but now massive funds are being provided to distribute them for free. Should the company more aggressively pursue this strategy? What are the benefits and detriments to P&G and the PuR brand? To the people in these countries?

Teaching notes for this case are available from Greenleaf Publishing. These are free of charge and are available only to teaching staff. They can be requested by going to:

www.greenleaf-publishing.com/oikos2_notes

Appendix A: Existing Water Treatment Solutions

Exhibit 1 Point-of-Use Solution Comparison Table

Source: Center for Sustainable Enterprise, The University of North Carolina at Chapel Hill, "Water for the Masses: An Assessment of Point-of-Use Water Treatment Solutions," January 2004.

Treatment	Key Strengths	Key Limitations	Initial cost outlay for users	Single user price per year	User price per liter	Estimated production cost to price ratio
Bottled	• Convenience • Avoid water treatment	• Unknown source risk	$.10 - $.30	$22 - $220	$.03 - $.30	30%
Filtered	• Availability and range of filter types • Effective with some contaminants • Can provide some aesthetic improvement	• Results vary dramatically with filter type and condition • Need for equipment maintenance • Need for education	$5 – $25	$10 - $50	$.01 - $.07	70%
Chemical	• Clinically proven • Chlorine availability • Effective with most pathogens • Residual disinfection • Works with turbid water	• Time required for treatment • Not effective with certain strains of contaminants • No visual indicator of treatment success • Treatment changes taste and odor • Need for education	$.10 - $.60*	$.10 - $1.20	$.0002 - $.002	30%
Combined Chemical	• Clinically proven • Effective with most pathogens • Neutralizes organic/inorganic contaminants (i.e., metal) • Residual disinfection • Visual proof of treatment	• Several steps and time required for treatment • Need for education	$.035 - $.10*	$2.50 - $7.30	$.0035 - $.01	30%
Ultraviolet	• Addresses some hard to treat contaminants • Does not address taste, color, smell • Can treat large quantities quickly	• High material cost • Water must be stored and consumed quickly due to contamination regrowth • Need for equipment maintenance	$810	$2 - $20	$.002 - $.027	70%
Solar	• Clinically proven • Effective with most pathogens • Does not address taste, color, smell • Material availability	• Weather dependency • Oversight required • Must be stored and consumed quickly • Not effective with some contaminants • Need for education	$0 - $1	$0 - $1	$.001	N/A

* User costs for several solutions take into account both subsidized (low end of price range) and unsubsidized (upper end of price range) retail prices.

Appendix B: PuR Purifier of Water

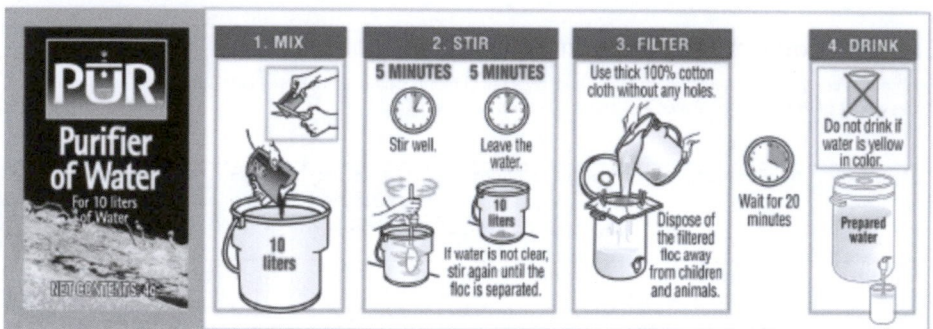

Appendix C: The Cost Recovery Model

Approximate Cost Per Sachet	Explanation
$0.035*	Cost to manufacture sachet in Pakistan
$0.005	Cost to ship product in other countries
$0.01	Typical duty/tariff to import
$0.01	Margin for PSI overheads/infrastructure
$0.03	Margin for distributor/wholesaler/retailer or local NGO selling to provide profit incentive
Total $0.09	Final cost to end-user.

Humanitarian groups can purchase PuR sachets labeled in English at a subsidized cost of $0.035 per sachet plus shipping from P&G. The current minimum order quantity is 1.14 million sachets which is the amount that fits in a 20 foot sea container.

Appendix D: Jemima's Story

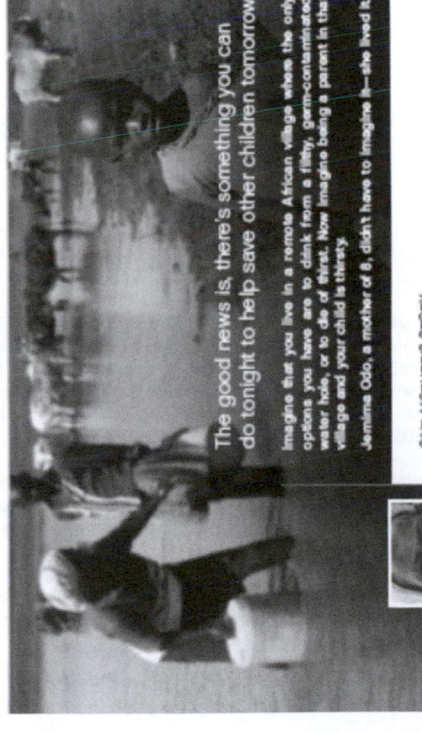

4,000 children worldwide died today of disease caused by drinking water like this.

The good news is, there's something you can do tonight to help save other children tomorrow.

Imagine that you live in a remote African village where the only options you have are to drink from a filthy, germ-contaminated water hole, or to die of thirst. Now imagine being a parent in that village and your child is thirsty.

Jemima Odo, a mother of 8, didn't have to imagine it—she lived it.

Jemima Odo is now an ambassador of courage and hope

ONE MOTHER'S STORY

The Odo family lived in a small village in the western hills of Kenya next to a brown, muddy water hole. Like most of the waterways running through this part of the country, the water was contaminated with a variety of parasites, germs and viruses, making it unsafe for human consumption. Most of us would not walk through this water with bare feet, but Jemima and her family drank it every day—they had no other choice.

Like other families in the village, the Odos did what they could to make the water safer to drink, but their best efforts were ineffective. Illness was rampant in the village. The healthiest adults were able to withstand the challenges to their immune system, but the young, the weak and the sick would often succumb to disease and death. Two of those victims were Jemima's children.

Already weakened from HIV, Jemima fell victim to the unsafe water. Her weight dropped to 78 pounds and her resolve started to crumble. Yet despite her illness and grief, Jemima remained hopeful in the face of a hopeless situation. And then the breakthrough happened. New technology in the form of a simple water purification system, PŪR Purifier of Water, turned the water taken from the village water hole from a deadly enemy to a life-giving resource.

With the help of the technology—and an enduring commitment from Procter & Gamble (P&G) in the form of the Children's Safe Drinking Water (CSDW) program—the situation in Jemima's village changed dramatically.

"Only two years ago, I was weak and bedridden," Jemima said. "Today, I'm healthy, strong and 40 pounds heavier. PŪR and CSDW have become blessing to not only my family, but the community as well."

With every purchase of a PŪR Water Filtration System, P&G is donating a portion of the proceeds to expand the Children's Safe Drinking Water program in Kenya.

A PŪR SOLUTION: CHILDREN'S SAFE DRINKING WATER PROGRAM

The World Health Organization calls safe drinking water "one of the world's greatest needs." Every day approximately 4,000 children worldwide—the population of a large US high school—die because they don't have safe water. Kenya, in particular is one place where clean water is still only a dream in some villages.

The breakthrough that helped make water purification possible in places like Kenya PŪR Purifier of Water—a technology borne of the collaboration between P&G Health Sciences Institute and the US Centers for Disease Control and Prevention. PŪR Purifier of Water is a powdered product that effectively reduces parasites, bacteria and other contaminants found in water—and has been proven to dramatically reduce diarrheal illness in children.

The program that brought Purifier of Water to Kenya was CSDW. Working since 2003, P&G as part of its corporate cause, Live, Learn and Thrive", partners with emergency relief workers in villages in developing nations and helps the people there establish safe-water practices. Using PŪR Purifier of Water, the villagers learn how to treat their local water supply and safely store it for water use. To date, CSDW has provided enough product to produce more than 500 million liters of clean drinking water for children and their families in need around the world. But there are still many more people to help. Fortunately, there is a way you can help today.

PROVIDING PŪR FILTERED WATER FOR YOUR FAMILY NOW MEANS CLEAN WATER FOR FAMILIES IN KENYA

With every purchase of a PŪR Water Filtration System filter, P&G is donating a portion of the proceeds to expand the CSDW program in Kenya. These donations will go toward P&G's goal of contributing $5 million by the end of 2007 to help improve the current unsafe drinking water problem in Africa. Won't you help?

WHAT ARE YOU DOING TONIGHT?

As parents, we marvel at the fragility of our children when they come into the world. And as we cradle them close to us at night and rock them to sleep, we whisper a promise that parents around the world also make to their children, "I will protect you, little one, no matter what"

By purchasing a PŪR Water Filtration System filter today, you not only help keep your promise, but you also help parents half a world away keep theirs.

Appendix E: Excerpt

MEMORANDUM OF UNDERSTANDING

Developing a Strategic Collaboration for Improving Health between the Center for Communication Programs of the Johns Hopkins University Bloomberg School of Public Health and the Procter & Gamble Health Sciences Institute

This Memorandum of Understanding (hereinafter referred to as "MOU") defines the strategic collaboration between the Johns Hopkins University Center for Communication Programs and its affiliates, hereinafter "JHU/CCP", and The Procter and Gamble Health Sciences Institute and its affiliates, hereinafter "P&G/HSI" for improving the health of people in the developing world. As used herein, the term "AFFILIATES" means any corporation or other legal entity (including joint ventures) controlling, controlled by, or under common control with The Procter & Gamble Company or BOARD OF TRUSTEES through stock ownership or other equity interest, direct or indirect.

. Objectives of the Strategic Collaboration

The ultimate objective of the strategic collaboration is to improve the health and lives of people in the developing world. We intend to accomplish this objective by developing and implementing action-oriented and sustainable programs that result in measurable behavioral change and improved health status. Under this strategic collaboration both JHU/CCP and P&G/HSI wish to promote healthy behaviors in developing countries.

II. Guiding Principles of the Strategic Collaboration

This strategic collaboration is based on the highest principles of integrity, cooperation, and mutual respect shared by both organizations. Thus, to ensure that the integrity and credibility of both JHU/CCP and P&G/HSI are maintained, the strategic collaboration is based on key principles, which will guide our actions and decisions:

1. Both parties share a common vision to improve the lives of people in the developing world. We believe we can achieve this vision by developing and implementing effective programs that promote positive health behaviors.

2. We believe that our collaboration will be complemented by the different strengths which each organization provides, including: a) JHU/CCP's communication and program experience and established working relationships with donor organizations & counterparts in key developing countries; and b) the innovation provided in certain P&G/HSI health products developed for consumers in the developing world and the extensive consumer-oriented distribution networks utilized by P&G/HSI to assure availability.

3. The strategy and activities of the collaboration will be based upon solid scientific standards that can be explained and endorsed by both organizations. This will ensure that the collaboration and resulting program activities can be sustained and defended, whether internally or in response to an external challenge.

4. Any and all P&G/HSI products used to complement the communication messages developed as part of this collaboration will be of high and consistent quality and with adequate evidence to support

health related claims/benefits. JHU/CCP will not endorse specific products and no endorsement by JHU should be implied through this collaboration.

5. JHU/CCP and P&G/HSI will begin to identify opportunities in specific countries for strategic collaboration activities upon signing of this MOU. Both organizations will agree on collaboration activities prior to the start of any specific activity in any given country. This may include collaboration in a full range of JHU/CCP activities funded by USAID and/or other donors.

III. Examples of Strategic Collaboration Activities:

JHU/CCP and P&G/HSI through this strategic collaboration will contribute to the implementation of initiatives, activities and programs in the area of health. Specifically, we will seek opportunities to collaborate and cooperate in a variety of activities such as:

1. Developing and implementing communication programs, campaigns, and messages to educate the public on positive health behaviors. This activity may include the development of brochures, public service advertisements/announcements, social dramas and/or other entertainment-education programs/ events and other venues that harness the expertise of either organization.

2. Sponsoring scientific symposia to present key technological advances in health care products and public health advances in order to encourage scientific exchange and raise awareness/knowledge of health care professionals/providers.

3. Participating in media events to raise awareness of specific health issues and to announce health communication programs, campaigns, and materials designed to respond to these issues and generate positive impact on health behaviors and health status.

4. When appropriate and consistent with USAID/donor funded goals, guidelines and regulations, facilitating the distribution of P&G health care products which complement the communication objectives in government and/or NGO health care programs, schools, and other venues in order to help counterparts reach specific populations most in need of these products. P&G will not use JHU's name to promote its products or in any other way without specific permission of JHU.

5. Seeking other counterparts and/or collaborators, as appropriate and additional funding from their organizations, if needed, to further leverage the programs and efforts of our strategic collaboration.

6. Measuring the impact of the programs, communication campaigns, and messages on selected audience behaviors and health status.

IV. Joint Roles of Each Organization in the Strategic Partnership

This strategic collaboration agreement will begin upon signature of the MOU and last for a period of five (5) years from the date it is signed. Both JHU/CCP and P&G/HSI will identify 2 representatives (each) who will serve on a "leadership committee" providing technical guidance and managerial oversight for all joint activities under the MOU. The "leadership committee" will meet periodically during each year, to maximize collaboration opportunities, identify and plan new activities and to review on-going collaborative programs. The strategic collaboration will be evaluated annually, according to the success measured jointly and set by both parties, to determine if the objectives of the collaboration are being met. After each evaluation, the strategic collaboration may be revised or terminated based upon the mutual written consent of both parties. In addition, this MOU agreement may be renewed upon mutual written consent of both parties.

Case 10

Trevor Field and the PlayPumps of Africa[1, 2, 3]

Debapratim Purkayastha

IBS Center for Management Research, Hyderabad, India

If I can make money and do good at the same time, that's great. I'm a philanthrapreneur.[4]

> Trevor Field, Founder and Director, Roundabout Outdoor, in 2007

We believe that the PlayPump system, due to its practical, economic, and social viability, is a progressive and creative way to provide free fresh drinking water to rural communities ... With the PlayPump we can make children happy, reduce the workload for women, make a visible step forward in rural water development, and slow down the spread of HIV/AIDS.[5]

> Buyelwa Sonjica, Water Affairs Minister, South Africa, in 2005

1 This case © 2009 IBS Center for Management Research. All rights reserved.
2 This case was compiled from published sources, and is intended to be used as a basis for class discussion rather than to illustrate either effective or ineffective handling of a management situation.
3 This case won the first prize in the oikos Global Case Writing Competition 2009 (Social Entrepreneurship track), organized by oikos Foundation for Economy and Ecology, University of St. Gallen, Switzerland.
4 "PlayPumps Founder Has Unique Name for His Work," www.wdi.umich.edu, January 15, 2007.
5 Nicholas McDiarmid, "Borehole Pumps While Children Go Roundabout," www.search.sebinet.co.za, August/September 2005.

ICMR
IBS Center for Management Research
www.icmrindia.org

Water, Sustainability and Child's Play

In 2007, the PlayPump Water System (PlayPump) was nominated for the prestigious National Design Award, presented by the Smithsonian's Cooper-Hewitt, National Design Museum. Though the water system failed to win the design award, it had won many hearts across the world ever since its launch in the mid-1990s, due to its ability to solve one of the most pressing problems in peri-urban and rural areas of Africa—water (refer to Exhibit I for a brief note on the water problem).

In Africa, the water crisis is quite severe with around 40 percent of Africans lacking access to potable water supply. In addition to the deaths and economic loss caused by the lack of access to water, women and girls, on whom the burden of obtaining water for the family falls, have to trek long distances and spend hours collecting water from dams, springs, rivers, streams, and farm reservoirs. Where such traditional sources of water are not available, they have to rely on bore-wells, toiling hard over hand pumps. While this is back-breaking work, alternatives such as use of diesel, petrol or electric pumps are too costly to install and maintain.[6] They have also to contend with the fact that hand pumps break down often and remain unrepaired for a period of time. "By some estimates, 35 percent of Sub-Saharan Africa's improved water sources are out of service at any given time, mainly due to hand pump breakdowns. When broken pumps aren't repaired, communities are forced to return to unsafe water sources,"[7] wrote Geoff Hopkins, an operations analyst for the International Finance Corporation (IFC) in Johannesburg, South Africa.

Since this responsibility is linked to gender, women and girls spend a disproportionate part of their time hauling water—time that could be better spent with family or on economic activities, or in school.[8] According to experts, in many regions of sub-Saharan Africa, women and girls have to trudge an average of 8 kilometers to the nearest water source every day, and haul back containers of water weighing about 40 pounds. The absence of improved water supply has not only led to gender inequality but also affected the growth potential of the region, they said.

The PlayPump was a child's roundabout (merry-go-round) attached to a water pump, a storage tank, and a tap. As children played on the merry-go-round, the system pumped water to the storage tank and communities living nearby could use this clean water. The four surfaces of the storage tanks also doubled up as billboards for commercial and public education/social messages. Revenue earned from the advertising helped maintain the water systems for up to a decade. "It's a win–win situation … Children enjoy riding on it, particularly as these are places with no toys. Villagers no longer have to walk hours to the nearest well … The beauty of the

---

6 Nicholas McDiarmid, "Borehole Pumps While Children Go Roundabout," www.search.sebinet.co.za, August/September 2005.
7 Geoff Hopkins, "Kids Play, Water Pumps: A Sustained Investment," www.casefoundation.org.
8 Geoff Hopkins, "Kids Play, Water Pumps: A Sustained Investment," www.casefoundation.org.

roundabout pumps is that they are really simple, low-tech, and exactly what Africa needs,"[9] said Trevor Field (Field), the social entrepreneur who visualized the concept and gave up his well-paid job with an established publishing house to pursue it.

Roundabout Outdoor Pty Ltd. (RO), a for-profit organization with a social mission co-founded by Field, installed and maintained these PlayPumps while Play-Pumps International (PI), a non-profit organization also co-founded by Field, helped arrange the funds for installing the water systems. Over the years, RO and PI were able to build innovative partnerships with individuals, corporations, governments, foundations, and non-governmental organizations (NGOs) to donate Play-Pumps to African communities.[10]

The PlayPumps and the business model that Field adopted attracted the attention of experts who felt that it was both innovative and sustainable. They felt that in addition to solving the problem of clean drinking water, the system addressed the closely-related health, education, gender, and economic issues. It was often cited as an example of the emerging trend in sustainable development that applied business solutions to social problems.[11] Moreover, they said that tackling global challenges such as the water crisis required a collaborative approach such as the one that Field had adopted.

By early 2008, while Field had succeeded in installing more than 1,000 PlayPumps in five countries in Southern Africa, he also faced significant challenges in scaling up its operations further in order to achieve his objective of installing 4,000 Play-Pumps in ten African countries by 2010.

Background Note

The Birmingham-born Field had a career in advertising and marketing. He had also worked extensively in the printing and publishing industries, both in South Africa and the UK. Between 1971 and 1974, he worked with British Telecom and trained as Senior Technician in transmission. The following year, he emigrated to South Africa and later settled down in Johannesburg. He had initially come to South Africa to install TV microwave links at a time when there was no TV in South Africa. Thereafter, he joined the publishing house First General Media (FGM) in 1980 and was National Sales Manager for the Penthouse Magazine both in South Africa and the US.[12]

9 Christina Lamb, "The Drought-busting Magic Roundabout," www.timesonline.co.uk, April 17, 2005.

10 www.guidestar.org/pqShowGsReport.do?partner=amex&ein=04-3839391.

11 "The PlayPump: Business Solutions to Social Problems," southsouthnews.wordpress.com, August 1, 2006.

12 www.mbaswithoutborders.org.

Field soon took a liking to the life and people in the country, but he was distressed to see the hardships that people, especially those in the rural and peri-urban areas of South Africa had to go through to get drinking water. The plight of women and girls was especially troubling as they had the burden of collecting the water. They often had to trek long distances carrying heavy buckets. As he saw them toiling day after day for this precious resource, it became Field's burning desire to do something to solve this problem.

In 1989, on a casual visit to an agricultural fair in Pretoria (on the outskirts of Johannesburg) with his father-in-law, Field chanced upon a roundabout designed by an engineer and professional borehole-driller Ronnie Styver (Styver) that had a water pump attached to it. As it turned, the small roundabout pumped water from beneath the ground. Field soon realized that this innovation could be used to benefit millions of lives. He carried the idea around in his mind, thinking of improvements he could make. And he came up with the concept of a water system with a big water storage tank that could provide four spaces for outdoor advertising.[13] "I had seen 100 people battling to obtain water in various parts of the country. And I just thought it was a really good idea in a very simple way, and an environmental friendly way of providing water to people. If you look at rural African schools, they haven't got swing sets and the kind of playground equipment that European and American kids have got. So it was like killing two birds—or, since then, about six birds—with one stone. That's what turned me on to pursue it,"[14] explained Field.

Field worked with Styver to design a much bigger version of the roundabout and also brought about further improvements. For instance, one of the initial versions moved in only one direction but the children wanted it to move in both directions. In 1994, Field received funding from the Umgeni Water Company to set up the first two water systems in Masinga.[15] Consumer packaged goods major Colgate-Palmolive came forward to advertise its toothpaste on the storage tanks. The installation of the pumps was supervised by Field's wife, a therapist by profession, as Field was caught up with his regular job. "I had no idea how it would work … It was pretty crude to start with,"[16] Field recalled. However, the system caught the imagination of the people in Masinga. Field decided to give up his job with FGM in 1995 and dedicate all his time and effort to providing such water systems to disadvantaged communities.

In 1996, Field convinced his long-term business colleagues, Paolo Ristic and Sarel Nienaber, to invest in the water system. Together they obtained the license

13 Michael Lang, "Play-Pump Merry-Go-Round Provides Life Saving Water to the World," www.thelangreport.com, December 26, 2007.
14 "PlayPumps Founder Has Unique Name for His Work," www.wdi.umich.edu, January 15, 2007.
15 Masinga district is one of the most remote areas in the KwaZulu-Natal Province of South Africa.
16 Christina Lamb, "The Drought-busting Magic Roundabout," www.timesonline.co.uk, April 17, 2005.

for the product from the inventor, patented it, and started a small venture called 'Roundabout Outdoor Pty Ltd.' (RO) to market the product in 1997.[17]

Roundabout Outdoor and PlayPumps International

RO was a for-profit organization with a social mission. Subsequently, Field and his colleagues made more changes in the PlayPump's features and named the product 'PlayPump Water System', which they registered as a trademark. "We have trademarks in every country where we believe it will be used in the world,"[18] said Field. For most of the 1990s, the promoters worked tirelessly to improve the water system's functionality and durability. This was important as RO had to leave it in a rural community and there would be a lot of problems if the system was prone to breakdown or rapid wear-and-tear.

Another challenge was that the poor people for whom the water system was meant were unable to afford the system that cost around US$10,000 including installation then. Thus, RO had to be funded by private investment and international agency funds.[19] Its business model used donations to underwrite the installation of the water system while revenues from advertising funded maintenance. However, the company did not find raising the funds easy in the initial years.[20]

By 1997, 20 PlayPump water systems had been installed in South Africa. While RO looked after the marketing of the PlayPumps and the training of local teams to maintain the pumps, the manufacturing was done by a South African company Outdoor Fabrication and Steelworks (OFS).

In 1999, Nelson Mandela, then president of South Africa, attended the ceremonial installation of a PlayPump at a school in Rietfontein and was impressed by the water system. This paved the way for the installation of more such pumps in other parts of rural South Africa. The same year, RO entered into a public–private partnership (PPP) with South Africa's Department of Water Affairs & Forestry (DWA&F) to assist the department in its mission to deliver water to all of South Africa by 2008.[21] Under the terms of the agreement, RO had permission to access groundwater and distribute it free of charge on the condition that it would also maintain the water systems.[22]

The following year, RO won the World Bank Development Marketplace award for the system's ability to deliver water as well as HIV/AIDS prevention messag-

17   www.mbaswithoutborders.org.
18   John Eastman, "Trevor Field of PlayPumps International," blackandwhiteprogram.com, April 14, 2008.
19   www.nextbillion.net.
20   Yolandi Groenewald, "Collecting Water is Child's Play," *Mail & Guardian*, November 6, 2003.
21   Gareth Knight, "Roundabout Outdoor Shortlisted for Alcan Prize for Sustainability," www.oneafrikan.com, September 8, 2005.
22   Nicholas McDiarmid, "A Straightforward Roundabout Solution," IMIESA, July 2005.

es.[23] While the funds from the World Bank (US$165,000) came in handy, the award also provided more visibility to RO and the company received additional funding from non-profit foundations such as the Henry J. Kaiser Family Foundation (KFF), and other companies. For instance, KFF provided RO with its first large grant for carrying public health advertisements concerning HIV/AIDS, requiring it to raise matching funds through DWA&F. The South African electricity supply company, Eskom, too joined in the effort and sponsored 40 PlayPump units by the end of 2003.[24] "Without World Bank funding we'd still be in our infancy,"[25] said Field.

In 2003, RO with Eskom and the DWA&F won the *Mail & Guardian* Investing in the Future Awards for effective use of partnerships offering innovation and social relevance. In 2004, Field co-founded Roundabout PlayPumps (the name was later changed to PlayPump International), a South African NGO, to forge partnerships with corporations, foundations, governments, and individuals and raise funds for the installation of PlayPump water systems. In 2006, PI was also incorporated as a US 501(c)3 (non-profit) organization.

In 2005, RO was one of the ten companies shortlisted for the US$1 million Alcan Prize for Sustainability[26] by The Prince of Wales International Business Leaders Forum (IBLF).[27]

As RO entered into more partnerships, it continued to scale up; it installed around 700 PlayPump systems by the end of 2005, providing clean drinking water to more than one million people. Since the mid-2000s, it also started expanding into some other countries in sub-Saharan Africa.

During this time, the founders of Case Foundation, Jean and Steve Case, saw a PlayPump in Boikarabelo, South Africa, and joined in the organization's effort to install more such water systems throughout Africa.[28] Their support proved crucial in roping in US First Lady Laura Bush (Bush) to support the venture. On September 20, 2006, Bush announced a US$16.4 million PPP to install more PlayPumps including US$10 million from the US government, US$5 million from the Case

23 HIV/AIDS is another huge problem facing sub-Saharan Africa. This region had the highest population of HIV/AIDS victims in 2008. Multinational beverage company Coca Cola was one of the early supporters that put up anti-HIV/AIDS messages in the PlayPump billboard.

24 Yolandi Groenewald, "Collecting Water is Child's Play," *Mail & Guardian*, November 6, 2003.

25 "Tapping the Energy of Children at Play to Produce Clean Water and Promote HIV/AIDS Awareness," web.worldbank.org, 2004.

26 The prize is created by Alcan Inc, a leading aluminum and packaging company, in 2004 to recognize outstanding contributions to the goal of economic, environmental, and social sustainability by not-for-profit, non-governmental, and civil society organizations. The prize is managed by IBLF.

27 Gareth Knight, "Roundabout Outdoor Shortlisted for Alcan Prize for Sustainability," www. oneafrikan.com, September 8, 2005.

28 www.casefoundation.org.

Foundation, and US$1.4 million from The MCJ Foundation.[29] "[W]hen I told all my friends that I was going to make a children's roundabout that pumps water. And I was going to change the affliction of Africa, they all laughed at me. All of them. But when Laura Bush announced the 16.4 million dollar investment into my company, there was nobody laughing then,"[30] recalled Field. The Case Foundation continued its partnership with PI in its objective to raise a further US$45 million by 2010.[31]

RO did not make its financials public. However, PI in its Form 990, reported that for the year ending February 28, 2007, it had assets and income of US$3,055,739 and US$4,699,314 respectively (refer to Exhibit II for the organization's statement of financial position and Exhibit III for its statement of activities). By early 2008, more than 1000 PlayPump systems had been donated to schools and communities in Lesotho, South Africa, Mozambique, Swaziland, and Zambia. The company employed some 100 people—14 people in the office in Johannesburg who organized database and computer systems; 35 people in the factory manufacturing the product; the rest were contractors involved in the installation of the systems in various places in Southern Africa.[32] The installation crew lived in the provinces in which these water systems were installed.

PlayPumps—A Social Innovation

The PlayPump water systems were installed in places such as school playgrounds, clinics, and community centers. According to Field, "It's a positive displacement water pump, and as the children spin around, it transfers their energy into vertical or reciprocal motion, and that pumps water from an underground borehole or well to the surface where it's stored in a tank for future use."[33] The PlayPump was fitted with a 2,500-liter tank standing seven meters above the ground. Dozens of changes made to the design of the PlayPump over one decade ensured that the system was robust with maintenance costs being minimal. It could draw up to 1,400 liters (370 gallons) of water per hour at 16 revolutions per minute from a depth of 40 meters.[34] It was also capable of drawing water from up to a depth of

---

29 "The PlayPump: Business Solutions to Social Problems," southsouthnews.wordpress. com, August 1, 2006.
30 John Eastman, "Trevor Field of PlayPumps International," blackandwhiteprogram.com, April 14, 2008.
31 "South Africa: The Play Pump Turning Water into Child's Play," www.pbs.org, October 24, 2005.
32 John Eastman, "Trevor Field of PlayPumps International," blackandwhiteprogram.com, April 14, 2008.
33 "Why Pumping Water is Child's Play," www.news.bbc.co.uk, April 25, 2005.
34 Nicholas McDiarmid, "Borehole Pumps While Children Go Roundabout," www.search. sebinet.co.za, August/September 2005.

100 meters. It was less arduous and more effective than a hand pump, which could only draw 20–40 gallons per hour.[35]

The water drawn from underground went to the storage tank.[36] All these, while children were having fun playing on the roundabout, something they did not have access to earlier. "Once they're installed, you can't get the kids off of them … For these children who have never experienced a slide or a swing, they've never seen anything quite like it,"[37] said Field (refer to Figure I for PlayPump water system: how it works; and, Exhibit IV for a photograph of children playing on a PlayPump).

Figure I **PlayPump Water System: How it Works**

Source: www.playpumps.org

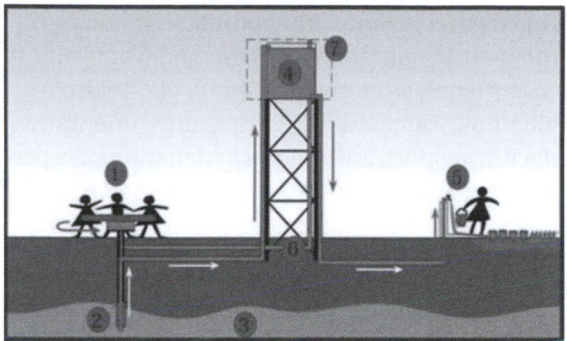

While children go round and round on the merry-go-round (1), clean water is pumped (2) from underground (3) into the tank (4). People can draw water from the tap (5) while excess water is diverted from the storage tank back down into the borehole (6). The four sides of the water storage tank (7) provides space for advertising.

All the four surfaces of the storage tank were leased out as billboards, with two sides for consumer advertising and the other two for health and educational messages. On these billboards, local companies as well as multinationals could advertise their products to the communities while the other two sides could be used to provide social/health awareness messages. For instance, in South Africa, these spaces were used to provide HIV/AIDS prevention messages of South Africa's national HIV/AIDS prevention program, LoveLife. RO had a policy that prevented products such as tobacco, liquor, or other products that were inappropriate for

---

35 "PlayPump: An Invention That Serves Humanitarian—by Trevor Field, Johannesburg, South Africa," www.trap17.com.

36 Michael Lang, "Play-Pump Merry-Go-Round Provides Life Saving Water to the World," www.thelangreport.com, December 26, 2007.

37 "Tapping the Energy of Children at Play to Produce Clean Water and Promote HIV/AIDS Awareness," web.worldbank.org, 2004.

children, from being advertised on these spaces. RO also saw to it that the content of the advertisements was culturally sensitive. It maintained the signages at regular intervals as part of its contractual obligations. The revenue generated from advertising was used for the maintenance of the water system for up to a decade. "We have shown that these water towers are the equivalent to television, billboards, and magazines in rural areas. A correctly placed ad can yield significant growth for a relevant product in these areas. The revenue we collect from this is ploughed straight back into [the] project,"[38] said Field. Each of these pumps worked for about 15–20 years before they needed to be replaced.

While the pumps were manufactured in Johannesburg, RO recruited and trained people in local communities on installing and maintaining the systems. According to RO, the cost of manufacturing one PlayPump was US$7,000.[39] The total cost of setting up a water system was US$14,000 that included the roundabout and pump, storage tank, 7 meter tank stand with boards, standpipe with tap and water runoff, and pipes. It also included set-up costs (such as country scoping, geo-hydro census, borehole assessment, site evaluation, water testing, community orientation, local crew training, specialized surface, transport, and system installation). Six percent of the cost went toward providing organizational support for the management of the US and South Africa offices.

"The PlayPump system makes water collection simple by providing an easy-to-use, sustainable source of water … The revenue generated from the advertising pays for the pumps' maintenance and ensures each installation's sustainability,"[40] said Hopkins. What's more, communities had access to water without having to pay any user fee. RO also worked with local governments and community leaders to ensure community involvement and ownership from an early stage.

The PlayPump and Sustainability

Experts felt that the PlayPump was a social innovation that was also sustainable. Herman Diale, Eskom's corporate social investment consultant, said, "Eskom decided to get involved because of the project's sustainability and the viability of improving the quality of life for rural communities. The project also holds social and environmental benefits … The PlayPumps are an innovative way of introducing sustainable, inventive technology to draw water."[41]

38 Nicholas McDiarmid, "A Straightforward Roundabout Solution," IMIESA, July 2005.
39 "PlayPump: An Invention That Serves Humanitarian—by Trevor Field, Johannesburg, South Africa," www.trap17.com.
40 Geoff Hopkins, "Kids Play, Water Pumps: A Sustained Investment," www.casefoundation.org.
41 Yolandi Groenewald, "Collecting Water is Child's Play," *Mail & Guardian*, November 6, 2003.

PlayPumps provided access to clean drinking water, contributing to public health by improving sanitation and hygiene and decreasing the risk of water-related diseases. Clean water and sanitation were very important for people living with HIV/AIDS to remain in good health and to take medicine. What made the PlayPumps even more attractive was that they offered a renewable, self-sustaining way of providing improved supply of water with minimum wastage. They did not require electricity or diesel to operate. And as they were operated manually in the day time, the borehole had time to replenish its water resources during the night. With electricity or diesel-powered systems there was also the risk of the system being accidentally left on, leading to wastage. Another important benefit was proper storage, which prevented contamination and reduced wastage due to spillage and evaporation.

There were other benefits too. The PlayPumps helped remove the barriers to education as children could go to school and stay longer as they did not have the chore of fetching water. They also had access to safe drinking water, latrines, and hand-washing facilities and school days were not lost due to water-related diseases. The PlayPumps promoted gender equality as girls could also attend schools.[42] And the children had an added motivation to go to school—the roundabout on which they could play to their heart's content.

The system also promoted play in regions where there were few safe playgrounds or access to play equipment. This was important as play is considered vital for physical, social, and cognitive development.[43]

Women could spend more time on more productive activities or with their family. As they did not have to haul water over long distances, they were less likely to suffer an injury.[44] "African and Asian women spend up to six hours a day walking to collect water … If we put a PlayPump in, if you look at the saving on time alone it's phenomenal, and it does have a massive impact on the health of children and people in general,"[45] explained Field.

Advertising revenue generated from leasing out of the billboard spaces not only helped maintain the water system but also helped provide social/health education messages, particularly HIV/AIDS prevention messages[46] that were so important in regions struggling with this pandemic. These messages raised awareness and also helped reduce the stigma associated with HIV/AIDS. Billboard spaces such as these were quite rare in some of the communities served by PlayPumps.

According to experts, with all these benefits, the water systems also led to economic development and a foundation for sustainable growth. For instance, in some

---

42 Lim Kong Soon, "Utilizing Children's Play for Clean Water," english.ohmynews.com, July 12, 2008.

43 "The PlayPump: Business Solutions to Social Problems," southsouthnews.wordpress.com, August 1, 2006.

44 Michael Lang, "Play-Pump Merry-Go-Round Provides Life Saving Water to the World," www.thelangreport.com, December 26, 2007.

45 "Why Pumping Water is Child's Play," www.news.bbc.co.uk, April 25, 2005.

46 Nicholas McDiarmid, "Borehole Pumps While Children Go Roundabout," www.search.sebinet.co.za, August/September 2005.

schools in South Africa, some children had even begun growing their own vegetable gardens.[47] In addition to this, RO created jobs in manufacturing, installation, and maintenance. It created jobs in rural areas where PlayPumps were installed. According to PI, its water system helped achieve the UN's Millennium Development Goals[48] (refer to Exhibit V for how the PlayPumps help in achieving the Millennium Development Goals).

Scaling Up

Many investors were attracted by the simple yet ingenious technology and the business model that supported the installation of PlayPumps, and since the late 1990s, RO was able to scale up significantly. PI worked collaboratively with government agencies, corporations, NGOs, and individuals to raise funds for the various projects.

The government provided logistical assistance such as finding suitable locations, safe drinking water, and getting approval from the local community.[49] Once a community had agreed that it wanted a pump, a community liaison was appointed. Then RO went about its job of installing the water systems in collaboration with various government departments and agencies engaged in bore-well drilling.

PPP with the DWA&F and funds from companies such as Eskom helped RO scale up significantly in South Africa. By mid-2005, over 600 installations had been completed, a large percentage of these at primary schools.[50] RO also started venturing out of South Africa into Mozambique and Swaziland. In Mozambique, loans and technical assistance from IFC helped it to install many PlayPumps while its installations in Swaziland were sponsored by UNICEF and the telecom company MTN.[51] IFC supported Roundabout to set up PlayPumps in primary schools in Mozambique through IFC loan and grant financing of US$125,000 and US$90,000, respectively.[52] "Roundabout [RO] is an example where the innovation and experience of a

47 Syspro, "The Trickle Down Effect," www.itweb.co.za.

48 The Millennium Development Goals are eight international development goals that 189 United Nations member states and other international organizations have agreed to achieve by the year 2015. They include halving extreme poverty, reducing child mortality rates, fighting disease epidemics such as AIDS, and developing a global partnership for development.

49 Yolandi Groenewald, "Collecting Water is Child's Play," *Mail & Guardian*, November 6, 2003.

50 Nicholas McDiarmid, "Borehole Pumps While Children Go Roundabout," www.search.sebinet.co.za, August/September 2005.

51 Christina Lamb, "The Drought-busting Magic Roundabout," www.timesonline.co.uk, April 17, 2005.

52 IFC Sustainability Report 2004.

private sector firm are leveraged to deliver big results at the grassroots level,"[53] said Richard Ranken, director of IFC's Africa Department.

After the setting up of PI in the US, funds started to flow more smoothly and RO made more elaborate plans to expand in other countries of Southern Africa namely, Mozambique, Swaziland, and Zambia.[54] RO generally started with a pilot program of 100 pumps within a 150 km radius in the countries it expanded into before scaling up further. Before starting operations, PI had to secure government commitments for bore-wells that would be matched by funding for pumps by private donors.[55] "[We] insist on putting an MOU, which is a Memorandum of Understanding between ourselves and the government. So that they [allow] free passage through their border posts with this equipment. There's no way we're going to pay import duty like gift. So they clear that import duty problem out of the way. They also help us with their Department of Water Affairs to identify certain boreholes or institute drilling programs for people who are disadvantaged,"[56] explained Field.

By mid-2007, the number of PlayPumps installed had grown to over 900. The presence of PI in the US ensured that the initiative received additional funds from other companies in addition to the US$16.4 million committed by Bush. It also received support from Alexandria-based Motley Fool financial services firm, schools such as T.C. Williams High School, and celebrities such as rapper Sean "Jay-Z" Carter and tennis star Nicole Vaidisova (Vaidisova). Bill Mann, adviser to Motley Fool Global Gains (Motley Fool), said, "We found very few organizations that were able to create such an unbelievable change in people's lives for such a small investment."[57] Jay-Z helped raise funds through concerts, and his MTV documentary *Diary of Jay-Z: Water for Life* raised awareness about the water crisis with a part of the proceeds going to PI, while Vaidisova acted as the international spokesperson for PI.[58] On June 28, 2007, Bush celebrated the installation of the US government's first PlayPump at a primary school in Lusaka, Zambia.[59]

53 "The PlayPumps Partnership," www.casefoundation.org/c/document_library/get_file?repository_id=1&file_path=%2Farticles&file_name=IFC-PlayPumps.pdf.
54 "The PlayPump: Business Solutions to Social Problems," southsouthnews.wordpress.com, August 1, 2006.
55 "The PlayPump: Business Solutions to Social Problems," southsouthnews.wordpress.com, August 1, 2006.
56 John Eastman, "Trevor Field of PlayPumps International," blackandwhiteprogram.com, April 14, 2008.
57 Melissa Frederick, "D.C. Charity Helps Kids Pump Clean Water in Africa," www.examiner.com, May 23, 2007.
58 " '100 Pumps in 100 Days' Campaign to Launch on World Water Day," www.playpumps.org, March, 2007.
59 "First Lady Laura Bush Launches the PlayPump™ Water System in Zambia," www.playpumps.org, June 28, 2007.

By early-2007, PI had donated more than 800 PlayPump water systems in South Africa, Mozambique, Swaziland, and Zambia.[60] On the occasion of World Water Day,[61] PI launched the "100 Pumps in 100 Days" campaign in partnership with Save the Children USA.[62] The campaign called upon individuals, schools, faith-based organizations, and other community groups to mobilize funds for the installation of 100 PlayPumps in African communities. People could contribute to the campaign by raising funds or donating (refer to Table I for the donation levels). On July 25, 2007, PI announced that it had raised US$1.5 million to donate 111 Play-Pumps.[63] Motley Fool helped raise funds for 3 PlayPumps. UK-based organization One Water that sold ONE Water bottled water product, under the slogan "When You Drink ONE, Africa Drinks Too" directed 100 percent of the proceeds from sales to the campaign.[64]

Table I **100 Pumps in 100 Days: Donation Levels**

Source: www.playpumps.org

US$14,000	Sponsors an entire PlayPump system and brings clean drinking water to 2,500 people.
US$300	Gives a classroom of children playground equipment and clean water for drinking and hand washing.
US$60	Provides ten people with access to clean water for up to ten years.
US$36	Helps a family get the water it needs for good health and hygiene.
US$6	Provides one child with access to clean water for up to ten years.

In early 2008, Sandra Hayes (Hayes) of PI said, "Pilot projects will also be soon commenced in Lesotho, Malawi, Ethiopia, Kenya, Tanzania, and Uganda."[65] Entry into all these countries was to be achieved by the end of 2008, except Ethiopia where the organization planned to enter in 2009. In 2008, the second version of the "100 Pumps in 100 Days" campaign helped raise funds for another 109 pumps[66,67] which

60 " '100 Pumps in 100 Days' Campaign to Launch on World Water Day," www.playpumps. org, March, 2007.
61 United Nations General Assembly has declared March 22 as the World Water Day.
62 "PlayPumps International Challenges Amateur Filmmakers Worldwide to Film Call to Action," www.playpumps.org, May 17, 2007.
63 "Playpumps International Exceeds '100 Pumps In 100 Days' Goal," www.playpumps.org, July 25, 2007.
64 Jenni Lukac, "All's Well that Ends Well," www.triplepundit.com, August 25, 2006.
65 Sam Aola Ooko, "Water is Child's Play, But You Gotta Spin!" ecoworldly.com, February 23, 2008.
66 "PlayPumps International Surpasses Goal with Second '100 Pumps in 100 Days' Effort," www.playpumps.org/site/apps/nlnet/content2.aspx?c=hqLNIXOEKrF&b=2603343&ct= 5655795.
67 Lim Kong Soon, "Utilizing Children's Play for Clean Water," english.ohmynews.com, July 12, 2008.

included PlayPumps installed in Lesotho (refer to Exhibit VI for a map of Africa showing countries where PlayPumps were installed and future expansion plans).

In addition to the partners just mentioned, RO and PI partnered with hundreds of organizations and individuals to scale up its operations (refer to Exhibit VII for a list of PI's partners). PI's mission was to donate and install 4,000 PlayPump in these ten countries, which would provide access to clean drinking water for up to 10 million people by 2010.[68] After Southern Africa, RO wanted to enter Western and Central African countries.

Harnessing the Power of New Media

Another factor that attracted the attention of analysts was PI's use of the Internet and social networks to mobilize funds to meet its objective. They noted that it was not an easy task for PI to raise funds as there were many stories about African poverty competing for the funds. However, PI used its website to promote its mission and help raise funds quite effectively. The website was well organized with plenty of information; it contained interactive Google maps that showed the location of pumps,[69] and visitors could download action kit for raising funds, or connect to a number of popular social networking sites. In the second half of 2007, it started the "KnowH2O!" campaign to teach students about the global water crisis and how they could help solve the problem.[70] The KnowH2O site had content relevant to students, teachers, and other groups and individuals. They could download free lesson plans, take a water quiz, and create their "Sponsor a PlayPump" page.

The major changes came post-2005, when to achieve its objective, PI moved its website from its South African host to one in the US. It also hired Net strategist Garth Moore to help it develop an "everyman" approach to raising online donations.

By mid-2007, PI had built up a following of more than 500 Facebook members, most of them at colleges, to support small-scale fundraising operations.[71] Similar online communities were set up on Think MTV, Razoo, Change.org, and MySpace. In addition to this, its use of Kintera's technology platform for content management in 2007 helped it to increase online donations and increased the subscriber base for its newsletter.[72] "Before, there was overseas interest in PlayPumps but most of our donors were still local to Africa. The new use of the Web has made a

---

68 www.guidestar.org/pqShowGsReport.do?partner=amex&ein=04-3839391.

69 Dan Sauter, "Changing the World on the Web," www.dynamittechnologies.com, July 8, 2008.

70 "Playpumps International Exceeds '100 Pumps In 100 Days' Goal," www.playpumps.org, July 25, 2007.

71 Tom Watson, "Facebook Generation: Will Social Networks Change the Nature of Philanthropy?" www.huffingtonpost.com, June 18, 2007.

72 "PlayPumps International Increases Efficiency and Results Using Kintera," www.kinterainc.com, 2007.

huge difference,"[73] said Hayes. Experts felt that the overall aim of PI's digital initiatives was 'sustainability through a network of linked supporters'.[74]

Challenges

Experts felt that RO and PI faced various challenges in meeting its stated mission. The challenges started with finding groundwater sources. This was followed by rigorous testing to ensure that the quality of water was good and that the bore-well recharge was sustainable. If the tests failed, the drilling costs were sunk.[75] The cost of installations was not uniform across different countries and even in different provinces. Inflation in some African countries added to the challenges.

Expansion into a new country also involved a lot of challenges. The organization had to conduct initial country analysis and secure the necessary commitments from the respective government. RO's teams had to conduct on-the-ground research, needs assessments, water testing, site evaluations, and consult with other groups and stakeholders in the area in order to find the best sites. It took months of groundwork before a single PlayPump could be installed in a new country.

Another challenge was dealing with political instability in neighboring countries when thinking of expansion. For instance, Field wanted to install his pumps in Zimbabwe but could not do so due to the volatile political situation in the country with Robert Mugabe at the helm. Field explained, "We've been wanting to help them for a very long time. But you can't go into the place. We haven't been there because we didn't want [to] put any of our installation crews at risk for political harassment or worse, number one. Number two, they wouldn't allow us to bring the equipment in without charging us a 32% import duty, which was never going to happen in my lifetime. And number three, you know, their own [...] basic system. They go uphill. You can't shove a truck up with diesel. You can't go anywhere."[76] Field added, "It makes me sick that we can't; they're our neighbor ... But I can't risk what small amount we have in a war."[77]

Another challenge was emerging competition and protecting its IPRs. A South African for-profit entity had developed a similar water system. RO had to intimate the company through its patent attorney that the company was infringing on its

73 Tracie McMillan, "Charity Makes Waves with Web Word of Mouth," www.msnbc.msn. com, January 28, 2008.
74 Tom Watson, "Facebook Generation: Will Social Networks Change the Nature of Philanthropy?" www.huffingtonpost.com, June 18, 2007.
75 Syspro, "The Trickle Down Effect," www.itweb.co.za.
76 John Eastman, "Trevor Field of PlayPumps International," blackandwhiteprogram.com, April 14, 2008.
77 "PlayPumps Founder Has Unique Name for His Work," www.wdi.umich.edu, January 15, 2007.

IPRs. Field said that a similar system had also been developed in India but he felt that the system may not work as efficiently.

However, according to Field, funding still remained the biggest challenge.[78] Lack of adequate funds was the major hurdle in its way of scaling up throughout Africa and beyond. It had no lack of people from around the world wanting to volunteer and get involved in the installation projects. But the company was unable to accommodate such requests. "It's all very noble. But we've got African people that actually need those jobs … And also, we have a problem guaranteeing the safety and well-being of foreigners in rural communities, working in areas that they're not familiar with,"[79] he said.

Looking Ahead

By mid-2008, PI/RO had set up more than 1,000 PlayPumps in five countries and was in the process of expanding to five more in sub-Saharan Africa. It was committed to reaching its ambitious target of setting up 4,000 pumps by 2010 and serving 10 million people.[80] According to the company, moving into new countries was proving the viability of its business model for sub-Saharan Africa.

Field spent a lot of the time giving presentations in educational and other institutions in order to generate funds. According to him, he was engaged in a commercial activity but with the aim of "giving back to the society" and this gave him a lot of satisfaction. However, he regretted the fact that he could not install PlayPumps in all the regions in and outside Africa that required such water systems. He was especially bothered about his inability to enter neighboring Zimbabwe. But with the environment showing signs of improvement in 2008, he said he was hopeful of venturing into Zimbabwe in the future.

Experts said that PlayPumps were simple yet innovative, sustainable, and capable of providing huge benefits to the disadvantaged communities. Its business model which was based on collaboration was also praised. It provided corporations with a chance to get involved as a part of their corporate social responsibility agenda. Moreover, many people who came to know about the concept said that it was very inspirational and had moved them to action—either by way of donating funds or by helping raise funds for the project. Some experts were also taking keen interest to see whether the concept could be moved to a broader commercial model.

Some people said that regions in Asia and Latin America should also benefit from this model and were unhappy that Field wasn't doing enough to extend the

78 "PlayPumps Founder Has Unique Name for His Work," www.wdi.umich.edu, January 15, 2007.
79 John Eastman, "Trevor Field of PlayPumps International," blackandwhiteprogram.com, April 14, 2008.
80 Syspro, "The Trickle Down Effect," www.itweb.co.za.

benefit to disadvantaged communities in these regions. Field, however, believed that installing PlayPumps in Africa would take all of his life. "I'd like to export to other countries but Africa takes up too much of my time."[81] However, this did not stop him from exploring his alternatives. He said, "We're working with all sorts of different people. We're looking for partners in all sorts of different countries … if we could put out a model together in such a way that we can take it to Nigeria, Ghana, Côte d'Ivoire, Congo, India, Dinah, the Pacific Rim countries. If we could franchise the concept and the know-how and the IP to other groups. That they could work on it and we could change this water shortage problem that the world is facing in a much bigger fashion than what we would be able to do on our own."[82]

References and Suggested Readings

Lim Kong Soon, "Utilizing Children's Play for Clean Water," english.ohmynews.com, July 12, 2008.

Dan Sauter, "Changing the World on the Web," www.dynamittechnologies.com, July 8, 2008.

John Eastman, "Trevor Field of PlayPumps International," blackandwhiteprogram.com, April 14, 2008.

Nii Simmonds, "PlayPumps International—Children Power Clean Water Technologies," nubiancheetah.blogspot.com, April 7, 2008.

Sam Aola Ooko, "Water is Child's Play, But You Gotta Spin!" ecoworldly.com, February 23, 2008.

Tracie McMillan, "Charity Makes Waves with Web Word of Mouth," www.msnbc.msn.com, January 28, 2008.

"PlayPumps International Increases Efficiency and Results Using Kintera," www.kinterainc. com, 2007.

Michael Lang, "Play-Pump Merry-Go-Round Provides Life Saving Water to the World," www. thelangreport.com, December 26, 2007.

"Play Pumps," www.i-genius.org, August 7, 2007.

"Playpumps International Exceeds '100 Pumps In 100 Days' Goal," www.playpumps.org, July 25, 2007.

"First Lady Laura Bush Launches the PlayPump™ Water System in Zambia," www. playpumps.org, June 28, 2007.

"Playpumps: Child Powered Merry-go-rounds Bring Drinking Water to South Africa," www. colorado.edu, June 24, 2007.

Tom Watson, "Facebook Generation Will Social Networks Change the Nature of Philanthropy?" www.onphilanthropy.com, June 13, 2007.

Melissa Frederick, "D.C. Charity Helps Kids Pump Clean Water in Africa," www.examiner. com, May 23, 2007.

81 "PlayPumps Founder Has Unique Name for His Work," www.wdi.umich.edu, January 15, 2007.

82 John Eastman, "Trevor Field of PlayPumps International," blackandwhiteprogram.com, April 14, 2008.

" '100 Pumps in 100 Days' Campaign to Launch on World Water Day," www.playpumps.org, March, 2007.

"PlayPumps Founder Has Unique Name for His Work," www.wdi.umich.edu, January 15, 2007.

Nicole Wallace, "Blending Business and Charity," philanthropy.com, September 28, 2006.

"The PlayPump: Business Solutions to Social Problems," southsouthnews.wordpress.com, August 1, 2006.

Stephen C Smith, "What Works," www.sojo.net, February 2006.

"South Africa: The Play Pump," www.pbs.org, October 24, 2005.

Gareth Knight, "Roundabout Outdoor Shortlisted for Alcan Prize for Sustainability," www.oneafrikan.com, September 8, 2005.

Nicholas McDiarmid, "Borehole Pumps While Children Go Roundabout," www.search.sebinet.co.za, August/September 2005.

"Why Pumping Water is Child's Play," news.bbc.co.uk, April 25, 2005.

"Pumping Water is Kid's Play," www.sagoodnews.co.za, April 20, 2005.

Christina Lamb, "The Drought-busting Magic Roundabout," www.timesonline.co.uk, April 17, 2005.

FMO, Annual Report 2005.

IFC Sustainability Report 2004.

"Tapping the Energy of Children at Play to Produce Clean Water and Promote HIV/AIDS Awareness," web.worldbank.org, 2004.

Yolandi Groenewald, "Collecting Water is Child's Play," *Mail & Guardian*, November 6, 2003.

Scott Smith, "Getting Wet in Rural South Africa," www.iafrica.com, September 2, 2002.

Sheila Kinkade, "Energy-Producing Playground," www1.worlbank.org, 2002.

"Play Pumps—South Africa," www.handsontv.com, January 2000.

"Case Foundation, U.S. Government Partner to Bring Clean Water to Africa," www.casefoundation.org.

"Design Like You Give a Damn," www.architectureforhumanity.org/designlikeyougiveadamn/AFH_blad.pdf.

"South Africa: The Roundabout Outdoor Playpump," www.worldbank.org, November 2002.

Gary Hamel, "Management Innovation in Action: World Bank," www.managementinnovationlab.com.

Geoff Hopkins, "Kids Play, Water Pumps: A Sustained Investment," www.casefoundation.org.

"PlayPumps International Increases Efficiency and Results Using Kintera," www.kinterainc.com/site/c.owL8JoO7KzE/b.3367803/k.9A2B/PlayPumps_International_Increases_Efficiency_and_Results_Using_Kintera.htm.

"Roundabout Outdoor Play Pump, South Africa," www.changemakers.net.

Syspro, "The Trickle Down Effect," www.itweb.co.za.

"The PlayPumps Partnership," www.casefoundation.org/c/document_library/get_file?repository_id=1&file_path=%2Farticles&file_name=IFC-PlayPumps.pdf .

"Water—Pump as You Play!" www.stepin.org.

www.casefoundation.org

www.causemarketingforum.com

www.guidestar.org/pqShowGsReport.do?partner=amex&ein=04-3839391

www.nextbillion.net

www.playpumps.org

Exhibit I **The Water Problem**

Compiled from various sources.

Clean drinking water is vital for human survival and economic well-being but many communities in developing countries in Africa, Asia, and Latin America have problems getting a regular supply of potable water. The scarcity of clean water forces these people to rely on water from sources that may be contaminated. Lack of clean drinking water is a leading cause of death in the developing world and is responsible for 80 percent of all sickness in the world.[a] It has been estimated that water-borne diseases (such as, cholera, diarrhoea, and hepatitis) account for 6,000 lives lost per day and one child dies from preventable, water-related disease every 15 seconds.[b] According to experts, the chances of survival of these people can be increased by 50 percent if they are provided with access to improved supply of water.[c]

According to the World Health Organization (WHO), reducing the proportion of people that lack access to safe water and adequate sanitation the world by half would save nearly US$90 billion annually. "The World Health Organization estimates that if everyone had access to basic water and sanitation services, the health sector would save more than US$11 billion in treatment costs, and people would gain 5.5 billion productive days each year due to reduced diarrheal disease,"[d] said Vanessa J. Tobin, Water, Environment and Sanitation, UNICEF. In addition to disease and death related to water, experts estimate that 40 billion hours are lost annually to hauling water.[e]

a Michael Lang, "Play-Pump Merry-Go-Round Provides Life Saving Water to the World," www.thelangreport.com, December 26, 2007.

b "PlayPumps International Selected by The Motley Fool's Global Gains Investment Service for "100 Pumps in 100 Days" Campaign," www.playpumps.org, May 17, 2007.

c Lim Kong Soon, "Utilizing Children's Play for Clean Water," english.ohmynews.com, July 12, 2008.

d www.playpumps.org/site/c.hqLNIXOEKrF/b.2603385/k.53B9/About_Us__More_Quotes.htm.

e Michael Lang, "Play-Pump Merry-Go-Round Provides Life Saving Water to the World," www.thelangreport.com, December 26, 2007.

Exhibit II **PI's Statement of Financial Position: Fiscal Year Ending February 28, 2007 (In US$)**

Source: aidafrica.org

ASSETS	
Cash	2,403,305
Pre-paid expenses and other assets	648,714
Pledges receivable, net of US$41,582 discount	3,720
Total Assets	3,055,739
LIABILITIES AND NET ASSETS	
Liabilities	
Accounts payable and accrued expenses	112,597
Grants payable, net of US$23,404 discount	795,596
Total Liabilities	908,193
Net Assets (Deficit)	
Unrestricted net deficit	(279,739)
Temporarily restricted net assets	2,427,285
Total Net Assets	2,147,546
Total Liabilities and Net Assets	3,055,739

Exhibit III **PI's Statement of Activities: Fiscal Year Ending February 28, 2007 (In US$)**

Source: aidafrica.org

	Unrestricted	Temporarily Restricted	Total
Revenue and Support			
Contributions	1,221,971	3,472,085	4,694,056
In-kind contributions	817,460	-	817,460
Interest income	4,592	-	4,592
Net assets released from restrictions	1,044,800	(1,044,800)	-
Total Revenue and Support	3,088,823	2,427,285	5,516,108
Expenses			
Program services			
Water systems	2,108,044	-	2,108,044
Support Services			
Fundraising	324,323	-	324,323
Management and general	119,401	-	119,401
Unallocated in-kind services from affiliated organizations	816,794	-	816,794
Total support services	1,260,518	-	1,260,518
Total Expenses	3,368,562	-	3,368,562
Change in Net Assets	(279,739)	2,427,285	2,147,546
Net Assets, beginning of period	–	–	–
Net Assets (Deficit), end of period	(279,739)	2,427,285	2,147,546

Exhibit IV A Photograph of Children Playing on the PlayPump

Source: Nicholas McDiarmid, "Borehole Pumps While Children Go Roundabout," www.search.sebinet.co.za, August/ September 2005.

Exhibit V PlayPump Water Systems: How they Help Achieve UN's Millennium Development Goals

Source: www.playpumps.org/site/c.hqLNIXOEKrF/b.2603319/k.E203/
The_PlayPump_System__Millennium_Development_Goals.htm

1. Eradicate extreme poverty and hunger

- Providing water close to home frees up time for more productive activities, and far fewer school/workdays are lost due to ill health.
- A water supply helps ensure a robust garden and healthier livestock in times of drought.
- Community water supplies can also lead to income generation activities such as brick-making, etc.

2. Achieve universal primary education

- A water supply ensures that children, especially girls, are more able to attend school and teachers more willing to work at a school with such basic facilities.
- Children that regularly suffer diarrhoea and other water and sanitation-related diseases miss classes.
- Children stay away from school because they are needed to carry out domestic chores or tend animals while their mothers are collecting water.
- UNICEF estimates that more than half of the world's schools lack drinking water, clean toilets, and hygiene lessons for school children. Safe water and sanitation are essential to protect children's health and their ability to learn in school.
- Children, particularly girls, are denied their right to an education because they are busy fetching water.

3. Promote gender equality and empower women

- The burden and drudgery of collecting water is mostly borne by women and especially girls.
- In underserved African communities, women often walk up to 6 miles each day to collect just one bucket of water. Providing water close to home frees up women's time for more productive use, such as tending kitchen gardens or working in cottage industries. Income generation also leads to increased status for women.
- Involving women in water projects is a direct means of empowerment. They are often involved in the management and maintenance of community water systems.

4. Reduce child mortality

- Diarrhoeal disease associated with water and sanitation leads to 2.1 million deaths each year—the majority of which are children.
- It has been estimated that 5,000 children die every day from water and sanitation related diseases.
- Children are most vulnerable to disease resulting from contaminated or inadequate quantities of water for drinking and personal hygiene.
- Malnutrition, which is the most significant cause of immunodeficiency, is associated with about half of all child deaths.
- Frequent bouts of diarrhoea lead to further deterioration in nutritional status and ability to resist disease.

5. Improve maternal health

- Carrying heavy loads of water leads to spinal deformation that can result in obstruction of the birth canal, putting both the mother's and infant's life at risk.
- Anaemia is common in pregnant African women, and it is exacerbated by the continued heavy work of water collection. This has the potential to impair foetal growth and adversely affects the quantity and quality of breast milk. It is not uncommon for pregnant women to continue collecting water until the day they give birth.
- Good hygiene of expectant mothers and safe delivery spaces are impossible without an accessible source of water.

6. Combat HIV/AIDS, malaria, and other diseases

- Infected people are more vulnerable to opportunistic pathogens which cause diarrhoea and skin diseases. This can be controlled to some extent by safe water and sanitation.
- Diarrhoea is a major cause of morbidity for people living with HIV/AIDS.
- Water used for food security and improved nutrition also helps people to remain healthy.
- Safe water is essential for ingesting any medications.
- Less time spent on fetching water allows caregivers, who are usually women and girls, more time and energy for coping with the disease or for working outside the home.
- In many of the countries in the world most affected by the HIV/AIDS pandemic, water and sanitation services are extremely limited. With the shift of focus from HIV/AIDS prevention efforts to treatment options, more attention must be given to improving water services.

7. Ensure Environmental Sustainability

- Integrate the principles of sustainable development into country policies and programs; reverse loss of environmental resources.

- Reduce by half the proportion of people without sustainable access to safe drinking water.
- Achieve significant improvement in lives of at least 100 million slum dwellers, by 2020.

8. Develop a global partnership for development

- Community water supply programs represent an entry point to the development of democratic society, leadership, and good governance.
- A water supply program can be the catalyst for this process because there is a need for the community to organize a representative management committee.
- Building a water system involves the community in an enormous amount of decision-making, and this continues after project completion as the community assumes responsibility for the installation.
- Very often, a water supply project is the first time that a community learns how to administer a communal utility.
- There are a wide variety of new skills learned in this process including technical, managerial, and leadership.
- It is a confidence building experience for the community as a whole and often leads the community to undertake other projects entirely of its own initiative.

Exhibit VI **Countries Where PlayPumps Were Installed And Future Expansion Plans**

Source: PlayPump International, 'Action Kit," www.playpumps.org.

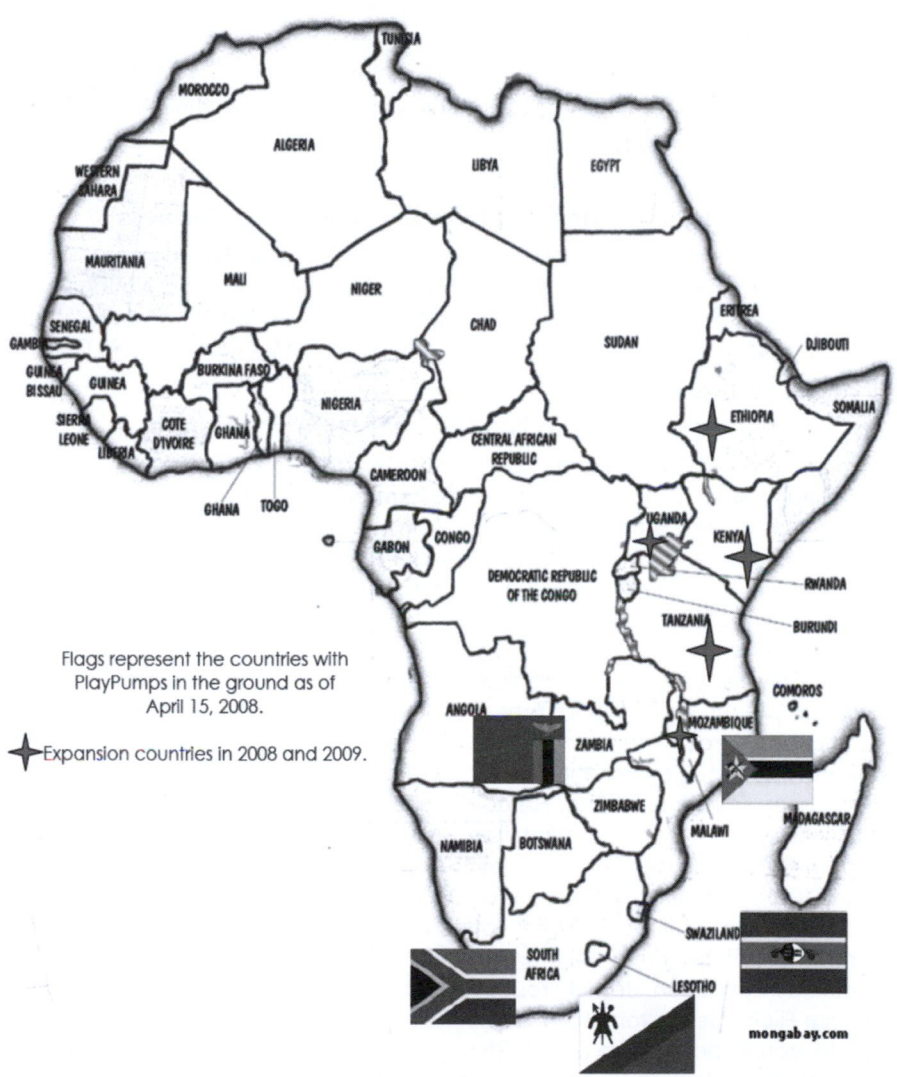

Flags represent the countries with PlayPumps in the ground as of April 15, 2008.

Expansion countries in 2008 and 2009.

mongabay.com

Exhibit VII **A List of RO and PI's Partners***

Source: www.playpumps.org.

Featured Partners

Anheuser-Busch, The Case Foundation, The Film Connection, Flashbags, The Motley Fool, National Geographic Kids, One water, Save the Children USA

PI Programmatic, Government, Media and Education Partners

Cool Globes, Hasbro/Playskol, Lesotho Ministry of Natural Resources, Museum of Natural History (New York), National Geographic Kids, National Geographic Wild Chronicles, National Youth Leadership Council, Philani Maswati Charity, Save the Children USA, The Film Connection, Think MTV

PlayPumps International Funding Partners (1 pump or more)

Adam and Caleb Tuckman and Jessica Reisman, Alamo Heights Independent School District, Albany Friends of PlayPumps, Anheuser-Busch, Anonymous, Assumption Catholic Church, Bill Ward, Bob and Joyce Beyers, Bristol-Myers Squibb Foundation, Campbell Family Fund, Centenary United Methodist Church, CityBridge Foundation, City of Richmond's Department of Parks, Recreation and Community Facilities After School Program, Coca-Cola Africa Foundation, Coke USA, Dave Sirulnick, David Brand and Family, Deen Day Sanders, Dick Waterfield, Dozoretz Family, Edmonds United Methodist Church, Ellen Wood, Ernest Greer, Euan and Bethany Menzies, Giving Express from American Express, Glastonbury School District, Glen Rock Poverty Project, Glencoe School District, Google Consumer Product Team, Gregg Drilling & Testing, Harbor Road Foundation, Heidrick & Struggles, Horace W. Goldsmith Foundation, Hurlbut-Johnson Fund, IHSAN, In Honor of Bruce Paltrow (Gwyneth Paltrow), In Honor of Christopher Kefalas (Blake & Darcy Anderson), In Honor of George Grosz, In Honor of David and Lucille Cole, In Honor of Mike Hoffman (Kaplan Philanthropic Fund), InsureMe Charitable Fund, Ira Moreland, Jane Griner, Jean R. Romoser Charitable Foundation, Jewish Youth Philanthropy Institute of DC, John & Rebecca Richardson, Jonathan D. Krist Foundation and Music with a Mission, Joseph Pope, Joshua & Jodi Press, Just Give, Lauth Family Foundation, Lesley and Joanne Hogan, Link Foundation, Louise McIlhenney, Marin Jewish Community Teen Foundation, Mark and Sarah Stegemoeller, Mark Ronson, Martin LB Walter, Mary Mellon, McCullough Intermediate School, Mike & Maggie Hoffman Foundation, Miles Gilburne & Nina Zolt, Montesorri CA, Moondance Fund, Neighbors Keeper Foundation, Nicholas LaMonica, Nicole Vaidisova, One Water, Oswald Family Foundation, Pat and Astrid Merriman Family Fund, Paul and Gail Taylor, Peggy and Jim Lientz Family, Philip & Rebecca Hochman, Project Redwood Foundation, Reebok Human Rights Foundation, Rick Smolan and Jennifer Erwitt, River Valley

Community Church, Rob and Jennifer Pace, Roth Family Foundation, Sarita Kennedy East Foundation, Scarsdale Middle School Human Rights Club, Sean "JAY-Z" Carter, Slauson Middle School, South Peninsula Jewish Community Teen Foundation, St. Gregory Catholic Church, Susan DeSimone, Ted and Lynn Leonsis, The Case Foundation, The Draw Academy, The MCJ Foundation, The Michael and Susan Dell Foundation, The Motley Fool, The Peggy and Jim Leintz Family, The R. K. Mellon Family Foundation, Theo and Kristina Ratliff, Tom & Beth Eckert, Universal Music, Warner Music, West Family Foundation, Western Union Foundation, Wingra School (Wisconsin), Young Family, Zyman Family Foundation

RO Partners

The Nelson Mandela Foundation, All advertisers, past and present (Clearwater Project, Colgate Palmolive, Highveld Steel, KFF, loveLife, Omidyar Network, Sesame Workshop, The World Bank)

* The list is not exhaustive.

Teaching notes for this case are available from Greenleaf Publishing. These are free of charge and are available only to teaching staff. They can be requested by going to:

www.greenleaf-publishing.com/oikos2_notes

Case 11

WaterHealth International

Providing Safe Drinking Water to the Bottom of the Pyramid Consumers[1, 2, 3]

Hadiya Faheem and Debapratim Purkayastha
IBS Center for Management Research, Hyderabad, India

Introduction

In February 2009, Irvine, California-based WaterHealth International Inc. (WHI) received a funding of US$15 million from the International Finance Corporation[4] (IFC) to expand its operations in India. With the funding, it was expected that

---

1 This case © 2010 IBS Center for Management Research. All rights reserved.

2 This case was written by Hadiya Faheem, under the direction of Debapratim Purkayastha, IBS Center for Management Research, IBS Hyderabad. It was compiled from published sources, and is intended to be used as a basis for class discussion rather than to illustrate either effective or ineffective handling of a management situation.

3 This case won the third prize in the oikos Global Case Writing Competition 2010 (Social Entrepreneurship track), organized by oikos Foundation for Economy and Ecology, University of St. Gallen, Switzerland.

4 The International Finance Corporation was established in 1956. It promotes economic growth in developing countries by mobilizing capital in the international financial markets, financing private sector investment, and providing advisory services to businesses and governments.

ICMR
IBS Center for Management Research
www.icmrindia.org

more than 600 communities in India would be able to set up WaterHealth Centers[5] (WHCs) with a capacity to serve over 3 million people. On receiving the funding, Tralance Addy (Addy), founder of WHI, said, "In response to the need to address the urgent problem of water-borne diseases, WaterHealth plans to expand rapidly. As we continue to do so as a result of strong demand, our need for capital to help communities finance these systems also increases. We are pleased, particularly in these challenging economic times, that IFC has elected to strengthen its relationship with WHI."[6]

Ever since its launch in 1996, WHI had been involved in dealing with one of the most pressing problems in developing countries worldwide—scarcity of potable water. It was estimated that more than 2 billion people lacked access to clean drinking water in developing countries. These people, therefore, often relied on water resources that were contaminated. It was reported that nearly 60 million children suffered from diminutive growth due to water-borne diseases. In addition to deaths and economic loss, women and girls, on whom the burden of obtaining water for the family fell, had to trek long distances and spend around six hours of their time fetching water—time that could be better spent with family or on economic activities.[7]

WHI aimed to alleviate the suffering caused by water-borne diseases and the associated economic loss through its innovative and breakthrough UV Waterworks (UVW) technology. The UVW technology was invented by Ashok Gadgil (Gadgil), an Indian-born senior physicist at the Lawrence Berkeley National Laboratory[8] (Berkeley Lab) in 1993, for disinfecting water from harmful pathogens and microbes with the help of ultraviolet light (UV). The result was safe and clean drinking water that exceeded the World Health Organization's[9] (WHO) water standards and was

---

5 WaterHealth Centers are the main offering of WHI which harnesses the company's proprietary UV Waterworks technology to provide a water facility for communities. An average WHC can provide a community of 3,000 residents with up to 20 liters of potable water per person per day.

6 "WaterHealth International Announces $15 Million Financing by IFC," www.reuters.com, February 16, 2009.

7 "Statistics Illustrate the Challenge of Clean Water Access around the World," www.waterhealth.com/water-crisis/statistics.php.

8 Established on August 26, 1931, the Lawrence Berkeley National Laboratory is located at the University of California. The lab was founded to conduct scientific research.

9 Headquartered in Geneva, the World Health Organization (WHO) is a specialized agency of the United Nations. The main task of the WHO is to coordinate with other institutions on international public health programs.

sold to bottom of the pyramid[10] (BoP) consumers.[11] As of 2009, WHI operated through subsidiaries in India, the Philippines, and Ghana. WHI water systems were also installed in a number of countries including Mexico, Bangladesh, Sri Lanka, and some parts of Africa.

Over the years, Addy,[12] as the CEO of WHI, played a crucial role in refining the business model of the company in an endeavor to make its services relevant to the target segment and also ensure returns for the investors. After meeting with limited success while trying to sell the UVW technology in the form of a product, WHI changed its business model to offer it as a service. WHI helped arrange loans for communities to finance the installations of its water systems and the beneficiaries had to pay a nominal user fee to avail of the service.

WHI's UVW technology and the business model it adopted to serve the underprivileged communities living in rural and peri-urban areas attracted the attention of experts who felt that it was innovative and sustainable. Experts felt that, in addition to solving the water problem, the company addressed issues related to health, gender, education, and economic losses associated with the water problem. It also generated employment for local people besides indirectly improving earnings in rural households. Experts said that tackling global challenges such as the water crisis required a collaborative approach like the one adopted by WHI.

As of mid-2009, more than 600 WHCs had been installed, providing safe water to more than one million people around the world. WHI's aim was to take the UVW technology to needy communities throughout the world by establishing a global presence (refer to Exhibit I for WHI's vision and values). While experts appreciated WHI's efforts to provide potable supply of water to underprivileged communities in developing countries and also appreciated its sustainability-driven business model, they felt that going forward the company would have to address various challenges.

Gadgil's Initial Efforts

An outbreak of cholera in West Bengal, India, in 1992 provided the impetus for the development of the UVW technology. Since the surface protein on this particular

---

10 In economics, the bottom of the pyramid is the largest, but poorest socio-economic group. There are an estimated four billion people in the world who live on less than US$2 per day (mostly in developing countries) that come under this group. Many companies, cutting across industries, are developing new business models to target this group.

11 "WaterHealth International, Inc. (WHI) Today Announced ICICI Bank's Funding Commitment for WHI's Development of Community Water Facilities in Rural India," www. politicalfriendster.com, December 12, 2008.

12 As of 2009, Addy was a member of the board of directors.

strain of cholera was a little different, several vaccines which had been used to cure cholera till then were ineffective. This led to the death of thousands of people in India. The strain soon spread to Bangladesh and Thailand. Gadgil was well aware of the water problem that communities in India faced and he desperately wanted to do something to help solve the issue, which, he knew, plagued other developing countries as well. But he could not do anything constructive because of the other projects he was involved in at Berkeley Lab.

Distressed by the loss of human life caused by the epidemic in his home country, Gadgil began to constantly think about ways in which the issue of water-borne diseases could be addressed. In 1993, he started working evenings and weekends and began his research with a mechanical engineering student and researcher in the Life Sciences Division of Berkeley Lab, Derek Yegian, to devise a system that would disinfect water using UV light. In his initial years, he did not have any funding for his project. He only had access to a colleague's expertise and the equipment offered by Berkeley Lab. During his research, he found that the UV light could disinfect one ton of contaminated water for five cents.[13] "It took two years to make it simple, simple, simple—and as low-maintenance as possible. It was extraordinarily inexpensive—about 4 cents to 5 cents per person per year. That got me excited. I thought, 'We can make a profit, but with a social mission,'"[14] said Gadgil. Several scientists were amazed by the technology invented by Gadgil as it was simple yet ingenious, and capable of addressing the water problem in developing countries. Daniel Kammen, Professor at UC Berkeley's Energy and Resources Group, Goldman School of Public Policy and Department of Nuclear Engineering, said, "The general idea of using UV light in a tube to kill pathogens has been around since the 1970s, but Ashok really pioneered the use of the technology for low-cost applications in developing countries."[15]

While Gadgil's research was on, cholera continued to be a problem in India. It was reported that from May to August 1994, nearly 2,200 people had lost their lives to the disease.[16] This led Gadgil to launch his prototype. The same year, he received some funding from federal and private sources. Using this money, he developed a prototype that was efficient and low in cost. The working model could disinfect eight gallons of water per minute for a price of two cents per ton, which included the annual capital cost of the unit, consumables, and electricity.[17] The model was taken to a village in India for field testing. It was tested using a car battery since the area had no electricity. The feedback from the tests revealed that the technology

---

13   "Success Stories: Start-Ups—WaterHealth International Inc.," www.lbl.gov/tt/success_stories/articles/WHI_more.html.

14   Colin Stewart, "Changing the World, One Gallon at a Time," www.ocregister.com, May 24, 2007.

15   "Researchers Help Bring Clean Water to Households in Developing Nations," www.universityofcalifornia.edu, February 6, 2003.

16   Ashok Gadgil, "UV Waterworks: Reliable, Inexpensive Water Disinfection for the World," eetdnews.lbl.gov, 1996.

17   Martha Davidson, "Innovative Lives," invention.smithsonian.org, February 26, 1999.

could be improved further. The villagers said that the model was too efficient for small villages and rural communities of India since the system purified water much faster than they could store and supply it. They also pointed out that they lacked the kind of water resources required. Moreover, they felt that the system was too big, bulky, and expensive.

In 1995, Gadgil decided to revise the prototype after obtaining feedback from the villagers. It was at this time that Edas Kazakevicius (Kazakevicius), a Lithuania-based physics student, expressed an interest in working with Gadgil on his UVW project. In late 1995, Gadgil in conjunction with Kazakevicius built a revised prototype which was compact in size and weighed only 15 pounds.[18] The system could disinfect four gallons of water at four cents per ton utilizing 40 watts of electricity.[19] This smaller model matched the 3.5 gallon capacity hand pumps supplied by the UNICEF[20] in many parts of the developing world, according to Gadgil.

The UVW system was retailed at US$800 and could last for 15 years. The full vending station including filters, pumps, and tanks cost about US$7,000. The water disinfected by the UVW system could be stored for up to 36 hours for consumption.[21]

Having developed the prototype, Gadgil decided to patent and license the technology. Berkeley Lab's Technology Transfer Department played a significant role at this stage of the prototype. It received funds from the US Department of Energy's[22] Office of Science for developing this technology to a stage where it could be licensed. According to Viviana Wolinsky, the Licensing Manager at Berkeley Lab, "Gadgil worked with the Technology Transfer Department to devise a strategy for a technology that everyone realized had the potential to offer significant, widespread social benefit. To foster the broadest distribution of the technology, Berkeley Lab decided to patent and license it."[23]

Several companies bid for Gadgil's UVW technology and WHI was one of them. The University of California which runs Berkeley Lab licensed the UVW technology to WHI.

18 Martha Davidson, "Innovative Lives," invention.smithsonian.org, February 26, 1999.

19 Ashok Gadgil, "UV Waterworks: Reliable, Inexpensive Water Disinfection for the World," eetdnews.lbl.gov, 1996.

20 Established by the United Nations in 1946, UNICEF is the acronym for United Nation's Children's Fund. It works for children's rights, their survival, development, and protection.

21 Suzanne Snell, "Water and Sanitation Services for the Urban Poor," waterwiki.net, December 1998.

22 The US Department of Energy is a government department set up with the mission of promoting and advancing energy technology in the US.

23 "Success Stories: Start-Ups—WaterHealth International Inc.," www.lbl.gov/tt/success_stories/articles/WHI_more.html.

About Waterhealth International

In 1996, Addy, a Ghana-based entrepreneur, set up WHI. The organization's stated aim was to "invest in business that aids society". By setting up this organization, Addy planned to address the water problem faced by communities in developing countries. He said that he often felt the need to do something for people in water-stressed communities where women and girls travelled long distances to haul water. He also cited the example of his childhood days in Ghana where he had to wait in long lines to fill water from the tap. According to him, providing safe and clean drinking water was one of the best ways to impact the lives of the BoP communities.

Addy's focus on doing something for the BoP customers grew while he was working at Johnson & Johnson[24] (J&J). While working there, Addy looked at a number of technologies that could address the water problem. He then licensed the UVW technology from Berkeley Lab. In 1998, WHI collaborated with UNICEF to integrate a solar-powered hand pump with the UVW system since several villages in developing nations had no access to electricity.[25] Though that did not materialize, Addy planned to continue with the existing model. J&J executives, however, did not show any interest in the UVW technology and said, "Look, this is really interesting. This is really great, but it's just a little too weird for us. We don't see this being at Johnson & Johnson Company."[26] Hence, Addy decided to start a company of its own and resigned from J&J in 2001. He also brought in Gadgil as the vice president, R&D, and Chief Technology Officer of WHI.

Despite the benefits offered by the UVW systems, WHI was unable to sell the number of units needed for the company to break even. By 2002, the company had made investments of around US$6 million, but was able to sell only 300 units at a price of US$1,000 each.[27] This led to the company filing for bankruptcy. However, Addy's venture management company Plebys International LLC[28] (Plebys) initiated a buy-out and restructured the company. Subsequently, it also restructured the ownership of shareholders from seventy shareholders to a core group of nine shareholders (refer to Table I for WHI shareholding pattern after restructuring in 2002).

---

24 Johnson & Johnson, one of the premier healthcare companies, was founded by the Johnson brothers in 1887. The company is engaged in the manufacture and sale of healthcare products in more than 57 countries across the world through more than 250 operating companies.

25 Suzanne Snell, "Water and Sanitation Services for the Urban Poor," waterwiki.net, December 1998.

26 "Peter Hamilton—Interview—Plebys," www.e-clips.cornell.edu.

27 Colin Stewart, "Changing the World, One Gallon at a time, www.ocregister.com, May 24, 2007.

28 Plebys International LLC is a venture management and development company that sets technology-based enterprises with the stated aim of serving underserved markets worldwide.

Table I **WHI's Shareholding Pattern after Restructuring in 2002**

Source: "Project Sponsor and Major Shareholders of Project Company," www.ifc.org

Company	Percentage
Plebys International, LLC	78.46
Elwyn Ewald	7.31
Johnson & Johnson Corporation	5.18
Monsanto Corporation	3.23
Eric Lemelson	2.84
Richard Cortese	1.4

With the help of Plebys, WHI raised investments of US$16 million from SAIL Venture Partners,[29] Dow Venture Capital,[30] the IFC, and Acumen Fund[31] in 2002.[32]

In 2004, Plebys invested another US$2 million in WHI.[33] According to Addy, the company had failed initially since it had focused on marketing a product rather than the service. Addy maintained that a market for clean water did exist and decided to adopt a new approach to market its UVW technology. WHI partnered with several non-governmental organizations (NGOs) to educate rural consumers about the significance of drinking clean water. He built up a network of professionals who were trained to maintain and service the equipment. He also set up a financing structure that enabled the communities to make a down payment of around 30 to 40 percent with the rest of the amount being paid through a loan arranged by WHI.[34]

Following the investment from Plebys, IFC and Acumen Fund also invested US$1.8 million. "These investments highlight growing recognition of the importance of WHI's technology and business models and our ability to get things done to provide safe drinking water even in challenging environments around the world,"[35] added Addy. The UVW units were field tested in USA, Mexico, the Philippines, South Africa, and India. They were produced in California, USA, and at Mumbai in India. Over the following years, the company refined its business model and set up

---

29 Founded in 2002, SAIL Venture Partners is a venture capital company with offices in Washington DC and Southern California.

30 Dow Venture Capital invests in start-up companies in Asia, Europe, and North America.

31 Acumen fund is a non-profit venture fund that aims to serve the underserved communities globally through market-oriented and innovative approaches.

32 "Ventures WaterHealth International," www.plebys.com/ventures/waterhealth.htm.

33 Nitasha Tiku, "Do-Good Capitalist of the Year," www.inc.com, December 2007.

34 Ibid.

35 "WaterHealth International Receives New Funding Totaling $1.8 Million," www.allbusiness.com, November 22, 2004.

its water systems in many countries. Analysts felt that since 2004, the focus of the company had been more on India.

Being a privately held company, WHI did not disclose its revenue. However, its typical installation reportedly brought in as much as US$50,000 and the company expected to break even in 2008.[36] For the year ended 2008, WHI revenues were estimated to be US$17.3 million.[37] It had an employee strength of around 125 people. Its prominent shareholders were Acumen Fund, Dow Venture Capital, IFC, SAIL Venture Partners, and Plebys.

Creating a Sustainable Business Model

WHI installed its UVW system in places such as schools, hospitals, and local communities. It also installed the systems at homes and in apartment buildings. Its flagship offering was WHCs (also called Community Water Systems). A standard WHC was approximately 55 square meters in size with an additional area for social use. The WHC was designed to act as a place for social gathering for the village people. The village residents collected water from these WHCs. In some of the communities, local entrepreneurs delivered water to some houses at a fee. A standard system offered 20 liters of water for one person per day and served up to 3,000 people. The system required maintenance only once in three months and thus this did not significantly add up to the cost of owning or operating the system.[38]

The land for setting up the WHC and water resources was given by the local governments (for instance, the village *panchayat*[39] in India).[40] The equipment, sourced from vendors, was provided by WHI. The company took the responsibility of installing the capacity equipment. After taking approval from the local community, the WHCs sourced water from perennial water sources. In the dry season, the company entered into contracts with water vendors or water tankers to supply water to their WHCs in order to ensure uninterrupted water supply.

WHI offered a financing program to the communities after criteria such as community size, user interest, and compliance to repay the loan had been met. The company collaborated with financial institutions to help with the finances for the communities. The village leadership, local government, NGOs, or private sponsors made the down payment and the remaining costs were then financed by the

---

36 "Go Green, Get Rich," money.cnn.com, April 4, 2007.

37 www.zoominfo.com, 2009.

38 Ashok Gadgil, "The Rosenfeld Effect," www.energy.ca.gov, April 29, 2006.

39 *Panchayat* is a political system followed in the villages of India, Pakistan, and Nepal. In a *panchayat*, five elders assemble and settle disputes taking place between individuals and villages. They receive funds from local body grants and state governments, etc.

40 "WaterHealth International, Inc. (WaterHealth Ghana)," www.aquaya.org/files/ nairobi.../Mawunyo_Puplampu.pdf.

company. The fee collected from sale of water was then used to repay loans. After the loans were repaid, the WHCs became income-generating assets for the local communities. The proceeds were sufficient to cover the expenses of the UVW system in addition to the cost of tanks, controllers, valves, pumps, civil structures, and maintenance of the equipment.[41] Moreover, the proceeds were used for improvements in villages. The communities shared the net revenues gained from the user fees with WHI if the system had been financed by the company.[42]

In addition to helping with the finances to set up WHCs, WHI also educated the communities about the threat from water-borne diseases. Addy added, "Now we build the key technical components, provide financing, educate customers about the devastating impact of water-borne diseases, and provide a financial method for collecting money and putting it into the bank."[43] (Refer to Box I for services offered by WHI.)

Box I **Services Offered by WHI**

Source: www.waterhealth.com/products/community-water-systems.php

---

- Site assessment and preparation
- Conveyance of raw water from source to treatment facility
- Turnkey assembly, installation, and validation of water treatment equipment and civil works
- Building a modern, aesthetically designed and landscaped civil structure that also serves as a gathering place for the community
- Provision of specially designed water containers that minimize the potential for recontamination during customer use and storage
- Extended maintenance contracts to keep quality and operating standards high
- Recruitment, hiring, and training of local residents to operate facilities
- Overall management of WHCs
- Ongoing education programs on health and hygiene

The water for the WHCs was sourced from the pond through buried high density polyethylene pipes. People were offered training on safety, health, and the environment in order to ensure that the WHCs were run in accordance with the policies and procedures of WHI. The company persuaded people to buy clean water by advertising the financial benefits to the poor communities. Experts appreciated WHI's efforts at advertising the benefits of potable water to the poor. According to

---

41 Nachiket Mor, D Chattanathan, and Rajiv Panthary, "Enhancing the Flow of Credit and Managing Risks in Agriculture," www.icrier.org/pdf/mor%20paper.pdf.
42 "WaterHealth International, Inc.," www.aquaya.org, June 26, 2009.
43 Colin Stewart, "Changing the World, One Gallon at a Time," www.ocregister.com, May 24, 2007.

Robert Katz, a staff member at the World Resources Institute,[44] "Poor people care about feeding, clothing, and housing the family. If people are missing work because they are getting sick from water-borne diseases, you can show them how much money they are losing."[45]

In March 2006, WHI developed a franchise model, making marketing and distribution easy for local entrepreneurs. The entrepreneurs who bought the franchise model were assured of a marketing and service model with ongoing checks being done for quality and maintenance. On an average, the franchisees received a return on investment within 12 to 18 months, according to WHI.[46] Experts felt that the franchise model was an attractive business value proposition for local entrepreneurs and non-profit organizations interested in revenue generation.

Experts felt that WHI had developed a cost-effective technology for serving the poor. They also commended the company for its approach to social marketing and distribution. Several industry observers were of the opinion that the WHI's business model was unique since it was a combination of social marketing expertise, knowledge about local markets, financing skills, and one of the world's best technologies that purified water from bacterial contamination (refer to Box II for salient points of WHI's business model).

Box II WHI's Business Model: Salient Points

Source: WaterHealth International, Inc. (WaterHealth Ghana), Presentation at the AQUAYA Workshop in Nairobi Kenya 26th June 2009.

Direct WHC sales (assessment/equipment/facility/support)

- Community provides land and access to water
- Community makes cash down payment of 10% and above
- Bank finances remainder—arranged through WHI

Maintenance service contracts

- Mandatory service contract for 8–10 years (loan term)
- Service charges paid to WHI from user fees
- Sale of service contracts after loan term

Management fees

- Share of net user fee revenues if system financed
- Contracted services if system purchased outright

---

44 The World Resources Institute is a non-profit organization that works with the mission of protecting the environment and improving the lives of the people.

45 "The Why Files," whyfiles.org, November 15, 2007.

46 "Water Health International: Water Supply Franchising," timbuktuchronicles.blogspot. com, March 12, 2006.

Some experts felt that the model was sustainable since the system could treat surface water from lakes, ponds, and rivers. In case of any water shortage, WHI entered into deals with water tankers to source water for their WHCs. WHI through its UVW technology provided access to clean drinking water, contributing to public health by improving sanitation and hygiene and decreasing the risk of water-borne diseases. Moreover, the UVW technology offered a renewable, self-sustaining way of providing an improved supply of water with minimum wastage. It did not require fuel and also contributed to keeping the environment safe as it did not have to use biomass fuel for boiling water. Proper storage prevented water contamination and reduced wastage due to spillage and evaporation. What's more, the water supplied met WHO standards at lower costs than other methods of water purification (refer to Exhibit II for a note on how the UVW technology works; to Exhibit III for a typical system configuration of a WHI system; to Exhibit IV for photographs of WHCs; and to Exhibit V for WHI's investment cost advantage vs. other options).

WHI removed education barriers since the children did not have the chore of fetching water. They also had access to safe drinking water and several communities provided free water to schools. Moreover, children did not miss school due to water-borne diseases. Women could spend time on economic activities rather than wasting their productive hours on fetching water. According to experts, with all these benefits, the UVW systems also led to economic development and a foundation for sustainable growth. For instance, it generated employment for people in rural areas where WHI installed its water disinfection systems. The people employed were responsible for installing, cleaning, and maintaining the equipment. The local residents were also hired for selling and distributing water to remote areas.[47]

WHI was successful in its venture in several countries. By January 2007, around 500 systems had been installed in Asia, Central America, and Africa and served around 500,000 people.[48] WHI and Gadgil received several awards and recognition for the UVW technology (refer to Exhibit VI for a list of awards and recognition received by the UVW technology). In 2007, Addy was also profiled by the *Inc. Magazine* as 'Do-good Capitalist of the Year'.[49]

Some experts opined that while the company had received immense recognition, it still had to reap profits. A few venture capital firms opined that the company should expand its business worldwide in order to have a return on investment. Commenting on WHI's approach to business, Henry Habicht, Managing partner, SAIL Venture Partners, said, "It's very important to make money like any other business."[50] Reiterating his commitment to running WHI as a for-profit enterprise, Addy said, "We're motivated to do what we're doing because of a huge need and

47 Achintya Madduri, "Water Water Everywhere?" floatingsun.net, November 3, 2007.
48 Go Green, Get Rich," money.cnn.com, April 4, 2007.
49 *Inc. Magazine* is a New York-based monthly magazine. The magazine is targeted at people who run growing companies.
50 Colin Stewart, "WaterHealth: Changing the World, One Gallon at a Time," www.ocregister.com, May 24, 2007.

huge suffering. Unless we can bring private capital to bear on these problems, the solutions will not be sustainable … We are very much a for-profit company."[51]

Experts often cited WHI as an example of a social enterprise. Some of them opined that the WHI could do more for poor people if it operated as a business that made profits rather than as a donor-backed organization.

WHI's Worldwide Operations

As of 2009, WHI operated through subsidiaries in three countries—India, the Philippines, and Ghana. The company's prime focus had been on India where more than 200 of its water facilities had been installed. The company also had UVW systems installations in some other countries.

WHI in India

WHI contended that India was a major market for targeting the BoP consumers since the adverse impact of unsafe water on health was a continuing story, causing diseases like diarrhoea, cholera, etc. In India, the monsoon was the time when there was a spurt in water-borne diseases, as drinking water became mixed with sewage and animal waste. Unhygienic practices during collection and storage and limited access to sanitation facilities also brought about the transmission of water-borne diseases in humans. According to the WHO, diarrhoea was the single largest cause of death of over 700,000 Indians in 1999—over 1,600 deaths per day.[52] The situation highlighted the need for focused interventions to prevent the occurrence of water-borne diseases. Despite the public investments in water and sanitation infrastructure, many low-income rural communities in India lacked access to safe drinking water because of the population of more than 1 billion with 70 percent of people living in rural areas.[53] Many of the people living in rural areas had no access to potable water. In 2004, it was estimated that around 10 million people residing in rural areas were affected by diarrhoea. The reasons cited were unsafe drinking water contaminated by water-borne diseases.

In 2004, IFC made equity investments of US$1.2 million in WHI since it had combined its UVW technology with a commercial approach. IFC further catalyzed co-investments of US$1.35 million, enabling WHI to set up operations in India.[54] WHI carried out its operations in India through its subsidiary WaterHealth India (WHIN).

---

51 "WaterHealth," www.whatsbubbling.com, June 12, 2007.
52 www.intwot.org
53 "WaterHealth India," www.waterhealth.com.
54 "Sustainability Business Innovator Annual Report 2008," www.ifc.org, September 2008.

The immense potential provided by the Indian rural market prompted WHI to launch a pilot project in Bomminampadu[55] with the aim of preventing water-borne diseases and supplying clean drinking water to the poor in 2005. WHI set up a CWS in association with the NAANDI Foundation[56] (NAANDI). According to Gadgil, "We team up with local organizations because they understand the language and the culture. People in the villages trust them."[57]

WHI sold coupons to families that could be redeemed at CWS for potable water. Some families preferred water to be delivered to their houses for an extra amount. This opened up opportunities for local entrepreneurs who delivered water to houses for some extra money. As part of the CWS, an educational program was conducted by the NGOs that taught the villagers about issues related to health and hygiene and also encouraged them to use potable water.

According to WHI, the cost of this turnkey operation was US$50,000 which was comparatively lower than similar capacities such as bore wells. In India, the financing for the installation of the CWS was done through ICICI Bank.[58]

The village had a population of 3,200 and the launch of the water disinfection system was adopted by 60 percent of the households. The villagers and the local leaders noted that there was a drastic reduction in people getting affected by water-borne diseases. On seeing the improvement in the village, M Ganga Bhaima, Sarpanch (Head) of the village, said, "I feel as if I have given a new lease of life to my village. By drinking this good water, they will enjoy good health and live a good life."[59] In addition to providing potable water, WHI also generated employment for the local community. Each CWS had three part-time employees—two technical workers and a social worker for educating the community on health issues.

In 2005, WHI installed its CWS at another village, Akividu.[60] WHI conducted health campaigns in the village in an attempt to educate villagers about the benefits of using clean water. The community leaders also supplied clean drinking water to school children. The beneficiaries and people who partnered with WHI were all praise for these water systems as they had not believed that it was possible to have a solution to the problem of unsafe water that was both reliable and affordable.

Buoyed by the acceptance of the UVW technology, students at Berkeley Labs started conducting similar experiments to carry out water purification projects in the underserved communities of Mumbai in 2005. In the following year, WHI's

55 Bomminampadu is a village in the Krishna district of the Southern Indian state Andhra Pradesh.
56 NAANDI Foundation is a public trust that works in affiliation with the government, the society, and the several corporate houses for serving the underprivileged.
57 David Pescovitz, "Community Water Works," www.coe.berkeley.edu, April 1, 2005.
58 ICICI Bank is the second largest bank in India. It is a private sector bank started in 1994 and has subsidiaries and affiliates in the areas of investment banking, life and non-life insurance, venture capital, and asset management.
59 "The Village of Bomminampadu is a Clean-water Pioneer," www.waterhealth.com/worldwide-operations/study1.php.
60 Akividu is a village in the West Godavari district of Andhra Pradesh.

operations in India got a significant boost with ICICI Bank deciding to support the company's expansion in India. On October 10, 2006, ICICI Bank extended around US$865,000 for setting up CWSs in India.[61] In 2006, 50 CWSs were set up in Andhra Pradesh.

On February 9, 2007, WHI launched the 'Blue Revolution' initiative in India. The aim of the initiative was to eventually supply safe water to more than 2 billion people who had either little or no supply of potable water. The initiative was launched in association with several private companies, NGOs, and government organizations in a bid to solve the health crisis at a global level. WHI's Blue Revolution in India was inspired by the success of the Green Revolution[62] in the country. Commenting on the launch, Addy said, "India has been a touchstone for WaterHealth International to demonstrate the sustainability and viability of its clean water initiatives. We hope to have the same impact on India as the Green Revolution did on agriculture, and we intend to make this a global initiative."[63]

WHI encouraged local franchisees, entrepreneurs, and village organizations in Andhra Pradesh to set up CWSs. It sold the equipment to NAANDI which took the responsibility of marketing the units. For local entrepreneurs, the cost of setting up a CWS was estimated at Rs. 2–2.3 million.[64] Funding of nearly Rs. 1.5 million was offered through financial institutions while the remaining was funded by WHI. WHI offered water to rural consumers in 15 liter cans at Rs. 1.50.[65] Using this money, the entrepreneurs repaid the loans (refer to Exhibit VII on WHI's operational structure in India).

Subsequently, WHI scaled up its operations in India at a rapid pace. On July 21, 2007, WHI announced that over 100 CWS had been set up in Andhra Pradesh. These centers were operational in Krishna and West Godavari districts[66] and offered potable water to over 250,000 people.[67] The number of CWSs installed in India had increased to over 200 by 2009. For its future installations, WHI planned to integrate rainwater harvesting capabilities to its UVW systems.

61 "ICICI Bank Funds WaterHealth International's India Initiative," www.waterhealth.com, October 10, 2006.

62 The term Green Revolution is used to refer to the period from 1967 to 1978. India, post independence, struggled with food security. The Green Revolution, started in 1967, is a term coined to denote the use of modern agricultural practices like double cropping, use of synthetic pesticides, using hybrid seeds, etc. adopted to solve the food crisis.

63 "WaterHealth International Announces the Launch of the Blue Revolution," www.indiaprwire.com, February 9, 2007.

64 As of October 2009, US$1 approximately equals Rs. 45.85.

65 Nachiket Mor, D Chattanathan, and Rajiv Panthary, "Enhancing the Flow of Credit and Managing Risks in Agriculture," www.icrier.org/pdf/mor%20paper.pdf.

66 "WaterHealth Announces More than 100 WaterHealth Centres in Andhra Pradesh," www.waterhealth.com, July 21, 2007.

67 "Global Philanthropy 2007 Year in Review," www.zicklincenter.org, 2007.

WHI in the Philippines

WHI had started its worldwide operations by setting up a subsidiary at Manila, the Philippines, in 1997. The company offered its franchisee model to local entrepreneurs in the Philippines so that they could sell potable water to the poor. The model enabled proprietors of 'mom and pop' stores to own and operate branded WHI water stores called 'Aqua Stores'. Moreover, they could benefit from the know-how of WHI—such as location of setting up a water store, expected level of delivery and foot traffic, and managing finances and technical services.

The franchisees had to pay US$8,000 as a fee to set up a franchise and for the turn-key operation. The Philippine government regulated the water stores. A WHI store could occupy 20 to 30 square meters of storefront. The stores were given access to well water or municipal water and electricity. Experts felt that the franchise model offered by WHI established a commercial model and also offered entrepreneurship opportunities for people who planned to own and operate businesses on their own. The franchisees were offered training by WHI professionals on operating the stores in compliance with sanitary and quality standards.

The UVW system was purchased by the state government and a private entrepreneur took up the responsibility for distribution and installation and also provided follow-up maintenance of the system. The Rotary Club[68] also gave access to finances by offering loans to the local communities for installation of the UVW systems in Manila. The systems were installed in places where a centralized water piping system was expensive for local governments and chlorination was not a feasible option due to its maintenance costs.

The UVW systems were installed in three different approaches. In Manila, 90 units were installed on a for-profit basis. The Rotary Club installed 10 units in and around the slums of Manila by offering a revolving loan. After having targeted the rural areas, WHI also tapped the potential in the urban areas of the Philippines. In 1999, WHI set up a few WaterHealth Philippines and Aqua Sure Water Store franchises for offering clean water at affordable prices to more than 100,000 people living in urban areas.

By May 1999, the WHI distributor in the Philippines had 37 'Aqua Sure' water stores in urban areas and 30 water centers in rural areas. Nearly 50,000 people had access to safe and drinking water offered by WHI at one-third of the price of bottled water. In 1999, the Rotary Club allotted funds for setting up of UVW systems in nine schools in the Philippines. WHI's Manila operations resulted in income generation for workers and local entrepreneurs.

In 2003, WHI entered into a joint venture (JV) with Bendix Sales Corporation[69] (Bendix) in the Philippines and formed WaterHealth Philippines with WHI holding 65 percent of the shares and the rest by Bendix. With this JV, WHI aimed to enter

---

68 The Rotary Club facilitated access to loans thereby helping in the establishment of a sustainable water disinfection system for people of Manila.

69 Bendix Corporation was WHI's private partner in Philippines that facilitated the purchase of UVW units.

the water service provider market in the Philippines. By 2007, Manila had nearly 50 WHI franchisee water stores. Most of them were installed through the Rotary Club.[70]

WHI in Ghana

On December 12, 2007, WHI launched its first WHC in Ghana through its subsidiary WaterHealth Ghana. The water facility was located at Afuaman, a rural community in Ghana. After launching the WHC, Addy said, "I am pleased to witness our first endeavor in Ghana come to fruition. As a son of Ghana, this project holds special significance for me. This has been truly a team effort among government officials, World Vision Ghana, and WaterHealth and I am confident that it will be the first of thousands in the country and West Africa."[71]

Addy saw potential in Ghana since there was a population of around 2 million people with around 50 percent of the population having no access to potable water. It was also estimated that around 70 percent of illnesses were due to water-borne diseases in Ghana.[72] WHI had worked with the local communities in Ghana to train them on the installation of water disinfection systems. The company also conducted several education campaigns for educating the community members on the significance of health and hygiene. WHI's initiative to supply potable water to the people of Ghana was embraced by the government.

As of mid-2009, there were six WHCs in Ghana, five of which were funded by SafeWater Network.[73]

WHI Installations in Other Countries

In 1998, WHI started its operations at Guerrero, Mexico. The Guerrero Department of Health (DoH) bought 60 UVW systems from WHI.[74] In 1999, the State Government of Guerrero purchased and installed 75 units in the rural areas of Mexico.[75] The UVW systems were installed near locations such as schools, households, and health clinics. The communities were entrusted with the responsibility of main-

---

70 "Mobilizing Science-Based Enterprises for Energy, Water, and Medicines in Nigeria (2007)," books.nap.edu, 2007.

71 "First WaterHealth Centre Inaugurated in Afuaman," www.waterhealth.com, December 12, 2007.

72 "WaterHealth Ghana," www.waterhealth.com/worldwide-operations/ghana.php.

73 Headquartered in Westport, Connecticut, Safe Water Network is a non-profit organization founded with the stated aim to provide potable water to the poor.

74 Carol Kolb deWilde, Anita Milman, Yvonne Flores, Jorge Salmerón, and Isha Ray, "An Integrated Method for Evaluating Community-based Safe Water Programmes and an Application in Rural Mexico," heapol.oxfordjournals.org/cgi/content/abstract/czn01.

75 "Ultraviolet (UV) Waterworks," www.pi.energy.gov/documents/ EWSLmexicoPhilippinesUVW.pdf.

taining the system and paying for any replacement of parts and for the electricity required by the system.

The installations of disinfection systems in Mexico adopted a public–private approach where the state government purchased the system and a private entrepreneur took care of the process of installation, maintenance, and distribution. The DoH entered into a contract with an engineer to visit places where the UVW systems were installed four times a year in order to make technical repairs if required and deliver replacement consumables.

By 1999, WHI had installed over 175 UVW units in rural villages of Guerrero in Mexico and Manila in the Philippines to provide safe drinking water to more than 300,000 people, according to WHI.[76] According to WHI, the total investment for setting up water stores at Guerrero and Manila was US$5,690,000 of which 80 percent was invested by the private sector organizations like Bendix (US$1,000,000), WHI (US$3,500,000), and Pew Charitable Trust,[77] Mertz-Gilmore Foundation,[78] and Rockefeller Foundation[79] (US$105,000). The remaining funding was done by public sources such as Guerrero State with US$750,000 and the United States Agency for International Development[80] (USAID) and United States Department of Energy (USDoE) with US$335,000.[81]

In February 1999, a UVW system was installed at a rural health clinic, Greenock Clinic, located near Dundee, KwaZulu-Natal, South Africa. The clinic mostly diagnosed children for diarrhoea caused due to drinking of contaminated water. The installation was funded by the USDoE through Berkeley Lab and the US South Africa Binational Commission.[82] The UVW units were donated by WHI.[83]

In early 1999, WHI installed its first UVW system in Bangladesh with the support of the USDoE. The company sourced surface water to disinfect and purify it since

---

76 "Ultraviolet (UV) Waterworks," www.pi.energy.gov/documents/
    EWSLmexicoPhilippinesUVW.pdf.
77 Pew Charitable Trust is a US-based organization that adopts a rigorous approach to encourage civic life and improve public policy. The company partners with several public and private organizations that work for the benefit of the society.
78 Mertz-Gilmore Foundation is a New York-based private organization that promotes and supports health communities, human rights, sustainable environment, and performing arts.
79 Established in 1913, Rockefeller Foundation is a US-based philanthropic organization that funds intractable challenges faced worldwide.
80 The United States Agency for International Development is a US-based federal government organization that provides humanitarian and economic assistance across the world.
81 "Ultraviolet (UV) Waterworks," www.pi.energy.gov/documents/
    EWSLmexicoPhilippinesUVW.pdf.
82 Founded in March 1995, the US South Africa Binational Commission facilitates a bilateral cooperation between the US and South Africa to make sure that the key mutual concerns are discussed at the highest level of the government.
83 "UV Waterworks Field Installations," eetd.lbl.gov/iep/archive/uv/pdf/XBD9905-01059.
    pdf.

the water resources were heavily contaminated with arsenic. UVW systems could not remove arsenic from the water. The system provided water to nearly 2,000 people daily.[84]

In September 2008, WHI in association with IFC started a project to offer 50 UVW systems in Sri Lanka. As part of this project, WHI aimed to offer potable water to nearly 100,000 people affected by the Tsunami.[85,86] WHI utilized private and public resources to identify the needs of the local consumers, provide training to local operators and partners, and maintain the systems. Over time, WHI intended to scale up its operations in the country by moving to permanent locations and increasing the access to clean and safe drinking water.

WHI's water systems were also installed in countries such as Tanzania, El Salvador, Nepal, Tibet, Uganda, Haiti, Nicaragua, and the Honduras in different configurations.[87, 88]

Scaling Up

Many investors were attracted by the business model and ingenious technology adopted by WHI. This led to WHI scaling up significantly after it emerged from bankruptcy in 2002. It worked collaboratively with the local communities, government, and private sponsors to raise funds for installing the water purification systems in several places worldwide. Experts felt that the system could be easily scaled up to provide potable water to a broad range of population groups. The innovative UVW technology attracted several investors and this helped WHI in scaling up its business model.

The government provided support to WHI for setting up WHCs. In some countries, the government also provided funding.[89] The financing was offered through banks too in some countries. At a time when the global economic scenario was becoming grimmer, WHI was able to attract funds to fuel its expansion. In January 2007, (WHI) received funds of more than US$11 million in venture capital from

---

84 "UV Waterworks Field Installations," eetd.lbl.gov/iep/archive/uv/pdf/XBD9905-01059. pdf.

85 On December 26, 2004, an earthquake (measuring 9.3 on the Richter scale) in the Indian Ocean occurred off the coast of northwest Sumatra, Indonesia unleashed a tsunami that caused massive destruction and death across coastlines of Thailand, Indonesia, Sri Lanka, India, Maldives, and even distant Somalia.

86 "WaterHealth International Tsunami Relief Effort," www.waterhealth.com.

87 Patricia Sullivan, "Rx for H2O, in Two Parts," umassmag.com, Fall 2006.

88 "Global Water Solutions through Technology," www.calumet.purdue.edu, October 23, 2008.

89 "Drinking Water Treatment Becomes More Affordable with U.S. Help," www.america. gov, January 12, 2009.

Dow Venture Capital, ICICI Bank, SAIL Venture Partners, and Plebys.[90] In September 2007, WHI received loan guarantees of US$30 million from Dow Venture Capital to expand its operations in India.[91] Experts felt that the company would set up nearly 2,000 WHCs using these funds.[92]

In September 2008, IFC signed a mandate with WHI for an equity investment of US$25 million for WHIN. WHI planned to install CWSs in more than 2,000 villages, serving a population of 10 million rural consumers by the end of 2009.[93]

In January 2009, WHI received funding of US$10 million in venture capital from Dow Venture Capital to expand its operations globally.[94] This marked the first close of its Series D funding for scaling up its operations. According to Addy, "We are pleased by the confidence exhibited in WaterHealth by our current investors. As we move to rapidly expand the number of communities we serve and achieve unprecedented scale, access to capital is critical to our continuing success."[95]

In February 2009, WHI entered into an agreement with IFC to fund over 600 communities for the purchase of UVW systems over a period of 18 months. IFC offered a funding of US$15 million to serve over 3 million people in India.[96]

The funds helped WHI to scale up and, as of January 2009, the company had installed around 600 water systems in developing nations worldwide.[97] "Today, Water Health International serves over 350,000 paying customers in over 200 villages. And so we have a model that we know can be sustainable, that we know can scale and now we face a whole different set of choices around [...] supporting the company to help the government see if there are possibilities for outsourcing. Using it as a model for replication in other countries, in other areas, and using the company to scale itself,"[98] said Jacqueline Novogratz, founder and CEO of Acumen Fund. (Refer to Table II for number of WHC installations: 2005–2008.)

90 Lauren Abendschein, "Major Investments Open New Markets for Water Services," www.nextbillion.net, January 10, 2007.
91 "Sustainability Business Innovator Annual report 2008," www.ifc.org, September 2008.
92 "Dow & WHI to Provide Water Systems for 11 Million People in India," news.dow.com, October 2, 2007.
93 "Sustainability Business Innovator Annual Report 2008," www.ifc.org, September 2008.
94 "O.C. Clean-water Firm Gets $10 Million Investment," www.ocregister.com, January 19, 2009.
95 "WaterHealth International Announces First Close of Series D Funding," www.waterhealth.com, January 13, 2009.
96 "WaterHealth International Announces $15 Million Financing by IFC," www.reuters.com, February 16, 2009.
97 "WaterHealth Completes $10 m Series D Funding," www.financialexpress.com, January 16, 2009.
98 David Serchuk, "Debriefing Jacqueline Novogratz," www.forbes.com, May 5, 2009.

Table II **Number of WHC Installations: 2005–2008**

Source: WaterHealth International, Inc. (WaterHealth Ghana), Presentation at the AQUAYA Workshop in Nairobi Kenya 26th June 2009.

Year	New sites
2005	2
2006	>40
2007	>140
2008	>300

The Challenges

WHI had to negotiate various challenges over the years. Some of these still posed significant obstacles in the way of its achieving its mission. WHI's initial challenges lay in the cost of its UVW system since most of the communities targeted by WHI were under-served and lacked adequate capital to install the system. Moreover, a few villagers were unhappy that they had to pay for drinking water which, till then, had been free. It was also reported that several local residents still fetched water from contaminated resources despite the availability of potable water. "The old water is free,"[99] said Dhana Lakshmi, a local resident in a village in India. To tackle this problem, Addy partnered with several NGOs to educate villagers about the significance of drinking clean water. This also led Addy to advocate the use of a financing structure that required communities to make a 30 to 40 percent down payment while the rest of the amount was arranged as a loan by WHI.[100]

Critics also felt that the UVW systems were expensive. Verghese Jacob (Jacob), lead partner at the Byrraju Foundation,[101] which installs water purification systems in the villages of India, said that his plants cost less than that of WHI's and that they also charged less for water. Jacob added, "WaterHealth has good intentions, but unless they can bring the costs down, it's not really sustainable."[102] But Addy argued that the model adopted by Byrraju Foundation was not sustainable as it depended on subsidies. However, some of WHI's investors too believed that WHI's business

99 Peter Wonacott, "Behind One Effort to Tap into India's Water Market," online.wsj.com, August 14, 2007.

100 "WaterHealth Lands $10M for UV Water Purification," www.greentechmedia.com, January 14, 2009.

101 Founded in July 2001, by Satyam group of companies, Byrraju Foundation is a philanthropic organization.

102 Steve Hamm, "A For-Profit Brings Clean Water to the Poor," www.businessweek.com, November 25, 2008.

model was expensive. According to Brian Trelstad, chief investment officer for Acumen Fund, "The business model is still a little too expensive to be easily affordable for villages, but we think it will work long-term."[103]

In addition to the installation costs, experts contended that the system did not address risks associated with post-contamination. They said that there was no residual disinfectant in water that could address this challenge. Moreover, the UV lamps required electricity to operate the system, which was challenging since most of the rural communities had little or no access to electricity. The company addressed this concern in Ghana by including a solar panel with the WHCs. However, this option was not configured in WHCs in other countries.

Another significant challenge was that the UVW system was not suitable for brackish and saline water. Also, it could not purify arsenic and fluoride from water. However, the company said it was making efforts to address this issue. According to WHI, "WaterHealth is continually innovating, as well as evaluating, new technologies that will eventually enable us to reduce the salt content of brackish water in addition to disinfecting it."[104] As of 2009, Gadgil was leading the company's effort in this area.[105]

Outlook

By mid-2009, WHI was providing safe drinking water to more than one million people around the world. The company was successful in attracting capital for scaling up its operations despite the economic situation continuing to be grim.

Experts felt that WHI's efforts at providing potable water to the poor would significantly contribute to achieving the UN Millennium Development Goals (MDG) by 2015. They also noted that various organizations with different business models had come up to address the problem of providing safe water to needy communities (refer to Exhibit VIII for some business models adopted by organizations operating in the safe water sector). WHI contended that the BoP segment offered a lot of opportunities for competitors to tap the segment since it was estimated that there were nearly 2 billion people who lacked access to clean water. According to Addy, "We want to play a leadership role in delivering clean water, but the market opportunity is certainly large enough to accommodate a number of players."[106]

103 Steve Hamm, "A For-Profit Brings Clean Water to the Poor," www.businessweek.com, November 25, 2008.

104 www.waterhealth.com/water-crisis/faq.php.

105 "Global Water Solutions through Technology," www.calumet.purdue.edu, October 23, 2008.

106 "Go Green, Get Rich," money.cnn.com, April 4, 2007.

As of 2009, WHI was led by a professional management team with Sanjay Bhatnagar[107] as the CEO. Addy was a member of the board of directors while Gadgil acted as the scientific advisor to WHI (refer to Exhibit IX for WHI's management team and board of directors). The management team planned to expand WHI's reach globally. According to WHI, "WaterHealth plans to develop its business on a worldwide basis. Our choices for near-term market entry will be influenced by the areas of greatest need, where our business approach and market conditions will allow rapid deployment of our systems to make a meaningful impact on water-borne diseases on a sustainable basis. Beyond our current initiatives in India, the Philippines, and West Africa, we are evaluating needs and opportunities in other parts of the world, including the U.S., Latin America, and several Asian countries."[108] WHI was also designing a Home/Institutional system that would bring potable water to homes at affordable prices. Experts opined that such point of entry (POE) systems were suitable to institutions or homes that lacked a connection to a municipal water system. Furthermore, WHI was engaged in developing an Emergency Relief Unit (ERU) that had the ability to be deployed in any place across the world for supplying clean drinking water in cases of any emergencies or natural disasters.

Experts too felt that WHI should ramp up its presence since there was tremendous potential to be tapped in the safe-water sector. According to experts, in the estimated US$400 billion global water industry, billions of people remained underserved.[109] (Refer to Table III for the underserved rural population worldwide.)

Table III **Underserved Rural Population Worldwide**

Source: WaterHealth International, Inc. (WaterHealth Ghana), Presentation at the AQUAYA Workshop in Nairobi Kenya 26th June 2009

Country	Rural population (million)	Villages (approximately)
India	800	650,000
China	740	600,000
Africa	600	500,000
Rest of the World (excluding North America and Europe)	1,000	>750,000

107 Sanjay Bhatnagar is also the founder of the THOT Capital Group (TCG), a private equity firm based in New York. Prior to setting up TCG in January 2001, Sanjay was the CEO of Enron Broadband Services for the Middle East and Asia. He was also Chairman and CEO, Enron South Asia. Before this, he worked for Schlumberger as an engineer and manager in several countries worldwide.

108 www.waterhealth.com/water-crisis/faq.php.

109 "WaterHealth International, Inc. (WaterHealth Ghana)," www.scribd.com/doc/53231816/Mawunyo-Puplampu, June 26, 2009.

Experts opined that WHI, with its unique offering and business model, was well placed to take advantage of the opportunities before it. However, they also pointed out that the road ahead would not be easy. Part of the challenge was to further improve its offering to make it more relevant to the target segment and also make them realize that spending a small amount of money for such a vital resource was well worth the investment. Obtaining the capital to help more communities finance these water systems, so as to ultimately achieve significant scale relative to the magnitude of the problem, was another challenge.

References and Suggested Readings

"WaterHealth International, Inc. (WaterHealth Ghana)," www.scribd.com/doc/53231816/ Mawunyo-Puplampu, June 26, 2009.
David Serchuk, "Debriefing Jacqueline Novogratz," www.forbes.com, May 5, 2009.
"WaterHealth International Announces $15 Million Financing by IFC," www.reuters.com, February 16, 2009.
"O.C. Clean-water Firm Gets $10 Million Investment," www.ocregister.com, January 19, 2009.
"WaterHealth Completes $10 m Series D Funding," www.financialexpress.com, January 16, 2009.
"WaterHealth Lands $10M for UV Water Purification," www.greentechmedia.com, January 14, 2009.
"WaterHealth International Announces First Close of Series D Funding," www.waterhealth. com, January 13, 2009.
"Drinking Water Treatment Becomes More Affordable with U.S. Help," www.america.gov, January 12, 2009.
"WaterHealth International, Inc. (WHI) Today Announced ICICI Bank's Funding Commitment for WHI's Development of Community Water Facilities in Rural India," www. politicalfriendster.com , December 12, 2008.
Steve Hamm, "A For-Profit Brings Clean Water to the Poor," www.businessweek.com, November 25, 2008.
"Global Water Solutions through Technology," www.calumet.purdue.edu, October 23, 2008.
"Sustainability Business Innovator Annual Report 2008," www.ifc.org, September 2008.
"First WaterHealth Centre Inaugurated in Afuaman," www.waterhealth.com, December 12, 2007.
Nitasha Tiku, "Do-Good Capitalist of the Year," www.inc.com, December 2007.
"The Why Files," whyfiles.org, November 15, 2007.
Achintya Madduri, "Water Water Everywhere?" floatingsun.net, November 3, 2007.
"Dow & WHI to Provide Water Systems for 11 Million People in India," news.dow.com, October 2, 2007.
Peter Wonacott, "Behind One Effort to Tap into India's Water Market," online.wsj.com, August 14, 2007.
"WaterHealth Announces More than 100 WaterHealth Centres in Andhra Pradesh," www. waterhealth.com, July 21, 2007.
"WaterHealth," www.whatsbubbling.com, June 12, 2007.

Colin Stewart, "Changing the World, One Gallon at a Time," www.ocregister.com, May 24, 2007.

"Go Green, Get Rich," money.cnn.com, April 4, 2007.

"WaterHealth International Announces the Launch of the Blue Revolution," www.indiaprwire. com, February 9, 2007.

Lauren Abendschein, "Major Investments Open New Markets for Water Services," www. nextbillion.net, January 10, 2007.

"Global Philanthropy 2007 Year in Review," www.zicklincenter.org, 2007.

"Mobilizing Science-Based Enterprises for Energy, Water, and Medicines in Nigeria (2007)," books.nap.edu, 2007.

"ICICI Bank Funds WaterHealth International's India Initiative," www.waterhealth.com, October 10, 2006.

Patricia Sullivan, "Rx for H2O, in Two Parts," umassmag.com, Fall 2006.

Ashok Gadgil, "The Rosenfeld Effect," www.energy.ca.gov, April 29, 2006.

"Water Health International: Water Supply Franchising," timbuktuchronicles.blogspot.com, March 12, 2006.

David Pescovitz, "Community Water Works," www.coe.berkeley.edu, April 1, 2005.

"WaterHealth International Receives New Funding Totaling $1.8 Million," www.allbusiness. com, November 22, 2004.

"Researchers Help Bring Clean Water to Households in Developing Nations," www. universityofcalifornia.edu, February 6, 2003.

Martha Davidson, "Innovative Lives," invention.smithsonian.org, February 26, 1999.

Suzanne Snell, "Water and Sanitation Services for the Urban Poor," waterwiki.net, December 1998.

Ashok Gadgil, "UV Waterworks: Reliable, Inexpensive Water Disinfection for the World," eetdnews.lbl.gov, 1996.

Carol Kolb deWilde, Anita Milman, Yvonne Flores, Jorge Salmerón, and Isha Ray, "An Integrated Method for Evaluating Community-based Safe Water Programmes and an Application in Rural Mexico," heapol.oxfordjournals.org/cgi/content/abstract/czn01.

International Finance Corporation, "Safe Water for All: Harnessing the Private Sector to Reach the Underserved," www.ifc.org/ifcext/sustainability.nsf/Content/ Publications_Report_SafeWaterforAll.

Nachiket Mor, D Chattanathan, and Rajiv Panthary, "Enhancing the Flow of Credit and Managing Risks in Agriculture," www.icrier.org/pdf/mor%20paper.pdf.

"Peter Hamilton: Interview—Plebys," www.e-clips.cornell.edu.

"Statistics Illustrate the Challenge of Clean Water Access around the World," www.waterhealth. com/water-crisis/statistics.php.

"Success Stories: Start-Ups—WaterHealth International Inc.," www.lbl.gov/tt/success_sto- ries/articles/WHI_more.html.

"The Village of Bomminampadu is a Clean-water Pioneer," www.waterhealth.com/world- wide-operations/study1.php.

"Ultraviolet (UV) Waterworks," www.pi.energy.gov/documents/EWSLmexicoPhilippine- sUVW.pdf.

"UV Waterworks Field Installations," eetd.lbl.gov/iep/archive/uv/pdf/XBD9905-01059.pdf.

"Ventures WaterHealth International," www.plebys.com/ventures/waterhealth.htm.

"WaterHealth Ghana," www.waterhealth.com/worldwide-operations/ghana.php.

"WaterHealth India," www.waterhealth.com.

"WaterHealth International Tsunami Relief Effort," www.waterhealth.com.

floatingsun.net/udai/files/Water%20Water%20Everywhere.ppt
www.intwot.org
www.lbl.gov/tt/success_stories/articles/WHI_more.html
www.nsf.gov
www.waterhealth.com
www.zoominfo.com

Teaching notes for this case are available from Greenleaf Publishing. These are free of charge and are available only to teaching staff. They can be requested by going to:

www.greenleaf-publishing.com/oikos2_notes

Exhibit I WHI's Vision and Values

Source: www.waterhealth.com/company/vision.php

The WaterHealth Vision

- To be a part of a focused, long-term solution to the global water crisis.
- To find sustainable and affordable ways to provide safe water to the underserved, worldwide.
- To inspire business success and innovation, with a core social purpose.

Commitment to the Environment

WaterHealth is committed not only to reach safe water to the underserved but also to recharge and replenish the global water table in a mission to return to the environment what humankind is taking from it. We provide solutions that minimize negative impact on the environment and see a greater role today and in our future in the sphere of green economics.

Commitment to Human Health

Products and services from WaterHealth stem from a powerful sense of concern about the impact of unsafe water on human life. We believe that those deprived of safe water are deprived in the truest sense of the term and we are guided by a commitment to these millions of underserved, everywhere. We constantly innovate to seek out solutions that can be afforded by even the underserved poor.

Commitment to the Future

The future is a fundamental raison d'être for us at WaterHealth. We bank on our uncompromising ethical considerations above all else and this, with our constant endeavors to define new standards in quality, makes us a sustainable, future ready business ecosystem. A thriving force that inspires and empowers our employees, beneficiaries and all stakeholders.

Exhibit II **How the UVW Technology Worked**

Compiled from various sources.

The UVW technology included a UV disinfection system that delivered UV light for inactivating microorganisms by disrupting their DNA. The small-scale, energy-efficient, and low-maintenance design of the UVW unit was a uniquely affordable and effective device. It operated using the equivalent of a 60-Watt light bulb at a cost of 4–5 cents per ton of water to provide drinking water to 2,000 people. The flow of water into the UV chamber was powered by gravitational force. It purified 15 liters of water per minute. It deactivated 99.995 percent of the microbial contaminants with the help of a germicidal UV lamp which employed a UV dosage of 120 mJ/cm^2, disabling the DNA of the micro-organisms in the water. This UV dosage was three times higher than the 40 mJ/cm^2 prescribed by the Environmental Protection Agency[b] (EPA) and the National Science Foundation[c] (NSF). This very high safety margin ensured that communities had an adequate amount of purified drinking water even when their only drinking water source was one which was highly contaminated.

The UVW unit required very little maintenance and was designed in such a way that in case of any malfunction, an electrical valve would shut down the entry port to the device, so that water did not enter it.

WHI tested its UVW technology in third-party laboratories in order to know its efficacy across several viruses, bacteria, and parasites causing water-borne diseases. It received certification from the State of California as a 'Class A device'. It also received validation in South Africa, the Philippines, Mexico, and India.[d] Experts felt that the UVW system was an absolute water disinfection system that removed bad taste, odors, and silt in addition to killing microorganisms causing waterborne diseases. The water purified through this technology exceeded the WHO standards of potable water.

WHI's UVW technology differed from conventional UV systems, ozonation, reverse osmosis, and chlorination. The benefits of the technology included high efficacy combined with high throughput, a small footprint, and long-term reliability. The modular design meant that systems could be scaled to serve communities of various sizes. Non-proprietary components that were coupled with UVW in WHI's installations were readily available in most parts of the world. Ease-of-use and low maintenance requirements meant that the systems could be deployed even in the most remote locations. It released no by-products, no toxic waste, and no water waste. Moreover, it was robust and long-lasting (refer to Table for a comparison between WHI and other technologies for water purification). WHI's water purification system had a modular design that had the ability to scale itself depending upon the need to serve the communities (refer to Figure for a diagram of WHI's UVW system).

Table **WHI and Other Technologies for Water Purification**

Factor	WHI Technology	Conventional UV	Reverse Osmosis	Ozonation	Chlorine
Suitable for treating bacteria & viruses	Yes	Yes (if sufficient UV dose)	No (if low-pressure household unit)	Yes	Yes
Suitable for treating cysts	Yes	Yes (if sufficient UV dose)	Yes	Yes	No
Cost/performance ratio	Low	High	High	High	High
Operations & maintenance needs	Low	High	High	High	High
Energy use	Very Low	Low	High	High	Very Low
Inventory, storage & transport needs	Low	Low	Low	Low	High
Overdose risk	No	No	No	No	Yes
Harmful by-products in water	No	No	No	No (unless bromide is present)	Yes
Requires Pressurized System	No (unless pumps are required)	Yes	Yes	No	No

The UVW system had several applications. It could source surface water from lakes, ponds, rivers, and could also access groundwater resources. WHI was also developing solutions which could remove arsenic and fluoride from water.

Figure **WHI's UVW System**

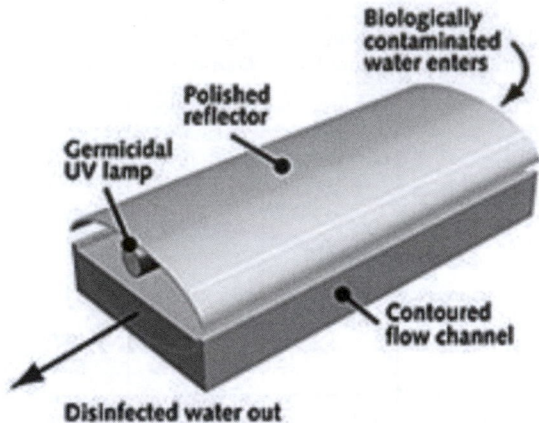

a   www.lbl.gov/tt/success_stories/articles/WHI_more.html.
b   Headquartered in Washington, the Environmental Protection Agency is set up to protect the environment and human health.
c   Founded in 1950 by the US Congress, the National Science Foundation is a federal agency set up "to promote the progress of science; to advance the national health, prosperity, and welfare; to secure the national defense …" (Source: www.nsf.gov).
d   "Frequently Asked Questions," www.waterhealth.com.

Exhibit III A Typical System Configuration of a WHI System

Source: WaterHealth International, Inc. (WaterHealth Ghana) Presentation at the AQUAYA Workshop in Nairobi Kenya 26th June 2009.

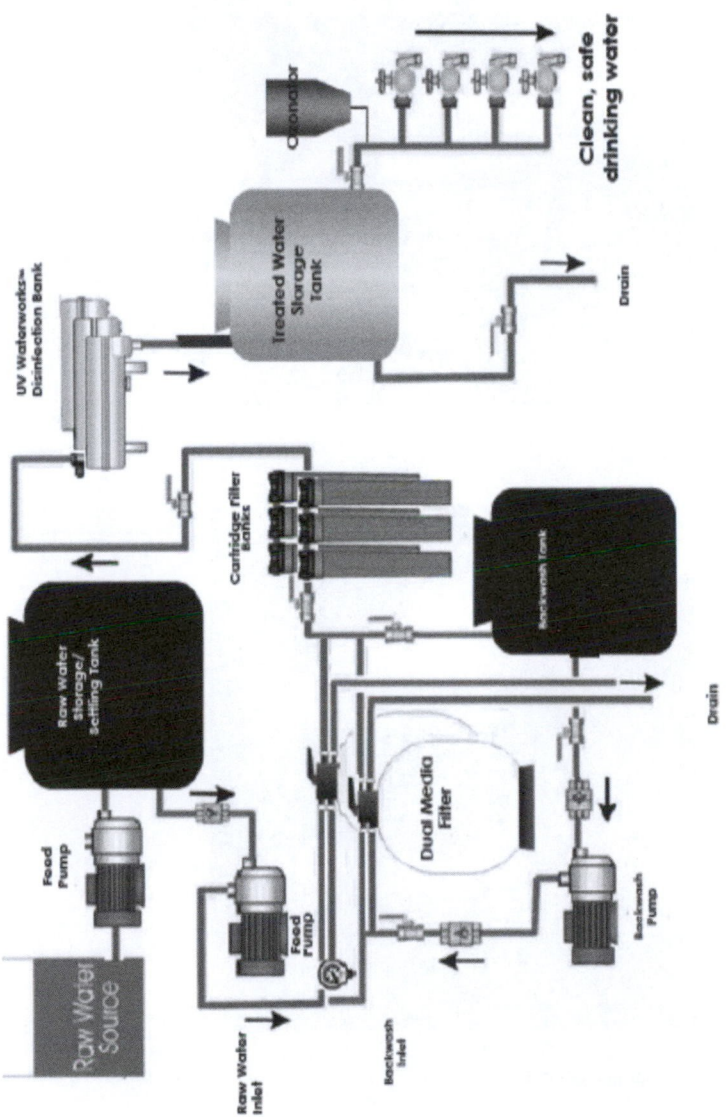

Exhibit IV **Photographs of WHCs**

Source: floatingsun.net/udai/files/Water%20Water%20Everywhere.ppt.

A WaterHealth Center in AP, India

A WaterHealth Center in Amasaman, Ghana

Exhibit V   WHI's Investment Cost Advantage vs. Other Options

Source: "Global Water Solutions through Technology," www.calumet.purdue.edu, October 23, 2008.

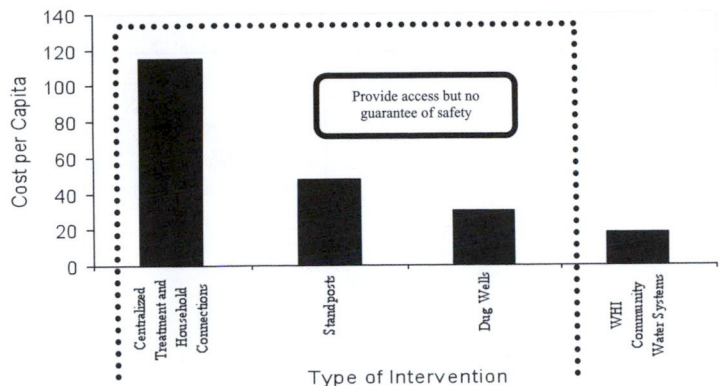

Exhibit VI **List of Awards and Recognition Received by Gadgil and his UVW Technology**

Compiled from various sources.

1996	UVW technology was named as the 'Best of What's New' by *Popular Science* magazine.
	Gadgil received an award for technology innovation by *Discover Magazine*.
1997	UVW technology listed in US News and World Report's '20 Ways to Save the World'.
1999	*Discover Magazine* honored the UVW invention as 'Best of the Decade'
2004	Gadgil received the Tech Museum Awards Laureate for inventing a new technology for the benefit of mankind.
	Gadgil received the Affymatrix Health Award as part of Tech Museum Awards.
2005	Gadgil was named Trendsetters and Heroes of Public Works by *Public Works Magazine*.
2006	Gadgil was included in the 'Modern-day da Vincis' list by the Chicago-based, Museum of Science and Industry.
2007	WHI listed in the 'Ten to Watch' list of 'The Clean Tech Revolution', a Harper Collins Publication book.
2007	Business 2.0 profiled WHI in an article titled 'Saving the planet has suddenly become good business'
2007	Toshiba Green Innovation Award by Toshiba America Inc.[a] and Orange County Innovation[b] (OCI)
2007	Listed in Clean Tech Revolution's 'Ten to Watch'

a Toshiba America Inc. is one of the leading manufacturers of electronic and electrical products.

b Orange County Innovation is an association of service, academic, and business leaders devoted to promote the OCI as an innovation powerhouse.

Exhibit VII **WHI Operational Structure in India**

Source: Nachiket Mor, D. Chattanathan and Rajiv Panthary, "Enhancing the Flow of Credit and Managing Risks in Agriculture," www.icrier.org/pdf/mor%20paper.pdf.

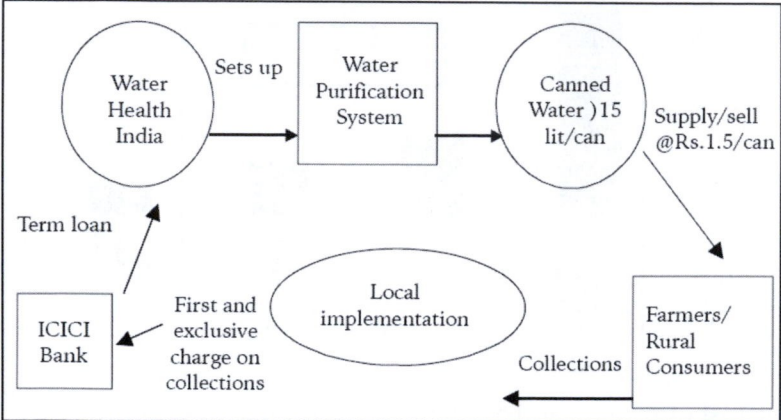

Exhibit VIII **Some Business Models Adopted by Organizations Operating in the Safe Water Sector**

Source: International Finance Corporation, "Safe Water for All: Harnessing the Private Sector to Reach the Underserved," www.ifc.org/ifcext/sustainability.nsf/Content/Publications_Report_SafeWaterforAll

Business Model	Definition	Examples	Key Risks
Earned income—unit sales	Revenue from volume or unit sales of product	Hindustan-Unilever Packaged-water vendors (such as those found in Ghana, the Philippines, and Indonesia)	Creating aspirational demand through branding, pull-marketing; competition from knock-offs; rural distribution
Earned income—advertising and leasing revenue	Revenue from sale of advertising space and easing of retail space	Iko-toilet	Maintaining high visibility of facilities
Earned income—microfinance	Deferred payment for product	Safe Water and AIDS Project ACCESS AED/POUZN	Transaction costs; interest rates; long payback period; MFIs' capacity and reputation; credit default
Earned income—franchising	Income from licensing branded water-vending service	Odanthurai Packaged Drinking Water Federation IKOtoilet	Maintaining consistent quality and execution among franchisees
Earned income—blended	Fees from products and services	IKOtoilet WaterHealth International	Maintaining adequate revenue mix
Contributed income	Indirect beneficiary (e.g., government or NGO) pays for product or service	Vestergaard-Frandsen	Donor dependence; competing technologies
Hybrid blended income	Earned and contributed income sources	International Development Enterprises Population Services International NAANDI Foundation	Donor dependence; market distortion from subsidies; balancing cash flows from different sources; maintaining sustainable ratio of donor versus market revenue sources

Exhibit IX WHI's Management Team and Board of Directors

Source: www.waterhealth.com

Management Team

- Sanjay Bhatnagar: Chief Executive Officer, Global
- Vikas Shah: Chief Operating Officer, WaterHealth India
- Ranabir Dutt: Chief Financial Officer—Global
- Thomas Weil: General Counsel
- Andrew L. Lux: Vice President, Worldwide Operations and R&D
- Mawunyo Puplampu: General Manager, WaterHealth Ghana
- Donaldo I. Palomar: General Manager, WaterHealth Philippines

Board of Directors

- F. Henry Habicht II, (Managing Partner of SAIL Venture Partners)
- Dennis Merens, (Director of Corporate Venture Capital)
- Richard C. Nell (a J&J Veteran)
- Sanjay Bhatnagar
- Tralance Addy

Part V
Scaling, Legitimacy and Profit Challenges for Mission-Driven Organizations

Case 12

Business Model Innovation by Better Place

A Green Ecosystem for the Mass Adoption of Electric Cars[1, 2, 3]

Ramalingam Meenakshisundaram and Besta Shankar
IBS Center for Management Research, Hyderabad, India

> After a century of being joined at the hip, the car industry and the oil industry are headed for a divorce. Cars are about to leave behind the dirty fuel—in this case, gasoline—that has powered them. It's going to have dramatic consequences throughout the energy and car industries.[4]
>
> Vijay Vaitheeswaran, Correspondent at *The Economist* and co-author of *Zoom: The Global Race to Fuel the Car of the Future*

2 This case was written by Besta Shankar, under the direction of Ramalingam Meenakshisundaram, IBS Center for Management Research. It was compiled from generalized experience, and is intended to be used as a basis for class discussion rather than to illustrate either effective or ineffective handling of a management situation.
3 This case won the third prize in the oikos Global Writing Competition 2010 (Corporate Sustainability Track), organized by oikos Foundation for Economy and Ecology, University of St. Gallen, Switzerland.
4 Francesca Di Meglio, "Eyeing a Future of New-Fuel Cars," www.businessweek.com, October 4, 2007.

It's a subscription system much like cellular providers have. You sign up for a certain number of miles a month.[5]

Shai Agassi, Founder and CEO of Better Place

It makes so much sense from the environmental point of view as well as the business point of view.[6]

Idan Ofer, Chairman of Israel Corp[7] and Board Chairman of Better Place

When I first heard about it, I thought it was just another crazy idea. It sounded far-fetched. Then I sat down and listened, and it just might make sense … [However] Change doesn't happen quickly in the auto sector.[8]

Stephen Girsky, Managing Director, Centerbridge Partners[9]

Introduction

Better Place, formerly Project Better Place, a start-up company founded in October 2007 in Palo Alto, California, in the US, was a winner of the 2009 AMR Research Sustainable Leadership Award for Clean Technology.[10] According to *Wired* magazine,[11] Better Place was the fifth largest start-up in the history of business ventures till March 2009.[12] Shai Agassi (Agassi), the company's founder and CEO, was ranked

---

5 Chuck Squatriglia, "Shai Agassi Wants to Sell Electric Cars Like Cell Phones," www.wired.com, October 30, 2007
6 Steve Hamm, "$200 Million for Electric Cars?" www.businessweek.com, October 29, 2007.
7 Israel Corp, the largest holding company in Israel, has diversified interests—in fertilizers and specialty chemicals, energy, shipping, and transportation. It derives 70 percent of its revenues from international trade. Source: www.israelcorp.com, accessed June 1, 2009.
8 Steve Hamm, "$200 Million for Electric Cars?" www.businessweek.com, October 29, 2007.
9 Centerbridge Partners, New York, founded in the year 2006, is one of the leading private equity firms in North America. It makes investments mostly in North America-based companies. Source: investing.businessweek.com, accessed June 1, 2009.
10 This award recognized companies that are "trailblazers in clean technology development including alternative energy, clean tech market service provision, grid delivery systems, smart technology and information, energy storage devices and platforms, and other enabling technologies." Source: "Dell, HP, Better Place, Tririga Earn Sustainability Awards," www.environmentalleader.com, May 29, 2009.
11 *Wired* is a monthly magazine in English published from San Francisco. It covers topics related to business, lifestyle, and leadership. Source: www.wired.com
12 Rachel Pulfer, "Venture Capital: A Modern Midas," www.canadianbusiness.com, March 16, 2009.

third in the list of '100 Most Creative People 2009'[13] prepared by Fast Company,[14] New York. He was also included in the '2009 Scientific American 10', a list of 10 people selected by the *Scientific American* magazine[15] for their endeavors to ensure that technological evolution contributed to the betterment of society.[16]

Agassi, who resigned from SAP AG[17] as the President of its Products and Technology Group in March 2007, started Better Place with the ambition of setting up an ecosystem—including a 'smart grid' of charging stations and battery swapping facilities—for electric vehicles. These charging stations were to be powered by electricity generated from renewable sources such as solar energy and wind energy. Consumers could swap their batteries at the swapping facilities in less time than it would take to fill a car's fuel tank with gasoline (gas) at a conventional gas station. Such a grid was expected to encourage widespread adoption of electric vehicles, reduce the dependence on fossil fuels,[18] and contain the levels of environmental pollution.

Better Place intended to become "the premier global provider of electric vehicle services, accelerating the transition to sustainable transportation."[19] Agassi took a cue from the business model of the telecom industry where consumers could choose a subscription plan with a certain number of minutes per month, with the handset cost being subsidized based on the tenure of the plan to which the consumer had committed himself/herself. Better Place's innovative business model proposed to offer transportation services to consumers through miles per month subscription plans, with the cost of the electric car being subsidized based on the tenure of the plan.

13 www.fastcompany.com.
14 *Fast Company* is a US-based business magazine (10 issues per year) in English covering areas such as innovation, digital media, technology, leadership, design, and social responsibility of the companies. It is known for reporting on individuals who come out with creative ideas in the marketplace. Source: www.fastcompany.com, accessed June 3, 2009.
15 *Scientific American* magazine is published from New York. The magazine, which was started in August 1845, is one of the oldest publications in the US. It reports on innovations in research. Source: www.scientificamerican.com.
16 "Scientific American 10: Guiding Science for Humanity," www.scientificamerican.com, June 2009.
17 SAP AG, headquartered in Walldorf, Germany, is one of the world's leading software services companies and has a focus on Enterprise Resource Planning (ERP) software products. It earned revenues of €11.58 billion for the financial year 2008 and had a customer base of over 82,000 spread across in more than 120 countries. Source: www.sap.com, accessed June 2, 2009.
18 Coal, oil, and natural gas, found in the top layer of the earth's crust, are known as fossil fuels. These fossil fuels are formed by the decomposition of animal and plant remains buried over million years ago. Fossil fuels are not renewable energy sources as they cannot be replenished once they have been used. Source: www.nripc.org.
19 "Fifty Best Tech Start-ups: The Next Google?" www.businessweek.com.

By June 2009, nations such as Israel, Australia, Denmark, Japan, and some states of the United States and Canada had taken initiatives to provide a favorable regulatory environment for electric vehicles and partner with the company to build the required infrastructure.

Background

Automobiles contributed to a significant share of the global demand for fossil fuels (refer to Exhibit I for the increasing share of the transportation sector in global oil consumption). The internal combustion engines (ICE)[20] in the vehicles made use of gasoline or diesel, which were derived from petroleum. Overdependence on the finite reserves of fossil fuels forced many nations to explore ways to increase the fuel efficiency of automobiles and also to find alternatives to fossil fuel.

Further, there was a growing concern over the harmful emissions caused by burning fossil fuels for transportation. According to the International Energy Outlook 2009 released by Energy Information Administration (EIA)[21] of the US Government, worldwide carbon dioxide (CO_2)[22] emissions from the combustion of various fossil fuels such as coal, oil, and natural gas were expected to exceed 40 billion metric tons by 2030 (refer to Exhibit II for the projected trend in worldwide emissions of carbon dioxide from 2006 to 2030).

The large-scale adoption of electric vehicles for transportation, especially in the passenger vehicles segment (cars and utility vehicles), was seen as a way to reduce the dependence on fossil fuels. Electric vehicles were both fuel-efficient and environment-friendly to run. Automakers had come up with several innovations such as hybrid electric cars, plug-in hybrid electric cars, and pure electric cars (refer to Table I for an overview of these three types of electric cars).

20 Internal combustion engines are engines in which the combustion of fuel (like gasoline) produces high energy. This energy is used to run the components such as pistons, which in turn, generate the required mechanical energy to move vehicles such as cars and scooters. Source: www.howstuffworks.com.
21 Energy Information Administration (EIA), Washington, D.C., is an independent statistical organization under US Department of Energy providing data and forecasts on energy related matters. It was established in 1977 by the US Government to assist policy making regarding the economy and environment. Source: www.eia.doe.gov, accessed June 2, 2009.
22 Fossil fuels are hydrocarbons; on combustion of hydrocarbons, CO_2 is a main product. It is one of the greenhouse gases that trap heat in the atmosphere. Greenhouse gases are responsible for global warming, leading to an increase in the average temperature of the earth.

Table I **Hybrid, Plug-in Hybrid, and Pure Electric Cars**

Compiled from www.fueleconomy.gov, www.thegreencarwebsite.co.uk, www.herelectricvehicle.com, www.projectgetready.com, and www.wikipedia.org.

Type	Description	Examples
Hybrid electric	Hybrid cars possess internal combustion engines (ICE) and a rechargeable energy storage system. Hybrid cars use most of the power from the ICEs and electric motors provide additional power when needed. The energy storage system is recharged automatically by the engines (when the load is low) and from regenerative braking.	Honda Insight Toyota Prius
Plug-in hybrid electric	Plug-in hybrid cars have internal combustion engines and electric batteries. Battery power is used instead of ICEs at low speeds at which ICEs are less efficient. The batteries can be recharged from an external power source.	BYD Auto's F3DM (China)
Pure electric (battery electric)	Pure electric cars do not contain internal combustion engines but run solely on the power from the rechargeable batteries. They are environmentally friendly vehicles which do not produce harmful emissions or heavy noise.	Tesla Roadster (USA) Th!nk City (Norway) Reva (India) BMW Mini-E

Although hybrid electric vehicles and plug-in hybrid electric vehicles made use of the energy storage system or battery, they could contribute only to a limited extent to the twin objectives of reducing dependency on fossil fuels as well as eliminating emissions from fossil fuel combustion in automobiles. However, pure electric vehicles that were powered solely by the battery could contribute to a great extent to the achievement of these twin objectives. In some countries, the government started subsidizing the purchase of electric cars. Countries like Israel, which were greatly concerned with energy security[23] issues, realized the potential of the electric cars and initiated measures to increase the percentage of such vehicles on the road.

Although electric cars proved to be fuel-efficient and environment-friendly, they had some limitations from the consumer perspective (refer to Table II for the advantages and disadvantages of electric cars).

23 National governments are concerned about gaining uninterrupted access to energy sources to meet their current and future energy requirements for sustained economic growth and development. When a nation is able to meet all its energy requirements without importing energy or energy sources, it is said to be energy independent.

Table II **Advantages and Disadvantages of Electric Cars**

Adapted from "How Better Place Plans to Revive the Electric Car," www.cnet.com.au, February 11, 2009; and other sources.

Advantages	Disadvantages
• Zero direct emissions of greenhouse gases (However, electric vehicles contribute to indirect emission of greenhouse gases, if the batteries are charged by electricity generated from fossil fuels) • High energy efficiency when compared to vehicles run on petrol or gasoline. • Very low noise emission while operating	• Limited driving range (about 100 km to 160 km) per charge • Time consuming to recharge the batteries, in the range of 4 hours to 8 hours • Absence of a widespread network of charging stations at convenient locations in the city and along highways • Expensive to replace the batteries; increased total cost of ownership. An electric car (including the battery) was expected to cost about US$50,000 in the US, while a comparable fossil-fuel based car was priced at less than US$20,000. • Low speed limit when compared to automobiles with internal combustion engines.

These limitations hindered the mass adoption of electric cars globally. In earlier electric cars, lead batteries were used and the disposal of depleted batteries posed an environmental hazard. The adoption of lithium-ion[24] batteries addressed this concern to some extent; it also improved the driving range per charge and the lifetime of the batteries. However, the inconvenience of long-distance travel, the time taken to recharge the batteries, and the absence of a widespread network of charging stations continued to inhibit the growth in demand for electric cars.

Better Place's Business Model

The aim of Agassi's innovative ecosystem for electric cars was to facilitate mass adoption of this cleaner technology by consumers by making it more affordable and convenient to own as well as operate an electric car. In this disruptive business model, consumers could sign up with Better Place for subscription plans under which they had to use a certain number of miles a month for a certain number of years. In turn, they received an electric car on lease. And in cases where the consumer signed up for a long-term subscription plan such as for six years, the

---

24 Batteries made from lithium (Li), a light and highly reactive metal, which were mostly used to power cell phones, laptops, etc. They possess high energy density, more rechargeable cycles, and long life; and they lose charge slowly when not in use. Due to the above features, they were regarded as a suitable choice for electric cars.

company was even ready to give a free car. The cars were provided with lithium ion batteries which were believed to be the best in battery technology available for electric vehicles when Better Place commenced operations.

The unique selling proposition of this scheme was that the consumer could choose to either charge the batteries at a vast network of charging stations at convenient locations or simply swap the drained batteries for new ones at designated battery swapping facilities. Moreover, each car was equipped with a global positioning system (GPS) device for determining the geographical location and intelligent software that could alert the driver as to the level of battery charge, the estimated distance that the car could travel with the available charge, and the locations of nearby charging stations and swapping facilities in the Better Place grid. As a result, a Better Place consumer could enjoy the advantages of electric cars but not suffer from the associated limitations. Commenting on the technology that enabled this innovative ecosystem, Evan Thornley, Head for Better Place in Australia, said "What it means for the world is there is now a viable technology for mass adoption of electric vehicles (EVs)."[25]

By using renewable energy sources to power the charging stations wherever possible, Better Place attempted to eliminate even the indirect emissions of greenhouse gases due to the operation of electric cars. Thus the Better Place ecosystem for electric cars was positioned as not only consumer-friendly but also environment-friendly, making the world a truly 'better place' to live in. However, it required a high level of start-up capital for building the infrastructure for the smart grid. Agassi raised US$200 million[26] initially for this new venture by convincing investors about the viability of the business model and its contribution to environmental sustainability: Israel Corp invested US$100 million while the remaining amount was contributed by multiple investors including VantagePoint Venture Partners,[27] a leading investment firm in cleaner technology.[28]

Better Place entered into alliances with electric car manufacturers, battery manufacturers, and renewable energy producers. Such alliances were seen as win–win opportunities for all the concerned entities. Steve Howard, CEO, The Climate Group,[29] said, "This project will bring electric vehicles to life in a truly low carbon

25 Peter Alford, "'Cars all electric in 20 years': Evan Thornley," www.theaustralian.news.com. au, May 13, 2009.

26 Steve Hamm, "$200 Million for Electric Cars?" www.businessweek.com, October 29, 2007.

27 Vantage Point, based in California, is one of the leading US venture firms that make investments in the sectors of clean technology, information technology, and healthcare with a special focus on Asia. As of June 2009, it had capital amounting to US$4.5 billion. Source: www.vpvp.com, accessed June 3, 2009.

28 "Venture Fund Bets Billion on Cleantech," www.thestar.com, December 1, 2008.

29 The Climate Group is a not-for-profit organization that works internationally to find solutions to the climate change. It is headquartered in the UK and has offices in the US, Europe, Australia, China, Hong Kong, and India with a membership of over 50 that

Figure IA **The Better Place Business Model and the Consumer**

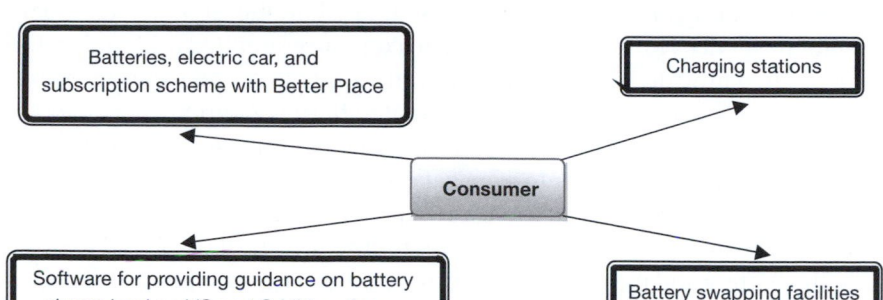

way. It will demonstrate how the electric vehicle and renewable energy industries can act in synergy to strengthen the economic argument for both."[30]

It also partnered with governments, parking lot operators, and companies to install charging stations. Commenting on the innovative business model of his company, Agassi said "Existing technology, coupled with the right business model and a scalable infrastructure can provide an immediate solution and significantly decrease carbon emissions."[31]

Figure IB **The Better Place Business Model and the Alliances**

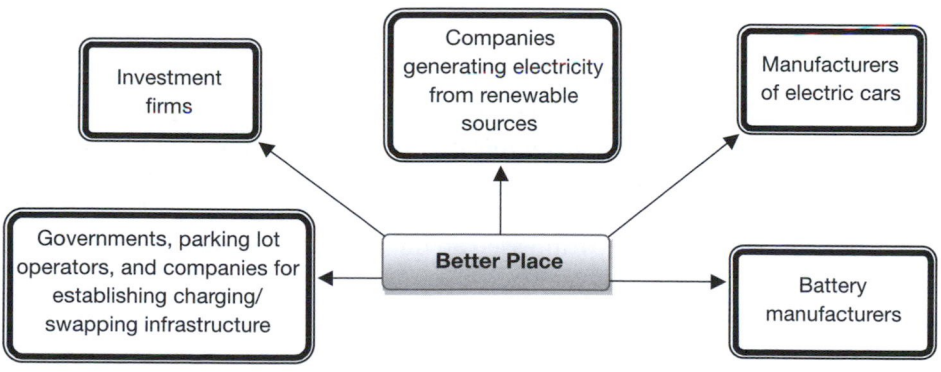

includes companies, governments, and other regional organizations. Source: www. theclimategroup.org, accessed June 1, 2009.

30 www.betterplace.com.
31 Karin Kloosterman, "Making Electric Cars Sell Like Cell Phones," www.treehugger.com, November 23, 2007.

The Smart Grid

Better Place's network consisted of integrated charging stations and battery replacement services for its subscribers. The company supplied lithium ion-based batteries which provided extended life time and long range and were environmentally safe. Better Place claimed that its automated battery swapping facilities could replace depleted batteries with charged batteries within three minutes and that there was no need for the driver to even get out of the car.

The software used in the electric cars, which was designed and developed by Better Place, ensured complete information for the drivers. It displayed the energy level in the battery and the nearest battery recharging and swapping facilities available. It calculated the distance traveled by the cars for which they were charged by the company. It also had a provision for the drivers to handle their parking and charging spots conveniently, and was able to book the charging spot in advance.[32] Customers needed to pay for the electricity consumed at the existing commercial rates. Better Place claimed that cost per unit distance traveled by its electric cars would be just $1/7$th of the cost for vehicles powered by ICEs.[33]

Global Presence

A favorable regulatory environment was a pre-requisite for this business model to be successful in any geographic region. This could be in terms of funds for setting up the smart grid, tax incentives to the various partners in the Better Place ecosystem, and tax incentives to consumers who subscribed to the electric car transportation services of Better Place. The company entered into agreements with two densely populated but small countries—Israel and Denmark, and a sparsely populated big country—Australia. The states of California and Hawaii in the USA, and the province of Ontario in Canada took the initiative in this regard within their respective countries. Japan too expressed an interest in the unique business model proposed by Better Place.

Better Place in Israel

Although situated in the Middle East region, Israel was poor country in terms of oil reserves and depended heavily on oil imports for its energy requirements. Due to its political enmity with a few countries, it faced oil supply ban from those coun-

---

32 "Electric Cars Make for a Better Place," www.roadtraffic-technology.com, December 19, 2008.

33 Derek Fung, "How Better Place Plans to Revive the Electric Car," www.cnet.com.au, February 11, 2009.

tries. Israel had a vision of becoming energy independent by 2020 by reducing its oil dependency to zero.

As of 2008, nearly 90 percent of the car users in Israel drove about 45 miles a day.[34] Also, the average distance between urban centers in Israel was less than 100 miles, making it easier to establish a nationwide smart grid. With effect from August 1, 209, the government gave tax exemptions and subsidies for the purchase of electric cars, and increased the import duties on fossil fuel-based cars.

In December 2008, Israel agreed to partner with Better Place to build the charging network. It was estimated that the Better Place business model would bring down the average monthly fuel expenditure for an Israeli from US$250 per month to US$80 per year.[35] Israel generated a vast amount of renewable energy from solar power which could be utilized to feed the smart grid.

Better Place planned to have 100,000 electric cars on Israel's roads by 2011. It partnered with the Renault–Nissan alliance[36] to market the electric cars in Israel once the infrastructure was put in place.[37] In the initial stage, the company wanted to roll out several models of electric cars with different subscription pricing packages, and to subsidize the cars to reduce the total cost of ownership.

Better Place in Denmark

Denmark is a small country with a good population density and an established infrastructure for wind power.[38] On an average, every Dane travelled a distance of 41 km daily.[39]

Denmark had been at the forefront in taking initiatives to reduce its impact on the environment and it was among the top nations that had shown strict compliance to various environmental agreements.[40] It adopted an Energy Policy in February 2009, with the main goal of reducing Denmark's dependence on fossil fuels. The key features of this policy were:

34 "Electric Cars Make for a Better Place," www.roadtraffic-technology.com, December 19, 2008.

35 Karin Kloosterman, "Making Electric Cars Sell Like Cell Phones," www.treehugger.com, November 23, 2007.

36 The Renault–Nissan Alliance, formed in 1999, is a partnership between French automaker Renault and Japanese automaker Nissan Motors. The alliance has emerged as a strong contender in the global automotive sector. By the end of the financial year 2008, this alliance was the third largest in terms of sales in the world, and had a market share of 9 percent globally. Source: www.renault.com, accessed June 3, 2009.

37 "Renault–Nissan, Project Better Place Announce First Electric Vehicle Mass Market," www.japancorp.net, January 21, 2008.

38 Electricity generated from wind energy.

39 "Statistical Yearbook 2009," www.statbank.dk.

40 "Environmental Agreement Compliance (Most Recent) by Country," www.nationmaster.com.

- Goal of increasing of renewable energy constitution to 20% in gross energy consumption by 2011

- Reducing the gross energy consumption by 4% by 2020 compared to 2006

- Tax exemptions for electric cars extended until 2012 starting from 2008

- Framing of policies by the end of 2009 to promote plug-in-hybrid cars.

In pursuing its environmental initiatives, Denmark promoted the adoption of electric cars through various subsidies, taxes, and environmental projects. Among the various types of taxes levied on cars, registration tax accounted for more than half of the on road price of the cars. Denmark exempted electric cars from registration tax until 2012, bringing down the price drastically. Electric cars were also exempted from others taxes such as ownership tax, vehicles excise duty, countervailing charges, and road taxes. There were no tax exemptions for hybrid cars in Denmark as of September 2009. According to Shai Agassi, the price of the electric car in Denmark was expected to come down from US$60,000 to US$20,000 due to these tax exemptions.[41]

In Denmark, Better Place signed up with DONG Energy which had wind power installations. The electric vehicles were to be supplied by the Renault–Nissan alliance. Anders Eldrup, CEO of DONG Energy, said, "With this project, we hope to contribute substantially to reducing CO_2 emissions from Danish cars. At the same time, we will achieve a new way of storing the unstable electricity output from wind turbines, as electric vehicles are typically charged during the night, when the exploitation of power generation is low. This provides optimum exploitation of our resources for the benefit of the environment."[42]

Better Place in Hawaii

Hawaii, a small island state, provided a favorable environment for Better Place to set up its infrastructure. Further, the state government had a vision of increasing the contribution of pollution-free sources to energy generation to as high as 70 percent.[43]

By the end of 2008, Hawaii had tied up with Better Place to electrify its transportation by building the necessary infrastructure such as a charging network and swapping facilities. Better Place signed a Memorandum of Understanding with electricity generating companies in Hawaii for the supply of renewable energy to

---

41 "Tax Exemption Attracts Automakers to Denmark," www.wellsphere.com, November 7, 2008.

42 "Project Better Place to Sell Electric Cars in Denmark," www.greenbang.com, March 27, 2008.

43 Jeff St. John, "Better Place Goes to Hawaii," www.greentechmedia.com, December 2, 2008.

their charging stations, and planned to place the electric cars manufactured by the Renault–Nissan Alliance in the market by 2012.[44]

Better Place in Australia

As of October 2009, Australia was ranked seventh highest in the world in terms of per capita car ownership, with approximately 15 million cars in use.[45] Unlike Israel, Denmark, or Hawaii, Australia was a large landmass with urban centers separated by huge distances. Further, it had a low population density. There were doubts about the viability of the Better Place model under such unfavorable conditions. However, the company went ahead with its plans for Australia. "We figured out it's time to pick a bit of a bigger island to demonstrate our ability to scale,"[46] said Agassi in reply to a question on the company's venture into Australia.

Better Place planned to construct several charging/swapping stations in the three big cities of Melbourne, Sydney, and Brisbane. The company also planned to construct a charging station every 25 miles on the highways connecting these three cities. For sourcing electricity for the network, it tied up with AGL Energy, one of the major electricity producers in Australia. To meet the necessary investment for building the infrastructure, it collaborated with Macquarie Capital Group,[47] Sydney. Better Place aimed to release the electric cars supplied by the Renault–Nissan alliance on Australian roads by 2012.

As of 2009, Australia's expenditure on fossil fuels for transportation ranged between AUS$20 billion and AU$30 billion per annum.[48] Better Place estimated that the replacement of fossil fuels by renewable energy in the transportation sector would drastically reduce its expenditure on energy to about AU$4 billion per year.[49]

Better Place in California, USA

Better Place entered into an agreement with the state of California in the US to build the charging infrastructure for the electric cars. The company planned to complete the infrastructure and launch its electric vehicle services in the state by 2012.

44 "Better Place Electric Cars head to Hawaii," www.reuters.com, December 2, 2008.
45 David Ehrlich, "Better Place to Charge Up Australia," cleantech.com, October 23, 2008.
46 David Ehrlich, "Better Place to Charge Up Australia," cleantech.com, October 23, 2008.
47 Macquarie Capital Group is a global provider of banking, financial, advisory, investment, and fund management services. As of March 2009, it operated in over 70 countries and had an employee strength of nearly 12,700. It managed assets worth AU$243 billion. Source: www.macquarie.com.au, accessed June 10, 2009.
48 The wide range was largely due to the fluctuation in the price of crude oil in terms of US dollars, and the fluctuations in the currency conversion exchange rate between the US dollar and the Australian dollar.
49 Derek Fung, "How Better Place Plans to Revive the Electric Car," www.cnet.com.au, February 11, 2009.

The Bay Area that envelops the San Francisco Bay in California, famed for its high-technology businesses, took the lead in promoting electric cars as the primary mode of personal transportation. To make San Francisco the electric vehicle capital of the USA, regulatory authorities gave incentives for the companies that permitted the installation of charging stations on their premises and incentives to consumers for purchasing electric cars, besides encouraging public agencies to replace the existing cars in their fleet with electric cars.[50]

Better Place in Ontario, Canada

Better Place entered into an agreement with the government of Ontario in Canada to establish its smart grid in that state. At the same time, the government was evaluating various policy initiatives to encourage the mass adoption of electric vehicles in the province. Bullfrog Power, a renewable energy generation company, signed up as Better Place's partner for powering the smart grid.

Challenges to the Business Model

The Better Place business model faced many challenges in terms of consumer preferences, market suitability, competitors/substitutes, and the threat of technology changes.

Consumer preferences

Analysts said it was likely that consumers who had got used to the luxury provided by big, ICE-powered automobiles and their various features, would not be too impressed by the electric cars that would operate in the Better Place ecosystem. Moreover, the big automakers were developing plug-in hybrid cars to be launched in the market by 2010 or 2011, before Better Place could entrench itself in the market. These cars, such as the Toyota Prius (plug-in hybrid version) and the Chevrolet Volt were expected to match conventional automobiles in terms of features while providing the additional convenience of using either battery and/or gasoline according to the needs of the situation. On the other hand, subscribers of Better Place's services would have only a limited range of electric cars to begin with. Further, consumers could find it inconvenient to swap batteries at regular intervals during long trips.

50 Ucilia Wang, "Better Place to Charge up California," www.greentechmedia.com, November 20, 2008.

Market suitability

According to analysts, the Better Place business model was best suited for small countries or big metropolitan areas, with a high population density. These places offered scope for scalability of the charging network. But in very large countries, establishing the network would be a cumbersome task and the return on investment might not be commensurate with the risks involved. Installation of charging stations needed the active support of institutions such as municipalities, parking lot operators, and companies, with many implications for the existing infrastructure. Moreover, renewable energy occupied a small proportion of total electricity generation in many countries, making it difficult for the environmental objectives of the business model to be achieved.

Competition and substitutes

As the market for electric cars was estimated to grow, companies such as Coulomb Technologies Inc., Itron Inc.,[51] and GridPoint Inc.[52] were independently working toward establishing networks of charging stations in the US (refer to Exhibit III for a profile of Coulomb Technologies Inc.). As these companies facilitated charging for any type of electric car, it was expected to boost the customer choice to a wide range of brands in electric cars. Public policy-makers in many countries could find this model more attractive in order to protect consumer interests and encourage open competition rather than support a closed ecosystem managed by a single company (or a single group of companies).

Their business model was simpler than that of the Better Place ecosystem: they offered subscription plans that were beneficial to repeat users, but subscription was not a prerequisite for using their services. Moreover, they too preferred renewable energy sources for powering their charging network, and could claim to be as eco-friendly as Better Place in eliminating greenhouse gas emissions.

The Better Place ecosystem faced competition from global automakers who had plans to manufacture plug-in hybrid electric vehicles and pure electric vehicles and did not belong to this ecosystem (refer to Exhibit IV for various developments in the US market for electric cars).

The Better Place ecosystem also faced competition from automobile manufacturers such as BYD Auto of China, which had world-class R&D expertise in battery technology and was willing to set up its own charging infrastructure with

---

51 Itron Inc is a Washington-based company offering products and services to the energy and water industries globally. Its portfolio included intelligent metering, data collection, and software solutions. As of July 2009, about 8,000 utilities across the world used its solutions. Source: www.itron.com, accessed July 24, 2009.

52 GridPoint Inc is a Virginia-based technology company providing software solutions to the utilities to efficiently manage electricity supply and demand. It solutions were focused on load handling, renewable energy management in the total supply, and solutions for electric vehicles charging. Source: www.gridpoint.com.

rapid charging facility. In January 2009, Wolfgang Bernhart, Senior Researcher, Roland Berger Strategy Consultants GmbH,[53] commented, "BYD Auto is probably the closest … to becoming the first Chinese auto maker to crack the Western auto markets."[54] (Refer to Exhibit V for BYD Auto's global ambitions in the market for electric cars.)

Threat of changes in battery technology

If there was any disruptive breakthrough in battery technology with a longer range and a faster recharge, the smart grid infrastructure of Better Place, with its emphasis on battery swapping, may become redundant. In March 2009, the US government, led by the President, Barack Obama, unveiled an energy plan that included an outlay of US$2 billion for battery research for electric cars.[55]

Future of the Industry and the Business Model

Faced with depleting reserves of fossil fuels, volatility in the price of crude oil, and increasing concerns about environmental pollution and greenhouse gas emissions, the global automotive industry was gradually moving toward electricity as the source of power for automobiles, at least in a hybrid form.

In the United States, the bankruptcies of Chrysler Corporation[56] and General Motors Corporation[57] in 2009 and the government's stimulus package for the industry were expected to accelerate the push for eco-friendly vehicles. The energy plan unveiled by the US government in March 2009 had an outlay of US$150 billion toward developing alternative and clean energy sources, with the government aiming to promote one million plug-in hybrid cars by 2015.[58] The plan provided

---

53 Headquartered at Munich, Roland Berger Strategy Consultants GmbH is one of the leading global players in strategy consultancy. By the end of 2008, it had offices in 27 countries with employee strength of 2,100 people and annual revenues of 670 million Euros. Source: www.rolandberger.com, accessed August 18, 2009.

54 Norihiko Shirouzu, "Technology Levels Playing Field in Race to Market Electric Car," online.wsj.com, January 12, 2009.

55 "US Government to Distribute $2 billion in Grants for Car Battery Research," www.automonster.ca, July 23, 2009.

56 Chrysler Corporation is a Detroit-based automotive company that manufactures cars, minivans, sports utility vehicles, and light trucks.

57 General Motors Corporation, one of the leading automakers based in Detroit, US, was founded in 1908. As of June 2009, it possessed manufacturing plants in 34 countries, had 244,500 employees, and sales and services outlets in 140 countries. From June 1, 2009, the company pursued reorganization and conducted operations under the US Government's Bankruptcy laws. Source: www.gm.com, accessed June 4, 2009.

58 Patrick E. Meyer, "Obama's Ambitious Energy Policy," www.todaysengineer.org.

federal tax exemptions ranging from US$2,500 to US$7,500 on the purchase of plug-in hybrid electric cars and pure electric cars.[59] Owners installing alternative fuel equipment received tax credits up to 50 percent of the cost of the equipment; for residential equipment purchase, consumers got up to US$2,000 tax credit.[60]

In Europe, the electric cars market was estimated to exceed 250,000 units by 2015,[61] according to a study by Frost & Sullivan in October 2008. Among emerging nations, observers expected China to take the lead in electrification of road transportation.

Corporations and entrepreneurs were looking forward to a concrete agreement at the of the United Nations Climate Change Conference—Copenhagen 2009 (COP15) that would facilitate new business opportunities related to becoming a 'low carbon economy' (refer to Exhibit VI for the roles of government and business in controlling climate change). Increasing fund allocation for producing renewable and clean energy such as solar energy and wind energy was expected to augur well for the electric vehicle charging network facilitators. The predictability of the cost of electricity generation from renewable sources was another positive factor in this regard. Increased pressure on corporations to be more socially and environmentally responsible was expected to induce many of them to install charging stations on their premises. Given such a favorable environment, electric cars and charging networks, which served the cause of environmental sustainability, appeared to have a bright future. However, the question remained: would Better Place's innovative business model be commercially sustainable in the long run?

References and Suggested Readings

1. Andrew Williams, "Nissan to Build Massive Electric Car Factory in US," gas2.org, June 22, 2009.
2. "Nissan Plans to Build EVs and Batteries in USA," gm-volt.com/2009/06/20/nissan-plans-to-build-evs-and-batteries-in-usa, June 20, 2009.
3. Richard S. Chang, "Five More Electric Cars from Mitsubishi," greeninc.blogs.nytimes.com, June 18, 2009.
4. Zack Newmark, "Renault to Unveil Three Electric Car Concepts in Frankfurt," www.worldcarfans.com, June 18, 2009.
5. "Scientific American 10: Guiding Science for Humanity," www.scientificamerican.com/article.cfm?id=scientific-american-10&page=2, June 2009.
6. "International Energy Outlook 2009," www.eia.doe.gov/oiaf/ieo/highlights.html, May 27, 2009.

59 "US Government to Distribute $2 billion in Grants for Car Battery Research," www.automonster.ca, July 23, 2009.
60 www.afdc.energy.gov.
61 "The Global Oil Paradox," awbriefing.com, October 2008.

7. Gerard Wynn and Anna Ringstrom, "Green Industry Demands Low-Carbon Dollars," www.reuters.com, May 26, 2009.
8. Tomoko A. Hosaka, "Palo Alto's Better Place Unveils New Battery Technology for Electric Cars," www.mercurynews.com, May 14, 2009.
9. Peter Alford, "'Cars All Electric in 20 Years: Evan Thornley," www.theaustralian.news.com, May 13, 2009.
10. Richard Lowenthal, "Being Smart about Your Electric Vehicle Infrastructure," gas2.org, May 4, 2009.
11. Gavin Newsom, "The Race to an EV Future: Being First to an Electric Vehicle Grid," gas2.org, April 29, 2009.
12. Josie Garthwaite, "Better Place Pops the Hood, Gears Up for All-or-Nothing Rollout," earth2tech.com, April 23, 2009.
13. "The Reality of Electric Dreams," www.smh.com.au/environment/energy-smart/the-reality-of-electric-dreams-20090409-a28c.html?page=fullpage#contentSwap1, April 10, 2009.
14. Chuck Squatriglia, "We Drive Nissan's Electric Car, and It's Sweet," www.wired.com, April 2, 2009.
15. Alun Taylor, "Honda Executes 180° Turn on Plug-In E-Cars," www.reghardware.co.uk, April 28, 2009.
16. Jonathon Ramsey, "Tesla Model S: $50,000 EV Sedan Seats Seven, 300-Mile Range, 0–60 in 5.5 s," www.autoblog.com, March 26, 2009.
17. Jim Motavalli, "EV Manufacturers are Plugging into Available Federal Money," industry.bnet.com, March 17, 2009.
18. Rachel Pulfer, "Venture Capital: A Modern Midas," www.canadianbusiness.com, March 16, 2009.
19. Jennifer Sullivan, "Governors Envision Eco-Friendly Fuels at I-5 Rest Stops," seattletimes.nwsource.com, March 8, 2009.
20. "Project Get Ready," www.onelectriccars.com/tag/paul-mitchell, February 25, 2009.
21. Sharon Wrobel, "Local Firms to Help Better Place," www.jpost.com, February 24, 2009.
22. "Ford Sneaks up on Electric Car Future," www.hybridcars.com/news/fords-sneaks-electric-car-future-25557.html, February 19, 2009.
23. Derek Fung, "How Better Place Plans to Revive the Electric Car," www.cnet.com.au, February 11, 2009.
24. Donna Fuscaldo, "Better Place Wants to Make Owning an Electric Car More Convenient," www.foxbusiness.com, January 30, 2009.
25. David Ehrlich, "Better Place Raises Financing for Denmark Electric Car Project," earth2tech.com/2009/01/27/better-place-raises-financing-for-denmark-electric-car-project, January 27, 2009.
26. Ucilia Wang, "Better Place Grabs 103M, Names New Danish CEO," www.greentechmedia.com, January 27, 2009.
27. David Ehrlich, "Better Place Raises Financing for Denmark Electric Car Project," earth2tech.com, January 27, 2009.
28. Helen, "Better Place Electric Cars Coming to Ontario," greengta.ca, January 19, 2009.
29. Dennis Hollier, "Charging Ahead: Hawaii Looks beyond Oil," www.hawaiibusiness.com, January 2009.
30. Sebastian Blanco, "Better Place Answers Questions about Home Charging, Obama's Interest," www.autobloggreen.com, December 23, 2008.
31. "Vantage Point Venture Partners Cleans Up with $435 billion," dealbook.blogs.nytimes.com/2008/12/23/vantagepoint-venture-partners-cleans-up-with-435-million, December 23, 2008.

32. Lisa Sibley, "Charging Ahead with Plug-In Stations," sanjose.bizjournals.com, December 19, 2008.
33. "Top 10 Private Companies to Watch in 2009," energytechstocks.com/wp/?p=2049, December 17, 2008.
34. Martin LaMonica, "It Takes a Village to Sell an Electric Car," news.cnet.com, December 16, 2008.
35. Lindsay Riddell, "Palo Alto Startup Better Place Looks to Electric Car Recharging Stations," eastbay.bizjournals.com, December 12, 2008.
36. Tyson Herberger, "REVA Electric Cars May Soon Be for Sale in Israel," greenprophet.com, December 12, 2008.
37. "The Inspired Auto Bailout of Tom Friedman's Dreams," www.huffingtonpost.com/2008/12/10/the-auto-bailout-tom-frie_n_149868.html, December 10, 2008.
38. Rory McCarthy, "Israel Pilot's Electric Car Network," www.guardian.co.uk, December 9, 2008.
39. "Hawaii Planning Statewide Electric Car Network," hardware.slashdot.org/article.pl?sid=08/12/05/1915212, December 5, 2008.
40. "Better Place Electric Cars Head to Hawaii," www.reuters.com/article/bondsNews/idUSN0229573020081203, December 2, 2008.
41. "Making Hawaii a Better Place: Electric Cars Are in Our Future,"
42. www.maui.com/news/200901143.cfm, December 2, 2008.
43. Tyler Hamilton, "Venture Fund Bets Billion on Cleantech," www.thestar.com, December 1, 2008.
44. Karin Kloosterman, "San Francisco Partners With Shai Agassi's Electric Car Scheme, A $1 billion Project," www.huffingtonpost.com, November 27, 2008.
45. "When Will Auto Industry Reach 'Better Place'?" seekingalpha.com/article/108121-when-will-the-auto-industry-reach-a-better-place?source=feed, November 26, 2008.
46. Ucilia Wang, "Portugal, Renault-Nissan Set Electric-Car Plan," www.greentechmedia.com, November 25, 2008.
47. Stacy Feldman, "San Francisco Joins 'Better Place' Electric Car Project," solveclimate.com, November 21, 2008.
48. Chloe Albanesius, "Bay Area Cities Agree to Power Electric Cars," www.goodcleantech.com, November 21, 2008.
49. Ucilia Wang, "Better Place to Charge Up California," www.greentechmedia.com, November 20, 2008.
50. Jeremy Korzeniewski, "Renault Plans Three Electric Cars for the Future," www.autoblog.com, November 10, 2008.
51. "Project Better Place Expands into Australia," www.triplepundit.com/pages/project-better-1.php, October 24, 2008.
52. John Reed, "Australia Backs Recharging Network for Electric Cars," www.ft.com, October 22, 2008.
53. Tom Young, "France to Build Electric Car Infrastructure by 2011," www.businessgreen.com, October 13, 2008.
54. "The Man who Resuscitated Electric Cars," www.thebudgetecoist.com/archive/the-man-who-resuscitated-the-electric-car, October 4, 2008.
55. Sam Abuelsamid, "Hyundai to Deliver First Electric Car in New Zealand," www.autobloggreen.com, September 26, 2008.
56. "The Road Ahead," www.economist.com/business/displaystory.cfm?story_id=12070722, September 4, 2008.
57. Adam Stein, "Plug In and Drive," www.terrapass.com, August 26, 2008.

58. "Portugal and Renault–Nissan Alliance Partner Directly on EVs; Consumer Sales Begin in 2011," www.greencarcongress.com/2008/07/portugal-and-re.html, July 9, 2008.

59. Katie Fehrenbacher, "Daimler Working on Electric Mercedes, Electric Smart Car, & Project Better Place," earth2tech.com, June 23, 2008.

60. Karin Kloosterman, "A Reader Responds to Project Better Place Getting Wired," www.treehugger.com, May 5, 2008.

61. Alex Zaharov-Reutt, "Denmark Signs Deal to Implement Israel's Electric Car Project," www.itwire.com, March 28, 2008.

62. "Think Ox Electric Car—Think Global," www.theirearth.com/index.php/news/think-ox-electric-car-think-global, March 18, 2008.

63. Shai Agassi "The Future of Transportation—Part 1," www.egovmonitor.com, February 4, 2008.

64. Micheline Maynard, "Toyota Will Offer a Plug-In Hybrid by 2010," www.nytimes.com, January 14, 2008.

65. Karin Kloosterman, "2010: The Year We Make Electric Contact," www.treehugger.com, December 17, 2007.

66. Chuck Squatriglia, "Shai Agassi Wants to Sell Electric Cars Like Cell Phones," www.wired.com, October 30, 2007.

67. Steve Hamm, "$200 Million for Electric Cars?" www.businessweek.com, October 29, 2007.

68. UN Global Compact Office and Dalberg Global Development Advisors, "Champions of the Low Carbon Economy: Why CEOs are Ready for a Global Climate Agreement," www.unglobalcompact.org, September 2009.

69. Alan Salzman, "Shai Agassi," www.time.com/time/specials/packages/article/0,28804,1894410_1893209_1893476,00.html.

70. Kathy Jackson "Hyundai Plans Plug-In Hybrid for 2012 in United States," www.autoweek.com/article/20090402/carnews/904029989.

71. "Battery Swapping Technology Set for Electric Cars," www.brisbanetimes.com.au/technology/battery-swapping-technology-set-for-electric-cars-20090514-b3me.html.

72. "City Of San Francisco Unveils Charging Station For Electric Cars," www.coulombtech.com/press_releases/release_20090218.php.

73. "Chevy Volt: The Future is Electrifying," www.chevrolet.com.

74. "Denmark's Electric Avenues," www.plentymag.com/blogs/edge/2008/03/denmarks_electric_avenues.php.

75. "Ford Escape Hybrid—What the Auto Press Says," usnews.rankingsandreviews.com/cars-trucks/Ford_Escape-Hybrid.

76. "Sign Up and Charge! Coulomb Technologies Announces First Charge Point Network Availability for Electric Vehicles Drivers," www.coulombtech.com/press_releases/release_20090106.php.

77. "Switched on Highways," www.newsweek.com/id/178851/page/2.

78. www.fastcompany.com/100/2009/shai-agassi.

79. www.scientificamerican.com/article.cfm?id=scientific-american-10&page=2.

80. www.thegreencarwebsite.co.uk/glossary-jargon-buster.asp.

81. www.fueleconomy.gov/feg/hybridAnimation/hybrid/hybridoverview.html.

82. www.pluginamerica.org/plug-in-vehicle-tracker.html.

83. www.greencarcongress.com.

84. www.betterplace.com.

Exhibit I **Worldwide Total Oil Consumption by Various Sectors**

Adapted from Key Energy Statistics 2009, www.iea.org.

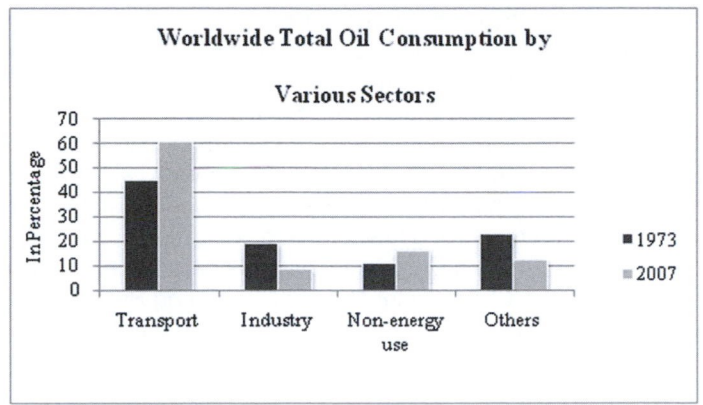

Exhibit II **Projection of CO_2 Emissions Worldwide**

Adapted from International Energy Outlook 2009, www.eia.doe.gov, May 27, 2009.

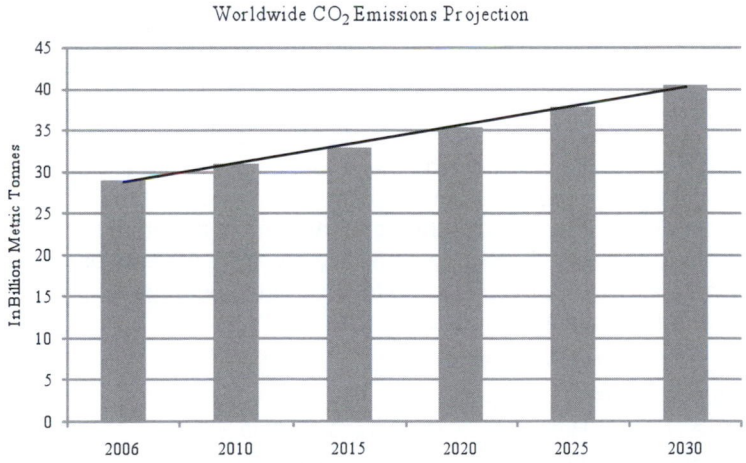

Coulomb Technologies Inc, a California-based company, was founded in 2007 with the objective of providing charging infrastructure services for electric vehicles. From the United States, it expanded its operations to Europe, the Middle East, and Africa by partnering with various distributors in those areas. The company's offerings included selling, installing, and servicing the charging infrastructure which it called ChargePoint Network.

The ChargePoint Network included charging stations and the network operating system to control them. The charging network was divided into local groups of charging stations which were again controlled through a single gateway charging station. A gateway charging station supported communications for nearly 100 charging stations. This gateway charging station communicated with the ChargePoint Network Operating System which was hosted on a remote server of the company. This operating system established communication with the charging stations for user authentication and access to the network and also provided the customers with web-based portal access. This network automatically informed the drivers of electric vehicles—through SMS or e-mail—about vacant charging stations in their vicinity, provided easy access to charging for non-members of the network, gave timely information on the charging status of the batteries, and sent alerts on depletion of the charge of the batteries.[a] However, the company did not provide any charging facilities at customers' homes.

Its offerings catered to both business-to-business (B2B) and business-to-consumer (B2C) markets. In the B2B market environment, it supplied charging infrastructure to municipalities, parking lots, and parking infrastructure owners. In the B2C market, it offered subscription-based charging facilities to the drivers of electric cars. Electric car drivers were offered flexible recharging options that made them use the network by paying for the charging session or by subscribing for a monthly plan that suited their charging requirements. Subscribers had the flexibility of using any charging station irrespective of the local group to which they belonged.

The company's clients included:

- City Hall, City of San Francisco
- Rampart Casino, Las Vegas[b]
- Sierra Nevada Brewing Co.,[c] Chico, California
- City of Amsterdam, the Netherlands (45 charging stations in the first phase by May 2009, growing to 200 charging stations by 2012)

As the network facilitated charging of batteries for any type of electric vehicle, it was expected to gain from the roll-out of electric cars from many companies.

a www.coulombtech.com/products.php.

b Rampart Casino is one of the famous casinos in the city of Las Vegas. It offers facilities such as four star hotels, a casino, restaurants, and a spa complex. Source: www.rampartcasino.com.

c Sierra Nevada Brewing Co. is one of the leading microbreweries in America and has earned many accolades for its international standard ales and lagers. It was started in 1980 and since its inception, had come up with many innovations to conserve energy resources.

Exhibit IV Developments in the US Market for Electric Cars

Compiled from various sources

In the US, among the cars that used electric batteries for fuel efficiency, hybrid cars had shown an upward trend; by 2008, they had gained about 2.5 percent share of the annual market for light vehicle sales. Toyota Prius had a dominant share of the hybrid cars sales in 2008, followed by Honda Insight. As there was more preference for fuel efficient cars from consumers to shield against the volatile gasoline prices, many of the major automakers in US also planned to release plug-in hybrid electric vehicles (PHEVs) and pure electric cars. General Motors was expected to release its much anticipated Chevy Volt by 2011 and had partnered with battery suppliers to hasten the process of releasing the car for sale. Other leading automotive companies such as Toyota, Ford Motor Company[a], Chrysler Group LLC[b], and Honda were also in the process of producing plug-in hybrid or pure electric models (refer to Table A for planned releases of electric cars in the US by major automakers).

Table A Electric Cars to be Released for Sale in the US by Major Automakers

Automaker	Brand	Vehicle Type	Expected Year of Release in the US
General Motors	Chevy Volt	PHEV	2010
Toyota Motor Corporation, Japan	Plug-in Prius	PHEV	2012
Nissan Motor Co. Ltd., Japan	Leaf	Pure electric	2010
Chrysler Group, LLC	Dodge Circuit EV	Pure electric	2010
Ford Motor Company	Yet to be named	Pure electric, PHEV	2011: pure electric 2012: PHEV
Daimler AG,[c] Germany	Smart Car	Pure electric	2012
BMW, AG, Germany.	MINI E	Pure electric	May 2009

As of 2009, there were no US automakers in the pure electric car manufacturing segment except Tesla Motors, Inc., which exclusively catered to this segment with its Sports Utility Vehicle (SUV), Roadster. With a 53 kWh battery, the Tesla Roadster had a range of 244 miles (390 kilometers); the car was priced above US$100,000. By 2011, Tesla Motors planned to launch its Model S with a range of 300 miles (480 kilometers) and priced just below US$50,000.

GM invested US$25 million to establish a battery lab to facilitate speedy development of the hybrid, PHEV, and pure electric cars from the company. GM also tied up with LG Chem Ltd[d] to supply battery for its Chevy Volt model and collaborated with LG Chem and Compact Power, Inc.,[e] toward improving the technology. Further, the company had worked with University of Michigan in developing curriculum for engineering related to battery technology. "The new global GM battery lab will benefit consumers across America by helping us advance the development of battery technology in the United States and put cleaner, more efficient vehicles on the road more quickly and affordably,"[f] said Fritz Henderson, CEO, General Motors.

a   Based at Detroit, Ford Motor Company was one of the leading multinational automotive companies in the world. It manufactured cars, trucks, and SUVs; and by the end of financial year 2008, it had employee strength of over 200,000 people worldwide. Source: www.ford.com, accessed July 24, 2009.

b   Founded in 1925, Chrysler Group LLC, Detroit, was an automotive company that manufactured cars, minivans, SUVs and light trucks.

c   Germany-based Daimler was one of the leading manufacturers of cars and trucks in the world. For the financial year 2008, it earned revenues of over 95 billion Euros and employed more than 273,000 people. Source: www.daimler.com, accessed July 24, 2009.

d   It is a Seoul-based manufacturer and exporter of chemicals and polymers, industrial materials, and electronic components. Source: www.lgchem.com.

e   Compact Power, Inc. is a Michigan-based subsidiary of LG Chem Ltd in North America that manufactures lithium-ion batteries for the automotive and non-automotive segments. Source: www.compactpower.com.

f   "GM's 'Reinvention' Starts With $25 Million Battery Lab," www.mixedpower.com, June 16, 2009.

Teaching notes for this case are available from Greenleaf Publishing. These are free of charge and are available only to teaching staff. They can be requested by going to:

www.greenleaf-publishing.com/oikos2_notes

BYD Auto, which had its origins in the BYD Company, a manufacturer of lithium-ion and other rechargeable batteries, was regarded as the world's first mass producer of plug-in hybrid electric cars. BYD Company had entered the automotive sector in 2003 by acquiring Qinchuan Motors, Xian, and renaming it as BYD Auto. Beginning 2005, BYD Auto released a series of models based on internal combustion engine technology into the Chinese market. By the end of 2008, its F3 was one of the top car models being sold in China.

Under the leadership of its founder Wang Chuanfu, BYD Auto ventured into the design, development, and manufacture of different types of electric cars by leveraging its expertise in battery manufacturing. In December 2008, it released its first plug-in hybrid electric car model F3DM in the Chinese market. Also in the pipeline for BYD Auto was the E6, a pure electric car scheduled for release by late 2009 in China.

As of July 2009, the Chinese government was in the process of promoting electric vehicles through various subsidies and tax exemptions to address the twin concerns of environmental sustainability and energy security. China had committed US$2.2 billion in 2009 to promoting low emission vehicles in the country. According to an assessment by Bain & Company, if the electric cars were priced less than US$15,000, their annual sales were expected to reach 1.5 million worldwide with sales of 200,000 units coming from China. However, China did not have adequate infrastructure for charging electric car batteries. BYD Auto planned to provide recharging facilities for its batteries by establishing charging stations.

In 2008, BYD Company had attracted worldwide attention when Warren Buffett, CEO of Berkshire Hathaway Inc, acquired a 10 percent stake in it for US$230 million. BYD Auto had plans of introducing electric cars in the US by 2011. The electric vehicles segment was an emerging market in the US and it offered a level playing field for BYD Auto to compete with well-established giants in the global automotive industry. Further, the US was the second largest emitter of greenhouse gases, with China occupying the top slot.

BYD Auto planned to release the electric cars in the US at a price of about US$22,000, well below the prices of other major automakers such as GM and Toyota. Its proprietary battery technology for electric cars was expected to be more energy-efficient. With the use of electrodes made of iron phosphate[a], these batteries were also less susceptible to catching fire compared to conventional lithium-ion batteries. Further, the company could provide quick recharging facilities for its batteries: a user could recharge more than half of a battery in 10 minutes.[b] However, this quick recharging facility required 100 amperes of current whereas households provided only 20 amperes.

a   Iron phosphate was chosen because of its thermal stability and safety features.

b   "BYD in Pole Position to Dominate Electric Car Market," www.climatesuccess.org, June 2, 2009.

Exhibit VI **Controlling Climate Change—The Roles of Government and Business**

Source: UN Global Compact Office and Dalberg Global Development Advisors, "Champions of the Low Carbon Economy: Why CEOs are Ready for a Global Climate Agreement," www.unglobalcompact.org, September 2009.

In the run-up to the December 2009 summit at Copenhagen on climate change, heads of several large corporations called for a strong global climate agreement that could become the foundation for them to transition their businesses into low-carbon businesses. The following excerpts are from the executive summary of a report co-published in September 2009 by the UN Global Compact Office.

There is tremendous economic opportunity in addressing climate change

The mandate to revolutionize how we produce and consume provides one of the greatest value creation opportunities the world has ever seen. Many believe this potential could surpass even the value created in the information technology revolution. The opportunity is not restricted to either newcomers or incumbents, but is instead open to anyone ready to find solutions.

This opportunity can only be unleashed with regulatory certainty and a price on carbon

While many companies are already moving to a lower carbon economy, they are poised to invest massively more. What they require to make the investments is a regulatory environment that is stable, and sends the market a clear signal on how to price carbon. A price on carbon, established globally, ensures a level playing field without competitive distortions or disruptions to trade.

A low carbon economy is attainable, and business is a critical part of the solution

The CEOs profiled in this report highlight that the transition to a low carbon economy is within reach. All that is needed is a framework within which business can move forward with the transition. Not only do we have the necessary solutions today, an agreement would spur further innovation. As the implementers of a move to a low carbon economy, business has a critical role to play.

Climate change needs to be addressed by governments now

Not ten years from now, not five years from now, but now. The effects of climate change are already evident. The transition to a low carbon economy, if advanced now, can deter the worst human and financial costs. The current economic crisis should not prevent us from moving ambitiously on an agreement. Moving on an agreement now will reduce the risks of climate change and create a more secure economic future for all.

Case 13
Noir/Illuminati II[1,2]

Benoit Leleux

International Institute for Management Development, Lausanne, Switzerland

Case A: Defining Socially Responsible Affordable Luxury Clothing

Peter looked out of his window. *His* window. He liked the sound of that. It had taken him 15 years of discipline and hard work to reach this point. Of course, he had enjoyed more prominent and remarkable views and offices in the past, but for the first time it was his name on the lease contract, his office and his company. And 2007 was going to be the year of Noir/Illuminati II. So far, after nine months, it looked very promising.

Peter Ingwersen had founded the companies in February 2005. The two entities were like Siamese twins; Noir designed and produced luxury clothing for women, while Illuminati II was set up to produce high-quality cotton fabrics both for Noir and other leading fashion brands. Together, they provided the basis for a totally new concept in fashion. Over the years, Peter had attended many fashion shows all over world and had become both aware and very concerned by the total lack of "social

1 This case Copyright © 2008 by IMD—International Institute for Management Development, Lausanne, Switzerland. All rights reserved. Not to be used or reproduced without written permission directly from IMD, Lausanne, Switzerland.

2 Professor Benoit Leleux, S. Schmidheiny Professor of Entrepreneurship and Finance, prepared this case with the assistance of Barbara Scheel Agersnap, IMD MBA 2001, as a basis for class discussion rather than to illustrate either effective or ineffective handling of a business situation.

substance" of many of the major fashion companies. Was fashion just the ultimate personalization of some of the worst aspects of human behavior? Was it all about egocentrism and showing off? Could something be done to bring back meaning and substance to the world of fashion? Corporate Social Responsibility (CSR) was making its way into most other industries: why could it not infiltrate fashion? Was there any way to improve the "feel good" factor of beautiful clothes with a clear social responsibility message? Could egocentrism rhyme with eco-friendliness?

Conceptually it was very clear: Noir/Illuminati II would define socially responsible affordable luxury clothing. Putting the concept into operation was the real challenge. Building a brand on social awareness, or the guilt of conspicuous consumption, could clearly be a two-edged sword. Would customers buy the story? Even more pressing, would investors follow him in this venture?

He went back to his hotel and, after a very long shower, he started to put the action plan together.

Defining the Idea and Analyzing the Market

Peter's experience in the fashion industry, both in Europe and the US, was quite extensive (refer to Exhibit 1 for Peter Ingwersen's biography). After completing his training at the Danish School of Arts and Crafts, he joined Levi's Nordic Region as a designer in 1986, rapidly moving up the ranks in creative positions. By 1999, he was the global brand manager for Levi's Vintage Clothing and Red labels and the brand director for the EMEA[3] region. He left Levi's in 2002 to join an up-and-coming fashion company, Day Birger & Mikkelsen, as managing director. This was not enough: he was after a completely novel way to approach fashion, a new paradigm for the industry, something that would radically change the way people look at clothes consumption.

During his many years in the industry, he had grown more and more aware and concerned about the lack of social and environmental substance in the world of fashion. Nobody seemed to care much about the broader implications of creating and buying expensive clothes. In a way, conspicuous consumption seemed to belong to the sphere of indulgence, an area free of social guilt and responsibilities. Whereas other industries were rapidly gaining consciousness and accepting responsibility for their actions on the world, fashion seemed to remain very much immune to these higher callings.

That would soon become Peter's crusade. Could he bring back meaning and substance to the world of fashion? Was there any way to improve the "feel good" factor of beautiful clothes with a clear social responsibility message? It is with this in mind

---

3 EMEA: Europe, Middle East and Africa.

that he started to hash out the principles behind Noir/Illuminati II, the company that would also provide the channel for the realization of his dream.

Noir/Illuminati II would rest on three key pillars:

- **A very specific niche, in terms of price, appeal and design.** Peter had neither the interest nor the financial resources to start another mass market fashion company. The focus would be on the socially conscious and responsible affluent clientele.

- **A strong message and rationale to encourage the purchase decision.** For most people in the developed Western world, clothes, especially luxury ones, are not necessities; most people own enough clothes to keep themselves warm for the rest of their lives.

- **A sustainable company.** This ruled out focusing on some short-term fads; the company had to be established on solid, durable foundations so as to contribute over the long term.

Peter planned every part of the marketing parameters before he brought the company to life. Positioning, Products, Pricing, Placement, and Promotion, the infamous five Ps of fashion, were all conceptualized early on. He added a sixth P of his own: Profitability. The latter was critical for sustainability and a successful exit.

Exit was most likely to happen through a trade sale to one of the leading luxury brands, such as Louis Vuitton Moet Hennessy (LVMH) or Pinault-Printemps-Redoute (PPR). To be of any interest to them, it was essential to create a unique niche product absent from their portfolios. Big groups were always on the prowl for the imaginative addition to their product line-ups, for that new product that would leverage their competences and brand capital. After a careful segmentation of their portfolios, Peter identified what he considered to be their biggest "market holes": (1) most did not have a product with a strong Corporate Social Responsibility (CSR) profile; and (2) they did not have an affordable luxury clothing brand. The two concepts, affordability and luxury, were still often perceived as totally antagonistic. A minor antagonism certainly was not going to stop Peter: Noir Illuminati/II would be socially responsible affordable luxury clothing.

To reach his objectives, Peter realized that he had to build a strong brand. From his time at Levi's he knew how important high intangible value was. When Levi's ran into economic turmoil in the 1970s, it was able to borrow some US$500 million on the back of the company's little red logo. That gave it the fuel to fix its issues rapidly and effectively. Corporate Social Responsibility would be the fuel to his brand.

In a 2004 report, the Boston Consulting Group estimated that the market for luxury goods would reach $1 trillion by the year 2010.[4] With new and increasing buying power, especially in places like China, Russia and the Middle East, the market would become even more attractive. A further segmentation revealed a sweet spot

---

4 www.bcg.com/publications/files/New_Luxury_Creators_and_the_Forces_That_ Support_Them Apr_04.pdf.

for goods that were not as expensive as luxury products from Cartier, Chanel and Dior, for example, but somewhat more affordable. Peter refined his vision:

> We want to endorse meaningful consumption for the luxury consumer. We will be the new "ethics chic".[5]

Convert Luxury Sinners!

Peter always loved a good story, and to some extent he found inspiration in a 16th-century Catholic Church practice called the "letters of indulgence." Buying letters of indulgence as a punishment for sins was a popular way to clear one's conscience, even though most sinners of the time felt no remorse for the sins they had committed and had no intention of changing their ways.[6] That became one of the leading points of contention for Luther, who believed that sinners needed to carry remorse throughout their lives, not buy their way out of trouble.

For Peter, this concept of indulgence was still very much alive today, redefined in a more politically correct way as charity. By definition, luxury products were the ones that consumers did not really need, at least in their most extravagantly expensive forms. Hence, the consumption of luxury products bred guilt, albeit unconsciously. If he could find a way to generate a strong "positive association" with the act of conspicuous consumption, the guilt would be reduced and the attractiveness of the product would be that much stronger. The new trendsetter would have to be the one with enough free time and money to devote to responsible activities, such as caring for others or the environment. That trend was most visible in the huge appeal of movements such as Greenpeace and Friends of the Earth, the emergence of an organic product culture, the large increase in the number of charitable foundations, etc. These activities were becoming the ultimate status symbols, the ways to differentiate from the crowd and show you had reached the highest echelons of purpose and achievement. Giving and caring were in; conspicuous spending was out. Noir would be the first brand specifically engineered to bring social responsibility to luxury clothing.

Translating Purpose into Style

Once the strategic objective was laid out, it needed to be translated into a style of its own, i.e. a "red thread" in the design that would immediately identify a Noir

---

5 www.aoifehegarty.com/2006/09/seeing-red.html.
6 unterkunft.wittenberg.de/e/seiten/ablass.html

product. Themes had to be defined to give internal consistency to the collections and continuity to the product offering. What would define a Noir piece of clothing in the street? Peter went back to its original storyline. What would the new trendsetters really miss? They gave up conspicuous consumption for meaningful spending. Somewhere, they elected to tone down their inner tendencies for more socially acceptable ones. But this was not about atonement: they did not give up on expressing their personalities, on making brash statements about how they felt about themselves … Noir's style would have to bring back that missing element of provocation, to spice up the offering. Meaningful spending, but personally rewarding and ego satisfying! For Peter, it was clear the key driver would have to be sex appeal. Clothes would have to make people look and feel attractive. They would mix masculine and feminine accents and consist mostly of suits with delicate tops, shirts and blouses. A few other designers, such as Helmut Lang, Jil Sander and Raf Simons, had tried something similar but they had all been acquired by the Prada Group and lost some of their original identity in the transactions. Noir would produce two collections per year consisting of 50 to 60 designs each, and they would be the personalization of attractiveness and sex appeal.

Building Conscience: Illuminati II, the Responsible Cotton Brand

Today, emphasis is on fashion that carries a greater and deeper meaning. Clothing is more than protection against the weather; it is a means of establishing the personal identity. In a world where we often take and seldom give, Noir is aimed at both the fashion and social conscience of the consumer, who can thus endorse consumption and give a little back to the world by purchasing clothing that supports sustainable business processes in the Third World.

Peter Ingwersen

Style and pricing would clearly define the brand positioning, but evidently the product itself would also have to be set apart on the social responsibility map. Peter decided to focus on the textiles that would be used. A new brand, Illuminati II, was created to produce the finest sub-Saharan textiles from organically grown Ugandan cotton. The cotton would be weaved and further processed in Europe for Noir exclusively. Noir would then sell it around the world to leading luxury brands.

The name Illuminati derived from the Latin word *illumina*, meaning glow or light. The light was to be in sharp contrast to Noir. Illuminati II was to be the luxurious fabric brand that would supply the highest-quality cotton fabrics to Noir and other luxury brands. It would operate under the umbrella of the most stringent fair trade and socially responsible organizations, such as the United Nations Global Compact Principles (www.unglobalcompact.org) and ILO's production guidelines (www.ilo.org). Illuminati II's vision was to deliver organic and Fair Trade cotton fabrics whilst ensuring sustainability of The Humane Business Model from the heart of Africa. A Noir Foundation would also be established to recycle a percentage of the firm's revenues and profits to support the African cotton workers. The support would be conveyed to them through an NGO in the form of essential medicines and healthcare.

Peter originally approached a number of Sub-Saharan governmental organizations with his idea. Only Uganda showed interest, and the interest was mutual. The business model for cotton in Uganda (as in most developing countries) was solely price driven: producers were competing primarily on price, even though the cost of growing high-quality cotton was very similar as for the lower-quality product. The price for 1 kg of short staple[7] cotton fibers was $0.95; the high-quality extra-long staple fetched $3.40. Peter wanted the farmers to start growing the extra-long staple cotton and do it organically. Until then, organically grown cotton was mostly produced in India, China and the US.

It took almost a year from the initial approach in 2005 to find the right local partners and to get ready for production. All farming in Uganda was done on government-owned land. A Danish public-sector investor[8] helped the company negotiate the deal. In early 2007 the work of testing and identifying the best possible locations and the best long-staple cotton seeds for the area were completed. Some 500 acres along the Nile were sown. Harvesting would be done by hand so as to create employment opportunities twice a year for about 500 local people. Initially, the raw cotton would be shipped to Europe to be woven but the long-term plan was to develop all processing locally and increase the local value added.

The plan called for the commercial launch of Illuminati II fabrics in July 2008 for the Spring 2009 collections, but this would of course depend on the final quality of the harvest. While all the elements were in place, and agriculturalists were extremely optimistic about the prospects for the high-end organic cotton, the proof would come none too early.

Making Corporate Social Responsibility Sexy!

Corporate Social Responsibility is the continuing commitment by business to behave ethically and contribute to economic development while improving the

---

7 Staple refers to the average length of cotton fibers: Short Staple (less than 25 mm), Medium Staple (25 to 30 mm), Long Staple (30 to 37 mm) and Extra-Long Staple (37 mm and above). The longer the staple, the higher the quality of the final cloth.
8 www.ifu.dk.

quality of life of the workforce and their families as well as of the local community and society at large.[9]

Noir and Illuminati II were from the start two components of the same global concept. Illuminati II was the socially responsible enabler of the affordable luxury clothing Noir would produce. Illuminati II would be the business-to-business brand, the "Intel inside" of high-end cotton. Noir would be the business-to-consumer end.

CSR had become a way of addressing relationships with customers, employees, suppliers, governments, local communities and the environment in a holistic manner. By engaging more pro-actively in society and acting in a responsible manner, companies were seen as interacting in a positive way to create value not only for themselves but also for society in a broader sense. There was no defined correct way of performing CSR. Like marketing, it was a discipline that could be used strategically—but with no guarantee of results. The benefits of CSR extended way beyond the strict financial bottom line; they also included an improved brand perception, reduced risks of pollution, better staff attraction and retention if the corporate philosophy matched that of the employees, etc. Peter Ingwersen remarked:

> I believe there is a tendency that people are starting to be a little less focused on themselves only. Instead of living in a world of "me-me-me", people are now looking at how to shape their world around "me-me … and others."

Engaging in responsible actions was also a way of minimizing a company's risks. Companies present in countries where governments were unwilling or unable to fulfill their responsibilities by creating norms and laws often operated in troubled water themselves, ultimately bearing the image responsibility if something went wrong. The Mattel toy recalls in the summer of 2007 due to lead paint contaminations were examples of the public relations disaster that could ensue. In an attempt to help such companies analyze their situation and social performance, the OECD produced guidelines for multinational enterprises operating in what it described as "weak governance zones." These guidelines included CSR questions a company should ask when looking at investments in such zones.[10] The UN produced its Global Compact Principles,[11] and the International Chamber of Commerce[12] its principles on issues from anti-corruption to intellectual property.

Examples of pro-active programs include the oil and gas companies' environmental management programs, such as BP working with scientists and academics in Angola to explore deep-sea eco-systems and understand better the impact of the company's operations on the environment. Companies such as Coca-Cola and

---

9 Phil Watts and Lord Holmes. "CSR: Meeting Changing Expectations." World Business Council for Sustainable Development, 1999.

10 For more details see www.oecd.org/dataoecd/26/21/36885821.pdf.

11 www.unglobalcompact.org.

12 www.iccwbo.org.

McDonald's volunteered activities within health, wellness and the environment, educating children in schools to healthy eating, pioneering eco-friendly packaging solutions, removing sugar-loaded products from easy access, etc.

Adopting a CSR policy did not guarantee that a company played fair or that it would obtain endless positive PR and attract the best employees. For Peter, however, a well thought out CSR policy should be an integral part of the company's overall strategy. It would act as the very visible "glue" running through the company, the symbol of a deep-running set of values held by the firm—about how the clothes were supposed to be produced, the cotton harvested, etc.—without compromising design, quality and appeal. Or, as he explained:

> We want to be the company that turns CSR sexy.

But was the strategy unique? While Peter was writing his business plan, Edun, a New York-based "socially conscious clothing company" founded by, among others, U2's lead singer Bono, was launched. Edun clothing was also produced from 100% organic cotton originating from African countries.[13] Worried by this potential competitor, Peter jumped on a plane to New York to meet with the people behind Edun. It turned out they were not in the luxury segment and that they, in many ways, would be complementary to, rather than competing with, his own ideas. Edun would sell mostly basic wares, like T-shirts without prints. On the face of it, two great fashion firms pushing the socially conscious ticket was probably better than one, as Edun was likely to help pay the cost of educating customers about the new concept.

Uniforms?!

In 2006 Novo Nordisk, a global pharmaceutical company from Denmark, asked Noir to design its new company uniforms. Novo Nordisk was in the process of redesigning its entire corporate image, from reception areas (to create more customer-friendly interiors) to new uniforms for all "contact" staff. Novo Nordisk was a pioneer in the promotion of CSR, having integrated the principles in its strategy very early on. It was only appropriate for them to select a clothing company that was equally CSR-conscious. And since Noir was also Danish, the choice was obvious.

Noir designed and produced uniforms for all Novo Nordisk's offices around the world. To satisfy such a large order, the company rapidly expanded its staff and dedicated it entirely to the task. The order was a critical turning point for Noir, not only financially but also strategically: 30% of Noir's turnover in 2006 originated from that single Novo Nordisk order. Strategically, the order initiated a whole new line of business for Noir. In 2007 it also designed uniforms for Georg Jensen,[14] an international luxury brand offering a wide range of products from jewellery to gift articles. More corporate clients were expected to follow in the footsteps of these two famous brands. Even though it was difficult to slot uniforms into the socially responsible affordable luxury clothing category, it did make sense as a product category within the Noir lineup: the production numbers were large so that development costs could be spread over many units, leaving quite attractive margins for the company.

An added bonus was the fact that Novo Nordisk mentored Noir on CSR issues; it opened its books and shared its experiences within this relatively new field. For example, it introduced Noir to its CSR audit practices, which facilitated Noir's acquisition of an ILO certification for its production sites in Portugal.

Pricing 'Affordable Luxury'

Socially responsible affordable luxury clothing may sound like an exciting slogan; it is also a potent oxymoron,[15] or contradiction in terms: how can luxury be affordable? Clearly, it would require a delicate balance of strong cost controls and responsible pricing. To control costs, Noir would have to set its quality just right; it had to be "high-end", but it was impossible to envision the type of 100% Italian handmade production of Prada, Givenchy or Gucci. This would break the bank and place the products outside the "affordable" bracket. For this reason, Peter opted for Portugal as a production base; it vouched for European craftsmanship and quality but was significantly less expensive than Italy. To maintain a reasonable price status, Noir would position itself just above large-scale brands such as Zara or middle-of-the-range names such as Donna Karan (DKNY) and Dolce & Gabbana (D&G) but below such luxury leaders as Prada. This would translate into an average $2,000 price tag for a Noir suit, significantly less than the $3,000 required for an equivalent suit from Prada.

Location, Location, Location

Peter designed a two-tier strategy for placing Noir products. The first few years were of course critical for the perception of the brand, so it was important to be in

14 www.georgjensen.com.
15 An oxymoron is a figure of speech that combines two normally contradictory terms. *Oxymoron* comes from the Greek *oxy* (sharp) and *moros* (dull). Thus the word *oxymoron* is itself an oxymoron … (en.wikipedia.org/wiki/Figure_of_speech).

all the right luxury stores initially—other stores and shops would follow. For Noir, the "right" luxury stores were located in top fashion cities: Paris, London, New York, Berlin, Milan, Moscow and Hong Kong. Ideal store names would include for example Barneys in New York and Harvey Nichols in London.

To reach the purchasers in these stores it was important to get their attention and become the talk of town. With this in mind, Peter contacted an old friend who worked as deputy editor at *Harper's Bazaar*, the biggest fashion magazine worldwide. He flew to New York simply to have lunch with her and tell her the story behind Noir/Illuminati II. She loved it, and in September 2005 an article featuring Peter, the company and its philosophy hit the streets. The article was added to the letters of introduction Peter sent to the 30 luxury stores he was targeting for his collection. The power of the endorsement was amazing. All 30 stores responded to the cold letter and bought pieces of the collection.

The objective was to have Noir in 30 stores the first year, 60 stores the following year and 150 stores by 2010. This was probably the maximum in order to maintain the cachet of luxury and exclusivity; the aim then would switch to increasing the volume per store. A dedicated Noir flagship store was not planned, at least not within the first five years. This would become a possibility later, with New York or Paris the most likely locations. The flagship store would serve as a PR booster. It was not anticipated that it would create channel conflicts with the other high-end stores selling Noir products.

Interestingly, Peter did not approach a single Danish purchaser at this time, in spite of being based in Copenhagen. The vision for Noir was global from the start—everything in the company had to be global. While most companies find it important to prove their products in their home markets, Noir wanted to have immediate exposure to international buyers.

All initial sales were handled by Peter himself. He believed it was important to build personal relationships with every single purchaser. After the first year, a number of agents were appointed. All existing and target customers were individually called before each fashion show and offered tickets to the events. The majority of the sales took place behind the stage straight after the shows: it was critical to get the collection to the stores before the next season and the next collections.

Promotions

Peter believed in a strategy of aggressive press coverage. He carefully planned all interviews and generated campaigns based on editorials and word of mouth rather than pure advertising. Editors from *Vogue*, *Elle* and other big fashion magazines were given exclusive interviews and the articles were published in top markets—Italy, France, Russia, Japan, China and the US. More trendy fashion magazines, such as *Numéro* and *Surface*, were also important, and even newspapers such as the *Financial Times*, *Süd Deutsche* and *Le Figaro* ran articles featuring Noir and Peter. (Refer to Exhibit 2 for some Spring 2007 designs.) This strategy allowed Peter to communicate directly with both the purchasers and the end-consumers. The pull strategy worked beautifully, with consumers emptying the shelves rapidly and forcing the stores to call urgently for replacement stock.

Peter also relied on "ambassadors" for his clothes, mostly celebrities and politicians. Celebrities got extensive media coverage, and a photo with a movie star in a Noir dress at the première of a new film would generate more and better PR than any advertising budget could buy. Peter was still working on getting endorsements from Angelina Jolie, Elizabeth Hurley and Sharleen Spiteri, the lead singer from the rock band Texas. (Refer to Exhibit 3 for some fashion magazine coverings of Noir collection in Spring 2007.)

Building a Team

To make things happen, Peter had to assemble a remarkable team of professionals. Early on, he relied on a team of six people: a designer, a production manager, a CSR specialist, a marketing expert, a sales expert and a tailor. Most of them had international experience and were "old hands" in the industry. They were more expensive to hire than rookies right out of school, but Peter believed it was the best investment to make to put the right knowledge to work immediately. By September 2007, the total number of staff had reached 15, of which 2 were freelancers. Peter did not believe in hiring friends, but wanted each individual to somehow "fit" the group at different levels: socially, culturally and professionally. His standards of professionalism were extremely high. A deal was a deal, a deadline a deadline, internally as well as externally. Customers and suppliers were to be treated with the utmost respect and CSR in general meant decent behaviors were expected toward all members of society.

Raising the Necessary Financing: Rounds 1 and 2 ...

In 2005, the launch year, Noir managed a turnover of DKK2.9 million.[16] In 2006 the turnover more than doubled to DKK6.9 million (€925,000), of which 70% originated from Noir collections and the balance from company uniforms. The target for 2007 was DKK12 million (€1.6 million), of which 70% again would be Noir-generated

---

16 Or some €388,000 on the exchange rate (1 DKK = €0.134) prevailing on 30 December 2005.

and the balance come from contract sales. Novo Nordisk alone would account for 80% of the uniform sales, or some 24% of the total turnover for the year.

Although Noir had been extremely well received initially, growth consumed resources and Peter struggled to finance the company. The quest for funds started right at the beginning of the company and never really stopped. In March 2005, he engineered the first round of financing. He was ready to give up 50% of the company in order to bring on board the "right" investor—someone not only able to finance the company but also to offer relevant competences and networks. He found what he was looking for in a Danish textile company called GGT. While Peter knew a lot about designing and producing clothes, he knew little about growing cotton or producing and selling textiles, so GGT's skills would complement his own nicely. The company was 50% owned by one of the biggest Danish private equity funds, another interesting connection to establish. In July 2005, GGT and Peter signed the term sheet on the basis of a formal business plan. Both parties agreed that a specialist accounting firm should look at the valuation of Noir, based on the pro forma figures provided. A number of sensitivity analyses were also conducted to account for the uncertainties in some of the assumptions in the model. (Refer to Exhibit 4 for valuation details.) The combined valuation of Noir/Illuminati II came to around DKK70 million, or some € 9.4 million.

Unfortunately, the private equity investor suddenly decided to sell its stake in GGT, which left the company uncertain about its own future and not really in a position to invest in Noir. This was a tough blow for Peter, who had spent almost three months and DKK3 million (about €400,000) trying to finalize the deal. The effort was now in vain. Finding new investors turned into a question of survival. Doubling up his efforts, Peter went back to everyone he knew in the industry, both individuals and corporates and was able to sign up two angel co-investors. One of them, Thomas Lavkorn, had relevant experience in the clothing industry, having previously built a fashion company and taken it public through an IPO. Jointly, the two partners invested DKK3 million for an equity share of 49%, for a pre-money valuation of about DKK3 million (about €400,000), nowhere close to the earlier valuation envisioned with GGT. This investment was also clearly insufficient to cover the burn rate for long, but it was essential to give the company a breathing space of about six months to bring in the additional financing needed.

In December 2005, Peter met Mrs. Nash at a dinner party in London. Mrs. Nash was born in Kenya and was passionate about fashion. She was married to Noel Nash, the CEO and founder of a London-based European private equity group. Noel was actively looking for new opportunities within the start-up arena to place some of his private money. Two months later, the Nash couple, who were attracted to the idea of combining CSR and luxury fashion, visited Peter in Copenhagen to conduct the due diligence. A formal investment proposal came out of the process. Simultaneously, another wealthy private individual in Denmark heard about Noir through the fashion grapevine. He took the initiative to contact Peter and undertook his own separate due diligence, also resulting in a separate investment proposal.

Peter decided to bring the two investors together on a common term sheet. The total investment would be around DKK10 million (€1.34 million). The agreement was signed in July 2006. One of the original investors asked out, so after the second round, the equity was equally shared between the two second-round investors (20% each), the remaining original investor (10%) and Peter (50%).

Leveraging the Financing ... and Preparing for the Next Rounds

While DKK10 million was a nice injection, it would not last forever under a forecasted monthly cash burn of around DKK700,000 and only a small profit expected in 2006. Noir was able to obtain a short-term bank loan of DKK5 million, but it was clear that another round of financing would have to be finalized by the spring of 2007.

Two groups of potential investors materialized for the third round. First, the existing lead investors expressed an interest in coming back with a group of young individuals who owned a leading Scandinavian agency specialized in online content. As lead investors of round three, the investors would offer Noir services for web design at cost. Noir, for its part, would have to promise to use the agency for three years. The other potential investor was a well-known UK-based Nordic professional investor, Balder Group, investing in retail, property and media in Northern Europe. The Balder Group offered a convertible loan, with conversion tied to Noir delivering on set milestones over a three-year period. The Balder Group already owned several clothing companies and department store chains in Nordic countries and the UK.

Both investor groups were committing to invest the same amount of money to Noir, but their profiles could not have been more different. The current investors were known entities, had deep pockets, a very strong interest and their media agency would be very valuable to the brand. The new Icelandic investor offered some interesting distribution channels and extensive retail experience. The latter could become particularly interesting for Illuminati II when the cotton textiles were ready to be sold, in particular if the brands within the Balder Group were ready to pay for the high quality. This was a big assumption at this point since most of these clothing-related companies were currently not in the luxury segment.

Peter leaned back in his chair and took a deep breath. He had never been naive about the work and challenges he would be faced with. But right now there were many issues to consider:

- How strong was the product positioning? Affordable luxury was very much an oxymoron, but then again these kinds of conflicts never prevented brands from becoming successful. Did Noir's price/quality positioning really make sense in the competitive fashion industry?

- Did it make sense to push two brands (Noir and Illuminati II) at the same time? Was the original rationale still strong enough?

- From a placement strategy point of view, did it make sense to go global from the start or was there value in testing the home market first?

- Are uniforms for large corporate clients supporting or hindering the development of the brand and its perceived positioning in the market?

- Which investor would be best for Noir Illuminati II to accelerate the business as well as to support the company, its basic values and principles in the long run?

- Did he have the right team to grow the business?

- Was the envisioned market entry strategy sufficient to support the planned growth?

- How attractive would Noir Illuminati II be to companies like Gucci and LVMH from a portfolio point of view? Why would they possibly want to acquire him? If that exit route was really unlikely, then how would he best prepare for the next alternative route for exit?

- Would the Illuminati cotton be ready for launch as planned? Would it sell?

There was still much to organize before the board meeting the following day. It was going to be yet another very long night. The future of the company lay in the balance, so sleep would clearly have to wait …

Exhibit 1 **Peter Ingwersen's CV**

Date of Birth: 10.10.62
Birthplace: Copenhagen, Denmark
Nationality: Danish

Education

School of Arts & Crafts, Kolding, Denmark, 1982–1986
Specialization: Clothing Design, Retail Trends, Concept Development and
Consumer Attitudes.
The school is the local equivalent to St. Martin's School of Art in the United
Kingdom

Professional Experience

2002–2004:   Managing Director Day Birger et Mikkelsen (www.day.dk)
1999–2001:   Global Brand Director for Levi's Vintage Clothing & Levi's
                 RED
                 Member of the Levi's® Brand Management Leadership Team
                 Full P&L Accountable, reporting to the President of the
                 Levi's® Brand
                 Global Brand Director, Levi Strauss Europe, Middle East and
                 Africa, Bruxelles
                 Responsible for brands such as Levi's® Europe, Levi's® US
                 and Levi's® Japan
1998–1999:   Strategist. Part of team of six asked to redesign and reposi-
                 tion Levi's® Europe.
1995–1998:   Marketing Innovations Manager, Levi Strauss Europe, Middle
                 East & Africa.
1990–1995:   Creative Manager, Levi's® Nordic
1986–1990:   Head of Design, Levi's® Nordic Region

Exhibit 2 **Examples of Noir Design, Spring 2007 Collection**

Exhibit 3 **Sample Press Coverage of Noir Fashion—*Vogue*, *Bazaar*, *Cover*, *The Times***

Exhibit 4 **2005 Valuation Model: Earnings Projections**

Assumptions for the forecasting period, 2005-2014:
The forecasted results are based on NOiR's budgets and businessplan
For the period 2011-2014 an annual growth of 10% p.a. is assumed
For the period 2011-2014 the gross margin is reduced by 5% p.a., from 50% in 2011 to 35% in 2014 to reflect growing competition
For the period 2011-2014 expenses to PR, advertising, sales and distribution as well as administration is estimated to be 17% of the turnover
Tax is 28%

Assumptions for the terminal period, 2015-2016:
Gross margin 30%
Expenses to PR, advertising, sales and distribution as well as administration is estimated to be 17% of the turnover
Tax is 28%
Growth is estimated at 3%

(DKK)	Forecast 2005	2006	2007	2008	2009	2010	2011	2012	2013	2014	Terminal Period 2015	2016
Turnover	-	5,088,000	16,879,000	51,720,000	65,670,000	100,398,000	110,437,800	121,481,580	133,629,738	146,992,712	151,402,493	151,402,493
COGS	150,000	2,694,000	8,589,000	26,010,000	32,985,000	50,349,000	55,383,900	66,814,869	80,177,843	95,545,263	105,981,745	105,981,745
Gross Result	(150,000)	2,394,000	8,290,000	25,710,000	32,685,000	50,049,000	55,053,900	54,666,711	53,451,895	51,447,449	45,420,748	45,420,748
Sales, General & Administration	4,841,000	8,336,000	12,202,000	14,124,000	15,868,000	17,268,000	18,994,800	20,894,280	22,983,708	25,282,079	26,040,541	26,040,541
EBITDA	(4,991,000)	(5,942,000)	(3,912,000)	11,586,000	16,817,000	32,781,000	36,059,100	33,772,431	30,468,187	26,165,370	19,380,207	19,380,207
Write offs												
EBIT	(4,991,000)	(5,942,000)	(3,912,000)	11,586,000	16,817,000	32,781,000	36,059,100	33,772,431	30,468,187	26,165,370	19,380,207	19,380,207
Tax	(1,397,480)	(1,663,760)	(1,095,360)	3,244,080	4,708,760	9,178,680	10,096,548	9,456,281	8,531,092	7,326,304	5,426,458	5,426,458
Net Income	(3,593,520)	(4,278,240)	(2,816,640)	8,341,920	12,108,240	23,602,320	25,962,552	24,316,150	21,937,095	18,839,066	13,963,749	13,963,749
Gross margin	N.A.	47%	49%	50%	50%	50%	50%	45%	40%	35%	30%	30%
EBITDA margin	N.A.	-117%	-23%	22%	26%	33%	33%	28%	23%	18%	13%	13%
EBIT margin	N.A.	-117%	-23%	22%	26%	33%	33%	28%	23%	18%	13%	13%

2005 Valuation Model: Discounted Cash Flow Model and Select Sensitivities

Assumptions:
Cashflow is estimated based on turnover etc - above
Suppliers are paid immediately
Capital expenditures = 0
WACC at 25%

(DKK)	Forecast 2005	2006	2007	2008	2009	2010	2011	2012	2013	2014	Terminal Period 2015	2016
EBIT	(4,991,000)	(5,542,000)	(3,912,000)	11,586,000	16,817,000	32,781,000	36,059,100	33,772,431	30,468,187	26,165,370	19,380,207	19,380,207
Adjusted tax	1,397,480	1,663,760	1,095,360	(3,244,080)	(4,708,760)	(9,178,680)	(10,096,548)	(9,456,281)	(8,531,092)	(7,326,304)	(5,426,458)	(5,426,458)
EBIT after tax	(3,593,520)	(4,278,240)	(2,816,640)	8,341,920	12,108,240	23,602,320	25,962,552	24,316,150	21,937,095	18,839,066	13,953,749	13,953,749
Write offs	-	-	-	-	-	-	-	-	-	-	-	-
Gross cash flow	(3,593,520)	(4,278,240)	(2,816,640)	8,341,920	12,108,240	23,602,320	25,962,552	24,316,150	21,937,095	18,839,066	13,953,749	13,953,749
Changes in Working Capital	-	(848,000)	(1,965,167)	(5,806,833)	(2,325,000)	(5,788,000)	(1,673,300)	(1,840,630)	(2,024,693)	(2,227,162)	(740,010)	-
Changes in Fixed Assets	-	-	-	-	-	-	-	-	-	-	-	-
Free Cash flow	(3,593,520)	(5,126,240)	(4,781,807)	2,535,087	9,783,240	17,814,320	24,289,252	22,475,520	19,912,402	16,611,904	13,213,739	13,953,749
Discount factor, WACC @ 25%	0.89	0.72	0.57	0.46	0.37	0.29	0.23	0.19	0.15	0.12	0.10	0.10
NPV of FCF	(3,214,142)	(3,668,039)	(2,737,266)	1,160,935	3,584,162	5,221,126	5,695,070	4,215,846	2,988,055	1,994,226	1,269,026	6,091,343

Sensitivity Analysis (DKK)

The table below illustrates the effect when changing the following factors and assumptions:
Sales
EBITDA margin
WACC
Growth (terminal period)

	Sales Index					
	98	99	100	101	102	
EBITDA margin	-4%	13,751,150	14,149,101	14,566,299	15,003,478	15,461,398
	-2%	16,857,428	17,368,264	17,903,303	18,463,501	19,049,845
	0%	19,963,707	20,587,427	21,240,307	21,923,523	22,638,252
	2%	23,069,985	23,806,590	24,577,311	25,383,546	26,226,739
	4%	26,176,264	27,025,753	27,914,315	28,843,569	29,815,185

	WACC (%)					
	21%	23%	25%	27%	29%
Growth in Terminal Period	2.0%	29,975,797	24,997,813	20,960,509	17,640,546	14,879,303
	2.5%	30,252,717	25,190,364	21,097,194	17,739,298	14,951,734
	3.0%	30,545,392	25,392,803	21,240,307	17,842,332	15,027,081
	3.5%	30,855,172	25,605,921	21,390,297	17,949,920	15,105,517
	4.0%	31,183,566	25,830,552	21,547,654	18,062,361	15,187,226

Case B: Greenwash and Anorexic Models

Peter could not believe his eyes. He was just sifting through comments posted on the Inhabitat[1] website following the London and New York Fashion Weeks. While the articles themselves were very supportive of his strategy and Rikke Wienmann's collections, the website's readers' comments were direct attacks on his sustainability rationale, basically labeling it "greenwash," very critical of his choice of models—too skinny by today's standards—and expressing concerns about anorexia.

Once the shock had worn off, he tried to understand what the implications of such rash customer perceptions could be for the brand and its positioning. Maybe this was just an isolated incident from disgruntled British and American customers, overexposed to the issues and hence over-sensitive to them. But maybe it also reflected a turning point in the Corporate Social Responsibility movement. Were people really starting to feel that way? Were they starting to question these CSR labels and how much they really did for people in Africa? Was this the beginning of the dreaded backlash against the new green political correctness? Was CSR now also spreading to issues such as people's weights?

The responses from the fashion editor and other readers were encouraging, but maybe it was time to prepare for similar questioning of the underlying philosophy of the company. It was time for sure to shed more light on Illuminati II's contributions to Uganda's farmers …

---

1 Inhabitat.com is a weblog devoted to the future of design, tracking the innovations in technology, practices and materials that are pushing architecture and home design toward a smarter and more sustainable future. Inhabitat was started by NYC designer and graduate architecture student Jill Fehrenbacher as a forum in which to investigate emerging trends in product, interior and architectural design. Emily Pilloton is the managing editor; Sarah Rich and Evelyn Lee and Jorge Chapa are senior contributing editors.

Inhabitat

London Fashion Week: Noir Fall 2007,[2] by Jill Danyelle, March 4th, 2007

Noir is a relatively new label founded by Copenhagen native Peter Ingwersen and designed by Rikke Wienmann. The label has been burning up the runway with its hot looks, but Noir's sexiness is based in sustainability. They are connected with Illuminati-II, a textile company that will launch in 2008. The company was created to brand, market and sell high-level, organic cotton fabrics and Noir is being built as the vessel. Their first collection, Spring 2006, contained 30% certified fabrics. This has been increased seasonally to 70% with their most recent collection. The certified fabrics range from silks to cottons to wools. The certification standards are either Oeko-Tex or EU Eco Label. Additionally, Illuminati II is a member of the United Nations Global Compact and supports ILO, The International Labour Organization, ICC's Business Charter for sustainable development and UN's Universal Declaration of Human Rights. Finally, the Noir foundation will contribute to secure the workers in Uganda and ensure that the needs for things such as wells and medicine are met.

Peter Ingwersen recently stated, "Illuminati II is created to prove that organic and ethical fabrics can be used in luxurious and sexy designs as proven in the Noir collection."

Season after season, the label continues to illustrate just that. Its recent show during London fashion Week was no exception. It closed the show with two stunning

2 www.inhabitat.com/2007/03/04/london-fashion-week-noir-fall-2007.

gowns, leaving little excuse for not going green on the red carpet. What came beforehand was perhaps its most ambitious collection yet. It had plenty of Noir's signature "darkness", but also included crisp white shirts and soft neutrals in plenty of wearable styles that continue to adhere to its inspiration of strong tailoring that is often a feminine interpretation of the masculine armoire.

Noir's Fall 2007 Raven collection

Fall 2007 images courtesy style.com[3]

3 style.com.

Responses to 'London Fashion Week: Noir Fall 2007'

April 4th, 2007 at 10:26 pm
Blake says:

> Does anyone find it a bit repulsive that this brand is basically tying its sales to the plight of poor African farmers? Basically "Buy our clothes or they go hungry". There is plenty of fair trade and organic cotton already on the market to choose from if serious about helping people so no need to start some new organizations at some future date as long as you keep buying.
>
> Noir is heavily marketed as sustainable, eco, etc. yet up to this latest season they used mostly regular cotton and a lot of leather. The crazy part is that this is stated and yet they are still being highlighted everywhere as the line to save the world. Certified Oeko Tex 100 does not mean sustainable. It only means that the dyes (which are still bad) are free of heavy metals and controlled instead if dumped in the environment. Almost all dyeing in Europe is Oeko Tex 100 these days.
>
> Can anyone recognize greenwashing anymore? If someone makes a big noise about how much good they are doing in the world then this deserves to be scrutinized. No free passes just because there is the occasional exposed nipple.

April 27th, 2007 at 3:04 pm
Jill Danyelle, fashion editor, says:

> Blake,
>
> I clearly view Noir differently. I don't think that they are trying to get you to buy their clothes so that you won't feel guilty about the plight of poor Africans. I think they are trying to be supportive of the people that support the cotton industry. It is difficult to start a huge agricultural project overnight. I feel Mr. Ingwersen was very open and transparent about the company's current production and future goals. Illuminati is also one of the few companies to focus on producing quality eco-textiles for the apparel industry. We need these companies in the supply chain to support the industry.
>
> At this point, certified fabrics are better than nothing. Additionally, there may not be plenty of fair trade and organic cotton on the market, especially if you are talking about finished textiles for high end designs. We need eco-design in all levels of the apparel market.
>
> As the sustainable bubble rises, yes, we will see more greenwashing. However, I believe transparency is key. It is up to the media (and consumers) to educate themselves. As you noticed, I did ask questions about the fabric. I am not sure many other fashion journalists could even tell you what SKAL or ISO 1400 means. I don't see Noir trying to earn points and customers as much as I see them trying to raise awareness in an industry that has been very slow to tip. One way to get a fashionista's attention is to design a stellar collection.

September 10th, 2007 at 4:25 pm
Ksrline Says:

> What Noir is doing is very important. They are not greenwashing, they are the real deal. They may be new on the American market but Peter Ingwersen has been director of a very respected high end fashion label in Denmark. He is a first mover- trend setter. Noir is spreading the awareness amongst fashionistas around the world (especially in northern Europe) about the story about how the clothes are made. This is helping create the demand for sustainable and fairtrade labels and items. If you work in design you know that finding sustainable materials is a challenge. We need the demand and awareness for the development of high quality products and process to happen. Fashion is an important and powerful factor. Fashion is communication. Please support Noir for being part of leading the way.

New York Fashion Week: Noir Spring 2008,[4] by Jill Danyelle, September 9th, 2007

Yesterday, the Danish label NOIR held its first show during New York Fashion Week. The socially and environmentally conscious label was a welcomed addition to the slowly growing, yet still miniscule contingent of designers showing eco-friendly options here. NOIR worked with model Shalom Harlow for their spring campaign (above). The model is well known for her support of eco-friendly fashion. Continue reading for details on the collection and images from the show.

For Spring 2008, their fifth collection, the line was dedicated to 'transparency'. The duality of this concept for NOIR was expressed physically with the launch of their Nu NOIR lingerie collection, while also being woven into their CSR business model. While the collection kept within the overall dark and sexy theme the label has become known for, there were some touches of lightness and color, such as the bright pink dress in a double layer of African cotton and silk. The continued use of leather won't win over any vegans, but there were plenty of other fabrics that could garner the respect of environmentalists in general. The collection was comprised mainly of organic and African cottons, silks and oeko-tex certified fabrics in caviar grays, black and white.

Hopefully, the added presence of another eco label at the shows will underscore the diversity we can see in eco-fashion. Fashion companies and designers may begin to realize that designing with the environment in mind has little to do with adhering to any one aesthetic.

Responses to "New York Fashion Week: Noir Spring 2008"

September 10th, 2007 at 7:11 pm
Rachelblue says:

> Can't designers use real people as models—people who occasionally smile, eat and think real thoughts? Sigh! Good on Noir for their environmental and social principles but these designs seem quite dull to me—not very inspiring—same old same old—yawn!

September 11th, 2007 at 12:25 am
Mel says:

> Wow, you seem a bit cynical, Rachelblue. Models are, in fact, actual people who eat, smile, and think and it irritates me when people judge them based on what they've seen them do for 30 seconds on a catwalk. Being pretty and slim doesn't make them idiots. And you do realize that it is the designers who instruct the models not to smile?
>
> That said, I agree about the designs. They're definitely more high-fashion than a lot of environmentally conscious brands, but the styles are pretty 'done'.

Case 14

The ReUse People
Turning Scrap into Sales[1,2]

William G. Powell and Charles J. Corbett
University of California, Los Angeles (UCLA), USA

Introduction

In June 2007, Ted Reiff, co-founder and president of The ReUse People (TRP), sat in his warehouse cubicle and pondered over the future of his nonprofit organization. He had just watched a truck unload a beautiful hardwood floor that his organization had salvaged, and he felt proud that he had been able to save such pristine materials from an untimely and unnecessary landfill grave.

According to its Web site at the time, "The ReUse People reduces the solid waste stream and changes the way the built environment is renewed by salvaging building materials and distributing them for reuse."[3] In other words, TRP specialized in deconstruction, the process of dismantling a building and salvaging the materials. It was at a critical juncture in its growth. Thus far, it had offered services spanning the entire deconstruction value chain: deconstruction, logistics, and retail. The company's warehouse in Oakland, California, which was used for storage and retail

---

1 This case © 2010 The Regents of the University of California.
2 This case was prepared by William G. Powell (MBA, 2006) and Professor Charles Corbett, with assistance from Kate Winegar, as a basis for classroom discussion rather than to illustrate either effective or ineffective handling of an administrative situation. This case was awarded 2nd prize in the Social Entrepreneurship Track of the Oikos Case Writing Competition 2009.
3 The ReUse People's Web site, "News Room," www.thereusepeople.org/NewsRoom, accessed December 31, 2007.

sales, was nearing capacity. TRP had more deconstruction jobs than it could handle, and it was shipping salvaged material across the United States and into Mexico. With such high levels of demand, the TRP board of directors knew that it should grow the organization, but the members didn't agree about how to do so.

Some company managers argued that TRP should become the leading deconstruction contractor by entering new cities, hiring its own deconstruction crews, and operating its own warehouses. TRP's profit margins on deconstruction jobs were very high, and supporters of this view felt that TRP should raise the funds for expansion into one new city at a time and focus on profit margins. Other managers believed that an early mover advantage would be critical for TRP's success, and that the company should become a leading authority on deconstruction by training and certifying other demolition contractors in deconstruction. The differences had large implications for the organization, how it was run, and how it fulfilled its mission. If the organization chose to focus on growing as a deconstruction contractor, it would have to open new warehouses, hire staff, and compete with local demolition contractors. If it chose to begin certifying demolition contractors, it would have to focus on training and evangelism.

Reiff saw the merit in both strategies, but was unsure which to pursue. Ultimately, he would be responsible for leading the organization down whichever path he and the board of directors chose, and with an important board meeting coming up, he knew that the decision would be made fairly soon.

Company Beginnings

Ted Reiff

Ted Reiff was a serial entrepreneur who had started companies in four different industries throughout his career. A graduate of Ohio State University with a major in business, he began his career working for the data processing consulting firm Management Horizons. When PricewaterhouseCoopers acquired Management Horizons, Reiff took an entrepreneurial position at Raytheon, and later started his own investment bank in San Diego focusing on biotechnology, artificial intelligence, and defense technology. When the investment bank did not perform to his liking, he closed the San Diego location and started a similar bank in Mexico City. He returned to the United States in 1993.

In early 1993, Reiff gave a lecture on US–Mexican joint ventures to contractors in Tijuana, Mexico. At that event, Judy Bishop saw him speak. Bishop was working on a relief effort for the victims of flooding in northwestern Mexico where an estimated 10,000 people had fled their homes. Bishop spoke to Reiff after his lecture and asked for help in sending building materials across the US–Mexican border to help rebuild the thousands of flood-damaged homes. Bishop and Reiff collaborated and convinced the city councils of San Diego and Tijuana to allow a shipment of building materials to cross the border without tariffs. By April 1993, Bishop organized a shipment of 400 tons of donated building materials from San Diego to Tijuana. According to Reiff, this was the largest private donation that had ever occurred between the two countries.

The success of the donation spurred Reiff and Bishop to continue to collaborate. Reiff wrote a business plan for the resale of building materials to Mexican contractors. The business plan originally called for the organization to be a for-profit enterprise, but difficulty in fundraising persuaded Reiff and Bishop to incorporate as a nonprofit. Bishop and Reiff were very excited about their business idea, but nonprofit incorporation was a lengthy process, and they did not want to wait the year it would take for the government to register their organization. In the process of discussing the difficulties of incorporating a nonprofit with his friends, Bishop found out that one friend had a registered, but non-operational nonprofit. Since the friend had already paid for the registration and was recognized by the government as having 501(c)3 tax status, Reiff took over the nonprofit and changed its name to The ReUse People. While their original plan called for a profit-generating revenue stream, the rewritten nonprofit business plan incentivized building-materials donors with a tax-deductible donation.

Reiff had strong opinions about the role of an entrepreneur in the early stages of growing an organization. A fervent believer in planning, he carefully crafted the TRP business plan and mission statement to ensure relevancy for several years. It was important to Reiff that he and his managers made decisions according to the agreed-upon plan. Upon hiring new managers, he looked for a candidate's interest in sticking to a plan, even after it became clear that the plan had some faults. "Every plan is going to have problems," Reiff commented. "Most entrepreneurs come up with a plan and then change it when their next-door neighbor points out a problem. I like to hire people who stick with a plan." Reiff also instilled in his employees the need to be salespeople. "Each employee's number-one priority on a daily basis should be to sell people on The ReUse People's mission." Sales, Reiff argued, would lead to top-line revenue growth—his second priority after selling.

TRP's Early Days

TRP's first materials donor was Home Depot. Home Depot retail locations had a liberal merchandise returns policy, but they often had difficulty reselling returned items and discarded those that did not sell quickly. TRP began taking these discarded items and shipping them to Mexico where they would be reused. In return, Home Depot received a tax deduction for the donation. Shortly thereafter, TRP began deconstructing homes in San Diego.

Recognizing that there was a larger market and more sympathetic municipal governments in northern California, Reiff moved TRP to Alameda County, across the bay from San Francisco. TRP received a grant to open its first retail warehouse to sell its salvaged materials, and opened the lot to the public in 2000. By mid-2000, TRP offered, according to Reiff, the industry's most comprehensive set of services related to deconstruction and materials reuse in the country. No other organization at the time offered deconstruction services, shipping and logistics, and retail.

Company Operations

The Deconstruction Process

Based in a warehouse in Oakland, California, TRP began its service cycle with an estimate of a deconstruction job opportunity. The company often competed against demolition contractors, so its salespeople had to educate the homeowner and the general contractor about deconstruction, its environmental impact, and its financial benefits.

Demolition was the traditional method of tearing down a building. It took one to two days to tear down a typical residence, and required a bulldozer or excavator and a crew equipped with sledgehammers. By contrast, deconstruction took longer, was more organized, required more people, and created much less waste. Despite its benefits, however, deconstruction could cost the homeowner two to three times as much as demolition. (Exhibit 1 contains information about the financial benefits of deconstruction versus demolition.) At the time, the average cost of deconstruction in the Bay Area was $12 per square foot.

Most residential deconstruction firms were incorporated as nonprofits, allowing the homeowner to gain a tax advantage from donating the salvaged materials. This tax advantage outweighed the higher cost of deconstruction services. A deconstruction team could often salvage $80,000–$100,000 of materials and appliances from a larger home, as shown in Exhibit 2. Depending on his or her tax bracket, the average homeowner could earn about 30% of the value of the donated salvaged materials. In addition, homeowners who chose to demolish their homes also had to pay a landfill fee, which was about $60–$80 per ton in the Bay Area.[4] A typical project for TRP would be a 2,500 square foot residence, but they had done projects as large as 500,000 square feet. Two particularly large projects were the sets of the film sequels The Matrix 2 and 3, and the deconstruction of the Dayview Terrace complex in National City in San Diego County. The latter consisted of 618 living units, of 750 square feet each, and some other buildings. Deconstruction had been planned to take two years, but in the event only two months were available; Reiff recalls how they were able to salvage all the doors and other key parts, despite being practically chased around the site by the bulldozers.

---

4 Bob Falk and Brad Guy, *Unbuilding: Salvaging the Architectural Treasures of Unwanted Houses* (Newtown, CT: The Taunton Press, 2007), 12. "A simple raised wood-floor, wood-framed older house can weigh 50 lb. per sq. ft. A 1,500-sq.-ft. light wood-frame building can therefore weigh more than 37 tons or the volume of about three 40-cu.-yd. container loads."

TRP's main hurdle in selling services to homeowners was the cost of the deconstruction, which was much higher than demolition. It simply took longer for TRP salespeople to educate homeowners and general contractors about the financial and environmental benefits of deconstruction. Reiff argued that there would be an inflection point at some time in the future when the cost of deconstruction would be surpassed by the cost of demolition. The financial incentive for homeowners to choose deconstruction over demolition would be a straightforward calculation that did not require estimations of tax breaks to offset higher direct fees. When this occurred, TRP and others would have the option of changing their tax status from nonprofit to for-profit.

Successful deconstruction required careful planning and preparation. Assessing whether deconstruction could be performed safely was a first and critical step. Some buildings were not suitable, either due to insurmountable structural deficiencies or an excess of hazardous materials. Wood structures were the most suitable for deconstruction, as steel and concrete were more likely to be recycled than reused.[5] If deconstruction appeared feasible, a walk-through yielded an inventory of materials, and the contractor needed to decide which to salvage.

Once TRP's estimate was complete, the homeowners hired a third-party specialist to appraise the value of the materials that would be salvaged. (Exhibit 2 contains examples of appraised values of materials salvaged from TRP deconstruction projects.) This appraisal later served as the dollar amount the donating homeowners could deduct from their taxes that year. If anything happened to the materials after they were donated (rain damage, for example), TRP assumed all liability and the homeowner could still declare the original appraised value for tax purposes.

Once a deal with a homeowner was finalized, a TRP area manager walked through the house with a voice recorder, placing numbered stickers on items he thought were salvageable. Arthur Renaud, the area manager for West Los Angeles, explained that this recorded information was turned into an inventory list, which included all the items, their numbers, and corresponding descriptions. Each worksite had a binder that described the steps TRP expected the crew to follow, and in which sequence. Some crews did not adhere to the precise schedule, but as long as the end result was good, Renaud did not mind.

The deconstruction process took TRP 10 to 20 days to complete, and varied according to the size of the home and the number of crew members on the job. The crew began with the home interior, removing cabinets, lighting, and other cosmetic details. The roofing was then dismantled, followed by the sheathing, rafters, and ceiling of the home. Finally, the wall coverings, siding, and the studs, flooring, and floor joists were removed. The crew spent the last few days cleaning up the site and loading the trucks to tow away the salvaged materials. They hauled debris separately to a materials-recovery facility or landfill.

---

5   Falk and Guy, *Unbuilding: Salvaging the Architectural Treasures of Unwanted Houses*. This paragraph draws heavily from this reference.

Before deconstruction started the contractor decided where and how to store the salvaged material and debris. Because many items were worth much more as a set than individually (e.g. doorknobs, kitchen cabinets, vintage lighting fixtures, hardwood floors, etc.), and pristine items were more valuable than damaged ones, careful storage during the deconstruction process was critical. Every time items were moved they risked being damaged or separated, so preparing a plan before deconstruction started helped to avoid costly and time-consuming movements later in the process.[6]

Renaud stressed the importance of keeping a clean workplace, as "it represents us." This included staging the salvaged materials carefully, so they could be loaded quickly and correctly. Needless to say, this had to be done without damaging the materials. If a deconstruction crew seemed to be causing too much breakage, Renaud reminded them of the importance of proceeding carefully.

TRP had a few deconstruction crews of its own, but for most projects it worked with traditional demolition companies with which it had close relationships. On such projects, the demolition crews operated according to TRP's guidelines, and were trained and closely monitored by TRP. Reiff was also exploring an arrangement with the California Conservation Corps, under which TRP would train young adults working with the CCC in deconstruction, after which the CCC would have licensed deconstruction crews in their midst. Reiff saw this as a way to combine environmental and social goals, as such an arrangement would provide young adults with the skills needed for other jobs they might take upon leaving the CCC, including exposure to an actual workplace.

Logistics

From the very beginning, Reiff saw logistics as the key to successful deconstruction. "No contractor in the world likes to throw something away; they just don't know what to do with it." Sometimes there were stores for salvaged materials, but they did not take everything that a contractor saved, and even big stores filled up during the peak summer season so they simply could not accept any more materials. Reiff's goal was to open multiple warehouses so they could move materials to where they were in demand, and to be able to tell everybody that "we'll never be full, you bring your stuff to us and we'll find a home for it." Shipping materials between TRP's warehouses was not cheap; Reiff noted that once they started doing this they no longer made money, but they did not lose money either. He gave the example of hollow core doors, which were widely used, but nobody wanted to reuse them. TRP removed the doorknobs and hinges, which "we can sell all day long," and stacked the doors in a semi-trailer. The company then sent them to Mexico, where they sold

---

6 Falk and Guy, *Unbuilding: Salvaging the Architectural Treasures of Unwanted Houses*, p. 108. This page gives sample site layouts for different configurations of the house and the lot.

them for a dollar a door, enough to cover the freight. "What's important," says Reiff, "is that we're keeping a very low-value, high-volume item out of landfill."

Retail Operations

After performing a residential deconstruction, TRP either shipped the salvaged materials to a prearranged buyer or to its warehouse. Prearranged orders came from a variety of sources: TRP consistently received orders from Mexican contractors for lumber and raw materials; and it had a standing order for all high-quality lumber from a specialty-furniture manufacturer based in Berkeley, California, called The Wooden Duck. Reiff estimated that the average shipping costs were 1.0–1.5% of the total appraised value of the salvaged materials.

The warehouse was open to the public, and a mix of contractors and consumers shopped its aisles. The majority of the materials that reached its warehouse were sold within two months, and many items were donated to other local nonprofit organizations or sent to Mexico for the cost of shipping. Because TRP priced materials to move quickly, and donated a lot to local nonprofits, there was no connection between appraised value and sales price. Even some warehouse items sold for as little as 5% of their appraised values.

At the rate TRP sold items through retail, Reiff estimated that the warehouse could hold materials from about seven deconstruction jobs per month. TRP needed resources from three to five deconstruction jobs per month in order to cover all warehouse costs, including rent ($0.50 per square foot), personnel, and utilities. The TRP warehouse in Oakland had historically generated a 20% operating profit margin.

Marketing

TRP did not invest much money in marketing. The organization instead relied on word-of-mouth referrals, fliers posted near its warehouse, and its website. Reiff made sure each of his employees—regardless of their function within the company—promoted deconstruction whenever possible. TRP also sold bumper stickers and t-shirts containing humorous quotes such as, "I bought your grandmother's commode at The ReUse People."

Reiff was also efficient at generating media interest. In addition to several news articles, he and TRP were featured in a 30-minute Public Broadcasting Service program hosted by Huell Howser. To create a sense of community, Reiff published a semiannual newsletter titled *The Velvet Crowbar* and distributed it to former and potential clients, general building contractors, architects, and building department employees of local municipalities.

Industry Considerations

The Deconstruction Industry

In 2004, deconstruction was still a fledgling industry in the United States despite increasing landfill fees. Industry experts estimated that construction and demolition produced approximately 30% of all solid waste in the United States in 2003, while only about 20–30% of that waste was recycled.[7] Furthermore, the Institute for Local Self Reliance projected that deconstruction could redirect almost 24 million tons of waste per year from landfills back into the economy.[8]

By contrast, the deconstruction industry in Europe had been forced to evolve earlier than in the United States due to higher landfill fees and pricier building materials. Homeowners had to find ways to reduce waste during home construction. Governments, anticipating diminishing landfill space, created incentives to encourage materials reuse. The United Kingdom was the most advanced in reusing construction materials. In 2005, almost 24% (60 million tons) of 250 million tons of construction material used in the United Kingdom was recycled. The Netherlands and Germany recycled 14% and 10%, respectively.[9] In 2006, The Dutch government required that all materials be reused when contractors tore down a building, and that no debris was allowed.[10] In many European countries, materials manufacturers were responsible for managing their supply chain to ensure that recycled materials had an aftermarket.[11]

Despite the fact that about 245,000 residential structures were demolished each year in the United States,[12] deconstruction was more common in commercial and government sectors than in the residential sector. Industrial-grade materials, such as steel beams and cinder blocks, were easier to reuse since they were durable and modular. Commercial real estate companies and government agencies also had the financial and industry resources to make a deconstruction project worthwhile. A commercial real estate developer had the industry contacts to quickly identify another party interested in an order of reusable steel beams, and had the financial resources to ship it. Government entities, such as the Army Corps of Engineers, had long been advocates of deconstruction and published widely on its feasibility and importance. So far, though, this was not a market that TRP had focused on.

---

7 Deconstruction Institute, *A Guide to Deconstruction*, prepared by Bradley Guy and Eleanor M. Gibeau, January 2003.

8 Diane Greer, "Building the Deconstruction Industry," *BioCycle*, November 1, 2004.

9 "The classic image of demolition is of a building crumbling under the blow of a wrecking ball," *Contract Journal*, March 15, 2006.

10 Barbara Knecht, "Designing for Disassembly and Deconstruction" *Architectural Record*, October 1, 2004.

11 Ibid.

12 Deconstruction Institute, *A Guide to Deconstruction*, prepared by Bradley Guy and Eleanor M. Gibeau, January 2003.

Within the residential sector, deconstruction was most common in areas of the country where salvaged materials had historical value. Firms across the United States specialized in removing moldings, statues, stained glass windows, and other high-value architectural elements found in older buildings. Deconstruction of basic materials, such as bricks, lumber, doors, and windows was much less common.

Deconstruction services were often performed by firms that also did demolition. The demolition industry was a regional business where contractors would bid on projects. Since design, color, and warranties were not part of the requirements for demolition contractors, homeowners usually hired the lowest bidder. The resulting bidding warfare drove prices down to the point where margins for demolition contractors were very slim. Deconstruction, with its higher price tag, was often a more attractive, higher-margin service for demolition contractors to provide.

Industry Components

There were three primary components to the deconstruction industry: building deconstruction; shipping and logistics for the salvaged materials; and retail sales of the salvaged materials. At the time, TRP was the only organization that performed all three functions, with other firms specializing in only one or two.

The US Building Materials Reuse Association (BMRA), a deconstruction industry association in the United States, estimated in 2004 that the retail portion of the deconstruction industry was $40 million, but the organization did not report revenue for the other two components. The BMRA did, however estimate that the entire industry grew about 30% over the five-year period 1997–2002.

Retail stores for salvaged construction materials provided an outlet for building materials not directed to a contractor. The nonprofit home construction organization Habitat for Humanity created retail locations, called ReStore, for reused building materials. The first ReStore opened in Winnipeg, Canada, in 1989. Habitat for Humanity subsequently opened new stores across the United States and Canada. In 2004, an industry expert estimated that ReStores generated about $38.4 million in revenue annually. Donated materials for ReStores came from building supply stores, contractors, demolition crews, and individuals.[13] Proceeds from ReStores were channeled to local Habitat for Humanity construction projects. Donated materials included most of the materials a homeowner would need for new construction, including lumber, doors, windows, cabinetry, and appliances.

By 2004, many more stores selling reused building materials existed. Several, such as Urban Ore and Ohmega Salvage, were located near TRP's Oakland facility and competed directly with it. Reiff saw the hierarchy of competition as follows: "Our biggest competition is the bulldozer. Next, in California and some other areas in the US, there are material recovery facilities (MRFs) that take material and grind it up for various uses, or for energy recovery. When legislation requires diversion

---

13 Habitat for Humanity, "Habitat ReStores," www.habitat.org/env/restores.aspx, accessed October 24, 2008.

from landfill, sending material to a MRF satisfies that requirement, and it's a lot cheaper than we are. The next level of competition is organizations such as Habitat for Humanity. They do what we call a skim, they take only the high-grade materials, they don't have the necessary licenses and insurance to do a full deconstruction. They usually do their work for free, with volunteers, and only take the custom doors, custom hardware, cabinets, etc. There are firms that do deconstruction and resale of lumber only. Nobody does the full spectrum of deconstruction and reuse that we do."

Industry Groups and Government Agencies

Some industry groups and government agencies lobbied for regulation of the deconstruction industry. The BMRA, whose mission it was to educate and influence government agencies about the benefits of deconstruction and materials reuse, encouraged government regulation through the US Environmental Protection Agency (EPA). In a 2006 report, the EPA had set forth plans to begin regulating the deconstruction industry. This plan singled out materials reuse in Section 3.1.1, titled "Decrease Waste Generation and Increase Recycling," which read, "Through 2011, reduce adverse effects to land by diverting materials from disposal through increased material reuse and recycling."[14] Included among the strategic targets for the EPA in this plan were a decrease in the total amount of waste in landfills and an "increase in the reuse and recycling of construction and demolition debris."[15]

Reiff and TRP favored a free-market approach to deconstruction. Reiff indicated a number of reasons why the "Feds would screw things up," including unnecessary and costly requirements and certifications, strict process requirements, IRS limitations on materials donations, and restrictions on materials containing lead-based paint.

The BMRA and the EPA were both wary of reusing materials containing lead-based paint. While there were laws in place in 2005 governing the use and disposal of lead-based paint in residences and offices, there were no national standards concerning the reuse of building materials containing lead-based paint. The BMRA and the EPA were creating some standards, however, including a manual for deconstruction.

Reiff projected that the vast majority of the doors and windows salvaged from deconstruction projects across the United States contained lead-based paint. Stricter regulations would slow the industry's growth and would affect TRP directly. Reiff estimated that the majority of the windows and doors in the TRP warehouse at any point in time were covered in lead-based paint. "Without sales of materials containing lead-based paint, we will have to rethink our business model," Reiff commented. However, he also noted that:

---

14 US Environmental Protection Agency, *Draft 2006–2011 EPA Strategic Plan Architecture Public Review Draft February 14, 2006*, p. 13.
15 Ibid.

> Material with lead-based paint can still be sold, but it has to be handled and treated in a very particular and safe way. The beauty of deconstruction is that we're not creating dust. The lead stays with the material; it does not get released into the air or water as dust. If it's on a board, you can turn it over, like siding, so the lead-based paint is on the inside, or you can paint over it, so it's also encapsulated. Both are EPA-approved procedures.

Another government issue companies in the industry wrestled with concerned the IRS. Homeowners were often donating materials and getting tax deductions as high as $80,000. Reiff worried that too many homeowners with such large tax deductions would prompt the IRS to investigate or create roadblocks preventing homeowners from realizing the full value of the donation. Such a move would be disastrous for the deconstruction industry.

Not all government agencies, however, threatened the future of TRP. The California State Assembly passed AB 939 (The Integrated Waste Management Act) in 1989, which required all municipalities to divert up to 25% of their waste from landfills by 1995 and 50% by the year 2000. BMRA President Brad Guy argued that AB 939 greatly increased interest in this sector in California and this in turn generated programs, ordinances, etc., that have become models for the rest of the United States.

TRP at a Crossroads

Growth Options

Reiff had a clear sense of where he thought the deconstruction industry was heading and how TRP could become a dominant player in that scenario. For starters, he knew the industry would grow. It had to, he figured, because landfill fees were likely to continue rising.

However, the past 10 years of rapid growth was taking its toll. In January 2007, TRP temporarily lost its credit line because Reiff's travel schedule had caused him to miss a paperwork deadline. Reiff summarized it succinctly: "I was dropping balls."

To capitalize on the future industry growth, and to uphold TRP's mission statement, Reiff and his board of directors knew that the company should move into new geographic regions. The question was how to do this.

One option was to certify other contractors to perform deconstruction services, or it could stick with its core competency and increase its own capacity to do so. Deconstruction services commanded higher profits than certifying third parties, but growth would be slower and the risks much higher.

The process of certifying contractors in deconstruction would require several steps. First, to raise awareness, Reiff and his team would have to educate demolition experts about the fundamentals of deconstruction. TRP would then have to train selected demolition contractors to perform deconstruction on residences.

Reiff estimated that a TRP team member would have to spend about four hours with a crew six to eight times before that crew could be certified in deconstruction. With turnover in demolition companies running high, Reiff assumed that his team would have to perform annual training sessions for the certified contractors. Once a contractor finished deconstructing a home, he would be responsible for shipping the salvaged materials to either a new construction site or to the TRP warehouse.

By contrast, the process of expanding TRP's own operations was conceptually simpler, though not easy to execute. It would require hiring additional crews, training them, and finding work to keep them busy enough to cover the associated fixed costs. This would be difficult to do within a confined geographic area, but branching out beyond TRP's traditional regions would make it correspondingly harder. Reiff currently spent a large portion of his time traveling up and down the San Diego–Los Angeles–San Francisco Bay Area corridor, and the prospect of extending his commute to Oregon, Washington, Arizona, and beyond, was not appealing.

So far, TRP's unsystematic approach had led it to work with certified contractors in other parts of the country, but Reiff questioned whether the company should keep going down that path. In May 2007, TRP was about to start a project in Seattle, and it had already done three in the Boulder/Denver area. It was also likely to start projects in St. Louis and Chicago. Reiff explained how the Chicago project illustrated the opportunistic nature of TRP's growth thus far:

> We did a job for someone in San Diego six months ago, and they were happy with us. Later his uncle in Chicago called. He was doing his house in six months and wondered if we could help him. We had also been written up nicely in a magazine around that time, which triggered a call from a contractor in Chicago who wanted to be a certified contractor for us. We were already contemplating expanding into a range of other cities but not yet Chicago, but I couldn't resist the combination so I told the uncle I'd be there in six months.

Some aspects of the deconstruction process were the same everywhere in the country, while others were location-specific. For instance, houses in St. Louis and Chicago had much more brick than those in California. Reiff was aware of an underground brick-cleaning economy in Chicago, where demolition contractors paid homeless people a small amount per brick cleaned.

Reiff estimated that each new location would require an investment of $250,000. In total, he identified about 25 markets in the United States where he would like to open new TRP locations, requiring a total upfront investment of $5–6 million. Instead of asking foundations for the capital, he planned on contacting corporations. Many corporations, he argued, would want to align themselves with TRP for publicity and strategic purposes.

In addition to geographic expansion, TRP was also penetrating deeper into their existing markets. Reiff recalls how, a few years ago, they considered closing down the Los Angeles operation, as it was proving too hard to get jobs. After bringing in a regional manager, who in turn hired Arthur Renaud and others to run parts of the Southern California market, TRP did 54 projects in the region in 2007. Exhibit 7 shows a breakdown of the number of projects by region.

Reiff's Decision

Reiff knew that the future path of this company would be decided at the upcoming board meeting. Regardless of which growth path they decided to pursue, he would need a systematic way of evaluating and entering new geographical areas, as well as an operational infrastructure that made sense. He would also have to hire additional employees, including regional managers to develop the new geographic markets, and additional back office staff at TRP's headquarters. Reiff was unsure about the attributes he should focus on in evaluating candidates. Moreover, TRP's financial position, though generally on track, sometimes limited Reiff's ability to pursue the ambitions he had for TRP as quickly as he would like.

Teaching notes for this case are available from Greenleaf Publishing. These are free of charge and are available only to teaching staff. They can be requested by going to:

www.greenleaf-publishing.com/oikos2_notes

Exhibit 1 **Homeowner Financial Comparison of Deconstruction Versus Demolition**

Source: thereusepeople.org/Deconstruction, accessed May 1, 2007.

The example below is a composite based on actual jobs and used here to make an economic comparison between deconstruction and demolition. This composite is a single-story, 2,200 square foot house plus garage, with 3 bedrooms, 2 baths, raised foundation, composite shingles, single-paned windows, carpeting, hardwood floors, and a 12 × 40 foot wood deck. The costs do not include removal of concrete slabs, sidewalks, foundations or asphalt, but do include the site being left in a rake clean condition (no debris).

In the demolition scenario, the owner pays $10,100, but in the TRP deconstruction scenario, the homeowner receives $4,702 in after-tax benefits. In other words, the owner would be financially better off in the amount of $14,802 ($4,702 received in tax benefits versus paying $10,100 in demolition costs).

	TRP Deconstruction[b]	Demolition
Physical lowering of house	($17,238)	($6,000)
Disposal of trash & debris	($4,100)	($4,100)
Appraisal of salvaged materials	($3,000)	$0
Total costs	**($24,338)**	**($10,100)**
Donation value[a]	**$88,000**	**$0**
Tax savings* (after-tax value of donated materials)	$29,040	$0
Total costs	**($24,338)**	**($10,100)**
After-tax benefit/ (Out-of-pocket cost)	**$4,702**	**($10,100)**
The after-tax difference between the two methods is $14,802.		

a Total materials (lumber, plywood, cabinets, plumbing and electrical fixtures, doors, windows, etc.) would usually appraise for $77,000 to $112,000 in good usable condition. Assuming a tax bracket of 33% (federal only—this will be larger in states with an additional income tax), the after-tax cash value, based on a typical appraisal value of $88,000, is $29,040.

b Figures vary depending on location, age and condition of the home and materials, topography, type of siding and interior walls, distance from TRP, landfill rates, etc. Still, the analysis almost always favors TRP deconstruction over demolition.

Exhibit 2 **Actual Appraised Donation Values from The ReUse People Deconstruction Projects**

Source: thereusepeople.org/Deconstruction, accessed May 1, 2007.

City	Square Feet	Appraised Donation Value ($)
California:		
Rancho Santa Fe	4,900	168,465
Newport Beach	6,771	333,000
Manhattan Beach	4,400[a]	110,000
Santa Monica	1,400	46,694
Pacific Palisades	4,500	162,600
Sherman Oaks	2,200	74,000
Santa Barbara	2,100 [a]	57,000
Santa Cruz	3,342	137,712
Los Gatos	3,696	140,040
Palo Alto	2,488	94,849
Woodside	8,600	326,863
Atherton	5,523	182,346
Fremont	2,220 [a]	65,000
Oakland	1,400	74,144
Orinda	4,275	137,940
Larkspur	2,304	129,425
Napa	2,804 [b]	102,025
Healdsburg	2,772[a]	174,315
Colorado:		
Boulder	3,300	114,000

a Complete gut.
b House and barn.

Exhibit 3 **The ReUse People's Balance Sheet, 2004–2007**

	Dec 31, 04	Dec 31, 05	Dec 31, 06	Dec 31, 07
ASSETS				
Current Assets				
Checking/Savings	15,042.80	(8,351.46)	1,258.49	11,468.04
Accounts Receivable	71,489.50	52,448.60	163,645.02	102,260.06
Other Current Assets				
Inventories	112,000.00	112,000.00	112,000.00	129,748.00
Prepaid Expenses	522.84	10,882.46	8,835.17	11,264.03
Total Other Current Assets	112,522.84	122,882.46	120,835.17	141,012.03
Total Current Assets	199,054.94	166,979.60	285,738.68	254,740.13
Fixed Assets				
Leasehold Improvements	-	-	12,106.71	12,106.71
Rolling Stock	87,238.76	79,113.36	145,534.20	147,594.94
Furniture & Fixtures	20,614.14	22,354.14	45,269.66	67,897.24
Accumulated Depreciation	(23,249.00)	(44,309.00)	(61,609.39)	(112,714.96)
Total Fixed Assets	84,603.90	57,158.50	141,301.18	114,883.93
Other Assets				
Deposits	3,107.00	3,105.00	14,560.69	13,435.50
Rent Deposit	650.00	7,075.00	12,075.00	11,075.00
Total Other Assets	3,757.00	10,180.00	26,635.69	24,510.50
TOTAL ASSETS	287,415.84	234,318.10	453,675.55	394,134.56
LIABILITIES & EQUITY				
Liabilities				
Current Liabilities				
Accounts Payable	93,301.70	105,197.27	86,084.26	140,634.03
Other Current Liabilities				
NFF LOC	-	-	-	7,584.51
Deductions payable	240.18	72.13	2,646.93	1,322.23
Payroll Payable	-	-	-	6,057.00
PR Taxes Payable	10,080.31	18,288.69	27,060.47	763.57
Sales Tax Payable	13,248.17	10,521.66	(2,093.85)	11,886.38
Total Other Current Liabilities	23,568.66	28,882.48	27,613.55	27,613.69
Total Current Liabilities	116,870.36	134,079.75	113,697.81	168,247.72
Long Term Liabilities				
Chase Bank (auto loan)	-	-	19,166.67	9,166.63
Computer Purchase	1,962.09	634.15	136.84	-
Copier	5,241.00	3,936.38	1,186.94	2,000.47
OBD Truck Loan	45,555.30	26,625.13	20,558.95	21,936.60
Toyota Forklift	-	-	19,304.19	18,996.18
Total Long Term Liabilities	52,758.39	31,195.66	60,353.59	52,099.88
Total Liabilities	169,628.75	165,275.41	174,051.40	220,347.60
Equity				
Retained Earnings	159,344.58	75,764.23	73,489.25	120,674.26
Net Income	(41,557.49)	(6,721.54)	206,134.90	53,112.70
Total Equity	117,787.09	69,042.69	279,624.15	173,786.96
TOTAL LIABILITIES & EQUITY	287,415.84	234,318.10	453,675.55	394,134.56

Exhibit 4 The ReUse People's Profit & Loss Statement, 2004–2007

	Jan - Dec 04	Jan - Dec 05	Jan - Dec 06	Jan - Dec 07
Income				
Cash Donations	-	-	-	485.00
Consulting/Commissions	-	5,194.00	7,193.00	26,545.00
Deconstruction Fees	967,372.21	896,756.53	610,457.30	517,874.00
Project Coordination Fees	65,834.00	156,670.95	338,749.00	343,855.40
Wholesale Sales	43,958.20	39,051.51	95,048.35	100,403.99
Warehouse Sales	355,797.78	369,183.51	453,032.78	525,266.78
Grants received	-	8,500.00	-	17,000.00
Other Income	748.60	-	-	13.98
Total Income	1,433,710.79	1,475,356.50	1,504,480.43	1,531,444.15
	Jan - Dec 04	Jan - Dec 05	Jan - Dec 06	Jan - Dec 07
Expense				
ADMINISTRATION				
Advertising	10,541.66	7,408.97	5,143.12	14,800.89
Auto Allowance	269.85	13,563.11	-	11,470.64
Bad Checks	(34.00)	10,053.71	2,236.85	-
Bad Debts	9,982.34	-	-	-
Bank Charges		1,327.62	2,514.76	3,105.07
Conferences & Meetings	-	-	-	839.38
Contributions				
Cash Donation	100.00	300.00	-	-
Materials Donation	2,605.00	-	-	-
Total Contributions	2,705.00	300.00	-	-
Depreciation	-	6,948.00	6,711.00	18,100.00
Dues & Subscriptions	1,119.95	1,139.00	1,580.49	229.00
Employee Welfare	-	-	1,500.00	3,740.50
Insurance - Liability	3,543.48	5,410.88	3,933.95	1,277.25
Insurance - Medical	4,476.00	2,871.00	4,257.24	6,307.21
Insurance - Vehicle	-	-	1,871.39	3,088.23
Licenses and Permits	5,103.40	30.00	1,654.83	2,713.66
Medical Expenses	3,287.94	(200.12)	-	3,125.60
Office Supplies - Admin	8,000.63	11,918.39	9,528.78	8,342.74
Postage & Delivery	1,908.67	1,706.80	2,552.34	2,857.95
Professional fees				
Computer & website	5,153.64	10,915.30	14,548.40	3,979.52
Consulting & Training	8,444.21	10,466.41	27,352.00	29,498.25
Legal, Acct'ing, Pension Mgt	16,474.77	2,501.85	15,158.35	11,079.00
Payroll Processing	4,515.59	3,897.27	6,322.29	16,209.75
Total Professional fees	34,588.21	27,780.83	63,381.04	60,766.52
Rent	6,620.00	12,071.39	11,237.39	11,115.00
Repairs & Maintenance	3,802.52	3,132.35	6,263.56	1,887.12
Telephone	24,058.37	6,253.29	13,778.63	15,257.35
Tools	-	-	8.80	843.37
Travel	21,064.08	39,408.47	54,410.41	64,378.39
Utilities	379.22	5,387.81	4,026.27	4,125.62
Wages - Officer	37,015.45	49,684.43	20,500.00	39,396.00
Wages - Operations Mgr	-	-	-	22,269.12
Wages - Office	29,799.26	38,644.91	41,495.19	53,434.98
Payroll Taxes Fed & State 100	5,114.40	7,959.28	6,227.04	8,491.33
Worker's Comp - 100	1,439.24	1,863.33	2,616.94	4,084.43
Miscellaneous	1,094.38	(377.00)	3,300.00	-
Total Administration	241,820.45	254,286.45	276,698.90	379,409.66

	Jan - Dec 04	Jan - Dec 05	Jan - Dec 06	Jan - Dec 07
Deconstruction Program				
Advertising	11,898.11	3,224.08	1,739.39	2,688.90
Auto Allowance	3,025.00	6,875.00	6,600.00	6,600.00
Depreciation	-	-	2,040.00	3,074.00
Disposal	126,519.64	79,010.83	46,470.58	55,078.43
Employee Welfare	7,539.00	8,874.61	5,997.00	117.00
Equipment Rental	38,300.12	4,887.25	1,510.24	1,288.41
Freight Out - Decon	6,066.00	4,762.28	104,700.42	-
Insurance - Liability	29,341.67	23,927.24	24,170.59	25,276.58
Insurance - Medical	800.00	1,149.80	1,354.11	1,407.64
Insurance - Vehicle	-	3,866.75	2,775.23	2,109.80
Office Supplies	-	-	1,153.14	505.86
Permits	2,118.20	182.20	300.00	357.00
Postage & Delivery	-	-	106.53	39.00
Rent	-	583.00	567.00	636.00
Subcontractors	153,110.37	177,546.00	60,370.81	-
Telephone	(24.12)	5,507.76	5,672.12	5,639.50
Tools & Supplies	18,349.01	15,472.62	4,738.75	8,046.99
Travel	17,387.09	23,271.14	7,474.53	385.89
Truck Expenses & Rental	14.00	12,878.49	7,632.50	15,064.28
Wages-600 Decon Mgr				
Base-600 Decon Mgr	42,151.29	26,380.00	28,970.39	28,600.00
OT-Incentive-600 Decon Mgr	30,687.02	36,127.59	26,586.39	25,785.00
Total Wages-600 Decon Mgr	72,838.31	62,507.59	55,556.78	54,385.00
Payroll Taxes Fed & State 600	(409.03)	6,128.45	4,205.56	4,657.21
Worker's Comp 600	-	2,420.23	1,528.85	1,888.39
Wages - Crew	216,732.17	80,992.28	-	-
Wages - Outsourced Crew 300	-	134,359.08	46,731.50	140,910.80
Casual Labor Crew	8,500.09	1,219.00	94.11	-
Payroll Taxes Fed & State Crew	24,977.08	11,386.31	-	-
Worker's Comp - Crew	92,408.78	51,063.95	-	-
DECON PROGRAM - Other		15.32		-
Total Deconstruction Program	827,491.49	722,111.26	393,489.74	330,156.68

	Jan - Dec 04	Jan - Dec 05	Jan - Dec 06	Jan - Dec 07
Project Coordination				
Advertising & Promotion	3,678.59	8,937.66	8,637.25	9,857.19
Auto Allowance	11,041.90	13,974.03	29,200.00	22,875.00
Consulting	-	-	10,922.50	10,500.00
Depreciation	-	8,112.00	8,112.00	5,857.00
Employee Welfare	-	-	900.00	575.00
Equipment Rental	-	-	1,161.45	1,662.94
Freight - Inter Region	-	340.00	1,650.00	1,206.25
Freight - Project	12,711.86	8,357.76	5,487.50	2,756.25
Insurance - Liability	-	-	6,519.17	3,063.22
Insurance - Medical	364.00	1,098.00	4,339.33	6,737.69
Insurance - Vehicle	-	-	1,030.11	917.40
Office Supplies	4,040.40	3,924.95	3,238.29	1,605.51
Permits - PC	612.35	-	90.00	387.00
Postage & Delivery	670.41	1,336.27	901.79	932.38
Rent	1,650.00	3,002.00	4,889.50	2,246.00
Subcontractors	8,800.00	-	-	-
Telephone	639.26	6,690.84	6,990.39	8,382.75
Tools & Supplies	-	-	1,224.98	1,493.46
Travel	6,883.41	3,180.43	3,056.51	1,537.89
Yard/Trailer Space Rent	1,601.74	3,523.25	4,759.50	14,682.20
Wages - Area Manager				
Base-Area Mgr	2,554.00	27,510.00	65,788.40	59,001.80
OT-Incentives	-	21,460.86	48,723.50	49,598.50
Total Wages - Area Manager	2,554.00	48,970.86	114,511.90	108,600.30
Wages - Regional Mgr				
Base-Reg Mgr	25,765.13	21,200.00	39,823.51	80,096.47
OT-Incentive-Reg Mgr	11,731.80	21,145.20	11,278.00	13,267.10
Override-Reg Mgr	-	1,117.20	18,251.00	10,662.00
Total Wages - Regional Mgr	37,496.93	43,462.40	69,352.51	104,025.57
Payroll Taxes Fed & State PC	2,654.97	8,966.48	14,850.16	15,294.77
Worker's Comp - PC	1,386.27	4,527.61	5,669.90	7,999.43
Total Project Coordination	96,786.09	168,404.54	307,494.74	333,195.20

	Jan - Dec 04	Jan - Dec 05	Jan - Dec 06	Jan - Dec 07
Retail Sales Program				
Advertising	13,939.88	10,778.11	10,392.17	11,441.17
Credit Card Fees and Rental	3,820.67	4,964.27	6,191.01	7,417.24
Depreciation		6,000.00	6,237.00	6,805.00
Disposal Fees	5,229.09	6,977.23	11,683.75	6,780.37
Employee Welfare	-	-	715.00	409.26
Freight	3,236.94		10,245.62	3,011.78
Insurance - Liability	9,026.04	16,419.67	11,178.55	3,696.77
Insurance - Medical		1,315.00	1,187.96	1,202.58
Insurance - Vehicle	8,875.65	3,939.75	4,000.25	5,198.04
Maintenance & Repairs	1,029.11	7,971.73	2,212.30	9,902.35
Merchandise - Consign/Purchase	5,510.75	(98.68)	5,441.00	3,000.00
Office Supplies	-	-	2,137.63	3,605.85
Postage & Delivery	-	-	185.62	366.46
Rent	45,134.78	46,673.54	52,025.11	72,793.25
Returned Checks	-	-	587.68	-
Telephone	-	3,999.55	5,154.16	8,087.16
Tools & Supplies	5,599.90	9,356.44	4,708.81	6,911.71
Travel	748.00	549.01	-	227.00
Truck & Equip Rental	9,124.58	9,414.91	1,044.01	4,076.74
Utilities	7,480.94	4,067.11	3,723.40	3,679.39
Vehicle Expenses	2,718.50	177.00	3,453.06	5,650.41
Wages-500 Retail Mgr				
Base-500 Retail Mgr	26,384.08	30,000.36	31,051.93	31,173.43
OT-Incentive-500 Retail Mgr	34,666.04	12,663.90	30,665.52	20,151.40
Total Wages-500 Retail Mgr	61,050.12	42,664.26	61,717.45	51,324.83
Worker's Comp - 500		967.29	1,647.96	3,125.45
Payroll Taxes Fed & State 500		2,516.62	3,508.68	5,782.09
Wages - Asst Mgr 400				
Wages - Outsourced 400	-	24,762.70	61,281.73	37,974.68
Base-Asst Mgr 400	18,115.41	11,015.00	4,569.60	6,730.00
OT-Incentive - Asst Mgr 400	11,636.42	7,598.41	-	9,887.60
Total Wages - Asst Mgr 400	29,751.83	43,376.11	65,851.33	54,592.28
Wages-400 Labor				
Wages - Outsourced 400	-	-	-	134,918.73
Base-400 Labor	24,666.46	60,604.20	69,201.84	-
OT-Incentive-400 Labor	11,716.28	8,534.45	9,974.48	17,712.00
Total Wages-400 Labor	36,382.74	69,138.65	79,176.32	152,630.73
Casual Labor 400	6,412.00	5,533.00	270.00	3,852.00
Payroll Taxes Fed & State 400	9,522.44	6,175.26	-	-
Worker's Comp - 400	40,637.18	17,960.20	-	-
Total Retail Sales Program	305,231.14	320,836.03	354,675.84	435,569.91
Interest & f/c,late fee Exp	3,939.11	16,439.76	10,801.77	13,362.31
Total Expense	1,475,268.28	1,482,078.04	1,343,160.99	1,478,331.45
Net Surplus (Deficit)	(41,557.49)	(6,721.54)	206,134.90	53,112.70

Exhibit 5 **The ReUse People Organization Chart, as of December 31, 2007**

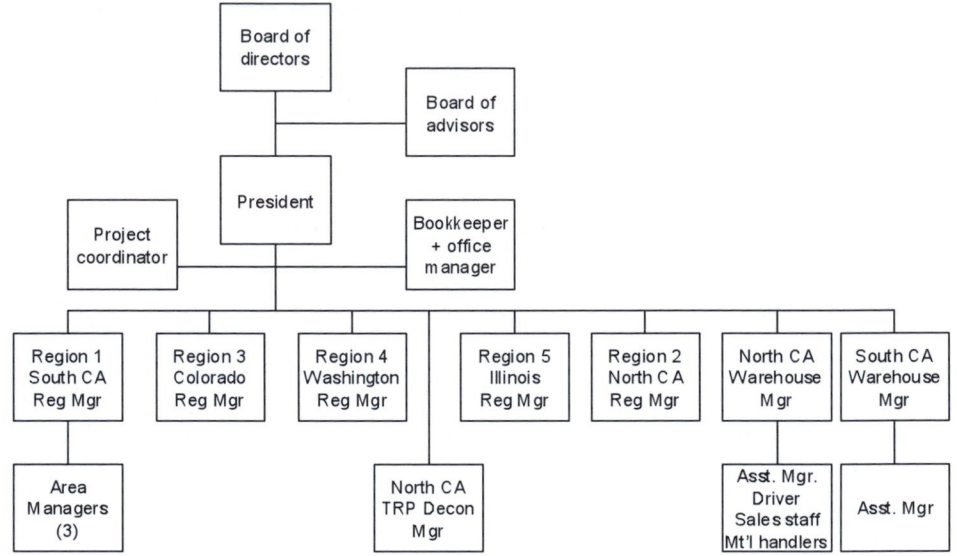

Exhibit 6 **Sample Deconstruction Project**

Reproduced from *The Velvet Crowbar*, Spring 2005, p. 2.

The TRP Mission:
TRP of California reduces the solid waste stream and changes the way the built environment is renewed by salvaging building materials and distributing them for reuse.

A crew of Habitat volunteers at Santa Clara site

With offices serving the San Francisco Bay Area, Eastern Sierras, L.A., Orange County & San Diego Phone toll-free: 888-588-9490

Anatomy of a Job
by Ted Reiff

Joint Project with Habitat Volunteers Proves Productive and Fun

Several months ago I had a meeting with the Silicon Valley affiliate of Habitat for Humanity. The purpose of the meeting was to explore the possibility of opening a warehouse similar to ours in Alameda. During the meeting, the folks from Habitat mentioned that they were acquiring a piece of property in Santa Clara on which stood an older home that had to be removed. They said they would provide all the volunteers necessary to deconstruct the building if TRP would provide the supervision, safety guidelines and training. In exchange, TRP would receive all the materials. I was reluctant at first, because I was concerned about safety issues using untrained volunteers and had reservations about productivity, or the lack of it. The home in question was built in the 1950s, had been vandalized and would not yield much reusable material. Plus, I was hesitant to give up a key supervisory person for up to two weeks.

I reluctantly accepted the assignment because I believe that if you are going to get into a partnering arrangement with a person or organization, the best way to get to know each other is to jump into a short term project that has the potential for conflict with minimal risks. That way you can test the mettle and tenacity of the prospective partner with little exposure. Besides, since the volunteers were to be provided by Cisco Systems, Habitat colleagues who had worked with the organization before, I fig-

ured the productivity curve would rise quickly.

Then Ted Becker at Habitat let the other shoe drop. Not only would there be a new crew every four hours—absolutely no repeats —the crew size would be from 10 to 15. Our crew size for a 1,700 square-foot house is five people—all trained and experienced in deconstruction and working as a unit. Now we had up to 15 inexperienced people most of whom had not worked together before.

So much for the productivity curve! Let's see, in our first four hours we spent 45 minutes on training, took one 15-minute break and indulged in a little Cisco shop talk. Add a bathroom break and at least one cellphone call. Ok, what the heck, we still had three hours to work.

Now the good news: we had a great time, the job got done in a little over two weeks, I met some great Cisco people and there were no serious injuries (two people stepped on nails and needed tetanus shots).

Working with the Habitat staff through the various issues of scheduling, coordination, personnel, training, deconstruction and materials handling was more fun than I could have imagined. I was impressed with their "can do" attitude and ability to forge positive relationships in the community.

On our side of the ledger, we demonstrated our ability to step into the breach and do what we said we would do, and we got some decent materials out of the job, including an old horse-drawn plow, which now sits

—continued on back page

Examples of Recent Jobs

Job Type	Owner/Contractor	Sq Ft	Tons Salvaged
Commercial building	Northstar Ski Resort	25,000	175.1
Wood-frame house and barns	A. J. Johnson, owner	3,200	48.2
2-story wood frame house	Shanley Construction	2,500	25.8
Wood-frame, single-story house	Talmage Construction, Inc.	3,770	43.8
2 1/2-story 1980 house interior only	Epoch Development	4,400	18.2

2

Continued from page 1 — Cool Remodel

potential use. He assured me that the kitchen cabinets would sell quickly, along with the remaining doors and other salvageable items.

From the first moment TRP began to lovingly dismantle my house, the entire remodel proved a remarkable experience. With Spectrum's guidance, I was able to incorporate many sustainable features, such as tiles handmade from recycled glass by Fireclay in San Jose; sustainable flooring materials like cork, linoleum and farm-raised oak from Carpeteria in Mountain View; energy efficient appliances from Dacor; custom-made cabinets constructed of plywood rather than particle board; insulation with no formaldehyde; and a tankless hot water heater.

The ReUse People took the very important first step in renovating my little "tear-down" into a home that is not only beautiful, but a meaningful part of the community.

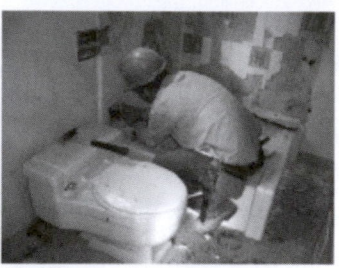

A TRP crew member carefully removes antique decorator tiles from the around the bathtub. They were later incorporated in Jesse Cool's new bathroom.

Continued from page 2 — Anatomy of a Job

in front of our warehouse, 1,500 used bricks, each individually cleaned by a desk jockey or computer geek, and some well-seasoned lumber.

Thanks Habitat for Humanity of Silicon Valley. I certainly would do it all again if the opportunity arose.

Jesse Cool is owner/chef of Flea Street Café and jZcool Eatery & Catering Company, both in Menlo Park, and The Cool Café on the Stanford University campus. She is the author of six cookbooks, including *The True and Real One Pot Cookbook* (Chronicle Books, 2005), *Breakfast in Bed* (Harper Collins, 1997) and *Your Organic Kitchen* (Rodale Press, 2000), numerous articles, and regular produce columns in *Peninsula Magazine* and the *San Jose Mercury News*. For more information, visit www.cooleatz.com.

Visit these TRP outlets:

TRP ReUse Bazaar
2100 Ferry Point, #150, Alameda, CA 94501
(510) 522-2722; toll-free 888-588-9490

Habitat Home Improvement Store
17700 S. Figueroa (corner of 182nd),
Gardena/Carson CA 90248
(310)-323-5665

Silver Lake Yards
1086 Manzanita Street, Silver Lake, CA 90026
(323) 667-2875

The ReUse People

2100 Ferry Pt. #150
Alameda, CA 94501
510/522-2722
Phone toll-free: 888/588-9490
www.thereusepeople.org
e-mail: info@thereusepeople.org

Exhibit 7 **Number of Projects by Region**

Year	Northern California		Southern California	Colorado	Washington	Illinois	Total
	TRP decon	TRP contractor					
2005	30	48	18	0	0	0	96
2006	20	50	59	0	0	0	129
2007	28	55	54	2	5	5	149

Case 15
LivingHomes[1,2]

Rebecca Henn and Andrew J. Hoffman
University of Michigan, USA

> Now comes the hard part, which is creating a sustainable business.[3]
>
> Steve Glenn, Founder and CEO, LivingHomes

In March 2007, Steve Glenn put down the phone and stared outside at his thirsty yard. He was still living under a temporary occupancy permit after eight months, and the new plants had to be hand-watered daily. Los Angeles County officials said they couldn't find a "mountain or rural inspector" to review the design of his gray-water system for permit approval and system startup.[4] If he was having these problems in a progressive city like Santa Monica, what would happen to his customers across the country? Would they encounter the same delays and barriers? Would these challenges discourage them from buying his prefabricated green homes? Would the homes' green features be disabled because of inexperienced zoning and

---

1 This case © 2010 University of Michigan, Erb Institute for Global Sustainable Enterprise and Rebecca Henn. Research Associate Rebecca Henn prepared this case under the supervision of Professor Andrew J. Hoffman with the assistance of Grace Augustine and Dave Vannette, as the basis for class discussion rather than to illustrate either effective or ineffective handling of an administrative situation.

2 The case was made available by GlobaLens, the publishing division of The William Davidson Institute at the University of Michigan. For reproduction and distribution of this case please contact Permissions@GlobaLens.com or call 1.734.615.9553. To link directly to the case, go to globalens.com/casedetail.aspx?cid=1428714.

3 Anderton, Francis. "LEEDing the way." *Dwell* Nov. 2006: 99-104.

4 Yoshihara, N. "Drought-busters Hit a Hurdle." *Los Angeles Times* 29 Mar. 2006. A gray-water system typically irrigates landscape with waste water from baths and sinks.

building code inspectors? This was no small issue. Even before construction, Santa Monica's zoning laws and height limits reduced the size of the home's modules and required a split-level foundation.[5] And these were just a few of the concerns when tapping into the emerging green building market. Glenn wanted to revolutionize the home building industry in the United States by merging product attributes of high-end style and green design with process attributes of home prefabrication and delivery. While each of these may have had independent market representation, few companies linked them all in one offering. He wanted the process of home construction to be not only quicker and less expensive, but also green and beautiful.

LivingHomes' target market included people who "drive Priuses, buy Bosch appliances and Design Within Reach furniture, shop at Whole Foods, and give money to the [Natural Resources Defense Council]."[6] To serve these customers, LivingHomes selected brand-name architects who specialized in a modern aesthetic. The homes' luxury provided every convenience for the high-end consumer. The homes' "green" attributes provided higher performance, less material and water waste, a healthier environment to live in, and greater energy efficiency than normal construction. And prefabrication embraces mass-production and scale benefits through the notion that customers should be able to buy a house no differently than the way they buy a car—in choosing a product that matches their market segment.

Glenn's thoughts were interrupted by the doorbell and another prospective customer tour of his modern, Ray Kappe designed home. This was the first LivingHomes structure, and was "installed" in an astonishing eight hours.[7] The 2,480 square foot house received the very first Platinum Level LEED® for Homes Certification by the US Green Building Council (USGBC), which is the highest possible level of certification in the LEED system.[8] Glenn loved showing off both the modern, luxurious design and sustainable features, from the photovoltaic panels on the roof to the recycled denim insulation (see Exhibit 1). He was sure that a better environment could be achieved through building low-energy, non-toxic, healthy homes like his, and to his pleasure, others agreed. His home was featured in dozens of newspapers and magazines in recent months—*Business Week, Forbes, Life, Los Angeles Times, House & Garden, Vogue Men's, TreeHugger, Inhabitat, Environmental Design and Construction, Residential Architect, Dwell, Wired, The Times* and *Financial Times* in London, and even France's *Le Monde*. The American Institute of Architects' Com-

5 Newman, Morris. "Green-Fab House." *The Architect's Newspaper* 7 June 2006: 18.

6 "Innovative, Start-Up Home Builder Makes Green Living a Reality with a New Line of Architectural Prefab Homes." Living Homes—Press Release. www.livinghomes.net/pdf/pressRelease_2006.04.272.pdf, accessed 27 Apr. 2006,

7 Ibid.

8 "The USGBC LEED for Homes Program Awards LivingHomes the First-Ever Platinum Rating in Residential Sustainable Design." Living Homes—Press Release. www.livinghomes.net/viewPress.html?id=1, accessed 16 Aug. 2006

mittee on the Environment selected the home as one of the Top Ten Green Buildings for 2007, while *Men's Journal* designated it as one of "97 Perfect Things."[9]

Despite this acclaim, Glenn struggled with code inspectors, costs that were hard to keep under control, an uncertain housing market, and a more affluent target consumer who might not see prefabrication, high-end luxury, and "green" as a consistent value proposition. He was not only trying to build sustainable homes, he also needed to build a sustainable business with its own niche in the US housing market.

The Housing Industry

In the United States, the American Dream is epitomized by home ownership.[10] In 1999, 70% of Americans lived in a single-family home. Though most people live in pre-owned homes, the market for new, single-family, detached homes has increased through population growth and consumers' desire for both larger homes and newness itself.[11]

In 2006, almost 1.5 million new homes were built in the United States. As Exhibit 2 shows, the market has historically gone through cycles of increasing and decreasing volume. The 2006 average sales price of new single-family homes sold (including land) was $305,900 (an 84% increase from $166,400 in 1996). With an average new home size in 2006 of 2,469 square feet, the critical number for calculating home value—the price per square foot—was $91.99 in the US Regionally, it was most expensive to build in the West[12] at $120.66 and least expensive to build in the South[13] at $80.32.[14] Exhibit 3 highlights additional characteristics of new housing in 2006.

9 Scanlon, J. "Objects of Desire. The Prefab Luxury Home." *Men's Journal* 16 Sept. 2007: 116-7.

10 "American Dream Downpayment Initiative." US Department of Housing and Urban Development [HUD]. www.hud.gov/offices/cpd/affordablehousing/programs/home/addi, accessed 28 Aug. 2007.

11 Cohen, L. *A Consumers' Republic: The Politics of Mass Consumption in Postwar America.* New York, NY: Random House, 2003.

12 Washington, Oregon, California, Idaho, Montana, Wyoming, Utah, Colorado, New Mexico, Arizona.

13 Texas, Oklahoma, Arkansas, Louisiana, Mississippi, Alabama, Tennessee, Kentucky, West Virginia, Virginia, Maryland, Delaware, North Carolina, South Carolina, Georgia, and Florida.

14 "Highlights of Annual 2006 Characteristics of New Housing." US Census Bureau. www.census.gov/const/www/highanncharac2006.html, accessed 28 Aug. 2007.

Housing Market Segments

The purchase of a home is "one of the most difficult economic decisions of a whole domestic life-cycle, a decision fraught with enormous consequences."[15] The three main tasks involved in building a new home—property selection, home design, and home construction—are rarely taken on solely by the homeowner. Instead, delivery systems have evolved to meet the demand of different consumers, with each system having different levels of price, quality, and speed (or delay).

Homes can be entirely "manufactured," and are primarily purchased by lower-income buyers. After purchase, they are typically delivered and placed on rented lots in clusters fittingly termed "parks." Traditionally, middle-income homeowners who are interested in a new home can either buy a finished speculative (or spec) home or customize pre-purchased construction plans for an individual lot. Generally, the level of customization is limited to a choice of colors, materials, finishes and a pre-selected list of options for cabinets and appliances. Within this market, one could work with either a small-scale home builder who completes as few as five houses per year, or a large-scale developer who creates developments in the hundreds or thousands of units per year. Affluent consumers who are not content with a standardized home can hire an architect to provide a thoroughly original, unique design. These are truly custom homes, where wealthy clients typically find their own property and hire an architect and contractor separately. LivingHomes wanted to provide the better aesthetic qualities of this latter affluent segment to the upper financial end of the middle-income market. The two major players in this arena were large-scale developers and small-scale custom home builders.

Homes Built by Developers

KB Homes and Toll Brothers, two of the largest home building development companies in the United States, offered a turnkey product within narrowly stratified communities—residents often share economic, aesthetic, and even generational similarities.[16] These and other home building companies wielded increasing control over the home building industry in the early 2000s. In 1986 they provided 65% of new homes; by 2006 that figure rose to 78%.[17] See Exhibit 4.

Since one of the most significant considerations in choosing a home is the neighborhood into which one moves and lives, developers ensure uniformity within the

---

15 Bourdieu, Pierre. *The Social Structures of the Economy*. Malden, MA: Polity Press, 2005. 19.

16 "Hampton Oaks." KB Home. www.kbhome.com, accessed 28 Aug. 2007.

17 This percentage represents homes "built for sale" (i.e. "the builder is offering the house and the developed lot for sale as one transaction") completed in 2006. "Comparing New Home Sales and New Residential Construction." US Census Bureau. 2006. 28 Aug. 2007; www.census.gov/const/www/salesvsstarts.html. "Highlights of Annual 2006 Characteristics of New Housing." US Census Bureau. 2006. www.census.gov/const/www/highanncharac2006.html, accessed 28 Aug. 2007.

neighborhoods they create by purchasing large greenfield sites (usually farmland, but almost always previously undeveloped property) on the edge of more urban areas.[18] They then hire a planning consultant to determine individual lot sizes, median home prices (based on local marketing studies), standard floor plans, options, and styles of homes to be built. Once approved by local zoning officials, the developers begin to market the homes. Customers then simply mix-and-match plans and building sites.

Developers also craft a set of restrictive property-use agreements regarding what future owners may or may not do with their property and homes. These neighborhood agreements historically included limitations such as paint colors, material choices for additions, fencing types and configurations, garden ornaments, vehicle parking, yard maintenance, mailbox styles, solar panels, and even approved outdoor activities. While some homeowners balk at this level of control, the neighborhood's homogeneity entices many buyers. Perceived property values are protected by eliminating neighbors with dilapidated recreational vehicles on blocks, or a yard full of garden gnomes. Depending on the location and market, home prices in one of these developments ranged from $125,000 to $1,000,000 and higher in the mid-2000s.

These builders are able to keep costs low (and profits high) because volume production of homes (often called "tract homes") resembles an assembly line, with houses so similar that crews are able to stay in a predictable sequence. Further, the use of prefabricated parts of homes (such as roof trusses and wall panels, as well as windows, doors and cabinetry) produces major cost savings through shorter production times, reduced weather delays and damage to homes under construction, and simplified scheduling of labor. This standardized method of house production successfully limits the variables that could otherwise slow the construction of a unique home—such as compliance with zoning laws and building codes, as well as ease of product acquisition since most pre-selected products (appliances, doors, hardware, etc.) are already in stock at the local supply companies.

Additionally, larger development firms provide home financing, thus offering a total solution to potential buyers. In 2006, 90% of all new single-family homes sold were financed by a mortgage, up from 55% in 1986.[19] However, constraining consequences of buying a developer's home result in accepting both the limited aesthetic styles and typically forgotten environmental concerns in the home's creation.

Toll Brothers considered itself "America's Luxury Home Builder" and in 2007 offered homes well above $1 million. Its average delivered home price was $690,000 in 2006.[20] KB Homes teamed up with Martha Stewart in 2005 and Disney in 2007

---

18 Jacovino, Edward J. "From Open Farmland to 1,500 Units?" Courant.com. www.courant. com, accessed 13 Aug. 2007.

19 Highlights of Annual 2006 Characteristics of New Housing." US Census Bureau. 2006. www.census.gov/const/www/highanncharac2006.html, accessed 28 Aug 2007.

20 "2006 Toll Brothers Annual Report." www.tollbrothers.com/homesearch/servlet/ HomeSearch?app=IRannual, accessed 1 Oct. 2007.

to create branded communities, and began to offer a green product to its consumers by integrating its myEarth program.[21] Customers of these home builders buy a product instead of a process: they need not deal with zoning, codes, or outside mortgage lenders or designers. While architects may dismiss developers' custom homes as McMansions that display "architectural and historical malapropisms,"[22] developers successfully market the homes with titles reminiscent of the old world Europe, such as Essex, Stratford, Vienna, and Windsor—regardless of whether their location is Texas, Michigan, or Pennsylvania.

Custom Designed Homes

A custom home designed by an architect is typically an expensive proposition, representing only 3–5% of new homes in the United States in 2006. Designing a home from scratch can require from one to two years of full-time attention from an architect. Architectural fees typically range from 10–20% of the home's total construction cost. This total cost can be an intimidating financial prospect for one family—especially since the total fee is often unknown until the design work is complete, the bids for construction are received, or even until the house is complete. Additionally, a unique design introduces variables that are purposely avoided by developers. Having the "perfect" granite for a kitchen countertop could delay construction for weeks, and owner-requested design changes in the middle of the process could grind construction to a halt. Numerous aspects of architectural homes hold this possibility, since these homes are, by most definitions, unique creations—essentially building a prototype with every home design. Economies of scale are not available to provide financial savings.

However, the value of architecture may lie more in its cultural capital, and in some cases, the quality of its structure or spatial environment. For example, the Frank Gehry brand carries certain cachet—what homeowner would not impress her friends by hiring the same architect who designed the Guggenheim Museum in Bilbao and the Disney Concert Hall in Los Angeles? The clients of Frank Lloyd Wright, a well-known American architect, were known as patrons, as in the art world, rather than simply homeowners. The term "starchitect" (a combination of star and architect) has emerged as a few personalities have become coveted brands.[23] The stylistic range of these personalized creations is as divergent as the people who sponsor them—from the radical forms of Herzog and de Meuron to the "superbly wrought

21 "KB Homes to Feature Disney Designs." *The Wall Street Journal* 26 Sept. 2007: B3. It is also worth noting that KB Homes' stock price tripled from 2001 to 2006: "2006 KB Homes Annual Report." investor.kbhome.com/annuals.cfm.

22 Huxtable, Ada Louise. *The Unreal America: Architecture and Illusion.* New York, NY: The New Press, 1997.

23 Deamer, Peggy. "Branding the Architectural Author." *Perspecta* 38 (Winter 2006).

wood structures"[24] of Bill Gates' family compound by James Cutler and Bohlin Cywinski Jackson. These homes, often without wide cultural precedent, stand in stark contrast to the more mass-produced options of a developer.

Green Buildings

Buildings and the Environment

Commercial and residential buildings leave a very large footprint on the environment in the United States. According to the Center for Sustainable Systems, "urbanized land consumes natural space and agricultural land at a rate 2.6 times the population growth in the United States" as of 2007.[25] Further, buildings consume 40% of the world's materials, 55% of the wood cut for non-fuel use,[26] 12.2% of the total water consumed, 40% of the world's energy, and create 36% of the carbon dioxide emissions that cause global warming.[27]

When one focuses specifically on the housing sector, there is evidence for even greater environmental concern. For example, the average size of a single-family home in the United States increased from 983 square feet in 1950, to 2,492 square feet in 2006 (more than 2.5 times larger), while the average number of occupants per household decreased from 3.37 to 2.62 over the same period (a 22% reduction). This equates to significantly more material and energy used per person. In 1950, 9% of housing units were occupied by only one person. By 2005, that number increased to 27%. As a result, total residential CO_2 emissions increased by 26% from 1990 to 2006, while the population increased only 20%.[28] Exhibit 5 shows more details of the environmental impacts of the residential sector.

Beyond the external environmental impacts of homes, the interior environment also merits consideration. As of 2007, Americans spent 90% of their time indoors, and the EPA reported that indoor air often contained pollutant levels two to five

24 Ivy, Robert. "Genius Loci: Jim Cutler's Design Embraces Northwest Place and Culture." *Architectural Record.* archrecord.construction.com/people/interviews/archives/0502JimCutler-1.asp, accessed 16 Aug. 2007.

25 "Fact Sheet: Residential Buildings." Center for Sustainable Systems—University of Michigan. css.snre.umich.edu/css_doc/CSS01-08.pdf.

26 Roodman, D.M., N.K. Lenssen, and J.A. Peterson. *A Building Revolution: How Ecology and Health Concerns Are Transforming Construction.* Washington, DC: Worldwatch Institute, 1995.

27 Kulman, J., and J. Schurke. *Sustainable Design.* Washington, DC: National Council of Architectural Registration Boards, 2001.

28 "Fact Sheet: Residential Buildings." Center for Sustainable Systems, University of Michigan. css.snre.umich.edu/css_doc/CSS01-08.pdf.

times higher than outdoor air.[29] These pollutants come from well-known sources such as radon and tobacco smoke, but also emanate from less well known sources such as formaldehyde in exterior wall plywood sheathing, furniture, or fiberglass in insulation. Dust particles from vinyl floors, wallpaper, fire retardant fabrics, and vinyl siding can give off other pollutants such as phthalates. Further complicating matters, efforts towards sealing a home for energy efficiency trap these pollutants inside. These efforts can also seal in water (in the form of condensation or leaks), promoting mould growth, which is in turn linked to respiratory problems and headaches. Responsibilities to the environment and human health, as well as greater mainstream acceptance of sustainability principles have prompted some members of the construction industry to pursue green buildings.

Green Buildings

Green building is a term encompassing strategies, techniques, and construction products that are less resource-intensive or pollution-producing than status quo construction. In some cases, this involves merely doing without extra space, finishes, or appliances. In others, it simply substitutes a less polluting product for more polluting ones (e.g., low-VOC paint).[30] More integrated strategies actually configure the shape of a space to take advantage of unique site attributes (e.g., facing glass towards the sun path to use natural or passive solar heat gain instead of using natural gas or electricity to heat a space). Experimentation of more unusual techniques caused green building to be seen by some as a fringe activity in the 1970s, when the oil crisis and inflation prompted efforts towards energy efficiency (e.g. rammed earth or straw bale house construction, composting toilets, and "cheese wedge" house forms where homes tilted towards the sun for passive solar gain).[31]

While the flush 1980s and low energy costs pushed many green approaches from mainstream interests, the early 2000s saw a resurgence. With concern for climate change, the American addiction to oil, and terrorism in the oil-producing regions, environmental concerns hit an all time high in the mid-2000s. And one area where this concern yielded the greatest change was green construction, which emerged as a more mainstream topic. "Green" was becoming fashionable with *Elle*, *Vogue*, *Vanity Fair*, and other magazines featuring green issues, while new magazines such as *Natural Home*, *Plenty*, and *Organic Style* gained in popularity. By 2006, Energy Star, the US government-backed energy performance rating system which des-

---

29 "The Inside Story: A Guide to Indoor Air Quality. EPA 402-K-93-007." US Environmental Protection Agency [EPA]. www.epa.gov/iaq/pubs/insidest.html, accessed 30 Aug. 2007.

30 VOC is an abbreviation for volatile organic compounds, which are harmful pollutants. Depending on the specific formulation, VOCs can include carcinogens, greenhouse gases, or ground-level ozone reactants.

31 Rybczynski, Witold. "Green Unseen: Environmentally Friendly Buildings Don't Need to Look Like Cheese Wedges." *Slate*. 16 July 2007. www.slate.com/id/2170511, accessed 19 Nov. 2007.

ignates homes that are at least 15% more energy efficient than standard homes, had reached a national market penetration of 12% for site-built, single-family new homes.[32] Nearly 200,000 new homes earned the Energy Star in 2006, bringing the total number of qualified homes across the nation to almost 750,000, though this penetration was not uniform (see Exhibit 6).

With this rush of excitement, accusations of "greenwashing" were not always unfounded, as every company wanted to join the marketing hype. In response to these charges, a few organizations created rating systems for green buildings. These systems codified environmental goals, and provided a measurement system for each. To achieve certification, one must meet a minimum number of the stated goals.

Green Building Rating Systems

US Green Building Council

In 1998, the United States Green Building Council (USGBC) introduced the LEED (Leadership in Energy and Environmental Design) rating system for new institutional and commercial construction. In this system, adhering to environmental goals earned points toward four certification levels: Certified, Silver, Gold, and Platinum. The goals for new construction (NC) were grouped into six categories: sustainable sites, water efficiency, energy & atmosphere, materials & resources, indoor air quality, and innovation & design process. LEED-NC Certified projects, like Energy Star homes, enjoyed variable popularity in states around the country (see Exhibit 7). LEED was the dominant standard for green building certification as of 2007, and attendance at USGBC's annual conference, Greenbuild, rose from 4,200 in 2002 to 20,500 in 2007—a five-fold increase in five years.[33] Subsequent to the success of LEED-NC adoption, the USGBC offered specialized rating systems for existing buildings, commercial interiors, core and shell, schools, retail, healthcare, neighborhood development and homes.

LEED for Homes

LEED for Homes began as a pilot study in August 2005. Unlike other LEED projects, which had to be certified by the USGBC office in Washington, DC, locally

32 "Energy Star Qualified New Homes Market Indices for States." *US EPA Energy Star*. 1 May 2007. www.energystar.gov/index.cfm?fuseaction=qhmi.showHomesMarketIndex, accessed 1 Oct. 2007.

33 US Green Building Council. "Greenbuild 2005: Is Georgia on your mind?" *Southface*. 2005. 1 Nov. 2005. www.southface.org/web/resources&services/publications/journal/sfjv105/sfjv105-greenbuild.htm, accessed 19 Nov. 2007. "Greenbuild 2007 Draws Record Attendance." *Floor Daily*. www.floordaily.net/Search/SearchItem.aspx?article=11649, accessed 16 Nov. 2007.

based LEED for Homes Providers certify residential projects.[34] This diffusion of responsibility was a welcome change from the LEED-NC backlogs that were encountered as LEED's popularity grew much faster than expected. The LEED for Homes rating system expanded its list of resource categories from six to eight to measure the overall performance of a home.[35] Exhibit 8 is a sample scoring sheet for LEED Homes certification. The USGBC also launched The Green Home Guide website in November 2007 to educate the target market (see Exhibit 9).[36]

Green Building Initiative

In 2005 the Green Building Initiative (GBI) launched a competing system for all building types called Green Globes.[37] The GBI was "originally conceived as a way to bring green building into the mainstream by helping local Home Builder Associations develop green building programs modeled after the National Association of Home Builders' (NAHB) Green Home Building Guidelines."[38] The organization also provided a Green Globes rating system for commercial projects, which appealed to those frustrated with the difficult and protracted LEED process.[39] GBI's advantage over LEED was in its "simpler methodology, employing a user-friendly interactive guide for assessing and integrating green design principles."[40] The point system also differed in allocation emphasis; GBI gave more credit than LEED to energy saving efforts. Regardless of the initiative's usability, critics complained that GBI did not hold the same credibility as LEED because it was both developed and overseen by one member of the industry—the NAHB.

34 "LEED for Homes." US Green Building Council. www.usgbc.org/DisplayPage. aspx?CMSPageID=147, accessed 28 Aug. 2007.

35 "LEED for Homes Program Pilot Rating System Version 1.11a." US Green Building Council. Jan. 2007. www.usgbc.org/ShowFile.aspx?DocumentID=2267, accessed 19 Nov. 2007.

36 "The Green Home Guide." US Green Building Council. www.greenhomeguide.org/index. html, accessed 19 Nov. 2007.

37 Smith, Timothy, Miriam Fischlein, et al. "Green Building Rating Systems: A Comparison of the LEED and Green Globes Systems in the US. Carpenters Industry Council." *Forest Health*. Sept. 2006. www.foresthealth.org/pdf/LEED%20Comparison%20Study.pdf, accessed 19 Nov. 2007.

38 "Origin and Non-profit Status." Green Building Initiative. From www.thegbi.org/gbi/ originandstatus.asp, accessed 28 Aug. 2007.

39 Podkul, Cezary. "Green Globes Certification Rises as Alternative to LEED." *Philadelphia Business Journal*. 17 Aug. 2007. philadelphia.bizjournals.com/philadelphia/ stories/2007/08/20/focus5.html, accessed 28 Aug. 2007.

40 Smith, Timothy, Miriam Fischlein, et al. "Green Building Rating Systems: A Comparison of the LEED and Green Globes Systems in the US. Carpenters Industry Council." *Forest Health*. Sept. 2006. www.foresthealth.org/pdf/LEED%20Comparison%20Study.pdf, accessed 19 Nov. 2007.

The Economics of Green Buildings

Overall, the full cost–benefit analysis of green building is a moving target. Some argue that adopting LEED forces the project to add expensive features (green roofs, photovoltaics, gray water systems) to meet LEED criteria. Indeed, a 2004 study by the US General Services Administration found that the anticipated construction premium for new federal courthouses would range from negative 0.4% for a low-cost LEED Certified facility to a high of 8.1% for a high-cost LEED Gold Certified courthouse. The GSA also cited additional soft costs ranging from $0.41–$0.80 per square foot for LEED-related requirements that went beyond GSA's standard project scope. A 2006 study by Building Design+Construction cites perceptions of higher up-front costs as the top barriers to incorporating green design into building projects.[41] But a 2006 report by Davis Langdon compared the cost of 83 LEED certified buildings with 138 conventional buildings and found that "many projects achieve sustainable design within their initial budget, or with very small supplemental funding … the costs per square foot for buildings seeking LEED certification fall into the existing range of costs for buildings of similar program type."[42] Exhibit 10a presents the results of several studies on the cost premiums for building green.

The reality is that some green building strategies may require increased up-front costs. High-efficiency equipment or low-VOC paints and adhesives often cost higher than their standard counterparts. Additionally, the costs of certifying a building can include application fees from $1,500 to $7,000, additional paperwork preparation, building commissioning, and energy modeling.[43] But such strategies can result in long-term financial savings. Exhibit 10b presents the results of studies on the economic benefits of building green. These include hard financial savings through reduced energy and water consumption, construction waste disposal costs, and more efficient or smaller mechanical equipment. A waterless urinal, for example, may cost more to purchase, but it costs less to install, and saves as much as $161–$192 per year in water/wastewater costs (at 2006 prices). Green buildings may also result in soft financial benefits through more rapid leasing of space, easier employee recruiting, reduced employee turnover, and reduced liability risk.[44] There are also suggestions that green buildings improve human performance for their occupants. Studies claim that students in schools with more natural light perform significantly

41 "Green Buildings and the Bottom-Line." *Building Design+Construction* Nov. 2006.

42 Matthiessen, Lisa Fay, and Peter Morris. "The Cost of Green Revisited." Davis Langdon. www.davislangdon.com/USA/Research/ResearchFinder/2007-The-Cost-of-Green-Revisited, accessed 21 Nov. 2007.

43 Building commissioning is the systematic process of ensuring that a building's complex array of systems is designed, installed, and tested to perform according to the design intent and the building owner's operational needs. This process is rewarded in the LEED point system. Definition retrieved from: Energy Design Resources. www.energydesignresources.com/category/commissioning, accessed 21 Nov. 2007.

44 Wilson, Alex. "Making the Case for Green Building." *Environmental Building New*s 14.4 (Apr. 2005).

better on exams,[45] retail sales are higher in day-lit stores,[46] office workers perform better when their workspace includes a view out a window,[47] and improved ventilation and views to the outdoors speed patient healing in hospitals.[48]

By analyzing the entire life of the building in light of these hard and soft benefits, long-term financial savings can cover initial costs at varying payback rates. In a case study of a 60,000 square foot building containing 40 apartments in New York,[49] the following costs and benefits in 2006 were found:

- Install solar panels: cost $19,000; payback 15 years

- Install fluorescent bulbs: cost $1,120; payback 3 years

- Install motion sensors: cost $11,000; payback 2 years

- Replace an old boiler with the most efficient gas unit: cost $50,000; payback 8 years

Clearly, as the prices of energy and water vary in both time and locale, these payback periods will be shorter or longer. See Exhibit 11 for nationwide variances.

LivingHomes

Steve Glenn created LivingHomes in Santa Monica, California, sixteen miles west of Los Angeles. He was no stranger to starting companies—his first was started as an undergraduate at Brown University, and was quickly sold to Apple. But after thirteen years of founding successful internet technology companies such as PeopleLink, Glenn wanted to return to a longstanding fascination—architecture. He had given the profession a try in college, attending a summer Career Discovery program at Harvard's Graduate School of Design. However, he had left there with the realization that he "lacked both the talent and temperament to be an architect."[50] Still, this did not diminish his interest or fascination, which he had developed as a child while playing with Legos and reading books on Frank Lloyd Wright. At Harvard,

45 Heschong, Lisa, Douglas Mahone, et. al. "Daylighting in Schools: An Investigation into the Relationship Between Daylighting and Human Performance." Heschong Mahone Group. 20 Aug. 1999.

46 Heschong, Lisa. "Daylight and Retail Sales." P500-03-082-A-5 (Oct. 2003). California Energy Commission.

47 Heschong, Lisa. "Windows and Offices: A Study of Office Worker Performance and the Indoor Environment." P500-03-082-A-9 (Oct. 2003). California Energy Commission.

48 Wilson, Alex. "Making the Case for Green Building." *Environmental Building News* 14.4 (Apr. 2005).

49 Tarquinio, J. Alex. "The Cost of Saving Energy." *New York Times* 15 July 2007: 11-1, 9.

50 "Steve Glen—People." LivingHomes. www.livinghomes.net/viewPerson.html?id=1, accessed 30 Aug. 2007.

Glenn quickly realized that a developer held more control in the building process, and therefore more power to "wed profit and purpose" by creating "responsible developments."[51] He could hire his favorite architects to "do some good in the world," just as his role model Jim Rouse had done with the revitalizations of Faneuil Hall Marketplace in Boston and South Street Seaport in New York City. Regardless, Glenn's official title on the LivingHomes' Web site is "Wannabe Architect." See Exhibit 12 for Glenn's bio.

Glenn approached LivingHomes in the same way he approached his other start-ups—plain and simple, he "loved developing products."[52] He wanted to make a "portfolio play" with a product line that met a range of customers' needs. After a long look into the sustainable real estate market, he decided that the time was ripe for this product in this market sector. Just like developing consumer products, his business plan outlined the target customer needs, and matched them to his proposed product strategies and features.

Product Differentiation

The business plan for LivingHomes rested on four central pillars. The first pillar was to select world-class architects. Glenn recognized that he did not possess the "starchitect" cachet to make LivingHomes a coveted brand, so he developed working relationships with a few well-known architects.[53] At the end of 2007, his company was working with two architects, Ray Kappe and David Hertz, with plans to announce a third, Kieran Timberlake. Each architect was to hit a different price point to provide customers with a suite of options. See Exhibit 13 for Kappe's profile from the LivingHomes' website. Kappe created four designs for LivingHomes, ranging from 1,690 to 4,000 square feet with a base price between $350,000 and $868,000[54] as well as LivingHomes' first, 2,480 square foot model. The homes' aesthetic style has been described as "environmental modernism," combining "the light, volume and linear forms ... [of] a modern space" with the "warmth and detail" found in a more traditional home. The design has been called fun, functional, flexible and practical.[55] Glenn felt that the success of the first home lay in "not screwing up" Kappe's design. In short, his approach was to "get great architects and get the hell out of the way."[56]

The second pillar was the use of prefabrication techniques to build the house in a controlled environment, and deliver it to the site as complete as possible. This was

51 Glenn, Steve. Personal Communication. 31 Dec. 2007.
52 Glenn, Steve. Personal Communication. 8 Nov. 2007.
53 "FAQ." LivingHomes. www.livinghomes.net/faq.html, accessed 30 Aug. 2007.
54 "Configure." LivingHomes. www.livinghomes.net/configure.html?model=rk1&step=0, accessed 15 Jan. 2008; Newman, M. "Green-Fab House." *The Architect's Newspaper* 7 June 2006, 18.
55 "Environmental Modernism: Form, Function, and Ecological Fidelity." LivingHomes. www.livinghomes.net/formFunction.html, accessed 28 Aug. 2007.
56 Glenn, Steve. Presentation at Greenbuild. 7 Nov. 2007.

not a new idea. In 2006, 40,000 new single-family homes were built in a modular fashion.[57] But connecting prefabrication to high-end green homes was new. It was prodded by the kind of thinking that asks, "Why can't you produce houses the same way Apple produces iPods?"[58] The idea is that a house should be stylish, sexy, easy to use, and mass produced. LivingHomes' models comprised prefabricated steel frames including pre-installed electrical systems, heating and cooling ducts, and insulation; they could weigh as much as 25,000 pounds and were stacked much like Legos to provide quick assembly. Further, homeowners could buy additional modules for home expansion after the home was complete and inhabited.

LivingHomes claimed that modular prefabrication produced "higher quality homes faster and for less money than traditional, 'stick-built' [site-built] methods."[59] The imminent work with Kieran Timberlake involved using a flat-pack system, where wall panels instead of whole modules were shipped to the site. This innovation could create a more compact delivery system and faster fit-out, which would be important for scaling the business. As John Quale, an assistant professor at the University of Virginia School of Architecture said, "It doesn't make sense to ship air."[60]

The third pillar was environmental sustainability. The company felt that this goal was synergistic with prefabrication as "modular fabrication supports sustainable building practices," creating only 4–5% material waste in construction, compared with the 30–40% material waste of site-built homes.[61] Exterior walls were made from sustainable wood siding and metal-framed glass doors and windows. The standard-order homes were guaranteed to reach a minimum of LEED Silver rating, though they had the capability to build to the Platinum level, as shown in their prototype.

Glenn's goal with LivingHomes was to build with "as close to zero negative impact on your health and on the environment."[62] The company strove to meet what they termed the "6Zs," or "Six Zeros of Sustainability: Zero Water, Zero Energy, Zero Waste, Zero Emissions, Zero Carbon, and Zero Ignorance." These were inspired by McDonough and Braungart's Cradle-to-Cradle ethic, where less bad does not mean good.[63] Each of these six categories delineated a green strategy that could then be

57 "Quarterly Starts and Completions." US Census Bureau. 2006. www.census.gov/const/quarterly_starts_completions_cust.xls, accessed 30 Aug. 2007 .

58 Yudelson, J. "Green Buildings and iPods." *Environmental Design + Construction* Apr. 2006.

59 Glenn, Steve. Personal Communication. 31 Dec. 2007.

60 Wendt, A. "Prefabricating Green: Building Environmentally Friendly Houses Off Site." *Environmental Building News* 16.10 (2007).

61 "Building for Superior Quality, Lower Cost and Less Waste." LivingHomes. www.living-homes.net/modularConstruction.html, accessed 30 Aug. 2007.

62 "Six Zeros of Sustainability." LivingHomes. www.livinghomes.net/zeros.html, accessed 30 Aug. 2007.

63 McDonough, William and Michael Braungart. *Cradle to Cradle: Remaking the Way We Make Things*. New York, NY: North Point Press, 2002.

counted in the LEED for Homes Certification process. "Zero Ignorance" involved education of the homeowner and a computerized dashboard in the kitchen that displayed real-time energy and water use. Glenn confessed to playing the dashboard like a videogame, trying to get a better score every day by using less energy and water. He compared this to hybrid car owners trying to get better gas mileage with their real-time dashboard readout.[64] Similarly, each home came with a Sustainability Scorecard of LEED Points, just like a nutritional label for food. LivingHomes wanted to be sure that their commitment to sustainability was both transparent and rigorous, and they believed that despite their "Six Zeros" goals, LEED certification was still necessary to give credibility to their green efforts and "keep [them] honest." But for the prototype home with the "6Z" goals, Glenn was the first to admit, "We're not quite zero on anything ... The point was to minimize these as much as possible, and we came extremely close."[65]

The fourth pillar was distribution. LivingHomes aimed to distribute the homes through a network of builders and developers, believing that they could deliver homes "better, quicker, and cheaper than [the builders/developers] could do themselves," and provide them with "the LivingHomes marketing playbook, including a skinnable Web site." This was a franchise model, whereby LivingHomes would develop partnerships with local builders and developers already established in communities having a large number of "cultural creatives" (Boulder, Austin, Raleigh–Durham, Seattle, etc.). LivingHomes could then direct national customer inquiries to its local partners. These partners would then provide LivingHomes with the ability to scale its business more quickly, which would provide both greater volume and better pricing.[66]

The company created a list of partners—companies that passed LivingHomes' internal review for alignment with the core values of the company ("building warm, functional, modern homes that strive to achieve minimal negative impact on the health of homeowners and their communities")—and could therefore be considered for possible inclusion in the homes. The list included mainstream companies like Best Buy, Bosch, GE Security, Herman Miller, HP, Jacuzzi, Klipsch, Kohler, and Panasonic as well as lesser known companies like 3Form,[67] Ecosmart Fire,[68] and EnviroGLAS Products Inc.[69] When the second LivingHome was built, potential customers could visit a *Wired* magazine website[70] and see a video of the installation, "Shop the Home" by purchasing items that the home contained (bath fixtures, lighting, furniture, salad bowls, clothing, and even the vodka), or sign up for events and lectures.

64 Glenn, Steve. Presentation at Greenbuild. 7 Nov. 2007.
65 Blum, A. "Plug+Play Construction." *Wired* 15.1 (Jan. 2007).
66 Glenn, Steve. (2007). Personal Communication. December 31.
67 3Form Material Solutions. www.3-form.com, accessed 30 Aug. 2007.
68 Ecosmart Fire. www.ecosmartfire.com/USA/home.php, accessed 30 Aug. 2007.
69 EnviroGLAS. www.enviroglasproducts.com, accessed 30 Aug. 2007.
70 *Wired* Home. www.wired.com/promo/wiredlivinghome/index.html, accessed 30 Aug. 2007.

The dual aims of high design and comprehensive environmental program raised the costs of the LivingHomes product, something that Steve Glenn was acutely aware of. At the beginning of 2008, base prices were between $250 and $280 per square foot (excluding foundation and transportation), which was far above the average of $120.66 (all included) in the western United States. At these price points, a 2,500 square foot house (similar in size to Steve Glenn's own LivingHome) would run more than $700,000 plus the cost for transportation, foundation, installation, construction management, design fee (8% of base plus foundation costs), and per-mitting—all together estimated at $70–$90 per square foot for a flat lot. Transpor-tation costs were an estimated $20 per square foot in Los Angeles (~$50,000) and foundations could cost upwards of an additional $125,000 for a site like Glenn's ($35–$190/sf), leading to a total cost of over $1,000,000. This was for an "off the shelf" home with no options or upgrades. Customers could further customize the house for a higher base price and additional hourly fees.

Some reports suggest that in Steve Glenn's house, "green features added an esti-mated 20 percent over a comparable prefab place, but resulted in a house that makes its own power, automatically irrigates plants using gray water (wastewater from the showers and sinks), and leaves almost no carbon footprint."[71] Glenn's first LivingHome was estimated to cost about $1 million. In June 2007 *Wired* magazine, with a reader base of cultured tech-savvy consumers, announced a joint venture with LivingHomes to build a 4,057 square foot, LEED Gold, "Wired LivingHome" co-sponsored by BMW CleanEnergy.[72] The home opened for ten days of limited tours in November 2007, and was offered for sale for $4 million. This was clearly a home for the upper-income and discerning green client. However, Glenn's eventual goal was to bring down the LivingHomes price to $150–$200 per square foot (not including land costs, designer fees, etc.).

Product Acquisition

Curious consumers could visit the company Web site (www.livinghomes.net) and configure their own home based on five standard models, then select finishes and options to produce a total estimated budget. See Exhibit 14 for a configuration example. Though customers could customize their homes online as they could a computer, the overall process was still very personalized. After initial conversa-tions, the company completed a site feasibility study to determine whether the cli-ent's site met logistical and legal criteria. Once confirmed, LivingHomes staff could proceed to customize the home based on site zoning and customer specifications. This customization included engineering and design modifications, all based on

71 Scanlon, J. "Objects of Desire. The Prefab Luxury Home." *Men's Journal* 16 Sept. 2007: 116-7.
72 "Introducing the Wired LivingHome by Wired Magazine + LivingHomes." Jetson Green. jetsongreen.typepad.com/jetson_green/2007/06/wired_livinghom.html, accessed 18 June 2007.

the prefabricated modules. Clients were charged an additional hourly fee for customization services.

LivingHomes initially purchased its Lego-like prefabricated steel modules from Profile Structures, Inc. of Santa Fe Springs, California (roughly 10 miles southeast of Los Angeles). This required careful coordination to maintain high standards of quality. Ray Kappe's design, for example, encountered "a fair amount of compromise and change" to conform to the "usual techniques and materials" of Profile Structures' steel models.[73] The internal staff at LivingHomes would then coordinate the orders for all equipment, cabinetry, lighting, etc. Foundation work was required before frame delivery. Clients could hire LivingHomes to manage foundation construction, or hire a contractor on their own. After installation day, LivingHomes committed itself to completing the installation of all equipment and finishes (kitchen cabinets, plumbing fixtures, etc.) in four weeks or less. For customers who wanted a more turnkey solution, Glenn was also taking a play from the books of larger developers, and building a community of homes to take advantage of the neighborhood qualities of like-minded customers. He acquired a plot in Joshua Tree National Park, and began pre-selling homes there.

Due to the expected learning curve associated with developing a new product and process, in 2007 LivingHomes was only delivering homes in the lucrative, yet competitive area of California.[74] Further, the nature of prefabricated homes requires that home delivery be within an economical range of the manufacturing site. The company also committed to working only with clients who were looking to have a LivingHome within twelve months of the initial inquiry.

LivingHomes Organization

LivingHomes employed a small team of Glenn, four architects, one project manager, one head of product management, and one office manager. See Exhibit 15 for the Team Profiles. The company described the team as nimble, the atmosphere as creative, and the skill sets as being drawn from "the worlds of technology, design, and construction management."[75] A key value that they tried to instill in their work force is a desire to "marry profit and purpose," and "co-opt capitalism to be a positive agent of change."[76] They also stressed that the work environment was fun and laid-back. According to the company:

> If you met [our employees] on the street, they'd probably talk to you about snowboarding, dogs, or some chair they're making … Plus we're near the beach, so we like morning runs, bike rides and surf sessions (when the waves are good). Two other things of note: ours is a dog-

73 Newman, Morris. "Green-Fab House." *The Architect's Newspaper* 7 June 2006: 18.
74 "FAQ." LivingHomes. www.livinghomes.net/faq.html, accessed 30 Aug. 2007.
75 "Living Homes: Not Your Typical Office." www.livinghomes.net/employment.html, accessed 30 Aug. 2007.
76 Glenn, Steve. Presentation at Greenbuild. 7 Nov. 2007.

friendly environment and Steve Glenn's grandmother brings lots of baked goodies.[77]

Product Market Segment

A survey by McGraw-Hill identifies green homeowners by the following attributes: Seventy-one percent are female; two-thirds have an annual income over $50,000; the average age is 45; more likely married and highly educated.[78] While this is in part the target of LivingHomes' product, Glenn wanted to go further. LivingHomes was targeting America's growing class of cultural creatives—people who value design, health and ecological sustainability in the products they purchase. Glenn maintained that a mass-produced, prefabricated green home would give people like himself and his friends—this creative class—a home to match their lifestyle. This class, unlike their parent's generation, did not want to sacrifice space and comfort for ecological performance. The LivingHome products were designed with this in mind, blending attributes such as high-end audio and theatre equipment into the home.

Members of the cultural creative class not only differ from hippies, but they were also strikingly different from the moderns (or yuppies) of the 1980s. While the moderns valued achievement, style, and economic progress, cultural creatives valued authenticity, nature, and community. However, this ostensibly diminished focus on success does not mean that they are not affluent. The creative class was estimated to have an average income between $25,000 and $75,000 (1995 figures).[79]

This group's marketplace was described as LOHAS—Lifestyles of Health and Sustainability. In 2000, this represented an estimated $230 billion US industry "for goods and services focused on health, the environment, social justice, personal development and sustainable living."[80] Figures also showed that this class was growing. In 2001, it was estimated that it represented 50 million people, approximately 25% of American adults, and by 2003 that figure had grown to 68 million Americans, or about 33% of the adult population.[81]

The cultural creatives were careful consumers who preferred their home to be located "far away from tract houses in treeless suburbs." They rejected "fake, imitation, poorly made, throwaway, cliché style or high fashion." In terms of décor,

---

77 "Living Homes: Not Your Typical Office." www.livinghomes.net/employment.html, accessed 30 Aug. 2007.

78 "The Green Homeowner: Attributes & Preferences for Remodeling and Buying Green Homes." Bedford, MA: McGraw Hill Construction, 2007.

79 Ray, Paul. H. and Sherry Ruth Anderson. *The Cultural Creatives: How 50 Million People Are Changing the World.* New York, NY: Three Rivers Press, 2001.

80 "About LOHAS." LOHAS. www.lohas.com/about, accessed 1 Oct. 2007.

81 Cortese, Amy. "Business; They Care About the World (and They Shop, Too)." *The New York Times* 20 July 2003. query.nytimes.com/gst/fullpage.html?res=9E01E3D8103CF933A1575 4C0A9659C8B63, accessed 1 Oct. 2007 .

status display happened inside the house not outside. They wanted the building to fit "into its proper place on the land," and they were conscious consumers who wanted to know "where a product came from, how it was made, who made it, and what will happen to it when they are done with it."[82] As Glenn pointed out, "our customers make uneconomic decisions in this space."[83]

LivingHomes Financials

For LivingHomes, capital was necessary to set up its office, develop marketing materials, pay salaries and develop contractual relationships with architects, suppliers, contractors and prefabricators. Glenn's model of pre-selling homes mirrored that of larger developers, where construction (or fabrication) did not start until the client agreement was completed. Glenn started the company with his own funds, but was soon working with venture capitalist Vinod Khosla, founding CEO of Sun Microsystems and former partner of the venture capital firm Kleiner Perkins. Still, Glenn retained significant ownership and control, and was confident of his expertise at raising significant investment to assure a successful product launch.[84]

Other Niche Players in the Green Building Industry

Marmol Radziner Prefab

The architectural firm Marmol Radziner, started by California idealists Leo Marmol and Ron Radziner, recently established a separate design/build practice in Los Angeles for their prefabricated products. The firm produced their first sustainable prefabricated prototype home in 2005, titled The Desert House, in Palm Springs, California. The company's construction crew numbered over 40 people, and the associated architecture firm, established in 1989, employed more than 60 architects, landscape designers, and fabricators. Clients could either order a custom prefab home, or select one of five base models and customize the fixtures and finishes. The homes were designed to achieve LEED Certification. In 2007, they were also constructing a subdivision-like development in Joshua Tree National Park.

Marmol Radziner was unusual among architects in that it already had a vertically-integrated factory doing millwork and detailing, so it was a natural step to expand to completely prefabricated houses. Green aspects of their buildings

82 Ray, Paul. H. and Sherry Ruth Anderson. "Lifestyles of the Cultural Creatives." *Cultural Creatives*. culturalcreatives.org/lifestyles.html, accessed 1 Oct. 2007.

83 Glenn, Steve. Presentation at Greenbuild. 7 Nov. 2007.

84 Glenn, Steve. Personal Communication. 31 Dec. 2007.

included responsible wood choices, structural insulated panels, solar panels, natural cooling, recycled steel construction, and of course, efficient factory built construction.[85] In 2007, the founders were spreading the word of their new product offering. They spoke at both the Dwell on Design conference and the Design Within Reach's showrooms in Pasadena, California.[86] See Exhibit 16 for images of Marmol Radziner's designs.

MKD (Michelle Kaufmann Designs)

MKD, founded by Michelle Kaufmann, debuted in 2004 with the Glidehouse (shown in Exhibit 17). It was prefabricated in a factory, using modern and environmentally-friendly building methods and materials. The Oakland, California company offered five models and custom homes in 2007. As of July 2007, Kaufmann had built seventeen prefab homes and had an additional seventy-five moving through the pipeline. She bought her own factory near Seattle, a location she chose because it was close to the mills that produced her framing, cabinetry, and flooring. The factory could complete a Glidehouse in a month. Kaufmann's houses cost between $185 and $250 per square foot, depending on the model and location, and she wanted them to be even cheaper. Her goal was to reach the middle-class market. MKD was featured in Sierra magazine and described as "The Henry Ford of Green Homes." The article compared the process of ordering one of MKD's "solar-ready, sustainably built, water- and energy-efficient modular homes" to ordering a pair of customized Nike shoes online.[87] So far, MKD had been able to convince some middle and high-income customers that prefabrication could be used to produce a desirable and eco-conscious home.

Next Steps

As Glenn finished the latest tour of his green home, the group followed Glenn to the roof, chattering excitedly about the features of the home. Their interest was palpable, and Glenn felt a surge of renewed optimism. A young couple approached him, gushing about the house. "We're getting married in two months and this is exactly the sort of place where we want to raise a family. If you offered a more affordable model, we would sign a contract today. Do you have something a bit less lavish, but still just as progressive?" Another couple intimated that cost was not a

---

85 Alter, Lloyd. "CA Boom Prefab: Marmol Radziner." *treehugger*. 21 Mar. 2007. www.treehugger.com/files/2007/03/ca_boom_prefab.php, accessed 12 Oct. 2007.

86 "News and Events." Marmol Radziner Prefab. www.marmolradzinerprefab.com, accessed 30 Aug. 2007.

87 Slater, Dashka. "Innovators: The Henry Ford of Green Homes." *Sierra Club*. July/Aug. 2007. www.sierraclub.org/sierra/200707/innovators.asp, accessed 30 Aug. 2007.

problem. However, the woman also commented that she could not bring herself to live in such a fishbowl, and her husband wanted a wood-burning fireplace—one that Glenn warned could cause indoor air pollutants, unlike the denatured alcohol fireplace installed in the LivingHome. As he led the group out the door, he turned around and saw his beautiful home. Could he really merge the pillars of high-end style, prefabrication, green, and distributed delivery?

Sales were starting to come in. By November 2007, LivingHomes had sold thirteen homes, and scheduled to install four of those within 4–9 months.[88] Glenn was confident about this market, and noted that even if his niche were a rounding error in new homes, he would have adequate sales. He hoped to learn more to perfect his home delivery process as these homes came online. Still, the high installed price was a genuine concern and he was "absolutely committed to aggressively reducing costs."[89] But he also defended the costs as providing a better product to his customers:

> We're currently at the higher end of the range of modern, prefab homes—and certainly those of us at this range are expensive vis-à-vis typical construction in many parts of the country—but it's important to do a fair comparison. We believe our homes represent a 20–40% reduction in the cost of similarly constructed, stick-built home. By 'similarly constructed,' we mean a steel-framed home, designed by a world-class architect that features substantial amounts of floor-to-ceiling glass, decking, and environmental finishes and energy systems. We will introduce homes in the future that have lower per square foot costs.[90]

Beyond getting costs down, Glenn faced other difficult questions:

- Was his target market large enough to really provide the economies of scale necessary to reap the benefits of prefabrication?

- Would prefabrication and mass production reduce the signature brand value of the LivingHome?

- Should he contract with more architects to create a more diverse product offering?

- How could he control transportation costs?

- Should he branch out geographically and develop relationships with other fabricators around the country? Should he acquire his own prefabrication plant?

88 Scanlon, J. "Objects of Desire. The Prefab Luxury Home." *Men's Journal* 16 Sept. 2007: 116-7.

89 Williams, J. "Letter to *LA Times* Editor on LivingHomes." [Steve Glenn's letter to the editor.] Curbed Los Angeles. 7 Aug. 2006. la.curbed.com/archives/2006/08/letter_to_la_ti.php, accessed 30 Aug. 2007. "Tour." LivingHomes. www.livinghomes.net/tour.html, accessed 30 Aug. 2007.

90 "FAQ." LivingHomes. www.livinghomes.net/faq.html, accessed 30 Aug. 2007.

- Would competitors emerge that could provide a similar product better, faster, or cheaper?

- And then, of course, how could he deal with zoning laws and the building inspectors who were unfamiliar with the innovations he was introducing?

Glenn knew that to provide a cost-competitive consumer product, he had to scale his business quickly to take advantage of the economies of scale of prefabrication. But knowing exactly how to do this with a 2,000–4,000 square-foot home was certainly different than doing it with software, or even a hand-held iPod. "Our focus, ultimately, is on builders ... We want to sell this [LivingHomes concept] to builders and developers. They'll be able to buy these from us."[91] Making this transition could prove to be the biggest challenge. Merging his short and long-term concerns, Glenn wondered, could he create a sustainable business by building sustainable homes?

91 Crouch, Alison. "Making a Living." *Innovative Homes* 34 (Fall 2006).

Exhibit 1 **Images of the First LivingHome**

Source: LivingHomes. www.livinghomes.net/gallery.html, accessed 30 Aug. 2007.

Exhibit 2 Annual Housing Starts (1978–2006)

Source: National Association of Home Builders. www.nahb.org/generic.aspx?centionID=130&genericContentID=554 &print=true, accessed 24 Nov. 2007.

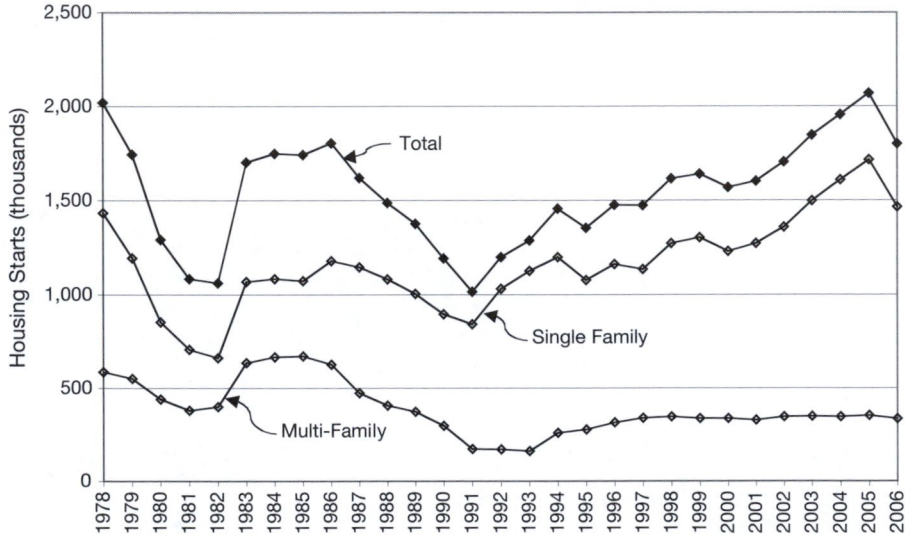

Exhibit 3 Highlights of Annual 2006 Characteristics of New Housing

Source: "Highlights of Annual 2006 Characteristics of New Housing." www.census.gov/const/www/ highanncharac2006.html, accessed 24 Nov. 2007.

In 2006:

- The average single-family house completed had 2,469 square feet, 769 more square feet than in 1976.
- 78% of all new single-family homes completed were speculatively-built (house and land are sold together as part of the same transaction), up from 65% in 1986.
- 39% of new single-family homes completed have four or more bedrooms, almost double the rate of just 20 years ago.
- 26% of new single-family homes sold have 3 or more bathrooms, almost triple the rate from 1986.
- Half of all single-family homes were completed in the South region, up 10 percentage points from 1976.
- Approximately 90% of all single-family homes completed have air conditioning!
- Approximately 95% of new single-family homes sold have at least a 1-car garage or carport.

- In the Northeast and Midwest 75% of the homes completed have a basement, but in the West only 20% have a basement and that drops to 10% in the South.
- Across the country, over half (53%) of all single-family homes sold have at least 1 fireplace.
- 25% of new single-family homes completed have a deck, down from 34% in 1996.
- Almost 70% of all new single-family homes sold use gas as the primary source of heating fuel and approximately 30% use electricity as the primary source.
- Attached single-family homes account for nearly 15% of all new single-family homes sold, up from 11% in 1996.
- Currently vinyl siding is the most common principal exterior material at 30% of new single-family homes sold. In 1996 wood was 22% of the share. It has now reduced to 5% in 2006. Regionally the exterior wall material of preference is: Vinyl—Northeast (86%) and Midwest (67%); Brick—South (41%); and Stucco—West (62%).
- 90% of all new single-family homes sold were financed by a conventional loan, up from 55% in 1986.
- The average sales price of new single-family homes sold (including land) was $305,900. In 1996, the average sales price was $166,400. This is an increase of over 84%!
- The average price per square foot for new single-family homes sold was $91.99, up from $64.38 in 1996. Regionally, it is most expensive to build in the West at $120.66 and least expensive to build in the South at $80.32.
- Over a tenth (12%) of all new single-family homes sold were built on lots of at least 22,000 square feet (approximately a half an acre); this is virtually unchanged from 1986 and 1996.
- 40,000 new single-family homes were modular homes, up 3,000 units from 1996. This represents about 2% of all homes completed; however, this method of construction is most prevalent in the Northeast, with nearly 10% of its units built this way.
- For more than 3/4 of all new single-family homes sold, closing costs were excluded from the sales price. This estimate has remained relatively stable over the past 20 years.
- Multi-family construction has decreased dramatically over the last 20 years from 636,000 units, in 1986 to 153,000 units in 1993. It rebounded 325,000 units in 2006.
- The average multi-family unit completed had 1,533 square feet, 173 more square feet than in 1999.
- The percentage of apartments completed being built to be sold was 39.2. This is second only to the record 39.6% set in 1982.

Please note that the estimates shown here are based on sample surveys and subject to sampling variability as well as non-sampling error.

Exhibit 4 New Housing Units Completed, by Type

Source: US Census Bureau. www.census.gov/const/quarterly_starts_completions_cust.xls, accessed 30 Aug. 2007 from

Year	Total	Built for Sale	Contractor Built	Owner Built	Median Square Footage	Average Square Footage
2000	1,242	883	192	126	2,057	2,266
2001	1,256	906	189	122	2,103	2,324
2002	1,325	967	195	123	2,114	2,320
2003	1,386	1,038	185	119	2,137	2,330
2004	1,532	1,170	191	125	2,140	2,349
2005	1,636	1,288	190	118	2,227	2,434
2006	1,654	1,293	198	124	2,248	2,459

Exhibit 5 Residential Building Factsheet

Source: Center for Sustainable Systems, University of Michigan. css.snre.umich.edu/css_doc/CSS01-08.pdf, accessed 24 Nov. 2007.

Center for Sustainable Systems

University of Michigan
440 Church Street, Ann Arbor, MI 48109-1041
phone: 734-764-1412   fax: 734-647-5841
email: css.info@umich.edu
http://css.snre.umich.edu

factsheets

Residential Buildings

Patterns of Use

Proven climate-specific, resource-efficient house design strategies exist, but due to lack of market incentives and political will, per capita materials and energy consumption continue to increase. Likewise, between 1950 and 1990, urbanized land expansion grew at a rate 3 times the rate of population growth.[1]

Size and Occupancy[2]

A majority of Americans live in single-family houses – in 2005, 64% of the 109 million U.S. households were single-family. Some unsustainable residential building trends to consider:

Average size of a new U.S. single-family house:
- 1950   983 ft^2
- 1970   1,500 ft^2
- 2000   2,200 ft^2
- 2005   2,434 ft^2 **a 148% increase from 1950**

Average area per person in a new U.S. single-family house:
- 1950   292 ft^2 per person
- 1970   478 ft^2 per person
- 2000   840 ft^2 per person **a 188% increase from 1950**

Average number of occupants per U.S. household:
- 1950   3.37
- 1970   3.14
- 2000   2.62 **a 22% decrease from 1950**

- In 1950, 9% of housing units were occupied by only one person. By 2005, this increased to 27%.[3]
- Americans spend on average, 90% of their time indoors.[4]

Energy Use

- A new single-family house in Michigan – as studied in 1998 by CSS – consumes 1.3 GJ per square meter annually.[5]
- A similar study of 3 houses in Sweden built in the 1990's shows annual energy consumption of 0.49 – 0.56 GJ per square meter – less than half the energy consumed in the Michigan house.[6]
- Between 1990 and 2006, total residential CO_2 emissions increased by 26% while population increased by only 20%.[7]
- The residential sector accounts for 21% of the total energy consumption in the U.S.[8] The breakdown of this energy consumption is shown in the figure to the right.

Average Size of a New U.S. Single-Family House

1970
1,500 ft^2

2005
2,434 ft^2

62%
Increase

Average U.S. Residential Energy Consumption[9]

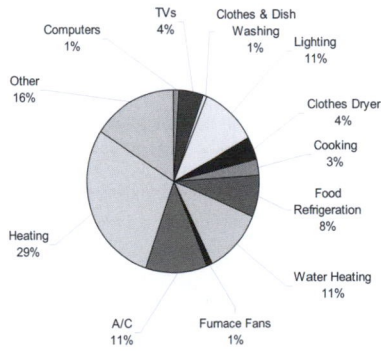

Computers 1%
TVs 4%
Clothes & Dish Washing 1%
Lighting 11%
Other 16%
Clothes Dryer 4%
Cooking 3%
Food Refrigeration 8%
Heating 29%
Water Heating 11%
A/C 11%
Furnace Fans 1%

[1] Rusk, D. (1999) *Inside Game Outside Game: Winning Strategies for Saving Urban America.* Washington, D.C. Brookings Institution Press.
[2] National Association of Home Builders (2007) *Housing Facts, Figures and Trends,* U.S. Census Bureau and Wilson, A. and J. Boehland (2005) "Small is Beautiful, U.S House Size, Resource Use, and the Environment." *Journal of Industrial Ecology.* Vol 9, No. 1-2, 277-287.
[3] U.S. Census Bureau (2004) *Historical Census of Housing, Tables Living Alone* and (2006) *American Housing Survey for the United States: 2005.*
[4] Wilson, S. (2004) "Design for Health: Summit for Massachusetts Health Care Decision Makers." Presentation September 2004.
[5] Blanchard, S. and P. Reppe (1998) *Life Cycle Analysis of a Residential Home in Michigan* (CSS98-05).
[6] Adalberth, K. (1997) "Energy use during the Life Cycle of Single-Unit Dwellings: Examples." *Building and Environment,* Vol. 32, No. 4, 321-329.
[7] Energy Information Administration (EIA) (2007) *U.S. Carbon Dioxide Emissions from Energy Sources 2006 Flash Estimate.*
[8] EIA (2007) *Annual Energy Review 2006* Report No. DOE/EIA-0384(2006).
[9] EIA (2007) *Annual Energy Outlook 2006 with Projections to 2030.*

Life Cycle Impacts[5]

The Center for Sustainable Systems conducted a case study to inventory life-cycle energy consumption from manufacturing, construction and operational phases of a new 2,450 ft^2 single-family house built in Ann Arbor in 1998.

- The case study house required 172 tons of concrete, 24 tons of wood and wood products.
- 90% of the life cycle energy consumption occurred during operation; only 10% went into building and maintaining the house.
- Top contributors to the primary energy consumption of the case study house were polyamide for carpet, concrete in foundation, PVC for siding, window frames and pipes, and asphalt roofing shingles.
- 75% of the materials in the case study house are currently recyclable; however, the U.S. average recycling rate of building materials from demolition and construction is only 20-30%.[10]

The following off-the-shelf energy efficiency strategies were then modeled to quantify the resulting life-cycle energy savings:

- wall and ceiling insulation increased from R-15 to R-35 and R-23 to R-49 respectively; building infiltration (leakage) reduced by half
- wooden basement walls instead of concrete; basement thermal insulation increased from R-12 to R-39
- double-glazed windows upgraded to include low-e treatment and argon fill
- energy-efficient appliances chosen; stove & dryer switched from electricity to natural gas
- energy-efficient lighting (fluorescent) adopted throughout
- building-integrated shading (overhangs) created on south-facing windows
- hot-water heat recovery installed
- air-to-air heat recovery used with ventilation system
- glass fiber thermal insulation replaced with recycled cellulose
- recycled-materials roofing shingles (wood/plastic)

- A 63% building life-cycle energy reduction was achieved through the above measures, all with readily available technology.
- Life cycle greenhouse gas emissions were reduced from 1,013 to 374 metric tons of CO_2-equivalent, over the 50-year lifetime of the house.
- Despite the additional material requirements, the total embodied energy was reduced by about 4%.
- Installation of a high efficiency HVAC system and cellulose insulation ranked as the most effective strategies in reducing annual energy costs.

Solutions and Sustainable Alternatives
Reduce operational demand of the home
From a life-cycle perspective, energy and water consumption during the life of a building contribute much more to its environmental impact than do building materials. The following suggestions can significantly reduce operational energy demand:
- Use passive heating methods – passive solar, waste heat from disposed hot water.
- Make use of passive cooling – night-flushing, shading.
- Use adequate insulation – recommended R-values in the Midwest climate: attic R-49, walls R-18.[11]
- Add ceiling fans, and the A/C can be comfortably set about 5 degrees higher.
- Maximize day-lighting – sky lights, south facing windows.
- Consider decentralized, "passive" sanitary services – compost toilet, living machine, rainwater use for toilets, greywater for gardening.
- Convert appliances from electric to natural gas, reducing primary energy consumption by about 75%.
- Install a low-flow showerhead – less than 2.5-gallons-per-minute – to save both water and energy.
- Save 40% of hot water heating energy with a simple wastewater heat exchanger.

Select durable and/or renewable materials
Building materials with long lives may have greater upfront cost, but long-term savings and reduced environmental impact are achieved by avoiding replacement. Renewable building materials also offer potential environmental advantages.
- Durables to consider: cork or hardwood vs. carpet, standing-seam roofing vs. asphalt shingles
- Renewables to consider: cork, linoleum, wool carpet, certified wood and plywood, strawboard, cellulose insulation, straw-bale
- Substituting asphalt shingle roofing with recycled plastic/wood fiber shingles can reduce embodied energy by 98% over 50 years

Resources
Blanchard, S. and P. Reppe. (1998) *Life Cycle Analysis of a Residential Home in Michigan* (CSS98-05)
Keoleian, G. A., S. Blanchard and P. Reppe (2001) "Life Cycle Energy, Costs, and Strategies for Improving a Single Family House", *Journal of Industrial Ecology* 4(2), p. 135-156. (CSS00-11)

---

[10] U.S. EPA (1998) *Characterization of Building-Related Construction and Demolition Debris in the United States* Report No. EPA530-R-98-010.
[11] U.S. Department of Energy, Energy Efficiency and Renewable Energy (2006) "Energy Savers: Tips on Saving Energy & Money at Home. Insulation." http://www1.eere.energy.gov/consumer/tips/insulation.html

Exhibit 6 **Energy Star Market Penetration: Energy Star Qualified New Homes, by State**

Source: United States. Environmental Protection Agency. "Energy Star Qualified New Homes Market Indices for States." *US EPA Energy Star*. www.energystar.gov/index.cfm?fuseaction=qhmi.showHomesMarketIndex, accessed 25 Nov. 2007.

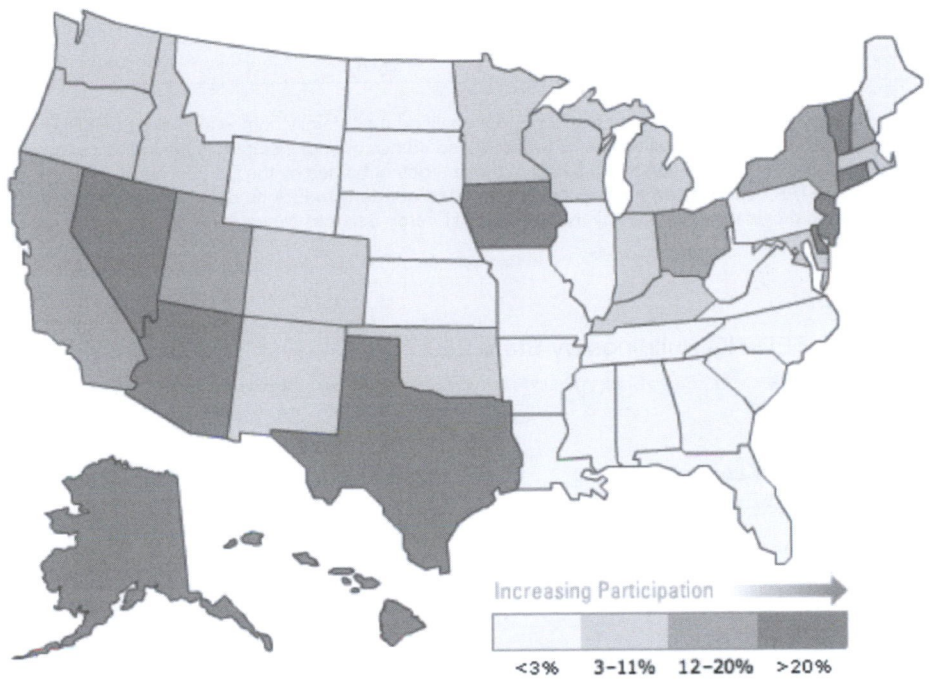

State	2006 Energy Star Qualified New Homes[a]	2006 One-unit Housing Permits	2006 Energy Star Market Penetration
Alaska	1,024	1,612	64%
Arizona	20,101	55,633	36%
California	18,105	107,714	17%
Connecticut	1,606	7,107	23%
Delaware	1,217	5,015	24%
Hawaii	2,086	5,597	37%
Iowa	5,866	10,250	57%
Nevada	18,891	26,722	71%
New Hampshire	820	4,826	17%
New Jersey	5,351	17,113	31%
New York	2,569	19,981	13%

State	2006 Energy Star Qualified New Homes[a]	2006 One-unit Housing Permits	2006 Energy Star Market Penetration
Ohio	3,462	27,514	13%
Texas	60,839	162,750	37%
Utah	3,554	22,595	16%
Vermont	501	2,071	24%

a In addition to site-built, there are ENERGY STAR qualified multi-family homes as well as ENERGY STAR qualified manufactured homes. However, these homes are not included in the indices because of differences in the definition and tracking of these types of homes by the US EPA and Census. ENERGY STAR qualified new homes data is submitted quarterly to EPA on behalf of builders by third-party rating providers accredited by the Residential Energy Services Network (RESNET).

Exhibit 7 LEED-NC Buildings by State 2006

Source: "About USGBC." US Green Building Council. www.usgbc.org/ShowFile.aspx?DocumentID=3376, accessed 25 Nov. 2007

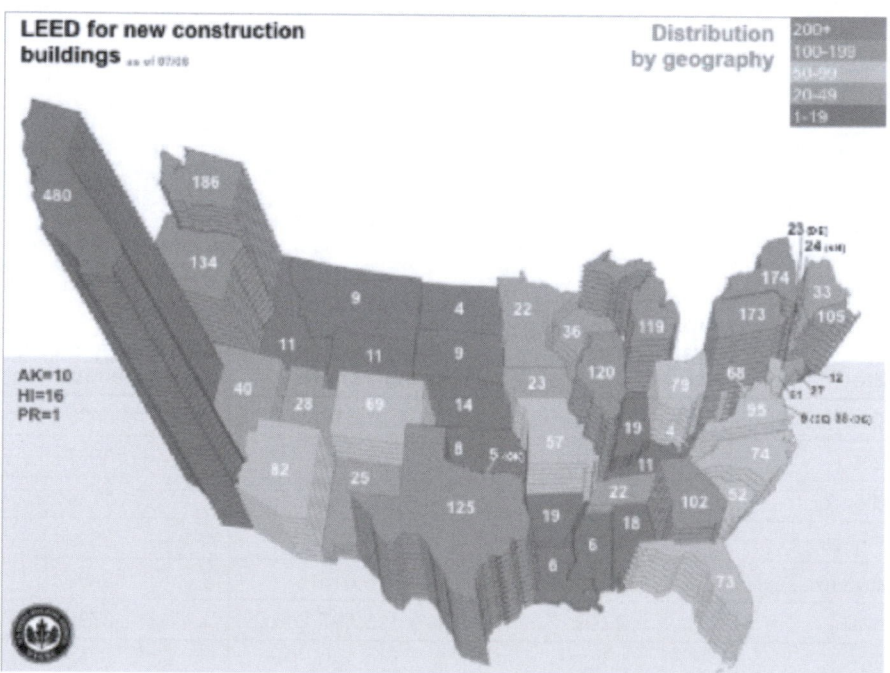

Exhibit 8 **LEED for Homes Checklist**

Source: US Green Building Council. (2007). LEED for Homes Program Pilot Rating System Version 1.11a. www.usgbc.org/ShowFile.aspx?DocumentID=2269, accessed 24 Nov. 2007.

Project Checklist
LEED for Homes

for Homes

Builder Name:	
Responsible Party (if different):	
Home Address (Street/City/State):	

Input Values: Click here if you're experiencing problems

No of Bedrooms: **4** ▾   Floor Area (SF): **2400** ▾

Minimum No. of Points Required:
Certified: **45**   Silver: **60**   Gold: **75**   Platinum: **90**

Detailed information on the measures below are provided in the companion document "LEED for Homes Rating System"

Max Points Available

Y / Pts No N/A			Section	Measure		Max Points
			Innovation and Design Process (ID)	(Minimum of 0 ID Points Required)		**9**
			1.1 **Integrated Project Planning**	Preliminary Rating		Prerequisite
		↘	1.2	Integrated Project Team		1
		↘	1.3	Design Charrette		1
		↘	2.1 **Quality Management for**	Durability Planning; (Pre-Construction)		Prerequisite
			2.2 **Durability**	Wet Room Measures		Prerequisite
			2.3	Quality Management		Prerequisite
			2.4	Third-Party Durability Inspection		3
		↘	3.1 **Innovative / Regional Design**	Provide Description and Justification for Specific Measure		1
		↘	3.2	Provide Description and Justification for Specific Measure		1
		↘	3.3	Provide Description and Justification for Specific Measure		1
		↘	3.4	Provide Description and Justification for Specific Measure		1
0			Sub-Total			
Y / Pts No N/A			**Location and Linkages (LL)**	(Minimum of 0 LL Points Required)	OR	**10**
			1 **LEED-ND Neighborhood**		LL2-5	10
		↘	2 **Site Selection**	Avoid Environmentally Sensitive Sites and Farmland	LL1	2
			3.1 **Preferred Locations**	Select an Edge Development Site	LL1	1
			3.2	OR Select an Infill Site	LL1	2
			3.3	Select a Previously Developed Site	LL1	1
			4 **Infrastructure**	Site within 1/2 Mile of Existing Water and Sewer	LL1	1
			5.1 **Community Resources**	Basic Community Resources / Public Transportation	LL1	1
			5.2 **& Public Transit**	OR Extensive Community Resources / Public Transportation	LL1	2
			5.3	OR Outstanding Community Resources / Public Transportation	LL1	3
			6 **Access to Open Space**	Publicly Accessible Green Spaces	LL1	1
0			Sub-Total			
Y / Pts No N/A			**Sustainable Sites (SS)**	(Minimum of 5 SS Points Required)	OR	**21**
			1.1 **Site Stewardship**	Erosion Controls (During Construction)		Prerequisite
			1.2	Minimize Disturbed Area of Site		1
		↘	2.1 **Landscaping**	No Invasive Plants		Prerequisite
		↘	2.2	Basic Landscaping Design		2
		↘	2.3	Limit Turf		3
		↘	2.4	Drought Tolerant Plants		2
		↘	3 **Shading of Hardscapes**	Locate and Plant Trees to Shade Hardscapes		1
		↘	4.1 **Surface Water Management**	Design Permeable Site		4
		↘	4.2	Permanent Erosion Controls / Professional Design of Erosion Control		2
			5 **Non-Toxic Pest Control**	Select Insect and Pest Control Alternatives from List		2
		↘	6.1 **Compact Development**	Average Housing Density ≥ 7 Units / Acre	LL1	2
		↘	6.1	OR Average Housing Density ≥ 10 Units / Acre	LL1	3
		↘	6.3	OR Average Housing Density ≥ 20 Units / Acre	LL1	4
0			Sub-Total			
Y / Pts No N/A			**Water Efficiency (WE)**	(Minimum of 3 WE Points Required)	OR	**15**
		↘	1.1 **Water Reuse**	Rainwater Harvesting System		4
		↘	1.2	Grey Water Re-Use System		1
		↘	2.1 **Irrigation System**	Select High Efficiency Measures from List		3
			2.2	Third Party Verification		1
		↘	2.3	OR Install Landscape Designed by Licensed or Certified Professional	WE 2.2	4
			3.1 **Indoor Water Use**	High Efficiency Fixtures (Toilets, Showers, and Faucets)		3
			3.2	OR Very High Efficiency Fixtures (Toilets, Showers, and Faucets)	WE 3.1	6
0			Sub-Total			

Project Checklist (cont'd)

HERS Index Value Achieved: 85
IECC Climate Zone: 1

EA 1.2 Pts Achieved: 0.0

Y / Pts No N/A	Energy and Atmosphere (EA)	(Minimum of 0 EA Points Required)	OR	38
	1.1 **ENERGY STAR Home**	Meets Performance Requirements of ENERGY STAR for Homes		Prerequisite
	1.2	Exceeds Performance of ENERGY STAR for Homes	EA 2-10	34
	7.1 **Water Heating**	Improved Hot Water Distribution System		2
	7.2	Pipe Insulation		1
	11 **Refrigerant Management**	Minimize Ozone Depletion and Global Warming Contributions		1
0	Sub-Total (or Sub-Total from Addendum A - Prescriptive EA Credits)			

Y / Pts No N/A	Materials and Resources (MR)	(Minimum of 2 MR Points Required)		14
	1.1 **Material Efficient Framing**	Overall Waste Factor for Framing Order Shall be No More than 10%.		Prerequisite
	1.2	Advanced Framing Techniques		3
	1.3	OR Structurally Insulated Panels	MR 1.2	2
	2.1 **Environmentally Preferable**	Tropical Woods, if Used, Must be FSC		Prerequisite
	2.2 **Products**	Select Environmentally Preferable Products from List		8
	3.1 **Waste Management**	Document Overall Rate of Diversion		Prerequisite
	3.2	Reduce Waste Sent to Landfill by 25% to 100%		3
0	Sub-Total			

Y / Pts No N/A	Indoor Environmental Quality (IEQ)	(Minimum of 6 IEQ Points Required)	OR	20
	1 **ENERGY STAR with IAP**	Meets ENERGY STAR w/ Indoor Air Package (IAP)	IEQ2-10	11
	2.1 **Combustion Venting**	Space Heating & DHW Equip w/ Closed/Power-Exhaust	IEQ 1	Prerequisite
	2.2	Install High Performance Fireplace	IEQ 1	2
	3 **Moisture Control**	Analyze Moisture Loads AND Install Central System (if Needed)	IEQ 1	1
	4.1 **Outdoor Air Ventilation**	Meets ASHRAE Std 62.2	IEQ 1	Prerequisite
	4.2	Dedicated Outdoor Air System (w/ Heat Recovery)	IEQ 1	2
	4.3	Third-Party Testing of Outdoor Air Flow Rate into Home		1
	5.1 **Local Exhaust**	Meets ASHRAE Std 62.2	IEQ 1	Prerequisite
	5.2	Timer / Automatic Controls for Bathroom Exhaust Fans	IEQ 1	1
	5.3	Third-Party Testing of Exhaust Air Flow Rate Out of Home		1
	6.1 **Supply Air Distribution**	Perform Duct Design Calculations	IEQ 1	Prerequisite
	6.2	Third-Party Testing of Supply Air Flow into Each Room in Home		2
	7.1 **Supply Air Filtering**	≥ 8 MERV Filters, w/ Adequate System Air Flow	IEQ 1	Prerequisite
	7.2	OR ≥ 10 MERV Filters, w/ Adequate System Air Flow		1
	7.3	OR ≥ 13 MERV Filters, w/ Adequate System Air Flow		2
	8.1 **Contaminant Control**	Seal-Off Ducts During Construction	IEQ 1	1
	8.2	Permanent Walk-Off Mats OR Shoe Storage OR Central Vacuum		2
	8.3	Flush Home Continuously for 1 Week with Windows Open		1
	9.1 **Radon Protection**	Install Radon Resistant Construction if Home is in EPA Zone 1	IEQ 1	Prerequisite
	9.2	Install Radon Resistant Construction if Home is not in EPA Zone 1	IEQ 1	1
	10.1 **Garage Pollutant Protection**	No Air Handling Equipment OR Return Ducts in Garage	IEQ 1	Prerequisite
	10.2	Tightly Seal Shared Surfaces between Garage and Home	IEQ 1	2
	10.3	Exhaust Fan in Garage		1
	10.4	OR Detached Garage or No Garage	IEQ 1	3
0	Sub-Total			

Y / Pts No N/A	Awareness and Education (AE)	(Minimum of 0 AE Points Required)		3
	1.1 **Education for Homeowner**	Basic Occupant's Manual and Walkthrough of LEED Home		Prerequisite
	1.2 **and/or Tenants**	Comprehensive Occupant's Manual and Multiple Walkthroughs / Trainings		1
	1.3	Public Awareness of LEED Home		1
	2.1 **Education for Building Mgrs**	Basic Building Manager's Manual and Walkthrough of LEED Home		1
0	Sub-Total			

| **0** | **Project Totals** (pre-certification estimates) | *Estimated Performance Tier:* | | **130** |

for Homes

Project Checklist, Addendum A
Prescriptive Approach for Energy and Atmosphere (EA) Credits

		Detailed information on the measures below are provided in the companion document "LEED for Homes Rating System"				***Max Points*** *Available*
Y/Pts No N/A		**Energy and Atmosphere (EA)**	(Minimum of 0 EA Points Required)		OR	**38**
		2.1 **Insulation**	Third-Party Inspection of Insulation, At Least HERS Grade II		EA 1	Prerequisite
		2.2	Third-Party Inspection of Insulation, Grade I AND 5% above code		EA 1	2
		3.1 **Air Infiltration**	Third-Party Envelope Air Leakage Tested </= 7.0 ACH50 (CZ 1-2)		EA 1	Prerequisite
		3.2	Third-Party Envelope Air Leakage Tested </= 5.0 ACH50 (CZ 1-2)		EA 1	2
		3.3	*OR* Third-Party Envelope Air Leakage Tested </= 3.0 ACH50		EA 1	3
		4.1 **Windows**	Windows Meet ENERGY STAR for Windows (See Table)		EA 1	Prerequisite
		4.2	Windows Exceed ENERGY STAR for Windows (See Table)		EA 1	2
		4.3	*OR* Windows Exceed ENERGY STAR for Windows (See Table)		EA 1	3
		5.1 **Duct Tightness**	Third-Party Duct Leakage Tested </= 4.0 CFM25 / 100 SF to Outside		EA 1	Prerequisite
		5.2	Third-Party Duct Leakage Tested </= 3.0 CFM25 / 100 SF to Outside		EA 1	2
		5.3	*OR* Third-Party Duct Leakage Tested </= 1.0 CFM25 / 100 SF to Outside		EA 1	3
		6.1 **Space Heating and Cooling**	Meets ENERGY STAR for HVAC w/ Manual J & refrigerant charge test		EA 1	Prerequisite
		6.2	HVAC is Better than ENERGY STAR		EA 1	2
		6.3	*OR* HVAC Substantially Exceeds ENERGY STAR		EA 1	4
		7.1 **Water Heating**	Improved Hot Water Distribution System			2
		7.2	Pipe Insulation			1
		7.3 **Water Heating**	Improved Water Heating Equipment		EA 1	3
		8.1 **Lighting**	Install at Least Three ENERGY STAR labeled Light Fixtures (or CFLS)		EA 1	Prerequisite
		8.2	Energy Efficient Fixtures and Controls		EA 1	2
		8.3	*OR* ENERGY STAR Advanced Lighting Package		EA 1	3
		9.1 **Appliances**	Select Appliances from List		EA 1	2
		9.2	Very Efficient Clothes Washer (MEF > 1.8, *AND* WF< 5.5)		EA 1	1
		10 **Renewable Energy**	Renewable Electric Generation System (1 Point / 5% Reduction)		EA 1	10
		11 **Refrigerant Management**	Minimize Ozone Depletion and Global Warming Contributions			1
0		Sub-Total				

By affixing my signature below, the undersigned does hereby declare and affirm to the USGBC that the LEED for Homes requirements, as specified in the LEED for Homes Rating System, have been met for the indicated credits and will, if audited, provide the necessary supporting documents.

Responsible Party's Name		Company	
Signature		Date	

By affixing my signature below, the undersigned does hereby declare and affirm to the USGBC that the required inspections and performance testing for the LEED for Homes requirements, as specified in the LEED for Homes Rating System, have been completed, and will provide the project documentation file, if requested.

Rater's Name		Company	
Signature		Date	

By affixing my signature below, the undersigned does hereby declare and affirm to the USGBC that the required inspections and performance testing for the LEED for Homes requirements, as specified in the LEED for Homes Rating System, have been completed, and will provide the project documentation file, if requested.

Provider's Name		Company	
Signature		Date	

Exhibit 9 **Green Home Guide**

Source: Green Home Guide. 25 Nov. 2007. www.greenhomeguide.org.

U.S. GREEN BUILDING COUNCIL

THE GREEN HOME GUIDE

| WHAT MAKES A GREEN HOME | GREEN HOME PROGRAMS | GUIDE FOR GREEN RENOVATION | LIVING GREEN | RESOURCES | NEWS & EVENTS |

INTRODUCTION

Green Homes for Everyone

From Seattle to Des Moines to New York City, anyone can have a green home. Rented or owned, affordable or market-rate, single-family or multi-unit, urban, suburban or rural: If it's housing, it can be green.

Green Home Basics

Green Homes 101
LEED for Homes
Sustainable Lifestyle Tips
Incentives for Going Green

NEWS

The Green Market is Growing

The 2007 McGraw-Hill Construction SmartMarket Report on Attitudes & Preferences for Remodeling and Buying Green Homes shows a growing market for green homebuilding and green renovation, even amid a downturn in the housing market at large – and maybe even largely *because* of that downturn.
READ MORE...
MORE NEWS...

How Green is Your Lifestyle?

Figure out your personal CO2 emissions:
- **EPA Carbon Calculator**

Calculate how many Earths would be needed to sustain the world's population if everyone lived like you:
- **How Many Earths?**

SPOTLIGHT

This LEED-certified home is part of the Carsten Crossings neighborhood in Rocklin, Calif. Every home in the 144-home subdivision is certified, with unique features that save homeowners $1,400 a year on utilities.
READ MORE...

Founding Sponsor

Newland® COMMUNITIES

AT THE HEART OF GREAT LIVING

GREEN BUILD

Exhibit 10a Costs of Green Buildings

Sources: Kats, G. "The Costs and Financial Benefits of Green Buildings." *Capital E*. Oct. 2003. www.cap-e.com/ewebeditpro/items/O59F3259.pdf, accessed 25 Nov. 2007. Hershfield, Morrison. "Construction Forecast Monthly." Reed Research Group, Sept. 2005. Referenced in: "2005 Survey of Green Building." Turner Construction. www.turnerconstruction.com/greensurvey05.pdf, accessed 25 Nov. 2007.

The Kats Study			The Reed Research Group	
LEED Rating	**Sample Size**	**Cost Premium**	**LEED Rating**	**Cost Premium**
Platinum	1	6.50%	Platinum	11.50%
Gold	6	1.82%	Gold	4.50%
Silver	18	2.11%	Silver	3.10%
Certified	8	0.66%	Certified	0.80%
Average	–	1.84%		

Exhibit 10b Benefits of Green Buildings

Capital E Analysis

Source: Kats, G. "Green Building Costs and Financial Benefits." Capital E. Oct. 2003. www.cap-e.com/ewebeditpro/
items/O59F3481.pdf, accessed 1 Jan. 2008.

Category	20-year NPV/sf
Energy Savings	$5.80
Emissions Savings	$1.20
Water Savings	$0.50
Operations/Maintenance Savings	$8.50
Subtotal	$16.00
Average Extra Cost of Green Building	(−$3.00 to −$5.00)
Total 20-year Net Benefit	$11–$13

Energy Performance for a Building Meeting ASHRAE Standard 90.0-1999 with a High-Performance Green Building

Source: "The Business Case for Sustainable Design in Federal Facilities." US Department of Energy: Energy Efficiency and Renewable Energy—Federal Energy Management Program (FEMP). Oct. 2003. www1.eere.energy.gov/
femp/sustainable/sustainable_federalfacilities.html, accessed 1 Jan. 2008.

	Base Case Building Annual Energy Cost	Building Annual Energy Cost	High Performance Percent Reduction
Lighting	$6,100	$3,190	47.70%
Cooling	$1,800	$1,310	27.10%
Heating	$1,800	$1,280	28.90%
Other	$2,130	$1,700	20.10%
Total	$11,800	$7,490	36.70%

Exhibit 11 **Energy and Water Prices**

Source: "Residential Electricity Prices: A Consumer's Guide (2003)." Energy Information Administration. www.eia.doe.gov/neic/brochure/electricity/electricity.html, accessed 25 Nov. 2007.

Region	Energy $/kWh	Water $/1,000 gallons
New England	$0.17	$17.23 NJ
Northwest	$0.72	$13.60 ID
California	$0.14	$44.03 CA
Southwest/Rockies	$0.97	$17.23 NM
New York	$0.16	$31.61 NY
Mid-Atlantic	$0.13	$19.07 DE
Upper Midwest	$0.85	$11.60 MN
Alaska/Hawaii	$0.20	$17.23 HI
South/Southeast	$0.87	$10.46 AZ
Lower Midwest	$0.97	$22.05 IN

Exhibit 12 **LivingHomes' Profile of Steve Glenn**

Source: LivingHomes. www.livinghomes.net/viewPerson.html?id=1, accessed 30 Aug. 2007.

People

Steve Glenn is an entrepreneur committed to positive social change through both for- and non-profit organizations. He is the founder and CEO of LivingHomes, LLC—a developer of modern, prefabricated homes designed by world-class architects that feature healthy/green materials and energy systems, all at a great price value. A fan of architecture and an avid Lego enthusiast from a very young age, Glenn tried his hand at design in college only to find the he lacked both the talent and temperament to be an architect. Instead, Glenn concluded that the world could use more real estate developers like Jim Rouse who focus on projects that reflect a deep appreciation for the aesthetic, environment and communities in which they're created. From Lego to prefab, LivingHomes represents the fulfillment of a life-long ambition to create a company that aspires to 'wed profit and purpose' by developing homes that make great design, functionality, and sustainable design practical and affordable.

Glenn spent most of his career in technology. Glenn founded and served as CEO for PeopleLink, a leading provider of enterprise e-community solutions to clients which included Oracle, GE, MTV, Paramount, Reuters and CBS. He is also a founding Partner of idealab!, a business incubation firm that raised over $1 billion in equity, and founded or invested in a number of successful companies including GoTo/Overture (OVER), NetZero/United Online (UNTD), CitySearch (TMCS), Tickets.com (TKTS), eToys and CarsDirect. Prior to idealab!, Glenn worked for Walt Disney Imagineering as co-director of the Virtual Reality Studio.

Glenn is also involved with a number of non-profits. Prior to LivingHomes, Glenn worked for nearly two years with the William Jefferson Clinton

Foundation first managing the development of a $330 million program in Mozambique that will provide care and treatment to over 350,000 HIV+ individuals. He then managed the development of a childhood health initiative with the American Heart Association.

Glenn co-founded and serves on the board of the Sustainable Business Council, Kaia Parker Dance Fund, and the Hope Street Group. He is also a member of the board of directors for LA Works and the Brown University Entrepreneur Forum.

He holds a bachelor's degree with honors in Organizational Behavior from Brown University, and received a scholarship for the Career Discovery Program in Urban Planning at the Harvard Graduate School of Design. Glenn stills plays with Legos. A lot.

Exhibit 13 LivingHomes' Profile of Ray Kappe

Source: LivingHomes. www.livinghomes.net/rayKappe.html, accessed 30 Aug. 2007.

Ray Kappe: Warm Modernist

Ray Kappe, FAIA, is renowned for his residential architecture which has been characterized as 'the apotheosis of the California House.' His designs evince a mastery of warm, modern spaces, clearly expressed construction systems, and environmental sensitivity. "I've always sought out the edges, the views, and a feeling of expansiveness," Kappe said.

During his first ten years of practice, he completed fifty custom post-and-beam houses. Exploring modular systems, prefabrication, passive energy and active solar systems, Kappe has completed commercial, low-cost housing, condominium, hotel and college buildings. He has also been involved in urban design and planning, as well as social and community advocacy. Responding to a question about the ten most important principles that helped make him a successful architect, planner, and educator, Kappe included the following two: "Always be willing to explore, experiment and invent. Do not accept the status quo;" and "Maintain good moral and social values."

In 1972, after three-and-a-half successful years as Professor and Founding Chairman of the Department of Architecture at California Polytechnic State University, Pomona, Kappe resigned. With a group of faculty members and students, he started the Southern California Institute of Architecture (SCI-Arc). The SCI-Arc model of education encourages learning through creative discourse and supports diversity of opinion within the framework of a common vision. Today the school is 34 years old, with 3,000 graduates working and teaching all over the world. It is considered one of the top architecture schools in the country.

Kappe has received many awards including the Richard Neutra International Medal for Design Excellence, the California Council/AIA Bernard Maybeck Award for Design, and the Topaz Medal, the highest award in architectural education. His own residence was designated a Cultural

Heritage Monument by the City of Los Angeles in 1996. Stephen Kanner, President of the A + D (Architecture + Design) Museum in Los Angeles wrote, "Ray's own home may be the greatest house in all of Southern California."

Ray continues to design from his strengths, even as his work incorporates new technology. "I'm no different in my mind than when I first started," he says. "I'm doing the kinds of things now I would have done 50 years ago. I feel like a 25-year-old."

Exhibit 14 **Example LivingHomes Configuration**

Source: LivingHomes. www.livinghomes.net/configure.html?model=rk1&step=0, accessed 30 Aug. 2007.

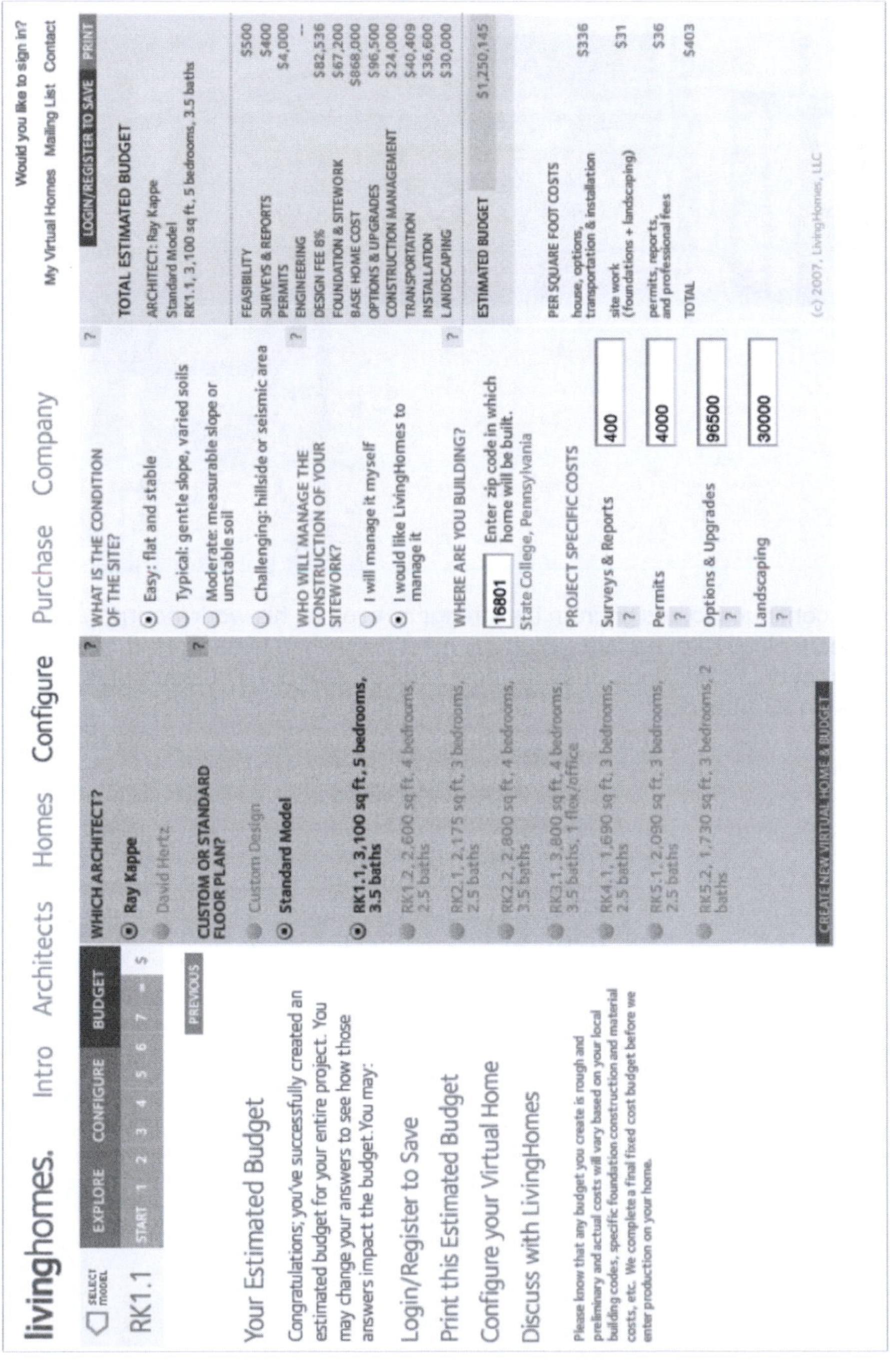

Exhibit 15 **LivingHomes' Team Profile**

Source: LivingHomes. 30 Aug. 2007. www.livinghomes.net/persons.html.

Amy Sims, Sous Chef

Architects I Like
Sverre Fehn, Renzo Piano , Rick Joy, Will Bruder, Bruno Mathsson

Buildings I Like
Norwegian Pavilion at the Venice Bienalle, Casa Malcontenta

Books That Inspire(d) Me
The Kite Runner, *Francesco Clemente Watercolors*, *Biomimicry*

Music I'm Listening To
The Be Good Tanyas, Shelby Lyn, Lilly Allen

Ways I Reduce My Ecological Footprint
Drive a Prius, capture and rescue my dishwater, recycle, renovated my 1922 house to include insulation, compost

Favorite Links
www.kcrw.org

Erich Volkert, Voice of Future LivingHomes Customers

Architects I Like
Eero Saarinen, Shigeru Ban, Charles Eames

Buildings I Like
Haga Sofia, the Glass House, old factories (open trusses/exposed brick), and bridges

Books That Inspire(d) Me
Cradle to Cradle, *The Tipping Point*, Crossing the Chasm, *The Age of Spiritual Machines*

Music I'm Listening To
80's, Massive Attack, Gotan Project, Chicane, and Radiohead

Ways I Reduce My Ecological Footprint
All my light bulbs are fluorescent, ride my bicycle to work, recycle, practice vermiculture

Favorite Links
www.gokgs.com, www.howstuffworks.com, www.popsci.com/popsci

Karen Bragg, Project Architect

Architects I Like
Murcutt, Piano, Sinan

Buildings I Like
La Tourette, Chapman Studios

Books That Inspire(d) Me
The Little Engine That Could

Music I'm Listening To
Tyson and Rita's music

Ways I Reduce My Ecological Footprint
Rapid 720

Favorite Links
earthquake.usgs.gov/eqcenter/recenteqsus, www.loslobos.org/site/player/index.
html?album=watch, www.howstuffworks.com

Exhibit 16 **Marmol Radziner**

Source: Marmol Radziner Prefab. www.marmolradzinerprefab.com, accessed 1 Oct. 2007.

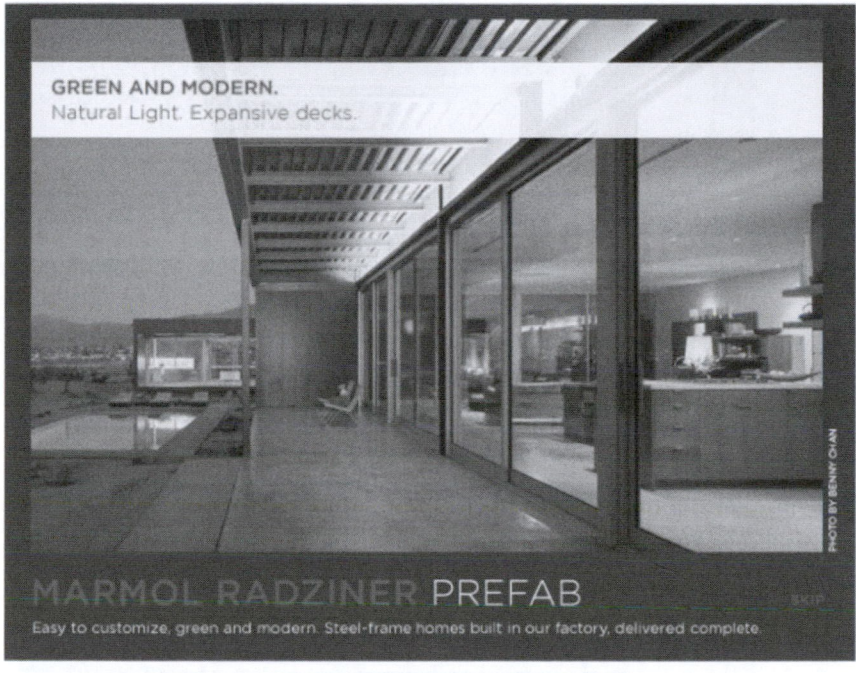

Exhibit 17 **Michelle Kaufmann Designs**

Source: Michelle Kauffman Designs. www.mkd-arc.com/homes/glidehouse, accessed 1 Oct. 2007.

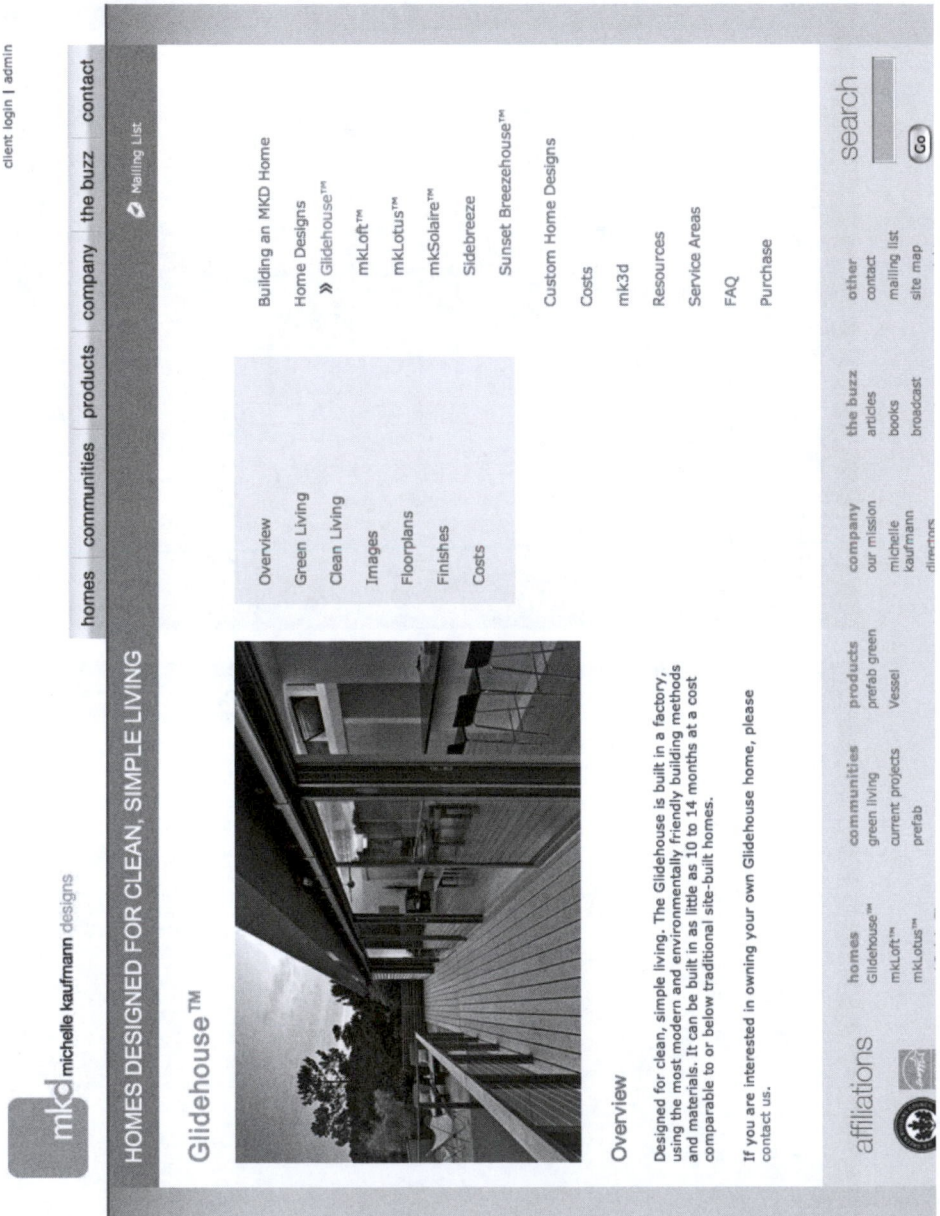

Part VI
Resources

Writing cases need not be an art. In fact, it is primarily a handicraft and there are a lot of helpful resources available—both on- and offline—that could help any writer to develop an excellent case. The following information builds on the first volume of the oikos case collection and is selected from a variety of sources. Most of the information in Chapter 6.3 was contributed by Prof. Kate Kearins, Auckland University of Technology. Thank you.

We thoroughly checked all links to online resources prior to publication. However, Internet links may change and if you face broken links we recommend you check the resources via keyword search in search engines such as Google. We welcome your comments on errors or additions: write to case@oikosinternational.org.

6.1
Guidelines for Case Writing

PennState University: Case Writing Guide

Opinions vary about what constitutes a good case. Jill L. Lane from PennState University's Schreyer Institute for Teaching Excellence offers a fine seven-page synopsis of guidelines for case writing. An excellent introduction.

www.schreyerinstitute.psu.edu/pdf/CaseWritingGuide.pdf

The Case Method Institute at Babson College

The Case Method Institute at Babson College offers a number of excellent online resources ranging from a three-page primer on "What is a Good Case and Teaching Note?" to "Merchandising Your Case: A Last Step in Publishing". The site also contains very informative links to other Internet resources.

www.casewriting.org

faculty.babson.edu/wylie/CWA_Resources

The European Case Clearing House (ECCH)

The European Case Clearing House (ECCH) is an independent, non-profit, membership-based organization dedicated to promoting the case method of learning. The ECCH case collection of management case studies and journal article reprints is the largest in the world. It is a unique and accessible resource for business school and university teachers worldwide. ECCH provides valuable online resources on how to write cases and how to use them in class.

www.ecch.com/about/completed-projects.cfm

6.2
International Case Writing Competitions

oikos Global Case Writing Competition (Switzerland)

The oikos Global Case Writing Competition aims to promote the development of new, high-quality case studies in the field of sustainability management and social entrepreneurship. Launched in 2003, it attracts submissions from leading management schools throughout the world. Apart from a substantial prize money (first prize: 5,000 swiss francs) the competition provides qualitative feedbacks for each case contributor within a double-blind case evaluation process.

www.oikos-international.org/academic/cwc/about.html

European Foundation for Management Development (EFMD) Annual Case Writing Competition (Belgium)

EFMD organizes an annual case competition with different categories, among them corporate social responsibility and inclusive markets. Case contributors may also submit cases in other mainstream categories such as entrepreneurship, family business, managing risk, and marketing. Each category winner is awarded with a prize money of €2,000. Cases are reviewed within a double-blind process. No feedback is given to case contributors. Winners are invited to the annual EFMD conference.

www.efmd.org/index.php/research-publications-a-awards/awards/case-writing-competition

European Case Clearing House (ECCH) Case Writing Competition (UK)

This competition focuses on two categories, "Renewable and Sustainable Energy, Technology and Development" and "New Case Writer: A First Teaching Case in Any Business Subject Area". For further details visit:

www.ecch.com/casecompetition

Dark Side Case Competition (Canada)

The Critical Management Studies (CMS) Interest Group and the Management Education Division (MED) of the Academy of Management are sponsors of the annual Dark Side Case Writing Competition. The competition is designed to encourage and acknowledge case writing that addresses the dark side of contemporary capitalism. According to the organizers, the award goes to the best case study—not to the worst offender.

group.aomonline.org/cms/Competition/Darkside/DarkSide%20Home.htm

CEEMAN: Central and East European Management Development Association (Slovenia)

CEEMAN is organizing an annual international case writing competition in partnership with Emerald Group Publishing Ltd. Besides funding the €1,500 CEEMAN/ Emerald prize for the author of the winning case, Emerald will publish the case in one of its journals and will also consider publishing other highly commended cases. As well as receiving a prize, the author of the winning case will be invited to the CEEMAN Annual Conference. The competition has no explicit relation to corporate sustainability issues.

www.ceeman.org

US Student Case Writing Competition (USA)

The US-based Society for Case Research is organizing in cooperation with Business Week an annual student Case Writing Competition. The competition is open to teams of up to five students attending a regionally accredited business or MBA program in the United States. Each team selected by its university will research and write a Case Incident (short case) based on a real-world business decision. The competition has no explicit relation to corporate sustainability issues. The annual call for cases is published via the Society for Case Research homepage:

www.sfcr.org

John Molson MBA International Case Competition (Canada)

This competition is not a case writing competition but in fact an international event dealing with case studies in real time. The John Molson MBA International Case Competition is an annual event organized by a team of MBA students from the John Molson School of Business (Canada). The competition is open to teams of four students from business schools worldwide, and is recognized as the largest competition of its kind. Its main purpose is to bridge the gap between corporate and academic worlds, which ultimately enriches both students and executives alike. The prize money for the winning team is CDN$10,000. This competition has no explicit relation to sustainability or corporate sustainability issues.

mbacasecomp.com

6.3
Case Collections and Journals

Case Collections

CasePlace.org (USA)

CasePlace.org is a free online resource for up-to-date case studies, syllabi, and innovative teaching materials on business and sustainability—from corporate governance to sustainable development. It is designed for business school faculty—to facilitate new curriculum development and new connections among faculty with aligned interests. However, the site is free and open to students, executive educators, and anyone interested in learning more about social and environmental issues in business and in connecting with others who share these interests. It is a non-commercial website, seeking to make as many materials as possible available for free. The site is run by the Aspen Institute.

www.caseplace.org

Duke University: Center for the Advancement of Social Entrepreneurship Teaching Cases

This site lists a number of teaching cases that explore the social entrepreneurship process, including issues related to economic strategies, social enterprise, scale, and entrepreneurial philanthropy. The site lists 30 teaching cases on social entrepreneurship which can be an important trigger for the development of a broader understanding of value creation processes.

www.caseatduke.org/knowledge/casestudies/index.html

ICFAI Center for Management Research (ICMR) (India)

The Institute of Chartered Financial Analysts of India (ICFAI)'s Center for Management Research (ICMR) holds Asia's largest online collection of management case studies. ICMR case studies are usually written from an industry or company perspective, rather than from the perspective of an individual decision-maker. In addition to training, these case studies are useful if you require information on industries, or on companies and their strategies. Though an increasing number of ICMR cases deal with corporate responsibility topics, the majority of cases do not have explicit links to corporate sustainability issues.

www.icmrindia.org

The European Case Clearing House (ECCH) (see Chapter 6.1)

ECCH is an independent, non-profit, membership-based organization dedicated to promoting the case method of learning. The ECCH case collection of management case studies and journal article reprints is the largest in the world. It is a unique and accessible resource for business school and university teachers worldwide. It has no explicit link to corporate sustainability topics but most oikos winning cases are also published within the ECCH case collection.

www.ecch.com

Other sources

A number of leading universities manage their own case collections, including IMD Lausanne (Switzerland), INSEAD Fontainebleau (France), Harvard Business School (USA), and Ivey School of Business (Canada).

Selected Research Journals on Case Studies[1]

Annual Advances in Business Cases

Published annually by the Society for Case Research (SCR). Cases must be presented at Society for Case Research annual workshop and successfully revised. Blind reviewed.

www.sfcr.org/aabc

---

1 We are grateful to Prof. Kate Kearins (Auckland University of Technology) who contributed this commented journal list to this volume.

Asian Case Research Journal

Published twice yearly, managed by the NUS Business School and published by World Scientific. Includes cases on Asian-based companies and non-Asian companies in Asian countries (the definition of Asian here includes Australia and New Zealand). Double-blind reviewed.

www.bschool.nus.edu/Research/journals/acrj/acrj.htm

The Business Case Journal

Published twice a year by the Society for Case Research (SCR) through McGraw-Hill Primis. Triple blind reviewed. Slightly broader in orientation than *The Case Research Journal*.

sfcr.org/bcj

The Case Research Journal

A leading North American case research journal, published quarterly by the North American Case Research Association (NACRA). According to the publishers: approximately eight cases per issue; double-blind peer-reviewed.

www.nacra.net/crj

The CASE Journal

Published online by The CASE Association 2–3 times a year. Cases also distributed by ECCH and Primis. Double-blind reviewed.

www.caseweb.org

International Journal of Case Method Research and Application

Founded in 2007, this new, refereed *International Journal of Case Method Research and Application (IJCRA)* is available online. The journal is being published by the World Association for Case Method Research and Application (WACRA). It follows a blind review process.

www.wacra.org/index.htm

International Journal of Case Studies in Management

Published quarterly online by the Centre de Cas, HEC Montreal, including cases in English, French and Spanish. Blind reviewed.

web.hec.ca/revuedecas/en/parutions/en_cours.cfm

The Journal of Applied Case Research

Published by the Southwestern Case Research Association. Double-blind reviewed.

www.swcrahome.org/JACR.html

The Journal of Critical Incidents

Initiated in 2008, published annually by the Society for Case Research (SCR). Critical incidents are seen as similar to cases, but shorter, usually less detailed and focused on more narrowly specific issues. Critical incidents must be presented at the Society for Case Research annual workshop and successfully revised. Blind reviewed.

www.sfcr.org/jci

The Management Case Study Journal (University of South Australia)

Founded in 2001, the journal is produced twice yearly online and contains cases that have application in graduate management education in the Asia Pacific context. It is published by the International Graduate School of Business at the University of South Australia (UNiSA) and it welcomes contributions that provide opportunity for critique and debate. Teaching notes are most welcome and encouraged to supply. The journal is double-blind reviewed.

www.ojs.unisa.edu.au/index.php/MCSJ

6.4

About the oikos Global Case Writing Competition

Concept and Award Committee

With the annual oikos Global Case Writing Competition oikos aims to promote the development of new, high-quality case studies in the field of sustainability management, and social entrepreneurship. Comprising two competition tracks (Corporate Sustainability Track, Social Entrepreneurship Track), the competition seeks to stimulate the production of cases that take on topics and situations of real-world organizations in the following areas:

- Corporate sustainability and strategy
- Social entrepreneurship
- Sustainability-driven business models
- Sustainability technologies and innovation
- Sustainability rhetorics and greenwashing
- Voluntary agreements and institutional change
- Organizational change and sustainability learning
- Corporate sustainability and corporate culture
- Sustainability as a business concept
- Sustainability networks and market development

The competition welcomes entries from all continents. The case studies should be suitable for use in management education and development, and should be related to managerial issues faced by organizations and individuals. Applicants may be teachers, research assistants or students of business administration (or related areas) at a registered university. Case entries may have more than one author, but each applicant may submit one case only. The case studies and associated material should concentrate on sustainability management or social entrepreneurship, be presented in English, be based on real cases, be focused on a recent situation or development, and be released by management of the subject organization/company for use by other business schools. oikos accepts electronic submitted cases only. Each case must be accompanied by a completed case submission form and a comprehensive teaching note.

Copyright ownership will remain with the author(s) and/or employer(s). Digests of the winning cases are published on the European Case Clearing House homepage (www.ecch.com). Inspection copies (without teaching note) will be published on the oikos international homepage (www.oikos-international.org/academic/case-collection/inspection-copies.html). Statutory authors retain full copyright to all originally created works.

All submissions are subject to a double-blind review process. The Award Committee pays particular attention to the concept and content: the integration of the different sustainability dimensions, the topic relevance, and its ability to create a learning experience.

Each case submission must be accompanied by a comprehensive teaching note of ten pages maximum. Apart from the innovativeness, the Award Committee pays particular attention to the style of writing, the quality of presentation and the clarity of data.

In each track (2010: Corporate Sustainability and Social Entrepreneurship) the top three cases are awarded with prize money. The annual first prize is 5,000 swiss francs (second CHF2,000, and third CHF1,000). The author of the winning case is invited to present the case at a leading conference. Details of the winning cases are also published on the oikos International homepage (www.oikos-international.org/projects/cwc) and the European Case Clearinghouse homepage (www.ecch.com). Each case contributor receives a written short feedback on the submitted case.

Since the inception of the competition in 2003, oikos has been working with leading international faculty members in the field of sustainability and strategy within the case competition project. In 2008–2010 the following faculty members comprised the Award Committee:

Corporate Sustainability track

- Prof. Oana Branzei, Ivey School of Business, Canada
- Prof. Frank M. Belz, Technical University of Munich, Germany

- Prof. Magali Delmas, University of California, USA
- Prof. Thomas Dyllick, University of St. Gallen, Switzerland
- Prof. Minna Halme, Helsinki School of Economics, Finland
- Prof. Andrew J. Hoffman, University of Michigan, USA
- Prof. P.D. Jose, Indian Institute of Management, Bangalore, India
- Prof. Steven J. Kobrin, The Wharton School, USA
- Prof. Bala Krishnamoorthy, NMIMS University, Mumbai, India
- Prof. Michael Lenox, Fuqua School of Business, Duke University, USA
- Prof. Renato Orsato, INSEAD, France
- Prof. Esben Rahbek Pedersen, Copenhagen Business School, Denmark
- Prof. Stefano Pogutz, Bocconi University, Milano, Italy
- Prof. Forest Reinhardt, Harvard Business School, USA
- Prof. Carlos Romero-Uscanga, EGADE Monterrey, Mexico
- Prof. Michael V. Russo, University of Oregon, USA
- Prof. Stefan Schaltegger, University of Lüneburg, Germany
- Prof. Christian Seelos, IESE Barcelona, Spain
- Prof. Claude P. Siegenthaler, Hosei University Tokyo, Japan
- Prof. Paul Shrivastava, Bucknell University, USA
- Prof. Friedrich M. Zimmermann, Karl Franzens University Graz, Austria

Social Entrepreneurship track

- Prof. Leo Bartlett, AISE Brisbane, Australia
- Prof. Gabriel Berger, University of San Andres, Argentina
- Prof. Marie Lisa M. Dacanay, AIM, The Philippines
- Prof. Gregory Dees, Duke University, USA
- Prof. Anil Gupta, IIM, India
- Prof. Roberto Gutiérrez, University de los Andes, Colombia
- Prof. Kai Hockerts, CBS Copenhagen, Denmark
- Prof. Kate Kearins, Auckland University of Technology, New Zealand

- Prof. Johanna Mair, IESE Barcelona, Spain

- Prof. Patricia Márquez, University of San Diego, California

- Prof. Sharon Oster, Yale University, USA

- Prof. Francesco Perrini, Bocconi University, Italy

- Prof. Jim Phills, Stanford University, USA

- Prof. Madhukar Shukla, XLRI Jamshedpur, India

- Prof. Chris Steyaert, University of St. Gallen, Switzerland

- Prof. Mark Swilling, University of Stellenbosch, South Africa

- Prof. Phil Auerswald, George Mason University, USA

- Prof. Julie Battilana, Harvard Business School, USA

- Prof. David Cooperrider, Case Western Reserve, USA

- Prof. Minna Halme, Helsinki School of Economics, Finland

- Prof. Cheryl Kernot, CSI, Australia

- Prof. Roger L. Martin, Rotman School of Business, Canada

- Prof. Alex Nicholls, University of Oxford, UK

Biographies of the Award Committee Members

Corporate Sustainability Track

Prof. Oana Branzei, Ivey School of Business, Canada

Prof. Oana Branzei is Assistant Professor of Strategy at the Ivey School of Business. Her current research initiatives explore the origins and processes of sustainable advantage, the formation of path-breaking strategies and capabilities, and the creation and diffusion of pro-poor, for-profit business models. She earned her PhD from the Sauder School of Business at the University of British Columbia, where she was an adjunct faculty and research fellow with the Forest Economics and Policy Analysis Research Unit, the Center for International Business Studies and the W. Maurice Young Entrepreneurship and Venture Capital Research Center. Prof. Branzei holds an HBA in foreign trade and international relations from "A. I. Cuza" University in Romania and got her MBA from the University of Nebraska. Prof. Branzei is a multiple research and teaching award winner, whose work has appeared in several leading academic journals.

Prof. Dr. Frank Martin Belz, TUM Business School, Munich, Germany

Prof. Frank-Martin Belz is full professor for Brewery and Food Industry Management at the TUM Business School, Technical University of Munich. His research focuses on sustainability innovations and sustainability marketing in consumer goods markets. He published a number of articles and books in these areas. Dr. Belz is also a member of the editorial board of the journal *Business Strategy and the Environment* and a reviewer for a number of other scientific journals. He has been acting as Managing Director of the oikos Foundation for four years (1999–2002) and was the president of the oikos Foundation for two years (2002–2004).

Prof. Magali Delmas, University of California at Santa Barbara, USA

Magali Delmas is Associate Professor at the Donald Bren School of Environmental Science and Management at the University of California Santa Barbara. Her research examines the interaction between business strategy and public policy. More specifically she analyzes how various forms of regulation impact organizational change and how firms can influence regulation. Previous to embarking on the academic career she worked at the European Commission at the Directorate for Industry. She received her MA in Political Science from the University of Paris, Sorbonne, and her PhD in Business Policy and Strategy from HEC Graduate School of Management, Paris.

Prof. Dr. Thomas Dyllick, Professor of Environmental Management, University of St. Gallen, Switzerland

Dr. Thomas Dyllick is Professor of Environmental Management at the University of St. Gallen, Managing Director of the Institute for Economy and the Environment and Vice President of the University. He serves on the Advisory Board of Gaia, Ecological Perspectives in Science, Humanities, and Economics and is a member of the Editorial Boards of *Greener Management International, Umweltmanagementforum* (*Environmental Management Forum; UWF*) and *Zeitschrift für Umweltpolitik und Umweltrecht* (*Journal of Environmental Law and Policy; ZfU*). His research interests are in the areas of sustainability and competitiveness, corporate sustainability strategies, and sustainability management systems.

Prof. Minna Halme, Helsinki School of Economics, Finland

Dr. Halme is Associate Professor at Helsinki School of Economics (HSE) and currently enjoys a five-year senior research fellowship of the Academy of Finland. Her current research focuses on business models for sustainable services and she is heading a project on material efficiency services to industry. She has worked with a number of European and national research projects on sustainable household services, sustainable organization cultures, actor networks and sustainable business strategies. She teaches masters', doctoral, and executive courses on corporate environmental management and social responsibility. She is also a visiting professor at the Seoul School of Integrated Sciences and Technologies, South Korea. Dr. Halme is a member of the editorial board of the journal *Business Strategy and the Environment* and reviews for a number of other scientific journals. She is member of the Administrative Board of WWF Finland 2005, of the Action Planning Committee of the Greening of Industry Network, and belongs to the Community of European Management Schools (CEMS) Faculty Group of Environmental Challenges for Business.

Prof. Andrew J. Hoffman, PhD, Holcim (US) Professor of Sustainable Enterprise, Co-Director of the Erb Institute, University of Michigan, USA

Andrew Hoffman is the Holcim Professor of Sustainable Enterprise at the University of Michigan (USA); he is also Professor at the Stephen M. Ross School of Business and the School of Natural Resources and Environment. In this role, Dr. Hoffman also acts as Associate Director of the Frederick A. and Barbara M. Erb Institute for Global Sustainable Enterprise. He has published five books and over 50 articles/book chapters on environmental and social issues as they relate to business. Recently he published the report *Getting Ahead of the Curve: Corporate Strategies that Address Climate Change* with the Pew Center on Global Climate Change (October 2006). He was awarded the 2003 Faculty Pioneer/Rising Star award from the World Resources Institute and the Aspen Institute. His book *From Heresy to Dogma* was awarded the 2001 Rachel Carson Prize from the Society for Social Studies of Science. He holds a PhD from the Massachusetts Institute of Technology, awarded jointly by the Sloan School of Management and the Department of Civil and Environmental Engineering. Prior to his career in academia, Prof. Hoffman worked for the US Environmental Protection Agency (Region 1), Metcalf & Eddy Environmental Consultants, T&T Construction & Design, and the Amoco Corporation. He serves on advisory boards of the Oakwood Healthcare System, University of Michigan Museum of Art, Earth Portal, Center for Environmental Innovation, and Canopy Partnership, as well as the editorial board of *Organization and Environment.*

P.D. Jose, Indian Institute of Management Bangalore, India

P.D. Jose is Professor in Corporate Strategy and Policy Area at the Indian Institute of Management Bangalore (IIMB). He is a Fellow of the Indian Institute of Management, Ahmedabad. He has a Postgraduate Diploma in Forestry Management from the Indian Institute of Forest Management, Bhopal and a Bachelor's in Science from the Institute of Science, Bombay University. Prior to joining IIMB, he was a member of the faculty at the Administrative Staff College of India, Hyderabad. He was also a Fulbright Fellow at the Massachusetts Institute of Technology, Boston and Kenan-Flagler Business School, North Carolina, during 1999–2000. In addition, he acted as consultant for several governmental agencies, state governments, and international organizations. Professor Jose has several publications in both international and national journals. He has presented papers and chaired special-interest sessions on environment and business in several international conferences as well as guest-edited a special issue of the journal *Business Strategy and the Environment*. He is a member of the International Planning Group of the Greening of Industries Network, which is a worldwide network of industries, international organizations, and universities.

Prof. Stephen J. Kobrin, Director, The Joseph H. Lauder Institute of Management and International Studies, Wharton School, University of Pennsylvania

Stephen J. Kobrin is the William H. Wurster Professor of Multinational Management at the Wharton School. He received his PhD in 1975 from the University of Michigan and holds an MBA from the University of Pennsylvania. His main research areas are focused on international political economy, globalization, global strategy, and the impact of the information revolution. He teaches Multinational Management and International Political Economy at the Management Department of the Wharton School at the University of Pennsylvania. He has published, for example, in the *Journal of International Affairs* and the *Oxford Handbook of International Business*. He is a member of the Consulting Editors Board of the *Journal of International Business Studies*. Stephen J. Kobrin is a Fellow of the Academy of International Business and the World Economic Forum.

Prof. Bala Krishnamoorthy, Professor and Head of Department, Business Policy and Environmental Management, NMIMS University, Mumbai

Dr. Krishnamoorthy holds a doctorate (PhD) in Management from JBIMS, University of Mumbai, and is a Postgraduate Diploma holder in Planning from the School of Planning, CEPT, Ahmedabad. She has 19 years' experience of training and research activities. She was a Fellow at USETI, Washington, DC, on Environmental Management and published a volume on *Environmental Management*. Recently she has received an International Felicitation in the area of Environmental Education and the WEE–IIEE–IAEWP Environmental Award. Her areas of interest areas include corporate environmental management, ethics, environmental management systems, ISO 14001, interpersonal relations, communication, leadership and managerial effectiveness, training for NGOs, and training for cooperative banks.

Prof. Michael Lenox, Fuqua School of Business, Duke University, USA

Michael Lenox is Associate Professor of Business at the Fuqua School of Business and has a secondary appointment as Associate Professor of Environmental Policy at the Nicholas School of Environment. Professor Lenox is the coordinator for the Strategy Area and he teaches the core MBA strategy course. Prof. Lenox's research focuses on technology, strategy and policy. He is in particular interested in the role of innovation for economic growth and firm competitive success. He is also interested in the interface between business strategy and public policy and in particular in institutional, or non-market, strategies of firms and prospects for industry self-regulation (especially with regard to environmental impacts). He has published in academic journals such as the *Strategic Management Journal, Academy of Management Journal, Management Science, Journal of Industrial Ecology,* and *Organization Science.*

Prof. Renato Orsato, INSEAD, France

Renato J. Orsato is a Senior Research Fellow at the INSEAD Social Innovation Centre, Fontainebleau (France). As a researcher, educator and consultant, in the past 15 years he has worked at academic institutions, such as Lund University (Sweden), University of Amsterdam (Holland) and University of Technology, Sydney (Australia), as well as with public organizations and private businesses in more than 20 countries. He holds a PhD in Management, a master's in Organization Studies and BA in Civil Engineering and Business Administration. He has written several book chapters and teaching cases, and published in academic journals such as *California Management Review, Organization Studies,* and *Journal of Industrial Ecology.*

Dr. Esben Rahbek Pedersen, CBS Copenhagen, Denmark

Esben Rahbek Pedersen (PhD) is a Research Fellow at the CBS Center for Corporate Social Responsibility. His research focuses primarily on corporate social responsibility; corporate citizenship; non-financial performance measurement; environmental, diversity and supply chain management; and lean management. More specifically, Dr. Pedersen is interested in how internal (organisational capabilities) and external factors (perceived environmental uncertainty) shape the adoption and use of non-financial performance measurement systems. He is published in a number of international journals, including the *Journal of Business Ethics,* the *Journal of Public Affairs,* and the *Journal of Corporate Citizenship.*

Prof. Stefano Pogutz, Bocconi University, Milano, Italy

Dr. Stefano Pogutz is Assistant Professor of Management and Coordinator of the Specialized Master Program on Economics and Environmental Management at Bocconi University, Milan, Italy. He is a Senior Researcher at SPACE, the Research Center on Risk, Occupational Health and Safety, Environmental and Crisis Management, Bocconi University. His current research interests include sustainable development, environmental management, innovation management and cleaner technologies, and corporate social responsibility. Prof. Pogutz participated in a number of research projects at national and international level collaborating, among others, with the Italian Ministry of University and Research, the Italian Ministry of Labor and Social Policies, and the EABIS (European Academy of Business in Society). Since 1996 he has been a member of the Faculty Group on Environmental Challenges for Business Management in Europe, Community of European

Management Schools, and a frequent lecturer within the CEMS Master in International Management (CEMS-MIM). In 2006 his latest book, *Developing Corporate Social Responsibility: A European Perspective* (with Francesco Perrini and Antonio Tencati), was published by Edward Elgar Publishing, Cheltenham, UK.

Prof. Dr. Forest Reinhardt, Harvard Business School, Boston, USA

Forest L. Reinhardt is the John D. Black Professor of Business Administration at Harvard Business School (HBS). He heads HBS's Business, Government, and the International Economy Unit. Reinhardt currently serves as the faculty chair of Harvard Business School's European Research Initiative. He is interested in the relationships between market and non-market strategy, the relations between government regulation and corporate strategy, the behaviour of private and public organizations that manage natural resources, and the economics of externalities and public goods. He is the author of *Down to Earth: Applying Business Principles to Environmental Management*, published in 2000 by Harvard Business School Press. Like that book, most of his articles and papers analyze problems of environmental and natural resource management. He has written numerous cases on these and related topics, used at Harvard and many other schools in MBA curricula and in executive programs. Reinhardt received his PhD in Business Economics from Harvard University in 1990. He also holds an MBA from Harvard Business School, where he was a Baker Scholar, and an A.B., cum laude, from Harvard College.

Prof. Carlos Romero-Uscanga, EGADE Monterrey, Mexico

Carlos Romero-Uscanga received his PhD degree in Management from ITESM Monterrey and a master's degree from ITAM Mexico City. He is Associate Professor for Strategy and Environmental Management at EGADE Monterrey where he is also the Dean of Graduate Programs. He has been a Visiting Professor in EMI (Bolivia), the University of San Diego, the University of Texas at Austin, and the University of North Carolina. His research interests include environmental strategy, decision-making processes, globalization, social enterprise, and environmental management. Carlos Romero-Uscanga is a Member of the Board of CEMS (Community of European Business Schools). In addition to his membership of the Award Committee of the oikos Case Writing Competition, he is also a case reviewer for the Social Enterprise Knowledge Network at Harvard Business School.

Prof. Michael V. Russo, University of Oregon, USA

Michael V. Russo is the Charles H. Lundquist Professor of Sustainable Management at the Lundquist College of Business at the University of Oregon. He also serves as Founding Director of the Sustainable Supply Chain Management Center at the Lundquist College. He came to Oregon after receiving his PhD from the University of California at Berkeley in 1989. He also serves on the editorial boards of the *Academy of Management Journal*, the *Strategic Management Journal*, and *Organization &*

Environment. Dr. Russo's academic research focuses on the interaction of national and international environmental, social, and political policies, and strategic management. His articles have appeared in leading academic journals, and his research on the bottom-line effects of corporate greening received the 1998 Moskowitz Prize in Social Investing. He has received funding from the National Science Foundation to study international voluntary environmental regulation under the ISO 14000 standards and from the Dreyfus Foundation to write business cases that incorporate green chemistry issues. One case written under the Dreyfus Foundation grant (*Seventh Generation: Balancing Customer Expectations with Supply Chain Realities*), won the 2007 oikos Case Writing Competition.

Prof. Stefan Schaltegger, University of Lüneburg, Germany

Dr. Stefan Schaltegger is full professor for Management and Business Economics, head of the Centre for Sustainability Management and the MBA Sustainability Management, and Vice-President of Research of the University of Lüneburg. He is or was a lecturer at various universities including the universities of Basel (WWZ, MSN), Bern (IKAÖ) (Switzerland), Distance-University of Hagen (Germany), Ho Chi Min City (Vietnam), Jyväskylä (Finland), the ETH Zürich (Switzerland), as well as the Norwegian School of Management (Oslo) and has taught different subjects including corporate sustainability management and corporate environmental management. Stefan Schaltegger is a member of the editorial board of international scientific journals including *Business Strategy and the Environment, Eco-Management and Auditing* and *Corporate Social Responsibility and Environmental Management*. Dr. Schaltegger is chairman of the Steering Committee of the European Environmental Management Accounting Network (EMAN), chairman of the board of Sarasin Sustainability Investments, member of the board of the R.I.O. Impuls Management Forum, member of the SustainAbility Faculty, London, member of the Lateral Think Tank (LTT) of the Swiss Academy of Technical Sciences (SATW), research fellow at the Norwegian School of Management (Oslo) and research fellow at the Center for Research in Economics, Management and the Arts (CREMA).

Prof. Christian Seelos, IESE Barcelona, Spain

Christian Seelos is Director of the IESE Platform for Strategy and Sustainability (IPSS) and a senior lecturer and senior researcher in the Strategic Management Department at IESE. He teaches MBA and executive courses in International Business, Global Strategic Management, Social Entrepreneurship and Strategy and Sustainability at various business schools in Europe, Africa and the United States. Prof. Seelos' research topics include poverty and inequality, new approaches at the "bottom of the pyramid", climate change, water stress, and emerging governance aspects. His research also focuses on innovative business models and social entrepreneurs that create new markets and foster economic and social development in the poorest countries. His insights on novel corporate strategies in emerging markets were recognized by the Strategic Management Society (best paper award for practice implications, 2007) and also won him the Gold Prize of the highly contested IFC-FT essay competition on private sector development in 2008. Also in 2008, he received the IESE Alumni Association Research Excellence Award in the category "best new course" for the MBA elective Entrepreneurial Strategies for Social Impact that he designed and teaches jointly with IESE Prof. Johanna Mair. Prof. Seelos also has a broad and varied professional experience. His previous positions include Director at FSG Social Impact Advisors in Geneva, a firm co-founded by Prof. Michael Porter; Contract Director at British Telecom Global Services; BT Ignite Head of Corporate Social Responsibility. Currently, he consults with a number of companies on topics of competitive strategy, innovation and sustainability issues.

Prof. Dr. Claude Patrick Siegenthaler, Hosei University, Tokyo

Since 2004 Claude Patrick Siegenthaler has held a tenure position as associate professor for environmental accounting at Hosei University Tokyo. He graduated as environmental economist from St. Gallen University in 1993 and completed his PhD in 2005. He has been a visiting researcher with AIST in Tsukuba, RISTEX and ICU in Tokyo, INSEAD in Fontainebleau, and with ETH Zurich. His current research concentrates on Business Education for Sustainable Development. In addition to his academic work, he has founded and served on the board of several for-profit and non-profit organizations in the sustainability field. Claude Siegenthaler received, inter alia, the Switzerland Technology Award 2000, the Environmental Award from the Vontobel Foundation, and the TOYP Award from the JC Global Network Osaka.

Prof. Dr. Paul Shrivastava, Bucknell University, USA

Prof. Dr. Paul Shrivastava's background combines academic work with significant entrepreneurial and senior management experience. Currently he is the Howard I. Scott Chair and Professor of Management at Bucknell University. Dr. Shrivastava has over 25 years of experience in management education, entrepreneurship and consulting to major multinational corporations. He has launched several entrepreneurial ventures. In 1976 he was part of the management team that launched Hindustan Computer Ltd., which today is one of India's largest computer companies. In 1985 he founded the non-profit Industrial Crisis Institute, Inc. in New York and published the *Industrial Crisis Quarterly*. He founded *Organization and Environment*, a journal published by Sage Publications. In 1998 he founded eSocrates, Inc. (and acted as its President and CEO until 2004), a knowledge management and online training/education software company based in Allentown, PA. Dr. Shrivastava received his PhD. from the University of Pittsburgh. He has published 15 books and over 100 articles in professional and scholarly journals. He has served on the editorial boards of leading management education journals including the *Academy of Management Review*, the *Strategic Management Journal, Organization, Risk Management*, and *Business Strategy and the Environment*.

Prof. Friedrich M. Zimmermann, Karl Franzens University Graz, Austria

In the 1970s and early 1980s, after his studies at the Universities of Graz and Munich, Dr. Zimmermann focused on research in the field of tourism development planning and prediction. Further to becoming a university lecturer in 1987, he was invited as a guest lecturer to the USA where he concentrated on integrative and sustainable regional research and development. After temporarily holding a chair at the University of Munich, he became a full university professor for geography and the head of the Institute for Geography and Regional Research at the University of Graz in 1997. Apart from his responsibilities as vice rector (since 2000), he is also a member of the Scientific Advisory Committee of Joanneum Research. In addition, he is the alternate president of the board of directors of the Technikum Joanneum GmbH (Styrian University Colleges) and the Austrian–Canadian Liaison Group.

Social Entrepreneurship Track

Prof. Leo Bartlett, AISE Brisbane, Australia

Leo Bartlett is currently the Executive Director of AISE, and Director of the Board of Social-e . He was the Foundation Professor, Foundation Dean, and Assistant Vice-Chancellor of Central Queensland University before returning to Brisbane as an Emeritus Professor in 2002 and undertaking the role of Planning Director of AISE. His principal interests have been in teaching and learning, research and evaluation, and community cultural and business development. Leo was appointed the Foundation Chair of the Board by Directors and the Queensland State Government in 1998, and was its Executive Chairman in 2000. He has also achieved the awards of a Certificate in Entrepreneurship (Archaeus Institute, based on an Australian Industry Development Corporation Scholarship for Entrepreneurship Training and New Business Development), the NxLeveL Instructor Certificate (US) in business development, and the certificate as Instructor of the National Foundation for Teaching Entrepreneurship (NFTE-US).

Prof. Gabriel Berger, University of San Andres, Argentina

Gabriel Berger is Professor in the Department of Administration at the Universidad de San Andrés where he teaches the Management of Social Purpose Organizations and Corporate Social Responsibility, and directs the Graduate Program in Non-profit Organizations. He has received his PhD in Social Policy from the Heller School for Social Policy and Management, Brandeis University, Boston, 1991. His main areas of interest are the management of non-profit organizations, corporate social responsibility, and social investments.

Prof. Marie Lisa M. Dacanay, AIM, The Philippines

Marie Lisa M. Dacanay is the President of the Institute for Social Entrepreneurship in Asia (ISEA), a consortium initiative set up in June 2008 by major social enterprise resource institutions, networks and academic institutions based in Singapore, India, Thailand, Indonesia, Vietnam, Japan and the Philippines. She is also an adjunct professor and leading researcher at the AIM. Prof. Dacanay holds a Master in Development Management from the Asian Institute of Management (1996). She received a Bachelor of Science in Statistics from the University of the Philippines (1983). Her recent published works include *Citizenship and Sustainable Development in the Philippines* (1999), *What Makes a Practice Exemplary?* (1999), and *Strategic Planning for Sustainable Area Development Intervention* (1999).

Prof. Gregory Dees, Duke University, USA

J. Gregory Dees is Professor of the Practice of Social Entrepreneurship and co-founder of the Center for the Advancement of Social Entrepreneurship at Duke University's Fuqua School of Business. He has published extensively on social entrepreneurship, including two books with Jed Emerson and Peter Economy, *Enterprising Nonprofits and Strategic Tools for Social Entrepreneurs.* In 2007, the Aspen Institute and Ashoka recognized his pioneering work with their first Lifetime Achievement award in Social Entrepreneurship Education. Professor Dees previously worked at McKinsey & Company, and taught at the Yale School of Management, at Harvard Business School, where he helped launch the Initiative on Social Enterprise and received the Apgar Award for Innovation in Teaching, and at Stanford's Graduate School of Business, where he served as the Haas Centennial Professor and as founding Co-Director of the Center for Social Innovation. While at Harvard, he interrupted his academic career with a leave of absence to work on entrepreneurial development in Appalachia. He serves on the board of the Bridgespan Group and on the World Economic Forum's Global Agenda Council for Social Entrepreneurship. He is on numerous advisory boards including Volans, REDF, Aflatoun, Business Leadership for Tomorrow, the Limmat Foundation, and the *Social Enterprise Journal.*

Prof. Anil Gupta, IIM, India

Dr. Gupta earned his PhD degree in Management from Kurukshetra University (India) in 1986 after his master's in Biochemical Genetics in 1974 from Haryana Agricultural University, Haryana. He is currently a professor in the Centre for Management in Agriculture. His unique work analysing indigenous knowledge of farmers and pastoralists resulted in his election to India's National Academy of Agricultural Sciences and recognition through Pew Conservation Scholar Award from University of Michigan. His professional experience includes the establishment of the National Micro Venture Innovation Fund, National Innovation Foundation, India (NIF) and Grassroots Innovation Augmentation Network (GIAN). Dr. Gupta also acted as President of the Society for Research and Initiatives for Sustainable

Technologies and Institutions (SRISTI), Chairperson of Ravi J Matthai Centre for Educational Innovation (Indian Institute of Management), Chairperson of Research and Publications (Indian Institute of Management) and Professor of the Centre for Management in Agriculture (Indian Institute of management).

Prof. Roberto Gutiérrez, University de los Andes, Colombia

Roberto Gutiérrez is Associate Professor at the School of Management at the Universidad de los Andes in Colombia. He is the coordinator of the Social Enterprise Knowledge Network (SEKN). Gutiérrez's research concentrates on social enterprise and education. He has received his PhD and MA in Sociology from the Johns Hopkins University. He has numerous publications in international journals such as *Harvard Business Review, Stanford Social Innovation Review, Journal of Management Education*, and *Social Responsibility Journal*.

Prof. Kai Hockerts, Copenhagen Business School, Denmark

Dr. Hockerts is Associate Professor at Copenhagen Business School where he is affiliated with the Center for Corporate Values and Responsibility. He holds a PhD in Management from the University St. Gallen (Switzerland) and a Diploma in Business Administration from the University of Bayreuth (Germany). Before joining Copenhagen Business School, Kai was Adjunct Professor and Senior Research Program Manager at INSEAD, Fontainebleau (France). Kai's business experience includes two years as a management consultant for Life Cycle Assessments and Eco-Design at Ecobilan S.A., Paris. He also worked at the New Economics Foundation, London, Dow Chemical Europe, Zürich-Horgen, and the Hamburger Umweltinstitut. As part of his research work Kai has presented papers at numerous conferences and academic workshops including the Academy of Management Conference and the Greening of Industry Network Conference. He is a co-organizer of the International Social Entrepreneurship Research Conference (ISERC) series, which in 2007 he brought to CBS.

Prof. Kate Kearins, Auckland University of Technology, New Zealand

Prof. Kearins is Professor of Management at the Auckland University of Technology (New Zealand). Her main areas of interest include corporate political strategy and social responsibility; stakeholder engagement and accountability; and environmental management and sustainability. Prof. Kearins completed her PhD in 1997 focusing on power relations in local government. Since, she has reoriented much of her research towards business engagement with sustainability. Prof. Kearins has co-authored a series of papers on business education for sustainability and authored over 100 academic papers, many of which have appeared in refereed journals. She has been joint-recipient of several international awards for case research. Prof. Kearins was Chair of the Academy of Management's US-based Organizations and the Natural Environment Division in 2006–2007. She serves on the editorial boards of *Business and Society, Business Strategy and the Environment, Journal of Business Ethics, Journal of Management Education, Management Communication Quarterly*, and *Qualitative Research in Accounting and Management*.

Prof. Johanna Mair, IESE Barcelona, Spain

Johanna Mair is Associate Professor in the Strategic Management department at IESE Barcelona. Prof. Mair's current research lies at the intersection of traditional strategy and entrepreneurship. More specifically she is interested in how institutions stifle and enable social and economic progress and the role of entrepreneurial actors in this process. Prof. Mair has received numerous awards for her outstanding research and publications. In 2007 she was recognized as a "Faculty Pioneer" by the Aspen Institute and received the "Ashoka Award for Social Entrepreneurship Education". Her research was awarded with the 2008 Gold Prize of the IFC–Financial Times Essay Competition and the 2007 Strategic Management Society "Best Paper for Practice Implications Award". She is co-author of two books on Social Entrepreneurship and author or co-author of numerous book chapters, peer-reviewed journal articles and articles for management practice. She serves on the editorial board of the *Strategic Entrepreneurship Journal* and reviews papers for numerous renowned journals and bodies, including the Academy of Management, the Strategic Management Society, the *Journal of Management*, and the *Journal for Business Venturing*. She has also published numerous case studies and teaching notes. Before earning her PhD in management with a specialization in strategy from INSEAD (France), Prof. Mair was directly involved in many aspects of the executive decision-making process in international banking. Today, alongside her academic responsibilities, she still carries out consultancy work for several multinational companies and international institutions such as the World Bank and serves on the advisory board of globally operating entrepreneurial companies, foundations and social venture funds.

Prof. Patricia Márquez, University of San Diego (California)

Patricia Márquez is Associate Professor of Management at the University of San Diego (USD) (California). Before coming to USD, Patricia Márquez was a professor at IESA Business School in Caracas, Venezuela. She was the Cisneros Scholar at the David Rockefeller Center for Latin American Studies (DRCLAS) at Harvard University and visiting professor at Harvard Business School for the academic year 2005–2006. She has taught graduate and executive education courses on leadership and organizational behavior, business initiatives at the base of the pyramid, corporate social responsibility, and social enterprise. Prof. Márquez earned her PhD and MA in Socio-Cultural Anthropology from the University of California, Berkeley. Prof. Márquez's current research is on the role business can play in alleviating poverty worldwide. She is an active participant of the Social Enterprise Knowledge Network (SEKN) coordinating SEKN's research project "Market-Based Poverty Reduction in

Iberoamerica" (2005–2009). She has published in international journals, such as *Business & Society, Harvard Business Review Latin America* and *Harvard Business School Publishing.*

Prof. Sharon Oster, Yale University, USA

Sharon M. Oster is Dean and Frederic D. Wolfe Professor of Management and Entrepreneurship at the Yale School of Management. Dean Oster joined the faculty at the Yale School of Management as Associate Professor of Economics and Management in 1982. She was the first recipient of the Yale School of Management Award for Excellence in Teaching, in 1988, and received this recognition a second time in 2008. Dean Oster has also served as Director of the school's Program on Social Enterprise, which supports work on non-profit and public organizations, as well as initiatives in the area of corporate social responsibility. From 2002 to 2005, Oster was co-director of the Yale School of Management–Goldman Sachs Foundation Partnership on Non-profit Organizations, in cooperation with the Pew Charitable Trusts. Dean Oster has consulted widely to private, public, and non-profit organizations, and currently serves on the boards of a number of for-profit and non-profit organizations, including Health Care REIT, Yale University Press, and Amistad Academy. She is a 1970 graduate of Hofstra College, from which she also received an honorary doctorate in 2001. She received her PhD in economics from Harvard University in 1974.

Prof. Francesco Perrini, Bocconi University, Italy

Francesco Perrini is Professor of Management and Corporate Social Responsibility at the Giorgio Pivato Management Department of Bocconi University, Milan, Italy. He is also Senior Professor of Corporate Finance at the SDA Bocconi School of Management. Since 1990 he has been a researcher at Bocconi, focusing on strategic and innovation management; management of corporate development processes (strategy implementation, acquisitions management; financial strategies and valuation; SMEs), and social issues in management (corporate governance, sustainability, corporate social responsibility [CSR], socially responsible investments [SRI], sustainable innovation and social entrepreneurship). Prof. Perrini is Director of CSR group at SDA Bocconi and the member of the Advisory Board of the SPACE Bocconi Research Centre for Studies on Security and Protection against Crime and Emergencies; member of the Board of Directors and Scientific Director of the Italian Centre for Social Responsibility (I-CSR), Milan; member of the Management Board of Finetica, a Research Centre on SRI, partnership between Bocconi and Pontificia Unversitas Lateranensis, Vatican, Rome; External Collaborator of the Multinational Enterprises Program at International Labor Organization (ILO), Geneva. He holds Postgraduate Degrees in Protection Management and Financial Management, Laurea Degree in Business Administration from Bocconi,

PIM from ESADE and ITP from NYU. He is on the Academic Board of EABIS and on the Membership Committee of SIM Division at the Academy of Management.

Prof. Jim Phills, Stanford University, USA

Jim Phills is the Claude N. Rosenberg Jr. Director of Stanford's Center for Social Innovation (CSI) and Professor of Organizational Behavior at the Stanford Business School. He directs a number of CSI's executive programs and teaches MBA electives on non-profit strategy and social entrepreneurship. His research focuses on strategic change, organizational learning, and social innovation. He is also Academic Editor of the *Stanford Social Innovation Review* and Faculty Director of the Executive Program for Non-profit Leaders, the Executive Program for Philanthropy Leaders, and Strategy for Non-profit Organizations. Prof. Phills is the author of a number of publications on learning and change in the private, public, and non-profit sectors. Prior to moving to Stanford, he was on the faculty at the Yale School of Management where he received the Alumni Association Award for Excellence in teaching in 1995. In addition to his research and teaching, Prof. Phills has consulted to a wide array of organizations for over 20 years. Prof. Phills is a magna cum laude graduate of Harvard College, holds a master's degree in Psychology and Social Relations from Harvard University, and received his PhD in Organizational Behavior from Harvard Business School and the departments of Psychology and Sociology.

Prof. Madhukar Shukla, XLRI Jamshedpur, India

Dr. Madhukar Shukla has been Professor at XLRI in the Organizational Behavior and Strategic Management areas since 1990. Prior to joining XLRI, he taught at Administrative Staff College of India, Hyderabad, and worked as Consultant with the National Productivity Council, India. During 1993–1994, he was Visiting Professor at ESADE, Barcelona (Spain). Dr. Madhukar Shukla earned his PhD in Psychology from IIT Kanpur (India) and MA in Psychology from the University of Lucknow (India). He is a member of the Advisory Board of the University Network for Social Entrepreneurship.

Prof. Chris Steyaert, St. Gallen, Switzerland

Chris Steyaert studied organization psychology at the Katholieke Universiteit Leuven, where he obtained his doctor's Degree in Psychology. After teaching courses in group dynamics and organizational behaviour at the Katholieke Universiteit Leuven, and teaching organization theory at the EHSAL (Economische Hogeschool) in Brussels, Chris Steyaert became in 1996 Visiting Associate Professor at the Copenhagen Business School, where he became tenured in 1998. In 1999, he joined ESBRI (Entrepreneurship and Small Business Research Institute) to study creativity and entrepreneurship in a societal perspective. Chris Steyaert has published in international journals and books in such areas as entrepreneurship and organizational innovation, human resource management, and language and translation.

Furthermore, he has been developing learning programs for SMEs and entrepreneurship, and has been working as process consultant in creativity projects for several companies.

Prof. Mark Swilling, University of Stellenbosch, South Africa

Prof. Mark Swilling is Division Head: Sustainable Development in the School of Public Management and Planning at the University of Stellenbosch, Academic Director of the Sustainability Institute, and a Senior Research Fellow at the Warwick Institute of Governance and Public Management, Warwick University (UK). He was co-founder, former Director and Professor of the Graduate School of Public and Development Management (P&DM), University of the Witwatersrand, 1993–1997. Prior to joining P&DM, Prof. Swilling worked for PLANACT, an urban development NGO which he helped establish in 1985. After a period as Senior Researcher at the Centre for Policy Studies in Johannesburg (1986–1990) where he focused on state security policy, he worked on a full-time basis for PLANACT, 1990–1993. Prof. Swilling is on the editorial boards of leading academic journals. He has published several edited and co-authored books, over 60 academic articles and contributed extensively to public debate in the popular press on issues related to development, democratization, governance and social movements. His most recent publication is *The Scope and Size of the Non-Profit Sector in South Africa* which brings together four years of research that was conducted in collaboration with the Comparative Nonprofit Sector Project at Johns Hopkins University (Baltimore, USA). He also helped initiate the Africa Human Genome Initiative. Professor Swilling holds his PhD from the University of Warwick and has a BA and a BA (Honors) obtained through the Department of Political Studies at the University of the Witwatersrand where he was also a lecturer from 1982–1987. He has received various merit awards, including election into the international Ashoka Fellowship.

Prof. Philip Auerswald, George Mason University, USA

Philip Auerswald is Assistant Professor at the School of Public Policy. Professor Auerswald's work focuses on linked processes of technological and organizational change in the contexts of policy, economics, and strategy. He is the co-editor of *Innovations: Technology | Governance | Globalization*, a quarterly journal from MIT Press about people using technology to address global challenges. He is the author and co-author of numerous books, reports, and research papers, including *Seeds of Disaster, Roots of Response: How Private Action Can Reduce Public Vulnerability* (Cambridge University Press, 2006) and *Taking Technical Risk: How Innovators, Executives, and Investors Manage High-Tech Risks* (MIT Press: 2001). Prior to joining the faculty at George Mason University, Professor Auerswald was a lecturer and Assistant Director of the Science, Technology, and Public Policy Program at the Kennedy School of Government, Harvard University. He has been a consultant to the National Academies of Science, the Commonwealth of Massachusetts, and the

National Institute of Standards and Technology. He holds a PhD in Economics from the University of Washington and a BA (political science) from Yale University.

Prof. Julie Battilana, Harvard Business School, USA

Julie Battilana is the Hellman Faculty Fellow and Assistant Professor of Business Administration in the Organizational Behavior unit at Harvard Business School. Professor Battilana earned a BA in sociology and economics, an MA in political sociology and an MSc in organizational sociology and public policy from École Normale Supérieure de Cachan, an MSc in management and economics from HEC Business School, and a joint PhD in organizational behavior from INSEAD and in management and economics from École Normale Supérieure de Cachan. Professor Battilana's research examines the process of institutional entrepreneurship. Her research received an honourable mention for best paper out of a dissertation from the OMT division of the Academy of Management in 2007. She has published or has articles forthcoming in *Strategic Organization, Organization, Research in Organizational Behavior* and *The Academy of Management Annals*, as well as in handbooks of organizational behaviour and strategy.

Prof. David Cooperrider, Case Western Reserve, USA

David L. Cooperrider is the Fairmount Minerals Professor of Social Entrepreneurship at the Weatherhead School of Management, Case Western Reserve University. Professor Cooperrider is past Chair of the National Academy of Management's OD Division and has lectured and taught at Harvard, Stanford, University of Chicago, Katholieke University in Belgium, MIT, University of Michigan, Cambridge and others. David is founder and Chair of the Center for Business as an Agent of World Benefit. David has served as advisor to a wide variety of organizations including the Boeing Corporation, Fairmount Minerals, Green Mountain Coffee Roasters, McKinsey, Parker, Sherwin Williams, Wal-Mart as well as American Red Cross, American Hospital Association, Cleveland Clinic, and World Vision. David has published 14 books and authored over 50 articles. He has published in journals such as *Administrative Science Quarterly, Organization and Environment, Human Relations, Journal of Applied Behavioral Science, Management Inquiry, The OD Practitioner*, and in research series such as *Advances in Strategic Management*.

Prof. Minna Halme, Helsinki School of Economics, Finland

Dr. Halme is Associate Professor at Helsinki School of Economics (HSE) and currently enjoys a five-year senior research fellowship of the Academy of Finland. Her current research focuses on business models for sustainable services and she is heading a project on material efficiency services to industry. She has worked with a number of European and national research projects on sustainable household services, sustainable organization cultures, actor networks, and sustainable business strategies. She teaches masters', doctoral, and executive courses on corporate environmental management and social responsibility. She is also a visiting professor at the Seoul School of Integrated Sciences and Technologies, South Korea. Dr. Halme is a member of the editorial board of the journal *Business Strategy and the Environment* and reviews for a number of other scientific journals. She is member of the Administrative Board of WWF Finland 2005, of the Action Planning Committee of the Greening of Industry Network, and belongs to the Community of European Management Schools (CEMS) Faculty Group of Environmental Challenges for Business.

Prof. Cheryl Kernot, CSI, Australia

Prof. Kernot is Associate Professor and Director of Social Enterprise at the Centre for Social Impact at the University of New South Wales (UNSW), Sydney. After a distinguished political career Cheryl Kernot has spent the last five years working in the UK as a Program Director at the Skoll Centre for Social Entrepreneurship at the Said Business School at Oxford University and as the Director of Learning at the School for Social Entrepreneurs in London. Her specialist role at the Skoll Centre was to assist and mentor start-up social businesses particularly in the delivery of innovative health services. Prof. Kernot has recently been elected Chair of the Fair Trade Association Australia & New Zealand. Since December 2007, she has been an honorary board member of Foresters Community Finance which is pioneering social investment in social enterprises, and is also on the founding committee of a UK charity which works to provide shelter and education for street children in Kampala, Uganda.

Prof. Roger L. Martin, Rotman School of Business, Canada

Roger Martin has served as Dean of the Rotman School of Management since September 1, 1998. He holds the Premier's Chair in Competitiveness and Productivity and is Director of the AIC Institute for Corporate Citizenship. Previously he spent 13 years as Director of Monitor Company, a global strategy consulting firm based in Cambridge, Massachusetts, where he served as co-head of the firm for two years. Prof. Martin received his BA from Harvard College, with a concentration in Economics, in 1979, and his MBA from the Harvard Business School in 1981. His research work is in integrative thinking, business design, corporate social responsibility and country competitiveness. He has written seven *Harvard Business Review* articles and published three books. He was named one of the 10 most influential business professors in the world (2007) and one of seven "Innovation Gurus" (2005) by *BusinessWeek*. He serves on the boards of Thomson Reuters, Research in Motion, The Skoll Foundation, the Canadian Credit Management Foundation, Social Capital Partners and Tennis Canada.

Prof. Alex Nicholls, University of Oxford, United Kingdom

Alex Nicholls is the first lecturer in social entrepreneurship appointed at the University of Oxford and was the first staff member of the Skoll Centre for Social Entrepreneurship. Nicholls' research interests range across several key areas within social entrepreneurship, including: the interface between the public and social sectors; organizational legitimacy and governance; the development of social finance markets; and impact measurement and innovation. Nicholls is widely published in peer-reviewed journals and is the co-author of a major research book on Fair Trade (with Charlotte Opal; Sage, 2005). His ground-breaking edition of a collection of key papers on the state of the art of social entrepreneurship globally was published by Oxford University Press in autumn 2006. In terms of network building, Nicholls organized the first Skoll World Forum in Social Entrepreneurship in 2004 and has subsequently co-organized the event. Furthermore, he is developing a web-based university social entrepreneurship academic network in partnership with Ashoka. Nicholls has held lectureships at a wide variety of academic institutions including: University of Toronto, Canada; Leeds Metropolitan University; University of Surrey; and Aston Business School. He has been a Fellow of the Academy of Marketing Science and Member of the Institute of Learning and Teaching. Nicholls also sat on the regional social enterprise expert group for the South East of England and is a Non-Executive Director of a major fair trade company.

6.5
About oikos

oikos is the International Student Organization for Sustainable Economics and Management, a leading reference point for the promotion of sustainability change agents. We aim to empower action competence for sustainable development among tomorrow's decision-makers. To target this objective, we strive to:

- Increase awareness for sustainability opportunities and challenges focusing on students of Management and Economics;

- Foster their ability not only to analyze long-term economic, environmental and social trends, but also implement sustainability-driven innovation;

- Create institutional support for these learning processes through the integration of sustainability issues in research and teaching at the world's faculties for Management and Economics.

oikos was founded as a local student group at the University of St. Gallen, Switzerland, in 1987. Ever since, oikos St. Gallen has organized workshops, conferences, simulation games, and educational events to integrate sustainability issues into teaching and research of economics and management. In addition, institutional innovation is part of the oikos concept. In 1990, the oikos Foundation was created. In 1997, oikos decided to internationalize its activities and to strengthen sustainability awareness—not only among students in Switzerland, but also within faculties of Economics and Management throughout the world. oikos International was born.

Today, oikos is a global network of local chapters all working towards the same mission. With 35 chapters in 15 countries, the oikos network has the potential to reach 50,000 students worldwide. All chapters are neutral, non-political platforms for open-minded sustainability discussion. Local chapters aim at enriching students' curricula at their respective universities with sustainability knowledge. The international oikos projects focus on teaching (e.g. oikos Winter School, oikos Model WTO, oikos Case Writing Competition), research (oikos PRI Young Scholars Finance Academy, oikos UNDP Young Scholars Development Academy, oikos Young Scholars Entrepreneurship Academy, oikos PhD Fellowship Program), and networking (oikos Spring and Autumn Meetings, oikos Award for Student Entrepreneurship in Higher Education).

The international oikos activities are funded by a circle of donors. Members of our circle of donors are actively engaged in the sustainable development dialogue. Organizations that have supported oikos in the past and present include ABB, Avina Foundation, BP (Switzerland), Corymbo Foundation, Deutsche Telekom, Ernst Schweizer AG, Helvetia, Fondation Looser, Foundation for the Third Millennium, the Dow Chemical Company, Gasser, KPMG, Knecht & Müller AG, Mercator Foundation Switzerland, oikos Foundation, Novo Nordisk, Rhomberg, UBS, the Shell Foundation, Toyota, Sustainable Asset Management (SAM) and WWF, among others.

The headquarters of oikos is in St. Gallen, Switzerland. Please refer to our website or the addresses below. More information about international oikos activities can be found at: www.oikosinternational.org.

Contact

oikos International
President 2011: Harriet Jackson
president@oikosinternational.org

Tigerbergstraße 2
9000 St. Gallen
Switzerland

Tel. +41 (0)71 224 26 98
Fax +41 (0)71 224 26 98

oikos Foundation
Managing Director:
Dr. Jost Hamschmidt
jost.hamschmidt@oikosinternational.org

Tigerbergstraße 2
9000 St. Gallen
Switzerland

Tel. +41 (0)71 224 2595
Fax. +41 (0)71 224 2722

6.6
Literature

Abel, D. (1997) "What Makes a Good Case?" *ECCHO: The Newsletter of European Case Clearing House* 17: 4-7.

Barnes, L.B., C.R. Christensen, and A.J. Hansen (eds.) (1994) *Teaching and the Case Method* (Boston: Harvard Business School Press, 3rd edn).

Boehrer, J., and M. Linsky (1990) "Teaching with Cases: Learning to Question." In M.D. Svinicki (ed.), *The Changing Face of College Teaching* (New Directions for Teaching and Learning, no. 42; San Francisco: Jossey-Bass).

Bolton, M.A., J.A. Erskine, M.R. Leenders, and L.A. Mauffette-Leenders (1981) *Teaching with Cases* (London, Canada: Research and Publications Division, School of Business Administration, The University of Western Ontario).

Clawson, J.G., and S.C. Frey (1986) "Mapping Case Pedagogy." *Organizational Behavior Teaching Review* 11: 1-8.

Friedman, T.L. (2001) *The Lexus and the Olive Tree: Understanding Globalization* (New York: Anchor Books).

Ghoshal, S. (2005) "Bad Management Theories Are Destroying Good Management Practices." *Academy of Management Learning and Education* 4(1): 75-91.

Gilmore, T.N., and E. Schall (1996) "Staying Alive to Learning: Integrating Enactments with Case Teaching to Develop Leaders." *Journal of Policy Analysis and Management* 15(3): 444-456.

Heath, J. (2006) *Teaching and Writing Case Studies: A Practical Guide* (Wharley End: ECCH, 3rd edn).

Hamschmidt, J. (ed.) (2007) *Case Studies In Sustainability Management and Strategy: The oikos Collection* (Sheffield, UK: Greenleaf Publishing).

Herreid, C.F. (1998) "What Makes a Good Case? Some Basic Rules of Good Storytelling Help Teachers Generate Student Excitement in the Classroom." *Journal of College Science Teaching*, December 1997/January 1998: 163-165; available online at sciencecases.lib.buffalo.edu/cs/pdfs/What%20Makes%20a%20Good%20Case-XXVII-3.pdf.

Hoffman, A. (2004) "Reconsidering the Role of the Practical Theorist: On (Re)connecting Theory to Practice in Organization Theory." *Strategic Organization* 2: 213-222.

Lane, J. L. (2007) *Case Writing Guide*; available online at www.schreyerinstitute.psu.edu/pdf/CaseWritingGuide.pdf.

Leenders, M., and J.A. Erskine (1989) *Case Research: The Case Writing Process* (Ontario: School of Business Administration, University of Western Ontario).

Leenders, M., J. Erskine and L. Mauffette-Leenders (2001) *Writing Cases* (Richard Ivey School of Business, University of Western Ontario, 4th edn).

McKeachie, W.J. (1994) *Teaching Tips: Strategies, Research, and Theory for College and University Teachers* (Lexington, MA: DC Heath).

McNair, M.P., and A.C. Hersum (1954) *The Case Method at the Harvard Business School* (New York: McGraw-Hill).

Mintzberg, H. (2005): *Managers, Not MBAs: A Hard Look at the Soft Practice of Managing and Management Development* (San Francisco: Berrett-Koehler).

Pfeffer, J., and C. Fong (2002) "The End of Business Schools? Less Success than Meets the Eye." *Academy of Management Learning and Education* 1(1): 78-96.

Reinhardt, F.L. (1998) "Environmental Product Differentiation: Implications for Corporate Strategy." *California Management Review* 40(4): 43-73.

Tapscott, D., and D. Ticoll (2003) *The Naked Corporation: How the Age of Transparency Will Revolutionize Business* (New York: The Free Press).

Wassermann, S. (1994) *Introduction to Case Method Teaching: A Guide to the Galaxy* (New York: Teachers College, Columbia University).

Wüstenhagen, R., et al. (2007) "The Social Acceptance of Renewable Energy Innovation." *Energy Policy*, Special Issue, 35(5) (May 2007).

Wüstenhagen, R., et al. (2008) *Sustainable Entrepreneurship and Innovation* (Cheltenham, UK: Edward Elgar).

Yaziji, M. (2004) "Turning Gadflies into Allies." *Harvard Business Review* 82(2): 110-115.

Zell, D. (2005) "Pressure for Relevancy at Top-Tier Business Schools." *Journal of Management Inquiry* 14(3): 271-274.

About the editors

Jost Hamschmidt is the Managing Director of the oikos Foundation, an international reference point for sustainability research and teaching in Business and Economics education. He is also a Lecturer at the University of St. Gallen, Switzerland. Jost received a master in Business Administration from the University of Kassel (Germany), a BA in Technology Management from the University of St. Etienne (France) and holds a PhD in Management from the University of St. Gallen. He has been a visiting fellow at the Haas School of Business, University of California, Berkeley (2001/2) and Harvard Business School (2007/8). In 2007 he edited the volume *Case Studies in Sustainability Management and Strategy: the oikos collection* (Greenleaf Publishing) and in 2008 he co-edited the volume *Sustainability Entrepreneurship and Innovation* (Edward Elgar). At oikos he is responsible for fundraising and leading the oikos academic programs. In his teaching, he focuses on action-oriented learning methods for creating sustainability-driven transformation processes in small and large organizations. He has worked with social entrepreneurial ventures such as Myclimate, South Pole Carbon Asset Management and Traktor AG. In 2010 he became founding member of The Hub Association Zurich, a Social Entrepreneurship incubator.

Michael Pirson is Assistant Professor at Fordham University, New York, and a Research Fellow at Harvard University. He is also the track chair of the oikos Global Case Writing Competition—Social Entrepreneurship track. Michael received his PhD in Organizational Behaviour from the University of St. Gallen, Switzerland. His research focuses on the conditions of stakeholder trust in organizational contexts. He is also examining the impact of organizational design on stakeholder well-being and looks at social enterprises as humanistic alternatives to traditional business design. In his teaching, he focuses on the management dilemmas in the 21st century, such as ecological and social sustainability, stakeholder trust, employee engagement and individual happiness. He also uses activity-based learning techniques to teach social entrepreneurship. Before receiving his doctorate, Michael worked in international management consulting for several years. He also gained experience in the political arena while working on Hillary Clinton's Senate campaign. Michael has started several social enterprises in the area of economic development and currently serves on the board of three social enterprises based in the USA.